Entrepreneurial Ecosystems Driving Economic Transformation and Job Creation

Muhammad Nawaz Tunio
The University of Sufism and Modern Sciences, Bhitshah, Pakistan

IGI Global
Scientific Publishing
Publishing Tomorrow's Research Today

Vice President of Editorial — Melissa Wagner
Managing Editor of Acquisitions — Mikaela Felty
Managing Editor of Book Development — Jocelynn Hessler
Production Manager — Mike Brehm
Cover Design — Phillip Shickler

Published in the United States of America by
IGI Global Scientific Publishing
701 East Chocolate Avenue
Hershey, PA, 17033, USA
Tel: 717-533-8845
Fax: 717-533-8661
Website: https://www.igi-global.com E-mail: cust@igi-global.com

Library of Congress Cataloging-in-Publication Data

Names: Tunio, Muhammad Nawaz, 1984- editor.
Title: Entrepreneurial ecosystems driving economic transformation and job creation / edited by Muhammad Nawaz Tunio.
Description: Hershey, PA : IGI Global Scientific Publishing, [2025] | Includes bibliographical references and index. | Summary: "This book delves into the multifaceted nature of these ecosystems, exploring their components, dynamics, and the profound impact they have on both local and global economies"-- Provided by publisher.
Identifiers: LCCN 2024049293 (print) | LCCN 2024049294 (ebook) | ISBN 9798369394861 (hardcover) | ISBN 9798369394878 (paperback) | ISBN 9798369394885 (ebook)
Subjects: LCSH: Economics. | Job creation. | Entrepreneurship.
Classification: LCC HB171 .E67 2025 (print) | LCC HB171 (ebook) | DDC 338/.04--dc23/eng/20250109
LC record available at https://lccn.loc.gov/2024049293
LC ebook record available at https://lccn.loc.gov/2024049294

British Cataloguing in Publication Data
A Cataloguing in Publication record for this book is available from the British Library.

Table of Contents

Detailed Table of Contents

This chapter explores the pivotal role of computational thinking in facilitating career transitions and entrepreneurship, particularly within the context of the evolving digital economy. As the boundaries between traditional employment and entrepreneurship blur, computational thinking emerges as a critical skill set that enables individuals to navigate these changes effectively. The chapter examines how computational thinking, characterized by problem-solving, logical reasoning, and algorithmic design, can empower individuals transitioning from established careers into entrepreneurial ventures. It also discusses the integration of computational thinking into educational curricula to foster a culture of innovation and adaptability, essential for both individual career development and broader economic growth. By highlighting case studies and real-world applications, this chapter demonstrates how computational thinking not only equips individuals with the tools necessary for entrepreneurial success but also drives organizational innovation and economic development.

Hybrid entrepreneurship, where individuals balance full-time employment with entrepreneurial ventures, is reshaping the gig economy. This evolving model provides significant benefits, including increased flexibility, diversified income sources, and enhanced innovation. However, it also presents challenges, such as the need for updated labor laws, tax regulations, and adequate support structures. As technology advances and the nature of work changes, hybrid entrepreneurs will play

It considers the mechanisms through which economic diversity will spur creative thinking to arrive at new business models and products. It gives case studies of successful startups to bring out real-life examples of how economic diversity has been the source of innovation. The chapter, therefore, highlights with tangible benefits accruing from diverse economic backgrounds. In a nutshell, it ends with the strategic recommendations for entrepreneurs and investors on how to harness economic diversity in enhancing innovation, building resilient business ventures, and gaining long-term success in competitive markets.

The chapter explores the intersection of creativity, innovation, and sustainability in entrepreneurship. Emphasis is given to the role of creative thinking in driving sustainable technological development in entrepreneurship. It explores the important role that creativity plays in identification and solving of complex challenges modern entrepreneurs face in developing technologies that are not only innovative but also environmentally and socially responsible. The chapter shows how entrepreneurs can use creativity to develop sustainable solutions that will help answer market demand while reducing their impact on the environment. This is a blend of theoretical insight with practical examples, important case studies of businesses that efficiently put sustainable practice into their technology innovation, hence providing a way forward for future entrepreneurs. This chapter aims to teach readers how to strategically utilize creative processes to drive technological innovation and achieve sustainable, long-term entrepreneurial success.

This chapter turned its focus on critical elements such as access to capital, infrastructure, collaborative culture, and government policies in line with effective

This research utilizes the framework of institutional theory to explore the dynamics between student entrepreneurial ambitions and the support mechanisms provided by their educational institutions. The study involves a survey of 420 students from a selection of universities in Haryana, chosen for their diverse entrepreneurial programs. The study employs structural equation modeling to analyze the data and test our theoretical propositions. This research contributes a novel perspective to the discourse on entrepreneurship education by underscoring the significance of the institutional environment, rather than individual entrepreneurial traits, as a determinant of entrepreneurial intent among students.

This chapter explores the critical relationship between an organization's innovation culture and its impact on employee engagement and retention. An innovation culture fosters an environment that encourages creativity, autonomy, and continuous development, which significantly influences employees' motivation and satisfaction. By examining key metrics such as engagement surveys, retention rates, performance metrics, and innovation outcomes, the chapter highlights how these factors interrelate to enhance organizational performance. Best practices for cultivating a supportive innovation environment, empowering employees, investing in professional development, and maintaining work-life balance are discussed. Additionally, strategies for recognizing and rewarding innovation and fostering collaboration are examined. Understanding these dynamics provides organizations with actionable insights to improve engagement and retention, ultimately driving long-term success and growth.

This chapter explores how employee ownership and profit-sharing arrangements blur the traditional boundaries between employment and entrepreneurship. It examines the historical evolution and various models of employee ownership, including stock options, ESOPs, and profit-sharing plans. By analyzing the entrepreneurial mindset fostered through these models, the chapter highlights their impact on organizational culture, employee engagement, and business performance. The discussion also covers the benefits, challenges, and limitations of implementing such models, supported by case studies from notable companies like John Lewis Partnership and Mondragon Corporation. Looking ahead, the chapter identifies key trends and implications for the future, including technological advancements, inclusivity, and regulatory developments. The findings underscore the potential of these models to transform work environments, enhance employee motivation, and drive organizational success.

Hybrid entrepreneurship, where individuals manage both full-time employment and entrepreneurial ventures, presents unique challenges and opportunities for achieving work-life balance. This paper examines the strategies and tools hybrid entrepreneurs use to manage their dual roles effectively. It explores the impact of technology, including project management software and scheduling apps, on balancing personal and professional responsibilities. The study also addresses common challenges such as time constraints, role conflict, and boundary issues, while highlighting future trends like advancements in technology and evolving work environments. By understanding these dynamics, hybrid entrepreneurs can enhance productivity, foster innovation, and maintain well-being. The findings offer insights into creating sustainable practices that support both personal and professional success.

Foreword

In today's rapidly evolving global economy, the role of entrepreneurship has never been more critical. The concept of entrepreneurial ecosystems—dynamic environments where a diverse set of stakeholders including entrepreneurs, investors, academic institutions, governments, and support organizations interact—has emerged as a powerful driver of economic transformation and job creation. These ecosystems are not merely collections of individual elements; rather, they are interdependent systems where each participant contributes to and benefits from the whole.

Entrepreneurial ecosystems thrive on innovation and collaboration, fostering the development of new businesses that challenge existing market structures and bring novel solutions to the forefront. By nurturing talent, facilitating access to capital, and providing the necessary support infrastructure, these ecosystems create an environment where startups can grow, scale, and succeed. They are the fertile ground in which ideas are cultivated into products and services that meet the needs of the market, thereby generating wealth and creating jobs.

One of the most significant impacts of entrepreneurial ecosystems is their ability to transform economies. In regions where traditional industries may be in decline, entrepreneurial activity can spark new growth sectors, leading to a more diversified and resilient economy. These ecosystems often become hubs of innovation, attracting talent and investment from around the world, and they can reposition entire regions as leaders in emerging industries. For developing economies, the establishment of a robust entrepreneurial ecosystem can be a critical factor in leapfrogging stages of development, enabling them to compete on a global scale.

Job creation is another vital contribution of entrepreneurial ecosystems. Startups and small businesses are significant engines of employment, often creating jobs at a faster rate than established firms. The collaborative nature of ecosystems means that as one business grows, it can create opportunities for others—suppliers, service providers, and partner firms—all contributing to a virtuous cycle of job creation and economic growth. Furthermore, ecosystems that promote inclusive entrepreneurship ensure that these opportunities extend to a broader segment of society, including underrepresented groups and marginalized communities.

However, the success of an entrepreneurial ecosystem is not guaranteed. It requires intentional design and continuous support. Policymakers, educational institutions, and private sector leaders must work together to remove barriers to entrepreneurship, whether these are regulatory, financial, or cultural. There is also a need for sustained investment in education and skills development to ensure that the workforce is prepared to meet the demands of a changing economy.

Entrepreneurial ecosystems are essential catalysts for economic transformation and job creation. They represent the intersection of innovation, collaboration, and opportunity, driving forward the industries of the future while providing tangible benefits to society today. As we look to the future, it is clear that fostering these ecosystems will be crucial to sustaining economic growth, creating jobs, and ensuring that the benefits of entrepreneurship are widely shared.

It is with great respect and admiration that we acknowledge the invaluable contributions of

Dr. Muhammad Nawaz Tunio, the esteemed editor of this volume. His unwavering dedication, deep expertise, and insightful guidance have been instrumental in shaping this book, "Entrepreneurial Ecosystems Driving Economic Transformation and Job Creation."

Dr. Tunio's vision and commitment to advancing our understanding of entrepreneurial ecosystems have brought together a diverse array of perspectives, fostering a rich dialogue on the critical role these ecosystems play in driving economic growth and job creation. His meticulous attention to detail, coupled with his profound knowledge of the subject, has ensured that each chapter resonates with relevance and rigor.

We extend our deepest gratitude to Dr. Tunio for his leadership and for the inspiration he has provided through this project. His work continues to influence and inspire countless scholars, practitioners, and policymakers, and it is an honor to have his guiding hand in the creation of this book.

Aamir Rashid

City University of New York, USA

Preface

In an era where global economic landscapes are continuously reshaped by innovation, technology, and shifting market demands, the role of entrepreneurship has gained unprecedented importance. The concept of entrepreneurial ecosystems has emerged as a vital framework for understanding how economies can foster innovation, spur job creation, and drive economic transformation. This book, "Entrepreneurial Ecosystems Driving Economic Transformation and Job Creation," delves into the multifaceted nature of these ecosystems, exploring their components, dynamics, and the profound impact they have on both local and global economies.

UNDERSTANDING ENTREPRENEURIAL ECOSYSTEMS

At its core, an entrepreneurial ecosystem is a complex, interconnected network of stakeholders that includes entrepreneurs, investors, support organizations, academic institutions, government bodies, and large corporations. These stakeholders interact within an environment that nurtures entrepreneurship, providing the necessary resources, networks, and support systems that entrepreneurs need to start, grow, and scale their businesses. The strength of an entrepreneurial ecosystem lies not just in the individual components, but in the synergies that arise from their interaction.

Entrepreneurial ecosystems are not homogeneous; they vary widely depending on factors such as geography, industry focus, cultural norms, and the maturity of the local economy. For instance, Silicon Valley is often cited as the quintessential entrepreneurial ecosystem, characterized by a high concentration of technology firms, a strong venture capital presence, and a culture that encourages risk-taking and innovation. However, entrepreneurial ecosystems can and do emerge in a variety of contexts, from bustling urban centers to remote rural areas, each with its unique strengths and challenges.

The Role of Innovation in Economic Transformation

Innovation is the lifeblood of entrepreneurial ecosystems. It drives the creation of new products, services, and business models that disrupt traditional industries and create new markets. This process of creative destruction, as described by economist Joseph Schumpeter, is fundamental to economic transformation. In entrepreneurial ecosystems, innovation is fostered through collaboration, knowledge exchange, and the continuous flow of ideas between different stakeholders.

One of the key ways in which entrepreneurial ecosystems drive economic transformation is by enabling the emergence of new industries. For example, the rise of the digital economy has been fueled by ecosystems that support tech startups, providing them with the resources needed to develop groundbreaking technologies such as artificial intelligence, blockchain, and the Internet of Things. These technologies, in turn, have had far-reaching impacts on traditional industries, from manufacturing to finance, leading to the creation of new economic sectors and opportunities for growth.

Moreover, entrepreneurial ecosystems are often at the forefront of addressing societal challenges through innovation. Social entrepreneurship, which seeks to solve social, environmental, and economic problems through market-based solutions, is a growing component of many ecosystems. By supporting social entrepreneurs, ecosystems contribute to inclusive economic growth and help address pressing global issues such as poverty, inequality, and climate change.

Job Creation and the Role of SMEs

Small and medium-sized enterprises (SMEs) are the backbone of most economies, and entrepreneurial ecosystems play a crucial role in supporting their development. SMEs are significant drivers of job creation, often accounting for a large proportion of employment in both developed and developing economies. The support systems within entrepreneurial ecosystems, including access to finance, mentoring, and networks, are essential in helping these businesses grow and thrive.

Startups and SMEs benefit immensely from being part of a vibrant entrepreneurial ecosystem. The networking opportunities, access to skilled labor, and proximity to other innovative firms create an environment where collaboration and knowledge sharing are encouraged. This not only helps businesses scale but also leads to the creation of high-quality jobs. As these businesses grow, they generate employment opportunities across various sectors, from technology to services, contributing to overall economic development.

The multiplier effect of job creation within entrepreneurial ecosystems cannot be overstated. As startups expand, they not only hire more employees but also stimulate demand for goods and services from other local businesses. This, in turn, leads to further job creation and economic activity, creating a virtuous cycle of growth. In regions where traditional industries are declining, entrepreneurial ecosystems can provide a much-needed boost by creating new employment opportunities and revitalizing local economies.

The Globalization of Entrepreneurial Ecosystems

In an increasingly interconnected world, entrepreneurial ecosystems are no longer confined to specific geographic locations. The rise of digital technologies and the globalization of markets have enabled ecosystems to transcend borders, leading to the emergence of global networks of entrepreneurship. These global ecosystems are characterized by the flow of talent, capital, and ideas across regions, creating opportunities for collaboration and innovation on a scale never before seen.

The globalization of entrepreneurial ecosystems has significant implications for economic transformation and job creation. It allows for the diffusion of best practices and the transfer of knowledge between ecosystems, enabling regions with less developed ecosystems to learn from and collaborate with more established ones. This can lead to the rapid development of new industries and the creation of jobs in regions that might otherwise struggle to compete in the global economy.

However, the globalization of entrepreneurial ecosystems also presents challenges. There is a risk that the benefits of these ecosystems may become concentrated in a few global hubs, leaving other regions behind. To ensure that the benefits of entrepreneurship are widely shared, it is essential to support the development of local ecosystems and to create policies that encourage inclusive growth. This includes investing in education and skills development, improving access to finance for underserved communities, and fostering a culture of entrepreneurship at all levels of society.

Policy Implications and the Role of Government

The success of entrepreneurial ecosystems is often closely tied to the policies and regulatory frameworks that govern them. Governments play a critical role in shaping the environment in which ecosystems operate. This includes creating policies that encourage innovation, reducing barriers to entrepreneurship, and providing support for startups and SMEs.

One of the key policy challenges is ensuring that entrepreneurial ecosystems are inclusive and accessible to all. This means addressing issues such as access to finance, particularly for underrepresented groups such as women and minority entrepreneurs. It also involves creating an education system that fosters entrepreneurial skills and mindsets from an early age, as well as providing ongoing support for adult learners who wish to enter the entrepreneurial space.

Governments also have a role to play in facilitating the growth of global entrepreneurial ecosystems. This can be achieved by promoting cross-border collaborations, investing in digital infrastructure, and ensuring that regulatory frameworks are conducive to international trade and investment. By creating an enabling environment, governments can help ensure that entrepreneurial ecosystems continue to drive economic transformation and job creation on a global scale.

CHAPTER OVERVIEW

Chapter 1 explores the growing importance of computational thinking as a tool for career transition and entrepreneurial success, emphasizing its integration into education to enhance adaptability and innovation. Chapter 2 delves into the rise of hybrid entrepreneurship, where individuals balance full-time jobs with entrepreneurial pursuits, reshaping the gig economy and presenting both opportunities and challenges for labor laws and regulations. Chapter 3 examines the role of emerging technologies, such as AI and blockchain, in driving economic diversification, with particular attention to sustainability and inclusivity in growth.

Chapter 4 discusses the impact of economic diversity on fostering innovation within startups, using case studies to illustrate how diverse economic backgrounds encourage creativity and resilience. In Chapter 5, creativity is highlighted as a crucial factor in developing sustainable technological innovations, providing insights on how entrepreneurs can address environmental and social challenges. Chapter 6 analyzes successful entrepreneurial ecosystems, drawing on global examples to demonstrate the importance of access to capital, supportive policies, and collaborative culture.

Human factors within entrepreneurial ecosystems are the focus of Chapter 7, emphasizing the role of behaviors, values, and attitudes in shaping successful ventures. Chapter 8 provides an analysis of how price dynamics impact entrepreneurship in Africa, offering policy recommendations to bolster economic stability and growth. Chapter 9 introduces crowdfunding as a valuable tool for solopreneurs, offering strategies for creating impactful campaigns that align with long-term financial planning.

Chapter 10 discusses strategic alignment in organizations, introducing the Balanced Scorecard as a comprehensive tool for enhancing performance. Chapter 11 examines networking and partnerships as essential to the success of hybrid entrepreneurs, especially in a digitally transforming business environment. Chapter 12 investigates the influence of educational institutions on student entrepreneurship, highlighting how institutional support shapes entrepreneurial intent.

Chapter 13 focuses on the benefits of fostering an innovative culture to enhance employee engagement and retention, providing strategies for building a supportive work environment. In Chapter 14, employee ownership and profit-sharing models are examined for their potential to bridge traditional employment with entrepreneurial empowerment, with case studies illustrating their impact on motivation and productivity. Finally, Chapter 15 addresses the challenges hybrid entrepreneurs face in achieving work-life balance and presents tools and strategies to manage dual roles effectively.

This preface sets the stage for a multifaceted exploration of entrepreneurship, innovation, and the evolving global economy, offering readers insights into the interconnectedness of individual, organizational, and governmental roles in shaping the future.

CONCLUSION

"Entrepreneurial Ecosystems Driving Economic Transformation and Job Creation" seeks to provide a comprehensive understanding of the complex and dynamic nature of entrepreneurial ecosystems. Through the contributions of leading experts and practitioners, this book explores the various components of ecosystems, the processes that drive economic transformation, and the critical role of entrepreneurship in job creation.

As we move forward in an increasingly uncertain and rapidly changing world, the importance of fostering vibrant entrepreneurial ecosystems cannot be overstated. They are the engines of innovation, the drivers of economic growth, and the creators of jobs. By understanding and supporting these ecosystems, we can build a more resilient and inclusive global economy that benefits all.

Muhammad Nawaz Tunio
The University of Sufism and Modern Sciences, Bhitshah, Pakistan

Acknowledgment

The creation of this book, "Entrepreneurial Ecosystems Driving Economic Transformation and Job Creation," has been a journey filled with collaboration, dedication, and support from numerous individuals and organizations. It is with deep gratitude that I acknowledge their contributions.

I am deeply grateful to the team at IGI Global for their professionalism, encouragement, and continuous support throughout the publication process. Their expertise in academic publishing, combined with their commitment to promoting knowledge and research, has made this book possible. Special thanks to the editorial and production teams for their meticulous attention to detail and their dedication to ensuring the highest quality of work.

A sincere thank you goes to the expert reviewers whose invaluable feedback and constructive criticism have greatly enhanced the quality of this book. Their expertise and thoughtful insights have helped to refine the chapters and ensure that the content is both rigorous and relevant.

Finally, I would like to thank all the contributors, researchers, and practitioners who shared their knowledge and experiences. Their dedication to advancing the understanding of entrepreneurial ecosystems and their impact on economic transformation and job creation has been inspiring.

This book is a testament to the collective efforts of everyone involved, and I am deeply appreciative of the support and collaboration that made it a reality.

Chapter 1
Innovating Education and Entrepreneurship Through Computational Thinking:
New Pathways for Economic Development

Muhammad Usman Tariq
https://orcid.org/0000-0002-7605-3040
Abu Dhabi University, UAE & University College Cork, Ireland

ABSTRACT

This chapter explores the pivotal role of computational thinking in facilitating career transitions and entrepreneurship, particularly within the context of the evolving digital economy. As the boundaries between traditional employment and entrepreneurship blur, computational thinking emerges as a critical skill set that enables individuals to navigate these changes effectively. The chapter examines how computational thinking, characterized by problem-solving, logical reasoning, and algorithmic design, can empower individuals transitioning from established careers into entrepreneurial ventures. It also discusses the integration of computational thinking into educational curricula to foster a culture of innovation and adaptability, essential for both individual career development and broader economic growth. By highlighting case studies and real-world applications, this chapter demonstrates how computational thinking not only equips individuals with the tools necessary for entrepreneurial success but also drives organizational innovation and economic development.

DOI: 10.4018/979-8-3693-9486-1.ch001

INTRODUCTION

The relentless progression of digital innovation is inducing a substantial transformation in the educational sector. Computational reasoning has become crucial in various educational paradigms, spanning STEM (Science et al.) and permeating non-STEM subjects. This section delves into many computational reasoning tools and platforms available to educators, emphasizing their role in altering teaching procedures. This chapter aims to enable educators to seamlessly integrate computational thinking into their instructional practices by providing a comprehensive guide.

Significance of Computational Reasoning in Education

Computational reasoning, characterized by problem-solving, logical thinking, and algorithmic design, transcends traditional disciplinary boundaries. It equips students with the ability to approach complex problems systematically, fostering critical thinking skills applicable across various domains. Students are better prepared for challenges and opportunities in the future when computational thinking is taught in schools to meet the needs of a world increasingly dependent on technology.

Overview of Computational Reasoning Instruments

Scratch and ScratchEd: Developed by MIT, Scratch is a visual programming language that empowers students to create interactive stories, games, and animations. An online community and resource centre called ScratchEd assists educators in incorporating Scratch into their classrooms (Resnick et al., 2009).
Code.org: A non-profit organization dedicated to expanding access to computer science, Code.org provides various resources, including coding examples, interactive tutorials, and teacher training programs (Partovi, 2014).
Micro: bit: A pocket-sized programmable computer, Micro: bit promotes problem-solving creativity by providing a hands-on approach to learning coding and computational thinking (BBC, 2016).
Google CS First: An initiative by Google, CS First offers free, ready-to-use coding lessons for teachers to introduce computer science concepts in a fun and engaging way (Google, n.d.).
TinkerCAD: Focused on STEM subjects, TinkerCAD allows students to create 3D designs and simulations, integrating computational thinking into design and engineering (Autodesk, 2021).
Kahoot!: Beyond traditional coding tools, Kahoot! gamifies the learning experience, making it a powerful platform for assessing and reinforcing computational thinking concepts through quizzes and interactive games (Kahoot!, 2020).

Blockly: Blockly is a visual programming language that uses blocks to represent code. It can be used to teach beginners how to code and serves as a bridge to more advanced programming languages (Google, n.d.).
Code with a Pen: Merging coding with art, Pencil Code allows students to visually see the results of their code in real time, promoting creativity and trial and error in programming (Pencil Code, n.d.).
Edpuzzle: Edpuzzle enables educators to add questions, comments, and insights to educational videos directly to incorporate computational thinking into video-based **lessons (Edpuzzle, 2021).**
Microsoft MakeCode: Offering a platform for programming microcontrollers and creating engaging projects, Microsoft MakeCode supports the integration of coding and computational thinking in various subjects (Microsoft, n.d.).

Challenges and Benefits

While these tools present exciting opportunities for educators, it is essential to recognize the benefits and challenges associated with their implementation. Benefits include increased student engagement, enhanced problem-solving skills, and improved critical reasoning abilities. However, obstacles may arise regarding access to technology, teacher education, and the need for ongoing updates to keep up with changing tools.

Professional Development Opportunities

To effectively utilize computational reasoning tools, educators require ongoing professional development opportunities. Studios, online courses, and collaborative networks, such as the Global Society for Innovation in Education (ISTE), can empower educators with the skills and knowledge necessary to integrate these tools into their teaching practices (ISTE, 2021).

Thus, preparing students for the complexities of the modern world necessitates incorporating computational thinking into education. Innovative teaching methods are made possible by educators' access to many tools and platforms, resulting in a generation with essential problem-solving and critical-thinking abilities. As innovation advances, teachers should embrace these tools and participate in continuous professional development to harness their full potential in transforming the educational landscape.

INTRODUCTION TO COMPUTATIONAL THINKING TOOLS

The educational landscape is transforming significantly due to the incorporation of computational thinking tools, a pivotal force in reshaping pedagogical approaches. These tools encompass a diverse range of software, applications, and digital platforms specifically designed to cultivate computational thinking skills among students. Computational thinking, characterised by problem-solving, algorithmic design, and logical reasoning, is acknowledged as a foundational skill set with broad applicability across disciplines and essential for navigating the intricacies of the modern world.

Categorisation of Tools

These tools can be systematically categorised based on their functionalities, target age groups, and educational objectives to facilitate a thorough exploration. One notable category includes visual programming languages such as Scratch, developed by MIT, which introduces coding concepts through a user-friendly interface, rendering it suitable for learners of all ages (Resnick et al., 2009). Another category encompasses platforms like Code.org, a nonprofit organisation offering various coding lessons and teacher resources, fostering global accessibility to computer science education (Partovi, 2014).

Educational Objectives

Integrating computational thinking tools aims to give students problem-solving skills, logical reasoning abilities, and proficiency in thinking algorithmically. For example, the micro: bit, a pocket-sized programmable computer, facilitates a hands-on approach to coding, stimulating creativity and proving a valuable tool for achieving these educational objectives (BBC, 2016). By incorporating these tools, educators can establish dynamic learning environments that transcend traditional teaching methods, nurturing a culture of innovation and critical thinking.

Real-life instances illuminate the tangible implications of integrating computational thinking tools into education. In the context of Scratch, students collaboratively create interactive stories, games, and animations, honing their coding skills and enhancing creativity and teamwork (Resnick et al., 2009). Code.org's impact is evident in initiatives like the "Hour of Code," a global movement introducing millions of students to coding, emphasising inclusivity and accessibility (Partovi, 2014).

The micro bit finds application in various educational contexts, such as the "Micro: bit in Space" project, where students coded messages transmitted to the International Space Station, illustrating the real-world implications of computational thinking (BBC, 2016). These examples underscore the transformative potential of computational thinking tools, transitioning from theoretical knowledge to practical, real-world applications.

Educators gain a comprehensive understanding of the technological landscape by categorising these tools based on functionalities, target age groups, and educational objectives. This understanding enables informed decisions about tool selection aligned with specific teaching goals and the diverse needs of students. TinkerCAD, for instance, allows students to create 3D designs and simulations, which aligns with objectives in science, technology, engineering, and mathematics (STEM) education (Autodesk, 2021).

Thus, the introduction to computational thinking tools lays the foundation for thoroughly exploring their integration into educational settings. Systematic categorisation based on functionalities, target age groups, and educational objectives provides a structured framework for educators navigating diverse tools. Real-life examples accentuate the practical impact of these tools, highlighting their transformative potential in cultivating computational thinking skills among students. As education continues evolving in the digital era, strategically incorporating these tools into pedagogical practices becomes imperative for preparing students to excel in an increasingly complex and technology-driven world.

Evaluating and Selecting Tools

The process of choosing computational thinking tools for classroom implementation is a crucial aspect of seamlessly integrating technology into educational settings. Educators are confronted with numerous options, each differing in functionalities, features, and suitability for various learning environments. This section delves into the fundamental principles and considerations educators should meticulously evaluate when selecting computational thinking tools.

Suitability

The suitability of a computational thinking tool is pivotal for its successful integration into the classroom. With their visual programming language, tools like Scratch provide an accessible entry point for younger students, fostering engagement and easing the learning curve (Resnick et al., 2009). However, educators must consider the adaptability of these tools. While Scratch is excellent for introductory concepts, advanced tools like Python may be more appropriate for older students or those with a deeper coding background, ensuring a gradual and challenging learning progression.

User-Friendliness

Usability is crucial to a tool's effectiveness in the educational setting. Code.org and Blockly, by emphasizing intuitive interaction points, cater to students at different skill levels (Google, n.d.; Partovi, 2014). Nevertheless, educators should critically assess the balance between simplicity and depth. More complex tools may need to be revised to delve into more advanced computational concepts. Striking a balance ensures that user-friendly interfaces maintain the educational depth for students to grasp fundamental **principles.**

Flexibility

Flexibility is fundamental in accommodating diverse teaching styles and classroom dynamics. Scratch's support for collaborative coding projects enhances flexibility by promoting collaboration and peer learning (Resnick et al., 2009). Educators should evaluate a tool's adaptability across various learning environments, ensuring it caters to individual and collaborative work. This flexibility ensures the tool remains relevant in different educational settings, fostering a dynamic and inclusive learning environment.

Educational Value

The educational value of a tool directly influences its impact on students' computational thinking skills. TinkerCAD's emphasis on 3D designs and simulations aligns with STEM subjects, enhancing the educational experience (Autodesk, 2021). However, educators should critically examine whether the tool complements existing curricular goals or introduces novel perspectives. Students' holistic development significantly benefits from tools seamlessly integrating computational thinking principles with educational content.

Cost

Cost considerations are crucial in tool selection, especially for educators and institutions with limited budgets. Open-source tools like Scratch and Blockly provide cost-effective solutions, ensuring widespread access to computational thinking education (Google, n.d.; Resnick et al., 2009). However, educators should balance a tool's price with its educational value and functionality. Computational thinking tools remain accessible without compromising effectiveness by striking a balance between features and price.

Accessibility

Inclusion features and compatibility with assistive technologies are aspects of a tool's accessibility beyond cost. Edpuzzle's direct integration of questions and comments into videos enhances accessibility, accommodating diverse learning styles (Edpuzzle, 2021). Nevertheless, educators should explore tools for their inclusivity features, language support, and adaptability to assistive technologies. Addressing these aspects ensures that computational thinking tools cater to a broad spectrum of students, irrespective of their evolving needs.

Compatibility with Existing Technologies

Compatibility with existing technologies within educational institutions is crucial for seamless integration. Microsoft MakeCode's compatibility with microcontrollers aligns with existing technologies while providing a dedicated platform for coding projects (Microsoft, n.d.). Educators should critically evaluate how well a tool integrates with other educational software and hardware. This ensures a cohesive technological environment in the classroom, minimizing disruptions and enhancing overall flexibility.

Alignment with Curriculum Standards

Alignment with curriculum standards ensures that computational thinking tools contribute meaningfully to educational objectives. Kahoot!'s gamified quizzes and interactive games assist in formative assessment and align with the goals of the curriculum (Kahoot!, 2020). Educators should critically analyze whether a tool complements or enhances existing curricular standards. This alignment ensures that computational thinking skills are seamlessly integrated into broader educational frameworks, maximizing their impact on student learning outcomes.

Thus, the comprehensive evaluation of computational thinking tools involves a nuanced assessment of suitability, usability, flexibility, educational value, cost, accessibility, compatibility with existing technologies, and alignment with curriculum standards. Balancing these considerations enables educators to make informed decisions, select tools that align with computational thinking and resonate with academic goals, and prepare students for the challenges of the 21st century.

INTEGRATING TOOLS INTO CURRICULA

The integration of computational thinking tools into existing educational programs is a multifaceted process that requires strategic planning, teacher training, and alignment with educational objectives. This chapter explores strategies and best practices for seamlessly incorporating these tools into formal and informal learning environments, emphasizing real-world case studies that highlight successful implementations across various educational settings.

Integration Strategies

Alignment with Learning Objectives

An essential strategy for successful integration is aligning computational thinking tools with specific learning goals within the curriculum. This ensures that the use of these tools is intentional and contributes to broader educational objectives. For instance, integrating Scratch into a primary school science curriculum can enhance students' problem-solving skills by creating interactive mathematical games (Resnick et al., 2009).

Comprehensive Professional Development

To ensure successful tool integration, educators need access to sufficient professional development opportunities. Workshops, training sessions, and online courses empower educators with the skills and confidence required to effectively integrate computational thinking tools into their teaching practices (ISTE, 2021). Real examples, such as those from the International Society for Technology in Education (ISTE), showcase the positive outcomes of comprehensive professional development initiatives.

Cross-Disciplinary Integration

Principles of computational thinking are not confined to STEM fields; they can be applied across disciplines. Approaches should encourage cross-disciplinary integration, allowing computational thinking tools to enrich diverse areas of study. For example, in higher education, incorporating coding practices involving Python in a social science course can enhance data analysis and critical thinking skills.

Gradual Integration

Rather than introducing computational thinking tools abruptly, a gradual integration approach is often more effective. This involves starting with simple tools and activities before progressing to more complex ones. The gradual introduction of tools like Blockly or Code.org ensures that students and teachers can build confidence and proficiency over time (Google, n.d.; Partovi, 2014).

Real-World Case Studies

Elementary School Case Study: Coding in Science

In an elementary school setting, a case study highlights the successful integration of coding exercises using Scratch to develop mathematical concepts. Students collaborated to create interactive projects that not only reinforced their understanding of mathematical concepts but also encouraged creativity and teamwork (Resnick et al., 2009).

Secondary School Case Study: Cross-Disciplinary Integration:

A secondary school case study embodies the cross-disciplinary integration of computational thinking tools. In a history class, students used coding platforms to analyze historical data and visualize trends. This innovative approach enhanced their ability to interpret historical events and developed computational thinking skills applicable beyond STEM subjects.

Higher Education Case Study: Data Analysis in Social Sciences:

At the higher education level, a case study demonstrates the successful integration of computational thinking tools into a social sciences course. Students used Python programming to analyze and interpret social data, gaining valuable insights into research methods and enhancing their quantitative reasoning skills.

Innovative Approaches

Project-Based Learning

Adopting project-based learning approaches enhances the integration of computational thinking tools. Students engage in hands-on projects, such as creating interactive simulations or developing coding solutions for real-world problems. This approach fosters creativity, critical thinking, and practical application of computational principles.

Educational Gamification

Gamifying the learning experience with tools like Kahoot! introduces an element of fun and competition into the educational process. In a higher education case study, gamified quizzes aligned with course content served as formative assessments, developing computational thinking concepts in an engaging manner (Kahoot!, 2020).

Community Collaboration

Establishing collaboratie communities, both within and beyond educational institutions, promotes the sharing of best practices and innovative approaches. Online platforms like CS for All Teachers provide educators with a space to exchange ideas, resources, and successful implementation strategies, fostering a culture of continuous improvement (CS for All Teachers, n.d.).

In conclusion, seamlessly integrating computational thinking tools into existing curricula demands a thoughtful and diverse approach. By aligning with learning objectives, providing comprehensive professional development, encouraging cross-disciplinary integration, adopting gradual implementation, and embracing innovative strategies, educators can ensure that computational thinking becomes an integral and enriching part of the learning experience. The real-world case studies provided illustrate the various ways in which these tools can enhance traditional teaching methods and prepare students for the challenges of the 21st century. Successful implementations of computational thinking tools across diverse educational settings, from elementary schools to higher education institutions, underscore the significant impact of these tools on traditional teaching methodologies. By highlighting real case studies, we gain insights into innovative approaches that have enhanced formal and informal learning environments, offering a glimpse into the potential of computational thinking tools in education.

Enhancing Student Engagement and Learning

The integration of computational thinking tools into educational settings has ushered in a paradigm shift, offering new avenues to enhance student engagement, foster creativity, and improve overall learning outcomes. This section delves into the interactive elements, gamification strategies, and hands-on activities that deepen students' understanding of computational concepts, examining the transformative potential of these tools in various educational contexts.

Learning with Interactive Elements

Computational thinking tools introduce interactive elements that resonate with the digital-native generation, capturing their attention and engaging learning. Platforms like Scratch enable students to create interactive stories, games, and animations, transforming passive learners into active creators (Resnick et al., 2009). This interactivity enhances understanding and fosters a sense of pride and ownership, making the learning experience more meaningful.

In higher education, interactive simulations powered by computational thinking tools have been implemented to teach complex concepts. For example, physics courses leverage PhET Interactive Simulations to allow students to experiment with virtual environments, providing an intuitive and interactive way of grasping intricate scientific principles (PhET et al.).

Gamification Strategies

Gamification, the integration of game elements into non-game settings, is a robust strategy used by computational thinking tools to enhance student engagement. Platforms like Code.org and Blockly employ gamified challenges and puzzles to teach coding concepts. Gamification transforms learning into a more enjoyable experience and introduces elements of competition and achievement, motivating students to persevere in problem-solving (Partovi, 2014).

An example of gamification in education is the Hour of Code initiative, which utilizes gamified coding tutorials to introduce programming to students of all ages. This global movement has successfully engaged millions of students in coding activities, breaking down barriers and demystifying the perception that coding is only for computer science experts (Code.org, n.d.).

Hands-On Activities and Project-Based Learning

Computational thinking tools facilitate hands-on activities and project-based learning, providing students with tangible experiences that extend their understanding of abstract concepts. In primary and secondary education, platforms like Scratch and TinkerCAD empower students to create and explore, turning theoretical knowledge into practical application (Autodesk, 2021; Resnick et al., 2009).

At the higher education level, project-based learning is widely adopted. Computational thinking tools, for instance, are used by students taking courses in engineering and computer science. This hands-on approach develops theoretical concepts and enhances problem-solving skills, preparing students for the dynamic demands of the workforce.

Case Studies and Examples

Scratch in Primary Education

Scratch has been utilised in an elementary school setting to enhance student engagement and learning. Students collaborated on creating interactive stories that incorporated coding elements. This project-based approach introduced computational thinking concepts and developed storytelling skills and collaboration (Resnick et al., 2009).

Code.org in Secondary Education

The gamified coding tutorials provided by Code.org have been successfully integrated into secondary education. A case study showcases how these tutorials were used in a high school computer science course, transforming coding from a theoretical concept into an engaging challenge. Students progressed through levels, earning badges and fostering a sense of accomplishment (Partovi, 2014).

PhET Interactive Simulations in Higher Education

The PhET Interactive Simulations platform has been instrumental in teaching physics concepts in higher education. Students engage in interactive simulations, manipulating variables and observing outcomes. According to PhET Interactive Simulations (n.d.), this method provides a virtual laboratory experience and enhances understanding abstract principles.

Hour of Code Global Initiative

The Hour of Code initiative represents a global example of gamification in action. Students worldwide participate in coding tutorials designed as games, demystifying coding and making it accessible to diverse students. The initiative's success lies in engaging students across age groups and backgrounds (Code.org, n.d.).

Catering to a Variety of Learning Styles

Recognizing that each student has preferences and strengths, computational thinking tools cater to various learning styles. Platforms like Blockly benefit visual learners, where visual elements can be dragged and dropped to create code. Kinesthetic learners thrive in hands-on coding activities, whereas auditory learners can engage with online tutorials and instructional videos (Google, n.d.; Edpuzzle, 2021).

The adaptability of computational thinking tools enables educators to differentiate instruction and personalize learning experiences for each student. This versatility is especially significant in inclusive classrooms where students may have varied learning styles and abilities.

Challenges and Considerations

While computational thinking tools offer numerous benefits, instructors must navigate challenges to maximize their effectiveness. Critical considerations include access to technology, teacher training, and equitable participation. Efforts to bridge the digital divide and provide equal opportunities to all students must be prioritized to prevent the exacerbation of educational disparities (Selwyn, 2016).

In conclusion, integrating computational thinking tools has transformed educational practices by enhancing student engagement, fostering creativity, and improving learning outcomes. Real-world case studies illustrate the impact of these tools in diverse settings, from elementary schools to higher education institutions. Effective pedagogical tools that not only teach computational concepts but also cultivate essential skills for the workforce of the 21st century include interactive elements, gamification strategies, and hands-on activities.

Addressing the diverse needs of learners through computational thinking tools has proven to be transformative in educational settings, revolutionizing student engagement, fostering creativity, and enhancing overall learning outcomes. This section explores the interactive features, gamification strategies, and hands-on activities embedded in these tools that deepen students' comprehension of computational concepts. The discussion revolves around the transformative potential of these tools in various educational contexts.

Learning with Interactive Elements

Computational thinking tools introduce interactive elements that resonate with the digital-native generation, capturing their attention and genuinely engaging learning. Platforms like Scratch enable students to create interactive stories, games, and animations, transforming passive learners into active creators (Resnick et al., 2009). This interactivity enhances understanding and instils pride and ownership, making the learning experience more meaningful.

In higher education, interactive simulations powered by computational thinking tools have been implemented to teach complex concepts. For example, physics courses leverage PhET Interactive Simulations to allow students to experiment with virtual environments, providing an intuitive and interactive way to grasp intricate scientific principles (PhET et al.).

Gamification Strategies

Gamification, integrating game elements into non-game settings, is a robust strategy used by computational thinking tools to enhance student engagement. Platforms like Code.org and Blockly employ gamified challenges and puzzles to teach coding concepts. Gamification transforms learning into a more enjoyable experience and introduces elements of competition and achievement, motivating students to persevere in problem-solving (Partovi, 2014).

An example of gamification in education is the Hour of Code initiative, which utilizes gamified coding tutorials to introduce programming to students of all ages. This global movement has successfully engaged millions of students in coding activities, breaking down barriers and demystifying the perception that coding is only for computer science experts (Code.org, n.d.).

Hands-On Activities and Project-Based Learning

Computational thinking tools facilitate hands-on activities and project-based learning, providing students with tangible experiences that extend their understanding of abstract concepts. In primary and secondary education, platforms like Scratch and TinkerCAD empower students to create and explore, turning theoretical knowledge into practical application (Autodesk, 2021; Resnick et al., 2009).

At the higher education level, project-based learning is widely adopted. Computational thinking tools, for instance, are used by students taking courses in engineering and computer science. This hands-on approach develops theoretical concepts and enhances problem-solving skills, preparing students for the dynamic demands of the workforce.

Case Studies and Examples

Scratch in Primary Education

Scratch has been utilised in an elementary school setting to enhance student engagement and learning. Students collaborated on creating interactive stories that incorporated coding elements. This project-based approach introduced computational thinking concepts and developed storytelling skills and collaboration (Resnick et al., 2009).

Code.org in Secondary Education

The gamified coding tutorials provided by Code.org have been successfully integrated into secondary education. A case study showcases how these tutorials were used in a high school computer science course, transforming coding from a theoretical concept into an engaging challenge. Students progressed through levels, earning badges and fostering a sense of accomplishment (Partovi, 2014).

PhET Interactive Simulations in Higher Education

The PhET Interactive Simulations platform has been instrumental in teaching physics concepts in higher education. Students engage in interactive simulations, manipulating variables and observing outcomes. According to PhET Interactive Simulations (n.d.), this method provides a virtual laboratory experience and enhances understanding abstract principles.

Hour of Code Global Initiative

The Hour of Code initiative represents a global example of gamification in action. Students worldwide participate in coding tutorials designed as games, demystifying coding and making it accessible to diverse students. The initiative's success lies in engaging students across age groups and backgrounds (Code.org, n.d.).

Catering to a Variety of Learning Styles

Recognizing that each student has preferences and strengths, computational thinking tools cater to various learning styles. Platforms like Blockly benefit visual learners, where visual elements can be dragged and dropped to create code. Kinesthetic learners thrive in hands-on coding activities, whereas auditory learners can engage with online tutorials and instructional videos (Google, n.d.; Edpuzzle, 2021).

The adaptability of computational thinking tools enables educators to differentiate instruction and personalize learning experiences for each student. This versatility is especially significant in inclusive classrooms where students may have varied learning styles and abilities.

Challenges and Considerations

While computational thinking tools offer numerous benefits, instructors must navigate challenges to maximize their effectiveness. Critical considerations include access to technology, teacher training, and equitable participation. Efforts to bridge the digital divide and provide equal opportunities to all students must be prioritized to prevent the exacerbation of educational disparities (Selwyn, 2016).

In conclusion, integrating computational thinking tools has transformed educational practices by enhancing student engagement, fostering creativity, and improving learning outcomes. Real-world case studies illustrate the impact of these tools in diverse settings, from elementary schools to higher education institutions. Effective pedagogical tools that not only teach computational concepts but also cultivate essential skills for the workforce of the 21st century include interactive elements, gamification strategies, and hands-on activities.

FUTURE TRENDS AND INNOVATIONS

This section presents a forward-looking perspective on emerging trends and potential future developments in computational thinking platforms and tools. As innovation continues to advance, the educational landscape is expected to undergo transformative changes, with additional opportunities arising from technologies such as artificial intelligence (AI), augmented reality (AR), and virtual reality (VR). The speculative discussions in this segment aim to explore how these advancements could further enhance computational thinking education, preparing students for the evolving demands of the 21st century.

Artificial Intelligence in Computational Reasoning

Artificial intelligence is poised to play a crucial role in the evolution of computational thinking education. Integrating AI technologies into computational thinking tools can enable personalised learning experiences. Adaptive learning platforms driven by AI algorithms can analyse individual student performance, identify strengths and weaknesses, and tailor educational content accordingly (Baker, 2010). For instance, an AI-driven coding tutor could dynamically adjust the difficulty of coding challenges based on the student's proficiency level, ensuring an optimal learning path.

Moreover, AI algorithms can provide real-time feedback and suggestions, guiding students through problem-solving processes. Natural language processing capabilities can enhance interactions with programming interfaces, allowing students to express coding intentions in natural language, with AI translating these into executable code (Alur et al., 2010). These advancements can make computational thinking education more accessible and adaptable, catering to diverse learning styles and abilities.

Augmented Reality (AR) Enhancements

Incorporating augmented reality (AR) into computational thinking tools can potentially transform students' engagement with coding concepts. By overlaying digital information in the real world, AR results in immersive and interactive learning experiences. In computational thinking, AR could empower students to visualise and manipulate code elements in real-time, fostering a deeper understanding of programming logic (Klopfer et al., 2009).

For example, AR applications could let students see virtual code snippets floating in their physical environment, interact with them using gestures, and observe the real-time execution of code changes. This hands-on and spatial approach to coding could enhance experiential learning for those who benefit from physical engagement with learning materials. AR could also facilitate collaborative coding projects, with students working in shared augmented spaces, promoting teamwork and peer learning.

Virtual Reality (VR) Immersive Experiences

Virtual reality (VR) has the potential to offer immersive and experiential learning environments for computational thinking education. VR platforms can simulate virtual coding labs, allowing students to explore complex algorithms, debug code, and experiment with programming concepts in a three-dimensional space. This immersive approach could enhance engagement and provide an intuitive understanding of abstract coding principles (Yu et al., 2018).

In a VR coding environment, students could virtually step into the execution flow of their code, visualising the data pathways and interactions between different program components. This spatial representation could broaden comprehension and provide a holistic view of how algorithms unfold. VR simulations could also mimic real-world applications, enabling students to apply computational thinking skills to practical scenarios, such as designing virtual models or solving coding challenges within a simulated environment.

Evolution of Gamification

While gamification has been an integral part of computational thinking tools, future trends may involve a more sophisticated and adaptive gamification approach. According to Hamari et al., AI-driven gamification could dynamically adjust the difficulty of challenges, tailor game elements to individual learning styles, and provide targeted feedback to enhance the learning experience (2014). For instance, a gamified coding platform could adapt its storyline, characters, and challenges to align with each student's unique preferences and progress.

Moreover, integrating blockchain technology could introduce decentralised gaming environments where students earn digital badges, tokens, or other rewards for completing coding tasks. This could create a gamified credentialing system, recognising and validating students' computational thinking achievements. Such developments could propel students through a more immersive and personalised gaming experience, promoting sustained engagement with coding activities.

Integration Across Disciplinary Lines

Future trends in computational thinking education may involve a deeper integration of coding principles across various academic disciplines. Computational thinking has the potential to become a foundational skill applicable to a wide range of fields as traditional boundaries blur. Tools that facilitate cross-disciplinary integration, such as coding platforms tailored for specific subjects, may emerge to enhance opportunities for application (Kafai et al., 2014).

Students could apply coding concepts in the context of real-world challenges in science, art, or language arts if computational thinking tools seamlessly integrate with these subjects' curricula. A science class might incorporate coding simulations for data analysis, an art class could explore creative coding for digital art projects and a language arts class could integrate coding for storytelling or creating interactive narratives. This cross-disciplinary approach aims to prepare students for a future where computational thinking is a crucial problem-solving skill across diverse professions.

Ethical Considerations and Inclusive Design

Ethical considerations and inclusive design are likely to be emphasised in future trends of computational thinking education. As these tools become more deeply embedded in educational practices, addressing ethical implications and ensuring inclusivity will be crucial. Teachers and developers may focus on designing culturally sensitive tools, avoiding reinforcing stereotypes, and promoting equitable access (Kanfer et al., 2019).

Additionally, discussions around the ethical use of artificial intelligence in educational settings will become more prominent. Ensuring algorithm transparency, safeguarding student privacy, and avoiding algorithmic bias will be essential. Tools that explicitly teach students the ethical considerations of technology, including the social impact of algorithms, data privacy, and responsible coding practices, may become essential components of computational thinking education.

Anticipated trends and developments in computational thinking tools promise to transform education by leveraging emerging technologies such as artificial intelligence, augmented reality, and virtual reality. These changes aim to make learning more adaptable, immersive, and inclusive, catering to diverse learning styles and preparing students for the growing demands of the 21st century. While these speculative discussions provide a glimpse into potential developments, approaching these innovations carefully, considering ethical implications, and a commitment to fostering an inclusive educational environment is essential.

Researching the Ramifications of Emerging Technologies on the Future of Education and Computational Thinking Pedagogy

The integration of emerging technologies, such as artificial intelligence (AI), augmented reality (AR), and virtual reality (VR), into computational thinking tools not only transforms educational practices but also has significant implications for the future of education. This section delves into the potential ramifications of these technologies, considering how they could shape the pedagogy of computational thinking. Stakeholders, including educators and policymakers, can gain insights into the evolving teaching and learning landscape by examining the advantages and challenges posed by these advancements.

Personalised and Adaptive Learning Opportunities

Incorporating artificial intelligence (AI) into computational thinking tools opens the door to highly personalised and adaptive learning opportunities. AI algorithms can analyse individual student data, track learning patterns, and deliver tailored content to address specific strengths and weaknesses. For instance, a coding platform powered by AI could dynamically adjust the difficulty of coding challenges based on a student's progress, ensuring an individualised learning path (Baker, 2010).

This personalised approach aligns with the principles of differentiated instruction, catering to diverse learning styles and abilities. As students engage with computational thinking tasks, AI-driven tools can offer real-time feedback, suggest relevant resources, and adaptively guide them through the learning journey. The pedagogical implications include a shift toward more student-driven and flexible learning opportunities, fostering independence and mastery.

Immersive and Experiential Learning Environments

Integrating augmented reality (AR) and virtual reality (VR) into computational thinking pedagogy holds the potential for immersive and experiential learning environments. AR overlays digital information onto the physical world, allowing students to interact with virtual coding elements in real-world settings. Conversely, VR provides fully immersive simulated environments where students can use three-dimensional coding scenarios (Klopfer et al., 2009).

Consider a scenario where students with AR glasses explore a park where virtual code snippets are scattered throughout. By interacting with these snippets, students can collaboratively solve coding challenges in a real-world setting. Students might find themselves in a virtual coding lab in virtual reality, where they can interact with code elements visually and spatially. A shift toward more hands-on, contextualised, and memorable learning experiences that foster a deeper comprehension of computational concepts are among the pedagogical implications.

Gamification and Incentive-Based Learning

The evolution of computational thinking tools towards gamification, supported by AI-driven adaptive features, introduces incentive-based learning strategies. Gamified elements like badges, rewards, and progress tracking may motivate students to participate actively in coding challenges. AI algorithms can personalise gamification elements, adjusting the difficulty of challenges and rewards based on individual learning trajectories (Hamari et al., 2014).

For example, a coding game could progressively introduce new levels and challenges tailored to a student's coding proficiency. As students progress, they earn virtual badges and rewards, creating a sense of accomplishment and fostering a growth mindset. Academically, this gamified approach aligns with motivational theories, emphasising the importance of intrinsic and extrinsic motivations in promoting sustained engagement and skill development.

Cross-Disciplinary Integration and Project-Based Learning

The implications of emerging technologies extend beyond the boundaries of computer science education, encouraging cross-disciplinary integration. Students can apply coding concepts in various settings by using computational thinking tools that seamlessly integrate with other academic subjects. Data analysis in a science class might be done with coding simulations, while creative storytelling projects in a language arts class might use coding (Kafai et al., 2014).

This cross-disciplinary integration aligns with the educational shift towards project-based learning. Students engage in hands-on, collaborative projects that require the application of computational thinking skills to solve real-world problems. The pedagogical implications include a shift towards a more holistic, interconnected, and practical approach to teaching and learning, preparing students for the interdisciplinary demands of the future workforce.

Education in Inclusive Design and Ethical Issues

As computational thinking tools advance, ethical considerations and inclusive design education are becoming increasingly important. AI algorithms used in educational settings must be transparent and bias-free and safeguard student privacy. The academic implications include integrating ethical discussions within computational thinking curricula, emphasising responsible coding practices, algorithmic bias awareness, and technology's societal impact (Kanfer et al., 2019).

Consider a scenario where students explore the ethical implications of AI decision-making within a coding context. They could discuss the importance of fairness, accountability, and transparency in algorithmic systems. Including ethical considerations in pedagogy promotes a deeper understanding of the societal implications of technology. It equips students with a responsible mindset as future creators and users of computational tools.

Teacher Professional Development and Technological Literacy

Integrating emerging technologies into computational thinking pedagogy necessitates ongoing teacher professional development to ensure that educators can effectively utilise these tools. Educators must cultivate technological literacy, understand how to incorporate these tools and guide students in their ethical and responsible use (Towers et al., 2012).

Workshops, online courses, and collaborative communities where educators can share best practices and learn from one another are examples of professional development programs. The pedagogical repercussions include a shift toward a more dynamic and ever-evolving teaching model, with educators taking on the role of facilitators and mentors in a technologically enhanced learning environment.

The implications of emerging technologies for the future of education and computational thinking pedagogy are multi-faceted. AI-driven personalised learning experiences, immersive environments facilitated by AR and VR, gamification strategies, cross-disciplinary integration, ethical considerations, and teacher professional development are significantly shaping the educational landscape. As these advancements continue to evolve, educators, policymakers, and stakeholders must collaboratively navigate the valuable opportunities and challenges to ensure that computational thinking education remains relevant and inclusive and prepares students for the complexities of the digital era.

CONCLUSION

In conclusion, the trajectory of contemporary education is intricately intertwined with the inevitable influence of computational thinking tools and platforms. This section has comprehensively explored these tools, spanning from their diverse functionalities to potential future developments. As the educational landscape continues to evolve, the section underscores the pivotal role of computational thinking in STEM and non-STEM subjects, asserting its status as a fundamental skill essential for students in the 21st century.

The evolution of computational thinking tools has been elucidated, emphasizing the dynamic interplay between education and technology. The educational journey has become increasingly enriched, from the fundamental concepts imparted by platforms like Scratch to the immersive experiences introduced by augmented reality and virtual reality. The integration of artificial intelligence has ushered in a new era of personalized learning, adapting to individual student needs and promoting a more tailored educational experience.

As key figures in this transformative process, educators are encouraged to adopt a proactive stance towards technological advancements. Staying abreast of the latest tools and platforms is not merely a professional requirement but a necessity for fostering an environment of innovation and relevance in the classroom. The examples throughout the section demonstrate how these tools can be seamlessly integrated into various educational settings, catering to a spectrum of evolving needs and preferences.

A central tenet is that educational methodologies should perpetually evolve. The digital landscape constantly changes, and educational paradigms must adapt to address the challenges and opportunities presented. This adaptability is exemplified by the shift toward personalized and adaptive learning experiences made possible by AI. Teachers are urged to explore innovative pedagogical approaches, embracing the gamified elements, immersive environments, and cross-disciplinary integration that computational thinking tools offer.

Furthermore, the section advocates for an ethical and inclusive approach to integrating emerging technologies. As computational thinking tools become more sophisticated, the responsibility to instil ethical considerations becomes paramount.

The inclusive design of these tools ensures accessibility for all students, regardless of their learning styles or abilities. Real-world case studies and examples have been presented to illustrate the positive impact of these tools across various educational settings, from elementary schools to higher education institutions.

In the broader context, the conclusion emphasizes the crucial role of computational thinking as a primary and essential skill for students. Coding is not the sole application of computational thinking; it encompasses problem-solving, critical thinking, and creativity. As the demands of the future workforce continue to evolve, students equipped with computational thinking skills are better prepared to navigate the complexities of a rapidly changing world.

In this spirit, the section concludes with an invigorating call for educational institutions, policymakers, and educators to collaborate in establishing an environment that nurtures computational thinking. Professional development opportunities, interdisciplinary collaboration, and a commitment to ethical considerations are integral components of this collaborative effort. By fostering an atmosphere where computational thinking is not just a subject but an ingrained mindset, education can truly prepare students for the demands of the digital age.

REFERENCES

Alur, R., Bodik, R., Juniwal, G., Martin, M. M. K., Raghothaman, A., Seshia, S. A., & Udupa, A. (2010). Syntax-guided synthesis. In *Proceedings of the 37th annual ACM SIGPLAN-SIGACT symposium on principles of programming languages* (pp. 637–650).

Angevine, C., Cator, K., Roschelle, J., Thomas, S. A., Waite, C., & Weisgrau, J. (2017). *Computational thinking for a computational world.*

Ausiku, M., & Matthee, M. (2021). Preparing primary school teachers for teaching computational thinking: A systematic review. In *Learning Technologies and Systems: 19th International Conference on Web-Based Learning, ICWL 2020, and 5th International Symposium on Emerging Technologies for Education, SETE 2020, Ningbo, China, October 22–24, 2020* [Springer International Publishing.]. *Proceedings*, 5, 202–213.

Autodesk. (2021). *TinkerCAD*. https://www.tinkercad.com/

Cansu, F. K., & Cansu, S. K. (2019). An overview of computational thinking. *International Journal of Computer Science Education in Schools*, 3(1), 17–30. DOI: 10.21585/ijcses.v3i1.53

Dagienė, V., Jevsikova, T., Stupurienė, G., & Juškevičienė, A. (2022). Teaching computational thinking in primary schools: Worldwide trends and teachers' attitudes. *Computer Science and Information Systems*, 19(1), 1–24. DOI: 10.2298/CSIS201215033D

Edpuzzle. (2021). *Edpuzzle*. https://edpuzzle.com/

Google. (n.d.). *Blockly*. https://developers.google.com/blockly

Grover, S., & Pea, R. (2013). Computational thinking in K–12: A review of the state of the field. *Educational Researcher*, 42(1), 38–43. DOI: 10.3102/0013189X12463051

Guenaga, M., Mentxaka, I., Garaizar, P., Eguiluz, A., Villagrasa, S., & Navarro, I. (2017). Make world, a collaborative platform to develop computational thinking and STEAM. In *Learning and Collaboration Technologies. Technology in Education: 4th International Conference, LCT 2017, Held as Part of HCI International 2017, Vancouver, BC, Canada, July 9-14, 2017* [Springer International Publishing.]. *Proceedings*, 4(Part II), 50–59.

Hamari, J., Koivisto, J., & Sarsa, H. (2014). Does gamification work?-A literature review of empirical studies on gamification. In *2014, the 47th Hawaii International Conference on System Sciences* (pp. 3025-3034). IEEE.

Hsu, T. C., Chang, S. C., & Hung, Y. T. (2018). How to learn and how to teach computational thinking: Suggestions based on a review of the literature. *Computers & Education*, 126, 296–310. DOI: 10.1016/j.compedu.2018.07.004

Kafai, Y. B., Burke, Q., Chen, J., Fields, D., Nelson, B., & Robinson, K. (2014). Connecting the dots: Developing STEAM literacies through creative collaboration. *Teachers College Record*, 116(6), n6.

Kahoot! (2020). *Kahoot!*https://kahoot.com/

Kalogiannakis, M., & Papadakis, S. (Eds.). (2020). *Handbook of research on tools for teaching computational thinking in P-12 education*. IGI Global. DOI: 10.4018/978-1-7998-4576-8

Kanfer, A., Schechter, A., Veeraraghavan, K., & Zou, J. (2019). Inclusive design in the creation of computer science education tools. In *Proceedings of the 2019 CHI Conference on Human Factors in Computing Systems* (pp. 1-13).

Klopfer, E., Squire, K., & Jenkins, H. (2009). Environmental Detectives—The development of an augmented reality platform for environmental simulations. *Educational Technology Research and Development*, 57(6), 1–22.

Lockwood, J., & Mooney, A. (2017). Computational thinking in education: Where does it fit? A systematic literary review. *arXiv preprint arXiv:1703.07659.*

Mannila, L., Dagiene, V., Demo, B., Grgurina, N., Mirolo, C., Rolandsson, L., & Settle, A. (2014, June). Computational thinking in K-9 education. In *Proceedings of the working group reports of the 2014 on innovation & technology in computer science education conference* (pp. 1-29). DOI: 10.1145/2713609.2713610

Microsoft. (n.d.). *Microsoft MakeCode*. https://www.microsoft.com/en-us/makecode

Oyelere, S. S., Agbo, F. J., & Sanusi, I. T. (2022, August). Developing a pedagogical evaluation framework for computational thinking supporting technologies and tools. [). Frontiers.]. *Frontiers in Education*, 7, 957739. DOI: 10.3389/feduc.2022.957739

Partovi, H. (2014). *Code.org*. https://code.org/

Resnick, M., Maloney, J., Monroy-Hernández, A., Rusk, N., Eastmond, E., Brennan, K., Millner, A., Rosenbaum, E., Silver, J., Silverman, B., & Kafai, Y. (2009). Scratch: Programming for all. *Communications of the ACM*, 52(11), 60–67. DOI: 10.1145/1592761.1592779

Rich, P. J., Bartholomew, S., Daniel, D., Dinsmoor, K., Nielsen, M., Reynolds, C., & Yauney, J. (2022). Trends in tools used to teach computational thinking through elementary coding. *Journal of Research on Technology in Education*, •••, 1–22.

Rijo-García, S., Segredo, E., & León, C. (2022). Computational thinking and user interfaces: A systematic review. *IEEE Transactions on Education*, 65(4), 647–656. DOI: 10.1109/TE.2022.3159765

Schwartz, L., Maquil, V., Johannsen, L., Moll, C., & Hermen, J. (2023). Teaching computational thinking with a tangible development platform: An exploratory field study at school with Kniwwelino. *Education and Information Technologies*, •••, 1–33.

Spires, H. A., Hervey, L. S., Morris, G. K., & Stelpflug, C. (2012). Energizing project-based inquiry in computational thinking: The development of an online professional development community. *Journal of Science Education and Technology*, 21(1), 15–25. DOI: 10.1007/s10956-011-9290-4

Su, J., & Yang, W. (2023). A systematic review of integrating computational thinking in early childhood education. *Computers and Education Open*, 4, 100122. DOI: 10.1016/j.caeo.2023.100122

Tang, X., Yin, Y., Lin, Q., Hadad, R., & Zhai, X. (2020). Assessing computational thinking: A systematic review of empirical studies. *Computers & Education*, 148, 103798. DOI: 10.1016/j.compedu.2019.103798

Yu, F. Y., Lin, Y. C., & Luo, S. Y. (2018). A study on learning motivation and effectiveness using multimedia materials for virtual reality. *Journal of Educational Technology & Society*, 21(1), 220–231.

ADDITIONAL READING

Tariq, M. U. & Sergio, R. P. (2025). Innovative Assessment Techniques in Physical Education: Exploring Technology-Enhanced and Student-Centered Models for Holistic Student Development. In M. Garcia (Ed.), *Global Innovations in Physical Education and Health* (pp. 85-112). IGI Global. https://doi.org/10.4018/979-8-3693-3952-7.ch004

Tariq, M. U. (2025). Leveraging Diversity and Inclusion for Enhanced Team Outcomes in Higher Education. In T. Burris-Melville & S. Burris (Eds.), *Developing Effective and High-Performing Teams in Higher Education* (pp. 479-512). IGI Global. https://doi.org/10.4018/979-8-3693-3852-0.ch017

Tariq, M. U. (2024). Navigating the Personalization Pathway: Implementing Adaptive Learning Technologies in Higher Education. In T. Minh Tung (Ed.), *Adaptive Learning Technologies for Higher Education* (pp. 265-291). IGI Global. https://doi.org/10.4018/979-8-3693-3641-0.ch012

Chapter 2
Role of Hybrid Entrepreneurship in the Gig Economy

Sandeep Kumar Singh
https://orcid.org/0000-0002-1741-7254
O.P. Jindal Global University, India

Parth Sharma
https://orcid.org/0000-0002-1955-9408
University of Petroleum and Energy Studies, India

Rohit
https://orcid.org/0009-0004-1796-5252
Gulf Medical University, Ajman, UAE

ABSTRACT

Hybrid entrepreneurship, where individuals balance full-time employment with entrepreneurial ventures, is reshaping the gig economy. This evolving model provides significant benefits, including increased flexibility, diversified income sources, and enhanced innovation. However, it also presents challenges, such as the need for updated labor laws, tax regulations, and adequate support structures. As technology advances and the nature of work changes, hybrid entrepreneurs will play a crucial role in driving economic growth and fostering new business opportunities. Addressing the regulatory and support needs of this growing workforce segment will be essential for maximizing the benefits of hybrid entrepreneurship and ensuring a balanced and resilient labor market.

DOI: 10.4018/979-8-3693-9486-1.ch002

INTRODUCTION

The world of work is undergoing severe changes. Some are due to technology, others due to changing values, and others still due to economic reformatting. One of these is that the gig economy has arisen, with its characteristic short-term contracts, freelance, and temporary work arrangements. This labour market gave birth to a new generation of entrepreneurs: borderline employment and its generation of businesses. This is termed hybrid entrepreneurship; that is, conducting full-time employment while being an entrepreneur on the side (Demir, Werner, Kraus, & Jones, 2020).

The prominence of hybrid entrepreneurship comes with the increase in the number of individuals who aim to have diversified sources of income, follow their passion, and build businesses without assuming full-time financial risks. This is why the Gig Economy, with its broad opportunities, will provide the best environment in which hybrid entrepreneurs could look into experimenting with new ideas, validating business models, and easing gradually from self-employment into employment if they so wish.

The chapter discusses the complex interplay of hybrid entrepreneurship with the gig economy. It identifies more closely the means through which flexibility in gig working allows the individual to supplement his or her primary employment, what motivates one to indulge in hybrid entrepreneurship, and what effect this has on the traditional models of employment. This chapter draws from real-life examples and cases to bring out opportunities and challenges that are met by hybrid entrepreneurs in the gig economy. It thus provides an insight into how this unique way of doing work lays out the future of entrepreneurship.

UNDERSTANDING HYBRID ENTREPRENEURSHIP

Hybrid entrepreneurship is a peculiar form of business ownership in which people hold full-time employment and at the same time work towards pursuing entrepreneurial venture part-time. Since these would-be entrepreneurs are in essence dual activity individuals, this type of entrepreneurship let them explore business opportunities while retaining their investment in security and accoutrements that accompany the conventional form of employment thoroughly (Bröckling,2015). A full-time holding of such first job lowers the risk associated with establishing a new business, including the strain of uncertain income and financial instability.

What Does it Mean?

Hybrid entrepreneurship refers to the process of owning one's business and, at the same time, being provisionally employed. It all stands in contrast to full-time entrepreneurship, in which people throw their full energy and resources into business projects and typically forgo a regular salary, too (Xi, Block, Lasch, Robert, & Thurik, 2017). Mode of entry into hybrid entrepreneurship: New venture start-up versus business takeover. The hybrid model, in such a case, offers an easier landing when somebody wants to come to entrepreneurship to test the waters before taking the plunge.

Among other essential characteristics, a hybrid entrepreneur involves: managing time, aversion to risk, and incremental growth. Hybrid entrepreneurs generally manage their time very well, working in a job while building their side business. This involves much juggling, requiring both planning and discipline in setting priorities. This is because hybrid entrepreneurs are never as risk-friendly as their full-time entrepreneur counterparts since they rely less on their business for money, thus giving them the privilege to make well-thought-out decisions. Lastly, the growth of the hybrid business is often incremental, with the entrepreneur gradually growing operations so they have time to become confident and experienced.

While both hybrid and full-time entrepreneurs will always work towards building a successful business base, the approach and many a time experiences happen to be very different. Full-time entrepreneurs devote all of their time, all their energy, and even all their resources to running and growing their business. This approach in most cases involves higher levels of risk and pressure, as the success of the business reflects back and determines the financial status of the entrepreneur.

On the other hand, hybrid entrepreneurs are lucky because they have some kind of security with a regular income. This reduces the pressure on them to go all out and be successful come what may. They can experiment with a number of different business ideas, take calculated risks, and learn from their mistakes without the fear of failure looming over them. However, the trade-off between the two indicates that while hybrid entrepreneurs might have a unique sense of time, s/he may not dedicate the same flavor of time and attention to the business as full-time entrepreneurs.

Motivations for Hybrid Entrepreneurship

Several factors motivate individuals to pursue hybrid entrepreneurship. For most people, the major reason is financial security (Tornikoski, Viljamaa & Varamäki, 2015). Keeping a stable income, having the business on the side, provides a kind of safety net that reduces personal and financial risks that pertain to entrepreneurship.

With this security, one can take the time to develop his businesses, hence ensuring they will be sustainable before moving possibly to full-time entrepreneurship.

Another major motivation is the urge for personal fulfilment (**Afshan, Shahid & Tunio, 2021**). Many hybrid entrepreneurs are therefore motivated through passion or an interest that is not fully satisfied from his day occupation. Through starting a side business, they are able to explore interests, creative pursuits, and some sense of fulfilment that is lacking in their regular employment. Thus, hybrid entrepreneurship can offer a clear route for attaining other long-term goals of the entrepreneur: financial independence and career diversification, or even a transition to full-time entrepreneurship.

More importantly, the gig economy powerfully motivates hybrid entrepreneurs as it provides flexibility, access, and low entry barriers to gig work in starting an entrepreneurial journey while working full-time. Broadly speaking, gig work could provide the probability to test business ideas, building networks, and gaining experience required for entrepreneurial success.

In other words, hybrid entrepreneurship is a more plausible and flexible solution to business ownership; a solution that lets people pursue entrepreneurial activity without losing protection from traditional employers (Tunio, Chaudhry, Shaikh, Jariko, & Brahmi,2021). This lowers risks that are attached to the act of entrepreneurship and at the same time increases personal and professional development, and therefore, this kind of employment will be considered most attractive in modern labour markets.

THE EMERGENCE OF THE GIG ECONOMY

The gig economy has evolved at breakneck speed, characterized by an increasing trend of flexibility and more opportunities for individuals with short-term, freelance, or contract employment. Brought by the influence of mainly technological advances, changes in the demographic structure of the workforce, and fluctuating economic conditions, the shift in the world of work from permanent to a more fluid, project-based labor market is reshaping comprehensively its frontline (PARILLA, & LIU, 2021). Appreciating the dynamics of the gig economy helps the critical underpinning that will provide a better understanding of the emergent space in hybrid entrepreneurship.

Background and Development

The idea of gig work is not new at all. It is said that many forms of short-term, on-call, freelance jobs have been seen in the past—such as in the entertainment, construction, and even the agriculture industry. But the gig economy, as we know it today, began in the late 20th and early 21st centuries thanks to the spurts in the internet and digital platforms that made connecting employees to jobs much more easy.

In the early 2000s, platforms like Elance, oDesk, and later, Upwork, Freelancer, and TaskRabbit had gained attention (Mizrahi, 2018), which enabled people to locate and perform freelance work from any point on the planet. In fact, these platforms were the first real things that could be thought of—much less a first thing—for which technology played an important role in effectively matching supply with demand in the labor market toward a new era. Gradually, as the internet and digital tools started becoming an increasingly accessible medium, this 'gig economy' began to transcend from freelance-type work in such areas as ride- and food-sharing, through professional consulting services and ending up at a creative workshop.

The global financial crisis in 2008 further fueled the rise of the gig economy. People flocked to gig work to make ends meet in an uncertain world, as traditional job markets were vanishing. Economic necessity aside, this period saw a cultural shift toward flexibility and autonomy over the security of full-time employment. This mix of economic necessity and new attitudes about work—the desire to value flexibility and autonomy over security in full-time work—on top of existing efforts to develop piecework into a working chaotic world, created a mix that was ripe for the gig economy.

Key Drivers in the Growth of the Gig Economy

Explosive growth in the gig economy, indeed last year, was driven majorly by:

1. Technological Advancements: The current explosion in smartphones, mobile applications, and the digitization of services is catalyzing the process of personal resource location and gig work transaction (Banik, & Padalkar,2021). The sources of these kinds of platforms derive from Uber, Airbnb, and Fiverr, which transformed their industries and enabled workers to connect directly with consumers. It became much easier in searching and performing gig work, with ease and lesser barriers to entry due to these kinds of technology, potentially bringing many more people into gigging, even from places located far from commercial centers.
2. Changing Workforce Demographics: The flexible need associated with the lifestyle of people has been making the workforce more flexible and diversified, with most of them applying for more work arrangements that better suit their people's lifestyles (Chappa, Varghese,& Chandler, 2017). Most Millennials and the Gen Z workforce pay a lot of attention to autonomy, work-life balance, and flexibility in engaging in a variety of interests. The

gig economy fits their preference, assuring a high level of flexibility that can suit individual needs.

3. Economic Conditions: The uncertainty of economic conditions and the erosion of traditional job security have also galvanized the gig economy. Many workers have found that it is a way to earn their subsistence in a world struck by economic difficulties, or as the main source of work itself, especially during any period post an economic downturn. The gig economy has opened up a relatively buoyant space for workers in pivoting fast and taking up developing opportunities.
4. Employer Demand for Flexibility: Firms are pressing for more elasticity in their labor force so they can respond more effectively to the changing marketplace and reduce their costs (Allon, Cohen, & Sinchaisri, 2023). Gig work is helping to provide those companies with a just-in-time labor supply to scale up or down as necessary. As companies sprint toward more elastic types of employment, the number of industries in which gig workers are in demand continues to rise.

The Gig Economy Supported by the Rise of Digital Platforms

At the core of the growing gig economy were digital platforms that served to mediate labor and consumers. These platforms enabled not only matching but also several unique business models that were emerging for the first time within the gig economy.

For example, ride-sharing platforms such as Uber and Lyft have revolutionized the transportation industry by allowing customers to earn money by driving passengers when they prefer and on their terms (Zwick, 2018). Likewise, platforms like Airbnb have disrupted the hospitality industry by enabling homeowners to rent out their properties to travelers. These kinds of platforms democratize access to opportunities that create income, which means that people can now monetize their assets and skills.

Most importantly, freelance work has now grown exponentially due to the development of websites like Upwork, Freelancer, and Fiverr. Freelancing sites encompass nearly every professional niche, from graphic designing and writing to programming and consultation. Freelancers can provide services across borders, which often yield very competitive pricing and greater discretion on whether to offer services that are of interest and fall within the skill set of the freelancer.

The growth in digital platforms has also ushered in new challenges related to issues of worker rights, job security, and income equality. With additional massification of the gig economy, many of these issues will require ethical concerns to safeguard rights and security measures for all participants so that they can access the benefits that characterize gig work.

In other words, the gig economy that has evolved from this wildcat segment of the labor market has become part of its mainstream force in reshaping working and living. In fact, gig economies are blossoming, and this has further been facilitated under the canopy of technological progress, changing workforce demographics, and economic conditions. With the rapid innovation and expansion of digital platforms, it is more likely that the gig economy will play a great role in the global economy within its coming years, offering a good number of opportunities and challenges for businesses and workers. Hybrid entrepreneurs can test some form of a business idea, develop streams of income, and eventually turn to full-time entrepreneurship using the gig economy to hybridize. This section explains the functioning of hybrid entrepreneurship within the gig economy, the kind of gig work that hybridizes, and some successful examples of hybrid entrepreneurs who have surged in the gig economy.

Hybrid Entrepreneurship: Strategy in Gig Economy

This makes the gig economy an ideal platform for hybrid entrepreneurship, where one can engage in business part-time yet not totally lose the employment revenue. Many people view hybrid entrepreneurship as a strategic way through which they can undertake entrepreneurship activities without moving out of their career. This involves low barriers to entry and flexible working hours, with a variety of opportunities to help one build business gradually.

Many use gig work as a testing ground for one's ideas. For instance, an individual who has a passion for photography might freelance as a photographer on Upwork or Fiverr while working a 9-to-5 job (Sinicki, Sinicki, & Ramachandran,2019). This way, they will get to learn about market demand, the necessity for skills, and build their clientele without financial pressure. If the sideline business gains traction, it is then up to the entrepreneur to decide if scaling up and eventually transitioning it to the main occupation is what he wants.

This strategic use of Gig also places them in a position to practice and learn entrepreneurial skills such as marketing, customer service, and financial management while still enjoying the security of conventional employment. With time, they can build an adequate business foundation, minimizing the potential risks that come with plunging fully into entrepreneurship.

Types of Gig Work Suited for Hybrid Entrepreneurs

Not all gig work is created equal for hybrid entrepreneurship; some types of gig opportunities are just better-suited to balancing with another full-time job. In reality, especially those with flexible time, remote jobs, and smiling capital, some of these gig works help in the ideal hybrid entrepreneurship, as illustrated below:

1. Freelancing: Freelance writing, graphic designing, web developing, and consultancy are all easily combined with hybrid entrepreneurship. All of these gigs are normally to facilitate flexible scheduling and can thus be done from home or any other place with an internet connection (De La Vega, 2020). Freelancers can take as much or as less load as their available time permits and thus make balancing it with a full-time job easier.
2. E-commerce: This is one of the most popular ways for hybrid entrepreneurs. Selling goods through an online store is done through, for example, Etsy, eBay, or Amazon. E-commerce can be very conveniently run during not-so-normal working hours, like automation, which takes care of most of the admin work in a business, such as inventory management and order processing.
3. Creation of Content: With the rise of social media and digital content spaces like YouTube, Instagram, and TikTok, even content creation is not an impossible gig for the hybrid entrepreneur (Gorissen, 2024). Content creation and gig-work in the platform economy: What contemporary sex work can teach us about the futures of digital labor. *The Information Society*, 1-20.. People can now produce and monetize content at their convenience, creating personal brands that could pay off through sponsorships, ad revenues, or direct sales.
4. Online Teaching and Tutoring: With the rise of online tutoring, another phenomenon of this century, entrepreneurial opportunities to teach courses online and provide tutoring or even coaching services have increased greatly (Curran, 2023). These online gigs allow workers to share knowledge and earn dollars while holding up the ability to teach when it's most convenient for them.
5. Gig Services: TaskRabbit or Thumbtack sites hold promise for the hybrid entrepreneur in the area where on-demand services like handyman work, event planning, or home organization. Many of these gigs offer flexible scheduling and are a way to turn hobbies or additional skills into sources of income outside of regular work.

Case Studies of Successful Hybrid Entrepreneurs in the Gig Economy

At the same time, multiple hybrid entrepreneurs have been able to leverage the opportunity found in the gig economy for their businesses while on full-time employment. The following are hybrid entrepreneurship case studies showing the different ways in which hybrid entrepreneurship can turn and how the gig economy provides a starting point for businesses.

1. The Part-Time Designer: Jane was working as a marketing professional on a full-time basis but always had a passion for graphic design. She began doing minor designs in platforms like Fiverr and Upwork in her free time (Blaising, Kotturi, Kulkarni, & Dabbish, 2021). Over the years, she developed the portfolio and had clients who would consistently more or fewer work. Later on, with experience and a good clientele base she was now able to switch from a full-time job to driving the business on her own – a hybrid entrepreneur.
2. The E-commerce Innovator: Mark was a full-time engineer but an exceptional sustainable fashion buff. He began a side gig based on his passion for eco-friendly attire and accessories: designing merchandise and operating an online store for it through Etsy in evenings and on weekends (Biemer, 2021). As Mark's e-commerce business took off, he dropped one day at a time from his engineering job—until he was entirely self-supporting via his innovative business.
3. The Content Creator: Sarah is a teacher by profession who ventured into making educational videos on YouTube just for fun. Her channel picked up, and eventually she started earning both on ads and through sponsored videos. Being an HEN, she was still working her full-time job as a teacher, but she built up her YouTube channel, which grew to be one of her main income-generating activities. Today, she manages teaching with content creation and a personal brand that has managed to capture hundreds of thousands of viewers.

These are but a few examples of how hybrid entrepreneurs work within the gig economy: using it for idea testing and skill development and, when appropriate, moving more fully towards entrepreneurship as a career. Having this platform, the flexibility, and spiky earning opportunities characteristic of the gig economy, a person who perhaps might not even have considered traditional entrepreneurship might find it interesting to consider an exploration of this type of economy as a stepping stone.

In conclusion, gig economy hybrid entrepreneurship offers a risk-mitigated approach to business start-ups. Capitalizing on flexibility and access to gig work, hybrid enterprises can be developed at a pace that both builds experience and further cements a solid foundation on which future success will grow.

Challenges and Opportunities

Hybrid entrepreneurship in the gig economy, therefore, offers a blend of opportunities and associated challenges. Entrepreneurial opportunities in this regard come from hybrid entrepreneurship intrinsically helping the process of exploration without requiring complete abandonment of the job in the first stage, as well as new doors that open on the face by being a hybrid entrepreneur. It also presents obstacles that have to be treaded carefully between the two. Understanding these challenges and opportunities is crucial for hybrid entrepreneurs looking to succeed in the dynamic landscape of the gig economy.

Challenges

1. Balancing Multiple Roles: Time Devotion to Another Full-time Job Perhaps the biggest challenge faced by hybrid entrepreneurs is the ability to balance responsibilities to a full-time job with the duties and running of a side business (Shevchuk, Strebkov, & Bögenhold, 2024). This can be demanding in time, whereby many people end up burning out under this arrangement. A hybrid entrepreneur must demonstrate strong time management skills and maximal boundaries so as guarding against the side business interfering with full-time employment. Additionally, the need for them to change personalities between being an employee to a business owner to possibly becoming a husband, wife, partner, father, or mother creates tension and usually impacts personal relationships.
2. Scaling and Limited Resources: Arguably usually time and cash will be in the short supply of a hybrid entrepreneur to sink into the venture. As such, this may limit the ability to scale on the side venture and take advantage of increased value metrics (Bögenhold, Klinglmair, & Kandutsch, 2017). Unlike full-time entrepreneurs who are free to fully dedicate all their time to their venture, hybrid entrepreneurs often have to make strategic decisions about where they allot their limited resources. This may dramatically and significantly slow business growth and indeed require solutions that might be quite creative: automation, the outsourcing of some operations, or even technology implementation in order to make sure that one's limited resources are used most effectively.
3. Legal and Financial Considerations: Hybrid entrepreneurs, on the other hand, will have to make sure that their side business is not conflicting with their main job, especially if they have signed an employment contract containing non-compete clauses or restrictions on doing outside work, for example. Another little thorny matter will be taking care of taxes related to both a full, formal salary and business income, which can entail financial planning down to the minutest detail, possibly with the intervention of a professional accountant. The hybrid entrepreneurs also need to consider factors which may be affected upon becoming a hybrid entrepreneur, such as health insurance, retirement plans, and other employment-related benefits (Cherry, & Aloisi, 2016).
4. Work-Life Balance: Work-life balance is one of the common issues faced by hybrid entrepreneurs. The two tasks of maintaining a full-time job and engaging in a second job can give no time for various personal activities, or for spending time relaxing with friends and family. This may further lead to burn

out, decreased productivity, and even health problems in the long term. Hybrid entrepreneurs should save some time to rest and care for themselves in order to keep working for the job and the business.

5. Market Competition and Differentiation: The gig economy is one that has much pressure considering the sheer number of people offering the same service or goods. In such an industry, it may be hard for hybrid entrepreneurs to stand out in a very simple marketplace where they may not invest as much time and energy in marketing and business development as the full-time entrepreneurs (Fos, Hamdi, Kalda, & Nickerson, 2019). It becomes very hard to differentiate one's offerings and establish a strong brand presence when operations are limited in terms of resources and time.

Opportunities

1. Financial Stability and Risk Mitigation: One of the greatest benefits of hybrid entrepreneurship is the financial stability that comes with having a steady income while building one's business (Alberti, & Varon Garrido, 2017). This kind of safety gives one the opportunity to take calculated risks without pressure that may have been experienced if the income were totally dependent on the business. An opportunity to try out different business ideas, to 'pivot' if necessary, and to invest in growth without risking personal finances, are valid avenues that ultimately lead to long-term success
2. Skill Development and Professional Growth: Hybrid entrepreneurship opens great opportunities for personal and professional growth. Entrepreneurship lets one earn a wide range of skills: problem-solving, marketing, customer relations, and financial management. These skills are not only facilitated by the wayside business but also improved in their performance at the primary job. Additionally, hybrid entrepreneurship opens opportunities in new industries, networks the professionals, and serves as experience that can later become an eye-opener for employment (Athalage, 2024).
3. Diversification of income A key advantage of hybrid entrepreneurial ventures is diversified income. With money flowing from a full-time job and a side business, hybrid entrepreneurs reduce financial dependence on one source of income. Such diversification enables one to buffer economic uncertainty, the risk of losing one's job, or an industry slump. It also opens up possibilities to save more, invest in growing the business in the future, or meet financial goals more quickly.
4. Testing Business Ideas at Low Risk: The gig economy offers a perfect setting in which one could test and validate business ideas without the necessity or requirement of any up-front investment of serious magnitude (Goswami, &

Underwood, 2022). Hybrid entrepreneurs can easily start up by offering their products or services small using gig platforms to test the demand and the feedback of customers. This way, they can tweak their offerings, build a customer base, and develop a more viable business model, further strengthening their argument to embrace full-time entrepreneurship. The opportunity to test ideas with minimal risk is all too potent and could permit better, more informed, and successful business decisions being made.

5. Flexibility and Autonomy: Hybrid entrepreneurship indeed allows them to have an adequate amount of flexibility and autonomy not available in traditional employment. The good thing about this would be that such an opportunity can allow partial entrepreneurs to work when, where, and how they please with part-time business ventures. This puts them in the position to be able to seek activities that mirror the interest and values that could be personal to them; this could be a passion project, a creative endeavor, the drawing out of a business idea that they want to shape by their vision. Autonomy related to hybrid entrepreneurship can finally prove to be very rewarding and empowering for overall job satisfaction and fulfillment.
6. Pathway to Full-Time Entrepreneurship: For many hybrid entrepreneurs, their side business serves as the pathway to full-time entrepreneurship. When their businesses grow and earn better, they might decide to do away with traditional jobs and concentrate completely on entrepreneurial venture. Such gradual steps to the real shift to entrepreneurship are much less problematic and risky because the hybrid entrepreneur has been able to establish a good base—good customers and a good model of business—previously. This will be a path to which the dream of full-time business will be paved.

Although hybrid entrepreneurship within the gig economy has its problems, it brings with it many opportunities for economic stability, personal growth, and entrepreneurial success. Done correctly, and with careful handling of potential pitfalls but grasping at opportunities, such a hybrid entrepreneur can establish really successful businesses that supplement their regular employment and eventually become a platform for more significant future entrepreneurial activities.

IMPACT ON TRADITIONAL MODELS OF EMPLOYMENT

Gig economy breeds hybrid entrepreneurship that is changing traditional models of employment. More and more people are becoming engaged in entrepreneurial activities besides their full-time jobs, and the border between traditional employment and self-employment has become very blurred. This shift has huge implications for both employers and employees, and for the labour market generally. This section, on the other hand, focuses on the challenge, as well as the potential for innovation and adaptation, that hybrid entrepreneurship could present to traditional models of employment.

Shifts in Employee Expectations and Work Preferences

Probably the most immediate impact of hybrid entrepreneurship to traditional employment is the shift in the expectation of the employees and which work preference they lean towards (Putra, & Ofosu, 2024). This is because, having the gig or entrepreneurship-based work does have the hallmarks of flexibility and independence – two that conventional rigid jobs do not provide. Workers who have such small enterprises tend to cherish self-scheduling, at-home work, and engaging in other hobbies or interests besides their primary occupation; thus, they are attracted to such characteristics within their full-time jobs.

Expectations have changed, hence more flexible arrangements with regard to remote work, flexible hours, and compressed workweeks are required. Companies not able to keep up with the new model, therefore, will find themselves at a serious disadvantage in the recruitment and retention of key competence, particularly the young generation, which is increasingly conscious about its work-life balance and self-fulfilment. Companies that provide support or flexibility for people who are entrepreneurial in spirit experience heightened job satisfaction, loyalty, and productivity.

Erosion of Job Loyalty and Long-Term Commitment

Hybrid entrepreneurship will eventually result in a reduction of job loyalty and long-term commitment among employees to that particular job (Battilana, Sengul, Pache, & Model, 2015). Having more than one source of income and the urge to succeed as an entrepreneur will in the long run imply a reduction in dependence upon jobs as the prime source of sustenance or professional development. Such diversification, related to sources of income and professional interests, would lower the commitment of employees toward staying around with the same employer for long.

For employers, the difficulty comes in the ability to maintain a stable and committed workforce. Long gone is the model where employees were beholden to a single organization for years, if not decades, in return for job security and various benefits. In contrast, the same traditional model is also said to be undergoing constant erosion in terms of the length of job tenures, fostering a much more temporary workforce model. Employers will have to revisit their strategies when it comes to employee engagement, retention, and career development. Creating opportunities for professional growth, supporting employee side ventures and maintaining an innovative company culture can enable the company to maintain the best talent when employees no longer demonstrate loyalty to jobs.

Redefinition of Roles and Career Paths

The increase in hybrid entrepreneurship is also triggering a redefinition of job roles and career paths within traditional employment models (Guo, Restubog, Cui, Zou, & Choi, 2019). With more and more employees being entrepreneurial on the side, their coming back with fresh skill sets, outlooks, and experiences to full-time engagements injects new ideas into the surrounding environment. Most likely, this cross-pollination of ideas usually leads to a more innovative and creative atmosphere, as the staff applies the entrepreneurial mindset in problem resolution, product development, or processes.

This will turn into a less conventional, linear, and more diverse kind of line of work. A worker looking for hybrid entrepreneurship won't, therefore, follow the usual path toward corporate advancement by sticking to one type of job in one company. They might seek such opportunities in project-based work or that will necessitate industry-hopping. Think about it, in order to successfully deal with these changing career aspirations, employers probably will have to offer even more diversified and flexible ways of career development, like lateral moves, cross-functional assignments, and short-term projects.

Challenges to Traditional Benefits and Compensation Structures

The growing hybrid entrepreneurship will also pose a challenge to the traditional benefits and compensation structures. For example, most traditional employment models were built assuming that full-time work for a single employer would be the norm, where many benefits, including healthcare or retirement plans, typically rely on that assumption. Hybrid entrepreneurs—or people who work a full-time job and maintain a business on the side—may have different needs related to their benefits and compensation.

Indeed, hybrid entrepreneurs will most likely have aspirations of more flexible benefits that can be addressed with their unique situations, such as portable retirement plans, health savings accounts, and gig economy platforms for additional income. Other forms of remuneration they would appreciate are bonuses and profit sharing, which would motivate them to contribute toward the success of the business without any obligations toward full-time commitment. Employers who can offer hybrid entrepreneurs personalized and flexible benefit packages are more likely to appeal to this group and to have a competitive advantage in the emerging labor market as well (Walsh, & Stephens, 2022).

Impact on Organizational Culture and Employee Engagement

Hybrid entrepreneurship can immensely touch on organizational culture and employee engagement. On one hand, workers engaging in entrepreneurship other than the workforce will bring energy, creativity, and innovativeness in their full-time positions, and these are positive characters of good company culture. If not managed right, hybrid entrepreneurship will lead to disengagement, divided attention, and lack of focus on the job at hand (Imperatori, & Imperatori, 2017).

Employers need to support and cultivate entrepreneurial culture within and even beyond the organization. Employers may establish internal innovation programs, avail resources and mentoring to the entrepreneurial employee, or just establish ways of appreciating and valuing the entrepreneurial success of the employees. An employer who aligns the culture to be in tandem with the entrepreneurial dreams of the workforce drives the levels of employee engagement upwards and creates a much more diverse and creative workplace.

INNOVATION AND THE GROWTH POTENTIAL OF THE BUSINESS

With the challenges addressed, hybrid entrepreneurship also brings with it immense opportunities for innovation and business growth potential within traditional models of employment. In most cases, employees engaged in entrepreneurial activities are usually leaders concerning new trends, technologies, and market opportunities. That is, by facilitating hybrid entrepreneurship, companies can benefit from a rich knowledge and experience base to stay competitive in today's fast-moving business environment of innovation that constantly changes (Davies, I. A., & Doherty, B. (2019).

For instance, companies might encourage employees to develop and present new business ideas, which then could be incubated within the company. Or employers might collaborate with employees' side businesses, using their products or services to mutual advantage. Companies treating hybrid entrepreneurship as a source of innovation can come up with new revenue sources, innovations, and a culture of continuous improvement.

Hybrid entrepreneurship, therefore, represents a redefinition of traditional forms of employment; there is much potential in this type of entrepreneurship, but at the same time, there are many challenges. As employees increasingly wish to become entrepreneurs in addition to holding their full-time jobs, the changed expectations require that organizations redefine the role of jobs to allow for flexible benefits and careers in a flexible structure of employment. At the same time, helping hybrid entrepreneurs while nurturing an innovative culture within companies manifests the creativity and entrepreneurial spirit of the employed labor—thus growing businesses and staying competitive in the fast-paced gig economy.

Policy and Regulatory Considerations

With hybrid entrepreneurship on the rise, it gives rise to a few very important policy and regulatory considerations. The convergence of formal employment with self-employment introduces nuances which expose the existing labor laws, tax codes, and modes of social protection to great complexities that they are wide of. This section draws out key policy and regulatory considerations associated with hybrid entrepreneurship and highlights areas where reform is necessary for the sake of equity, innovation, and protection of the workers and businesses.

Labor Classification and Worker Rights

Labor misclassification has been one of the prime regulatory challenges in hybrid entrepreneurship (Ang, 2023). Traditional labor laws usually classify workers as either employees or independent contractors, and different rights and protections are attached to these different classifications. On the other hand, hybrid entrepreneurs' straddle both camps: in one capacity, they may be working as employees, while in another, they may be third-party contractors or gig workers.

Such mixed application, in such situations, together with the labor rights and protection, would probably be hard to situate concretely. For instance, it is common for hybrid entrepreneurs to experience problems in acquiring benefits such as unemployment insurance, workers' compensation, and paid leave tied to their status as employees. While they often lack the autonomy and job flexibility associated with independent contractors, at other times they have a hard time getting the same benefits.

Policymakers will need to consider altering labor laws to better suit hybrid entrepreneurship. This may mean creating a new liminal category, in which policymakers recognize the unique positioning of hybrid entrepreneurs, giving them a bundle of rights and protections. Or it may mean that they are going to standardize benefits and protections by employees and independent contractors and, hence, give the essential social protection to all workers, not considering their status.

Taxation and Financial Reporting

These have often made tax obligations complex to hybrid entrepreneurs, as this involves reporting income from full-time employment and side business. This is prone to confusion and in some instances it even spirals into unintentional non-compliance with tax laws. In general, the tax system may lag in being accommodative enough to fulfill the needs of hybrid entrepreneurs to have clear ground on how to report their income, deduct business expenses, and comply with the tax regulations.

This necessitates tax authorities to also consider tax reforms to make tax-filing easier for hybrid entrepreneurs. This can be done by having simplified tax reporting that is available to the hybrid entrepreneur, clear guidelines of deductions that may be made, and even resources that these entrepreneurs may reference in order to be aware of their tax liabilities (Killian, Regan, 2019). In addition, they should have tax incentives or credits to promote entrepreneurship and enable small businesses to further develop through the potential that hybrid entrepreneurs bring to the scene, with their economic contributions appreciated.

Social Security and Benefits Portability

Social security arrangements in most countries are predicated on the nature of traditional employment, with a single employer making contributions to and withdrawals from their workers' social security systems. In addition the hybrid entrepreneur often spends their time revolving between several income sources, which therefore can make contributions to social security programs quite tedious and complex.

This might potentially be ameliorated by improved benefit portability, whereby workers' benefits can accumulate and be transferred among forms of employment. For example, a hybrid entrepreneur might be allowed to combine benefits between a full-time job and a side business to qualify for social security benefits. In addition to the above, policymakers could create portable benefits platforms that enable the workers to tote the management of their own benefits independent of the single employer to avoid the constant interrupt of coverage as workers shift between various forms of work.

Intellectual Property and Non-Compete Clauses

The side business of a hybrid entrepreneur might involve the development of innovative products, service, or technology/app in the quest, thereby bringing about legal ironies in implementing the intellectual property right and non-compete clause. This mostly occurs because employers usually have provisions in their policies that give them the rights to IP created by an employee, even when this is created outside of work hours. Likewise, a non-compete clause in an employment contract can put restrictions on employees not to go into business areas that may be considered to be in competition with the employer (Grant, 2023).

Such legal constraints constitute an enabling factor for hybrid entrepreneurs who would otherwise remain inhibited from pursuing further with a new venture because of worries about the ownership of an overbridging IP and possible future litigation from the current employer. Policy-makers may want to rethink some policies to spell out the rights of the hybrid entrepreneur in terms of intellectual property and non-compete clauses. This could mean setting clearer boundaries between work-related and personal IP, reigning the reach of non-compete agreements, or even offering legal immunities for employees who do.4 engage in entrepreneurial activities outside of their employment

Support for Entrepreneurial Education and Training

Policy support for training in entrepreneurship and business: most of these hybrid entrepreneurs are least informed about formal business training, so are experiencing challenges in areas like financial management, marketing, or regulation compliance (Cornforth, 2020). The development of skills by these hybrid entrepreneurs will thus be enhanced through resources, training programs, and mentorship opportunities that result from the support the government and educational institutions give.

Policymakers may regard such issues and maybe respond to them through entrepreneurial training grants or subsidies; promoting pubic–private sector programs on entrepreneurship or embedding entrepreneurial studies in the national schools' curricula. Such knowledge and skills development could also pay off to the gig economy at large since hybrid entrepreneurs are more likely to be educated or knowledgeable on most business-related issues or challenges that they may anticipate and strike out in advance.

Privacy and Security

Data privacy and data security are major concerns in hybrid entrepreneurship, as most hybrid entrepreneurs run their businesses online and through digital platforms (Bögenhold, 2019). Gig work platforms, payment processors, and other online services through which personal and business data is collected, stored, and circulated put hybrid entrepreneurs at risk of data breaches, identity theft, or unauthorized entry.

Regulators must provide for solid data privacy laws that can ensure the protection of, at least, the interests of the hybrid entrepreneurs, and which will promote innovation and development of the gig economies. This can take shape in setting explicit standards for data security, making digital platforms transparent about their data practices, and giving legal remedies to individuals in case of such practices. Further, hybrid entrepreneurs must be educated about the most effective ways of protecting their information and that of their customers.

Implications for Labor Regulation

The gig economy has also caused a reconsideration of the broader labor market regulations applied in the good old days, as hybrid entrepreneurship takes its rise. Conventional employment policies focused on full-time or long-term jobs can thus hold little water in a contemporary labor market characterized by flexible, project-based, and entrepreneurial work. The potential approaches toward labor market regulation changes are most likely to be in line with the several and varying ways in which persons work today.

This might mean going back to reassessment of the minimum wage, hours of work, and protection laws with regards to another regime of suitability and applicability to all work regimes, including hybrid entrepreneurship. Policymakers can also investigate how fair competition can be guaranteed within the gig economy, providing a level playing field for all hybrid entrepreneurs while safeguarding the workers against exploitation by such platforms and unethical employers.

In other words, challenges and opportunities for hybrid entrepreneurial growth in the gig economy accrue benefits to the policymakers or regulators. Governments help create a more dynamic, inclusive, and resilient economy by adjusting labor laws, the tax code, the social security system, and other regulations. At the same time, it is essential to ensure that these policies protect workers' rights, promote fair competition, and encourage innovation in the rapidly evolving world of work.

FUTURE TRENDS AND IMPLICATIONS

Likely changes in the structure of work are expected to occur as hybrid entrepreneurship matures within the gig economy, which will change the ways businesses operate and create policy. In that sense, knowledge of these future trends will provide invaluable input to workers, employers, policymakers, and society at large. This section highlights several important trends in the views of the future on hybrid entrepreneurship and the gig economy.

Increased Integration of Technology and AI

Perhaps the most conspicuous future hybrid entrepreneurship trend is the integration of technology and artificial intelligence (Kopalle, Gangwar, Kaplan, Ramachandran, Reinartz, & Rindfleisch, 2022). As technology continues to become more advanced, the hybrid entrepreneur will have many more tools at their disposal, both to enjoy and to help in automating work activities and managing a business. AI tools, for example, can make market data analysis easier by forecasting customer behaviors, optimizing businesses' marketing strategies, and streamlining operations that help scale ventures by hybrid entrepreneurs while keeping their main employment.

This is more than likely to trend toward the production of further hybrids that are a whole lot more tech-savvy: how they can leverage AI to recognize new business opportunities, cut down on operational costs, and, therefore, maintain a quality product or service. However, it also raises questions about the future of human labor in the gig economy. As AI becomes capable of doing more complex work, a nature of some work will die and in its place give rise to groups of totally new technology-oriented jobs. For both hybrid entrepreneurs and traditional employees, this will become a new way of life, thus adapting continuously with upskilling.

Blurring Boundaries Between Full-Time Employment and Entrepreneurship

The boundaries between full-time employment on the one hand, and entrepreneurship on the other, are only expected to further blur as this trend leads to many more workers becoming hybrid entrepreneurs (Bögenhold & Klinglmair, 2016). This is also likely to give rise to new modes of working in which elements of traditional work abound, mixed with an entrepreneurial operation. For instance, organizations may provide their employees the opportunity to contribute to intrapreneurial projects, which allow employees to innovate and work on other business ideas with the guarantee of protection and safety in their current full-time job.

This blending of roles would prove to make organizations more dynamic and innovative, as entrepreneurial thinking is naturally applied to daily work by employees. It may also result in a more fluid labor market as workers migrate between full-time employment, gigging, and entrepreneurship. However, in doing so, the new working models may also test existing labor market regulations, structures for benefits, and workplace cultures, demanding radical adaptations to accommodate these models of work.

Expansion of Hybrid Work Models

Hybrid entrepreneurship at a rise is likely to make hybrid work models expand by professionally combining remote work, flexible working hours, and project-based assignments. More workers will get more opportunities for full-time work that, at the same time, create room for gig work. This change will encourage more flexible work styles on the part of employers, such as remote work, job sharing, and multiple-job participation.

The trend is toward an increasing decentralization and diversification of the workforce, with workers geographically distributed and diversified across industries. Although this provides a potential opportunity to deliver a better balance between work and personal life, hence increasing job satisfaction, there are challenges associated with how to keep a team cohesive, how to manage remote employees, and how to ensure the constant flow of information. This mandates employer investment not only in technology and training but in appropriate management practices that can underpin these hybrid models of work and build organizational culture.

Emergence of New Support Structures for Hybrid Entrepreneurs

With the increasing hybrid entrepreneurship, there has consequently been an emergence of new support structures and ecosystems designed for hybrid entrepreneurs in mind (Reynolds, & Holt, 2021). These support structures might involve co-working spaces designed for people juggling full-time jobs with operating a side business, or even online community platforms, mentorship programs, and several other networking events taking into account their special needs.

Further, financial products and services designed for hybrid entrepreneurs should be developed properly, from generic flexible loans and insurance policies to retirement schemes—all shaped by multiple sources of income. Governments and academic institutions could also provide more specific support, including grants and training programs, as well as incubators, to help hybrid entrepreneurs develop their ventures without compromising their primary employment.

Greater Focus on Work-Life Integration

What this indicates is that, in the future, hybrid entrepreneurship may become more severe as people seek their balances among integrated and complex life domains. It is not about the separation of work from personal time, as found in tradition; rather, work-life integration allows for fluid boundaries where people may need to blend life and work attitudes in order to lead satisfying lives (Jeanne, 2017)

Hybrid entrepreneurs will continue to experiment with pull-out ways of integrating their work into life, whether that means aligning their side businesses with their passions or values they hold or through technology, like time management. Work is also supported by employers to integrate wellness programs, appropriate work arrangements, and a culture that supports employee well-being. However, work-life integration would have to be paid sustained attention to realize such objectives without permitting work to occupy every bit of the day, causing burnout, stress, and generally a denial of personal life to the detriment of the overall being.

Economic Growth and Innovation

Hybrid entrepreneurship, on the other hand, holds so much future economic potential and the prospect of abundant innovation because more and more people bring to entrepreneurial life the ideas they have while under full-time paid employment. This could increase the number of small business enterprises, start-ups, and new product/service introductions, boosting economic dynamism and job creation. The market gap and unsatisfied demand can be taken up by the hybrid entrepreneur, empowered with a heterogeneous perspective and déja présent experience from the full-time role.

This growth in hybrid entrepreneurship could also disrupt traditional industry and business models, leading to increased competition and a need for established companies to innovate or die. Thus, policymakers are facing the challenge of how to encourage this economic transition by ensuring that hybrid entrepreneurs have the necessary resources, funding, and regulatory environment in which to conduct their business. What is more, policies concerning equal conditions of competition and rights of employees are among the areas in which there may be a need for urgency as the labor market is dynamic and prone to the changes.

Education and Career Development Models Change in Course

Given that hybrid entrepreneurship is gradually forming, the education and career development models are bound to change providing a way out for individuals in the context of an emerging world of work. What this likely means is that more traditional systems of education will soon find themselves shifting toward having their learners move into the entrepreneurial features of economy. We are likely to see a rise in interdisciplinary programs, bootcamps and online courses, all increasingly teaching individuals how to manage multiple income streams, start a business and fit into a gig economy.

There will have to be corresponding changes in career development to accommodate the many and nonlinear career paths enabled by hybrid entrepreneurship. This could entail providing more sophisticated, adaptive functionality in career planning tools and mentorship programs or, more broadly, the landscape of lifelong learning and skill development opportunities. Employers may need to support employees in pursuing hybrid entrepreneurship through professional development resources and by valuing entrepreneurial experience as a part of career advancement.

The future of hybrid entrepreneurship in the gig economy, nevertheless, presents important times for the structure of work, business operation systems, and the design of policies. These trends are well understood, and they reveal a lot about the future landscape, meaning that stakeholders are presented with the urgent need to manage a successful transition to obtain the best mileage out of the current tendencies of hybrid entrepreneurship in adding value in the direction of a more dynamic, innovative, and inclusive economy.

CONCLUSION

Hybrid entrepreneurship in the gig economy is a major enabler of transition in work structures from a traditional wage labor framework toward more entrepreneurial pursuits. Diversification and flexibility give them the scope to create multiple strings of income while holding onto job security in one single place. Hybrid entrepreneurs are most likely furthering the cause of key agents in the drive of innovation and growing economies, supported by technological changes, changes in the regulatory environment, and shifts in social norms. However, with this move come the challenges that fall under the need for updated labor laws and tax regulations, as well as support structures. Addressing these challenges while leveraging the potential of hybrid entrepreneurship implies that resilient and dynamic workers will be demanded in the future. That future will need to balance a flexibility in work with adequate support systems to ensure that an environment is in place to whereby workers and businesses thrive.

REFERENCES

Afshan, G., Shahid, S., & Tunio, M. N. (2021). Learning experiences of women entrepreneurs amidst COVID-19. *International Journal of Gender and Entrepreneurship*, 13(2), 162–186. DOI: 10.1108/IJGE-09-2020-0153

Alberti, F. G., & Varon Garrido, M. A. (2017). Can profit and sustainability goals co-exist? New business models for hybrid firms. *The Journal of Business Strategy*, 38(1), 3–13. DOI: 10.1108/JBS-12-2015-0124

Allon, G., Cohen, M. C., & Sinchaisri, W. P. (2023). The impact of behavioral and economic drivers on gig economy workers. *Manufacturing & Service Operations Management*, 25(4), 1376–1393. DOI: 10.1287/msom.2023.1191

Ang, L. (2023). The Legal Classification of Human Capital in 'Markets, Hybrids and Hierarchies'. *The Chinese Journal of Comparative Law*, 11(3), cxae003. DOI: 10.1093/cjcl/cxae003

Athalage, K. C. (2024). THE IMPACT OF HYBRID WORKING ON EMPLOYEE WAY OF LIFE AND THE NEED TO RESHAPE THE EMPLOYEE VALUE PROPOSITION.

Banik, N., & Padalkar, M. (2021). The spread of gig economy: Trends and effects. *Форсайт*, 15(1, 1 (eng)), 19–29. DOI: 10.17323/2500-2597.2021.1.19.29

Battilana, J., Sengul, M., Pache, A. C., & Model, J. (2015). Harnessing productive tensions in hybrid organizations: The case of work integration social enterprises. *Academy of Management Journal*, 58(6), 1658–1685. DOI: 10.5465/amj.2013.0903

Biemer, J. R. (2021). *Our Environmental Handprints: Recover the Land, Reverse Global Warming, Reclaim the Future*. Rowman & Littlefield Publishers. DOI: 10.5771/9781538140666

Blaising, A., Kotturi, Y., Kulkarni, C., & Dabbish, L. (2021). Making it work, or not: A longitudinal study of career trajectories among online freelancers. *Proceedings of the ACM on Human-Computer Interaction, 4*(CSCW3), 1-29. DOI: 10.1145/3432925

Bögenhold, D. (2019). From hybrid entrepreneurs to entrepreneurial billionaires: Observations on the socioeconomic heterogeneity of self-employment. *The American Behavioral Scientist*, 63(2), 129–146. DOI: 10.1177/0002764218794231

Bögenhold, D., & Klinglmair, A. (2016). Entrepreneurship and hybrid self-employment. *Contemporary entrepreneurship: multidisciplinary perspectives on innovation and growth*, 127-140.

Bögenhold, D., Klinglmair, R., & Kandutsch, F. (2017). Solo-Self-Employment, human capital and hybrid labour in the gig economy. *Форсайт*, 11(4, 4 (eng)), 23–32. DOI: 10.17323/2500-2597.2017.4.23.32

Bröckling, U. (2015). The entrepreneurial self: Fabricating a new type of subject.

Chappa, C., Varghese, M., & Chandler, K. (2017). Shaping the gig economy. *Proceedings of the Northeast Business& Economics Association*, 70-73.

Cherry, M. A., & Aloisi, A. (2016). Dependent contractors in the gig economy: A comparative approach. *SSRN*, 66, 635. DOI: 10.2139/ssrn.2847869

Cornforth, C. (2020). The governance of hybrid organisations. In *Handbook on hybrid organisations* (pp. 220–236). Edward Elgar Publishing. DOI: 10.4337/9781785366116.00022

Curran, N. M. (2023). "More like a friend than a teacher": Ideal teachers and the gig economy for online language learning. *Computer Assisted Language Learning*, 36(7), 1288–1308. DOI: 10.1080/09588221.2021.1976801

Davies, I. A., & Doherty, B. (2019). Balancing a hybrid business model: The search for equilibrium at Cafédirect. *Journal of Business Ethics*, 157(4), 1043–1066. DOI: 10.1007/s10551-018-3960-9

De la Vega, J. C. A. (2020, July). Making the Gig Economy Work for Workers: An Exploration of Freelancing Platforms. In *Proceedings of the 33rd International BCS Human Computer Interaction Conference* (pp. 55-57). BCS Learning & Development. DOI: 10.14236/ewic/HCI20DC.13

Demir, C., Werner, A., Kraus, S., & Jones, P. (2020). Hybrid entrepreneurship: A systematic literature review. *Journal of Small Business and Entrepreneurship*, 34(1), 29–52. DOI: 10.1080/08276331.2020.1764738

Fos, V., Hamdi, N., Kalda, A., & Nickerson, J. (2019). Gig-labor: Trading safety nets for steering wheels.

Gorissen, S. (2024). Content creation and gig-work in the platform economy: What contemporary sex work can teach us about the futures of digital labor. *The Information Society*, •••, 1–20. DOI: 10.1080/01972243.2024.2381481

Goswami, S., & Underwood, Q. (2022). *The Young Entrepreneur: How to Start A Business While You're Still a Student.* Kogan Page Publishers.

Grant, B. A. (2023). Unleashing Corporate Entrepreneurship. *Brook. L. Rev.*, 89, 1031.

Guo, F., Restubog, S. L. D., Cui, L., Zou, B., & Choi, Y. (2019). What determines the entrepreneurial success of academics? Navigating multiple social identities in the hybrid career of academic entrepreneurs. *Journal of Vocational Behavior*, 112, 241–254. DOI: 10.1016/j.jvb.2019.03.003

Imperatori, B., & Imperatori, B. (2017). Engagement and disengagement at work: what's new. *Engagement and Disengagement at Work: Drivers and Organizational Practices to Sustain Employee Passion and Performance*, 5-18.

Killian, S., & O'Regan, P. (2019). Taxation and social enterprise: Constraint or incentive for the common good. *Journal of Social Entrepreneurship*, 10(1), 1–18. DOI: 10.1080/19420676.2018.1517103

Kopalle, P. K., Gangwar, M., Kaplan, A., Ramachandran, D., Reinartz, W., & Rindfleisch, A. (2022). Examining artificial intelligence (AI) technologies in marketing via a global lens: Current trends and future research opportunities. *International Journal of Research in Marketing*, 39(2), 522–540. DOI: 10.1016/j.ijresmar.2021.11.002

Meijerink, J., & Keegan, A. (2019). Conceptualizing human resource management in the gig economy: Toward a platform ecosystem perspective. *Journal of Managerial Psychology*, 34(4), 214–232. DOI: 10.1108/JMP-07-2018-0277

Mizrahi, O. (2018). *The Gig Is Up: Thrive in the Gig Economy, Where Old Jobs Are Obsolete and Freelancing Is the Future*. Greenleaf Book Group.

Putra, K. D., & Ofosu, S. D. (2024). FULL-TIME NOW OR LATER! Influence of Organizational Working Environment on Transition Intention.(Multi-case study of Hybrid Entrepreneurship in Indonesia).

Reynolds, N. S., & Holt, D. (2021). Sustainable development and profit? A sense-making perspective on hybrid organisations and their founders. *Business Strategy and the Environment*, 30(4), 2147–2159. DOI: 10.1002/bse.2737

Roche, J. The Hybrid Nature of Social Enterprises - Exploring possible tensions and sources of mission drift. Louvain School of Management, Université catholique de Louvain, 2017. Prom.: Janssen, Frank. http:// hdl.handle.net/2078.1/thesis:10953

Shevchuk, A., Strebkov, D., & Bögenhold, D. (2024). Work values and hybrid careers in the gig economy: The evidence from an online labor market. *Economic and Industrial Democracy*, 45(1), 138–163. DOI: 10.1177/0143831X221140153

Sinicki, A., Sinicki, & Ramachandran. (2019). *Thriving in the gig economy*. Apress.

Tornikoski, E. T., Viljamaa, A., & Varamäki, E. (2015). Hybrid entrepreneurship during retirement: Comparison of motives and aspirations. In *Entrepreneurship, self-employment and retirement* (pp. 187–208). Palgrave Macmillan UK. DOI: 10.1057/9781137398390_9

Tunio, M. N., Chaudhry, I. S., Shaikh, S., Jariko, M. A., & Brahmi, M. (2021). Determinants of the sustainable entrepreneurial engagement of youth in developing country—An empirical evidence from Pakistan. *Sustainability (Basel)*, 13(14), 7764. DOI: 10.3390/su13147764

Walsh, K., & Stephens, S. (2022). The Side-Hustle: An Emergent Typology of Entrepreneurs as Employees. *International Review of Entrepreneurship*, 20(2).

Xi, G., Block, J. H., Lasch, F., Robert, F., & Thurik, R. (2017). Mode of entry into hybrid entrepreneurship: New venture start-up versus business takeover.

Zwick, A. (2018). Welcome to the Gig Economy: Neoliberal industrial relations and the case of Uber. *GeoJournal*, 83(4), 679–691. DOI: 10.1007/s10708-017-9793-8

Chapter 3
Role of Innovation and Entrepreneurship in Economic Diversification

Ashutosh Pandey
https://orcid.org/0000-0002-8255-8459
FORE School of Management, New Delhi, India

P. G. S. A. Jayarathne
De Montfort University, UK

Amit Kumar Yadav
https://orcid.org/0000-0002-4565-5284
O.P. Jindal Global University, Sonipat, India

Ajay Chandel
https://orcid.org/0000-0002-4585-6406
Lovely Professional University, India

ABSTRACT

Innovation and entrepreneurship are essential drivers of economic diversification and growth. This chapter explores how emerging technologies, such as AI, blockchain, IoT, and 5G, are reshaping industries and creating new business opportunities. It highlights the role of sustainability and green innovation in fostering environmentally conscious solutions and examines the impact of remote work and digital nomadism on the traditional workplace. Additionally, the chapter discusses advancements in health and wellness, opportunities in global and emerging markets, and the importance of social impact and inclusivity in fostering equitable growth. By understanding and leveraging these trends, stakeholders can drive economic diversification and create a resilient, adaptable economic landscape.

DOI: 10.4018/979-8-3693-9486-1.ch003

INTRODUCTION

Economic diversification has been one of the important strategies followed by countries all over the world in order to increase resilience and sustainability in their economy. It refers to the spread and development of an economy by reducing over-reliance on a single industry or source of revenue, ensuring sensitivity and vulnerability decrease to any kind of shocks and fluctuations originating from a source (Ali et al., 2022). For many countries, especially those overly dependent on natural resources or a few dominant industries, diversification can be a way to achieve economic stability, to foster economic growth that is more sustainable, and to generate more opportunities that lead to more inclusive economies. Though the success of most economic diversification is pegged to the effective harnessing of innovation and entrepreneurship, these two serve as the fundamental drivers of new industries, technologies, and markets (Acs et al., 2013).

Innovation is needed for economic diversification because it is the process of providing new products, new processes, services, and ideas. It would mean to create new economic activities or transform existing ones, which in turn would enable an economy to develop new sectors and industries, letting the rest fall back a bit in the traditional ones. For example, most countries that have been able to diversify their economies have mainly done it by encouraging innovation within the sectors experiencing high growth, which could be technology, renewable energy, or even advanced manufacturing. Such a step not only creates new employment opportunities but also increases the competitive advantage of a country globally (Asem, 2024).

In another way, entrepreneurship complements an aspect of economic diversification by translating innovative ideas into practical businesses and industries. The entrepreneurs are generally the first to identify new opportunities and to test new and innovative business models, in terms of closing the path to market expansion (Boschma et al., 2017). They diversify through start-ups and small businesses likely to make incursions into new markets, thus providing new products and services. Added to these are economic activity creation, the generation of employment, and the ability to create a culture of innovation and risk-taking, all from a melting pot for a vibrant and diversified economy.

It is within this frame of economic diversification that the interaction between innovation and entrepreneurship becomes of prime importance. Together, innovation can succeed in a virtuous cycle in which the birth of new businesses is promoted by innovation, and then, those businesses contribute to the diffusion and commercialization of innovation. This synergy is noted by a simultaneous rise in entrepreneurial ecosystems (Corradini & Propris, 2015), which are an interconnected network of actors between entrepreneurs, investors, research institutions, and government, providing the enabling environment and resources supporting innovation-led economic diversification. These ecosystems create an enabling environment to foster the rise of innovations through startups and update new ventures capable of diversifying the economy (Cantner et al., 2019).

However, economic diversification through innovation and entrepreneurship is not easy. Many countries are burdened with obstacles such as lack of access to capital, poor infrastructure, and regulatory constraints, which can thwart any entrepreneurship initiatives or innovation. Inadequate available skilled labor and the absence of a culture according to which entrepreneurial risk could be promoted can, moreover, decelerate efforts toward diversification. Therefore, the onus is on the governments and policymakers to create an enabling environment that encourages innovation and entrepreneurship. These include policies promoting encouragement, access to finance, education and upskilling, and innovation culture (Cheng et al., 2023).

This chapter will present how innovation and entrepreneurship can serve as a lever in driving economic diversification; how these elements entail the development of new industries and their conversion into more resilient and sustainable economies. The chapter approaches the issue in the backdrop of documenting inter-linkages between the case studies and uses analysis to provide examples of innovation-driven and entrepreneurial-based diversification and the challenges, obstacles, policy measures, and institutional support that needs to be surpassed for the accomplishment of that (Damoah, 2020). The point of departure is based on the premise that it is only by grasping the dynamic interrelation among innovation, entrepreneurship, and economic diversification that we can truly fathom the potential these drivers hold to spur national economic growth and development in an increasingly dynamic global economy.

UNDERSTANDING ECONOMIC DIVERSIFICATION

Economic diversification is a process by which countries or regions increase their economic base by developing a diversified set of industries or other economic activities. Diversification is the key to breaking the cycle of overreliance that often results in vulnerability to external shocks, either through the fluctuations in prices of commodities or variations in geopolitical tensions or natural disasters. It would build better economic resilience, hence more stability and growth that is verily sustainable due to minimal exposure towards various kinds of risk (Grillitsch & Asheim, 2018).

Definition and the Goals of Diversification

Economic diversification is fundamentally shifting from mono-economy where an economy depends on one single sector such as oil, agriculture or even tourism for the lion's share of economic output and employment. An example of this is a drifting into a multi-sectoral economy as in the case of industries and services (Hassen, 2022). Main objective behind diversifications is to ensure an economy that is robust and has the wherewithal to sustain any external shocks. By developing multiple sources of income, countries can fall back on any one sector and avoid sector-specific slumps that hold negative implications on the economy. Further, diversification will facilitate sustainable economic growth, provide better employment opportunities, and become a foundation of better economic development; profiting from strengths and potentials in varied sectors (Harraf et al., 2020).

Historical Background and Examples of Economic Diversification

Historically, most countries around the globe have always learned the importance of pursuing economic diversification as a means of negating the over-reliance on a single commodity or an industrial sector. For instance, during the later part of the 20th century, many nations in the Middle East that rely on oil started to develop an understanding of the risks that come with the dependence on petroleum (Kim et al., 2013). For example in the gulf, UAE and Saudi Arabia have very high investment rates in tourism, finance, aviation, and technology. These efforts have gradually made their economies shift from purely oil-based to diversified and resilient. Concerning Asia, the transformation of Singapore from a tiny trading post into one of the global financial and technological hubs underscores success in economic diversification. Focusing on education, infrastructure, and strategic development of industry, Singapore could easily attract foreign investment and bring about innovation, hence impetus for economic growth in different sectors (He et al., 2022).

Benefits of Economic Diversification

The advantages that emanate from this entirety are enormous. To begin with, enhanced economic resilience is a key advantage. A diversified economy will have the ability to absorb shocks, since the downturn faced in a given sector may be cushioned by another sector's growth or stand on its two feet. This characteristic of diversity is most important since it can keep significant economic equilibrium from going to hash and therefore can scan the onset of severe recessions. Furthermore, diversification will lead to sustainable economic growth as it follows a more balanced development approach (Munir & Javed, 2018). This is the economy that, through diversification, can maximize the full potentials from various sectors—ranging from agriculture and even manufacturing to service and technology—thus making it strong at the base. There are also great job opportunities that can be created with such a scenario, in the mitigation of poverty through diversification in the employment sector. A more diversified economy will be offering additional jobs that will suit different skill levels and, in this, further reduce the potential of unemployment realized from any particular sector (Miniaoui & Schilirò, 2017).

Challenges and Obstacles to Economic Diversification

While there is promise in diversification, it begets challenges. In most countries, the obstacles towards diversification are very high, and it could be because of a lack of infrastructure, difficulty in finance, or inadequate human capital. For those endowed with natural resources, there is a very big challenge due to the "resource curse", that is, being over reliant on such resources, begetting both economic and political challenges. Besides that, it is met with resistance to change and vested interests (Shuaibu et al., 2018). In some cases, the lack of political will and well-defined policy frameworks hinders strategies aimed at diversification. Such barriers can only be overcome by a joint effort on the part of the government, the private sector, and other concerned stakeholders in creating an enabling environment for diversification, with the main instrument of investment in this regard being education, infrastructure, and innovation. How does Innovation and Entrepreneurship spur Economic Diversification?

"Innovation and entrepreneurship" are the two most important factors that create the diversification of economies. The core of innovation is that innovation assists in forming new industries and changing the existing industries. New markets will be created and it leads to the commercialization of innovation and hence diversification in economy. In a diversified economy, innovation does not stay limited to the realm of technology (Xiao et al., 2018), spread to health, and reach other opportunities regarding renewable energy and creative industries. This innovation is in turn billed forward by entrepreneurship, as it provides dynamism and flexible response to changed market circumstances and the pursuit of new opportunities. In sum, innovation and entrepreneurship together form the backbone of a diversified economy and thus help it move forward and thrive in progressively fast-moving and stimulated surroundings (Williams & Vorley, 2014).

When the details of economic diversification are grasped, it is all the more appreciated that the nature of innovation and entrepreneurship within this process adds value. Moving to the subsequent chapters, as we delve further into the mechanics of how these components have the potential to play out, it will be possible to see that economies can become much more resilient and stronger, with the capacity both to better withstand external shocks and at the same time to exploit new opportunities towards growth (Zhang, 2023).

The Role of Innovation in Economic Diversification

Innovation is a potent drive for economic diversification in general, which typically implies the generation, development, and commercialization of novel ideas, products, processes, or services with the capacity to bring about considerable improvements or change. Economies are pushed to enlarge their industrial bases by innovation, as they penetrate new markets and continue increasing their competitiveness in the global environment. Through continuous improvement and adjustment, it can become the basis for transforming the economic structure, overcoming dependence on traditional sectors, and ultimately achieving sustainable economic development (Afshan et al., 2021).

Definition and Types of Innovation

Different types of innovation can be generally identified as making unique contributions to economic diversification:

1. **Product Innovation:** It is the introduction of new or significantly improved goods or services. Laying down the creation of new products in such a way that they meet emerging needs or building an improved version opens new markets for businesses and attracts different customer segments (Tunio et al., 2020). For instance, electric vehicles have provided growth in the automotive industry, opening up new opportunities for manufacturers, suppliers, and service providers.
2. **Process Innovation:** This is the type of innovation that delves into the best methodologies of the production and delivery of goods and services. Process innovation makes businesses more competitive through gaining efficiency, cutting costs, and enhancing quality. For example, with the adoption of such state-of-the-art manufacturing technologies as 3D printing and automation, the production of complicated products has changed. The overall process has become faster and cheaper (Shaikh et al., 2021).
3. **Organizational Innovation**: Organizational innovation involves the implementation of changes in business practices, workplace organization, or external relations as regards the company so that it may upgrade its performance. Through changes in their management approach or operations organization, companies can further develop their adaptability and their

reactivity to the market. This hence becomes one of the most important innovations for diversification since there are potential entries in to sectors and new ways of conducting business (Shaikh et al., 2022).

4. **Marketing Innovation:** It refers to bringing new product design, changes in packaging, placement, promotion, and pricing strategy. This means companies are able to create differentiation and appeal to a new market of customers through marketing innovation (Acs et al., 2013). The successful marketing strategies open up new markets, thereby driving diversification by introducing products in new regions or demographics.

HOW INNOVATION DRIVES NEW INDUSTRIES AND SECTORS

Innovations are the key to the creation of new industries and sectors at the bottom of economic diversification. Innovation defines the boundaries set by technology and knowledge through the development of entirely new fields of economic activity (Ali et al., 2022). For instance, the digital economy gave birth, among other things, to such innovative developments in information technology and the Internet as e-commerce, digital marketing, cybersecurity, and many more. These have created millions of jobs and, by all means, contributed to economic growth in many countries (Asem, 2024).

Innovation also facilitates the transformation of other more traditional sectors, enabling them to diversify and go deep into new areas. For example, the agricultural sector has significantly diversified through innovations such as precision farming, which is used to attain maximum performance in crops with minimal resource use through the use of data analytics and probably GPS. The same way, the healthcare sector has diversified into new services with the development of services such as telemedicine and personalized medicine, enhancing the value addition to its clients (Boschma et al., 2017).

Case Studies of Innovation-Led Economic Diversification

The way innovation drives economic diversification is vividly demonstrated in many countries and regions:

- South Korea, which used to be dependent on agriculture and light industries, changed its economy through a focus on innovation. By making massive investments in the area of Research and Development and developing a front-ranking education system, South Korea crafted a robust innovation ecosystem. As a result, rapidly emerged worldwide competitive industries in the country have become electronics, automotive, and biotechnology, and the economy has been widely diversified, while the country has learned not to depend on the old types of industry (Cantner et al., 2019).

- Israel: Being termed the "Startup Nation," Israel has proudly used innovation and taken steps towards economic diversification. It has maintained more of its dependency on R&D, especially in the high-tech industries, for securing its base in cybersecurity, medical devices, and agritech—spawning an environment for innovating new industries with government support, venture capital, and a culture of daredevil risk-taking, placing Israel among the global leaders in innovation (Cheng et al., 2023).
- Germany: As mentioned the driver of this economic diversification in Germany has been innovation, especially for its "Mittelstand" of small and medium-sized enterprises. Through continuous innovation in industries like renewable energy, automotive technology, and industrial automation, the engineering and manufacturing abilities of the country have been sustained over a period of time. This has helped Germany to maintain its diversified economy at very competitive levels along with a very strong export base (Corradini & Propris, 2015).

Innovation and Competitive Advantage

Innovation offers great competitive advantages for economies and businesses in the world economy. It helps economies create products and services that would bear higher value, meet changing consumers' desires, and provide solutions in global challenges, such as digitalization and environmental protection (Damoah, 2020). Such competitive advantage is important for long-term economic growth and provision of means for economies to adjust to the global changes.

Innovations can be encouraged among the nations, and it can also encourage FDI since most investors are in a way attracted by the innovative and dynamic economy. FDI, in turn, contributes capital, technology transfer, and skill development and access to international markets, further adding to economic diversification (Grillitsch & Asheim, 2018).

Innovation Ecosystems and Diversification

At the same time, the innovation ecosystems were created around it: interconnected organizations, such as universities, research institutions, start-ups, and government bodies. It, therefore, offers proper structure, resources, and relevant helps to make innovation blossom. In a nutshell, they enable a collaborative culture of sharing and commercialization of new technologies upon which an enabling environment is created through innovation for new industries or a sector (Harraf et al., 2020).

For instance, the United States is characterized by its most vital innovation environment, witnessed in the Silicon Valley, which underlies the utmost degree of economic diversification. It elicited the broad development of such diversified industries as information technology and software, biotechnology, and clean energy by offering a fertile environment for innovation and entrepreneurship within a distance (Hassen, 2022).

Challenges of Innovation in Economic Diversity

While undoubtedly one of the key components of economic diversification, innovation faces a number of challenges. It includes inadequate levels of R&D financing, deficiency in skilled labor, poor infrastructure, and regulatory barriers. A predominant cultural factor against innovation lies in resistance to change and its opposite (He et al., 2022), risk aversion. Investments in education and skills development, supportive regulation, and an innovative paradigm shape the road to solutions.

It is in the process of economic diversification, where innovation helps the economy expand industrial bases, create new markets, and increase competitiveness. By understanding the types of innovation taking place and how they further economic diversification, policy rethinking and business can tap into the key power that will propel sustainable economic growth and development. Entrepreneurship as a Catalyst of Diversification: The key driver of economic diversification is entrepreneurship (Kim et al., 2013). It is a process of creating, managing, and scaling a new business one more based on ideas from innovation or only the discovery of a fresh market opportunity. Entrepreneurs play a very huge role in stimulating economic growth through the generation of startups, forming new products and services, and employment. They are at the leading frontiers of discovering and establishing new industries and, thus, help drive economies toward diversification. Through risk-taking, creativity, and problem-solving, they contribute to the diminution of the reliance of the economy on traditional sectors and the promotion of a more diversified economic landscape.

Definition of Entrepreneurship and its Characteristics

Entrepreneurship is defined by the pursuit of opportunity outside existing resources currently controlled. Very often, entrepreneurs identify gaps in markets, come up with creative solutions, and bring these solutions into being through new ventures. Key characteristics of entrepreneurship include innovation, the notion of taking risks, proactiveness, and the ability to adapt to changing conditions (Shuaibu et al., 2018). Unlike traditional companies that are likely again strapping in the old industry, entrepreneurship bears the characteristic of many a time being a growing fast and disruptive business. The disruption opportunity is very useful for economic diversification as it leads to the development of new industries and reshaping the old ones (Miniaoui & Schilirò, 2017).

Entrepreneurs either visualize the spirit to bring new things into existence, or they are compelled to do things in a manner different from the status quo. They would, in the process of doing this, take some form of risk, invest some resources, or even muscle their way through some challenges before attaining similar outcomes. This mentality turns out to be the driving force in the diversification aspect, since it calls for a new market, technology ventures, and alternative business frameworks. This implies that the economy is constantly evolving and dynamic with entrepreneurs consistently changing hands, hence making it flexible enough to withstand any economic changes at the international level (Munir & Javed, 2018).

The Role of Startups and Small Businesses in Economic Diversification

Startups and small businesses are what make economies diverse. Whether bringing new products and services to the market, entering and taking over niches, competition is created in the process. Unlike big corporations, which can be quite risk-aversive and are more interested in just preserving their existing market positions, startups and small businesses are more agile, being prepared to experiment with new and innovative ideas. It is this readiness to explore where there are new territories that become critical for economic diversification—pioneering the building of new industries while moving economic activity into new spaces (Williams & Vorley, 2014).

For example, in most developing countries, SMEs have been the driver towards economic diversification in economies that have traditionally mainly concentrated on agriculture or mining. Such enterprises have diversified into the areas of information technology, renewable energy, tourism, and manufacturing, among others, through value addition, and have contributed to increasing the GDP and employment opportunities. Startups and small businesses can support sustainable diversification, driving up from resources that are local and market conditions that are local (Xiao et al., 2018).

Moreover, the startups more often introduce new business models that might disrupt the public markets or even exclusively new markets. For instance, fintech startups have greatly diversified the financial services market through alternative finances and services, such as digital payments, peer-to-peer lending (Zhang, 2023), and blockchain-based solutions. These innovations have given new choices to consumers, have jolted competition and induced innovativeness amongst entrenched financial institutions.

Examples of Entrepreneurial Ventures Contributing to Economic Diversification

There exist countless examples from around the globe wherein entrepreneurial ventures have served as the impetus for economic diversification. Some of the notable examples include:

- Silicon Valley, United States: Arguably, Silicon Valley is one of the best examples of how an entrepreneurial ecosystem can contribute to real economic diversification. What was just a highly narrow economy that was based in defense and semiconductor manufacturing has evolved to be a global technology and innovation hub. The area is the home of Silicon Valley entrepreneurs, which is the frontier of some new industries such as software development, internet services, biotechnology, and artificial intelligence. It was motivated by an entrepreneurial culture, access to venture capital, and a very strong network of research institutions and universities (Afshan et al., 2021)
- Nigeria's Tech Scene: In the last decade, Nigeria has so far experienced rapid development in terms of technology start-ups, especially in the field of Fintech. In turn, these challenges occasioned imaginative solutions on the part of Lagos and other major cities entrepreneurs, notably in financial services and mobile payments (Shaikh et al., 2021), therefore, significantly diversifying an economy that was hitherto too reliant on the oil industry. Using technology and local skills, Nigerian entrepreneurs are in the process of developing new economic opportunities which could eventually weaken the stranglehold that the oil sector has over the country's economy (Tunio et al., 2020).
- India's Renewable Energy Industry: A number of entrepreneurs in India have led the country's drive to renewable energy. By first creating startups in the sectors of solar, wind, and bioenergy, these entrepreneurs helped diversify the country's energy sector, which was earlier dominated by coal and oil, into other renewable sources of energy. Government support and friendly policies added to the entrepreneurship and helped increase capacity in renewable energy very rapidly while generating job opportunities (Shaikh et al., 2022).

Entrepreneurial Ecosystems and Their Role in Diversification

These are networked, interconnected entities incorporating startups, investors, incubators, accelerators, universities, and government agencies in the process of supporting and fostering entrepreneurship (Boschma et al., 2017). An ecosystem is quite useful for economic diversification in that it provides a very conducive environment for innovation and business creation. These are environments that offer resources such as funding, mentorship, market access, and infrastructure necessary for the growth and scaling of startups (Ali et al., 2022).

Such an entrepreneurial ecosystem would rapidly enhance economic diversification due to the attraction of talent, innovation, and collaboration. For instance, the State of Israel's entrepreneurial ecosystem, known as the "Startup Nation," has led to the diversification of its economy from traditional sectors such as agriculture and textiles. An emphasis on technology and innovation in the ecosystem has seen the birth of new industries—cybersecurity, medical devices, and agritech—that have further strengthened the economy in terms of growth and resilience (Acs et al., 2013).

This knowledge sharing may further lead to the innovation of new industries and diversification of current industries within an ecosystem. Therefore, such ecosystems help connect entrepreneurs with investors, researchers, and industry experts in order to create a perfect ground where innovation (Cantner et al., 2019) and economic growth can thrive. Collaborative environment is important in overcoming the challenges associated with economic diversification, which involve access to finance and development of skills, among others (Asem, 2024).

Challenges That the Entrepreneurs Face in Promoting Diversification

While entrepreneurship can turn out to be a very powerful catalyst for economic diversification, entrepreneurs are often faced with a host of issues that may impede their efforts. Access to finance is one of the most common barriers—especially in developing countries where financial markets might be underdeveloped and the investors very risk-averse. Poor access to capital can prevent entrepreneurs from scaling their businesses and exploring new markets, which actually slows the pace down for diversification efforts (Corradini & Propris, 2015).

In this way, one of the most important obstacles to entrepreneurship can be regulatory hurdles and bureaucratic red tape. Extensive and tight regulations increase the cost of doing business, discourage investment, and finally reduce the ability of startups to innovate and grow. Furthermore, the lack of proper basic infrastructure in most developing nations, like reliable internet access, transport, and energy supply, may considerably hamper entrepreneurial activity and processes of diversification (Cheng et al., 2023).

Cultural factors, such as societal attitude to risk and failure, are yet another influence on entrepreneurship. In most cultures, there is a stigma attached to business failure, which by itself most often discourages a potential entrepreneur from following through with novel ideas. The only way to deal with these challenges head-on is by providing a policy environment that can support entrepreneurship, lower regulatory hurdles, and make finance and physical infrastructure available for them (Damoah, 2020).

Policies for Boosting Entrepreneurship for Diversification

Promote entrepreneurship and economic diversification; therefore, the government and stakeholders should work in consideration of the following targeted strategies aimed at countering these challenges to achieve an enabling environment for innovation and the growth of business. Among these are:

- Access to Finance: Provision of grants, loans, and venture capital targeted at supporting businesses to scale up and expand into new markets. Financial institutions that will fund startups and SMEs to build their capacity.
- Easy government rules and reduced bureaucratic red tape: These are seen to reduce the cost of doing business and support entrepreneurial activity. This includes providing protection for intellectual property and provision of appropriate legal frameworks that protect innovation and risk-taking (Grillitsch & Asheim, 2018).
- Investing in Education and the Development of Skills: There is a growing realization that developing an enterprise culture is an important ingredient for business, entrepreneurship, and innovation. The kind of skills needed for starting or growing businesses fully justifies investment by governments in these kinds of education and training programs.
- Building Entrepreneurial Ecosystems: In this direction, support should be given in developing entrepreneurial ecosystems that offer resources, mentoring, and networking opportunities to enable scaling and sustaining growth of the startups. Numerous governments and other stakeholders are working to build an ecosystem functioning as an enabler for collaboration, knowledge sharing, and innovation (Harraf et al., 2020).

First, entrepreneurship is an important catalyst to economic diversification. It does this by creating new industries, transforming others that are already in place, and causing increased activity in general within economies. In these ways, it gives rise to a dynamic and resilient economy—by way of the culture of innovation and risk—that will be able to adapt to changes that come about in the world at large (Hassen, 2022). Finally, targeted strategies and supportive policies can be adopted by governments and other stakeholders to promote entrepreneurship and its role in driving sustainable economic diversification.

INNOVATION-ENTREPRENEURSHIP SYNERGIES

Innovation and entrepreneurship are strongly interrelated drivers of economic diversification. When combined, the synergies created by the two factors become exceptional in driving new industries or changing the profile of existing ones, making them resilient and dynamic. Such synergies are very instrumental in understanding what policymakers, business leaders, and other stakeholders are doing and should be doing to make economic diversification a reality as a pathway to sustainable development (Miniaoui & Schilirò, 2017).

The Interdependency of Innovation and Entrepreneurship

Innovation and entrepreneurship go hand in glove. Innovation lays the bedrock for entrepreneurship in the form of new ideas, technologies, and processes to be harnessed and exploited by entrepreneurs in order to create value. In turn, entrepreneurship enables innovative ideas to hit the market, commercialize new technologies, and scale up novel solutions. This close relationship ensures that innovation does not exist in theoretical models or laboratories but is translated into concrete products and services answering market needs (Kim et al., 2013).

It is often the entrepreneurs themselves who act as catalysts of innovation, identifying gaps in markets and recognizing the potential of new technologies or processes. Equally, the ability to take risks, experiment, and pivot based on market feedback allows them to delve into innovative ideas that might have been otherwise ignored or dismissed by more risk-averse organizations (He et al., 2022). Besides, with the strength of entrepreneurs, they can create demand for innovation, by destroying the existing ways of operation and bringing new expectations from the consumers. For instance, innovation is triggered in the very case of an established organization, when it faces pressure arising from current market needs.

How Innovation Drives Entrepreneurial Ventures

Innovation is one of the most important drivers of entrepreneurial enterprises. It provides the means and ideas for entrepreneurs to differentiate their businesses from competitors' and set new market niches. Such innovation naturally stands a chance of offering a unique value proposition that attracts customers and brings advantages in their competitive nature, hence ultimately displacing old markets or establishing totally new ones (Shuaibu et al., 2018).

The surge of digital platforms has changed the nature of running and interaction in business with customers. Such entrepreneurs have launched ventures, harnessing new technologies such as AI, blockchain, and the IoT, to disrupt traditional models of business. Uber, Airbnb, and Zoom—companies that have changed the nature of respective industries with their new solutions (Zhang, 2023), reshaping consumer behavior and expectations. This is proof of how innovation can drive entrepreneurship, as it creates a plinth for new business opportunities while at the same time disrupting existing markets (Munir & Javed, 2018).

Innovation allows the entrepreneur to achieve a great amount of scalability for their venture. This helps a business get economies of scale from innovated processes and technologies that shall render operations efficient, with low cost and less wastage. More easily, this shall let their businesses scale up quickly and become more competitive than larger and more established ones. For instance, cloud computing made it easier for startups to access very strong computing resources without large upfront investments in IT infrastructure, which made it easy to see rapid growth and expansion (Williams & Vorley, 2014).

How Entrepreneurship Stimulates Innovation

Entrepreneurship stimulates innovation in a way that it opens up an environment open to experimentation, risk-taking, and creativity. More often than not, entrepreneurship is fueled by the passion held towards problem-solving (Xiao et al., 2018), unmet needs, and bringing about a positive change. Such a motive on the part of the entrepreneur makes them innovative at all times. This mindset creates a culture of innovation, where new ideas can be supported, experimented with, and honed.

Entrepreneurial ventures offer the ability for fast iteration and learning, which is critical in the development of novel ideas. Unlike large corporations where procedures and bureaucracy may eventually slow decisions and innovation, startups are generally far more agile and adaptable. This makes them agile at trying new concepts, listening to customer feedback, and varying their offerings in response to changes in market needs at amazing speed (Afshan et al., 2021).

More often than not, the entrepreneur collaborates with third-party researchers, investors, and industry experts in the development and commercialization of new technologies. The cross-pollination of these ideas sometimes results in innovative solutions that might not have been thought of within the boundaries of corporate silos (Tunio et al., 2020). With the integration of unique perspectives and expertise, entrepreneurship acts as a bridging concept that provokes a cooperative mode of thinking toward innovation, driving the creation of new products, services, as well as business models.

Examples of Synergies Between Innovation and Entrepreneurship

There are many around the world where the synergies between innovation and entrepreneurship have been the drivers of economic diversification. These include:

- Fintech Sector in Kenya: The case of Kenya's fintech sector provides a leading example of how both innovation and entrepreneurship can create new industry sectors. Entrepreneurs in Kenya created a novel mobile money transfer service named M-Pesa, which is altering the nature of financial services in the country. This entrepreneurial activity not only filled a significant gap in financial inclusion but also catalyzed further innovation in mobile banking, microfinance, and digital payments, which contributed to economic diversification (Shaikh et al., 2021).
- Biotechnology in Singapore: The biotechnology industry in Singapore exemplifies the coming together of innovation and entrepreneurship to unlock new pathways for the economy. The Singaporean government investment in R&D and setting up research institutions laid out the path for innovation in biotechnology (Shaikh et al., 2022). It was with these inventions that entrepreneurs after that capitalized to start biotech companies in drug development, diagnostics, and regenerative medicine. The entrepreneurial activity has diversified the economy of Singapore, which was based on manufacturing and finance, for the past and has made it a hub for biomedical sciences.
- Renewable Energy in Germany: Germany's renewable energy sector stands as an open case of how innovation and entrepreneurship can bring diversification to an altogether traditional industry. Innovative technologies in this very regard, whether of solar panels, wind turbines, or bioenergy, have been exponentially absorbed by entrepreneurs in Germany as they attempted to create novel energy solutions. The growth, in this respect, of the entrepreneurial firms has not only grown the renewable energy sector; it has also diversified the energy mix of the country, resulting in reduced dependency on fossil fuel and increasing the level of energy security (Acs et al., 2013).

Innovation-Driven Entrepreneurship in the Creation of New Markets

Innovation-driven entrepreneurship tends to be superior at the creation of entirely new markets and new industries. By developing products and services that are revolutionary and that either meet unsatisfied or previously unserved needs or actually create new demand, entrepreneurs can blaze frontiers in the economy. This process of creating a new market is at the heart of economic diversification as it broadens the base of the economy and consequently minimizes the economy's dependence on the traditional sectors (Ali et al., 2022).

For instance, companies like Tesla, which are into electric car manufacturing, have created a new market within the automobile industry. With their innovation in battery technology, vehicle design, and the integration of software (Asem, 2024), Tesla and other EV startups did not only disrupt the traditional market for automobiles but also spawned other industries in the process: battery manufacturing, charging infrastructure, and renewable energy. This innovation-driven entrepreneurship provides a strong impetus toward diversifying the automotive sector and, more generally, provides impetus toward economic diversification efforts.

The sharing economy, just as in the case of firms like Airbnb and Uber, has created new markets for accommodation and transportation. Such companies, through the force of their digital platforms and innovative business models, have managed to reframe traditional industries, creating thus new sources for economic activity and, more generally, diversifying the service sector (Boschma et al., 2017).

Fostering Synergies Between Innovation and Entrepreneurship

The enabling environment would support the maximization of innovation and entrepreneurship linkages. This would encompass the cultivation of culture, the availability of resources, and encouragement for collaboration among different stakeholders. The primary strategies toward this achievement include:

- Encourage R&D: R&D investment is needed to render new ideas and technologies that can be commercialized by entrepreneurs. It requires the joint mandate of governments, businesses, and academic institutions to develop strong R&D ecosystems that provide a consistent pipeline of technologies commercialized through venturing (Cheng et al., 2023).
- Collaboration and networking: When entrepreneurs, researchers, investors, and industry experts are brought together, it can facilitate the process of the creation and commercialization of innovative solutions. This allows the creation of networking events, incubators, accelerators, and innovation hubs (Cantner et al., 2019) to provide platforms through which stakeholders connect, share ideas, and collaborate in new ventures.
- Access to Finance and Resources: One of the key most critical ingredient factors for making an entrepreneurship driven by innovation is access to all relevant financial resources, infrastructure, and business support services by entrepreneurs. Governments and financial institutions need to innovate funding instruments, grants, loans, and venture capital, to support start-ups and scale-ups.

- Tweaking the regulatory environment to be more conducive: To create synergies between them, what is required is an institutional framework that promotes innovation and entrepreneurship (Damoah, 2020). This will essentially take in protection of intellectual property rights, reduction of redtapism, and a policy framework aimed at risk-taking and experimentation.
- Promote Culture of Innovation and Entrepreneurship: Culture of innovation and entrepreneurship should be developed for effecting economic diversification. This would in turn support creativity, taking risks, and learning at all societal levels, say from education systems to corporate environments (Corradini & Propris, 2015).

Mainly, strong synergies between innovation and entrepreneurship should, in most cases, form the central idea that lies behind economic diversification. Such interdependencies, when harnessed, will allow economies to grow new industries and transform the existing ones, thus shaping a dynamic and resilient economic landscape. Sustainability of economic growth and diversification can be effectively achieved by stakeholders using a number of strategies and policies that promote the synergy between innovation and entrepreneurship (Grillitsch & Asheim, 2018).

POLICIES AND INSTITUTIONAL SUPPORT FOR INNOVATION AND ENTREPRENEURSHIP

Effective policy and institutional support are required for engendering innovation and entrepreneurship, which act as the main drivers of economic diversification. By their actions, governments, international organizations (Hassen, 2022), and private sector institutions can do a lot towards creating an enabling environment that would foster innovation, facilitate entrepreneurial activities, and promote the development of new industries. These would be best advanced by focused policy, regulatory, financial, and infrastructure development acts, which are more likely to deepen linkages between innovation and entrepreneurship, hence finally leading to a more diversified and resilient economy (Harraf et al., 2020).

The Role of Government in Innovation and Entrepreneurship

Governments can play an important role in shaping the entire ecosystem of innovation and entrepreneurship. Either by stimulus or by their policies and regulatory frameworks, they will give rise to marshes and promote more new businesses in the commercialization of innovative ideas. A conducive policy environment will create an incentive and stimulus effect towards economic diversification and growth through a number of mechanisms:

- Building National Strategies for Innovation: A strong national innovation strategy outlines in the clearest terms possible the vision and approach of the government in fostering innovation within various sectors. Among other things, it may be based on investing in research and development, encouraging cooperation between academia and enterprise, and facilitating the commercialization of new technologies. The setting of clear priorities and objectives allows for a roadmap on innovation that aligns with broader goals of economic diversification (He et al., 2022).
- Financial Incentives and Support: The first stumbling block is the problem of access to the finance necessary for it. This can be taken care of by providing financial incentives in the form of grants, loans at friendly rates, and tax breaks to startups and small-scale firms that have engaged in innovative activities (Miniaoui & Schilirò, 2017). Examples include R&D tax credits to give firms incentives to engage in new product and technology development. Many governments can also create venture capital funds or public-private partnerships to provide financing in the early stages of startup that has high potential for growth (Kim et al., 2013).
- A Supportive Regulatory Environment: This will go in line with the first to enhance innovation and entrepreneurship. It basically involves reduction of bureaucratic aspects, easier ways of registration of business, and protection rights to intellectual property. Well-defined and transparent regulations that are consistent in application reduce barriers to entry for new businesses and enable risk-taking and innovation (Williams & Vorley, 2014).
- Investing in education and skill development: Education and skills are very central in creating a workforce that can really manage innovation and entrepreneurship. This would involve investment in education systems that put primary emphasis on creativity, critical thinking skills, and problem-solving. It will support vocational trainings and lifelong learning programs leading to the endowment of skills necessary for success in new industries (Shuaibu et al., 2018).
- Creation of Infrastructure for Innovation: Innovation and entrepreneurship require support in the form of physical as well as digital infrastructure. Governments can invest in created research laboratories or technology parks (Munir & Javed, 2018) or innovation hubs or investment in high-speed internet access. These provide entrepreneurs and innovators the required resources and environment to develop and scale their ideas. If we consider Silicon Valley as an example, the development of the valley was catalyzed by govern-

ment investment in infrastructure through defense research and investment in universities.

- Promotion of Innovation that is Inclusive and Entrepreneurship: With innovation and entrepreneurship inclusive, the chances of maximizing their impacts on economic diversification are high (Xiao et al., 2018). Consequently, governments can enable policies for underrepresented groups, such as women, minorities, and those from low-income backgrounds, to engage in entrepreneurship by way of targeted funding, mentorship, and access to networks that will help transcend entry barriers into the entrepreneurial ecosystem.

Institutions That Contribute to Innovation and Entrepreneurship

Other than the government, many other institutions are critical to helping innovation and entrepreneurship. They range from universities and research institutions, business incubators and accelerators, to financial institutions and non-governmental organizations. Each of these institutions has different resources, expertise, and support brought in the ecosystem necessary for the success of entrepreneurial ventures (Zhang, 2023).

- Universities and Research Institutions: Universities and research institutions represent some of the most significant sources of innovation. They conduct cutting-edge research, generate new knowledge, and train the next generation of innovators and entrepreneurs. Through this, HEIs can foster academia-industry collaboration in translating research findings into commercial products and services. Technology transfer offices, research parks, and innovation clusters are ways in which universities can contribute to the commercialization of research and the growth of new industries (Afshan et al., 2021).
- Business Incubators and Accelerators: These are organizations that act as means of helping startups and early-stage companies through assistance in mentorship, provision of resources, and networking opportunities. Incubators keep a nurturing environment for the startup to develop its idea and build up its business for a period of time. An accelerator is a short, intense program that takes in early-stage companies (Tunio et al., 2020) and fast-tracks them to grow. Both these types of organizations are very important in promoting entrepreneurship by providing it with access to capital, expert advice, and opportunity exposure to potential customers and partners.
- Financial Institutions and Venture Capitalists: These financial institutions, in particular banks and venture capitalists, are like backbone to fundraising for setting up and scaling up innovative industries (Shaikh et al., 2022).

Especially venture capital firms and angel investors invest in a very high risk but high reward venture; traditional banks may be too conservative to support. By investing in start-ups and early-stage companies, they are bringing out innovative ideas to the market and in turn contributing to diversification of the economy (Shaikh et al., 2021).

- Non-Governmental Organizations and Industry Associations: Most of the time, innovation and entrepreneurship are hatched by NGOs and industry associations. They offer training, mentorship, and advocacy services while creating networking opportunities for the entrepreneurs and innovators. For example, industry associations can organize events to give expo- sure to new technologies, create a platform for collaboration among mem- bers, or lobby for supportive policies. NGOs focus on social entrepreneurship or on underrepresented segments in the entrepreneurial ecosystems (Afshan et al., 2021).

Examples of Good Policy and Institutional Support for Innovation and Entrepreneurship

There are countries that have well-embraced good policies and institutional frameworks that give leeway to a lot of innovation and entrepreneurship towards economic diversification. These countries include:

- The Startup Ecosystem of Israel—Israel is referred to as the "State-Up Nation" being the start-up ecosystem that is nimble and entrepreneurial. The Israeli government has played an important role in the growth of this ecosystem through several policies such as generous R&D tax incentives, grants to even early-stage startups, and supporting venture capital funds (Asem, 2024). The great emphasis on education by the state of Israel in general, and particularly in science and technology, makes this country the originator of a highly professional workforce among users of innovation. Research and development are facilitated through institutions like the Israel Innovation Authority and the Office of the Chief Scientist, having contributed so much in ensuring that the academic world collaborates with the industry (Acs et al., 2013).
- Smart Nation Initiative of Singapore: Through good policies and initiatives, Singapore has been able to diversify its economy by fostering innovation as well as entrepreneurship. The Smart Nation initiative is essentially the government's plan to transform Singapore into a digital economy by using technology and data to drive innovation in ways that improve quality of life, create business opportunities, and deliver better government services. In its specificity, it is about investments in digital infrastructure, supporting startups and SMEs, and programs developing a skilled workforce. Institutions

such as A*STAR and EDB have consequently brought about innovation and also foreign direct investments (Ali et al., 2022).

- Growth of South Korea through Innovation: In a turning of only a few decades, this country has succeeded in transforming from its poor state into a high technic industrial giant due to having implemented the wise policy that has supported innovation and entrepreneurship. The government has made heavy investments in R&D in key industries, namely electronics, biotechnology, and renewable energy. Another crucial step has been policies promoting cooperation among large chaebols, SMEs, and startups. Institutions of higher learning and research, such as the Korea Institute of Science and Technology and the Korea Advanced Institute of Science and Technology, have been playing important roles in research and commercialization activities.
- Kenya's Silicon Savannah: With the government creating a friendly environment beyond its borders and a growing entrepreneurial spirit, Kenya's "Silicon Savannah" is an emerging digital innovation center. Besides, the Kenyan government has been spurred to encourage innovation by plans like Vision 2030 for national economic development. The likes of the iHub and Kenya National Innovation Agency (KENIA) are institutions that support tech start-ups through incubation, mentorship, and even funding. M-Pesa by Safaricom is another product – a mobile money transfer service -- emanating from Kenya that occasionally is used as an example worldwide, how innovation and entrepreneurship can lead to financial inclusion and economic diversification.

Challenges in Provide Policy and Institutional Support

Although the policy and institutional support provides a base for driving innovation and entrepreneurship, the effectiveness is marred by a number of hitches which include:

- Bureaucratic Inefficiencies: Over-bureaucratization and red tape may suppress innovation and entrepreneurship due to unnecessary entry and running-of-the-business costs. Governments need to work at reducing the process time and red tape in licensing and patenting within licensees for more conducive business-starting environments for innovators (Boschma et al., 2017).
- Poor Access to Finance: Governments do what they can, but there are still millions of entrepreneurs globally facing the challenge of a lack of access to finance, especially in developing countries. This challenge is usually compounded by risk-averse financial institutions and a shortage of venture capital, among other things. Mitigating such calls for focused interventions,

including government-backed loan-guarantees, seed-funding, and attracting private investment.

- Skill Gaps and Talent Shortages: Skilled labor shortages erode innovation and entrepreneurship in highly technology and knowledge—intensive sectors. The general investment in education and training programs by governments and institutions in the development of the right skills and capabilities is to support a dynamic and innovative economy (Cantner et al., 2019).
- Limited Collaboration and Networking: It is a fact that in innovation and entrepreneurship, there exists an ecosystem where stakeholders work in collaboration. But the reality is that platforms with effective networking and collaboration are largely wanting in the majority of regions. Networks and collaboration should therefore be built between entrepreneurs, researchers, investors, and other key players, fostered by the government and institutions which recommend it (Cheng et al., 2023).
- Resistance to Change: Cultural and social acceptance towards risk, failure, and innovation often creates barriers. In fact, in most cultures, there is a certain level of stigma associated with failing, which in itself may ward away potential entrepreneurs from such risks. Changes in these attitudes require efforts on the side of governments, learning institutions, and society at large to be changed by encouraging a culture of innovation, risk-taking, and lifelong learning (Damoah, 2020).

Supportive Policy and Institutional Strategies

Towards better policy and institutional support for innovation and entrepreneurship, the following strategies should be considered:

Comprehensive Policies on Innovation and Entrepreneurship: Governments should spell out and implement through policy, provisions that comprehensively develop innovation and entrepreneurship in all sectors of the economy. Such policies ought to have clear linkages to the broader national development goals and must have specific provisions for the underrepresented groups, collaborative endeavoring, and sustainability practices (Corradini & Propris, 2015).

- Enhance Public-Private Partnerships: The role that public-private partnerships could play in encouraging innovation is a very large one. More could be done to bring new opportunities to the public by these (Grillitsch & Asheim, 2018). Through the type of collaboration previously discussed, governments can access supplementary resources, expertise, and networking that are provided by private sector entities in supporting startups and innovators.

- Promotion of Regional and International Collaboration: The effectiveness of policy and institutional support for innovation and entrepreneurship would be very high in cases of regional and international collaboration. Knowledge, best practice in innovation, and entrepreneurial resources, therefore, circulate across countries; they thus learn from one another in their diversity to build strong and integrated innovation systems (Harraf et al., 2020).
- Continuous Monitoring and Evaluation: The policies and programs for care and support would be effectively implemented and carried out through mechanisms put in place for continuous monitoring and evaluation so that they work and are adjusted for better performance. Governments and institutions must establish mechanisms to continuously monitor the effects and impacts of their support measures.
- Encourage a Culture of Experimentation and Risk-Taking: The culture that allows or rather encourages experimentation and taking risks should be considered the major trend to follow in the developing innovation and entrepreneurship field. The government and institutions should lead by example, encouraging a mindset that does not fear uncertainty but is based on creative problem-solving (Hassen, 2022).

At the end of the day, good policies and institutional support are the key ingredients to spurring innovation and entrepreneurship, important agents of economic diversification. In this regard, governments and other stakeholders can, through specific policies in place and through enabling institutions, foster such an environment able to encourage new industry development and ensure a more diversified and strong economy (He et al., 2022).

Challenges and Barriers to Innovation and Entrepreneurship in Economic Diversification

As much as innovation and entrepreneurship are powerful drivers, they are often constrained by a number of challenges and barriers during the process of economic diversification. It is key for the policymakers, business leaders, and other relevant stakeholders to understand these obstacles as they put forward interventions that put into perspective an enabling environment (Kim et al., 2013). However, these challenges can be grouped into diverse domains such as financial, regulatory, cultural, infrastructural, and educational barriers. These barriers should call for a comprehensive approach that would be sensitive to the specificity of each of the economies and utilize both public and private sector support (Miniaoui & Schilirò, 2017).

Access to finance is one of the biggest barriers to innovation and entrepreneurship. Most entrepreneurs face the challenge of getting enough funds at both the seed and growth levels to start and scale their businesses. This holds particularly important in developing countries, where access to credit is low and financial markets are often underdeveloped (Munir & Javed, 2018).

- Lack of Access to Capital: Startups and small entrepreneurs are badly hobbled by the lack of access to capital from formal finance, particularly in their initial stages of growth (Shuaibu et al., 2018). It could be due to high perceived risk, lack of collateral, or even the fact that the business may not have a proven track record. Besides, in some places, the development of venture capital and angel investment networks is underdeveloped, thereby greatly constricting sources of seed and growth finance for innovative ventures.
- High Cost of Financing: Even when financing is is available, it could turn out to be costing the high for the startups and small enterprises. High-interest rates, tough conditions on loans, and cumbersome application procedures can discourage entrepreneurship from availing themselves reduced access to external funds. This barrier is especially hard for innovative startups that call for large upfront investments in R&D or technology (Xiao et al., 2018).
- Poorly Developed Alternative Funding Sources: Most regions are not well-developed in alternative funding sources through crowdfunding, peer-to-peer lending, and impact investing. The absence of these diverse funding mechanisms limits entrepreneurs to any kind of financial resources useful in innovating and growing businesses. In addition, most of the public mechanisms for funding businesses, like grants and subsidies, for instance, are limited and have a lot of bureaucracies to evade (Williams & Vorley, 2014).

Regulatory and Policy Barriers

The regulatory and policy environments are very central in configuring the innovation and entrepreneurship ecosystems. In many countries, however, such environments are normally oppressive and prohibitive, hence subjecting innovators and entrepreneurs to enormous challenges (Zhang, 2023).

- Bureaucratic Red Tape and Regulatory Complexity: Hurdles in establishing and running new ventures much more easily develop from strict regulatory requirements, over-bureaucratization, and excessively long approval procedures. Many entrepreneurs often report that such regulations present the highest hurdles, especially when obtaining permits, licenses, and certifications. These cumulatively retard the launch of new ventures and raise costs, lessening the overall appeal of starting a business (Afshan et al., 2021).

- Uncertain and Unpredictable Policies: The ever-changing face of government policies and regulations leads to an uncertain business environment that deters investment in innovation and entrepreneurship (Tunio et al., 2020). If entrepreneurs feel that this change in regulation will hurt their business model, when they feel more uncertain and less ready for investment in new ventures, in the long run, unpredictability will also make it difficult for businesses to serve the long-term planning purpose, such as investing in R&D or scaling operations.
- Poor Protection of Intellectual Property: There is no doubt that in the case of poor IP protection, it will become one of the greatest barriers to innovation, especially in industries like technology and pharmaceuticals, where a huge amount of knowledge becomes the center of innovation (Shaikh et al., 2022). The entrepreneur or innovator may shy away from investing in never-before concepts for fear that his or her intellectual property may not be protected from infringement or theft. Weak enforcement of IP would also weaken trust in the legal system, further discouraging innovation and investment (Shaikh et al., 2021).

Cultural and Social Barriers

Cultural and social factors may as well pose greater difficulties within innovation and entrepreneurship. The society's perceptions of risk, failure, and innovation affect the intensity to which people are willing to apply themselves to entrepreneurial activities and innovative ideas.

- Fear of Failure: In many cultures, failure carries a very strong stigma that paves the way to a person steering away from taking risks and also into venturing into new businesses. This kind of fear in turn strongly discourages many not to engage in entrepreneurship, especially into those avenues that seem high-risk in nature or have hazy chances of realisation. Encouraging an innovation and entrepreneurship culture that embraces failure as a learning opportunity is majorly attributed (Acs et al., 2013).
- Societal Risk Aversion Societal risk aversion may be a barrier to both innovation and entrepreneurship. In some cultures, there are people who would prefer assured, secure jobs in a firm than uncertain entrepreneurial activities (Ali et al., 2022). This is experienced when people lack social safety nets that may include unemployment benefits or health insurance, which might

make the risks in entrepreneurship looking humongous. In a bid to remove this barrier, entrepreneurship can be promoted as a good career option and all necessary support for risk-taking provided.

- Absence of Entrepreneurial Mindset and Skills: Most countries suffer from a general lack of awareness and understanding that entrepreneurship can be a probable career opportunity. This might be due to lack of entrepreneurial role models, entrepreneurial education, and training or cultural norms that seem to frown upon risk and innovation. Developing an entrepreneurial mindset and creating a culture that encourages creativity and innovative thinking is of most importance in case the country wants to see more entrepreneurship and economic diversification (Asem, 2024).

Infrastructural Barriers

A certain level of needed infrastructure is necessary to sustain innovation and entrepreneurship. Yet in most of the developing countries, infrastructural deficits are the most critical barriers to newly emerging ventures and industries.

- Limited Access to Technology and Digital Infrastructure: Due to the contemporary essence of entrepreneurship, especially in areas like e-commerce, fin-tech, and digital services, access to technology and digital infrastructure is a must. Yet, in most of these regions, not possessing high-speed internet or stable electricity (Boschma et al., 2017) and access to general advanced technologies are a deficit to the potential of any entrepreneur who desires to innovate and scale the business through the power of digital tools and platforms. Improved digital infrastructure and assured affordable access to technology will be key to fostering innovation and entrepreneurship.
- Poor Physical Infrastructure: Physical infrastructure in the form of transportation networks, logistics systems, and industrial parks is very important to sustain innovation and entrepreneurship. Inadequate infrastructure can increase the cost and complexity of business operations, particularly for start-ups and small businesses heavily reliant on effective supply chains and distribution networks. Investments in infrastructure development and their availability to the entrepreneurs are central to overall efforts in encouraging economic diversification (Cantner et al., 2019).
- Limited Access to Innovation Ecosystems: Research institutions, incubators, accelerators, and co-working spaces are an important part of innovation ecosystems; in other words, these entities serve as support institutions for entrepreneurs and innovators (Corradini & Propris, 2015). In most cases, these facilities are underdeveloped in the regions or, if developed, they become ag-

glomeration-based in major urban centers—meaning, very few entrepreneurs who do not reside in these areas will have access to such facilities. Access and diffusion of entrepreneur support ecosystems in general, and of incubators and accelerators in particular, are essential for developing a more inclusive entrepreneurial environment that is not restricted to businesses but also for social purposes (Cheng et al., 2023).

Educational and Skills Barriers

Education and competence development are the very basis of innovation and entrepreneurship. On the other hand, some of the biggest barriers to the establishment and growth of new industries and the development of new solutions are gaps in education and competence development (Damoah, 2020).

- Technical and Entrepreneurial Skills: An absence of technical skills in coding, data analysis, and engineering can easily thwart several business opportunities for entrepreneurs. Similarly, lack of entrepreneurial competencies in managing businesses, marketing, or financial literacy may overall mar the prospects of start-ups and small businesses surviving into larger and sustainable enterprises. Bridging these skill gaps through well-designed education and training programs would thus become critical in igniting innovation and entrepreneurship (Grillitsch & Asheim, 2018).
- Mismatch between Education Systems and Industrial Needs: Very many countries have education systems not aligned to the modern economy. Therefore, what the graduate has at the end of their school life will be different from what the employer will demand. This becomes instead a challenge to an entrepreneur as well as a business out to spread its tentacles. It will therefore be very necessary to reform the education systems so much at all levels to give more emphasis on STEM education and entrepreneurship and innovation to support economic diversification (Harraf et al., 2020).
- Limited Access to Quality Education and Training: A fundamental nature of this challenge is the inequality in access to quality education and training, particularly for the developing countries and the rural areas. In fact, such inequality can be extremely important as a barrier to innovation and entrepreneurship since access to skilled talent limits the drivers for setting up new ventures and thus developing innovative solutions (Hassen, 2022). This would translate into stepped-up support toward economic growth and diversification by increasing access to quality education and training, specifically in regions that are poorly served.

Market Barriers

In a similar way, market barriers can develop and pose huge challenges to innovation and entrepreneurship, in many cases with regard to access to the market, competition, and customer adoption.

- Limited access to markets: Market access is the door to any new venture or commercialization of innovative products and services (Miniaoui & Schilirò, 2017). However, in most countries, entrepreneurs have been facing challenges in accessing both local and international markets. These obstacles include trade barriers, lack of market information, and logistic challenges. Defeating these challenges requires a focus on increasing access to these markets through measures such as trade facilitation, market development programs, and support to export-oriented businesses (He et al., 2022).
- Much Competition and Saturation: Much competition and saturation in some of the fields make it really tough for a new entrant to establish himself and compete with old players. This is very typical in mature industries, where a few incumbents have high market power and huge resources. In this manner, competitiveness can be nurtured and an environment can be created to support innovation, hence fostering startup activities for a vibrant and diversified economy (Kim et al., 2013).
- Challenges in Customer Adoption of Innovative Products and Services: Many a time, though an innovative product or service is developed, it meets with friction from the customers, who are used to using traditional offerings (Shuaibu et al., 2018). Most customers feel a bit unreceptive and unwilling to shift to a new technology or a new solution because of the absence of information or realization of the "why" of innovation. Dealing with such a barrier calls for customer education, building trust in them, and making them realize the value offered by innovative products and services.

Strategies to Overcome Challenges and Barriers

The strategies for warding off the challenges and barriers to economic diversification are the strategies employed to overcome challenges and barriers in innovation and entrepreneurship.

- Increased access to finance: This is another point where governments, financial organizations, and development agencies have to, in common ground, try to enable easier access to finance for start-ups and small enterprises. This includes developing mechanisms that can provide relevant funding and financial products that are relevant for entrepreneurs (Munir & Javed, 2018).

- Simplifying regulatory frameworks: The governments should ease out complex regulatory frameworks and reduce bureaucracies, which result in a direct disincentive to private entrepreneurship and innovation. In this regard, it should be ensured that the business registration process is seamless, regulations are clear and consistent, and intellectual property registration is protected
- Promoting entrepreneurial culture: This would change the risk, failure, and innovation attitudes in societies. These programs include staging the success of entrepreneurship, provision of mentors and support groups, and teaching and training entrepreneurship (Xiao et al., 2018).
- Infrastructure Development Investment: Investments in physical and digital infrastructure are of essence in supporting innovation and entrepreneurship. This should be a collaboration between the governments and private sector partners to work on priority infrastructural projects in order to boost accessibility that supports connectivity, logistics, and enhances access to technology and innovation ecosystems (Williams & Vorley, 2014).
- Aligned education systems for catering to the new needs of the industry: This requires all education systems to reform in a manner that caters to new, modern needs of the economy, including adaptation of technical and entrepreneurial skills like STEM, entrepreneurship education, and lifelong learning.
- Bettering Market Access and Competitiveness: Measures to better market access and competitiveness should aspire to reduce the barriers arising for the developing markets, build competitiveness, and promote innovation. These include export-oriented firm support, facilitation of access to market information, innovative products, and service promotion (Zhang, 2023).

These stakeholders would only set the perfect situation for an enabling environment for innovation and entrepreneurship, economic diversification, and drive sustainable development if they seriously address these barriers and challenges (Afshan et al., 2021).

FUTURE TRENDS AND OPPORTUNITIES

Looking ahead, the future is engulfed by emerging trends and opportunities that can lead to new ways of innovation and entrepreneurship; these same factors can assure a diversified and growing economy. The future shall be driven by technological innovations, changes in global markets, and new social needs; each enables new entrepreneurial avenues and innovative solutions (Tunio et al., 2020).

Of these changes, the one standing at the forefront is **Digital Transformation** with Artificial Intelligence, Blockchain technology, the Internet of Things, and 5G, transforming all the industries while creating entirely new opportunities for businesses. In these regards, AI and machine learning give way to still greater heights of sophistication in data analysis and automation, leading to breakthroughs in such sectors as health, finance, and manufacturing. AI-powered startups providing personalized medicine and predictive analytics are just a few examples (Shaikh et al., 2022). Blockchain technology is constantly redefining trust and transparency, well beyond cryptocurrencies, through applications in supply chain management and digital identification verification. IoT is leading in the development of smart cities and connected devices. On the other hand, 5G technology promises to support much more enhanced connectivity and will allow new application realms through augmented reality and autonomous vehicles (Shaikh et al., 2021).

On the other hand, topics such as **sustainability and green innovation** have recently gained a lot of ground in the entrepreneurship agenda. Sustainability in business has also found time to grow, as the issues around the importance of the environment continue expanding. Innovations, therefore, thrive around the transitions that are being made to clean energy sources like solar and wind, and in renewables and energy storage systems (Ali et al., 2022). This is also true for the circular economy, which prompts innovations in biodegradable materials and waste-to-energy solutions—key areas of recycling and reducing waste. Another area of growth is in sustainable agriculture and food technology, with startups looking into vertical farming, alternative proteins, and precision agriculture to answer to the question of food security and environmental impact (Acs et al., 2013).

Remote work and digital nomadism are reshaping the status quo of the workforce, establishing new ways to innovate. The rising tidal wave of remote work has led to demands for an integrated set of solutions that will improve remote collaboration and productivity, from virtual collaboration tools to project management platforms (Boschma et al., 2017). With digital nomadism becoming more and more a way of life, new services accommodating remote workers—coworking spaces and freelance marketplaces—are growing as well. All these tendencies have converged to be seized on by entrepreneurs, who are now developing platforms supporting the infrastructure for remote work and digital nomad lifestyles (Asem, 2024).

Another such area with huge potential for economic diversification is **health and wellness innovation**. Innovation opportunities open up with these changes in health care delivery in the adoption of telemedicine and digital health technologies for telehealth platforms and the monitoring of patients remotely. Innovations have also highlighted mental health and wellness, leading to solutions for mental health apps and online counseling. Advancements in personalized medicine and genomics now make it possible to provide healthcare solutions through genetic testing and precision medicine that startups are currently focused on.

Furthermore, there are opportunities opened by **globalization and emerging markets**. New market growth and globalization provide more and more opportunities for innovation and entrepreneurship. Emerging markets have limitless opportunities for resourceful products and services. There are numerous opportunities brought by cross-border collaboration and trade. International partnerships and market expansion are opened to such startups, sometimes via joint ventures and global innovation challenges (Cantner et al., 2019).

The conceptualization of **social impact and inclusive innovation** becomes critical within the entrepreneurial ecosystem. Social entrepreneurship catalyzes the creation of positive social and environmental impact through opportunities like impact investing and sustainable development goals. Inclusive innovation works toward facilitating underrepresented groups in innovation and removing entry barriers to maximize the effect of entrepreneurship on more equitable growth (Cheng et al., 2023).

In summary, these future trends and opportunities hold great potential for innovation and entrepreneurship, entailing economic diversification and sustainable development. Taking advantage of the trends and associated opportunities would foster a dynamic and resilient economic landscape responsive to changing needs and advances.

CONCLUSION

Today, in a flexible global economy, the forces of diversification and growth are driven by innovation and entrepreneurship. The rise of emerging technologies such as AI, blockchain, IoT, and 5G is changing industries, creating new business opportunities, and an emphasis on sustainability plus green innovations. Increased remote work and the rise of digital nomadism are reshashing the conventional work environment, opening the doors to remote collaboration and digital services. Among them are focused health and wellness developments, as well as the study of international and market emergence arenas (Corradini & Propris, 2015), which provide opportunities for entrepreneurial activities. Social impact and inclusiveness attention remain top of mind priorities to ensure that the innovation process is harnessed for the pursuit of inclusive and sustainable development. The better stakeholders understand and respond to these shifts, the greater the resilience and diversity of an economic environment that will be crafted by the ability to adapt to challenges and capture opportunities tomorrow.

REFERENCES

Acs, Z., Szekeres, L., & Autio, E. (2013). *The role of entrepreneurship in economic development.*. DOI: 10.4337/9781782540427.00010

Afshan, G., Shahid, S., & Tunio, M. N. (2021). Learning experiences of women entrepreneurs amidst COVID-19. *International Journal of Gender and Entrepreneurship*, 13(2), 162–186. DOI: 10.1108/IJGE-09-2020-0153

Ali, A., Iftikhar, S., & Butt, S. (2022). Is innovation in pakistan driven by specialisation or diversity? *Pakistan Development Review*, , 705–714. DOI: 10.30541/v55i4I-IIpp.705-714

Asem, A. (2024). *Navigating digital transformation in alignment with vision 2030: a review of organizational strategies, innovations, and implications in saudi arabia.* Journal of Knowledge Learning and Science Technology Issn 2959-6386 (Online), 3(2), 21-29. DOI: 10.60087/jklst.vol3.n2.p29

Boschma, R., Coenen, L., Frenken, K., & Truffer, B. (2017). Towards a theory of regional diversification: Combining insights from evolutionary economic geography and transition studies. *Regional Studies*, 51(1), 31–45. DOI: 10.1080/00343404.2016.1258460

Cantner, U., Dettmann, E., Giebler, A., Guenther, J., & Kristalova, M. (2019). The impact of innovation and innovation subsidies on economic development in german regions. *Regional Studies*, 53(9), 1284–1295. DOI: 10.1080/00343404.2019.1639656

Cheng, F., Ji, S., & Chen, Y. (2023). The contract design of employee stock ownership plan and enterprise innovation investment: Evidence from china. *Sustainability (Basel)*, 15(3), 2601. DOI: 10.3390/su15032601

Corradini, C., & Propris, L. (2015). Technological diversification and new innovators in european regions: Evidence from patent data. *Environment & Planning A*, 47(10), 2170–2186. DOI: 10.1177/0308518X15599285

Damoah, O. (2020). Strategic factors predicting the likelihood of youth entrepreneurship in ghana: A logistic regression analysis. *World Journal of Entrepreneurship, Management and Sustainable Development*, 16(4), 389–401. DOI: 10.1108/WJEMSD-06-2018-0057

Grillitsch, M., & Asheim, B. (2018). Place-based innovation policy for industrial diversification in regions. *European Planning Studies*, 26(8), 1638–1662. DOI: 10.1080/09654313.2018.1484892

Harraf, A., Ghura, H., Hamdan, A., & Li, X. (2020). Formal institutions and the development of entrepreneurial activity – the contingent role of corruption in emerging economies. *Journal of Entrepreneurship and Public Policy*, 10(1), 15–37. DOI: 10.1108/JEPP-06-2020-0033

Hassen, T. (2022). A transformative state in the wake of covid-19: What is needed to enable innovation, entrepreneurship, and education in qatar? *Sustainability (Basel)*, 14(13), 7953. DOI: 10.3390/su14137953

He, D., Miao, P., & Qureshi, N. (2022). Can industrial diversification help strengthen regional economic resilience? *Frontiers in Environmental Science*, 10, 987396. Advance online publication. DOI: 10.3389/fenvs.2022.987396

Kim, S., Arthurs, J., Sahaym, A., & Cullen, J. (2013). Search behavior of the diversified firm: The impact of fit on innovation. *Strategic Management Journal*, 34(8), 999–1009. DOI: 10.1002/smj.2038

Miniaoui, H., & Schilirò, D. (2017). Innovation and entrepreneurship for the diversification and growth of the gulf cooperation council economies. *Business and Management Studies*, 1(1), 69. DOI: 10.11114/bms.v3i3.2594

Munir, K., & Javed, Z. (2018). Export composition and economic growth: Evidence from south asian countries. *South Asian Journal of Business Studies*, 7(2), 225–240. DOI: 10.1108/SAJBS-10-2017-0117

Shaikh, E., Tunio, M. N., Khoso, W. M., Brahmi, M., & Rasool, S. (2022). *The COVID-19 pandemic overlaps entrepreneurial activities and triggered new challenges: a review Study. Managing Human Resources in SMEs and Start-ups: International Challenges and Solutions*, 155-182.

Shaikh, E., Tunio, M. N., & Qureshi, F. (2021). Finance and women's entrepreneurship in DETEs: A literature review. Entrepreneurial Finance. *Innovation and Development*, , 191–209.

Shuaibu, M., Gwazawa, U., & Jega, A. (2018). Entrepreneurship development for diversification of nigerian economy. *Journal of Economics Management and Trade*, 21(6), 1–11. DOI: 10.9734/JEMT/2018/41679

Tunio, M. N. (2020). Role of ICT in promoting entrepreneurial ecosystems in Pakistan. [JBE]. *Journal of Business Ecosystems*, 1(2), 1–21. DOI: 10.4018/JBE.2020070101

Williams, N., & Vorley, T. (2014). Economic resilience and entrepreneurship: Lessons from the sheffield city region. *Entrepreneurship and Regional Development*, 26(3-4), 257–281. DOI: 10.1080/08985626.2014.894129

Xiao, J., Boschma, R., & Andersson, M. (2018). Industrial diversification in europe: The differentiated role of relatedness. *Economic Geography*, 94(5), 514–549. DOI: 10.1080/00130095.2018.1444989

Zhang, L. (2023). Examining the relationship between entrepreneurship education and job creation in china's post-pandemic economy. *Journal of Digitainability Realism & Mastery (Dream)*, 2(05), 45–52. DOI: 10.56982/dream.v2i05.119

Chapter 4
Economic Diversity and Innovation Analysis in Startups: Creativity in Business Ventures Through Entrepreneurship

S. Varalakshmi
Economics and Business Studies Department, Mazoon College, Muscat, Oman

Reem Ibrahim Al Farsi
https://orcid.org/0009-0004-6977-8272
Department of Business Studies, College of Economics and Business Administration, University of Technology and Applied Sciences, Oman

Ravi Vinod Kumar Sharma
Department of Business Studies, College of Economics and Business Administration, University of Technology and Applied Sciences, Oman

M. Umasankar
https://orcid.org/0000-0002-1346-7887
Department of Professional Studies, Christ University, Bangalore, India

D. Pavan Kumar
Department of MBA, Dr. D.Y. Patil Vidhyapeeth, Pune, India

ABSTRACT

The chapter focuses on the critical role of economic diversity in stimulating innovation and creativity in startup businesses. Bringing into discussion a number of economic contexts, it reveals how diverse economic conditions as a whole shape

DOI: 10.4018/979-8-3693-9486-1.ch004

entrepreneurial strategies and influence the development of innovative solutions. It considers the mechanisms through which economic diversity will spur creative thinking to arrive at new business models and products. It gives case studies of successful startups to bring out real-life examples of how economic diversity has been the source of innovation. The chapter, therefore, highlights with tangible benefits accruing from diverse economic backgrounds. In a nutshell, it ends with the strategic recommendations for entrepreneurs and investors on how to harness economic diversity in enhancing innovation, building resilient business ventures, and gaining long-term success in competitive markets.

INTRODUCTION

Innovation is currently viewed as a pillar of success in the quickly changing world of global enterprise startups. In most cases, the thin line separating two identical beginnings is their innovation power in coming up with newer products, services, or models of their business. However, innovation is not something going arm in arm with everything but is highly pinned on several external and internal factors. One of those critical factors includes economic diversity. Economic diversity is a gradient from which entrepreneurs emerge and which they inhabit—financial, social, and cultural diversity of contexts. Economic diversity has become another major factor affecting the way enterprise and innovation work for entrepreneurs. It is highly correlated to innovate activity in the start-up ecosystem and an influence on sources of both opportunity and funding. Studies look at the correlation of economic diversity and a detailed account of diverse economic backgrounds in problem-solving and creative ways of entrepreneurship. Economic diversity is a definition of the various economic environments, backgrounds, and conditions in which entrepreneurs and their businesses operate(Gompers & Wang, 2017).

This could take the form of differences in income levels, access to resources, cultural influence, or market conditions. In stark contrast, many startups see economic diversity as a challenge and an opportunity at the same time. Entrepreneurs representing different economic groups bring in special perspective, experience, and approach to remedy these challenges. Such diversity leads to great idea richness and better innovation capacity. In a startup, economic diversity is not about founders' backgrounds, but about the economic environments in which the startups operate(Brixy et al., 2017).

Very often, startups in economically diverse regions face challenges that are quite unique, including scarcity of resources and market instability, which may prove to be opportunities for innovation. For instance, a startup based in an emerging market is likely to develop solutions that are affordable in costs and scalable to a global level, while the one based in a more affluent area will probably major in the luxury or high-tech space. This diversity in economic contexts provides fertile grounds for entrepreneurial creativity, as individuals are forced outside the box if things are to go to work. Economic diversity plays one of the pivotal fostering roles in innovations within start-ups that stimulate the wide spectrum of ideas and approaches(Brixy et al., 2017). Entrepreneurs from varying economic backgrounds largely have different views towards market needs and customer behavior that form bases for creating innovative products and services. For example, an entrepreneur from a low-income background will definitely feel more at one with the needs of a cost-sensitive consumer and thus develops more affordable and scalable solutions. By contrast, for the entrepreneur from an affluent family background, the availability of capital and networks is much higher, thus enabling the pursuit of high-risk, high-reward innovations(Kofanov & Zozulov, 2018).

Moreover, economic diversity might be prone to cross-pollination of ideas. Having entrepreneurs together who have been working in different economic environments will allow them to share their special insights and experiences in their work, which actually enriches the idea exchange. Such cross-pollination quite often gives way to creativity and finally leads to the evolution of new business models targeting the capture of a wider spectrum of markets. For example, a startup team from both the developed and developing countries can pool their knowledge to produce a product that would be affordable yet technologically advanced enough to suit both markets (Gimenez-Fernandez et al., 2019). While this economic diversity has the power to spur innovation, it also comes along with several challenges. One of the major problems could be that there can be less harmony in terms of goals and expectations amongst people of diverse economic backgrounds. For instance, an entrepreneur from a high-income background will focus on long-term growth and scalability, while one from a low-income background will talk of short-term profitability and survival. Priorities like these can cause conflicts within the startup and hence can become a possible obstacle to innovation.

Furthermore, diversity can also complicate decision-making processes. It can give rise to divergent and, at times, very wide-ranging opinions related to financial management, investment strategies, and product development priorities arising from these diverse economic perspectives. These differences, though enriching to the decision-making process, will tend to slow it down if not managed properly. This means that the founders of the startup need to set out a common vision and clear communication channels to avoid economic diversity from acting as a point of friction rather than strength]. In spite of all the challenges, there are ways through which economic diversity can be used as a major competitive advantage for startups. In a globalized economy, one needs to understand and provide to different markets to have long-term survival. Those that do succeed in the global marketplace are the ones able to operate through different economic environments while meeting the needs of diversified customer bases (Pricopoaia et al., 2023). Economic diversity provides sets of instruments for a better adaptation of the changing market conditions, innovations of varied consumer demand, and the ability to open new opportunities.

Furthermore, too, diversity in the economy might be able to enhance startup resilience. It is reasonable to assume that startups accustomed to operating in several economic contexts are often more prepared to survive the possible downturns in the economy and changes in the market. They tend to have business models that would be easier to flex, as well as a higher innovativeness ability to pivot quickly when facing challenges. Thus, this adaptability factor may underlie long-term performance much more in modern volatile economic environments (Fitri & Pertiwi, 2019).

There is an advanced, many-tier play between economic diversity and innovation. The richness in views, experiences, and ideas from economic diversity enhances the creativity of the start-up ecosystem and feeds the supply of an innovative solution. While presenting some challenges, like synchronizing goals and decision-making processes, the benefits derived from economic diversity far outweigh any difficulties encountered. It is only those start-ups that welcome economic diversity that are able to be innovative, adjust easily to change, and become more resilient in the global competitive marketplace. This chapter provides a deeper look into how economic diversity impacts startup innovation, an overview of live examples of startups that have leveraged, real-life startups that have leveraged the use of economic diversity to their advantage, and some of the strategic recommendations for entrepreneurs and investors. Finding the key to using economic diversity, a startup will unlock a certain level of creativity that drives growth in this highly connected world (Barboza & Capocchi, 2020). Among other things, innovation and creativity stand out in entrepreneurship as some of the most critical drivers of success. Becoming more than mere buzzwords, these elements underpin the very capacity of startups: (1) to carve one's place in an over-competitive marketplace, (2) to solve complex problems, and (3) grow sustainably. Interpreting and realizing that the linkage of innovation with creativity to achieve success in entrepreneurship is very pertinent to budding and as much for already established entrepreneurs. Indeed, innovation within entrepreneurship can be broadly defined as a process that results in new ideas, products, services, or processes that have a market value.

It is the engine that runs a startup's ability to remain competitive, adaptive to dynamically changing market conditions, and responsive to the evolving needs of customers. Indeed, for entrepreneurs, the value of innovation is not an optional strategy. A startup that does not innovate is in danger of becoming irrelevant, in the sense that the risk of being quickly outcompeted by its more agile, thoughtful competitors is high. The first is that it develops pathways for new opportunities. Through the introduction of a new product or service category, the startup can establish a new category where it can create demand, attract customers, and position itself as a leader in its niche. Innovation allows any startup to tackle existing issues in novel ways, and in most cases, with better efficiency, lesser costs, and scale (Gimenez-Fernandez et al., 2019). For example, success enables innovation to disrupt complete industries, such as the emergence of financial technology start-ups that used technology as a means for doing banking in ways that traditional banks cannot. Innovation, in addition, lies very close to the ability to capitalize on market trends. An entrepreneur will be ready to introduce an innovation that will fit these changes in technology, consumer habits, and industry form. Such a proactive stance not only secures the relevance of the offering but also prepares the startup to ride new waves of growth opportunities.

While innovation involves giving life to new ideas, the truth is that creativity is really the ignition source for the whole process. Creativity in entrepreneurship implies thinking beyond set boundaries, challenging the existing state of affairs, and visualizing possibilities and alternatives that nobody else sees. It is the visual image of that feasible and meaningful thing that was previously untapped. Creativity, therefore, fuels innovation through providing fodder to ideas. This becomes more valuable in a startup environment, mostly constrained by resources. For example, a budget-constrained start-up would be creative in digital marketing strategies or partnering to achieve growth without a significant capital outlay. Further, creativity plays a critical role in engaging the customers (Kofanov & Zozulov, 2018). The ability to market its products creatively innovates, telling storylines of the brands, and the provision of experiences no one has ever encountered will be able to develop a strong relationship with its customers. This creative mode of engagement does not only help differentiate the startup with the others but also develops a much deeper connection with the target audience, which works toward long-lasting relationships. Innovation and creativity go hand in hand, the one reinforcing the other.

Creativity underpins innovation by producing non-existent ideas, and innovation introduces these ideas into useful, commercial solutions. They are a powerful duet in entrepreneurial accomplishment. Fostering such a culture that encourages not only creativity but also innovation is very important for startups. In order to do this, creating an environment in which members of the group feel free to think creatively, to investigate new ideas, and take measured risks is necessary. Such a culture would, therefore, not only ensure that the start-up would innovate but also ensure that it captures talent that respects and further enhances such dynamic practices. Conclusion Innovation and Creativity are key drivers of new venture success in entrepreneurship (Fitri & Pertiwi, 2019; Ojaghi et al., 2019). Starting with the two aspects thus, makes it easier for a start-up to more effectively handle the challenges in the market and differentiation from competitors and realize growth that is also sustainable. Through innovativeness and the development of creativity, the entrepreneur has great opportunities for attractiveness of the enterprise and high chances of the long-term success of the enterprise. This chapter is oriented toward the diversity of economy ranges in seeding innovation and creativity in start-ups (Guckenbiehl et al., 2021).

It explores how different economic backgrounds open up new entrepreneurial strategies, inspire creativity, and contribute to an innovative product and business model. The discussion being held involves different industry sectors and regions, and offers insights from a theoretical and practical perspective, by means of case studies. This chapter will therefore shed light on both challenges and opportunities in leveraging economic diversity in creating an enabling environment for start-up ecosystems, thus providing strategic guidance to entrepreneurs and investors. Ultimately, this will be useful to gain greater insights into how economic diversity fosters sustainable and innovative business ventures (Antonietti & Gambarotto, 2020; Barboza & Capocchi, 2020).

This chapter is mainly focused on the relationship between economic diversity and innovation in startup businesses. More precisely, its primary purpose is to determine how diverse economic environments influence entrepreneurial creativity in business model innovation. In addition, this chapter further seeks to explain the channel through which economic diversity triggers creative problem-solving, eventually creating resilience among business ventures. The chapter draws on case studies and brings forth strategic recommendations that would help entrepreneurs and investors in taking positive action toward the capture of economic diversity as a strong instrument for competitive advantage and long-term success within the dynamic context of startup ecosystems.

ECONOMIC DIVERSITY: A CATALYST FOR INNOVATION

The relationships are depicted in Figure 1, with economic diversity at the center. That means that economic diversity drives a number of other outcomes: creative problem-solving, cross-pollination of ideas, and inclusive business models. It also heralds enhanced innovation of unique solutions, increased market reach and business growth, competitive advantage, and global market opportunities, from the simple diversity-distinctiveness-utility-innovation chain. The long-term benefits that resilient ventures and international expansion offer are those that keep them on the path of success (Brixy et al., 2017; Gompers & Wang, 2017).

Figure 1. Relationships between economic diversity, its impact on innovation, and related elements

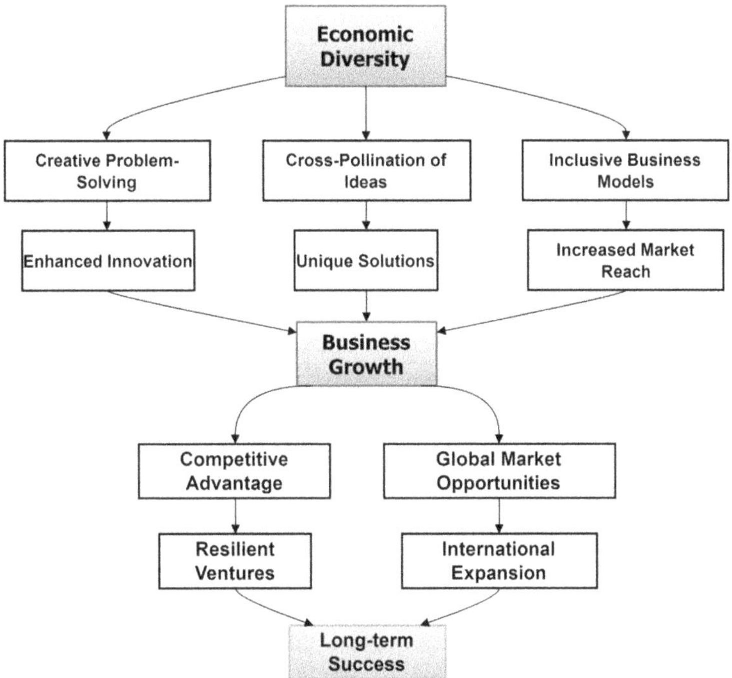

Defining Economic Diversity in the Startup Ecosystem

The economic diversity in the startup ecosystem has to do with a range of entrepreneurial economic backgrounds, environments, and conditions in which they operate. These diversities range accordingly, from differences in income, accessibility to resources, market conditions, and cultural inputs that determine the course of entrepreneurship. With global workforces, the startup space is now being influenced by entrepreneurship flowing from different economic contexts: developed metropolitan areas to emerging markets with characteristic challenges and opportunities. This diversity does not only lie in the financial status of the founders but also in the general economic environment, including local market dynamics, consumer behavior, and the availability of infrastructural and natural resources(Boopathi, 2024; Ravisankar et al., 2024).

This brings along manifold individuality in views, experiences, and approaches toward the solution of problems, and without which innovation becomes hard to chase. As such, entrepreneurs from different economic backgrounds may look at opportunities and challenges differently, resulting in richer sources of ideas. For example, while a lack of resources may stimulate innovation in a cost-effective and sustainable manner, another better-resourced setting may channel the effort into high-tech innovation. Basically, this means economic diversity within the startup ecosystem that begets a number of innovative ways that can suit different market needs.

The Impact of Diverse Economic Backgrounds on Startup Success

The economic background of the entrepreneur has huge effects on the trajectory of startups and how well they will be executed. Different economic backgrounds mean each entrepreneur brings different experiences into the mix, all of which can work either to strengthen or undermine them, depending on how they are harnessed. For example, entrepreneurs from low-income backgrounds may have developed in-depth knowledge about the needs of underserved or underrepresented markets that would motivate them to build solutions to solve real pain points within them. This could mean creating new products or services that will both be innovative and very socially impactful (Babu et al., 2022; N. et al., 2024; Pasumarthy et al., 2024).

On the other hand, entrepreneurs from wealthier backgrounds may have easy access to capital, networks, and mentorship, which could provide additional impetus to their ventures. Those entrepreneurs would be willing to take a risk or invest in an innovation of very high potential but at high cost—for instance, in advanced technology or huge marketing campaigns. At the same time, such entrepreneurs might not be able to relate to the needs of lower-income segment customers, and this could also potentially limit the market reach of innovations.

Their success, therefore, largely depends on how well they can leverage the economic diversity of their founding teams and target markets. Those startups that can combine insights from a variety of economic backgrounds tend to be more resilient and adaptive, capable of navigating diverse market conditions and addressing a wider range of customer needs. The ability to innovate across economic divides is a key determinant of long-term success within the competitive landscape of startups.

Economic Diversity and its Influence on Entrepreneurial Mindsets

Economic diversity therefore also means a lot in the shaping up of the entrepreneurial mindset. This will expose an entrepreneur since his formative years to the economic conditions that will give an all-round attitude towards the risk, resourcefulness, and innovativeness entailed. Entrepreneurs from economically challenged backgrounds might, however, develop a mindset driven by necessity into resilience and resourcefulness, often referred to as "necessity-driven" entrepreneurship. These entrepreneurs know how to stretch limited resources and, thus, are more likely to manage lean, scalable, and sustainable business models with a bias toward efficiency(Boopathi, 2024).

High-status background entrepreneurs take up a rather "opportunity-driven" entrepreneurial mindset. These entrepreneurs usually have greater leverage in trying out new fandangled ideas, investing in new, cutting-edge technologies, and other growth strategies that often entail much upfront investment. There usually is a high-impact innovation capable of disrupting whole industries, but also at higher risk.

The most powerful synergy might radiate in a startup team where these different mindsets converge. Necessity- and opportunity-driven entrepreneurs, in their collaboration, yield the dynamism of the need conjoined with ambition. Synergy would bring out innovative solutions that are viable and scalable—all the virtues of such development. Apart from this, a diversified entrepreneurial outlook further inculcates a culture of inclusiveness and flexibility into the startup process; meaning that the overall process is more prone to change in order to best cater to the situation that it is faced with or new opportunities presented to the stakeholder.

Therefore, economic diversity is a major key when it comes to instigating change in the startup community. Bringing in entrepreneurs from diversified economic backgrounds brings in a very diversified perspective, experiences, and approach to the game, leading to startups coming up with very unique solutions that focus on delivering results in very heterogeneous markets. The need to pilot through and leverage economic diversity will be a critical need for entrepreneurial success when it comes to the ever-increasing dynamism and globalization of the global economy. Only those startups that are able to absorb this diversity will end up surviving, innovating, and making a difference in the long run to an ever-changing world.

MECHANISMS OF INNOVATION DRIVEN BY ECONOMIC DIVERSITY

Figure 2. Mechanisms of innovation driven by economic diversity

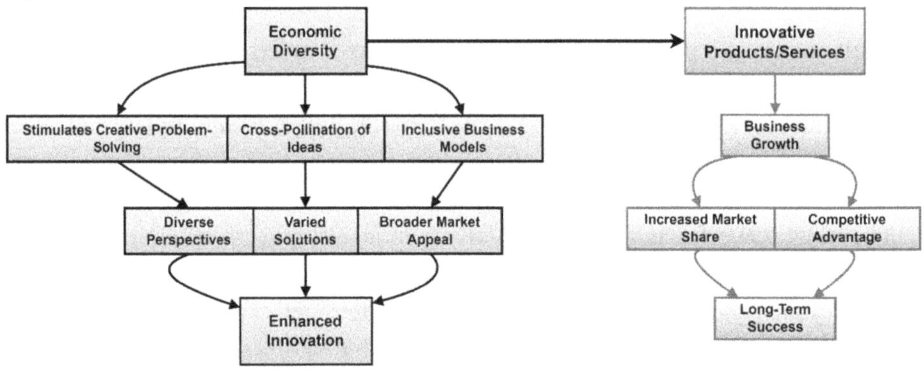

The figure 2 depicts the various mechanisms of innovation that are influenced by economic diversity. Economic diversity serves as a driver of innovation mechanisms by making room for creative problem solving and the cross-pollination of ideas. It will lead to diverse perspectives, varied solutions, and greater market appeal. This additional innovation in turn will come up with innovative products/services, increased market growth, enhanced market share, and competitive advantage. Long-term success can be achieved by means of increased market share and competitive advantage. The ultimate goal is broad appeal in the market and a competitive advantage (Almeida & Kogut, 1997; Audretsch et al., 2023; Kofanov & Zozulov, 2018; Marullo et al., 2018).

How Economic Diversity Stimulates Creative Problem-Solving

Economic diversity is an extremely strong driver in terms of creative problem-solving within startups. If entrepreneurs happen to come from other socioeconomic backgrounds, their team will carry a very wide range of perspectives, experiences, and approaches into the business. Such diversity can fuel creativity by challenging conventional thinking and encouraging the exploration of unconventional solutions. For instance, individuals coming from resource-constrained environments are usually highly frugal and effective in finding solutions to problems, many times finding the most diligent ways to leverage resources to gain the most output in relation to the input. People from relatively affluent backgrounds could, however, focus more on applying advanced technology and capital to attack problems at scale. These varied approaches will intersect to give a richer exercise of problem-solving, where these differing perspectives support more complete and innovative solutions.

This creative tension is rife when the kind of problem-solving needed is in many dimensions. When considering a start-up, where speed and creativity are of the essence, diverse economics also get its agility to help it prosper under many dynamic, uncertain circumstances, pivot strategies, and develop solutions that are both novel and effective. It breeds a culture of constant innovation in which diversity of thought and approach is not just tolerated but encouraged and infused into operations within a start-up.

Cross-Pollination of Ideas from Diverse Economic Contexts

It also cross-pollinates ideas from varied economic contexts into each other, thus leading to break-through innovations. When people with different economic backgrounds come together to work, they will be bringing knowledge and insights unique to their specific environments. Such cross-pollination can ignite new ways of thinking, allowing startups to develop products and services that create novelty and respond to huge niche market needs.

For example, an entrepreneur from a developing country might offer cost-effective and sustainable solutions that can be adapted to fit the needs of richer markets, while on the other hand, an entrepreneur from a developed economy is likely to bring state-of-the-art technological innovations adaptable to the improvement of life quality in less developed regions. This brings forth hybrid solutions that draw on the best in all different economic contexts to engender innovations that are both globally relevant and locally adaptable.

Moreover, the integration of ideas from such diverse economic contexts can illuminate new markets and customer segments not previously perceived. Embracing such diversity puts the startup in a better place to discover and exploit new opportunities for creating products and services that resonate in different economic contexts. This would enhance the competitive advantage of the startup and at the same time provide it with long-term sustainability and growth.

The Role of Inclusive Business Models in Enhancing Innovation

This is where an inclusive business model comes into action. It aims to encourage an inclusive way in which the innovated diversity can be accessible and helpful for a large stratum of economic stakeholders, mostly needy and deprived people. This, of course, will allow a startup to make sure that their innovations are relevant not to just one small segment of the market but are contributing to a broader social and economic impact(Gift et al., 2024; Sundar et al., 2024).

Inclusive business models drive innovation because they widen the circle of people who can both contribute to and benefit from the success of a startup. They drive the creation of products and services in a way that is affordable, accessible, and, in turn, scalable, hence very attractive to any client of the business. For example, a startup can be involved in the development of a digital platform focused on small businesses in emerging markets by giving access to affordable tools that will help them grow and hence power innovation at the grassroots level.

These models also advocate for the interaction of start-ups with diverse economic stakeholders in the innovation process. Customer, supplier, and partner engagement of different economic strata enables the start-up to co-create solutions more aligned with the needs of various markets. In this context, the efficiency built is between the relevance of innovation and key stakeholders to create a more inclusive and resilient business ecosystem.

Economic diversity is an extremely strong driver of innovation among startups: it stimulates innovative problem-solving and cross-pollination of ideas; therefore, it promotes inclusive business models and enhances the ability of a startup to innovate and be victorious in a competitive market. Those startups that manage this diversity more effectively are in a stronger position to come up with solutions that are both innovative and impactful, thus securing long-term success in a global economy characterized by diversity and dynamism.

STRATEGIC RECOMMENDATIONS FOR STARTUPS

Figure 3. Strategic recommendations for startups

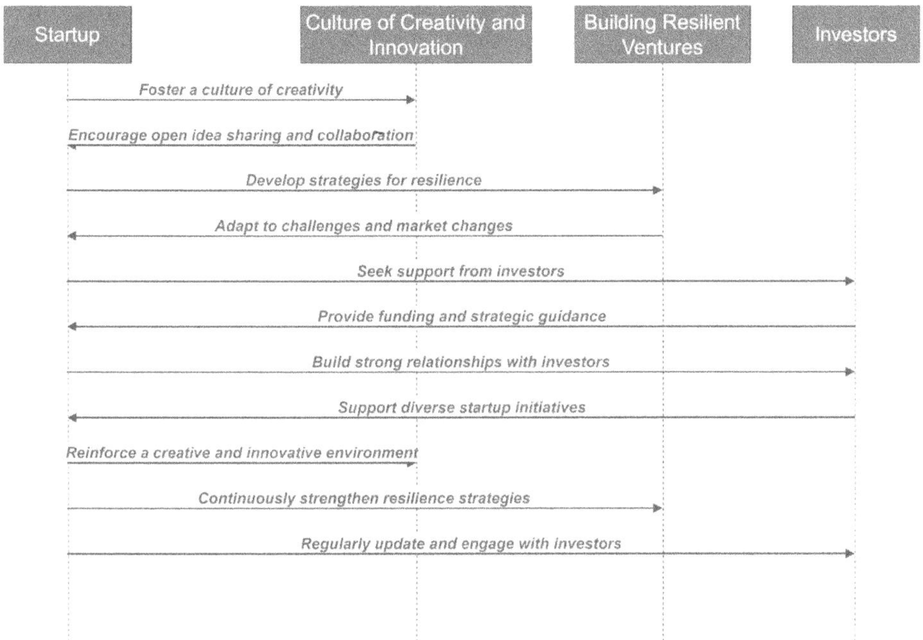

Mantras for creativity, encouragement for the free flow of ideas, approaches to start in order to become resilient, seeking help from investors, making good relationships, and sponsoring different initiatives in the startup should always be encouraged and complemented by creating such a creative and innovative atmosphere (Figure 3). Not only should start-ups devise strategies to keep the resilience of the firm increasing and update it on a regular basis, but they should keep their investors abreast with all follow-up actions. Investors provide the money and the counsel; consequently, the relationship with them is meant to be defined by robust dialogue and engagement. A culture of creativity, resilience, and a supportive environment will help the startup overcome challenges and reorient in the case of a shift in the market (Almeida & Kogut, 1997; Kofanov & Zozulov, 2018).

Fostering a Culture of Creativity and Innovation

Creating a culture that allows creativity to emerge and innovation to flourish is the key for startups to break through the competitive markets. An encouraging setting provides team members space for creative thinking, experimentation of the new, and taking calculated risks. Here are several strategies for creating that kind of culture:

Encourage Open Communication and Sharing of Ideas: Allow your people to air their views without the fear of criticism. This may be ensured through periodic sessions on brainstorming and idea-sharing. Feedback loops—whereby ideas are shared and refined—may be introduced to enhance the quality of innovations.

Diverse Perspectives Can Foster Creativity: The diversity of a team implies diverse perspectives, and these perspectives can lead to more innovative solutions. Recruit people from diverse backgrounds with different economic, cultural, and professional experiences. This kind of diversity in thought will actually trigger the discovery of new ideas and approaches that would not emanate in an otherwise homogeneous setting.

Allocate Time for Innovation: Give some, or afford for, some of your team members their very own time to pursue personal projects or license out new ideas. Google's famous "20% time" model, where employees are told to give 20% of their working week to projects they are passionate about, has seen the creation of major products like Gmail. Such opportunities can realize radical innovations.

Create a Safe Space for Experimentation: Encourage them to experiment by creating an environment of safety, meaning that failure will be looked at as a learning moment and not loss. Such a mindset will help teams to take bold steps without fear of failure, hence greater innovation. Prototypes or pilot programs could then be built to try out such ideas with a minimum of risk.

Celebrate and Reward Innovation: Do recognize and reward those employees who come up with innovative ideas or solutions. Whatever the magnitude of the success, it goes a long way in boosting the morale and motivating others to bring in creative input. Institutes, innovation awards, or bonuses for impactful ideas can be created to motivate creativity.

Building Resilient Ventures through Economic Diversity

The economic diversity can strengthen a startup with resilience and adaptability to the changing market and its challenges. Figure 4 identifies the importance of economic diversity in the maturing of resilient ventures. It points out some strategic ways through which this diversity can be effectively utilized.

Figure 4. Building resilient ventures through economic diversity

- **Understand and Capitalize on Diverse Market Needs:** A startup has to actively involve itself in the process of learning and understanding the various economic backgrounds of their target markets. This may include the knowledge of specific needs and preferences for different segments of the customers. Thus, products or services designed to cater to these broad ranges of economic conditions are more likely to succeed in different markets.
- **Inclusive Leadership and Teams:** Develop economically diverse leadership and provide an equal opportunity to contribute by all. The leadership team, itself diverse, brings in views from different perspectives and experiences that

could give rise to strategies and solutions that might be holistic in approach. Inclusive teams reflect the actual commitment of the startup towards diversity and increase its appeal to the wide world.

- **Embrace Resilient Business Models:** Design business models to give the enterprise resilience in different economic conditions. This might also include tiered pricing structures or solutions that can be customized to give relevance in different economic environments. Flexibility keeps startups relevant and competitive in various markets.
- **Strong Networks and Partnerships:** such relationships can nurture valuable resources, insights, and support from organizations to stakeholders across a diversity of economic backgrounds. Cooperation with organizations experienced in various economic environments opens up new opportunities and reinforces the market position for the startup.
- **Sustainability and Resource Efficiency:** Emphasize to them issues of sustainability and efficient use of the available resources, more so in resource-constrained settings. Products or processes that have sound economic and environmental reasons to be sustainable tend to give strength to the resilience and long-term survival of the startup.

Strategies for Investors to Support Diverse Startups

Investors can really help in the nourishment of a wide diversity of startups and building economic diversity in the entrepreneurial ecosystem(Boopathi & Khang, 2023; Mohanraj et al., 2024). It is to discuss some ways through which investors can contribute to efficiently supporting a diverse venture as follows:

- **Include Diversity as Part of the Investment Criteria:** Build diversity and inclusion into the investment decision-making process. Aggregate startups with diverse management teams or those that solve for underserved or diverse markets. Diverse teams usually are very innovative and often better placed in managing all categories of market needs.
- **Mentorship and Resources:** Apart from the money, provide mentorship and resources to diverse startups. Experienced mentors can help them in scaling, countering market challenges, and accessing additional funding. Resources in terms of networking opportunities and industry connections could be equally useful.
- **Inclusive Funding Models:** Research and promote inclusive funding models that improve the ability of a wide array of startups to access capital. This may include participating in crowdfunding, angel investing networks, or venture funds that pay more attention to underrepresented entrepreneurs. Such mod-

els might democratize access to funding and foster innovation in a number of economic contexts.

- **Advocate for Diversity and Inclusion Initiatives:** and participate in the same towards creating them within the startup ecosystem. For example, programs, events, and organizations set up to instill this quality in entrepreneurship deserve active support so that there can be a much more inclusive and vibrant entrepreneurial environment.
- **Impact Monitoring and Evaluation:** Periodically check the impacts the investment has on different startups. Analyze how investments made are able to contribute to economic diversity, innovation, and attainment of overall success. Use this information to improve how one invests and show the value of support for diverse ventures.

This will involve the cultivation of a culture of creativity and innovation and the creation of resilient ventures through economic diversity, while investing strategically in diverse startups. With these proposed steps, startups and investors can make effective contributions toward an innovative, inclusive, and resilient business environment that will be viable in the long term for success in entrepreneurship.

INNOVATION SUCCESS STORIES IN DIVERSE ECONOMIC ENVIRONMENTS

Case studies that follow show how, through an understanding of local needs, adaptation of models, use of technology, and formation of strong partnerships, a startup can thrive in economically diverse regions. The lessons learned from these successful entrepreneurs provide valuable insights into how diversity can be mobilized to drive business growth and innovation. Embracing and leveraging economic diversity would have important impacts and successes for startups in the global marketplace (Guerrero et al., 2021; Urmetzer & Pyka, 2020; Zhang et al., 2020).

Startups Thriving in Economically Diverse Regions

Jumia (Africa): Dubbed "the Amazon of Africa," this e-commerce platform has done an exemplary job in navigating the challenges associated with running operations in economically divergent regions across Africa. With the ability to unite local know-how and the possibility of forming partnerships with local business owners, Jumia has been able to overcome such logistical barriers and operate within a wide range of economic contexts. It focused on such localized solutions as mobile payments and regional warehousing, which helped it thrive in times of disparity across economies and levels of infrastructure within the continent.

Grameen Bank, Bangladesh: Grameen Bank is one of the pioneering microfinance institutions that offer very small loans to people in economically backward regions in Bangladesh. Dr. Muhammad Yunus founded it on the concept of 'banking for those not banked.' The success lies in its effort toward understanding and solving the economic problems of its clientele, hence fostering entrepreneurship and creating an economic environment with diversity and financial inclusion.

M-Pesa is the mobile money transfer and payment service developed by Safaricom, which has changed the way financial transactions are done in Kenya. It improved the low banking infrastructure and reduced the high costs of transaction costs in Kenya's economy. In both urban and rural settings, M-Pesa, through mobile technology, gave people the power to conduct financial transactions with ease. Its success story demonstrates that if such an innovation is based on local economic realities, then eventually it will alter access to financial services.

OYO Rooms, India: The Indian hospitality startup OYO Rooms has been very successful in catering to various requirements within the budget accommodation market. Taking the idea of standardization in a hotel experience at affordable rates, OYO has expanded vigorously across India and entered other international markets. How this company is in a position to replicate a business model across such diverse economic settings and yet stay focused on the twin parameters of quality and affordability emphasizes the importance of adaptability across different economic milieus.

Observations From Successful Entrepreneurs

Understand Local Needs: Successful entrepreneurs from different economic settings all emphasize the importance of this aspect. Jumia, Grameen Bank, and M-Pesa designed solutions to address very specific problems experienced in their target markets not to mention very many cases of same. This deep insight into local problems allows startups to develop solutions that are relevant and impactful.

Adaptability: Key is flexibility and adaptability to diverse economic environments. Thus, an entrepreneur must not hesitate to alter the shape and design of his business model, strategy, and operations in line with the existing economic environment. How OYO Rooms can standardize and yet adapt its offering across different regions will be a testimony to the importance of adaptability.

Technology is an enabler that helps one break barriers and fosters innovation across economically diverse regions. The success of M-Pesa showed how mobile technology could bridge a gap in financial services. On the other hand, Jumia uses digital platforms to address the logistics challenge in e-commerce. Using technology can help increase efficiency and achieve a wider reach.

Establish Strong Local Partnerships: Developing partnerships with local businesses and stakeholders avails orators of valuable insights and resources. Others include Grameen Bank's work with local communities and the partnering approach with success taken by hotel owners in OYO Rooms.

Analyzing the Role of Economic Diversity in Business Growth

This leads to the fact that economic diversity has many varied opportunities and challenges, thereby impacting business growth to a great extent.

Market Expansion and Opportunity: Economic diversity opens up possibilities for startups to engage in the solving of various market needs. Targeting several economic segments gives a means to several customer bases, thus increasing the market reach. For instance, the ability of M-Pesa to serve both the urban and rural populations in Kenya offers a fitting case study on how economic diversity can spur market expansion.

Higher Problem-Solving Capabilities: Different economic backgrounds ensure varied problem-solving approaches. If the people in a team belong to different economic backgrounds, then they will view the situation or problem differently, thus finding more innovative solutions. Diversity in problem-solving can be the reason for business growth by introducing and developing unique products and services.

Higher Resilience: Startups that operate in economically diverse environments usually become more resilient and adaptable. The experience of dealing with different economic conditions and responding to several challenges enhances the overall stability and growth prospects of a startup. Grameen Bank achieves success in providing financial services to unbanked people through economic diversity, which rendered resilience.

Social Impact and Brand Strength: Economic disparities can bring about improvement in social impact and brand strength for a startup. Those businesses working toward economic progress and inclusiveness often receive positive recognition and consumer and stakeholder support. A focus on local entrepreneurship at Jumia, and a commitment to affordable accommodation at OYO Rooms, highlight how addressing economic diversity can positively influence brand perception and growth.

CHALLENGES AND OPPORTUNITIES

Overcoming Barriers to Innovation in Diverse Economic Settings

While the challenges to navigating innovation across different economic settings are huge, they are at the same time very promising. Principal among these barriers are those related to differences in resources and infrastructure. Normally, a startup in an economically challenged region lacks access to capital, technology, or skilled talent. This normally retards their capacities for developing and scaling innovative solutions in most cases (Guckenbiehl et al., 2021; Ojaghi et al., 2019). The figure 5 illustrates the process of overcoming barriers to innovation in various economic settings. The resolution of these obstacles necessitates a comprehensive approach.

Figure 5. Overcoming barriers to innovation in diverse economic settings

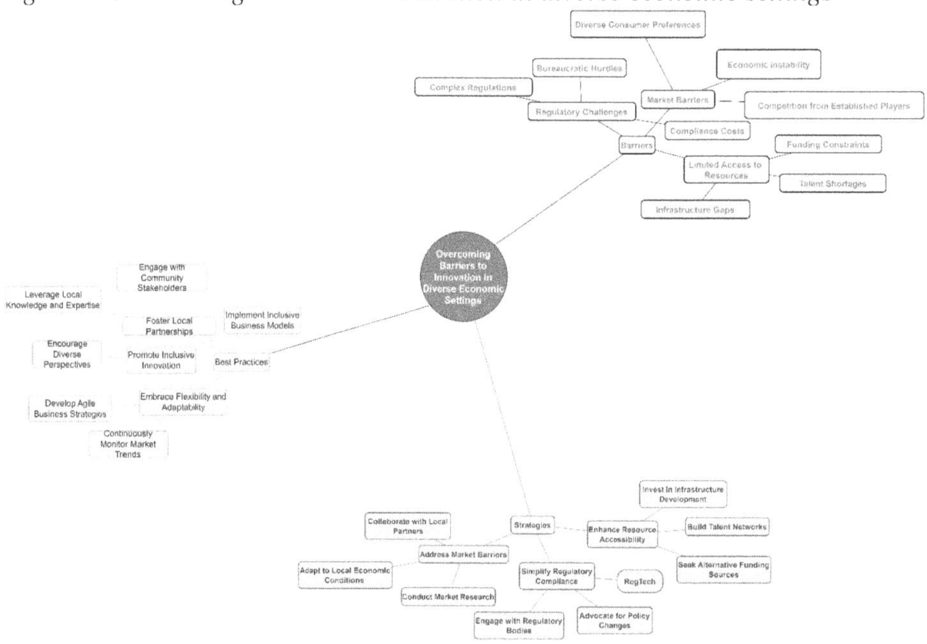

a. **Access to Capital:** The most prominent challenges in the startup settings, especially in less well-off settings, pertain to access to finance. This could be realized mainly through the following funding models: microfinance, grants, and impact investing. Strategic partnerships with venture capital firms or government programs that have some orientation toward economic development could prove very instrumental in terms of financial support.

b. **Infrastructure Development:** Limited infrastructure can constrain the growth of startups in economically constrained areas. Public-private partnerships in local infrastructure or investing in it can be achieved through mechanisms such as technology hubs and innovation centers that provide the necessary tools and environment for the startups.

   c) **Skill Development and Training:** The second major barrier is the lack of skilled talent. This can be overcome through partnerships with educational institutions and training centers, and providing them with the required skills and knowledge. Online and remote work facilities will also be of immense use in this matter by obtaining access to expertise from anywhere around the world.

      d. **Managing Regulatory Issues:** Different economic environments are generally governed by different regulatory regimes. The startups operate and have to comply with complex regulations that often vary significantly from region to region. Consulting local regulatory bodies and taking legal advice may go a long way in mitigating the possibility of legal issues by enabling the startups to understand and comply with the laws and regulations relevant to them.

Leveraging Economic Diversity for Competitive Advantage

While posing challenges, economic diversity opens several opportunities for a startup to build competitive advantage(Boopathi, 2024; Pasumarthy et al., 2024; S & Gopi, 2024). Economic diversity can be turned into a strategic tool to differentiate and add value to the startup:

a) **Innovative Solutions for Untapped Markets:** Economic diversity can enable startups to target new markets with unsatisfied needs. Many startups that have originated from an economically challenged background often realize very innovative solutions that precisely target unserved and underserved segments. By meeting the needs of these markets, one understands how to make high-impact products and services relevant to them.

b) **Multi-Dimensional Perspectives and Problem-Solving:** These are individuals who originate from different economic backgrounds, bringing along varied perspectives to the solution of a problem. It is through this that it creates an atmosphere of creativity and offers a chance to come up with solutions that may not be materialized out of a more homogeneous team. Such diverse viewpoints can fuel innovation and engender breakthroughs which set this startup apart from the competition.

c) **Global Market Opportunities:** Economic diversity can further contribute to the competitive advantage in the global market. Startups cognizant and responsive to various economic contexts may scale into the global environment by reaching heterogeneous consumers.

d) **Resilience and Adaptability:** Across various economic environments, the traits most usually acquired by any startup are those of resilience and adaptability. They have learned to sail through uncertainty and resource constraints very efficiently, thereby enjoying an added advantage in today's fast-paced and constantly transforming business environment. This helps them to be in a better position to pivot and adapt to new opportunities or challenges.

FUTURE TRENDS IN ECONOMIC DIVERSITY AND INNOVATION

Looking ahead, several trends shape how economic diversity and innovation are factored into the future:

a. **Growing Focus on Inclusive Innovation:** There is a growing realization that many innovations have to be inclusive to have relevance for large masses of diverse populations. Increased focus of startups in development of accessible and useful solutions to large economic segments can be seen. This trend is driven by growing focus on social impact and the value brought in by diversity in driving innovation.

b. **Growth of Digital Platforms:** It is the digital proliferation of platforms and technologies that fosters better economic inclusion and innovation. That is to say, startups today are using digital tools to extend activities into underserved markets, streamline operations, and even collaborate with partners worldwide. On that note, it will be easier for startups to leapfrog geographical and economic barriers with the new wave of e-commerce, online marketplaces, and remote work solutions.

c. **Rise of Impact Investing:** Interest in investing for the dual intent of creating social or environmental impact while having financial returns is on the rise. Already underway is the trend toward creating further interest amongst investors in funding and scaling startups that work on solving economic disparities and ensure sustainable development.

d. **Advancements in Technology and Innovation:** In this context, technological innovation, such as Artificial Intelligence, Blockchain, and the Internet of Things, drives innovation across diverse economic settings. This helps startups that can tap into these technologies to develop the most advanced solutions and sustain a lead over others. Moreover, democratization of technology is slowly and steadily making access to technology possible for startups from various economic backgrounds.

e. **Global Collaboration and Knowledge Sharing:** The future of economic diversity and innovation is likely to be characterized by enhanced collaboration and knowledge sharing at a global level. Networking, sharing of insights, and engaging in innovative projects will continue among startups and entrepreneurs across various economic settings. This would foster the cross-pollination of ideas and further accelerate the development of innovative solutions.

In that regard, while conquering the barriers to innovation set in different economic contexts is not easy, it also opens immense opportunities to a startup. The economic diversity can be leveraged and help the startup reap its competitive advantage, drive impactful solutions, and navigate the world market at large. Trends of economic diversity and innovation—which are most likely to define the future—seem to be inclusive innovation, digital, and collaborative globally. The startups that best understand and avail themselves of these trends stand a much bigger chance of succeeding and building a more vibrant, resilient entrepreneurial ecosystem.

CONCLUSION

This chapter has elaborated on the dynamic interplay between economic diversity and innovation in the startup ecosystem. Through this analysis, it has been underlined how economic diversity—that is, variation in economic backgrounds and conditions—acts as a spur and challenge for entrepreneurial ventures.

Economic diversity in the startup landscape gives views and experiences from all walks of life. This creates inventive problem-solving and drives innovation to answer various market needs. Those startups that negotiate and turn economic diversity to their good can help underserved markets, adapt to a variety of economic contexts, and rise in resilience. The Jumia, Grameen Bank, M-Pesa, and OYO Rooms case studies illustrate how nascent industries leverage this diversity within the economy to build solutions of impact and scale.

While diversity in the economy opens vistas of opportunity, it comes with challenges: resource constraints, infrastructural limitations, and regulatory complexities. This means that strategic ways of securing diverse funding sources, developing adaptable business models, and fostering cultures of innovation that are inclusive will be required to meet such challenges. Investors thus play a very significant role:

they support diverse startups and advocate for inclusive funding models that will be conducted to drive economic development and innovation.

Several trends have now emerged to define the future of economic diversity and innovation. Digital platforms, impact investing, and technological developments are rapidly expanding opportunities for startups across different economic contexts. Inclusive innovation and global collaboration are fast becoming central to drive progress and reduce economic disparities.

Thus, the economic diversity that exists is something which startups should know how to leverage in order to innovate and grow. Embracing diverse perspectives is how they can break through to use their strategic opportunities in hacking through complexities and getting to sustainable success. Endowed entrepreneurs and relevant case studies illustrate the power of economic diversity in driving innovation with resilience and meaningful impact. Tending to and harnessing the potential power of economic diversity will be key for entrepreneurship as the evolution of the startup ecosystem unfolds.

REFERENCES

Almeida, P., & Kogut, B. (1997). The exploration of technological diversity and geographic localization in innovation: Start-up firms in the semiconductor industry. *Small Business Economics*, 9(1), 21–31. DOI: 10.1023/A:1007995512597

Antonietti, R., & Gambarotto, F. (2020). The role of industry variety in the creation of innovative start-ups in Italy. *Small Business Economics*, 54(2), 561–573. DOI: 10.1007/s11187-018-0034-4

Audretsch, D. B., Belitski, M., Caiazza, R., & Siegel, D. (2023). Effects of open innovation in startups: Theory and evidence. *Technological Forecasting and Social Change*, 194, 122694. DOI: 10.1016/j.techfore.2023.122694

Babu, B. S., Kamalakannan, J., Meenatchi, N., Karthik, S., & Boopathi, S. (2022, December). Economic impacts and reliability evaluation of battery by adopting Electric Vehicle. In *2022 International Conference on Power, Energy, Control and Transmission Systems (ICPECTS)* (pp. 1-6). IEEE.

Barboza, G., & Capocchi, A. (2020). Innovative startups in Italy. Managerial challenges of knowledge spillovers effects on employment generation. *Journal of Knowledge Management*, 24(10), 2573–2596. DOI: 10.1108/JKM-08-2019-0436

Boopathi, S. (2024). Digital HR Implementation for Business Growth in Industrial 5.0. In *Convergence of Human Resources Technologies and Industry 5.0* (pp. 1–22). IGI Global. DOI: 10.4018/979-8-3693-1343-5.ch001

Boopathi, S., & Khang, A. (2023). AI-Integrated Technology for a Secure and Ethical Healthcare Ecosystem. In *AI and IoT-Based Technologies for Precision Medicine* (pp. 36–59). IGI Global. DOI: 10.4018/979-8-3693-0876-9.ch003

Brixy, U., Brunow, S., & D'Ambrosio, A. (2017). *Ethnic diversity in start-ups and its impact on innovation*. IAB-Discussion Paper.

Fitri, S., & Pertiwi, A. (2019). Innovation Mindset Model at the Early Stage Startup With Berkeley Innovation Index Approached. *Technology Management*, 4(13), 57–70.

Gift, M. D. M., Senthil, T. S., Hasan, D. S., Alagarraja, K., Jayaseelan, P., & Boopathi, S. (2024). Additive Manufacturing and 3D Printing Innovations: Revolutionizing Industry 5.0. In *Technological Advancements in Data Processing for Next Generation Intelligent Systems* (pp. 255–287). IGI Global. DOI: 10.4018/979-8-3693-0968-1.ch010

Gimenez-Fernandez, E. M., Bogers, M., & Sandulli, F. (2019). How the diversity of cooperation partners affects startups' innovation performance: An analysis of the role of cooperation breadth in open innovation. *Open Innovation and Entrepreneurship: Impetus of Growth and Competitive Advantages*, 9–35.

Gompers, P. A., & Wang, S. Q. (2017). *Diversity in innovation*. National Bureau of Economic Research. DOI: 10.3386/w23082

Guckenbiehl, P., de Zubielqui, G. C., & Lindsay, N. (2021). Knowledge and innovation in start-up ventures: A systematic literature review and research agenda. *Technological Forecasting and Social Change*, 172, 121026. DOI: 10.1016/j.techfore.2021.121026

Guerrero, M., Liñán, F., & Cáceres-Carrasco, F. R. (2021). The influence of ecosystems on the entrepreneurship process: A comparison across developed and developing economies. *Small Business Economics*, 57(4), 1733–1759. DOI: 10.1007/s11187-020-00392-2

Kofanov, O., & Zozulov, O. (2018). Successful development of startups as a global trend of innovative socio-economic transformations. *International and Multidisciplinary Journal of Social Sciences*, 7(2), 191–217. DOI: 10.17583/rimcis.2018.3576

Marullo, C., Casprini, E., Di Minin, A., & Piccaluga, A. (2018). 'Ready for Take-off': How Open Innovation influences startup success. *Creativity and Innovation Management*, 27(4), 476–488. DOI: 10.1111/caim.12272

Mohanraj, G., Krishna, K. S., Lakshmi, B. S., Vijayalakshmi, A., Pramila, P. V., & Boopathi, S. (2024). Optimizing Trust and Security in Healthcare 4.0: Human Factors in Lightweight Secured IoMT Ecosystems. In *Lightweight Digital Trust Architectures in the Internet of Medical Things (IoMT)* (pp. 52–72). IGI Global. DOI: 10.4018/979-8-3693-2109-6.ch004

N., S. P., Goritiyal, C., Ramana, N. V., Matcha, A., Sukania, P., & Boopathi, S. (2024). Economic Growth Study and Inferences From Developments in E-Mobility. In *Advances in Mechatronics and Mechanical Engineering* (pp. 178–199). IGI Global. DOI: 10.4018/979-8-3693-5247-2.ch010

Ojaghi, H., Mohammadi, M., & Yazdani, H. R. (2019). A synthesized framework for the formation of startups' innovation ecosystem: A systematic literature review. *Journal of Science and Technology Policy Management*, 10(5), 1063–1097. DOI: 10.1108/JSTPM-07-2018-0071

Pasumarthy, R., Mohammed, S., Laxman, V., Krishnamoorthy, V., Durga, S., & Boopathi, S. (2024). Digital Transformation in Developing Economies: Forecasting Trends, Impact, and Challenges in Industry 5.0. In *Convergence of Human Resources Technologies and Industry 5.0* (pp. 47–68). IGI Global. DOI: 10.4018/979-8-3693-1343-5.ch003

Pricopoaia, O., Busila, A. V., Cristache, N., Susanu, I., & Matis, C. (2023). Challenges for entrepreneurial innovation: Startups as tools for a better knowledge-based economy. *The International Entrepreneurship and Management Journal*, •••, 1–42.

Ravisankar, A., Shanthi, A., Lavanya, S., Ramaratnam, M., Krishnamoorthy, V., & Boopathi, S. (2024). Harnessing 6G for Consumer-Centric Business Strategies Across Electronic Industries. In *AI Impacts in Digital Consumer Behavior* (pp. 241–270). IGI Global.

S, B., & Gopi, S. (2024). Crafting Effective HR Strategies for the Modern Workplace: Navigating the Digital Frontier. In *Convergence of Human Resources Technologies and Industry 5.0* (pp. 23–46). IGI Global. DOI: 10.4018/979-8-3693-1343-5.ch002

Sundar, R., Srikaanth, P. B., Naik, D. A., Murugan, V. P., Karumudi, M., & Boopathi, S. (2024). Achieving Balance Between Innovation and Security in the Cloud With Artificial Intelligence of Things: Semantic Web Control Models. In *Advances in Web Technologies and Engineering* (pp. 1–26). IGI Global. DOI: 10.4018/979-8-3693-1487-6.ch001

Urmetzer, S., & Pyka, A. (2020). Innovation systems for sustainability. In *Decent Work and Economic Growth* (pp. 600–611). Springer.

Zhang, Y., Sun, J., Yang, Z., & Wang, Y. (2020). Critical success factors of green innovation: Technology, organization and environment readiness. *Journal of Cleaner Production*, 264, 121701. DOI: 10.1016/j.jclepro.2020.121701

KEY TERMS

OYO: (Oravel Stays Private Limited) is a global hospitality chain founded in 2013 by Ritesh Agarwal. It started as a budget hotel chain and has since evolved into one of the largest hotel and home rental networks worldwide.

Chapter 5
Creativity on Sustainable Technological Advancements in Entrepreneurship

Kaipa Raghu Ram
https://orcid.org/0009-0006-6186-9190
Department of Management, NSB Academy, Bengaluru, India

Sameena Begum
College of Economics and Business Administration, University of Technology and Applied Sciences, Oman

Vasmeen Sultana
Department of management and Commerce, Maulana Azad National Urdu University, Hyderabad, India

S. Padmavathy
https://orcid.org/0000-0002-1119-2963
Kongu Engineering College, India

D. Rakesh
JSS Science and Technology University, India

ABSTRACT

The chapter explores the intersection of creativity, innovation, and sustainability in entrepreneurship. Emphasis is given to the role of creative thinking in driving sustainable technological development in entrepreneurship. It explores the important role that creativity plays in identification and solving of complex challenges modern

DOI: 10.4018/979-8-3693-9486-1.ch005

entrepreneurs face in developing technologies that are not only innovative but also environmentally and socially responsible. The chapter shows how entrepreneurs can use creativity to develop sustainable solutions that will help answer market demand while reducing their impact on the environment. This is a blend of theoretical insight with practical examples, important case studies of businesses that efficiently put sustainable practice into their technology innovation, hence providing a way forward for future entrepreneurs. This chapter aims to teach readers how to strategically utilize creative processes to drive technological innovation and achieve sustainable, long-term entrepreneurial success.

INTRODUCTION

In the light of rapidly changing developments in the business world today, entrepreneurship lies at the very heart of economic growth and innovation. An entrepreneur, therefore, no longer just creates a new venture but takes on a very vital role in society, acting like an agent of change for advancing technology and driving market trends. However, with increasing awareness about the environment and societal impacts, this role of entrepreneurship has evolved to take on the responsibility toward sustainability. This dual focus on innovations and sustainability has provided a crucible in which a new paradigm has emerged: creativity as the activating agent in the concept of technologies that, at one and the same time, are both revolutionary and sustainable (Dana et al., 2022).

Creativity is normally viewed as the process of generating new and relevant ideas; it is one of the most cardinal factors in entrepreneurial success. It acts to drive innovation, thereby giving entrepreneurs the capacity to identify opportunities, resolve complex problems, and help distinguish their ventures within competitive markets. Within the context of sustainable entrepreneurship, it takes an even more significant role. Entrepreneurs would, in their creative moments, rise to solution-based thinking in trying to alleviate some of the pressing challenges on climate change, resource depletion, and social inequality. This chapter addresses the nexus of creativity, sustainability, and technology innovation, and highlights in what way creative processes can be put into action in driving invention in sustainable technologies with the purpose of contributing to both business success and societal well-being (Ogbeibu et al., 2021).

The entrepreneurial process should integrate well with sustainability to address the consequences of unsustained practices in the world. In this case, sustainability refers to the act of creating and devising products, services, and models of business that answer the present needs without compromising the ability of future generations to meet their own needs. For entrepreneurs, this should translate to considering the ecological, social, and economic impacts of their ventures right from the very beginning. Still, attaining sustainability is not about compliance or just satisfying regulatory provisions; instead, it is about totally rethinking one's approach toward innovation (Carayannis, 2020).

The creative entrepreneur may be at the forefront of the drive towards more sustainable technological development. It is within their potential to think unconventionally and challenge conventional wisdom that new ways to reduce waste, conserve resources, and develop products and services that positively affect society and the environment can be found. In turn, this ability empowers entrepreneurs to adjust to and go through the complexities and uncertainties involved in moving toward sustainability. This creativity will tap into the reservoir of sustainable innovation, be it in the area of the development of alternative materials, the design of energy-efficient processes, or the development of new business models in which the imperatives of the circular economy are taken into account (Ogbeibu et al., 2020).

In this chapter, we will consider ways through which creativity can be brought to the fore in driving sustainable technological advances in entrepreneurship. We first consider some of the theoretical underpinnings associated with creativity and its role in innovation. Drawing on insights from psychology, business, and design thinking: How can creative processes be applied in a systematic way to come up with novel ideas and solutions that meet the challenges of sustainability?. As well, we are going to look at barriers to creativity in entrepreneurship, including organizational culture, risk aversion, and resource constraints and propose strategies for overcoming them (Satalkina & Steiner, 2020).

Next, The idea of sustainable technology made a connection to entrepreneurship. Sustainable technology is about creating and using technical innovations that allow for social equity, economic sufficiency, and environmental conservation. Sustainable technologies range from renewable energy systems and green manufacturing processes to socially responsible digital platforms and sustainable supply chains. It will touch upon the features of technologies that could be qualified as sustainable, drivers for their adoption, and the role that creativity plays in developing these technologies. It will illustrate with the help of examples and cases that entrepreneurs were able to integrate issues of sustainability into their technological innovations and create business and societal value (Anjum et al., 2020).

The practical implications of how to create an enabling environment for sustainable innovation through creativity will also be addressed. This will comprise tools and methodologies that enable entrepreneurs to enhance their own creative thinking, such as design thinking, brainstorming techniques, and collaborative innovation platforms. We will further deliberate on the need to build a supportive ecosystem that fosters experimentation, risk-taking, and collaboration across boundaries. This may involve the creation of an organizational culture that values sustainability, investment in research and development, and mobilization of customers, suppliers, and other stakeholders—among them, key policymakers—to achieve sustainable results (Vrontis et al., 2022).

Finally, we will look at the future of sustainable entrepreneurship and how creativity will lead it. Indeed, as global challenges like climate change and social inequality continue to rise, the need for sustainable solutions will increase dramatically. Those entrepreneurs that can harness creativity to come up with innovative, sustainable technologies will be better placed to lead the way into the new era of business. By making sustainability a core aspect of the innovation process, these entrepreneurs will not only contribute to a more sustainable world but also secure a competitive advantage in an increasingly sustainability-conscious market (Sutrisno et al., 2023).

In this regard, the point at which creativity, sustainability, and technology intersect offers a very potent framework of entrepreneurial innovation. An embrace of creative thinking can, therefore, aid entrepreneurs in driving the development of sustainable technologies that will serve present needs without jeopardizing the future. This chapter is aimed at gaining an in-depth understanding of using creativity in a strategic manner for sustainable technological innovations backed first by theoretical insight, followed by certain practical tips for committed entrepreneurs who seek to leave a positive impact in the world (Thukral, 2021).

Scope: This chapter is supposed to look into the creativity aspect and how it influences sustainable technological innovation in the entrepreneurial context. It deals with a wide range of themes, among them theoretical underpinning of the creativity aspect in innovation, integrating sustainable practices into technology development, and the role an entrepreneur plays in putting across environmentally and socially responsible businesses. The chapter will provide examples and case studies from different sectors about the application of creative thinking in sustainable entrepreneurship. It will further elaborate on the challenges and opportunities connected with putting sustainable technologies into practice—a kind of comprehensive 'how-to' guide for entrepreneurs committed to long-term success.

Objectives: This chapter has the following objectives. The first is to analyze the role which creativity can play in driving sustainable technological advancements within an entrepreneurial venture. It will explore ways in which creative thinking can be harnessed and applied towards inventing solutions that consider environmental and social responsibilities. In addition, it will introduce practical strategies and frameworks by which entrepreneurs can incorporate the element of sustainability into technology innovation. The chapter will use case studies and examples of successful applications that have taken these strategies onboard to further afford practical insight. In the end, it is expected to inspire entrepreneurs to make sustainability part and parcel of the innovation process.

THEORETICAL FOUNDATIONS OF CREATIVITY AND INNOVATION

Figure 1. Theoretical foundations of creativity and innovation in entrepreneurial ventures

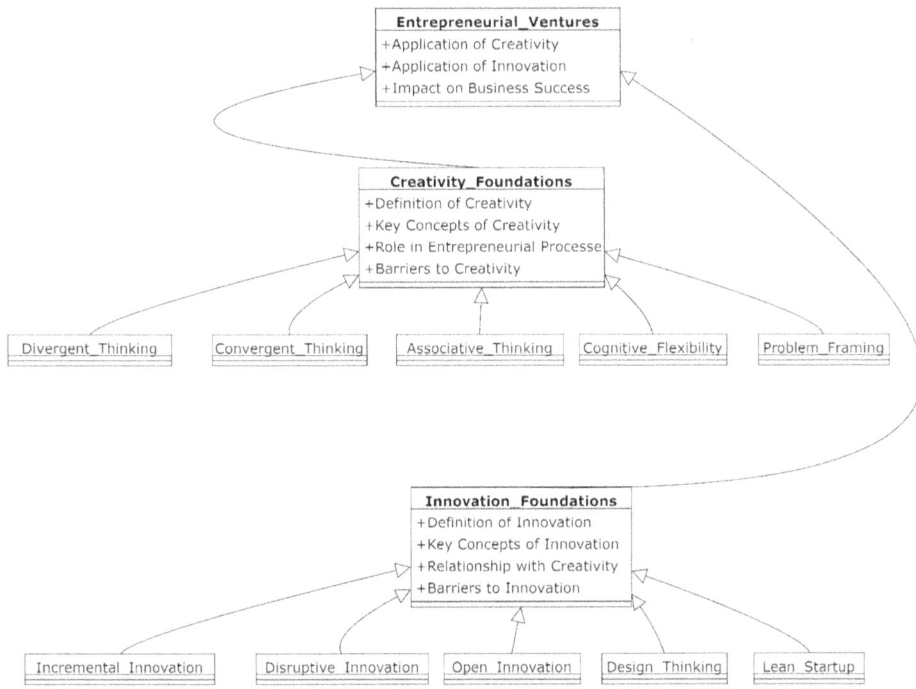

The theoretical foundations of creativity and innovation in entrepreneurial ventures are depicted in Figure 1. Creativity is conceptualised through divergent, convergent, associative, cognitive flexible, and problem framing. The role played in the entrepreneurial processes and the key concepts it contains conceptually define creativity. Incremental, disruptive, open, design, and lean startup methodologies are based on innovation. Creativity is quick at giving many ideas, whereas innovation is considered to form new markets by breaking the former existing ones. The diagram arranges these thinking and innovative types that show how they relate to the theoretical underpinning of entrepreneurial success. This diagram also represents one of the most important things: problem framing as a process through which creative definition and understanding of the problems take place (Terán-Yépez et al., 2020).

Understanding Creativity: Definitions and Key Concepts

Creativity is a multidimensional concept, crucial in different domains but at the centre of it, is the generation of something new and valuable which is pertinent in an original context. This is not about random thoughts but a deliberate cognitive activity involving knowledge, experience, and imagination. Creativity is at the core of innovation, as it supplies raw material—new ideas—that can be transformed into executable and novel solutions.

Central elements to understanding creativity are divergent thought-the ability to let the mind conceive of many possible solutions and routes-and convergent thought, which is essentially deciding which may be the most functionally solid solutions/ paths to a problem. Another important aspect drawn out is the creativity process, which actually seems to follow five stages, that include preparation, incubation, insight, evaluation, and elaboration. These stages describe how individuals move from identifying problems or opportunities to generating and refining ideas that can ultimately result in innovative solutions.

The Relationship of Creativity and Innovation

The execution of creative ideas, or an applicable idea is thus regarded as innovation. Creativity involves generating ideas whereas innovation is putting forward such ideas practically for the creation of value, either in the form of new products, services, processes, or a new business model. Creativity and innovation are thus symbiotic. Creativity gives a spark and innovation breathes life into the spark by putting it into effect and turning it commercial.

This becomes more decisive in entrepreneurship. Entrepreneurs need creativity to perceive opportunities in the marketplace, new things that could be done, and how their offerings can be clearly distinguished from those of the competition. However, creativity is not nearly enough; it is the ability to innovate that turns creative ideas into products or services into marketable economic goods. It implies one of the great challenges facing the entrepreneur: how to manage the transition from creativity to innovation by means of practical and economic ideas.

Creativity in Entrepreneurial Processes

Creativity comes in handy at every stage of the entrepreneurial process, from opportunity recognition to business model development and growth. At the opportunity recognition stage, creativeness is manifest in entrepreneurs identifying market voids, foreseeing trends, and coming up with products or services that would satisfy unmet needs. To do so, both the in-depth knowledge in the industry and in the wider social context in which it operates and an ability to think outside the box are demanded(Sundar et al., 2024).

In the development stage, creativity plays an important role in the design of innovative business models that will be sustainable in offering continued competitive advantage. Entrepreneurs have to be creative to crack the main problems, most of which arise from resource allocation, customer acquisition, and scalability. They might use creative problem-fighting techniques to figure out unique ways of delivering value to customers, optimizing operations, and differentiating the brand.

Creativity, too, is concerned with the domain of growth and the size of the enterprise. As the businesses grow, "the entrepreneur needs to keep on renewing and innovating persistently to maintain their competitive edge and accommodating changes in market conditions". It, therefore is required to come up with creative ideas continually and inculcate an "innovation culture" in the organization.

Creativity in an Entrepreneurial Process

Creativity in the entrepreneurial process is, however, thwarted by certain critical reasons. Firstly, it is the pressure for conformance to traditional norms and practices in an industry. Entrepreneurs can get bound by conventional wisdom or current market expectations that close the doors to thinking creatively. Furthermore, there is the fear of failure—typical problematics companies meet—which leads to risk aversion and, thus, additionally squeezes the room for searching. Resource limitations are another barrier. In most of the time the entrepreneurs have limited financial, human, and technological resources and this would be a barrier to trying out the new ideas that they have. Lack of enough resources will hinder investments into research and development, which is a fostering output creativity(Boopathi, 2024; Boopathi et al., 2023; Ravisankar et al., 2024).

The other barrier is the organizational culture. This holds the greatest role for nurturing or inhibiting creativity. It can be a stultifying presence in such an environment not oriented to innovation and one that does not put up adequate support for new ideas. The onus, therefore, becomes on the entrepreneur to ensure that a culture that allows experimentation is cultivated, a culture where failure is tolerated and a reward system that encourages creative thinking. Strategies that would help an entrepreneur to overcome these types of barriers include fostering collaborations, seeking diverse perspectives, and encouraging a growth mindset. They are able to create an environment that is likely to be involved in fostering creativity, which through successful innovation, will continue to keep them ahead of the competition in the market.

Currently, creativity and innovation are sauted lights on the process of being entrepreneurial. Knowing how to foster creativity is one of the imperative things every entrepreneur should know in creating innovative solutions that will answer the market's needs, thus eventually achieving entrepreneurial success. This is equally important to the overcoming the barriers of creativity, which allows an entrepreneur to make full use of the potential of the creative mind and channel this into meaningfully innovative output.

SUSTAINABLE TECHNOLOGY IN ENTREPRENEURSHIP

Figure 2. Main components such as drivers of adoption and the role of entrepreneurs

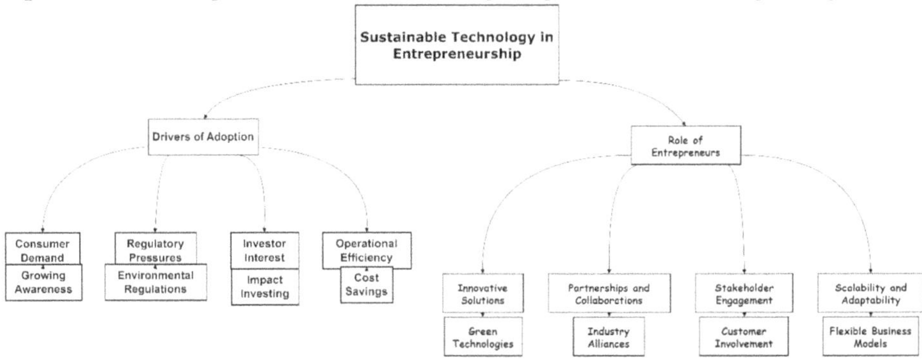

Main adoption components CBT regarded the role of entrepreneurs in entrepreneurship as a central topic driven by sustainable technology with such driving forces as driven by consumer demand, regulatory pressures, investor interest, and operational efficiency (Figure 2). Thus, while entrepreneurs contribute towards sustainable technology by developing green technologies, forming linkages with other organizations, and involving stakeholders, green solutions require scalability and adaptability for their growth or adaptation. You may move around the nodes and links to highlight any relevant lines of technology sustainability in entrepreneurship (Thukral, 2021).

Defining Sustainable Technology

Sustainable technology is simply the development and application of technological solutions to serve the needs of the present without detriment to the ability of future generations to meet their own needs. It is guided by the principles of environmental stewardship, social equity, and economic viability; that is, it seeks not only to minimize impacts on the planet but also to maximize benefits accruing to society. It is not only about creating green products but the wholesome approach, considering the entire lifecycle of a technology from design and production to usage and disposal.

In entrepreneurship, sustainable technology presents an opportunity to innovate in a way that business objectives are aligned with far more comprehensive societal objectives. When entrepreneurs develop technology with an entrepreneurship focus on sustainability, resource efficiency with climate protection, and community benefit, that avoids environmental degradation and positions business responsibly for the future, thereby creating brand reputation and customers' loyalty.

Characteristics of Sustainable Technologies

There are several distinctive features that set sustainable technologies apart from the conventional technologies (Elia et al., 2020):

Resource Efficiency: Sustainable technologies are designed to make optimum use of resources, whether energy, water, or raw materials. In that, the ways may include renewable sources of energy, recycled or biodegradable materials, and other processes reducing waste generation. Doing so helps conserve the natural assets of the planet by reducing non-renewable resource consumption.

Socially and Environmentally Optimized: Sustainable technologies minimize the profile on consuming as little strain as possible on the environment. Offset in this kind of effort covers the least possible level of emissions of greenhouse gases, least possible waste, and ecosystems' least possible harm caused by technologies. For instance, electric vehicles are sustainable because they produce no tailpipe emissions; therefore, they harm the environment less compared to conventional vehicles that use internal combustion engines. Similarly, a circular economy that practices recycling and upcycling manages to reduce general environmental footprints.

Scalability and Longevity: Sustainable technologies are those that exhibit scalabil-ity and longevity. They are adaptive and unbreakable, capable to be transformed with the fluctuating changes in the environment and market demands. It ensures the time value of technology by getting sustenance over time not just the short-term gains. Sustainable technology entrepreneurs think about scaling beyond their immediate application their innovation's effect and potential for enduring change.

Social Equity and Inclusivity: Besides the environmental impacts, sustainable technologies also have a place in addressing social issues with fairness and inclusivity. This could be in regards to the inclusiveness of developing technologies accessible for underserved population groups, which increases quality of life or is related to social justice. For example, where sustainable agricultural technologies will promote food security in developing regions, this shall be both socially impacting and environmentally sound. Sustainable technologies focus on an inclusive approach to bridging the gap and, in turn, ensure that the gains from innovation are widely shared.

Economic Viability: Whereas most talk in the line of sustainability bears the face of environmental and social goals, a very basic characteristic of sustainable technology is economic viability. Truly sustainable technology has to be economically workable and profit-making or at least self-sustaining in the long run. This would hence ensure that the technology is widely made in the market and sustained, deserving its meaning in being game-changers.

Hence, sustainable technology in entrepreneurship means those innovations that aim for the implementations or the applications that are meant to balance environmental, social, and economic issues. Such technologies are resource-efficient, have a low environmental impact, can be scaled and durable, provide for social equity, are economically sound. In simple words, developing and implementing sustainable technologies is a way of being sure that an entrepreneur is making a wealth contribution to this lovely planet and that his businesses are poised for long-term success in an increasingly sustainability-oriented world. Today, in the business world, the focus has turned functional, including sustainable technologies. This is because business has to strike a balance of economic growth with environmental and social responsibility. Sustainable technologies are such innovations that can meet the then current market demands while reducing negative impacts to the environment and to society at large. And the ones at the helm, again, are entrepreneurs, driving the development and adoption of such technologies to give solutions to global problems that entwine around climate change, resource scarcity, and social inequality.

Drivers of Sustainable Technology Adoption

Several key drivers are responsible for the adoption of sustainable technology in entrepreneurship. The surge in consumer demand for green products and services is one of the major forces. With the rise in consumer awareness about the environment, companies are increasingly being pushed into green technologies by consumers seeking companies that support sustainability. This consumer behavior shift is not a trend, but rather a robust market force that has to be acknowledged and conformed to by the entrepreneur for the sake of competitive survival (Gopal et al., 2024; Rahamathunnisa et al., 2024; Vijayakumar et al., 2024).

Other key drivers would be the regulatory pressures. Across the world, governments are enforcing much more stringent environmental regulations and policies to bring down the level of carbon emissions, enhance energy efficiency, and increase the percentage of renewable resources in their basket. We can already see several entrepreneurs benefiting because of first-mover advantage by being ahead of these regulations and avoiding penalties while welcoming incentives like tax breaks or subsidies for green initiatives.

More and more investors are becoming attracted to companies that have the attribute of being sustainable. Environment, social, and governance criteria have become core considerations for investment decisions, and most investors take a keen interest in companies that include sustainable practices. Those entrepreneurs who focus on sustainable technologies can thus attract investment from this fast-growing pool of socially responsible investors to acquire the financial wherewithal necessary to scale ventures.

Finally, the drive for operational efficiency and cost savings also encourages the use of sustainable technologies. Most sustainable technologies, such as energy-efficient systems and processes for waste reduction, provide long-term cost benefits. This can limit the use of resources and generation of waste, hence reducing operation costs, improving profitability, and enhancing sustainability generally in a business.

The Role of Entrepreneurs in Sustainable Innovation

This is crucial, as entrepreneurs play a tremendous role in developing sustainable innovation. Entrepreneurs are often the first movers who can develop new sustainable technologies for the market and challenge whole established industries or create new sectors altogether. Their attitude toward risk, experimentation with new ideas, and willingness to cross boundaries contribute to the creation of innovative solutions for the majority of the great social and environmental problems humankind faces today (Prasad et al., 2024; Venkateswaran et al., 2023).

The entrepreneurs are contributors to sustainable innovation, for the reason that they consider conditions for sustainability as part of the business models right from the start. This would mean the design of products and services that reduce environmental impact and resource-efficient processes in their operation, and business models which express circular economy principles by recycling, reusing, and waste reduction. By putting sustainability at the heart of the core ventures, the entrepreneur will be able to create long-term value for his business and provide positive value to society and the environment.

Thirdly, raising awareness and education on the benefits of sustainable technologies are massively aided by entrepreneurs. By showing the commercial strength of sustainable innovations, they are able to influence consumer behavior and shape standards in the industry while setting examples and encouraging other businesses to do same. It has been noticed that if an entrepreneur can show that he can actually conduct a business in a sustainable manner, he sets precedence for the rest to follow.

Sustainable technologies are thus part and parcel of modern entrepreneurship, motivated both by customers and under the coercion of regulators, attracted by investors, as well as in the search for operational efficiency. The entrepreneurship domain is one of the cornerstones in this revolutionary wave, practicing and embracing those distinctive sustainable innovations that cater to contemporary global problem solving. In the context of independent venturing and its use of sustainable technologies, it can be successful both economically and socially and/or environmentally responsible.

HARNESSING CREATIVITY FOR SUSTAINABLE TECHNOLOGICAL ADVANCEMENTS

In this case, creativity becomes the primary determinant in the development of sustainable technologies to be at par with the complex modern world. This makes creativity the prime mover for innovation: it is through this that entrepreneurs can develop effective yet environmentally responsible solutions. The road forward for incorporating creativity into research for the development of sustainable technology lies in understanding the creative procedure and some particular techniques and tools that are fabricated to enhance creative thinking (Gregori & Holzmann, 2020; Ogbeibu et al., 2020).

Figure 3. Structured approach to leveraging creativity for technological sustainability

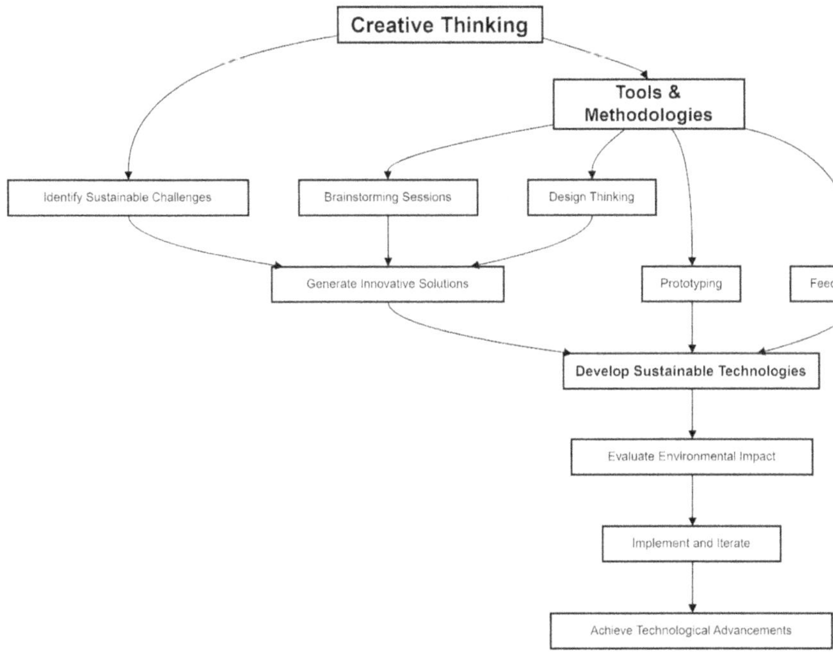

Figure 3 illustrates the process of generating innovative ideas, identifying sustainable challenges, generating solutions, developing eco-friendly technologies, evaluating environmental impact, implementing and refining the technology, and achieving technological advancements. Brainstorming sessions, design thinking, prototyping, and feedback loops are applied in generating ideas and assessing environmental impact, implementing and improving the technology, and achieving technological advancement. The approach is user-centered with continuous improvement and continuous improvement based on user input.

Creative Processes in Sustainable Innovation

Basically, the creative process in sustainable innovation has several stages, all important in the development of effective and impactful technologies. First of these is the process of problem identification: recognizing and defining which environmental or social issues are to be addressed. In terms of sustainable technology, this could be about problems dealing with resource depletion, pollution, or energy inefficiency. When the scope and particulars of the problem are clear, entrepreneurs are in a position to begin developing creative solutions that will resolve it (Satalkina & Steiner, 2020).

In the second stage, ideation with divergent thinking, it helps entrepreneurs to create alternate possibilities and their corresponding solutions. Tools like brainstorming, mind maps, and others to support ideation are also carried out in this stage in order to get diversity into the pool of possibilities. It actually becomes a stage for the nurturing of free thoughts and reasoning of unthinkable ideas since many a time sustainability makes a call for innovative solutions different from the normal stance.

Filtering of ideas takes place in the stage of concept development and evaluation. This is the part wherein the entrepreneur finds room for utilizing convergent thinking to sift through the ideas and identifies the most feasible and attractive ones. It comprises assessments of the ideas' practicability, environmental impact, and prototyping. Emphasis is put into turning creative ideas into practical and scalable solutions that are environmental-friendly.

Finally, the implementation state is simply actualizing the two developed concepts in the market. In this stage, the technology is designed, developed, and commercialized. Effective implementation is a collaborative and iterative process of testing with constant feedbacks for the technology to work accordingly and fit in the parameters of sustainability.

Tools and Methodologies for Enhancing Creativity

There are many tools and methodologies that exist within the domain of developing sustainable technologies, all of which have the potential to benefit creativity. One of the widely adopted methods is design thinking, a human-centered approach with an emphasis on empathy, ideation, and experimentation. Five stages form the core of design thinking: empathize, define, ideate, prototype, and test. Such focus on the needs of the end-user and iteration through prototypes aid entrepreneurs in developing technologies that are at once innovative and aligned with sustainability.

Brainstorming is another set of potent tools, either individually or in a group. There are techniques like reverse brainstorming, wherein participants think over how to cause the problem rather than solve it; this may uncover new views that may hold innovative solutions. Another technique is SCAMPER, which stands for Substitute, Combine, Adapt, Modify, Put to another use, Eliminate, and Reverse—a tool that encourages creative thinking by asking individuals to scrutinise and change existing technologies in a variety of ways.

It is also useful in organizing ideas and in visualization. Making a picture that links various ideas could help entrepreneurs discover their relationships and potential areas for sustainable innovation. It aids in the organization of ideas and generates new connections which, at times, might not be clear to linear thinking.

Accordingly, creativity in driving sustainable technological innovation requires a disciplined creative process and dedicated tools and methodologies. Working with design thinking, brainstorming, and mind mapping, among others, using collaborative tools in this regard will keep an entrepreneur on the right track to enhance their creativity in developing technologies serving pressing environmental and social problems. By such practices, creativity effectively drives sustainable innovation to impactful responsible technological solutions.

In order to manage the complex challenges of modern civilization, the integration of creativity in the process of developing sustainable technologies will be inevitable. By targeting creativity to be the force that drives innovation, entrepreneurs will have a better position to come up with relevant and effective solutions that respect the environment. To use creativity for sustainable technological innovation, one needs to master the creative process and apply dedicated tools and methodologies as specific enablers for creative thinking.

Creative Processes in Sustainable Innovation

The creative course in sustainable innovation generally has a few important steps in the creation of technologies that work and make a difference. First and foremost, there is the identification of problems. This critical step requires identifying and then defining any environmental or social issues that need attention. For sustainable technology, this could involve identifying problems in resource depletion or pollution and even issues tied to energy inefficiency. Grasping a view of the scope and specifics of a problem will help the entrepreneur focus his or her creative effort in that area.

The second stage is ideation, which is more divergent. Divergent thinking would allow the entrepreneur to generate many ideas and many solutions to problems. Here the process of brainstorming, mind mapping, or other techniques of ideation are taken and transferred in ways the entrepreneur considers each available option. This should be almost free thinking about and considering crazy ideas, as often the call for sustainability is for strategies that are innovative and can go off into other modes from the more traditional.

In the development of concepts, one takes the range of ideas that were generated in the preceding stage and refines them to allow for their evaluation. It is where convergent thinking is applied to narrow down the options and thus arrive at the most promising concepts. This shall comprise feasibility studies, environmental impact, and prototype studies. This will involve taking creative ideas and turning them into practical or scalable solutions that help realize set sustainability objectives.

The last stage, implementation, involves taking ideas developed to the market. Design, production, and commercialization also occur at this stage. A good implementation process requires collaborative action, iterative testing, and a continued feedback mechanism—all of which ensure that the working of the technology maintains intended requirements coupled with sustainability criteria.

Overcoming Barriers to Creative Thinking

Creativity has been added as a strong variable for sustainable technological development, enabling entrepreneurs to offer the market innovative solutions to environmental and societal issues. However, the successful use of creativity requires the removal of a number of barriers toward the creative process (Sutrisno et al., 2023; Trapp & Kanbach, 2021).

a. **Organizational Constraints:** Of these, rigid organizational structures and organizational cultures that are resistant to change are the most important ones. Overemphasis on processes and routines may depress creative thinking in organizations. To offset this, an entrepreneur has to inculcate a culture of experimentation, respect diverse perspectives, and have flexible processes and open culture to break up these constraints and stimulate creative thinking.
b. **Risk Aversion:** The pressure to keep the risk at a minimum and seek immediate returns often keeps entrepreneurs from engaging in innovative, but uncertain projects. Beat risk aversion by giving a safe space to experiment; failure is a lesson learned, not a setback. One can reduce fears associated with taking risks by promoting a growth mindset and being supportive of innovative projects.
c. **Constraints in Resources:** Resources in the form of time, money, or any other attribute, such as expertise, can impose a ceiling on the creativity by the entrepreneurs. This obstacle can be overcome by the entrepreneurs through partnering, collaborating, and crowdsourcing to obtain further resources and expertise. This would lead to the necessary help in overcoming resource constraints and gaining sustainable technological advancement with the help of open innovation platforms and involvement of stakeholders from outside.
d. **Cognitive Biases:** There are cognitive biases, like confirmation bias and the status quo bias, that can close in on creativity by making a person stick to familiar ideas and turn down novel ways. On the other side, entrepreneurs must motivate different perspectives and actually search for ideas that come outside the box. Techniques such as brainstorming, design thinking, and scenario planning might be helpful in giving a challenge to already operating assumptions and thus motivating more creative problem-solving.

Overcoming those creative-thinking barriers is therefore of essence in tapping creativity to develop sustainable technologies. The entrepreneur can unlock his or her creativity by imposing an open culture, embracing risk, leveraging resources, and achieving awareness about the ways of mitigating cognitive bias for the meaningful driving of advancements that can help make a more sustainable future possible.

BUILDING A SUPPORTIVE ECOSYSTEM FOR SUSTAINABLE INNOVATION

Another critical factor for an ecosystem that supports creating sustainable innovation is organizational culture that should promote creativity and strategic investments in R&D, or research and development. These are very core elemental factors for entrepreneurship in order to drive sustainable technological development (Lüdeke-Freund, 2020).

Figure 4. Building a supportive ecosystem for sustainable innovation

They collaborate in knowledge sharing with research institutions, seek funding and investment, and provide financial support. The community is engaged in developing solutions and provides validation; the advocate has supportive policies and implements supportive regulations and incentives. The policymakers bring together the entrepreneurs and the investors; the investors present the different types of investment that are open to stakeholders. The community provides moral support and validation for their solutions. All in all, what an entrepreneur needs to achieve sustainable innovation and growth is funding, financial support, involvement, and commitment of the community, support from policymakers (Volkmann et al., 2021).

The Importance of Organizational Culture in Promoting Creativity

The organizational culture is a very important factor in creating an environment that aids creative thinking and innovation. A culture of creative thinking may contribute importantly to an organization better able to develop and implement sustainable technologies.

Encourage Open Communication: Opening channels of communication can further advance creativity. Employees will contribute innovative solutions if they feel that their ideas are not subject to criticism. Forums for idea exchange in the form of regular brainstorming sessions or innovation workshops aid in open communication.

Rewarding Innovation: If in most cases employees are rewarded for their creative effort, then a system will benefit from that in many ways. It will create a culture where experimentation and risk-taking are encouraged. Success stories can be celebrated with the same zeal as learning from failures to reinforce a positive attitude towards creativity.

Collaborative behavior encourages teams to come up with ideas as various views and skill levels are combined. This is going to create innovative thinking and break down silos between departments. Offer opportunities for employees to work on interdisciplinary projects; this can result in new solutions and more efficient sustainable technologies.

Support Professional Development: Another important way to foster creativity is by increasing professional development among employees. This might consist of providing training programs, workshops, and creative problem-solving and sustainability resources in order to build employee competencies. This enables organizations to stay ahead in their innovation journey by continuously investing in human capital.

Investing in Research and Development for Sustainability

An organization that applies strategic investment in research and development for the advancement of sustainable technologies includes R&D of new ideas, innovative available solutions, and raising market insights. In that context, entrepreneurs benefit from this commitment in R&D to remain sustainable (Ciasullo et al., 2020).

Advancing Sustainable Technologies: R&D provides a chance to develop new materials, processes, and technologies that will save energy and reduce environmental impact. Through R&D investments, an entrepreneur can quickly develop state-of-the-art solutions associated with energy efficiency, renewable energy technologies, and environmentally friendly materials. Such innovation would help the business achieve its sustainability goals and may differentiate the business within the marketplace.

Competitive Advantage Improvement: An organization in a dynamic market needs to get ahead of the competition—really ahead—through innovation. R&D investments allow organizations to research new business models and cutting-edge technologies that provide them with their competitive advantage. Organizations focusing on sustainability-based R&D will drive industry leadership by developing solutions to meet consumer demand for environment-sensitive products and services.

Create Strategic Partnerships: The efforts of research institutions, universities, and other organizations can be aligned with the undertaking of R&D to make a greater impact. Such partnerships will have specialized skills, resources, and opportunities to attract funding sources. Such collaborations will, therefore, enable entrepreneurs to accelerate the development of sustainable technologies better suited to tackle these complex challenges.

Long-Term Value Created From R&D in This Regard: Although R&D investments mean a lot of upfront cost, it will give long-term value by encouraging innovation in the growth process. Technology-oriented sustainability from R&D shall reduce costs, bring more operational efficiency, and facilitate new streams of revenue. It can also enhance reputations and further attract investment from socially responsible investors.

Thus, creating an enabling environment for sustainable innovation means the development of an organizational culture that would advance creative activity and make strategic investments in R&D. By creating an environment where creativity is valued and supported, and by committing to research and development, entrepreneurs will be in the best position to advance the development of sustainable technologies to create business success and deliver positive societal impacts.

Creating an enabling environment that supports sustainable innovation is multi-layered, including collaborative innovation, stakeholder consultation processes, and strong policy and regulatory support. Each element together builds an environment in which sustainable technologies could be nurtured and provide long-term economic and environmental advantages.

Collaborative Innovation and Stakeholder Engagement

Indeed, collaborative innovation is one of the ways that take further sustainable technologies through putting a collection of diverse perspectives, competencies, and resources together. Partnerships and collaborations can help entrepreneurs and organizations to gain enormously from outside their immediate industry. For example, partnerships between start-ups, large companies, research institutions, and organizations with no purpose of making a profit may jointly conduct innovative work to integrate technologies or develop an innovative solution. This may take the form of knowledge sharing, joint research and development work, or co-created technologies so as to develop problem solutions on a sustainability plan (Bischoff, 2021).

Stakeholder engagement forms one of the most vital components in collaborative innovation. It is where entrepreneurial entities get to understand different needs and expectations from customers, suppliers, community members, and policymakers who could integrate such insights into their innovations. Involving stakeholders at very early stages of the development process might result in more efficient and more widely accepted solutions. For example, engaging customers in the design process could ensure that the end product will fit their needs and preferences, and consultations with local community organizations will ensure that technologies are more aligned with local environmental and social priorities.

The establishment of open innovation and knowledge-sharing platforms might also enhance collaboration. Innovation hubs, incubators, and accelerators for sustainability may provide networking for various entrepreneurs and stakeholders, while experimental and dialogic spaces are facilitated. This may also provide access to a range of resources—such as funding, mentorship, and technical support—needed to speed up development and the adoption process of sustainable technologies.

Policy and Regulatory Support for Sustainable Entrepreneurship

Policy and regulatory support are very important in creating an enabling environment for sustainable entrepreneurship. Governments and regulatory bodies can do a lot to promote sustainability through multiple mechanisms, including legislation, incentives, and standards (Volkmann et al., 2021).

Legislation can set out a clear framework of action for companies, particularly if it is aimed at reducing impacts and promoting sustainability. Regulations reducing carbon emissions or enhancing the share of renewable energy can drive innovation because they set performance standards, besides being clear and consistent, which helps businesses to understand what is expected and invest in technologies that will meet the standards.

Other incentives that can spur investment in sustainable technologies include tax credits, grants, and subsidies. In financing research, development, and implementation, lower entry barriers for entrepreneurs and uptake of innovative solutions are some of the ways through which governments can facilitate this. Programs offering funding to green projects or offering other rewards to reach pre-stipulated targets toward sustainability may also serve as incentives for business firms in environmentally friendly practices.

Standards and certifications can guide organizations toward sustainability. The regulators could establish standards for sustainable practices and products, so that innovations are aligned with rigorous environmental and social criteria. Setting regulatory standards for the introduction of sustainable practices and products could be quite useful. Certifications like LEED or Fair Trade allow consumers and investors to know that a company takes sustainability issues seriously and thus improves its reputation and marketability.

Government policies can thus be used to promote education and training in sustainability, thereby establishing a resourceful workforce that will drive innovation. Programmes oriented towards green technology, environmental management, and business sustainability can hence empower both entrepreneurs and employees with knowledge and skills for success in sustainable economic activity.

Such making of an enabling environment for sustainable innovation, therefore, calls for a holistic approach: collaborative innovation and stakeholder engagement, and policy and regulatory support. Fostering partnerships, stakeholder engagement, and policy support, entrepreneurs would be in a position to create an enabling environment which allows for the development and adoption of sustainable technologies. This only means advanced technological innovation but also a more sustainable and resilient future.

FUTURE DIRECTIONS IN SUSTAINABLE ENTREPRENEURSHIP

The field of sustainable entrepreneurship is turning increasingly dynamic, driven by emerging trends in technological innovation and increasing importance of creativity. With growing global emphasis on sustainability, it places entrepreneurs at the very forefront of developing and implementing solutions that ensure environmental and social sustainability while remaining economically viable. This comes with promising opportunities and challenges for the future of sustainable entrepreneurship (Boopathi, 2024; Ravisankar et al., 2024).

Figure 5. Sustainable technological innovation for sustainable entrepreneurship

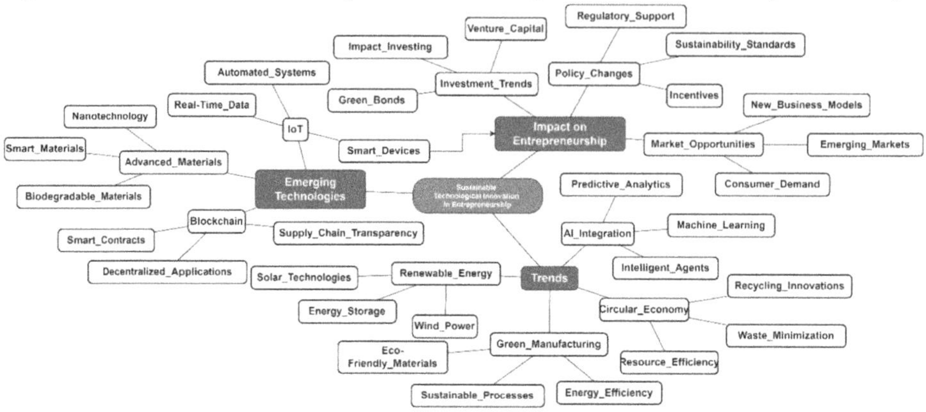

Figure 5 highlights the importance of sustainable technological innovation in entrepreneurship, focusing on key trends such as AI integration, machine learning, predictive analytics, intelligent agents, circular economy, waste minimization, resource efficiency, recycling innovations, renewable energy, green manufacturing, energy storage, and emerging technologies like blockchain, IoT, smart devices, real-time data, autonomous systems, and advanced materials. These trends are extremely relevant to entrepreneurship, including new business models, emerging markets, consumer demand for green products, investment trends. The map offers an overview of arising trends and implications for sustainable entrepreneurship, showing the interrelated factors of technology, market dynamics, and policy.

Emerging Trends in Sustainable Technological Innovation

a. **Circular Economy Models:** One of the biggest trends in sustainable technology is going to be circular economy models. As opposed to traditional linear ones, working on a "take-make-dispose" model of operation, circular economies are designed to squeeze out every last resource. This includes strategies for recycling, reusing, and refurbishing materials. More and more often, such technologies are being developed by entrepreneurs, including advanced recycling processes, modular product design, and systems for tracing material flows. All these innovations help reduce waste and resource consumption, promoting a more sustainable use of materials.
b. **Green Energy Technologies:** This sector is on the frontline of development. Innovations in areas such as solar, wind, and geothermal are continually getting cheaper and better due to improved materials science and engineering.

Moreover, emerging technologies in the fields of energy storage—like advanced batteries—to smart grids make it easier to integrate and have faith in renewable energy sources. In this direction, entrepreneurs test ways through which these technologies can be made more accessible and scalable, driving a shift away from fossil fuels and to a much cleaner energy system.

c. **Climate-Resilient Technologies:** As climate change impacts become more real, demand for technologies that enhance resilience and adaptation is increasing. These innovations range from climate-smart agriculture technologies to water management and disaster response. In light of this, entrepreneurs are engineering solutions that help communities adapt to the changing climate conditions, such as drought-resistant crops and water-saving irrigation systems, in addition to early warning systems against extreme weather events. These technologies of high importance in the reduction of the impacts of climate change and for supporting sustainable development.
d. **Digitalization and AI in Sustainability:** Digital technologies are fast integrating into the practice of sustainable entrepreneurship. This includes AI and machine learning, which may be applied in optimizing the use of resources to acquire efficiency and create new insights for sustainable practices. For example, AI algorithms can improve energy management in intelligent buildings, make supply chains sustainable, and project future environmental impact from a variety of activities. Such technologies are being captured by entrepreneurs to drive more compelling and data-driven ways of managing sustainability.

The Evolving Role of Creativity in Entrepreneurship

a. **Advanced Problem-Solving Capabilities:** Creativity remains the keystone of entrepreneurial success in business, more so in the domain of sustainability. With growing complexity in challenges, the need to offer solutions through creative problem-solving grew further. Today, entrepreneurs are joining the quest for sustainability with new creative ways of solving problems, from designing low-impact products to new business models driving circularity. This creative distortion enables entrepreneurs to look at problems from new vantage points and develop effective solutions that would not manifest through linear thinking.
b. **Cross-Disciplinary Innovation:** More cross-disciplinary approaches will characterize sustainable entrepreneurship in the near future. The integration of these knowledge bases—engineering, design, business, and environmental science—enables entrepreneurs to come up with solutions which are more holistic and effective. For instance, materials science insights can be integrated with design thinking in the development of new materials that have improved

properties and are sustainable. In this way, a person can attain an interdisciplinary approach that gives birth to creativity and innovation in the development of a solution that is at once technically superior and socially impactful.

c. **Consumer-Centric Innovation:** The question currently posed is how consumer-centric innovation plays an increasingly important role in the understanding and anticipation of consumer needs for sustainable entrepreneurship. Participatory design, co-creation, and other creative ways of engaging consumers are likely to create products and services more aligned with the values and preferences of the consumer. The possibility that entrepreneurship brings about an innovation that is both sustainable and well-received and adapted to the market will be ensured by involving consumers in the process. In this regard, a consumer-centric approach helps drive the success and scalability of sustainable technologies.
d. **Dynamic Business Models:** With the constantly changing landscape of sustainable entrepreneurship, business models should also be flexible and adaptive. Business strategies need to be continuously innovated based on market and regulatory environment changes and technological advances. Innovating business models—say, through subscription-based services on sustainable products or finding new revenue streams—keeps an entrepreneur competitive in the market and effectively works toward set goals on sustainability.

The upcoming trends in technological innovation and the changing role of creativity hold a promise for a brighter future of sustainable entrepreneurship. The adoption of circular economy models, evolvement of green energy technologies, and digitalization are among the high-impact drivers in sustainability by entrepreneurs. At the same time, creativity enhances problem-solving, facilitates collaboration across disciplinary boundaries, and aligns innovations with the needs of consumers. Such factors all combine to give a scenario of sustainable entrepreneurship that is dynamic and full of innovation, holding out great potential for solving pressing global challenges and promoting a more sustainable future.

CHALLENGES AND OPPORTUNITIES IN SUSTAINABLE ENTREPRENEURSHIP

Challenges

- **Scaling Sustainable Solutions:** Of the greater challenges in sustainable entrepreneurship, scaling innovations to wide practice stands as one of them. So many of the sustainable technologies often start as niche solutions that serve only a few. Scaling such innovations to reach wider markets faces a host of challenges related to production cost, regulatory barriers, and market resistance. It has to develop ways to scale the solution while keeping the sustainability credentials intact and handling increased complexity.

- **Funding and Investment:** The funding for sustainable enterprises is challenging due to the fact that investors are usually focused on short payback periods rather than taking a long-term perspective on environment and social impact. In the recent past, interest in impact investing has grown; however, securing capital for innovative and high-risk sustainable technologies remains challenging. That means that entrepreneurs shall have to come up with compelling business cases which prove the long-term value of their innovations in order to galvanize investment (Ravisankar et al., 2023).
- **Regulatory Uncertainty:** It is anticipated that the regulatory environment related to sustainable technologies will continue to evolve, thereby introducing uncertainty to the entrepreneur. The changes in policies, standards, and regulations may impact the feasibility and profitability of a sustainability-oriented venture. An entrepreneur needs to be aware of the tectonic shifts in regulation and has to be swift enough to adjust the strategy as requirements evolve.

Opportunities

- **Emerging Markets:** Sustainable entrepreneurship provides huge opportunities in emerging markets. This is because these regions are becoming potential markets due to rapid urbanization, industrialization, and growing consumer awareness, ultimately creating demand for sustainable solutions. If entrepreneurs can adapt innovations to special needs in these markets, they will be able to realize new growth opportunities and contribute to sustainable development in these regions.
- **Keeping Updated:** Knowing and keeping updated with all new technological developments in such areas as artificial intelligence, blockchain, or renewable energy represents further opportunities for sustainable entrepreneurship. The technologies might improve the effectivity and efficiency of solutions in sustainability. In turn, it gives the opportunity for entrepreneurs to create new products and services that would offer solutions to urgent ecological and social problems. These also could gain a new competitive edge and unlock new markets.
- **Consumer Trends:** The growing consumer demand for sustainable products and practices creates an enabling environment for sustainable entrepreneurship. Increasingly, most consumers reach out to those brands that can prove to have consideration for the environment and society. Those entrepreneurs who

can successfully align their products with such trends, and effectively communicate their efforts at sustainability, can capture market share and build brand loyalty.

Preparing for the Future: Strategies for Entrepreneurs

a. **Embrace Innovation and Technology:** For sustained leadership in the dynamic environment of sustainable entrepreneurship, the entrepreneur must continue seeking out and integrating new technologies and innovative practices. In this context, research and development and scanning technological trends could help to make use of digital tools, hence enhancing efficiency and impact of sustainable solutions. There is another dimension to partnerships with tech companies and research institutions: teaming up to leverage their expertise and resources.
b. **Emphasize Scalability and Adaptability:** Long-term sustainability requires dealing with scalable business models and strategies that are adaptable. While designing solutions, entrepreneurs must consider the scalability issues likely to be met during production, distribution, market expansion, or acquisition of customers. In addition, the flexibility to adjust in terms of a pivot—be it in terms of change in market conditions or regulatory requirements—would help ensure sustainable growth and impact.
c. **Strategic Partnerships:** This will bring stakeholders, investors, research institutions, NGOs, and the private sector together to develop strategic partnerships. The outlets for collaboration will allow the resources, know-how, and networks to be tapped for scaling the innovation and in regulatory barrier removal. Strong stakeholder relationships foster exchange of knowledge and collaborative problem-solving.
d. **Measure and Communicate Impact:** Showcasing the impact of sustainable innovations is critical for assuring investment, consumer trust, and long-term success. There is a need for entrepreneurs to develop robust frameworks through which to measure and report the environment and social impacts that are derived from solutions. Effective communication can then be aimed at creating credibility and market adoption in the marketplaces by differentiation of offerings.
e. **Be Informed and Engage in Policy Advocacy:** Being conversant with regulatory shifts and taking part in policy advocacy would enable entrepreneurs to effectively deal with an essentially changing regulatory environment. Actively participating in industry groups, contributing to policy discussions, and staying current with regulatory changes will position entrepreneurs to better anticipate and respond to changes that could affect their ventures.

It is from these great challenges that the future of sustainable entrepreneurship is created and, by them, unprecedented opportunities are given. Scalability, strategic partnerships, measurement, and communication of the impact—all based on innovation—are at the core and define the group of entrepreneurs that will outpace others in this fast-moving field. A proactive preparation for future directions is what will empower entrepreneurs in making real progress toward a more sustainable and resilient future.

CONCLUSION

There is a realization that if there has to be a change in the landscape of entrepreneurship towards sustainability, creativity and innovation will be indispensable. It explores how creativity can be harnessed to overcome several key barriers and unlock opportunities for sustainable technological development. By explicating and grounding theories of creativity and the challenges of scaling and financing sustainable solutions in theory, it positions entrepreneurs better for success.

It is in the collaborative nature of sustainable innovation that there exists a need to engage diverse stakeholders and to leverage collective expertise. Building an enabling ecosystem is as important—through partnerships and policy support—in order to build an environment in which sustainable technologies can thrive. Those entrepreneurs who proactively embrace technological change, focus on scalable solutions, and ride the wave of regulatory uncertainties with great agility will be powerfully positioned to lead in this space.

Looking ahead, there are challenges and opportunities in the future of sustainable entrepreneurship. Such entrepreneurs need to be agile, learn continuously from new trends, and be impact-driven toward sustainable growth and profitability. At this point, innovation, scalability, strategic partnerships, and communication will be very important in terms of an entrepreneur's contribution toward a more sustainable world.

The journey to sustainable entrepreneurship is dynamic and multi-dimensional. It encrypts a holistic approach that coalesces creativity, collaboration, and strategic foresight. It is through constant efforts and a commitment towards attaining sustainability that entrepreneurs can execute impactful solutions which not only drive technological progress but also positively contribute towards global environmental and social goals.

REFERENCES

Anjum, T., Farrukh, M., Heidler, P., & Díaz Tautiva, J. A. (2020). Entrepreneurial intention: Creativity, entrepreneurship, and university support. *Journal of Open Innovation*, 7(1), 11. DOI: 10.3390/joitmc7010011

Bischoff, K. (2021). A study on the perceived strength of sustainable entrepreneurial ecosystems on the dimensions of stakeholder theory and culture. *Small Business Economics*, 56(3), 1121–1140. DOI: 10.1007/s11187-019-00257-3

Boopathi, S. (2024). Digital HR Implementation for Business Growth in Industrial 5.0. In *Convergence of Human Resources Technologies and Industry 5.0* (pp. 1–22). IGI Global. DOI: 10.4018/979-8-3693-1343-5.ch001

Boopathi, S., Kumar, P. K. S., Meena, R. S., Sudhakar, M., & Associates. (2023). Sustainable Developments of Modern Soil-Less Agro-Cultivation Systems: Aquaponic Culture. In *Human Agro-Energy Optimization for Business and Industry* (pp. 69–87). IGI Global.

Carayannis, E. G. (2020). *Encyclopedia of creativity, invention, innovation and entrepreneurship*. Springer. DOI: 10.1007/978-3-319-15347-6

Ciasullo, M. V., Troisi, O., Grimaldi, M., & Leone, D. (2020). Multi-level governance for sustainable innovation in smart communities: An ecosystems approach. *The International Entrepreneurship and Management Journal*, 16(4), 1167–1195. DOI: 10.1007/s11365-020-00641-6

Dana, L.-P., Salamzadeh, A., Hadizadeh, M., Heydari, G., & Shamsoddin, S. (2022). Urban entrepreneurship and sustainable businesses in smart cities: Exploring the role of digital technologies. *Sustainable Technology and Entrepreneurship*, 1(2), 100016. DOI: 10.1016/j.stae.2022.100016

Elia, G., Margherita, A., & Passiante, G. (2020). Digital entrepreneurship ecosystem: How digital technologies and collective intelligence are reshaping the entrepreneurial process. *Technological Forecasting and Social Change*, 150, 119791. DOI: 10.1016/j.techfore.2019.119791

Gopal, M., Lurdhumary, J., Bathrinath, S., Priya, A. P., Sarojwal, A., & Boopathi, S. (2024). Energy Harvesting and Smart Highways for Sustainable Transportation Infrastructure: Revolutionizing Roads Using Nanotechnology. In *Principles and Applications in Speed Sensing and Energy Harvesting for Smart Roads* (pp. 136–165). IGI Global. DOI: 10.4018/978-1-6684-9214-7.ch005

Gregori, P., & Holzmann, P. (2020). Digital sustainable entrepreneurship: A business model perspective on embedding digital technologies for social and environmental value creation. *Journal of Cleaner Production*, 272, 122817. DOI: 10.1016/j.jclepro.2020.122817

Lüdeke-Freund, F. (2020). Sustainable entrepreneurship, innovation, and business models: Integrative framework and propositions for future research. *Business Strategy and the Environment*, 29(2), 665–681. DOI: 10.1002/bse.2396

Ogbeibu, S., Emelifeonwu, J., Senadjki, A., Gaskin, J., & Kaivo-oja, J. (2020). Technological turbulence and greening of team creativity, product innovation, and human resource management: Implications for sustainability. *Journal of Cleaner Production*, 244, 118703. DOI: 10.1016/j.jclepro.2019.118703

Ogbeibu, S., Jabbour, C. J. C., Gaskin, J., Senadjki, A., & Hughes, M. (2021). Leveraging STARA competencies and green creativity to boost green organisational innovative evidence: A praxis for sustainable development. *Business Strategy and the Environment*, 30(5), 2421–2440. DOI: 10.1002/bse.2754

Prasad, M. S. C., Dhanalakshmi, M., Mohan, M., Somasundaram, B., Valarmathi, R., & Boopathi, S. (2024). Machine Learning-Integrated Sustainable Engineering and Energy Systems: Innovations at the Nexus. In *Harnessing High-Performance Computing and AI for Environmental Sustainability* (pp. 74–98). IGI Global. DOI: 10.4018/979-8-3693-1794-5.ch004

Rahamathunnisa, U., Sudhakar, K., Padhi, S., Bhattacharya, S., Shashibhushan, G., & Boopathi, S. (2024). Sustainable Energy Generation From Waste Water: IoT Integrated Technologies. In *Adoption and Use of Technology Tools and Services by Economically Disadvantaged Communities: Implications for Growth and Sustainability* (pp. 225–256). IGI Global.

Ravisankar, A., Sampath, B., & Asif, M. M. (2023). Economic Studies on Automobile Management: Working Capital and Investment Analysis. In *Multidisciplinary Approaches to Organizational Governance During Health Crises* (pp. 169–198). IGI Global.

Ravisankar, A., Shanthi, A., Lavanya, S., Ramaratnam, M., Krishnamoorthy, V., & Boopathi, S. (2024). Harnessing 6G for Consumer-Centric Business Strategies Across Electronic Industries. In *AI Impacts in Digital Consumer Behavior* (pp. 241–270). IGI Global.

Satalkina, L., & Steiner, G. (2020). Digital entrepreneurship and its role in innovation systems: A systematic literature review as a basis for future research avenues for sustainable transitions. *Sustainability (Basel)*, 12(7), 2764. DOI: 10.3390/su12072764

Sundar, R., Srikaanth, P. B., Naik, D. A., Murugan, V. P., Karumudi, M., & Boopathi, S. (2024). Achieving Balance Between Innovation and Security in the Cloud With Artificial Intelligence of Things: Semantic Web Control Models. In *Advances in Web Technologies and Engineering* (pp. 1–26). IGI Global. DOI: 10.4018/979-8-3693-1487-6.ch001

Sutrisno, S., Kuraesin, A. D., Siminto, S., Irawansyah, I., & Ausat, A. M. A. (2023). The role of information technology in driving innovation and entrepreneurial business growth. *Jurnal Minfo Polgan*, 12(1), 586–597. DOI: 10.33395/jmp.v12i1.12463

Terán-Yépez, E., Marín-Carrillo, G. M., del Pilar Casado-Belmonte, M., & de las Mercedes Capobianco-Uriarte, M. (2020). Sustainable entrepreneurship: Review of its evolution and new trends. *Journal of Cleaner Production*, 252, 119742. DOI: 10.1016/j.jclepro.2019.119742

Thukral, E. (2021). COVID-19: Small and medium enterprises challenges and responses with creativity, innovation, and entrepreneurship. *Strategic Change*, 30(2), 153–158. DOI: 10.1002/jsc.2399

Trapp, C. T., & Kanbach, D. K. (2021). Green entrepreneurship and business models: Deriving green technology business model archetypes. *Journal of Cleaner Production*, 297, 126694. DOI: 10.1016/j.jclepro.2021.126694

Venkateswaran, N., Vidhya, K., Ayyannan, M., Chavan, S. M., Sekar, K., & Boopathi, S. (2023). A Study on Smart Energy Management Framework Using Cloud Computing. In *5G, Artificial Intelligence, and Next Generation Internet of Things: Digital Innovation for Green and Sustainable Economies* (pp. 189–212). IGI Global. DOI: 10.4018/978-1-6684-8634-4.ch009

Vijayakumar, G. N. S., Domakonda, V. K., Farooq, S., Kumar, B. S., Pradeep, N., & Boopathi, S. (2024). Sustainable Developments in Nano-Fluid Synthesis for Various Industrial Applications. In *Adoption and Use of Technology Tools and Services by Economically Disadvantaged Communities: Implications for Growth and Sustainability* (pp. 48–81). IGI Global.

Volkmann, C., Fichter, K., Klofsten, M., & Audretsch, D. B. (2021). Sustainable entrepreneurial ecosystems: An emerging field of research. *Small Business Economics*, 56(3), 1047–1055. DOI: 10.1007/s11187-019-00253-7

Vrontis, D., Chaudhuri, R., & Chatterjee, S. (2022). Adoption of digital technologies by SMEs for sustainability and value creation: Moderating role of entrepreneurial orientation. *Sustainability (Basel)*, 14(13), 7949. DOI: 10.3390/su14137949

KEY TERMS

AI: Artificial Intelligence

LEED: Leadership in Energy and Environmental Design

NGO: Non-Governmental Organization

SCAMPER: **S**: Substitute, **C**: Combine, **A**: Adapt, **M**: Modify (or Magnify), **P**: Put to another use, **E**: Eliminate, **R**: Reverse (or Rearrange)

Chapter 6
Entrepreneurial Ecosystems and Job Creation

Majdi Quttainah
https://orcid.org/0000-0002-6280-1060
Kuwait University, Kuwait

Ashutosh Pandey
https://orcid.org/0000-0002-8255-8459
FORE School of Management, New Delhi, India

Amit Kumar Yadav
https://orcid.org/0000-0002-4565-5284
O.P. Jindal Global University, Sonipat, India

Ajay Chandel
https://orcid.org/0000-0002-4585-6406
Lovely Professional University, India

ABSTRACT

This chapter turned its focus on critical elements such as access to capital, infrastructure, collaborative culture, and government policies in line with effective ecosystems. The chapter is based on case studies of the five entrepreneurial regions of Silicon Valley, Bangalore, Tel Aviv, Berlin, and Shenzhen, pointing out how each uses its unique strengths in building vivid entrepreneurial environments. A key place where the authors focus is on rising tendencies, such as models for working digitally, social entrepreneurship with a positive social impact, and the setting of technological advances to lead the way to future developments of these ecosystems. It also addresses bottlenecks other than financial constraints, which are regulatory

DOI: 10.4018/979-8-3693-9486-1.ch006

barriers, which underline the need for strategies adapted to these constraints and collaboration. This insight that can be garnered from these dynamics could empower stakeholders to make entrepreneurial ecosystems that are much more effective at supporting sustainable innovation.

INTRODUCTION

Over the past decades, entrepreneurial ecosystems have gained increasing importance in the modern context of economic growth, standing as a determinant factor in driving innovation and job creation. This complex interaction involves startups, small and medium-sized enterprises, investors, mentors, educational institutions, and government bodies, among others (Tunio et al., 2021). Policymakers, business leaders, and community stakeholders who hope to harness the full potential of entrepreneurship as an engine of economic development and as an effective means of delivering job opportunities must first understand how entrepreneurial ecosystems work and how they impact job creation. The heart of an entrepreneurial ecosystem is an environment that nurtures the creation of new ideas (Adelino et al., 2017). The resources available to the entrepreneurs in such ecosystems and the associated support mechanisms made available to them are the capital, mentorship, and network of their peers and experts. The resources enable the start-ups not only to survive the phase of development but also to scale and attain a competitive edge through providing employment. Synergy through symbiosis of various ecosystem components ensures that the benefits of entrepreneurship go beyond a single business and permeate through larger economic dynamics, contributing to job creation on a wider scale.

Creation of such jobs form one of the direct outcomes and perhaps among the most tangible of effects of a thriving entrepreneurial ecosystem. It is normally through upscale and startup operations inducing new jobs that innovative products and services emanate. The impact of entrepreneurial activity is, however, much more far-reaching because it generates indirect employment opportunities. For instance, the increase in startups will automatically trigger growth in ancillary industries and services, which include supply, marketing, and customer support. This is a multiplier effect and a testimony to the interrelatedness of entrepreneurial ecosystems and their eventual impact on employment (Ademilua et al., 2020).

Government and policy are very instrumental in determining the success of entrepreneurial ecosystems with the ability and potential to generate jobs. Governments may provide helping conditions to entrepreneurs through targeted policies and initiatives such as grants, tax incentives, and infrastructure development (Ahmed, 2022). Public-private partnerships may also help close gaps and open up synergies for the different stakeholders across the ecosystems. Policymakers are, therefore, capable of making improved impacts when these ecosystems get to shape the environment that is friendly to incubating entrepreneurship.

Educating and developing skills constitute some of the other essential components of entrepreneurial ecosystems. Although the role of educators and training programs is complementary in making people equipped with the necessary skills for entrepreneurial activity, entrepreneurial ecosystems create the breeding ground for entrepreneurial competence to develop. The educational ecosystem together with the entrepreneurship community ensures that there is alignment in the curricula and training programs that are aimed at industrial needs in order to further boost employability and start-up development (Anyadike-Danes et al., 2015).

Although entrepreneurial ecosystems offer good opportunities, they have numerous challenges and barriers that might undermine their offering in job creation. Access to capital, infrastructure, and regulatory issues may be some of the challenges that can potentially hinder the growth of start-ups and hence job creation. The addressing of these challenges requires team efforts from all the ecosystem stakeholder players in the formulation of strategies aimed at developing a more facilitative and inclusive entrepreneurial environment (Arabiyat et al., 2019).

In this light, therefore, entrepreneurial ecosystems play important roles in job creation and economic growth and provide encouraging innovation and startup support for the development of employment opportunities and, in general, economic benefits. Realizing this fully would involve understanding the dynamics of an entrepreneurial ecosystem and its ability to have an enabling environment for success. This, indeed, will help in developing a stronger and more resilient economy.

DEFINING ENTREPRENEURIAL ECOSYSTEMS

Entrepreneurial ecosystems are thus complex systems involving numerous interrelated elements that act together in encouraging emergence and survival of new foreign ventures. Ecosystems are not just a grouping of start-ups; on the contrary, they are dynamic environments where multi-various different elements interact amongst each other in supporting entrepreneurship and innovation (Bianchini & Pellegrino, 2017). A proper understanding of these core elements and their interplay in the ecosystem is core to the understanding of how entrepreneurial ecosystems function and contribute to the economic development process.

At the heart of any entrepreneurial ecosystem are the startups and entrepreneurs who drive innovation and business creation. With a leaning toward being risk-takers and creative, these people are determined to take ideas to market. Their ventures are the nucleus of an ecosystem that generates economic activity and jobs. The success of those startups often corresponds with how easily resources and support from other parts of the ecosystem can be garnered.

Support organizations are doing this in numerous ways to nurture startups, which means going out of the way to offer them much-needed resources and services. Key amongst these include incubators and accelerators, which provide support at the early stages. Incubators usually offer office spaces, administrative support, and networking to help startups overcome the difficulties that come with the problems of starting up at the initial stage (Doran et al., 2016). On the other hand, accelerators offer intensive, mentorship-oriented programs aimed at rapidly growing businesses—usually by way of seed funding and other resources. Coworking spaces also contribute by helping entrepreneurs share ideas and work in a shared environment that is conducive to productivity and best individual output through creative and innovative productivity.

Investment is also another turnkey in entrepreneurial ecosystems. Access to capital is what would literally breathe life into the startups—if the startups are to thrive and grow. Investors like venture capitalists and angel investors, together with crowdfunding platforms, provide the necessary funding that helps transform innovative ideas into viable business ideas. Venture capitalists often invest their money in start-ups with very high potentials for growth, in support areas—with the capital—found in the companies, and in experienced persons. Apart from capital, venture capitalists provide strategic support and networking opportunities to the start-ups. Angel investors often include persons with huge personal wealth who offer early-stage funding and mentorship (Duru & Anyanwu, 2019). Crowdfunding platforms serve in the democratization of access to capital, at the same time opening the floor to a multitude of individuals to access financial opportunities. Educational and research institutions are an indispensable part of the ecosystem, as they provide the knowledge, innovation, and a source of competent labor. This is often achieved as universities as well as research centres work closely with many start-up ventures to make it possible for them to apply practices researched commercially; such innovative technology transfer subsequently brings innovation. Besides, teaching programs as well as the training activities impart skills and knowledge to perhaps potential entrepreneurs to make them be able to succeed in the competitive business environment. Therefore, these institutions incubate many more entrepreneurial talents and make sure that new ideas and ventures survive (Mubaraki & Busler, 2014).

The government and policymakers have a great influence over the entrepreneur ecosystem through the set regulatory and economic environment. Entrepreneur-friendly policies on issues such as taxation, grants, and lean simplification of regulation, among others, go a long way toward making the ecosystem effective. The existence of infrastructure and services that facilitate the day-to-day operations of businesses—such as technology parks and innovation hubs—in which the government can invest is also in its capacity. Public/private partnerships will even better the ecosystem by merging the resources and efforts which ensure the move towards entrepreneurship and economic development (Duru & Anyanwu, 2019).

Mentors and advisors assist the start-ups in overcoming the challenges associated with business development. The valuable insights, ideas, and links are shared by the experienced entrepreneurs, industry experts, business consultants relevant to the new ventures. The mentors and advisors present a platform through which influencing factor is derived in the life of a start-up, mostly assisting the entrepreneurs to come up with the right and appropriate decisions on their businesses, which would otherwise have been responsible for making the most hard-headed decisions had they been without the help of a mentor.

The entrepreneurial ecosystems could be different, given their focus and characteristics. As in other aspects of tech-based hubs, key characteristics of tech hubs include a high density of technology-driven startups, research centers, and venture capital. Traditional industry clusters are built around manufacturing or agriculture, and support innovative startups in existing sectors (Gittell et al., 2014). Mixed model ecosystems allow for diversity that holds elements of high-tech and elements of the traditional industry. Emergent ecosystem: this is mostly the state of emergent regions or cities, with growing entrepreneurial activity nurtured by focused initiatives and investments for growth and innovation.

In conclusion, understanding the defining elements of entrepreneurial ecosystems and different types of ecological stakeholders comes next. Dynamic networks that draw and catalyse the creation of startups and hence also facilitate the creation of jobs. Each of them is a critical part of the system that encourages and fosters such an activity.

MECHANISMS OF JOB CREATION

Entrepreneurial ecosystems can promote job creation through several complex mechanisms, that could either be direct or indirect. Realization of the actual meaning of such mechanisms is, therefore, essential in appreciating the significance of entrepreneurship in job and economic development.

Direct Job Creation by Startups

Job creation by entrepreneurial ecosystems primarily happens at the outset by the jobs that are created directly by the individual startups. It takes a wide range of skills and knowledge to run businesses successfully, and more often than not, this would imply that a new venture would be at the stage of employing people at this stage for jobs ranging from product development to marketing, sales, finance to customer service (Arabiyat et al., 2019). For instance, a technology startup would engage the service of software developers, data analysts, and IT support while a manufacturing startup would engage the services of engineers, production workers, and quality control expert. The growth of these companies means new job creation, as well as the increase in employment in general in the local economy (Mohammed, 2022).

Indirect Job Creation Through Supply Chain

Aside from direct creation of employment, one of the most salient ways by which startups generate employment is through their supply chain and business network. As startups expand, they typically increase the demand for goods and services among other businesses; consequently, suppling, servicing as well as contracting job opportunities increase (Anyadike-Danes et al., 2015). For instance, an e-commerce company growing would increase the demand for logistics and storage services, which in turn might create jobs in these sectors. The ripple effects go through many industries: from IT services to marketing agencies and financial institutions, because startups are engaged with partners from a wide array of industries. Therefore, the development of one startup will eventually have a multiplier effect to create jobs in different parts of the economy (Mubaraki & Busler, 2014).

Economic Multiplier

The economic multiplier can help to give a proper insight into how an entrepreneur ecosystem can integrate the jobs in a better manner. The developed startups are designed through an influx of money and gradually boost economies by intensifying the general economic activities in one or several different regions. These augmented economic activities are likely to foster increased expenses, and hence it takes on the form of increased expenditure that can be promoted through organizing local business organizations and businesses. For instance, workers employed in thriving startups spend their earnings on acquiring goods, housing, and services, which increases the local markets' demand. Higher consumption might, therefore trigger job creation across other sectors of the economy such as retail, property, and even hospitality. Multiplier element emerges to outline elements indicating how the emergence of robust new business enterprises can help to accelerate other economic patterns and generate more or different jobs (Mwatsika, 2016).

Innovation and Industry Evolution

These ecosystems are built up to drive innovation, which might lead to completely new industry and employment categories. In terms of innovative realization and change of business models, these ecosystems often bring about new market opportunities with a pronounced disruptive impact (Osabohien et al., 2022). An illustration might be digital platforms, on which many apps are being developed, online marketing is shaping new activities, and digital content production processes are taking place. Such new innovations would both create new job rolls and drive the evolution from traditional industries to new form which significantly change employment patterns and new skill types.

Long-Run Employment Opportunities and Career Development

Among other elements, the rise of successful startups can also take to long-term career path opportunities and career development. There is often an opportunity to advance one's career within the company or through the strongly felt entrepreneurial dreams of many. Upon startup exposure, employees find themselves sharpening skills and networks that later feed into increased career opportunities. Moreover, exit of such successful entrepreneurs may reapply the knowledge and resource and mentor the new start-ups with the potential to generate jobs and skill set in the ecosystem (Santoleri, 2019).

Regional Economic Development

Entrepreneurial Ecosystem can contribute a larger pie in the regional economic development if it attracts talented individuals, investments and businesses to the region in question. Often, vibrant Entrepreneurial hubs become talent magnets as people from other regions or even other countries flock to these active Entrepreneurial centers (Stuetzer et al., 2017). This inflow of new skills and business-oriented people will therefore, in turn, create additional employment and economic development. Furthermore, strong entrepreneurial activity will make this place attractive for outside investors and companies, thereby increasing economic activities and additional employment opportunities

This broadly describes the mechanisms of job creations within entrepreneurial ecosystems; value chains created by direct creation, ripple effects through the supply chains, economic multiplier effects, industry evolution led by innovation, long-term career opportunities, and regional economic development derived from entrepreneurial activities. Realization of these mechanisms actually allows one to observe strong results in job creation out of entrepreneurial activities. The understanding of these mechanisms brings out the key role that entrepreneurial ecosystems play in the creation of jobs and support of economic development (Waruguru et al., 2017).

The Government and Policy

The role of government and policy in the entrepreneurial ecosystem is critical because it directly affects the environment in which the startups and businesses flourish. In other words, governments and policy drivers can create an environment that enables innovation, promotes entrepreneurship, and spurs employment opportunities. Governments can largely improve the efficiency of entrepreneurial ecosystems through a couple of ways.

Creating an Enabling Regulatory Environment

Encouraging business implies a regulatory regime which facilitates business while reducing barriers to entry with a view to the maximization of business undertakings. In this view, government's role would include making it easier to start and carry out business, making licensing more rational, and reducing bureaucracy and red tape. A pro-business regulatory environment reduces the initial barriers to entry to businesses for entrepreneurs through reducing upfront hurdles to starting enterprises (Gittell et al., 2014). Governments can facilitate it by mobilizing to requisition online registration systems and providing transparent regulatory framework for business compliance besides speeding up the processes and reducing the cost and time of regulatory approvals. In short, the governments may facilitate the means to open up multiple opportunities for individuals who can dare to be entrepreneurs in a more prolific manner (Zhang, 2023).

Provision of Financial Assistance and Incentives

Financial assistance from governments is yet another vital dimension related to the promotion of entrepreneurial ecosystems. It can offer them financial assistance through grants, subsidies, and tax incentives. It grants them grants, which need not be repaid and spent on supporting different research, development, and other activities at the initial stage. The subsidies can be for reducing the costs of hiring this labor or a subsidy for reducing the cost of buying technology. There can be other forms of tax concessions, in the nature of tax credits or deductions for expenses on research and development, thereby facilitating investment in innovation and growth. This financial support can reduce some financial strains on startups and thus make the idea of entrepreneurship more realistic (Zheng et al., 2015).

Investing in Infrastructure and Innovation

Governments are charged with the duty of investing in that type of infrastructure that is core to the development of entrepreneurship. This includes investments in innovation hubs, technology parks, and business incubators that support the development of real spaces and resources for startups. Further, digital infrastructure—high-speed internet and technology platforms—are crucial if startups are to be effective and agile in a global marketplace (Adelino et al., 2017). By creating and upgrading the elements of infrastructure, governments can that lend themselves to an environment that is amenable to entrepreneurship and innovation and attractive in the eyes of startups in their nascent stages.

Supporting Education and Training Programs

Education and training are at the core of developing a skilled workforce that will drive entrepreneurial success. The governments can pave the way for supportive entrepreneurial settings by investing in programs for entrepreneurship and business management, as well as in technical skills. This would practically mean the infusion of entrepreneurial learning within school curricula, support to create vocational education programs, and opening up more avenues, in various forms, for studying business and technology subjects at the level of higher education. Governments could also make sure that their citizens receive proper education and training on the matter; this would help create and develop a willing and able pipeline of entrepreneurs and employees, respectively, vital for the continuation of the ecosystem (Ademilua et al., 2020).

Facilitating Access to Networks and Mentorship

Governments can even make arrangements for events, from business conferences to networking meetups that link these start-ups into established networks and offer access to experienced mentors, potential investors, and industry experts. Such linkages are important for the start-up, seeking advice, partnerships, or funding. Likewise, governments can build spaces and forums for entrepreneurs to share knowledge, collaborate on ventures, and evolve relationships in the ecosystem.

Promotion of Public-Private Partnerships

Public-private partnerships present a form of bringing together resources and expertise from respective sectors in supporting the entrepreneurial ecosystem. In this case, the government will have to work in close collaboration with people in the private sector, such as corporations, venture capital, and business associations (Arabiyat et al., 2019). These will subsequently lead to creation of activities and events that bear fruits for start-ups. This can, therefore, go in line with developing opportunities for joint funding pertaining to different innovation labs and accelerator programs that offer support to entrepreneurs. Governments need to make sure that collaboration between the public and private sectors will improve and expand the effectiveness of entrepreneurial support initiatives (Ahmed, 2022).

Policy Evaluation and Adaptation

Governments have to continually check the policies in place to shape their relevance and effectiveness in pace-changing business environments, whereas policies must change in tandem with the needs and demands of entrepreneurs and the general citizenry. This concerns the following: monitoring the effect of the already existing policies; receiving feedback from the entrepreneurs and stakeholders on the trends and challenges flaring in the process of time; and making readjustments (Anyadike-Danes et al., 2015). Periodic evaluation will identify areas that might need improvement and also assure that government intervention is very much in the right order, advancing the growth and sustainability of entrepreneurial ecosystems.

Indeed, government and policy will fully play an active position toward the entrepreneurial ecosystem—a stance quite essential for its viability. This may encompass the development of a conducive regulatory environment, fiscal and capital allocational policies carried out through infrastructure investment, support for education and training, facilitation in the correspondent availability of networks and mentors, advocacy for private–public partnerships, and tailoring of policies (Anyadike-Danes et al., 2015).

Role of Government and Policy

The importance of government and policy to entrepreneurial ecosystems is foundational, affecting everything from regulatory frameworks and financial support to the development of infrastructure and educational initiatives. In this way, entrepreneurial ecosystems are greatly influenced by governments and policymakers in determining the environment within which startups either operate or grow. Their roles are pertinent in creating conditions where entrepreneurship advances, bringing forward innovation related to general economic growth.

Creating a Supportive Regulatory Environment

It that the other significant role that could be relevant to developing entrepreneurial ecosystems between the government and these businesses is to create a regulatory atmosphere that would allow businesses to easily run their operations. To a great extent, this will involve reducing the bureaucracy associated with starting and sustaining a business by lessening red tape and compliance costs (Arabiyat et al., 2019). Easy procedures for registering businesses, with clear and predictable regulations and efficient licensing procedures, might reduce barriers to entrepreneur entry. Governments can also ensure that there are regulations on intellectual property that are well laid and implemented to ensure that the inventions of the startups hit the market and further go an extra mile with a proper legal environment that is able to accommodate the ideas and inventions of the start-ups.

Providing Financial Support and Incentives

Governments can shape the financial pressure that is associated with startups by offering financial support and incentives. This could involve the granting of subsidies and grants for early-stage innovation and development, entailing tax incentives to companies for triggering investments in research and development, and facilitation of access to venture capital through public investment funds. The financial incentives can spread to tax breaks for startups or tax credits for businesses that hire from underrepresented groups. By lessening the financial crunches on start-ups, governments will enable more people to venture into entrepreneurship. This will continue enlarging and nurturing businesses that have already been established (Bianchini & Pellegrino, 2017).

Investing in Infrastructure and Innovation Hubs

Infrastructure is the backbone toward developing a favorable environment to support entrepreneurship. It is achievable by governments funding the contrasting of the innovation hubs, technology parks as well as business incubators which offer space and related physical facilities that meet the peculiar needs for the start-up of businesses. Such capacities would provide not just an office but also sources of high-speed internet, shared services, and networking opportunities (Doran et al., 2016). In fact, investments in the digital infrastructure that will drive a startup—broadband expansion and technology-enabled services—are critical in enabling it to effectively carry out its activities and access foreign markets. By providing such elements of infrastructure, governments usually facilitate conditions not only for the existence but also for the successful development and dynamism of startups and innovation.

Support for Education and Training Programmes

Education and training are important for the development of entrepreneurial talent for the establishment of a healthy and thriving entrepreneurial ecosystem. Governments can support entrepreneurship education by undertaking curriculum reforms in schools, providing vocational training courses, and investments in funding business and technology-related higher education. Additionally, such initiatives as scholarships, mentorship programs, and business plan competitions serve to give further incentives and prepare future individuals for entrepreneurship. Through adequate equipping the labour force with all the necessary entrepreneurial skills and knowledge, governments help set a pace of competent individuals who can effectively act as innovation sources and hence economic growth (Duru & Anyanwu, 2019).

Facilitating Access to Networks and Mentorship

Relationships and informal businesses can not only operate optimally without too much actively involved associations, and the government can be key in enhancing considerable interactions. It does so through events—industry conferences, networking meetings, and business plan competitions—that start to build the connections between investors, partners, and mentors (Gittell et al., 2014). Those connections are pure gold for any start-up that is seeking counsel, advice, feedback, or collaboration opportunities. Government-supported programs that match start-ups with mentors and advisors can then progress to provide highly valuable strategic guidance and support to clear bottlenecks and grow at scale with purpose and precision.

Foster Public-Private Collaboration

PPPs are the key mechanism for harnessing the resources and the expertise found in both sectors for the support of entrepreneurial ecosystems. Success cases in this—opportunity for the governments to corporately collaborate with private companies, venture capital firms, and business associations in the following ways: co-funding incubators/accelerators, joint research and development projects, and collaborative innovation labs. Through these partnerships, governments can share resources with the private sector, leverage the reach and impact of support programs, and 'drive' more effective outcomes for entrepreneurs (Mohammed, 2022).

Policy Evaluation and Adaptation

The ability of any government to successfully implement its policies to support entrepreneurial ecosystems lies in continuous evaluation and adaptation. Governments ought to review the impact of existing policies regularly and be able to make amends in line with emerging trends and challenges based on the feedback from entrepreneurs and other ecosystem stakeholders (Mubaraki & Busler, 2014). This policy review and fine-tuning process ensure that interventions remain current and effective in meeting the dynamic needs of the entrepreneurial community.

Governments can use the data and insights from such evaluations to pinpoint areas for improvement and how to ensure that the adopted incentives are realigned and that new re-designed interventions help better support job creation.

Fostering Inclusivity and Diversity

One way is in which the government supports entrepreneurial people to become more inclusive and diverse. It is through such policies and programs that targeted underrepresented groups, for example, women, minorities, and deprived communities, can be supported to create an ecosystem that is socially fairer and more vibrant. Such measures range from specific financial facilities, mentorship programs, to training programs aimed at addressing constraints to the target beneficiary identified earlier. In promoting inclusivity, therefore, governments ensure wide diffusion of the benefits accruing from entrepreneurship and that diverse perspectives help drive innovation and economic growth (Mwatsika, 2016).

In conclusion, the role of the government and its policy in an entrepreneurial ecosystem is multi-faceted, with each level playing a very critical role for the progress of the same. The building blocks through which governments can 'do' more in and for entrepreneurial ecosystems are: establishing a supportive regulatory framework, providing financial support, investing money in infrastructure and education and training (Osabohien et al., 2022), access to networks and mentoring, public-private partnerships, piloting and scaling, and inclusiveness. Involvement helps put in place all the relevant conditions under which startups can take off, become innovative, and support further economic development with additional jobs.

Educational and Skill Development

Entrepreneurship ecosystems are deeply rooted in education and competence development since they familiarize people with the right kind of knowledge, skills, and attitude needed to generate new ideas with social or economic value and subsequently build businesses around them. Accordingly, governments, educational institutions, and private organizations can collectively foster a culture in which entrepreneurship within the boundaries of education and training can lay the groundwork for entrepreneurial human capital development for the benefit of ecosystem vibrancy (Santoleri, 2019).

Embedding Entrepreneurship within Education

One important way in which education plays a part in entrepreneurial ecosystems is the fact that entrepreneurship itself is integrated into the curricula of formal education. This can be viewed in a number of ways: entrepreneurship is inculcated even starting at a very tender age in primary and secondary schools by the introduction of mere concepts of being an entrepreneur, which helps one to grow to develop an entrepreneurship mind at a tender age. With projects and various activities, the school is able to foster creativity, critical thinking, and collaboration skills that help in entrepreneurship (Doran et al., 2016). Under business, technology, and entrepreneurship, as students move to higher education, there are the specialized programs that are able to articulate issues in more detail on the topics. Courses can be organized in universities and colleges about business planning, venture management, innovation strategies, and market analysis which will give students an exposure on how to launch ventures, as well as manage them (Stuetzer et al., 2017).

Vocational Training and Professional Development

These vocational training and professional development programs are very crucial in ensuring that practical skills and competencies in the program areas are developed and delivered to suit the needs of entrepreneurs and start-up entities. In most cases, programs may focus on coding, digital marketing, financial management, and business operations, giving individuals the hands-on practical skills needed to support entrepreneurial activities. Vocational training colleges, Technical colleges and even online platforms can offer streamlined certifications and courses that can be applicable to the entrepreneurial efforts directly. Further, there can be professional development workshops and seminars which will enable existing entrepreneurs and professionals to remain abreast of the changes in the industry, new technologies, and emergent best practices (Waruguru et al., 2017).

Entrepreneurial Education and Incubators and Accelerators

Incubators and Accelerators have the most substantial role to play in entrepreneurial education by a way of offering the startup world structured programs where the best mentoring, resources, and training is provided in plentiful measure. Incubators and accelerators typically include workshops, seminars, and one-on-one coaching sessions that improve or build business skills, business model, market strategy, and investing in the business (Zhang, 2023). Besides enabling the business owner and entrepreneur learn by doing, and being mentored by the experienced professional in the specific field of business or entrepreneurship, the incubators and accelerators actively help these individuals to become problem-solving and efficient growing enterprises. All his educational programs are designed to the stage of development of the start-up, which is enriched with practical recommendations.

Developing Cooperation Between Educational Institutions and Industry

Responding to the needs for the real entrepreneurship, the closer cooperation should be established between educational institutions and industry. On the one hand, universities and business schools could work with start-up companies, mature companies and, on the other hand, with industry experts (Zheng et al., 2015). Through this activity, it could become more market-driven and up-to-date with the latest technology developments. Such partnerships may range from internships to project-based learning, whereby the students gain insights and practical experience in the entrepreneurial environment through collaborative research. In that sense, these partnerships seek to close the gap existing between academia and industry, thereby enabling the programs of education to meet modern requirements and students to attain capabilities relevant to success in the startup environment.

Promoting Lifelong Learning and Continuous Skill Development

Further, in the fast-paced entrepreneurial world, learning and upgrading skills must be an ongoing effort in order to always stay competitive and cutting edge in the industry. Within the power of governments and organizations closer to reality is the capacity to facilitate such learning throughout life by making available resources for education and training at all times (Adelino et al., 2017). It may take the form of classes that are online, workshops, and certification programs that would at least let entrepreneurs and professionals update their skills and knowledge, based on which industries reinvent themselves. Note also that "entrepreneurs could be prepared for innovations in new technologies, changing business practices, and for new market developments" etc.

Access to Resources and Tools

Allowing access to the resources and tools needed for entrepreneurial learning is a critical requirement. Resources involve giving online learning opportunities, educational materials among others and finances to support the learning endeavours (Zhang, 2023). Libraries, community centers, and online portals can provide various learning resources, such as books, research articles, and instructional videos. This is alongside grants and subsidies for education projects that will help reduce the cost barriers to any form of education acquisition and training.

Promotion of Mentorship and Peer Learning

Mentorship and peer learning are crucial components in entrepreneurial education. Mentorship programs provide valuable guidance and necessary support from experienced practitioners or industry experts to an aspiring entrepreneur in the way of facing challenges, how to make strategic decisions, and how to build networks. Learning through informal environments—such as entrepreneur meet-ups, study groups, and collaborative projects—provides the opportunity for individuals to learn from each other's experiences and share insights. All such informal learning environments may be meshed with formal education to provide practical insights and support (Zheng et al., 2015).

Evaluating and Enhancing Educational Programs

There is a need to innovate and improve educational programs to suit the updated needs of entrepreneurs and an entrepreneurial ecosystem. Feedback from students, faculty, and practitioners can be used in order to identify improvement areas and to ensure the increasing effectiveness and relevance of the programs (Arabiyat et al., 2019). Regular assessments and fine-tuning of these educational offerings by the institutions will support the entrepreneurial talent toward the successfulness of the ecosystem.

In other words, education and skills are at the core of any healthy and growing entrepreneurial ecosystem. Integrating entrepreneurship into education, offering vocational education, promotion and facilitation of entrepreneurial education through incubation and acceleration, promotion of cooperation between institution and industry, promotion of lifelong learning, resources, and programs complementation, promotion of mentorship, and continuous appraisal of programs are the core ingredients essential for the foundation of entrepreneurship success. The stakeholders can support a pipeline of brilliant people who would be the core of developing innovation to enhance growth in the economy through investing in education and skill formation (Adelino et al., 2017).

Challenges and the Barriers

Although entrepreneurial ecosystems are important to economic development and innovation, they experience different challenges and obstacles that constrain their effectiveness and growth. Understanding these barriers is important in the strategies for overcoming them to allow a friendlier environment for the entrepreneurs. Generally, the challenges can be categorized into financial, regulatory, structural, and socio-cultural barriers, all of them with a great influence on the vitality of the entrepreneurial ecosystem.

Financial Barriers

They face the challenge of raising capital, being its entrepreneurial ecosystems that have access to it. Most of the time, the ability of start-ups to raise funds is so hard, especially in the early stages of formation. Factors that can mitigate against entrepreneurs include low credit ratings attributed to the high level of the risks associated with their ventures, absence of equity or assets to be used as collateral, and inadequate record. In many regions, more so in developing countries, there is a lack of capital and investor networks, which may potentially impair the growth of many a promising startup. The complexity and stringency of funding applications, along with high costs in securing investment, also discouraged potential entrepreneurs from engaging in the businesses. Beating these economic challenges involves the mobilization, among other options of the use of government grants, the creation of crowdfunding platforms as well as the integration of investment networks (Ahmed, 2022).

Regulatory and Policy Hiccups

The establishment of appropriate regulatory and policy frameworks still stands as a critical ingredient in the realization of entrepreneurship ecosystems. The high-level bureaucracies and superfluous requirements by the government in the policy and regulatory framework often end up barring startups, given that high requirements call for a cost and time high requirement. This includes a great deal of inconvenience in business registration and licensing, high costs of meeting compliance, and tight labor regulations (Gittell et al., 2014). In some geographies, the quality of regulation is either too poor or inadequately responsive to today's needs of startups, piling more disadvantages on the would-be entrepreneurs. Governments and policymakers must work toward simplification, making regulations flexible to ease business setup and growth concomitantly, without jeopardizing fairness and efficiency in compliance processes (Arabiyat et al., 2019).

Structural and Infrastructure Constraints

Two major sections underpin the entrepreneurial ecosystem and support business development: human infrastructure and institutional infrastructure. An entrepreneurial ecosystem is, in a way, well-developed in physical and institutional terms in that it promotes business activities by startups; inadequacy in the presence of such facilities, for example, high-speed Internet being limited, is a hindrance factor (Mohammed, 2022). This is because the inadequate levels of office space and poor transport networks are a barrier to the operation of startups. On the other hand, underdeveloped innovation hubs, business incubators, and technology parks may hinder access to necessary resources and support services. Building and maintaining adequate infrastructural support for entrepreneurial activities to ensure that start-up entrepreneurs work in a supportive environment that yields success. This attraction of infrastructure in the form of a dedicated entrepreneurial spaces can tackle such structural barriers.

Socio-Cultural Barriers

Socio-cultural factors present actual challenges for entrepreneurial ecosystems. At some places, in the form of negative or discouraging social attitudes toward entrepreneurship, there is no respect for the entrepreneurial field, and consequently, no one is attracted towards entrepreneurship as a career choice. This is coupled with the fact that individual willingness to pursue entrepreneurial activities is often affected by cultural norms and biases, particularly on the cases of underrepresented groups (Doran et al., 2016). Lack of supportive networks and mentorship opportunities leaves the potential of the entrepreneurs unsupported and without guidance and motivation. Efforts to encourage and foster perceptions about entrepreneurship, diversity, and inclusion, and to develop good support networks among young entrepreneurs, can mitigate this kind of socio-cultural barrier.

Acquisition and Retention of Talent

Skilled talent that is available and retained is crucial to entrepreneurial ecosystems. In most cases, startups require specialized skills and expertise that are usually hard to find and, therefore, difficult to hire people with significantly high competency. High turnover and lack of competition for talent are among the circumstances that can challenge a startup to develop stable and effective teams. To address this, ecosystems need to invest in education and training programs based on industry needs and also create conditions and opportunities for lifelong professional growth. Moreover, they have to create such attractive working conditions that talent can be retained. Supply of skilled workforce is another benefit of the interface between education centers and industry (Duru & Anyanwu, 2019).

Market Access and Competition

Market entry and the ability to effectively compete can be heavy challenges for startups, especially in saturated or highly competitive industries. Therefore, simply reaching the customer and validating their offering proves to be a challenge, along with eventually establishing themselves in the market. Also, in some competitive and resourceful companies, the barriers to entry might be large. It is for this reason that the strategies of building access to the market, leveraging digital marketing tools, and creating unique value propositions turn out to be very important for startup survival in the face of such problems of entry and competition in their target markets (Gittell et al., 2014).

Economic and Political Instability

Economic and political instability can create a highly unpredictable and challenging environment for entrepreneurial activity. The incidence of risks and uncertainties may be imposed on startups by unfavorable conditions in the regions of their business, such as economic downturns, high inflation rates, or political unrest, therefore, affecting their operations and growth prospects (Mohammed, 2022). They discourage investment while at the same time dislocating supply chains and creating financial instability, in such a way that entrepreneurs may not squarely be able to plan and execute their business strategies. Overcoming these challenges would include efforts to stabilize the economic conditions, establishment of supporting policies, and provision of resources and guidance that would give rise to startups across uncertain environments.

Lack of Collaboration and Network Building

Effective collaboration and networking is vital in the expansion of entrepreneurial ecosystems. On some ecosystems, coordination and cooperation between different stakeholders such as startups, support organizations investors and government bodies can be missing. This can lead to fragmented efforts, duplicated resources, and significant opportunities for synergy and support that are missed (Mwatsika, 2016). Better collaboration through such means as networking events, joint programs, and collaborative projects enhances cohesion and galvanizes the supportive ecosystem within which more connections are made and resources are shared among stakeholders (Osabohien et al., 2022).

As a result, the challenges and barriers of an entrepreneurial ecosystem could be tackled through a mix of financial support, regulatory reform, infrastructure development, socio-cultural change, talent management, market access skills, economic stability, and more efficient networking processes. On the one hand, noticing and working on these barriers, the concerned parties, or the stakeholders, can create a more hospitable outlook for entrepreneurship and make some alterations, which will lead to innovation, job opportunities, and upward growth in economic dimensions (Santoleri, 2019).

Measuring Impact

Measuring the effectiveness of entrepreneurial ecosystems is key, on one hand, to understand how well they work, to guide policy decisions, and to indicate areas on which improvements may be made. Effective measurement has to be comprehensive in terms of assessing the various dimensions of performance of the selected entrepreneurial ecosystem, be it economic, social, or developmental lashes. This being so, stakeholders are more likely to benefit from the broad perspective of how entrepreneurial activities serve the larger economic and societal goals since it has to be done across metrics and methodologies (Stuetzer et al., 2017).

Economic Impact Assessment

One of the principal ways to measure an entrepreneurial ecosystem's impact is through economic assessment. This may involve the measurement of selected indicators like job creation, revenues generated, and levels of investment (Waruguru et al., 2017). The tool is used to track new business creation, the growth of earlier-stage startups they have invested in, and the holistic economic contribution attributable to an ecosystem. Equally, how much investment various startups are attracting—be it in the form of venture capital, angel investment, or government grants—will be an indicator of the financial health of the ecosystem. Added to that, the assessment of economic impact can handle productivity gains and new creation of markets due to entrepreneurial activity (Zhang, 2023).

Employment and Job Creation Metrics

Job creation is one of the key performance indicators of an entrepreneurial ecosystem. Measuring the number of jobs directly created by startups and overall employment impact on the local or regional labor market gauges, therefore, provide an idea of how much the activity of entrepreneurship contributes to economic growth and unemployment reduction (Osabohien et al., 2022). Hiding also in the measurement of the quantity of jobs created is the level of quality of these jobs. Job quality should be assessed by job quality, its level of stability, wage amounts, and career development opportunities. It is by tracking such indicators that stakeholders will be able to make a sense of how entrepreneurial ecosystems contribute to workforce development and support staying employment within the system (Zheng et al., 2015).

Innovation and Technological Development

Indicators for tracking the impact made by entrepreneurial ecosystems on technological development and innovation are put in place in such a way that the quantity of newly registered patents, the arrival of new products or technologies, or the business model that has been newly developed can be identified. This could be gauged through the degree to which startups contribute to technological and industry norm innovation. Measuring the relationships or research commercialization undertaken by startups from research institutions offers different insights on how the entrepreneurial activities promote technological innovation and knowledge spillover (Santoleri, 2019).

Social and Community Impact

Entrepreneurial ecosystems also have tremendous social and community impacts, which could be gauged through different vital metrics. It included the assessment of startup development to contribute to social matters, community development, and the overall level of well-being. Metrics on implementation of social impact initiatives (Arabiyat et al., 2019), the creation of products and services dealing with societal challenges, the participation of startups in local community activities, etc. combine to provide a full picture of their social contributions. Moreover, the ecosystem's diversity and inclusivity in terms of under-represented group participation or ecosystem people, more broadly, their representation also provides a measure of social impact how entrepreneurial venture has the potential for equitable growth (Stuetzer et al., 2017; Gilala et al., 2020).

Educational and Skill Development Outcomes

Complementing the previous section, the role that entrepreneurial ecosystems have in educational and skill development is another critical area that has to be assessed; it includes how better the educational programs, training, and mentorship opportunities, inter alia nurturing entrepreneurial talent better (Doran et al., 2016). It would be equally important to get metrics like the number of students and professionals enrolling for entrepreneurship-related courses, startup success rates amongst start-ups launched by program graduates and whether they have acquired the skills and the competencies imparted by the program. Equally important is tracking the long term career paths of those that have received entrepreneurial education and training to determine the broader impact on professional development (Duru & Anyanwu, 2019).

Infrastructure and Resource Utilization

The impact of infrastructure and resource availability on the entrepreneurial ecosystem can only be gauged through the level of utilization and resultant effectiveness of the support services of business incubation, acceleration, and innovation hubs. Metrics generally could be the number of startups using the resources, success rates of ventures supported through such facilities, and satisfaction of the users in regard to the services offered (Memon et al., 2022). Evaluating the effect of infrastructure investments in cultivating startup development and operational efficiency that, in turn, indicates the degree to which the resources are effective enough to support entrepreneurial activities (Bianchini & Pellegrino, 2017)

Long-Term Ecosystem Sustainability

Long term sustainability of an entrepreneurial ecosystem is dictated by the achievement of the increase of adaptation to the new emerging systems. Some metrics that show the sustainability of a start-up are the survival rate, years for which ventures remain successful, and its ability to retain talent and attract investment. Further, measuring how well and how quickly it can recover from economic downturns or technological disruptions, among other external challenges, is an indication of its resiliency and capability for long-term sustainability (Anyadike-Danes et al., 2015).

Feedback and Continuous Improvement

In order to get feedback regarding the realization and the areas for improvement, entrepreneurs, stakeholders, and participants in the ecosystem have to be surveyed via structured interviews, surveys, and focus group discussions. This will also include the gap analysis in the services to be offered, policy interventions, and resource allocations, all of which allow for the continuous improvement regarding feedback from the exercise and further adjustment of the strategies aimed at augmenting the applicability of the ecosystem (Mubaraki & Busler, 2014).

In essence, the ecosystem view measures a broader realm of impact, one that includes such things as economic valuations, employment numbers, innovation ratings, social effects, educational performance, infrastructure use, and long-term sustainability. By utilizing complementary metrics and methodologies (Zheng et al., 2015), stakeholders are better able to comprehend how the entrepreneurial ecosystem is doing and what is the way to make it more effective in the making of decisions and pursuing newer and innovative forms of ecosystem development for the provision of innovation, economic development, and community building (Mwatsika, 2016).

Case Studies and Examples

1. Silicon Valley, USA

Silicon Valley is arguably the most renowned model of an entrepreneurial ecosystem that functions correctly in the world. It is situated in the San Francisco Bay Area and represents the international frontier for what concerns technology and innovation. The reasons that lead to the success of Silicon Valley are several characteristics combined: a concentration of venture capital, culture of risk-taking and innovation, and a network of top-tier educational institutions such as Stanford University (Afshan et al., 2021). Its high focus on technology and entrepreneurship has seen numerous startups burgeon into success and big tech companies like Apple, Google, and Facebook. There exists a thick network of investors, mentors, and industry specialists within the ecosystem that propels tremendous growth and scaling for new ventures. Silicon Valley highlights the leading role that an ecosystem can possibly deliver with provisions in collaboration, knowledge sharing, access to capital, and driving innovation for economic growth.

2. Bangalore, India

Bangalore is widely known as the “Silicon Valley of India” for a reason. It enjoys a prime rank as the major tech and start-up hub in the country, powered by a fertile base of technical manpower and a small but active community of tech entrepreneurs, with government backing. In fact, it is this very crutch that the Karnataka Startup Policy provides, as does a string of incubation centers, amongst which is the very famous NSR Centre for Entrepreneurship located in Bangalore, sometimes providing the status as an IT company hub bringing in huge domestic and foreign investments. What you get to witness from the two take-off ventures by the name Flipkart, and Ola is Bangalore's role in defining India's tech space and how job creation through innovation can carve a career even in a swiftly moving market.

3. Tel Aviv, Israel

Tel Aviv is home to one of the liveliest and swiftest growing startup environments powered by a great culture and entrepreneurial zest. Research and development was mainly prioritized in Israel; therefore, through military technology and other governmental attempts such as the Office of the Chief Scientist, it has set up a conducive ground on which to launch tech companies. The city houses several venture capital firms, accelerators and incubators where The Junction and Startpbootcamp are based in Tel Aviv. Tel Aviv's ecosystem is more based on a culture of cooperating, startups, investors, and academic institutions support each other actively furthering the technological advancement. The success of modules of companies like Waze and Mobileye indicates that the city posits the potential of high-impact innovation, thus influencing and impacting significantly the whole of the high-tech world.

4. Berlin, Germany

Berlin is most frequently said to be the most startup-friendly city of Europe; it may be best described as diverse and creative. At the core of the city's attractiveness are affordability, rich culture, and an entrepreneurial-friendly environment. The Berlin ecosystem provides a large valuable resource set that includes something called the Berlin Startup Stipendium, which is monetary and mentor-based support for early-stage start-ups. The many co-working spaces, like WeWork and Factory Berlin, further boost networking and collaboration among entrepreneurs. As evidence of this, Berlin's success in fostering startups are better evidenced by companies such as Zalando and N26, which are now world-famous—both located in Berlin—making Berlin a successful entrepreneurial ecosystem.

5. Shenzhen, China

The innovation place growing the fastest is based in Shenzhen, positioned in China's south. Known as manufacturing mega-city, Shenzhen conducts numerous entrepreneurial communities in technology and electronic spheres that successfully built from the industrial base. The city's transformation is accompanied by many different government policies, such as the Shenzhen Innovation and Technology Plan, which spurs the investment in high-technology industry and startups. Shenzhen's ecosystem benefits further from the fact that through proximity to a vast network of suppliers and manufacturers along with remarkable infrastructure for tech development. These successes from companies like Huawei and DJI show the potential Shenzhen has to be a driving force behind technological innovation and economic growth through an increasingly supported entrepreneurial environment.

Joint Analysis

Altogether, the case studies on Silicon Valley, Bangalore, Tel Aviv, Berlin, and Shenzhen represent the diversity of approaches and factors leading to success in entrepreneurial ecosystems. These places, which are so diverse from each other in terms of geography and culture, share a lot in common that makes them tick with entrepreneurial success (Adelino et al., 2017).

Capital Access plays a critical role in any ecosystem. Every city is home to a strong network of VCs and angels who fuel the investment putting companies in the right trajectory for the next phase of growth and innovation. In this regard, for instance, Silicon Valley is highly identified with high venture capital (Ademilua et al., 2020). Similarly, this has been witnessed to be on the rise in the case of Bangalore as well, a factor supplementing the thriving tech industry. Financial capital is so important in an elevator that it is actually a commonality between elevators.

The other critical element present in each case study is Supportive Infrastructure – be it in the form of incubators, accelerators, or co-working spaces – each of these ecosystems offers resources and networking, which in turn support and enable start-up success. Berlin has many co-working spaces, while Bangalore supports innovation with many incubation centers (Ahmed, 2022).

It is in this way that every ecosystem presents its uniqueness: a collaborative culture. A focus on knowledge-sharing, mentorship, and partnership with the entrepreneur, investors, and academic makes for an atmosphere where innovation can flourish freely. The role played by the supportive community of Silicon Valley in taking risks and collaborating, the way Tel Aviv has combined military technology with research, and the rich creative scene in Berlin underline community collaboration leading to entrepreneurial success (Anyadike-Danes et al., 2015).

In this case, Government and Policy Support involve proactive regional authority efforts to generate an entrepreneurial environment. This, therefore, emerges in the government approach of formulating regulations that are most conducive to the region, an example being in Silicon Valley or innovation policies in Shenzhen. It is such a kind of common trend that underlines the truth of how indispensable strategic policy frames are to enhance the effectiveness of the ecosystem (Arabiyat et al., 2019).

Technological Changes are the propellants in every ecosystem, as areas use the latest technologies to promote some creative ideas. Tech-centricness in Silicon Valley, the R&D model in Tel Aviv, and the TechHub model in Shenzhen are some examples how technological integration helps startups grow and gain competitive advantage.

These are the emerging trends of the day that build inclusivity and globalization into increasingly addressing these ecosystems. Where Silicon Valley and Tel Aviv have long taken on a worldwide cast of technologists, Berlin is fast diversifying, and Shenzhen is growing with a much bigger lens on inclusivity and its place in the world. A push toward diverse and globally connected ecosystems reflects a broader trend to build more equitable and connected entrepreneurial environments (Doran et al., 2016).

To condense this, joint study from these case studies has ascertained that the most successful entrepreneurial ecosystems are those defined by strong financial support, robust infrastructure, a collaborative culture, effective government policies, technological innovation, increasing emphasis on inclusivity and globalization (Bianchini & Pellegrino, 2017). However, the understanding of the commonalities and regional variations should allow a facilitative and effective designing and supporting role by the stakeholders in the entrepreneurial ecosystems toward driving sustainable innovation and economic growth.

FUTURE TRENDS AND OPPORTUNITIES

There is a constant rapid change in the landscape of entrepreneurial ecosystems through technological developments, change in economic patterns, and social needs. Looking ahead, below is what we believe are some of the primary trends and opportunities that will define the context in which entrepreneurship does or doesn't succeed, influence the effectiveness of entrepreneurial ecosystems, and introduce key challenges that need to be appropriately managed (Duru & Anyanwu, 2019).

1. Emergence of Digital and Remote Work Ecosystems

The rise of digital technology and remote work is changing entrepreneurial ecosystems by leveling the playing field with fewer boundaries on where and how startups can operate. Today, with remote work, an up-and-coming entrepreneur can build and run a team without geographical limitations—thereby gaining access to a broader pool of available talent while incurring lower costs on overheads usually associated with physical office spaces (Gittell et al., 2014). This realignment will enable startups not only to access diversified talent from all over the globe but also to create inclusive workforces and innovate outside of geographic boundaries. Entrepreneurial ecosystems are increasingly being built on digital tools: platforms to enable remote work, virtual collaboration, and accessing global markets. The flexibility of this realignment will most likely be about the emphasis on technological ecosystems that enable remote and hybrid work models.

2. Rise of Impact and Social Entrepreneurship

Impact and social entrepreneurship are highly emphasized, with more and more startups rising to solve various problems in society, the environment, and ethical issues. More and more entrepreneurs have come up with business models that have a double bottom line of positive social impact at par with financial success, for example, social enterprise, sustainable business, and nonprofit (Mohammed, 2022). This trend is driven not only by increasing consumer demand for more responsible and ethical practices but also by growing awareness of global challenges like climate change and inequality. Entrepreneurial ecosystems evolve to meet this shift by offering support and resources for impact-driven ventures through incubators, funding opportunities, and networks specifically oriented toward social entrepreneurship. In this sector, one expects continuous growth in the future due to evolution and increased support of the ecosystems for ventures that pursue meaningful societal change.

3. Advancement and Innovations in Technology

The entrepreneurial ecosystems are mostly being changed by continuous technological innovation, opening new opportunities for innovation and further development. New technologies such as artificial intelligence, blockchain, IoT, and biotechnology drive new product and service development and business models. Startups are leveraging these technologies to build disrupting solutions, improve operational efficiencies, and solve complex problems (Mubaraki & Busler, 2014). As a result, the entrepreneurial ecosystems are increasingly interested in improving innovation in these technology sectors by research and development; access to state-of-the-art tools and resources; and finally, collaboration between the startups and technology providers. The future will have accelerated technological developments with increased impetus on beating new technologies into the entrepreneurial ventures.

4. Sustainability and Circular Economy

By gradually infusing the principles of sustainability and circular economy into entrepreneurial ecosystems and businesses, the impact on the environment will be less negative, and more on sustainable development. A culture of resource efficiency, low waste, and high rates of recycling and reutilization of materials underlines the model of the circular economy and opens up a wide field of innovation opportunities for product design, manufacture, and consumption (Mwatsika, 2016). An increasing number of startups design their business models under the principles of circular economy and offer product and service solutions for environmental sustainability. The entrepreneurial ecosystems react by supporting ventures oriented towards sustainability, enabling access to green technologies, and promoting practices corresponding to circular economy goals. In the future, much more strategies of entrepreneurship will integrate sustainability, and creation of eco-friendly resource-efficient businesses will be in the focus.

5. Rise of Global Startup Networks

Startup networks and ecosystems are increasingly growing outside traditional borders. Entrepreneurship today involves entrepreneurs seeking customer acquisition, sources of investment, and collaborative partnerships in international markets. Cross-border collaborations and startup hubs are arising that enable knowledge exchange, market entry, and scaling opportunities. This is a trend that entrepreneurial ecosystems are adapting to by promoting international partnerships, cross-border investments, and resources for global expansion. This growing trend in global startup networks will mean that, in the future, ecosystems will be increasingly connected and interrelated across regions and countries (Osabohien et al., 2022).

6. Inclusive and Diverse Ecosystems

In recent years, there has been a growing recognition of the role of inclusivity and diversity within entrepreneurial ecosystems. Currently underway are efforts to bring entrepreneurial opportunities and resources to underrepresented groups: women, minorities, and those from underserved communities (Stuetzer et al., 2017). This increasing trend in the types of initiatives aimed at creating more diversity in entrepreneurship—mentorship programs, funding opportunities, and community support—is just getting started. The more inclusive and diverse the startup ecosystem is, the better it will be to guarantee exposure to all kinds of perspectives, ideas, and talent. The future will be one of ongoing work in the construction of ecosystems that value diversity and offer fair opportunities to all entrepreneurs (Santoleri, 2019).

7. Evolution of Entrepreneurial Education and Training

The approach to entrepreneurial education and training is evolving to better meet the needs of today's entrepreneurs. Traditional education models are being supplemented by more flexible, hands-on, innovative learning opportunities such as online courses, bootcamps, and experiential learning programs. These new formats provide some of the skills, knowledge, and networks necessary for entrepreneurs to succeed in today's fast-changing business environment (Waruguru et al., 2017). Entrepreneurial ecosystems embrace these educational innovations, adding a full range of learning options, from specialized workshops to mentorship programs, to assist in entrepreneurial talent development. The future of entrepreneurship education will further evolve with the intent to provide more relevant and useful training methods that equip entrepreneurs for success.

8. Rise of Hybrid Business Models

Hybrid business models combine traditional and digital business models to leverage the startup ability to invent new ways of delivering value and engaging customers. Examples of this trend include omnichannel retail strategies, which fuse in-store and online experiences, and subscription-based models that blur the lines between product and service offerings. The entrepreneurial ecosystems are responding by supporting ventures that innovate hybrid approaches and furnishing resources for businesses to manage the complexity connected with the integration of different business models. The emergence of new hybrid business models will further be driven by evolving consumer preferences and continuous technological innovation in the future (Zhang, 2023).

CONCLUSION

Entrepreneurial ecosystems are a significant driver of innovation, economic growth, and new jobs; they drive the future character of industries and societies. To this complex interplay, many things matter: access to capital, supporting infrastructure, collaborative culture, and government policies. The case studies of Silicon Valley, Bangalore, Tel Aviv, Berlin, and Shenzhen are illustrations of how various regions mobilize distinctive strengths and resources in an attempt to sustain entrepreneurial milieus. Each ecosystem offers valuable insights into the elements that go into making up a vibrant, effective entrepreneurial landscape.

In the future, several key trends and opportunities will continue to shape entrepreneurial ecosystems. Digital and remote work models, impact, and social entrepreneurship will remain increasingly important, with changes in how technology comes about. The integration of sustainability and circular economy will lead to new definitions of business and innovation opportunities. Moreover, growth in global startup networks, focusing on inclusivity, is setting up more diversified and connected systems.

These trends are also bound, however, to pose some challenges in consideration to which proactive and adaptive strategies will be made. To this end, counterbalances to the trending expectations with the addressing of specified barriers related to financial constraints, regulatory hurdles, and infrastructure gaps will keep entrepreneurial ecosystems effective. Embracing new trends and conquering existing problems, stakeholders can create more resilient and robust ecosystems that foster entrepreneurship and drive positive impact on society.

Ultimately, entrepreneurial ecosystems succeed through collaborative effort between entrepreneurs, investors, policymakers, and community leaders. We can help unleash the full potential of entrepreneurship, hence offering our input to a thriving and dynamic global economy, working jointly to foster innovation and support the creation of emerging ventures that strive for inclusivity and sustainability. The continuous evaluation and adaptation to the evolving landscape should ensure that entrepreneurial ecosystems continue to thrive and result in meaningful outcomes for society.

REFERENCES

Adelino, M., Ma, S., & Robinson, D. (2017). Firm age, investment opportunities, and job creation. *The Journal of Finance*, 72(3), 999–1038. DOI: 10.1111/jofi.12495

Ademilua, V., Lasisi, T., Ogunmokun, O., & Ikhide, J. (2020). Accounting for the effects of entrepreneurial orientation on smes' job creation capabilities: A social capital and self-determination perspective. *Journal of Public Affairs*. Advance online publication. DOI: 10.1002/pa.2413

Afshan, G., Shahid, S., & Tunio, M. N. (2021). Learning experiences of women entrepreneurs amidst COVID-19. *International Journal of Gender and Entrepreneurship*, 13(2), 162–186. DOI: 10.1108/IJGE-09-2020-0153

Ahmed, E. (2022). The influence of entrepreneurial activity's innovation on job creation. *International Journal of Information Management*, 14(1), 506–514. DOI: 10.15282/ijim.14.1.2022.7247

Anyadike-Danes, M., Hart, M., & Du, J. (2015). Firm dynamics and job creation in the united kingdom: 1998–2013. *International Small Business Journal*, 33(1), 12–27. DOI: 10.1177/0266242614552334

Arabiyat, T., Mdanat, M., Haffar, M., Ghoneim, A., & Arabiyat, O. (2019). The influence of institutional and conductive aspects on entrepreneurial innovation. *Journal of Enterprise Information Management*, 32(3), 366–389. DOI: 10.1108/JEIM-07-2018-0165

Bianchini, S., & Pellegrino, G. (2017). *Innovation persistence and employment dynamics*. SSRN Electronic Journal. DOI: 10.2139/ssrn.2919290

Doran, J., McCarthy, N., & O'Connor, M. (2016). Entrepreneurship and employment growth across european regions. *Regional Studies, Regional Science*, 3(1), 121–128. DOI: 10.1080/21681376.2015.1135406

Duru, I., & Anyanwu, S. (2019). Entrepreneurship in small and medium enterprises: A catalyst for capacity building and sustainable youths' employment generation in the federal capital territory, Abuja, Nigeria. *International Journal of Social and Administrative Sciences*, 4(2), 277–296. DOI: 10.18488/journal.136.2019.42.277.296

Gilal, F. G., Gilal, N. G., Channa, N. A., Gilal, R. G., Gilal, R. G., & Tunio, M. N. (2020). Towards an integrated model for the transference of environmental responsibility. *Business Strategy and the Environment*, 29(6), 2614–2623. DOI: 10.1002/bse.2524

Gittell, R., Sohl, J., & Tebaldi, E. (2014). Do entrepreneurship and high-tech concentration create jobs? exploring the growth in employment in US metropolitan areas from 1991 to 2007. *Economic Development Quarterly*, 28(3), 244–253. DOI: 10.1177/0891242414530467

Memon, A. B., Meyer, K., & Tunio, M. N. (2022). Toward collaborative networking among innovation laboratories: A conceptual framework. *International Journal of Innovation Science*, 14(2), 282–301. DOI: 10.1108/IJIS-04-2021-0069

Mohammed, F. (2022). Impact of entrepreneurship development on employment generation in sabongari local government, kaduna state. *International Journal of Entrepreneurship and Project Management*, 7(1), 14–28. DOI: 10.47604/ijepm.1567

Mubaraki, H., & Busler, M. (2014). The importance of innovation in Europe: Swedish case study. *International Journal of Innovation and Knowledge Management in Middle East and North Africa*, 3(1), 51–63. DOI: 10.47556/J.IJIKMMENA.3.1.2014.3

Mwatsika, C. (2016). Measuring the number of jobs created through entrepreneurship training. *International Journal of Academic Research in Business & Social Sciences*, 6(7). Advance online publication. DOI: 10.6007/IJARBSS/v6-i7/2243

Osabohien, R., Worgwu, H., Adediran, O., & Soomro, J. (2022). Social entrepreneurship and future employment in Nigeria. *International Social Science Journal*, 73(250), 927–937. DOI: 10.1111/issj.12360

Santoleri, P. (2019). Innovation and job creation in (high-growth) new firms. *Industrial and Corporate Change*, 29(3), 731–756. DOI: 10.1093/icc/dtz059

Stuetzer, M., Audretsch, D., Obschonka, M., Gosling, S., Rentfrow, P., & Potter, J. (2017). Entrepreneurship culture, knowledge spillovers and the growth of regions. *Regional Studies*, 52(5), 608–618. DOI: 10.1080/00343404.2017.1294251

Tunio, M. N., Chaudhry, I. S., Shaikh, S., Jariko, M. A., & Brahmi, M. (2021). Determinants of the sustainable entrepreneurial engagement of youth in developing country—An empirical evidence from Pakistan. *Sustainability (Basel)*, 13(14), 7764. DOI: 10.3390/su13147764

Waruguru, M., Bwisa, H., & Kihoro, J. (2017). An assessment of the opportunity component of entrepreneurship policy in the youth, women, and uwezo funds in Kenya. *International Journal of Academic Research in Business & Social Sciences*, 7(1). Advance online publication. DOI: 10.6007/IJARBSS/v7-i1/2606

Zhang, L. (2023). Examining the relationship between entrepreneurship education and job creation in China's post-pandemic economy. *Journal of Digitainability Realism & Mastery (Dream)*, 2(05), 45–52. DOI: 10.56982/dream.v2i05.119

Zheng, L., Ding, T., & Li, J. (2015). Entrepreneurship and economic development in China: Evidence from a time-varying parameters stochastic volatility vector autoregressive model. *Technology Analysis and Strategic Management*, 27(6), 660–674. DOI: 10.1080/09537325.2015.1034676

Chapter 7
Human Factors in the Creation and Growth of Entrepreneurship Ecosystems

José G. Vargas-Hernandez
https://orcid.org/0000-0003-0938-4197
Tecnològico Nacional de Mèxico, ITS Fresnillo, Mexico

Francisco J. Gonzàlez-Àvila
Tecnològico Nacional de Mèxico, ITSF, Mexico

Omar C. Vargas-Gonzàlez
https://orcid.org/0000-0002-6089-956X
Tecnològico Nacional de Mèxico, Cd. Guzmàn, Mexico

ABSTRACT

This study aims to analyze the various human factors involved in the different processes of the entrepreneurship ecosystems. The analyses depart from the assumption that that the entrepreneurial ecosystem can be created and defined not only by broad geographies endowed by intentions but dependent of human factors. Th method employed is the meta-analytical supported by the descriptive based on the conceptual, theoretical and empirical literature review. The study concludes that human factors, such as behaviors and traits, values, attitudes and beliefs are relevant for the creation and growth of entrepreneurship ecosystems

DOI: 10.4018/979-8-3693-9486-1.ch007

INTRODUCTION

Research and study of entrepreneurship have focused more on the behaviors and characteristics of individuals and organizations (Shane & Venkataraman, 2000; Shane, 2003). Entrepreneurship ecosystems research emphasize human entrepreneurship factors, such as behaviors, traits, and skills (Frank, Lueger, & Korunka, 2007; Korunka, Frank, Lueger, & Mugler, 2003; Lehner & Harrer, 2019). At the micro-level the entrepreneurial ecosystem taxonomy model captures entrepreneurship initiatives associated with individual characteristics, traits, attitudes, beliefs, etc.

The entrepreneurship ecosystem literature aims to analyze specific entrepreneurship situations referred as the individuals exploring, discovering and evaluating opportunities with new goods and services to be exploited and add value (Stam & Spigel, 2017). Based on qualitative expert interviews the identified human factors influences the entrepreneurship ecosystems.

The entrepreneurship ecosystems literature is the laundry list of ecosystem human factors with clear reasoning of cause and effects of interdependent effects on entrepreneurship (Stam & van de Ven, 2021). Research on entrepreneurial ecosystems emerge from their changes in endogenous and exogenous human factors influencing them to be compared among regions (Levie & Autio, 2008). The entrepreneurship ecosystems geography literature provides insights into different human factors enhancing the regional prevalence (Bosma et al., 2011; Stam, 2010; Stam and Spigel, 2018; Sternberg, 2019).

Research findings of cases on entrepreneurship ecosystems are based on outputs of specific cases which contribute to the growth of the firms and to the market entry with financial autonomy and value propositions. Entrepreneurship outputs of unicorns are young firms are measured with data collected from CB insights (CB Insights, 2020). Scraping data can be obtained from historical web pages from the internet archive (Dealroom, 2020) and geocoding can be used to locate the unicorns only present in few regions, being selective in value measure of productive entrepreneurship (Aldrich & Ruef, 2018; Economist, 2019). The entrepreneurial ecosystem is defined through the unicorn businesses that reach a value of one billion in 10 years (Acs *et al.*, 2017).

The entrepreneurship ecosystem research is driven by disciplinary interests of objective value. The entrepreneurship ecosystem research approaches are concerned with delivering specific forms of value enabled from the elements of the ecosystem.

Research on entrepreneurship treats the creation of entrepreneurship opportunities as exogenous but considering to be part of the entrepreneurial process (Qian *et al.* 2013). Research on entrepreneurship evolves from a focus on spin-offs to a broader perspective to include the creation of start-ups (Siegel & Wright, 2015).

Further research is needed in the exploitation of data sources and methods to track the mobility of workers between the different types of firms in the entrepreneurship ecosystems aimed to provide perspectives on the transitions of the labor market in the human capital growth.

This analysis of the various human factors involved in the different processes of the entrepreneurship ecosystems begins with a conceptual review of the human factors, such as behaviors and traits, values, attitudes and beliefs that are relevant for the creation and growth of entrepreneurship ecosystems. Finally, some conclusions are offered.

HUMAN FACTORS

Entrepreneurship ecosystem is the set of interdependent and coordinated actors and human factors to enable productive entrepreneurship (Stam, 2015). Entrepreneurship ecosystems combine several human factors, processes, and agents with specific placed dynamics. Human factor orientation is defined by the Globe project and the components of humane entrepreneurship. A human orientation of individuals does not start entrepreneurship activities in new ventures due to they have fear to fail (Stephan & Uhlaner, 2010). Fear to fail is a deterring human factors and has negative effects on entrepreneurship initiatives. Numerous human factors are essential components comprising the entrepreneurial ecosystems which have been accepted as pillars.

Holistic perspective of entrepreneurship ecosystem focuses on the emergence and evolution differences in particular places influencing the manifestation of diverse forms of entrepreneurship, among other human factors. Path dependency is an essential ecosystem evolution in which the outputs and outcomes in a state shape the individual behavior and the ecosystem development (Brown *et al.*, 2016; Mack & Mayer, 2016; Auerswald & Dani, 2017; Lerner *et al.*, 2018; Radinger-Peer *et al.*, 2018; Schillo et al., 2016; Stephens et al., 2019). Entrepreneurship ecosystems is the set of interdependent human factors and actors coordinated to enable productive entrepreneurship in specific territories (Stam & Spigel, 2017). The interaction between the human individual and contextual factors are relevant in determining the entrepreneurial intention (Schmutzler *et al.*, 2019).

There are human factors that encourage or discourage the entrepreneurship practices and activities subject to different countries, regions, cultures, and language backgrounds requiring further. The interaction between the human individual and contextual factors are relevant in determining the entrepreneurial intention (Schmutzler *et al.*, 2019). Regional entrepreneurship systems approaches are based on the interactions of regional human factors influencing the discovery, creation, and exploitations of entrepreneurship opportunities (Qian et al., 2013). An entrepreneurship ecosystem identifies the domains of conducive culture, enabling leadership and policies, finance and human capital, venture markets and institutional support.

Human capital has a relevant role in entrepreneurship ecosystems for startups firms. Human capital availability in terms of individual agents may differ across the university entrepreneurship ecosystems leading to science and technology education entrepreneurship (Bolzani *et al.*, 2021). Firms that fail entrepreneurial recycling provide more resources for the redistribution of capital and human resources and capital. Blockchain technology has far-reaching effects on vulnerable entrepreneurship ecosystems practices and activities, affecting domains of policy, culture, finance, markets, human capital and supports (Rawhouser, *et al.* 2023).

The entrepreneurial self-efficacy is a personal factor influencing on entrepreneurial intention is (Barakat *et al.*, 2014; Bellò *et al.*, 2018; Rodríguez Gutiérrez *et al.*, 2019; Schmutzler *et al.*, 2019; Zhao *et al.*, 2005; Şahin *et al.*, 2019). There is a direct effect of entrepreneurship ecosystem human factors and self-efficacy on entrepreneurial intention and the mediating effect of entrepreneurship self-efficacy. The entrepreneurship ecosystem factors, and self-efficacy have a direct effect on entrepreneurship intention and a mediating effect on entrepreneurship efficacy. A bureaucratic entrepreneurship-unfriendly ecosystem due to factors such as unfavorable regulations of labor in local markets may drive to other jurisdictions. Market entry regulations as determinant of entrepreneurship ecosystem enhance firm establishment and growth.

Family circumstances: job and income security are emerging human factors resulting in burnout from the nature intense of entrepreneurship and time consuming. Entrepreneurship is considered a need for self-fulfillment that, as an intrinsic and systemic human factors of the entrepreneur, compromises an entrepreneurial dynamic between education and employment. Factors that motivate employees to enter entrepreneurship can also motivate entrepreneurs to return to employment. For example, monetary factors (Alstete, 2003; Wilson et *al.*, 2004) and family reasons (Verheul *et al.*, 2006) motivate employees to enter entrepreneurship while our findings show that monetary factors and family reasons also motivate a return to employment.

Internal motivations for autonomy and independence are relevant human factors for entrepreneurship (Gatewood et *al.*, 1995; Feldman & Bolino, 2000; Douglas & Shepherd, 2002; Hayter, 2015). Autonomy as a relevant factor for boomerang entrepreneurship to re-enter employment in contexts that have limited potential for corporate entrepreneurship. Changing of human motivation factors through the boomerang pathway aligns with changing motivations of entrepreneurship through serial entrepreneurship (Wright *et al.*, 1997). Pull factors draw people to entrepreneurship including demands, antecedents, challenges, family, job security, lifestyle, etc. to become at personal ability and experiential level.

There are gender differences in serial entrepreneurship impetus such us opportunities, nature of work, mentors, and human capital including education, managerial experience, employment, entrepreneurship capabilities etc. (Barnir, 2014). Significant disparities are appraised between entrepreneurship determinants such as the educational factor recognized as positive or contradictory influence on differentiated profiles. Investment in education and training reinforces creation and development of human capital leading to an entrepreneurship community with successful cases (Mueller & Thomas, 2001; Van Trang *et al.* 2019).

Beyond entrepreneurship is the offer of a prominent employment for high tec entrepreneurship firms that place value on attitudes and experience for corporate entrepreneurship motivating human factors (Adenfelt & Lagerström, 2006). Immigrant serial entrepreneurship who targets its ethnic community for contacts, increases human capital with (Dabić *et al.*, 2020).

Behaviors and Traits

Entrepreneurship is a challenging process starting with an intention which predicts entrepreneurial behavior translated into entrepreneurial action and without (Akinwale *et al.*, 2019; Liñán & Fayolle, 2015; Santos & Liguori, 2019). Social groups can participate in a multilevel entrepreneurship action model addressing the communities shaping entrepreneurship behaviors in specific entrepreneurship ecosystems (Kim *et al.* 2016; Jennings *et al.* 2013; Vedula & Kim, 2018; Roundy & Bayer, 2018). Building trust within a social ecosystem, share norms of behavior (Thomas & Autio, 2014).

The entrepreneurship cognition model describes the thinking and behavior of entrepreneurs (Sassetti *et al.*, 2018; Vlačić *et al.*, 2020). Upward and downward causality combined evidence the entrepreneurial behavior as a phenomenon at individual level shaping the systemic context and subject to systemic influences (Autio, 1997). Growth-oriented entrepreneurship has different behavioral make up (Baumol, 1996; Amit *et al.*, 2001). Serial entrepreneurship engages entrepreneurship behaviors in constant and sequential entrepreneurial activities (Amaral *et al.*, 2011). The entrepreneurship ecosystem quality has smaller impact on the venture of serial entrepreneurship behavioral addictions and capacity to recognize business opportunities and new ways of doing business (Vedula & Kim, 2019; Spivack *et al.*, 2014; Urban, 2009).

Entrepreneurship education increases intrinsic motivation and behaviors of business creation (Bongomin *et al.*, 2018). University entrepreneurship ecosystems has and intention to foment nurturing linkages with the entrepreneurship behavior to foster interactions with business (Salati Marcondes de Moraes, *et al* 2023). Intrapreneurial academic behavior generates an entrepreneurship climate as an antecedent of entrepreneurship behavior (Van der Sijde & Van Tilburg, 1998). University faculty entrepreneurship may establish supportive behaviors for organizational change (Whelan-Berry, Gordon, & Hinings, 2003).

Faculty behavior as educational leaders render in a long term a positive entrepreneurship evolution in students (Birdthistle, Hynes, & Fleming, 2007; Deakins, Glancey, Menter, & Wyper, 2005; Montecinos, Walker, & Maldonado, 2015; Tuytens & Devos, 2011). University entrepreneurship ecosystems evolution is based on behavioral responses to science opportunity commercialization mandates. Faculty members are potential intrapreneur agents responsible for creating platforms for social change by enabling behavioral shifts and modifying the settings concerning entrepreneurial incentives (Chiles, Bluedorn, & Gupta, 2007; Clark, 1998; Gurău, Dana, & Lasch, 2012; Mars & Rios-Aguilar, 2010).

To avoid distortion of entrepreneurship behavior should not be subsidies and grants. The opportunity commercialization of the co-evolution entrepreneurship ecosystem process is considered potential commercialization mandates enacted by agents based on their behavioral responses.

Entrepreneurship and corporate management have different personality traits, such as the openness to experience including curiosity and innovation, and conscientiousness including self-discipline and motivation, lower in neuroticism to tolerate stress (Zhao & Seibert, 2006).

Values

Entrepreneurship is an individual attitude that takes on objectives to advance new projects, innovating and adding value to existing business ventures, products, and services. Entrepreneurship is the process of discovering, identifying, exploring value-creating opportunities, and evaluating through innovation processes to produce goods and services (Shane, 2012). Different approaches to entrepreneurship challenge the evolving research leading to explore a framework on productive entrepreneurship ecosystems with respect to the creation of values (Pugh *et al.* 2021; Wurth *et al.*, 2021). Entrepreneurship produces the potential value generated by the interacting system elements. The bundled value attributes of a place-based ecosystem at the regional community study the influences and effects of entrepreneurship as change mechanism. Mechanisms can explain the prevalence of entrepreneurship ecosystems and economic development.

Cultural values have significant effects on entrepreneurship behavior (Shapero & Sokol 1982). A national culture is defined as a set of shared values, norms and practices subject to one country (House *et al.*, 2004). Culture have influences on the personal values and individual behaviors leading to entrepreneurship ecosystem. Cultural values compared with entrepreneurship behavior explains sensitive and conducive cultures, supportive of entrepreneurship ecosystems. Negative entrepreneurship activities are inevitable transitional development that is not well accepted and foster anti-entrepreneurship values.

Previous entrepreneurship experience of faculty and its impact is an open debate, while some studies confirm that the experience of professors in industrial activities are more committed to entrepreneurship initiatives, other support that experience is valued in entrepreneurship education engaging in innovative methods (Hindle, 2007; Abreu & Grinevich, 2013; Gulbrandsen & Thune, 2017; Lubango & Pouris, 2007; Moutinho, Fontes, & Godinho, 2007; Novotny, 2017; Diegoli, Gutierrez, & Salmones, 2018; Hopkins & Feldman, 1989; Stadler & Smith, 2017.

The integrated innovation entrepreneurship ecosystem coalesh around focal value technologies propositions in local systems in specific geographic regions for fostering entrepreneurship practices and activities (Adner, 2017; Hannah & Eisenhardt, 2018; Kapoor, 2018; Autio, Nambisan, Thomas, & Wright, 2018; Thompson, Purdy, & Ventresca, 2018)

Identification of the marketplace needs by the entrepreneurship to fulfill with value proposition is critical for success (Gaglio & Katz, 2001; Shane & Venkataraman, 2000).

The entrepreneurship ecosystems commitment of new financial actors creates value (Goswami, *et al.*, 2018; Kuratko, *et al.*, 2017). Venture capitals in serial entrepreneurship invest seeking profits in there are opportunities for employment, career progression, intellectual diverse team in management development, intellectual property rights and quality innovation to attend the marketplace, customer needs, wants and preferences and propositions change of value creation. Serial and habitual entrepreneurship as first-time entrepreneurs use to have a business plan that creates innovative marketplace options value.

The international entrepreneurship is a holistic organizational process that integrates the organization immersed in national cultures to explore opportunities in the international and global market to generate value (Dimitratos & Plakoyiannaki, 2003). Regional entrepreneurship ecosystems framework explains the variety of contextual dynamics leading to the objective value framing. The university ecosystem is composed by leadership, shared values, and norms. The university ecosystem has influence on the faculty commitment of entrepreneurship activities presenting a consistent model with explanatory value of commitment to support entrepreneurship.

Attitudes and Beliefs

The serial entrepreneurship is predisposed to start over again despite the gap between this attitude is hindered and boosted by individual characteristics, diversities, contingencies, etc. (Baù *et al.*, 2017; Barnir, 2014; Simmons *et al.*, 2019). Policy approaches are found in entrepreneurship education that promote positive attitudes towards the creation of entrepreneurship campuses ecosystems to support the creation of new business (Mason & Brown, 2014). The most positive attitude towards entrepreneurship is found in regions with high development of entrepreneurship ecosystems.

Cultural entrepreneurship is oriented towards change behaviors, mentalities, and attitudes using persuasive communication (Witter, 2011). Culture is a relevant feature of entrepreneurship ecosystems in issues such as sharing experiences and expertise, the inclusiveness philosophy, and the attitudes of giving before you get embedded in the start-up and failure to absorb the people involved in other start-up communities.

The entrepreneurial ecosystem can be explored using GEI dataset to analyze the aspects and the sub-indices of entrepreneurial attitude, entrepreneurial aspirations, and entrepreneurial abilities (Szerb & Trumbull, 2018). The Global Entrepreneurship Monitor (GEM) survey measures the entrepreneurship perceptions suggesting that attitudes are deeply engrained and should be stable over time requiring a generation to alter (Davidsson, 1991). The GEI dataset analyzes the entrepreneurial ecosystem from the entrepreneurial attitude, entrepreneurial aspirations, and entrepreneurial abilities (Szerb & Trumbull, 2018).

Beliefs about good entrepreneurship practices are in contradiction to do things differently compared to previous entrepreneurship generations (Smets *et al.* 2017). Entrepreneurship self-efficacy is an individual belief in his skills and abilities s linked to entrepreneurial activity (Barakat *et al.*, 2014). Entrepreneurship self-efficacy measures the personal beliefs in capabilities to implement the steps to start a business (Alammari *et al.*, 2019). Start-ups are believed to be good in such a way that the potential entrepreneurs need to be helped encouraging entrants and associated dead-weight (Vivarelli, 2004; Vivarelli, 2013; Quatraro & Vivarelli, 2015; Shane, 2009).

Creation and Growth

Entrepreneurship is the output of the system in which the entrepreneurs are the actors creating a healthy ecosystem (Stam, 2015). Entrepreneurship dynamics refers to lifecycle of startups creation, growth, stability and exit (Kazanjian, 1988). The term entrepreneurship ecosystem questions the assumption that cannot be created and defined by broad geographies endowed by intentions. Entrepreneurship is a process of vision, change, and creation that need energy and enthusiasm to develop and execute new ideas and creative solutions (Kuratko, 2016). Other elements of the entrepreneurship ecosystem include the availability of startup, culture and growth capital, the presence of universities, large firms, providers, etc.

Entrepreneurship has the function to reinforce and revolutionize the creation and development patterns by innovating, inventing, and proving technical possibilities to design, develop and produce new products or an old product in a new process, leading to provide new sources of materials, components and inputs, new organizational forms, etc. (Duarte & Ruiz, 2009). The creation of companies generates opportunities for the implementation of business projects that include the participation of other producers in the sector and families that improve their living conditions and contribute to the development of the community.

Entrepreneurship policy supports businesses with growth potential. Policies promoting high growth entrepreneurship must recognize the diverse nature of high growth firms rather than the stereotypes (Mason & Brown, 2013; Brown *et al*, 2014). Small business policies scattergun approach focusing on the number of business start-ups embedded as bad public policy that must be distinguished from entrepreneurship policies on the account of limited growth, survival and failure rates and displacement of start-ups (Shane, 2009; Nightingale & Coad, 2014).

People living in the region of an entrepreneurial ecosystem there are many that express they can create new firms (Jurvetson, 2000). Entrepreneurship is a function underlying force driving creative destruction (Schumpeter, 1976) in a regional entrepreneurship ecosystem context. The entrepreneurship practices arise from the entrepreneurial capabilities to exploit opportunities with the creation of good business (Bakar *et al.* 2017). The experience and insights of entrepreneurship allows to identify opportunities and to create and develop the market dynamics (Zahra, 2008). The growth of entrepreneurship activities in spin-off processes with employees leaving organizations to start their own firms are the source of further spinoff activities.

Educated and skilled Asian immigrants becoming entrepreneurs in nascent ecosystems at the birth phase who supported the growth of the Silicon Valley ecosystem and facilitating interactions with their home countries (Saxenian, 2002; Spigel & Harrison, 2018; Mack & Mayer, 2016). Entrepreneurship ecosystem diversity is revealed by the population of firms characterized by the growth-oriented entrepreneurship (Welter *et al.*, 2016). Skilled workers are resources for growth of entrepreneurship ecosystems. Technology workers leaving high technology firms can find work in growth startups in ecosystems opposing to migration to other regions and regional firms.

The scientific experimentation of lean startup philosophy transforms intuitive entrepreneurship processes into transactions steering and accelerated by management control systems (MCSs) characterized by startups and firms' growth-oriented leading to create new products and services under conditions of uncertainty (Blank, 2013; Ries, 2011). In the emerging entrepreneurship ecosystem perspective, the role of finance sources and determinants on entrepreneurship contributes to the aggregated wealth creation.

The entrepreneurship ecosystem emerges in the context for innovation in which participants are interdependent and can interact to co-create value (Nambisan & Baron, 2013; Adner & Kapoor, 2010; Jacobides, Cennamo, & Gawer, 2018). The growth of business and innovation in entrepreneurship ecosystems is accompanied by the increase on linkages and resources flows among the stakeholders and actors (McDermott *et al.,* 2013). The technologically innovative entrepreneurship ecosystems may decline eliminating opportunities and requiring large capital to invest on next generation of research and development which may be reflected in a new entrepreneurship model involving high skilled workforce in the creation and development of small firms not owned by them.

Technology creates market opportunities for the emergence of entrepreneurship ecosystems, new businesses and startups. Entrepreneurship ecosystems flourish in fertile spaces depends on disruptive technological advances and trajectory in industry conditions, creating discontinuities that produce new opportunities in which the technology might be exploited. Blockchain technology create opportunities and has opportunities for vulnerable entrepreneurship ecosystems that can benefit vulnerable communities and populations (Rawhouser, *et al.* 2023).

Firms, governments and citizens must intensify collaboration with programs to create and develop entrepreneurship ecosystems that enable resources for entrepreneurship innovations (Madzikanda *et al.*, 2021; Sitaridis & Kitsios, 2020). Public ecosystem architecture may support proactive stewardship including efforts with public agencies and communities to create and cultivate resources through top-down intervention favored by government to contribute to evolving entrepreneurship ecosystems by identifying connections that facilitate the inflow and recycling of resources. Entrepreneurship ecosystems is concerned with growth driven by entrepreneurial recycling processes (Mason & Harrison, 2006).

Public ecosystem architecture must create the conditions for cooperation among the stakeholders and actors to ensure the retention and recycling of resources. To create these conditions, the ecosystem architecture must cooperate with entrepreneurship ecosystem to position and identify the issues encumbering the evolution of the entrepreneurship ecosystem (Spigel & Harrison, 2018).

Public ecosystem architecture incentivize entrepreneurship to remain by advocating subsidies and tax rebates, creating opportunities for governance and mentoring contributions to new firms. Entrepreneurship ecosystems mut be incentivized to remain through advocating subsidies and tax rebates, creating opportunities for contributions in governance and mentoring. Regions with favorable tax regulations lead to increase of high growth entrepreneurship (Guzman & Stern, 2015). Policymaking focuses on promoting high growth firms (HGFs) (OECD, 2010; 2013). Policymaking recognizes the merit of a systems-based support for growth entrepreneurship. Gross domestic product (GDP) growth as an annual percentage is the dependent variable of entrepreneurship framework conditions in the model of Global Entrepreneurship Monitor (GEM, 2021)

An organizational culture of an anchor firm supporting an entrepreneurial organizational culture to attract workers with entrepreneurship mindsets leading to create and reproduce a regional entrepreneurship culture. Local founded firms in global competitive anchor firms tends to create local culture of entrepreneurship leading to become local models contributing to support other investors or mentors and entrepreneurships creating a broad community that coordinates the flow of resources throughout the entrepreneurship ecosystems (Spigel, 2013). These actions and activities improve the capacity to support firms and contribute to the health of the entrepreneurship ecosystem. A set of framework conditions can be developed to encourage the most favorable entrepreneurship activities aimed to enhance the ability to generate high growth firms (Napier & Hansen, 2011).

Anchor firms create new pools of entrepreneurship (Avnimelech & Feldman, 2010). Anchor firms and scale-ups attract entrepreneurship resources such as investment capital, skilled workers, etc. to be recycled in new rounds to strengthen the ecosystem that benefit its evolution by supporting new generations of startups, and growth of scaleups. Loss of an anchor firm catalyze ecosystem development, releasing skilled technical and managerial workers into the regional labor market, creating opportunities, and enriching the entrepreneurship resources.

Entrepreneurship university model is active in start-up creation, patenting, licensing, university-industry partnerships. Institutions of higher education, universities, and research centers are effective in being the convenor of entrepreneurship activities and groups, but the entrepreneurship programs located in business schools are not re-eminent due to that they are in the wrong place to be juxtaposed between professors and students to create and develop innovative ideas in computer and engineering sciences (Feld, 2012)

University entrepreneurship ecosystems are rooted in entrepreneurship culture of faculty, graduates and students associates and involved in start-up creation. The university entrepreneurship ecosystems initiatives may be disappointing in new firms' creation The effectiveness of university entrepreneurship initiatives for new firm creation is disappointing (Alves, Fischer, Schaeffer, & Queiroz, 2019). The entrepreneurship initiative turns into challenges in different entrepreneurship spheres, breakout and market growth potential. The academic entrepreneurship is a broader approach that includes entrepreneurship activities leading to the creation of firms including the high-tech and involving many stakeholders and actors in expanding dynamic regions (Matt & Schaeffer, 2016).

Harmonized datasets need to be created and developed to measure entrepreneurship ecosystems at the regional level. Entrepreneurship ecosystems measurement approaches focus more on start-ups and on inputs such as the levels of risk capital rather than on outputs as the levels of growth-ambition and high growth firms (HGF) (Mason & Brown, 2014). High growth firms at entrepreneurship ecosystems are frequently acquired by multinationals enterprises.

Entrepreneurship ecosystems is characterized by driven growth processes of recycling (Mason & Harrison, 2006). The entrepreneurship ecosystems recycling process is driven by premature exits because the inability to raise the required finances while senior management shareholders become wealthy not needing to work again to devote their energies to creating and supporting the entrepreneurship activity. Exit firms can recycle back founders and workers into the entrepreneurship ecosystem by creating new spin out firms and at existing scale-up firms. Recycling resources moving in entrepreneurship ecosystems are not bound to the firm that have created them.

CONCLUSION

This study analyzes the various human factors involved in the different processes of the entrepreneurship ecosystems, departing from the assumption that the entrepreneurial ecosystem can be created and defined not only by broad geographies endowed by intentions but dependent of human factors. The study concludes that human factors, such as behaviors and traits, values, attitudes and beliefs are relevant for the creation and growth of entrepreneurship ecosystems

A complex set of actors and human factors results in the outputs and outcomes of entrepreneurship ecosystems in regional and temporal setting. The entrepreneurship ecosystem framework provides a synthesis including a causal scheme to practitioners with the systemic conditions leading to entrepreneurship activities to create value as outcome._The spin-off process sets in motion a self-reinforcing process leading to the creation of an entrepreneurship ecosystem to support further entrepreneurship activities. Entrepreneurial ecosystems growth is more dependent on spin-off processes formed as a source for the future by the existing firms.

Policy may systematically create entrepreneurship ecosystems. Policymaking recognizes the principle that it cannot be created something from nothing. Intervention should be created by an entrepreneurship organization enabler with motivation and competence to enhance the ecosystem metrics for policymaking needed to intervene the entrepreneurship ecosystems to be measured. To identify systematic promotion and identification of faculty university intrapreneurial initiatives aimed to create and entrepreneurship culture.

Creating and developing entrepreneurship ecosystems takes an individualized perspective subject to the existing regional resources and assets. Serial entrepreneurship influences institutional policies in the development of new institutions to create cognitions, abilities and experiences overcome environmental limitations and stressors. People create start-ups that are likely to have little impact in low growth areas. Promotion of entrepreneurship ecosystems create internal and spatial inequalities between the winners and losers.

Entrepreneurship ecosystems are bridging assets serving to connect and share ideas, information, people, resources, talent and expertise, among individuals and organizations, investors, service providers, customers, stakeholders, able to realize the growth potential of firms. However, there are weak entrepreneurship ecosystems with a limited access to growth capital and public stock markets.

Future research in financial interactions of entrepreneurship ecosystems must pursue evolutionary approaches departing from mixed actors and human factors perspectives.

REFERENCES

Abreu, M., & Grinevich, V. (2013). The nature of academic entrepreneurship in the UK: Widening the focus on entrepreneurial activities. *Research Policy*, 42(2), 408–422. DOI: 10.1016/j.respol.2012.10.005

Acs, Z. J., Stam, E., Audretsch, D., & O'Connor, A. (2017). The lineages of the entrepreneurial ecosystem approach. *Small Business Economics*, 49(1), 1–10. DOI: 10.1007/s11187-017-9864-8

Adenfelt, M., & Lagerström, K. (2006). Organizational rejuvenation for knowledge exploitation: Exploring corporate entrepreneurship in an MNE. *Journal of International Entrepreneurship*, 4(2), 83–98.

Adner, R. (2017). Ecosystem as structure: An actionable construct for strategy. *Journal of Management*, 43(1), 39–58. DOI: 10.1177/0149206316678451

Adner, R., & Kapoor, R. (2010). Value creation in innovation ecosystems: How the structure of technological interdependence affects firm performance in new technology generations. *Strategic Management Journal*, 31(3), 306–333. DOI: 10.1002/smj.821

Akinwale, Y. O., Ababtain, A. K., & Alaraifi, A. A. (2019). Structural equation model analysis of factors influencing entrepreneurial interest among university students in Saudi Arabia. *Journal of Entrepreneurship Education*, 22(4), 1–14.

Alammari, A., Khalif, A. A., & DarougI, A. A. (2019). Restructuring the Libyan economy with available and unexploited resources of the tourism sector. *Volume II*, 398.

Aldrich, H. E., & Ruef, M. (2018). Unicorns, gazelles, and other distractions on the way to understanding real entrepreneurship in the United States. *The Academy of Management Perspectives*, 32(4), 458–472. DOI: 10.5465/amp.2017.0123

Alstete, J. (2003). On becoming an entrepreneur: An evolving typology. *International Journal of Entrepreneurial Behaviour & Research*, 8(4), 222–234. DOI: 10.1108/13552550210436521

Alves, A., Fischer, B., Schaeffer, P., & Queiroz, S. (2019). Determinants of student entrepreneurship: An assessment on higher education institutions in Brazil. *Innovation & Management Review*, 16(2), 96–117. DOI: 10.1108/INMR-02-2018-0002

Amaral, A. M., Baptista, R., & Lima, F. (2011). Serial entrepreneurship: Impact of human capital on time to re-entry. *Small Business Economics*, 37(1), 1–21. DOI: 10.1007/s11187-009-9232-4

Amit, R., MacCrimmon, K. R., Zietsma, C., & Oesch, J. M. (2001). Does money matter?: Wealth attainment as the motive for initiating growth-oriented technology ventures. *Journal of Business Venturing*, 16(2), 119–143. DOI: 10.1016/S0883-9026(99)00044-0

Auerswald, P., & Dani, L. (2017). Economic ecosystems. In Clarke, G., Feldman, M., Gertler, M., & Wojcik, D. (Eds.), *New Oxford Handbook of Economic Geography*. Oxford University Press.

Autio, E. (1997). New, technology-based firms in innovation networks symplectic and generative impacts. *Research Policy*, 26(3), 263–281. 00906-7DOI: <ALIGNMENT.qj></ALIGNMENT>10. 1016/ S0048-7333(96)

Autio, E., Nambisan, S., Thomas, L. D. W., & Wright, M. (2018). Digital affordances, spatial affordances, and the genesis of entrepreneurial ecosystems. *Strategic Entrepreneurship Journal*, 12(1), 72–95. DOI: 10.1002/sej.1266

Autio, E., & Thomas, L. D. W. (2014). Innovation ecosystems: Implications for innovation management. In Dodgson, M., Gann, D. M., & Phillips, N. (Eds.), *The oxford handbook of innovation management*. Oxford University Press.

Avnimelech, G., & Feldman, M. (2010). Regional Corporate Spawning and the Role of Homegrown Companies. *The Review of Policy Research*, 27(4), 475–489. DOI: 10.1111/j.1541-1338.2010.00452.x

Bakar, R., Islam, M. A., & Lee, J. (2015). Entrepreneurship education: Experiences in selected countries. *International Education Studies*, 8(1), 88–99.

Barakat, S., Boddington, M., & Vyakarnam, S. (2014). Measuring entrepreneurial self-efficacy to understand the impact of creative activities for learning innovation. *International Journal of Management Education*, 12(3), 456–468. DOI: 10.1016/j.ijme.2014.05.007

Barnir, A. (2014). Gender differentials in antecedents of habitual entrepreneurship: Impetus factors and human capital. *Journal of Developmental Entrepreneurship*, 19(1), 1–18. DOI: 10.1142/S1084946714500010

Baù, M., Sieger, P., Eddleston, K. A., & Chirico, F. (2017). Fail but try again? The effects of age, gender, and multiple–owner experience on failed entrepreneurs' re-entry. *Entrepreneurship Theory and Practice*, 41(6), 909–941. DOI: 10.1111/etap.12233

Baumol, W. J. (1996). Entrepreneurship: Productive, unproductive, and destructive. *Journal of Business Venturing*, 11(1), 3–22. DOI: 10.1016/0883-9026(94)00014-X

Bellò, B., Mattana, V., & Loi, M. (2018). The power of peers: A new look at the impact of creativity, social context and self-efficacy on entrepreneurial intentions. *International Journal of Entrepreneurial Behaviour & Research*, 24(1), 214–233. DOI: 10.1108/IJEBR-07-2016-0205

Birdthistle, N., Hynes, B., & Fleming, P. (2007). Enterprise education programmes in secondary schools in Ireland: A multi-stakeholder perspective. *Education + Learning*, 49(4), 265-276. https://doi.org/DOI: 10.1108/00400910710754426

Blank, S. (2013). Why the Lean Startup changes everything. *Harvard Business Review*, 91(5), 63–72.

Bosma, N., Stam, E., & Schutjens, V. (2011). Creative destruction and regional productivity growth: Evidence from the Dutch manufacturing and services industries. *Small Business Economics*, 36(4), 401–418. DOI: 10.1007/s11187-009-9257-8

Brown, R., Gregson, G., & Mason, C. (2016). A post-mortem of regional innovation policy failure: Scotland's intermediate technology initiative (ITI). *Regional Studies,* 50(7), 1260–1272. https://doi.org/. 2014. 985644DOI: 10. 1080/ 00343404

Brown, R., Mason, C., & Mawson, S. (2014) *Increasing the Vital 6%: Designing Effective Public Policy to Support High Growth Firms*, National Endowment for Science Technology &Arts (NESTA), London. Download from: https://www.nesta .org.uk/sites/default/files/working_paper_increasing_the_vital_6_percent.pdf

Chiles, T. H., Bluedorn, A. C., & Gupta, V. K. (2007). Beyond creative destruction and entrepreneurial discovery: A radical Austrian approach to entrepreneurship. *Organization Studies*, 28(4), 467–493. DOI: 10.1177/0170840606067996

Clark, B. R. (1998). *Creating entrepreneurial universities: Organisational pathways to transformation*. Pergamon Press.

Dabić, M., Vlačić, B., Paul, J., Dana, L. P., Sahasranamam, S., & Glinka, B. (2020). Immigrant entrepreneurship: A review and research agenda. *Journal of Business Research*, 113, 25–38. DOI: 10.1016/j.jbusres.2020.03.013

Davidsson, P. (1991). Continued entrepreneurship: Ability, need, and opportunity as determinants of small firm growth [November.]. *Journal of Business Venturing*, 6(6), 405–429. DOI: 10.1016/0883-9026(91)90028-C

Deakins, D., Glancey, K., Menter, I., & Wyper, J. (2005). Enterprise education: The role of head teachers. *The International Entrepreneurship and Management Journal*, 1(2), 241–263. DOI: 10.1007/s11365-005-1131-9

Dealroom, (2020). *European unicorns* [WWW Document]. URL https://app.dealroom.co/li sts/15129 (accessed 06.12.20) </Dataset>.

Diegoli, R. B., Gutierrez, H. S. M., & Salmones, M. M. G. (2018). Teachers as entrepreneurial role models: The impact of teacher's entrepreneurial experience and student learning styles in entrepreneurial intentions. *Journal of Entrepreneurship Education*, 21(1), 1–11. https://www.abacademies.org/articles/Teachers-as-entrepreneurial-role-models-1528-2651-21-1-138.pdf

Dimitratos, P., & Plakoyiannaki, E. (2003). Theoretical foundations of an international entrepreneurial culture. *Journal of International Entrepreneurship*, 1(2), 187–215. DOI: 10.1023/A:1023804318244

Douglas, E. J., & Shepherd, D. A. (2002). Self- employment as a career choice: Attitudes, entrepreneurial intentions, and utility maximization. *Entrepreneurship Theory and Practice*, 26(3), 81–90. DOI: 10.1177/104225870202600305

Duarte, T., & Ruiz Tibana, M. (2009). Emprendimiento, una opción para el desarrollo. *Scientia Et Technica*, 15(43), 326–331.

Economist (2019). *The trouble with tech unicorns - Tech's new stars have it all—except a path to high profits* [WWW Document]. URL https://www.economist.com/leaders 56.

Feld, B. (2012). *Startup Communities: building an entrepreneurial ecosystem in your city*. Wiley. DOI: 10.1002/9781119204459

Feldman, D. C., & Bolino, M. (2000). Career patterns of the self- employed: Career motivations and career out-comes. *Journal of Small Business Management*, 38(3), 53–67.

Frank, H., Lueger, M., & Korunka, C. (2007). The significance of personality in business start-up intentions, start-up realization and business success. *Entrepreneurship and Regional Development*, 19(3), 227–251. DOI: 10.1080/08985620701218387

Gaglio, C. M., & Katz, J. A. (2001). The psychological basis of opportunity identification: Entrepreneurial alertness. *Small Business Economics*, 16(2), 95–111. DOI: 10.1023/A:1011132102464

Gatewood, E. J., Shaver, K. G., & Gartner, W. (1995). A longitudinal study of cognitive factors influencing start- up behaviours and success at venture creation. *Journal of Business Venturing*, 10(5), 371–391. DOI: 10.1016/0883-9026(95)00035-7

GEM (2021) *Global Entrepreneurship Monitor*. Available at: https://www.gemconsortium.org/data/key-nes (accessed May 26, 2021).

Goswami, K., Mitchell, J. R., & Bhagavatula, S. (2018). Accelerator expertise: Understanding the intermediary role of accelerators in the development of the Bangalore entrepreneurial ecosystem. *Strategic Entrepreneurship Journal*, 12(1), 117–150. DOI: 10.1002/sej.1281

Gulbrandsen, M., & Thune, T. (2017). The effects of non-academic work experience on external interaction and research performance. *The Journal of Technology Transfer*, 42(4), 795–813. DOI: 10.1007/s10961-017-9556-1

Gurău, C., Dana, L.-P., & Lasch, F. (2012). Academic entrepreneurship in UK biotechnology firms: Alternative models and the associated performance. *Journal of Enterprising Communities: People and Places in the Global Economy*, 6(2), 154–168. DOI: 10.1108/17506201211228958

Guzman, J., & Stern, S. (2015). Where is Silicon Valley? *Science*, 347(80), 606–609. DOI: 10.1126/science.aaa0201 PMID: 25657229

Hannah, D. P., & Eisenhardt, K. M. (2018). How firms navigate cooperation and competition in nascent ecosystems. *Strategic Management Journal*, 39(12), 3163–3192. DOI: 10.1002/smj.2750

Hayter, C. S. (2015). Public or private entrepreneurship? Revisiting motivations and definitions of success among academic entrepreneurs. *The Journal of Technology Transfer*, 40(6), 1003–1015. DOI: 10.1007/s10961-015-9426-7

Hindle, K. (2007). Teaching entrepreneurship at university: From the wrong building to the right philosophy. In Fayolle, A. (Ed.), *Handbook of research in entrepreneurship education* (pp. 104–126). Edward Elgar. DOI: 10.4337/9781847205377.00013

Hopkins, T., & Feldman, H. (1989). Changing entrepreneurship education: Finding the right entrepreneur for the job. *Journal of Organizational Change Management*, 2(3), 28–40. DOI: 10.1108/09534818910145066

House, R. J., Hanges, P. J., Javidan, M., Dorfman, P. W., & Gupta, V. (Eds.). (2004). *Culture, leadership, and organizations: The GLOBE study of 62 societies*. Sage publications.

Insights, C. B. (2020). *The Global Unicorn Club* [WWW Document]. URL https://www. cbinsights.com/research-unicorn-companies (accessed 6.4.20).

Jacobides, M. G., Cennamo, C., & Gawer, A. (2018). Towards a theory of ecosystems. *Strategic Management Journal*, 39(8), 2255–2276. DOI: 10.1002/smj.2904

Jennings, P. D., Greenwood, R., Lounsbury, M. D., & Suddaby, R. (2013). Institutions, entrepreneurs, and communities: A special issue on entrepreneurship. *Journal of Business Venturing*, 28(1), 1–9. DOI: 10.1016/j.jbusvent.2012.07.001

Jurvetson, S. (2000). Changing everything: the internet revolution and Silicon Valley. In Lee, C. M., Miller, W. F., Hancock, M. G., & Rowen, H. S. (Eds.), *The Silicon Valley Edge: a habitat for innovation and entrepreneurship* (pp. 124–149). Stanford University Press. DOI: 10.1515/9781503619180-012

Kapoor, R. (2018). Ecosystems: Broadening the locus of value creation. *Journal of Organization Design*, 7(12), 1–16. DOI: 10.1186/s41469-018-0035-4

Kazanjian, R. K. (1988). Relation of dominant problems to stages of growth in technology-based new ventures. *Academy of Management Journal*, 31(2), 257–279. DOI: 10.2307/256548

Kim, P. H., Wennberg, K., & Croidieu, G. (2016). Untapped riches of meso-level applications in multi-level entrepreneurship mechanisms. *The Academy of Management Perspectives*, 30(3), 273–291. DOI: 10.5465/amp.2015.0137

Korunka, C., Frank, H., Lueger, M., & Mugler, J. (2003). The entrepreneurial personality in the context of resources, environment, and the startup process—A configurational approach. *Entrepreneurship Theory and Practice*, 28(1), 23–42. DOI: 10.1111/1540-8520.00030

Kuratko, D. F. (2016). Corporate entrepreneurship. *The Routledge Companion to the Makers of Modern Entrepreneurship*, 154.

Kuratko, D. F., Fisher, G., Bloodgood, J. M., & Hornsby, J. S. (2017). The paradox of new venture legitimation within an entrepreneurial ecosystem. *Small Business Economics*, 49(1), 119–140. DOI: 10.1007/s11187-017-9870-x

Lehner, O. M., & Harrer, T. (2019). Crowdfunding revisited: A neo-institutional field-perspective. *Venture Capital*, 21(1), 75–96. DOI: 10.1080/13691066.2019.1560884

Lerner, J., Schoar, A., Sokolinski, S., & Wilson, K. (2018). The globalization of angel investments: Evidence across countries. *Journal of Financial Economics*, 127(1), 1–20. .jfineco.2017.05.012DOI: <ALIGNMENT.qj></ALIGNMENT>10.1016/j

Levie, J., & Autio, E. (2008). A theoretical grounding and test of the GEM model. *Small Business Economics*, 2008(31), 235–263. DOI: 10.1007/s11187-008-9136-8

Liñán, F., & Fayolle, A. (2015). A systematic literature review on entrepreneurial intentions: Citation, thematic analyses, and research agenda. *The International Entrepreneurship and Management Journal*, 11(4), 907–933. DOI: 10.1007/s11365-015-0356-5

Lubango, L. M., & Pouris, A. (2007). Industry work experience and inventive capacity of South African academic researchers. *Technovation*, 27(12), 788–796. DOI: 10.1016/j.technovation.2007.05.013

Mack, E., & Mayer, H. (2016). The evolutionary dynamics of entrepreneurial ecosystems. *Urban Studies (Edinburgh, Scotland)*, 53(10), 2118–2133. DOI: 10.1177/0042098015586547

Mack, E., & Mayer, H. (2016). The evolutionary dynamics of entrepreneurial ecosystems. *Urban Studies (Edinburgh, Scotland)*, 53(10), 2118–2133. DOI: 10.1177/0042098015586547

Madzikanda, B., Li, C., & Dabuo, F. T. (2021). Barriers to development of entrepreneurial ecosystems and economic performance in Southern Africa. *African Journal of Science, Technology, Innovation and Development*, •••, 1–11.

Mars, M. M., & Rios-Aguilar, C. (2010). Academic entrepreneurship (re)defined: Significance and implications for the scholarship of higher education. *Higher Education*, 59(4), 441–460. DOI: 10.1007/s10734-009-9258-1

Mason, C., & Brown, R. (2013). Creating good public policy to support high growth firms. *Small Business Economics*, 40(2), 211–225. DOI: 10.1007/s11187-011-9369-9

Mason, C., & Brown, R. (2014). Entrepreneurial ecosystems and growth-oriented entrepreneurship. *Final Report to OECD*, Paris, 30(1), 77–102.

Mason, C. M., & Harrison, R. T. (2006). After the exit: Acquisitions, entrepreneurial recycling and regional economic development. *Regional Studies*, 40(1), 55–73. DOI: 10.1080/00343400500450059

Matt, M., & Schaeffer, V. (2012), The cooperative strategy of technology transfer offices: A longitudinal study. in Technology Transfer in a Global Economy, D. Audretsch, E. Lehmann, A., Link, A. Starnecker (Eds), special issue of the *International Handbook Series on Entrepreneurship* edited by Z. Acs and D. Audretsch, 55-72.

McDermott, G., Mudambi, R., & Parente, R. (2013). Strategic modularity and the architecture of multinational firm. *Global Strategy Journal*, 3(1), 1–7. DOI: 10.1111/j.2042-5805.2012.01051.x

Montecinos, C., Walker, H., & Maldonado, F. (2015). School administrators and university practicum supervisors as boundary brokers for initial teacher education in Chile. *Teaching and Teacher Education*, 49(1), 1–10. DOI: 10.1016/j.tate.2015.02.011

Moutinho, P., Fontes, M., & Godinho, M. (2007). Do individual factors matter? A survey of scientists' patenting in Portuguese public research organisations. *Scientometrics*, 70(2), 355–377. DOI: 10.1007/s11192-007-0207-4

Mueller, S., & Thomas, A. (2001). Culture and entrepreneurial potential. *Journal of Business Venturing*, 16(1), 51–75. DOI: 10.1016/S0883-9026(99)00039-7

Nambisan, S., & Baron, R. A. (2021). On the costs of digital entrepreneurship: Role conflict, stress, and venture performance in digital platform-based ecosystems. *Journal of Business Research*, 125, 520–532. DOI: 10.1016/j.jbusres.2019.06.037

Napier, G., & Hansen, C. (2011). *Ecosystems for Young Scaleable Firms*. FORA Group.

Nightingale, P., & Coad, A. (2014). Muppets and gazelles: Political and methodological biases in entrepreneurship research. *Industrial and Corporate Change*, 23(1), 113–143. DOI: 10.1093/icc/dtt057

Novotny, A. (2017). The heterogeneity of the academic profession: The effect of occupational variables on university scientists' participation in research commercialization. *Minerva*, 55(4), 485–508. DOI: 10.1007/s11024-017-9321-5

OECD. (2010). *High-growth enterprises: What governments can do to make a difference,* Pugh, R., Schmutzler, J., & Tsvetkova, A. (2021). Taking the systems approaches out of their comfort zones: Perspectives from under explored contexts. *Growth and Change*, 52, 608–620. DOI: 10.1111/grow

OECD. (2013). *Studies on SMEs and entrepreneurship*. Organisation for Economic Cooperation and Development.

Qian, H., Acs, Z. J., & Stough, R. R. (2013). Regional systems of entrepreneurship: The nexus of human capital, knowledge and new firm formation. *Journal of Economic Geography*, 13(4), 559–587. DOI: 10.1093/jeg/lbs009

Quatraro, F., & Vivarelli, M. (2015). Drivers of entrepreneurship and post-entry performance of newborn firms in developing countries. *The World Bank Research Observer*, 30(20), 277–305. DOI: 10.1093/wbro/lku012

Radinger-Peer, V., Sedlacek, S., & Goldstein, H. (2018). The path-dependent evolution of the entrepreneurial ecosystem (ee) – dynamics and region-specific assets of the case of Vienna (Austria). *European Planning Studies*, 26(8), 1499–1518. . 2018. 1494136DOI: <ALIGNMENT.qj></ALIGNMENT>10. 1080/ 09654313

Rawhouser, H., Vismara, S., & Kshetri, N. (2023). Blockchain and vulnerable entrepreneurial ecosystems. *Entrepreneurship and Regional Development*. Advance online publication. DOI: 10.1080/08985626.2022.2162979

Ries, E. (2011). *The Lean Startup: How Today's Entrepreneurs Use Continuous Innovation to Create Radically Successful Businesses*. Crown Business.

Rodríguez Gutiérrez, P. I., Pastor Pérez, M. D. P., & Alonso Galicia, P. E. (2019). University entrepreneurship: How to trigger entrepreneurial intent of undergraduate students. *Journal of Science and Technology Policy Management*, 10(4), 927–950. DOI: 10.1108/JSTPM-04-2018-0037

Roundy, P. T., & Bayer, M. A. (2018). Entrepreneurial ecosystem narratives and the micro-foundations ofregional entrepreneurship. *International Journal of Entrepreneurship and Innovation*, 20(3), 194–208. DOI: 10.1177/1465750318808426

Şahin, F., Karadağ, H., & Tuncer, B. (2019). Big five personality traits, entrepreneurial self-efficacy and entrepreneurial intention: A configurational approach. *International Journal of Entrepreneurial Behaviour & Research*, 25(6), 1188–1211. DOI: 10.1108/IJEBR-07-2018-0466

Salati Marcondes de Moraes, G. H., Brandão Fischer, B., Guerrero, M., Lopes da Rocha, A. K., & Rücker Schaeffer, P. (2023). An inquiry into the linkages between university ecosystem and students' entrepreneurial intention and self-efficacy. *Innovations in Education and Teaching International*, 60(1), 134–145. DOI: 10.1080/14703297.2021.1969262

Santos, S. C., & Liguori, E. W. (2020). Entrepreneurial self-efficacy and intentions: Outcome expectations as mediator and subjective norms as moderator. *International Journal of Entrepreneurial Behaviour & Research*, 26(3), 400–415. DOI: 10.1108/ IJEBR-07-2019-0436

Sassetti, S., Marzi, G., Cavaliere, V., & Ciappei, C. (2018). Entrepreneurial cognition and socially situated approach: A systematic and bibliometric analysis. *Scientometrics*, 116(3), 1675–1718. DOI: 10.1007/s11192-018-2809-4

Saxenian, A. (2002). Silicon valley's new immigrant high-growth entrepreneurs. *Economic Development Quarterly*, 16(1), 20–31. DOI: 10.1177/0891242402016001003

Schillo, R. S., Persaud, A., & Jin, M. (2016). Entrepreneurial readiness in the context of national systems of entrepreneurship. *Small Business Economics*, 46(4), 619–637. DOI: 10.1007/s11187-016-9709-x

Schmutzler, J., Andonova, V., & Diaz-Serrano, L. (2019). How context shapes entrepreneurial self-efficacy as a driver of entrepreneurial intentions: A multi-level approach. *Entrepreneurship Theory and Practice*, 43(5), 880–920. DOI: 10.1177/1042258717753142

Schumpeter, J. A. (1976), Capitalism, socialism, and democracy. *George Allen & Unwin* Ltd [1943].

Shane, S. (2003). *A General Theory of Entrepreneurship*. Edward Elgar. DOI: 10.4337/9781781007990

Shane, S. (2009). Why encouraging more people to become entrepreneurs is bad public policy. *Small Business Economics*, 33(2), 141–149. DOI: 10.1007/s11187-009-9215-5

Shane, S. (2012). The importance of angel investing in financing the growth of entrepreneurial ventures. *The Quarterly Journal of Finance*, 2(02), 1250009. DOI: 10.1142/S2010139212500097

Shane, S., & Venkataraman, S. (2000). The promise of entrepreneurship as a field of research. *Academy of Management Review*, 25(1), 217–226. https://www.jstor.org/stable/259271. DOI: 10.5465/amr.2000.2791611

Shapero, A., & Sokol, L. (1982). *The social dimensions of entrepreneurship*. University of Illinois at Urbana-Champaign's Academy for Entrepreneurial Leadership Historical Research Reference in Entrepreneurship.

Siegel, D. S., & Wright, M. (2015). Academic Entrepreneurship: Time for a Rethink? *British Journal of Management*, 26(4), 582–595. DOI: 10.1111/1467-8551.12116

Simmons, S. A., Wiklund, J., Levie, J., Bradley, S. W., & Sunny, S. A. (2019). Gender gaps and re-entry into entrepreneurial ecosystems after business failure. *Small Business Economics*, 53(2), 517–531. DOI: 10.1007/s11187-018-9998-3

Sitaridis, I., & Kitsios, F. (2020). Competitiveness analysis and evaluation of entrepreneurial ecosystems: A multi-criteria approach. *Annals of Operations Research*, 294(1), 377–399. DOI: 10.1007/s10479-019-03404-x

Smets, M., Aristidou, A., & Whittington, R. (2017). Towards a practice-driven institutionalism. In Greenwood, R., Oliver, C., Lawrence, T. B., & Meyer, R. (Eds.), *The Sage Handbook of Organizational Institutionalism* (pp. 384–411). Sage. DOI: 10.4135/9781446280669.n15

Spigel, B. (2013). Bourdieuian Approaches to the Geography of Entrepreneurial Cultures. *Entrepreneurship and Regional Development*, 25(9-10), 804–818. DOI: 10.1080/08985626.2013.862974

Spigel, B., & Harrison, R. (2018). Toward a process theory of entrepreneurial ecosystems. *Strategic Entrepreneurship Journal*, 12(1), 151–168. DOI: 10.1002/sej.1268

Spivack, A. J., McKelvie, A., & Haynie, J. M. (2014). Habitual entrepreneurs: Possible cases of entrepreneurship addiction? *Journal of Business Venturing*, 29(5), 651–667. DOI: 10.1016/j.jbusvent.2013.11.002

Stadler, A., & Smith, A. M. J. (2017). Entrepreneurship in vocational education: A case study of Brazilian context. *Industry and Higher Education*, 31(2), 81–89. DOI: 10.1177/0950422217693963

Stam, E. (2010). Entrepreneurship, evolution and geography. In Boschma, R., & Martin, R. L. (Eds.), *The Handbook of Evolutionary Economic Geography* (pp. 307–348). Edward Elgar. DOI: 10.4337/9781849806497.00014

Stam, E. (2015). Entrepreneurial ecosystems and regional policy: A sympathetic critique. *European Planning Studies*, 23(9), 1759–1769. DOI: 10.1080/09654313.2015.1061484

Stam, E., & Spigel, B. (2017). Entrepreneurial Ecosystems, forthcoming in: Blackburn, R., De Clercq, D., Heinonen, J. & Wang, Z. (Eds) *Handbook for Entrepreneurship and Small Business.* London: SAGE.

Stam, E., & Spigel, B. (2018). Entrepreneurial ecosystems. Blackburn, R., De Clerq, C., Heinonen, J. (Eds.). *The SAGE Handbook of Small Business and Entrepreneurship*. SAGE, London, pp. 407–422. DOI: 10.4135/9781473984080.n21

Stam, E., & van de Ven, A. (2021). Entrepreneurial ecosystem elements. *Small Business Economics*, 56(2), 809–832. DOI: 10.1007/s11187-019-00270-6

Stephan, U., & Uhlaner, L. (2010). Performance-based vs. socially-supportive culture: A cross-national study of descriptive norms and entrepreneurship. *Journal of International Business Studies*, 41(8), 1347–1364. DOI: 10.1057/jibs.2010.14

Stephens, B., Butler, J. S., Garg, R., & Gibson, D. V. (2019). Austin, Boston, Silicon Valley, and New York: Case studies in the location choices of entrepreneurs in maintaining the technopolis. *Technological Forecasting and Social Change*, 146(4), 267–280. DOI: 10.1016/j.techfore.2019.05.030

Sternberg, R., Bloh, J., & Coduras, A. (2019). A new framework to measure entrepreneurial ecosystems at the regional level. *Zeitschrift für Wirtschaftsgeographie*, 63(2-4), 103–117. DOI: 10.1515/zfw-2018-0014

Szerb, L., & Trumbull, W. N. (2018). Entrepreneurship development in Russia: Is Russia a normal country? An empirical analysis. *Journal of Small Business and Enterprise Development*, 25(6), 902–929. DOI: 10.1108/JSBED-01-2018-0033

Thomas, L. D. W., & Autio, E. (2014). The fifth facet: The ecosystem as an organizational field. *Proceedings - Academy of Management*, 2014(1), 10306. DOI: 10.5465/ambpp.2014.10306abstract

Thompson, T. A., Purdy, J. M., & Ventresca, M. J. (2018). How entrepreneurial ecosystems take form: Evidence from social impact initiatives in Seattle. *Strategic Entrepreneurship Journal*, 12(1), 96–116. DOI: 10.1002/sej.1285

Tuytens, M., & Devos, G. (2011). Stimulating professional learning through teacher evaluation: An impossible task for the school leader? *Teaching and Teacher Education*, 27(5), 891–899. DOI: 10.1016/j.tate.2011.02.004

Urban, B. (2009). Opportunity recognition: delineating the process and motivators for serial entrepreneurs: analysis of survey data. *Suid-Afrikaanse Tydskrif vir Ekonomiese en Bestuurswetenskappe*, 12(4), 513–532. DOI: 10.4102/sajems.v12i4.192

Van der Sijde, P., & Van Tilburg, J. (1998). Creating a climate for university spin-offs. *Industry and Higher Education*, 12(5), 297–302. DOI: 10.1177/095042229801200504

Van Trang, T., Hung Do, Q., & Luong, M. (2019). Entrepreneurial human capital, role models, and fear of failure and start-up perception of feasibility among adults in Vietnam. *International Journal of Engineering Business Management*, 11, 1–11. DOI: 10.1177/1847979019873269

Vedula, S., & Kim, P. H. (2018). Marching to the beat of the drum: The impact of the pace of life in US cities on entrepreneurial work effort. *Small Business Economics*, 50(3), 569–590. DOI: 10.1007/s11187-017-9908-0

Vedula, S., & Kim, P. H. (2019). Gimme shelter or fade away: The impact of regional entrepreneurial ecosystem quality on venture survival. *Industrial and Corporate Change*, 28(4), 827–854. DOI: 10.1093/icc/dtz032

Verheul, I., van Stel, A., & Thurik, R. (2006). Explaining female and male entrepreneurship at the country level. *Entrepreneurship and Regional Development*, 18(2), 151–183. DOI: 10.1080/08985620500532053

Vivarelli, M. (2004). Are all the potential entrepreneurs so good? *Small Business Economics*, 23(1), 41–49. DOI: 10.1023/B:SBEJ.0000026023.11752.a9

Vivarelli, M. (2013). Is entrepreneurship necessarily good? Microeconomic evidence from developed and developing countries. *Industrial and Corporate Change*, 22(6), 1453–1495. DOI: 10.1093/icc/dtt005

Vlačić, B., González-Loureiro, M., & Eduardsen, J. (2020). The process of the process of internationalization: Cognitive and behavioral perspectives in small ventures. *European Journal of International Management*, 1(1), 10027574. Advance online publication. DOI: 10.1504/EJIM.2020.10027574

Welter, F., Baker, T., Audretsch, D. B., & Gartner, W. B. (2016). Everyday entrepreneurship—A call for entrepreneurship re-s e a r c h t o e m b r a c e e n t r e p r e n e u r i a l d i v e r s i t y. *Entrepreneurship Theory and Practice*. Advance online publication. DOI: 10.1111/etap.12258

Whelan-Berry, K. S., Gordon, J., & Hinings, C. (2003). Strengthening organizational change processes. *The Journal of Applied Behavioral Science*, 39(2), 186–207. DOI: 10.1177/0021886303256270

Wilson, F., Marlino, D., & Kickul, J. (2004). Our entrepreneurial future: Examining the diverse attitudes and motivations of teens across gender and ethnic identity. *Journal of Developmental Entrepreneurship*, 9(3), 177–197.

Witter, M. (2011). Financing sustainable development in small island developing states. *Tools for Mainstreaming Sustainable Development in Small States*, 107

Wright, M., Robbie, K., & Ennew, C. (1997). Serial entrepreneurs. *British Journal of Management*, 8(3), 251–268. DOI: 10.1111/1467-8551.00064

Wurth, B., Stam, E., & Spigel, B. (2021). Toward an Entrepreneurial Ecosystem Research Program. *Entrepreneurship Theory and Practice*. Advance online publication. DOI: 10. 1177/10422

Zahra, S. A. (2008). The Virtuous Cycle of Discovery and Creation of Entrepreneurial Opportunities. *Strategic Entrepreneurship Journal*, 2(3), 243–257. DOI: 10.1002/sej.47

Zhao, H., & Seibert, S. (2006). The big five personality dimensions and entrepreneurial status: A meta- analytical review. *The Journal of Applied Psychology*, 91(2), 259–271. DOI: 10.1037/0021-9010.91.2.259 PMID: 16551182

Zhao, H., Seibert, S. E., & Hills, G. E. (2005). The mediating role of self-efficacy in the development of entrepreneurial intentions. *The Journal of Applied Psychology*, 90(6), 1265–1272. DOI: 10.1037/0021-9010.90.6.1265 PMID: 16316279

Chapter 8

Price Dynamics and Entrepreneurship in Africa:
What Public Policy Can Strengthen the Entrepreneurial Ecosystem?

Thomas Gahamanyi Niyonzima
University of Yaounde II Soa, Cameroon

Tchouassi Gérard
University of Yaounde II Soa, Cameroon

ABSTRACT

The aim of this chapter is to assess the effects of price dynamics on entrepreneurship in Africa. The dynamic specification was developed by Farahadi et al (2015 and reposted by Awoa et al. (2022). Data were collected on 35 African countries for the selected period from 2006 to 2018. The results of this chapter show that price dynamics have nuanced effects on entrepreneurship in Africa depending on the model and robustness applied. The IPC has a negative impact on entrepreneurship in Africa, while energy and non-energy prices have positive effects on entrepreneurship. Commodity price index have both positive and negative effects on entrepreneurship. Policy makers should develop strategies to reduce inflation by cutting public spending, raising taxes and introducing tight monetary policies, promoting better access to non-energy commodities by framing the beverage sector, implementing policies to strengthen the entrepreneurial ecosystem, reviving access to financing by popular banks and forcing FDI to partner with local entrepreneurs.

DOI: 10.4018/979-8-3693-9486-1.ch008

INTRODUCTION: BACKGROUND AND RATIONALE

For a long time, the question of how to effectively achieve economic development has been at the center of concerns of researchers, international organizations and political leaders (Pekarčíková et al., 2022; Afonso and Blanco-Arana, 2022; United Nations, 2010; Sen 2000). Interest in this question has been renewed with the succession of crises that the world economy has experienced since the beginning of this decade, with the levels of inflation never recorded, as well as the disparities observed in the development trajectories of the different regions of the world (Papcunová, 2023) Perkins & Allii, 2011). For these different reasons, the United Nations adopted the Sustainable Development Goals in 2015 in order to actively respond to these various global challenges linked in particular to poverty, inequalities, climate, environmental degradation, prosperity, to peace and justice. These goals are interconnected and, to leave no one behind, it is important to achieve each of them, and each of their targets, by 2030 (United Nations, 2020). Furthermore, given the levels of inflation recorded in recent years and the dependence of most developing economies on commodities whose prices are very volatile and determined on international markets, many authors argue that it would be important to take price dynamics into account more often in studies on the development of economies for the particular case of developing countries (Zhang and Wang, 2018; Addisu, 2020; Soffiantini, 2020; Abdallah, 2021). Indeed, the importance given to this subject is due to the fact that economic and infrastructural development is the basis of the well-being and quality of life of individuals living in a society through the creation of jobs and the increase in available resources. It also ensures a pleasant living environment while guaranteeing security, reducing poverty, facilitating access to health care and education (Cypher and Dietz, 2008; Ben Abdallah, et al. 2021, Voigt, 2019). However, in an increasingly liberalized global economic context, achieving economic development requires entrenching entrepreneurship in society. This makes it possible to extend the average lifespan of businesses and therefore, ultimately, to strengthen the capacities of families who experience precariousness or poverty on a daily basis (Doumbouya, 2011) and the increasing use of PPPs in French-speaking Africa (Doubogan & Aliha, 2020)

Although many authors support the benefits of economic development, the facts seem rather contradictory if we stick to a few traditional indicators (World Bank, 2022; World Economic Outlook, 2023). Indeed, the facts reveal a considerable gap between developed and developing countries when we consider, for example, indicators such as participation in global value chains, entrepreneurship and food security. Let us point out that the observation is the same when we compare the different levels of development by taking entrepreneurship into account. The same observation is also noted when examining the literature. Indeed, the literature on the entrepreneurial ecosystem reveals a diversity of approaches and models. Rather, we identify several definitions to understand the concept. In particular, Isenberg (2011) emphasizes that the entrepreneurship ecosystem "consists of a set of individual elements - such as leadership, culture, financial markets and open-minded customers - which combine in complex way." These elements integrated into a holistic system could stimulate growth and business creation in a specific location (Isenberg, 2011). Vogel P for his part (2013) defines it, as "an interactive community within a geographical region, composed of varied and interdependent actors (entrepreneurs, institutions and organizations) and factors (markets, regulatory framework, support framework, entrepreneurial culture, etc.), which evolves over time and whose actors and factors coexist and interact to promote the creation of new businesses. In the same vein, Mason, C. and Brown, R. (2014) define ecosystems as "an interconnected set of entrepreneurial actors (potential and existing), entrepreneurial organizations (companies, venture capitalists, business angels, banks), institutions (universities, public sector and financing agencies) and entrepreneurial processes (business creation rate, number of high-growth companies, number of gazelles, number of serial entrepreneurs, as well as the level of entrepreneurial ambition.

Subsequently, the latest report from the World Economic Forum as well as the global economic outlook published by the World Bank at the start of this year 2023 show that, compared to developed countries, the entrepreneurial ecosystem in developing countries is slow to take off. Due in particular to difficulties in accessing financing, low capacity for innovation, governance problems, lack of adequate infrastructure, lack of entrepreneurial culture but also the high vulnerability of small and medium-sized businesses to shocks (World Economics Outlook, 2023; OECD SME and Entrepreneurship Outlook, 2021). Furthermore, according to the ranking of the best countries in terms of entrepreneurship in the world in 2023, we can see that the Top 10 is ensured by advanced countries like Japan, Germany, the United States, the Kingdom United States, South Korea, Canada, Singapore, China and Switzerland, with most developing countries only occupying the bottom ranks (World's Most Entrepreneurial countries, 2021; World Economics Forum, 2022). Entrepreneurial activity in Africa results from various global shocks. The breakdown of the international system by different shocks offers ecopreneurial opportunities to circular economies, given the shortcomings of national sovereignties are exposed by protectionism. These shocks are of various orders. The entrepreneurship of immigrants (Tchouassi, G., 2009; Tchouassi, G., and Tagne, JS 2020) and of immigrants (Levy Thiery Tadjine, 2006), the entrepreneurship of internally displaced persons from wars and that of refugees from armed conflicts occupy most of today's entrepreneurial aspects Gérard, T., & Thomas, G. N. (2023). The question of entrepreneurship or entrepreneur has interested the scientific world since the conception of entrepreneurship as a field of research (Praag, 1999; Soltow, 1968; Akilimali

Ndatabaye Ephrem and McEdward Murimbika 2023). Researchers have debated and rejected the historical personality traits approach, arguing that entrepreneurs are not only born but can be created through participatory training (Tchouassi G. and Tchamanbe Djiné L., (2003), or an entrepreneurial exposure (Danil P. Forbes, 2017), (Henry et al., 2005; Herron and Robinson, 1993; Lopez- Núñez et al., 2020; McClelland, 1965; McCormick et al., 2019; Seikkula -Leino and Salomaa, 2020). Entrepreneurship is one of the main drivers of the economy (Tchouassi G.,2005), entrepreneurs invest, create jobs and contribute to increasing the standard of living for all. The work of the entrepreneur is to ensure that supply meets demand, make innovations available to consumers and also be able to market the fruits of his innovation (Bedard M., 2016), Gupta et al, 2022). Entrepreneurship seeks to solve problems of income inequality, unemployment, poverty and resilience after the advent of shocks. Among the factors of the entrepreneurial ecosystem, some researchers put economic, institutional and cultural factors at the forefront (Mateus Cerqueira et al., 2022). In the logic pursued by this chapter, there is a range of opinions around the relationship between inflation and entrepreneurship. This lack of consensus in the relationship between price dynamics and economic development indicators may in part be due to methodological problems. Indeed, we can note for example that this existing work has for the most part been concentrated in developed countries, although it is the developing countries and particularly Africa which most of the time suffer the effects of price variations. Furthermore, we can see that most of the work focuses on the prices of energy products and foodstuffs while putting to the margin the price of other goods and services whose dynamics can also affect the real variables of the economy such as than entrepreneurship. For these different reasons, this chapter aims to fill this gap by answering the following research questions: More specifically, What is the effect of price dynamics on entrepreneurship in African countries? To this question, the following hypothesis was formulated. Hypothesis: **Considering the theory in place, price dynamics would have a nuanced effect on entrepreneurship in Africa.**

LITERATURE REVIEW

Price Dynamics Would Have a Nuanced Effect on Entrepreneurship in Africa: Theoretical Framework and Literature Review

The problem of the effects of price dynamics on entrepreneurship in African countries has been the subject of numerous theoretical and empirical studies. The literature relating to this theme is not new in itself. However, to fully understand this relationship, it seems important to us to deal on the one hand with the theoretical foundations relating to this relationship and on the other hand, to highlight a brief review of the literature. Two major points are developed at this level. On the one hand we have the theoretical evolution of the notion of entrepreneurship and on the other hand the highlighting of the theoretical foundations. At this level we proceed in turn to the definition of the concepts. It is more precisely a question of defining price dynamics on the one hand and entrepreneurship on the other. The literature relating to price dynamics highlights two major concepts: the dynamics of inflation on the one hand, and that of the exchange rate on the other.

A. Theoretical Evolution of Entrepreneurship in the Face of Inflation

Conceptual analysis consists of immersing oneself in the concepts analyzed for a better understanding of the concepts studied. As for the transmission channels, it is organized around three factors. The theoretical evolution of entrepreneurship in a context of inflation can be analyzed around two aspects. First, we can observe the historical foundations of entrepreneurship based on classical approaches. Secondly, we can also illustrate contemporary theories of entrepreneurship.

1. Historical Foundations of Entrepreneurship

In the context of analyzing theories of entrepreneurship, it is necessary to focus on their origins. Most of these date back to the period dominated by classical economic analysis. These theories include: the theory of innovation and the theory of value creation.

1.1. The Theory of Innovation

According to this theory, entrepreneurs are the engine of economic growth and development. They are responsible for introducing new ideas, products and technologies that revolutionize the way we live, work and do business. Schumpeter believed that innovation is the key to long-term economic success and that it is the entrepreneur's ability to create and exploit new opportunities that drive innovation. The theory of innovation is based on this principle.

The theory of innovation, developed by Joseph Schumpeter, emphasizes the role of the entrepreneur as an innovator. According to Schumpeter, entrepreneurs are agents of economic change who introduce new ideas, products, processes or technologies to the market. This "creative destruction" is considered a key driver of long-term economic growth (Schumpeter, 1942). Schumpeter emphasized that entrepreneurs take risks by introducing new innovations, but that these risks are necessary to stimulate economic dynamics.

The Schumpeterian approach to innovation has profoundly influenced the understanding of economic processes and growth. By emphasizing the dynamic role of the entrepreneur as innovator, Schumpeter challenged traditional models of pure and perfect competition and emphasized the importance of creativity and disruption in economic development. This perspective also led to a reassessment of the role of the state in promoting innovation, recognizing that public policies can have a significant impact on the entrepreneurial environment and innovation (Schumpeter, 1942).

Schumpeter's theory of innovation has also been closely linked to the notion of economic evolution. By describing the innovation process as a disruptive force that challenges existing structures and creates new opportunities, Schumpeter highlighted the evolutionary and non-linear nature of economic development. This view has been particularly influential in the field of evolutionary economics, which emphasizes processes of learning, adaptation, and institutional change in the economy (Nelson and Winter, 1982).

The implications of Schumpeter's theory of innovation are broad and touch many areas of economics and business. By highlighting the central role of the entrepreneur as an agent of change and innovation, this theory has stimulated in-depth research on the determinants of entrepreneurial activity, policies favoring innovation, as well as the effects of innovation on business competitiveness and economic growth.

1.2. The Theory of Value Creation

Value creation theory focuses on the entrepreneur's ability to create economic value by combining resources in innovative ways. It emphasizes the entrepreneur's ability to identify undervalued opportunities and create value by exploiting them. This theory underlines the importance of innovation and entrepreneurial vision in the creation of economic wealth, and highlights the central role of the entrepreneur in this process (Baumol, 1968).

Value creation theory focuses on the entrepreneur's ability to create economic value by combining resources in innovative ways. However, in a situation of inflation, entrepreneurship faces several constraints which slow down its ability to create value. Inflation is the persistent increase in the prices of goods and services in an economy. This reduces the purchasing power of money and creates uncertainty in the market, making it difficult for entrepreneurs to plan and invest in long-term projects. One of the main constraints for entrepreneurship in an inflationary environment is increasing prices. We recall that the theory of value creation focuses on the entrepreneur's ability to create economic value by combining resources in innovative ways, even in contexts of high inflation. When an economy faces high inflation, entrepreneurs must be very creative in identifying undervalued opportunities and exploiting untapped market niches. In such situations, innovation becomes crucial to maintain the competitiveness of companies and ensure their survival.

Indeed, high inflation can lead to economic instability and a reduction in purchasing power, which creates new challenges for entrepreneurs. To face these challenges, entrepreneurs must innovate their business models, production processes and marketing strategies in order to maintain profitability and growth. In this context, the theory of value creation highlights the central role of the entrepreneur in the search and exploitation of economic opportunities, even in times of high inflation. Indeed, the ability of entrepreneurs to innovate and create value becomes essential to stimulate economic growth and mitigate the negative effects of inflation.

2. Contemporary Theories of Entrepreneurship

By continuing the theoretical analysis of the effects of price dynamics on entrepreneurship, we must also observe their evolution with contemporary issues. In this point, it is interesting to present these different contemporary theories.

2.1. Entrepreneurial Alert Theory

The theory of entrepreneurial alertness, developed by Israel Kirzner, offers a unique perspective on the role of the entrepreneur in discovering and exploiting profit opportunities in the marketplace. According to Kirzner, entrepreneurs are not simply passive actors who respond to market signals, but rather proactive agents constantly searching for undervalued opportunities and able to exploit them through their vigilance and alertness. Israel Kirzner, an Austrian economist, developed his theory of entrepreneurial alertness within the framework of the Austrian school of economics. This approach emphasizes the subjectivity of individual preferences, the dynamic and evolving nature of markets, and the central role of the entrepreneur in the economic process. For Kirzner, the function of the entrepreneur is above all that of discovering and exploiting profit opportunities that have not yet been fully realized by the market.

Alertness refers to the entrepreneur's ability to perceive opportunities that have escaped the attention of other market participants. This constant vigilance allows it to identify gaps between supply and demand, market inefficiencies or unmet needs, and to find innovative ways to respond to them. According to Kirzner, this ability to identify and exploit these undervalued opportunities is what truly distinguishes the entrepreneur from other economic agents.

The theory of entrepreneurial alertness highlights the active and creative role of the entrepreneur in the economic process. Unlike the traditional view of the entrepreneur as a simple organizer or manager of resources, this approach emphasizes the importance of entrepreneurial vision and the ability to identify profit opportunities where others do not see them. By emphasizing entrepreneurial alertness, Kirzner highlights the dynamic and evolving nature of markets, as well as the crucial role of the entrepreneur in this process. This perspective offers valuable insight into the nature of entrepreneurial activity and how entrepreneurs help drive innovation, economic growth and value creation.

2.2. Agency Theory

Agency theory examines the relationship between the owners (shareholders) and managers (entrepreneurs) of a company (Jensen and Meckling, 1976; Fama and Jensen, 1983). It highlights potential conflicts of interest between these two groups and seeks to understand how incentives can be aligned to ensure effective business management. This theory highlights the challenges associated with the delegation of control and monitoring of managers by owners, and explores mechanisms that can be put in place to mitigate these conflicts of interest.

Under agency theory, owners (shareholders) are the holders of the financial resources invested in the business, while managers (entrepreneurs) are responsible for leading and managing the business on a day-to-day basis. The interests of owners and managers can sometimes come into conflict, as the latter may be tempted to pursue their own objectives to the detriment of those of shareholders. For example, managers might seek to maximize their own compensation or job security instead of maximizing the value of the firm to shareholders.

One of the main challenges of agency theory is therefore to find mechanisms that encourage managers to act in the interests of shareholders. These mechanisms include performance-based remuneration, long-term incentives such as shares or stock options, and oversight by an independent board of directors. These mechanisms aim to align the interests of managers with those of shareholders, by providing them with incentives to maximize the value of the company.

In a context of inflation, these governance mechanisms may be subject to additional constraints. Inflation can affect the value of currency and distort economic incentives. For example, if manager compensation is tied to financial targets expressed in nominal terms (not adjusted for inflation), this could lead to opportunistic behavior aimed at maximizing nominal compensation at the expense of creating real value for shareholders.

Additionally, inflation can also affect the financial performance of the company, making it difficult to evaluate the performance of managers. In an inflationary environment, it becomes more difficult to distinguish actual company performance from that which is simply due to the effect of inflation on financial figures. This makes it more complex for shareholders and the board of directors to evaluate manager performance and make decisions about compensation and incentives.

Furthermore, inflation can also affect companies' investment and financing decisions. Contractors may face increasing costs, increased volatility in commodity prices and increased uncertainties regarding interest rates and macroeconomic conditions. This can make it more difficult for entrepreneurs to plan long-term and invest in profitable projects, as inflation introduces additional uncertainty about the future value of money.

Additionally, inflation can also affect the cost of capital and the availability of financing for businesses. Real interest rates can be impacted by inflation, making financing more expensive and reducing the ability of companies to raise funds for their investment projects. This can limit opportunities for entrepreneurs to expand and innovate, and lead to a less efficient allocation of capital in the economy.

B. Price Dynamics and Entrepreneurship: Lessons From the Literature

Two major aspects are addressed: the empirical results relating to the relationship studied on the one hand, on the other hand, we take into account the other determinants of entrepreneurship, and finally we finish with the transmission channels

1. Price Dynamics and Entrepreneurship: Controversial Results

The empirical literature examining the impact of price fluctuations (exchange rates and market prices) on international trade is divided into three groups: some authors provide evidence of a negative effect while others support the Although there is a positive influence, another group of researchers suggests a mixed effect. Bedard M. (2016) notes a correlation between economic freedom and entrepreneurship in the provinces of Canada. Inflation reduces economic freedom and consequently entrepreneurship since it makes long-term economic calculation more difficult. Furthermore, entrepreneurship constitutes a set of resilience strategies following crises, entrepreneurship as a judgment. This approach would seem to explain entrepreneurship in Africa instead of entrepreneurship taken as innovation, of vigilance. Khyared Mohammadi M. and Rostami N., (2021) show the negative effects of inflation on business start-up costs as well as the positive effects of inflation on the entrepreneurial ecosystem in countries focused on efficiency. short and long term. Orji Olo J., and Opualla -Charles S., (2022) demonstrate that there is a statistically less significant positive relationship between the inflation rate and business development in Nigeria. Oumari L. and Adamou Illou M, (2022) show that inflation has no impact on growth and indirectly on entrepreneurship in Morocco whether in the long term or in the short term.

2. Other Determinants

Bedard M. (2016) notes a correlation between economic freedom and entrepreneurship in the provinces of Canada. The size of the state, the burden of taxes, property rights, trade openness and economic regulations all have an effect on business creation, Bedard M. (2016). Khyared Mohammadi M. and Rostami N., (2021) show the negative effects of tax rates and FDI on business creation costs as well as the positive effects of unemployment and access to financing for entrepreneurial activities in a country. Orji Olo J., and Opualla -Charles S., (2022) demonstrate that there is a statistically significant positive relationship between the unemployment rate and private sector productivity while the inflation rate was consistent with expected signs but statistically insufficient to explain business development in Nigeria.

2.1. Price Dynamics in Africa

Inflation is an important economic phenomenon that can have significant consequences on the economic and financial stability of a country. Economic theory suggests that the quantity of money in circulation in an economy is one of the main determinants of long-term inflation (Andrianady R.Josue And Rajaonarison Njakanasandratra, 2023;Yves Jegourel and Philippe Chalmin, 2017)

In the oil sector, companies have increased exploratory investments and new deposits have been identified, particularly on the African continent – for example in Mozambique, Senegal and Uganda (Augé, 2015). De Meo (2013) believes that investors' enthusiasm for the raw materials sector and a policy of boosting infrastructure spending explain the strength of the price boom.

2.2. Entrepreneurship in Africa

The place of women in developing countries in the economic sector has long been achieved through the informal sector (Tchouassi, 2005;, Tchouassi and al, 2018; Catherine Nicole Fouda Biloa Fouda,2015). Indeed, through their culture, women have always carried out activities that contribute to the economic support of the family: agricultural, artisanal, commercial production, etc (Tchouassi, (2005) . In 1976, the International Labor Office (ILO) estimated that, in most African countries, the informal sector offered at least 50% of urban employment, all sexes combined. Women, in the informal sector, are mainly concentrated in commerce. This activity encounters various constraints to development. The constraints they face are: the weight of the socio-cultural environment or mentalities, legal constraints, constraints of managing their business and. regulatory constraints (Sakhraoui, 1996), (Tchouassi, (2002), weak entrepreneurial skills, difficulties in accessing credit, macroeconomic instability and the absence of support and support services. Dzaka and al., (2020),

Doumbouya (2011 Notwithstanding, entrepreneurship in Africa is dynamic and requires investment in formal African entrepreneurship (Severino et al 2021). Self-organization, rigor and perseverance constitute its strengths. Tchouassi ; 2004, Josée St Pierre et al. 2015). Faced with global shocks, entrepreneurial activities are developing in regions receiving migrants and internally displaced persons, Levy (2006).

3. Price Dynamics and Entrepreneurship: Transmission Channels

At the limit of our readings, the literature relating to the analysis of the relationship between price dynamics and entrepreneurship is not direct. However, without claiming any exhaustiveness, four transmission channels can be highlighted: these are financial development, foreign direct investments and commercial opening and the return of natural resources.

3.1. The Financial Development Channel

The first channel through which price dynamics can affect entrepreneurship is that of financial development. As noted by Lin (2010), (Rousseau and Wachtel, 2001), (Azariadis and Smith, 1996), (Boyd and Smith, 1998; Huybens and Smith, 1999 & Tchouassi, G., & Niyonzima, T. G. (2024).). When it comes to the relationship between financial development and entrepreneurship, there is a significant literature that links these two concepts. According to Gueye (2023), Gueye 2022), Khouri (2021), Schumpeter (1912), Ghanem and Achouche (2015) Levine (1997). Several other authors like McGowan et al. (2018) and Arnold and Flach (2017) indicate that financial sector reforms have a positive and significant effect on the density of entry into oil-producing countries of new companies by increasing the factor productivity of companies, which will ultimately lead to a better allocation of resources. In the same vein, Cole et al. (2016), Andrews and Cingano (2014). Buera et al. (2011).

3.2. The Foreign Direct Investment Channel

The second transmission channel through which price dynamics can affect the entrepreneurial ecosystem lies in foreign direct investments (Tchouassi, G., & Niyonzima, T. G. (2024). This relationship is justified by authors such as Nnadi and Soobaroyen (2015;Sayek, 2009). On the contrary, Obiamaka et al (2011) note that it is possible that inflation in the host country can have a positive impact on FDI inflows provided that it does not exceed a certain threshold. It is important to highlight that multinational enterprises (MNEs) are the main players in GVCs and local businesses through technology transfer and various mentoring activities. Thus, the country can create part of the value chain while not necessarily having all the skills upstream (Cattanéo et al., 2013). FDI can promote technological transfers as well as the integration of local SMEs into value chains (Allard et al., 2016). They can also lead to the emergence of new activities and have an incentive role on the quality of human capital through demand for specific labor or through apprenticeship (Avris et al., 2016).

3.3. The Commercial Opening Channel

The third channel through which price dynamics can affect entrepreneurship is through trade openness. If the exchange rate does not change, it encourages imports and discourages exports (Bittencourt, 2011). The harmful effects of inflationary pressures on export production are exposed by (Bittencourt, 2011), Gueye (2023), Gueye (2022) and this depends on the upstream or downstream integration of the economy under study (Okah, 2020). Instead of following a linear value chain, in which products move sequentially from upstream to downstream, adding value at each stage (Baldwin and Venables 2013), value creation in service value chains can occur as a network of activities, such as platform-based communication or transportation networks (Miroudot, 2016). Fernandez-Stark et al. (2011) assert that trade in certain services has an attractive power for FDI (logistics, finance, design and marketing services). This conclusion is shared by ADB et al. (2014) and (Okah, 2020). A positive and indirect effect is observable through trade openness, financial development and corruption control (Taghouti Abdelbaki (2023)

3.4. The Natural Resource Revenue Channel

The fourth channel through which price dynamics can affect entrepreneurship is in the revenue of natural resources. Richard Auty (1993) renewed by Mary Kaldor (2023) evoke the theory of the curse of natural resources. This theory states that developing countries with abundant extractive resources (oil, gas and minerals) perform worse than countries without resources, whether in terms of economic growth, governance or social indicators. Under the term "paradox of abundance." Terry Lynn Karl (2013). A negative effect is observable through the return of natural resources and entrepreneurship.

3.5. Price Dynamics and Entrepreneurship: Lessons From the Literature

The empirical literature examining the impact of price fluctuations (exchange rates and market prices) on international trade is divided into three groups: some authors provide evidence of a negative effect while others support the Although there is a positive influence, another group of researchers suggests a mixed effect. Bedard M. (2016) notes a correlation between economic freedom and entrepreneurship in the provinces of Canada, inflation reduces economic freedom and in turn entrepreneurship since it makes long-term economic calculation more difficult.

Furthermore, entrepreneurship constitutes a set of resilience strategies following crises, entrepreneurship as a judgment. This approach would seem to explain entrepreneurship in Africa instead of entrepreneurship taken as innovation, of vigilance. Khyared Mohammadi M. and Rostami N., (2021) show the negative effects of tax rates, FDI, inflation on the costs of starting a business as well as the positive effects of unemployment and access to financing entrepreneurial activities in countries focused on short and long term efficiency. Also the negative effects of tax rates, the unemployment rate on business start-up costs and the positive effects of inflation and access to financing and the absence of FDI in countries in the short and long term. Orji Olo J., and Opualla -Charles S., (2022) demonstrate that there is a statistically significant positive relationship between the unemployment rate and private sector productivity while the inflation rate was consistent with expected signs but statistically insufficient to explain business development in Nigeria. Oumari L. and Adamou Illou M, (2022) show that inflation has no impact on growth and indirectly on entrepreneurship in Morocco whether in the long term or in the short term.

METHODOLOGY

Estimation Model and Technique

The objective is to empirically assess the effects of price dynamics on entrepreneurship in Africa. For this purpose, we use the dynamic specification inspired by the work of Farahadi et al., (2015), and taken up by Awoa et al., (2022). It consists of evaluating the effects of natural resources on entrepreneurship by taking into account the conditional effect of economic freedom. We draw inspiration from this relationship by taking into account inflation as a variable capturing price dynamics. The specification is as follows: where represents the country, time, entrepreneurship measure, a vector of control variables and our indicator for measuring price dynamics.

The dynamic specification of equation (1) makes it possible to take into consideration the influence of initial entrepreneurship conditions on the decisions taken by agents during a given period. Specifically, introducing the entrepreneurship measure on the right side of the equation allows us to take into account the inertia observed in the evolution of entrepreneurship conditions. Regarding our vector of control variables, it includes a measure of the economic situation, financial openness, trade and natural resources.

Estimation Technique

Equation (1) is estimated using the generalized method of moments (GMM) in a dynamic panel. The choice of this technique is justified by the endogeneity problems inherent in the estimation and analysis of this relationship. These result in particular from several factors. The first is linked to the dynamic structure of the equation. The presence of the lagged dependent variable indeed leads to questioning the statistical inference based on the estimation of a regression by ordinary least squares (OLS) or Least Square Dummy Variables (LSDV), the autoregressive term being correlated with the individual specific effects, resulting in the autocorrelation of the residuals (Nickel, 1981). The second is based on the double causality between our dependent variable (entrepreneurship) and the explanatory variables because the latter influences the explanatory variables. This endogeneity bias seems to particularly arise in the case of this chapter, because as suggested by the work of Bergman et *al* . (2016), Maltritz and Wüste (2015) and Foremny (2014), economic performance and institutions could condition entrepreneurship options in countries. This problem of double causality cannot be excluded for certain of our control variables, trade openness and foreign direct investment. The GMM estimator makes it possible to correct these two endogeneity biases, and also has the advantage, unlike the instrumental variables estimator proposed by Anderson and Hsiao (1982), of generating internal instruments. The variables assumed to be endogenous are then instrumented by their lagged values. However, it should be noted that this method makes it possible to correct endogeneity in the weak sense, but not endogeneity in the strong sense. In the sense that it assumes that the explanatory variables can be affected by the past and present achievements of the dependent variable, but not by the future achievements of the latter. There are two types of dynamic panel GMM estimators: the system GMM estimator (GMM-SYS) and the first difference GMM estimator (GMM-DIFF). The GMM-DIFF estimator of Arellano and Bond (1991) consists for each period of taking the first difference of the equation to be estimated in order to eliminate the effects specific to the different countries, and then of instrumenting the explanatory variables of the equation in first difference by their level values delayed by at least one period. However, this method does not make it possible to evaluate the effect of time-invariant factors. Furthermore, Blundell and Bond (1998) showed that the GMM-SYS estimator provides better results than the first difference one using Monte Carlo simulations. Indeed, the latter gives biased results in finite samples when the number of instruments is not high. This bias is all the more important when the variables are invariant over time, or the study period is short, or when the specific effects are high. However, the GMM-SYS estimator allows this limit to be lifted. In fact, it combines the equations in level with those in difference. These two types of equations are estimated simultaneously. In the difference equations, the variables are instrumented by their first differences while for the level equations, we use additional moment conditions assuming that the explanatory variables are stationary. In view of these developments, the estimator used in this chapter is the GMM-SYS of Blundell and Bond (1998). Although the GMM-SYS estimator is more efficient than the GMM-DIFF estimator, one of the major problems when estimating using GMMs is the proliferation of instruments. Indeed, the number of instruments grows quadratically with the study duration T when estimates are made using GMMs, Roodman (2009). But despite this significant limitation in the estimations using the GMM method, very few studies have been able to identify the correction mechanisms (Bergman and Hutchinson, 2016). However, to correct this problem of instrument proliferation, we use the approach developed by Roodman (2009). According to the latter, in order to limit the proliferation of instruments we can limit the maximum delay of the instrumental variables or use the *collapse command* in Stata. But to ensure the relevance of the instrumentation method, we use a range of tests. The first is Hansen's (1982) J overidentification test . The second test carried out is a test of exogeneity of the instruments used for the GMM. This is the " *difference -in-Hansen* " test (or Hansen's C test). These different tests are supplemented by the residual autocorrelation test of Arellano and Bond (1991). Thus, the instrumentation technique is validated if the null hypothesis of autocorrelation of the residuals is rejected at the first order and not at the second, and if Hansen's J and C tests are not rejected.

Data and Study Period

The data for this chapter comes from 38 African countries over the period 2006 to 2018. The choice of the sample is driven by the fact that the continent is full of enormous potential in terms of self-employment on the one hand and on the other hand, the availability of data. The choice of different variables is made according to existing literature. We use the World Bank's new business density indicator to measure entrepreneurship. This indicator takes into account the creation of new businesses and activities that promote creative destruction (Djankov et al., 2010). Inflation (CPI) corresponds to the annual consumer price index. The CPI includes all goods purchased by consumers, including foreign goods if the country imports final goods. As such, it is an interesting measure of price variations when one wishes to focus the analysis on consumers only (De Soyres and Franco, 2019). Gross domestic product per capita helps monitor the level of development and growth of entrepreneurship in countries. Indeed, countries that have a high level of GDP have high levels of entrepreneurship (Harris et al., 2009). Regarding foreign direct investments, the choice of this indicator can be explained by one factor. When foreign companies engage in local markets, they provide individuals with rapid access to expertise, allowing them to explore and capitalize on their entrepreneurial opportunities. Finally, we include trade openness as a variable which is a driver of entrepreneurship in Africa. Indeed, an open economy increases its degree of competitiveness on the international market (Awoa et al., 2022).

Results

The analysis of the results of this chapter proceeds in two stages. The first consists of taking into account inflation as a measure of price dynamics and verifying its effects on entrepreneurship. In the second step, the aim is to verify the effects obtained using data from the World Bank's consumer price index base.

PRICE DYNAMICS AND ENTREPRENEURSHIP: TAKING INTO ACCOUNT THE CONSUMER PRICE INDEX

Table 1 presents the results of the effects of inflation dynamics on entrepreneurship in Africa. Before approaching the analysis of these results, it is important to remember that their approval requires validation of the instruments used at the end of our estimation. It is carried out jointly by the autocorrelation tests of Arellano and Bond (1991) and the tests of Sargan and Hansen. The statistics obtained at the end of the estimation of the different estimates described by relation 1 show that these four tests are conclusive. They therefore attest that the instruments we used for the various estimates are valid. In addition, the Wald test establishes that the model is overall significant at the 1% level in our various estimates.

Table 1. Effect of price dynamics on entrepreneurship in Africa

	(1)	*(2)*
Variables	***Entrepreneurship rate***	***Number of records***
L.Entrepreneurship rate	*0.795****	
	(0.053)	
L. Number of records		*0.858****
		(0.066)
CPI	***-0.067*****	***-0.070*****
	(0.029)	***(0.031)***
IDE	*-0.011****	*-0.013****
	(0.002)	*(0.002)*

continued on following page

Table 1. Continued

	(1)	(2)
GDP	0.091	0.036
	(0.106)	(0.122)
Commercial opening	0.067	-0.253*
	(0.074)	(0.145)
Natural resources annuity	0.046	0.070
	(0.043)	(0.061)
Constant	-0.839	2.204***
	(0.846)	(0.582)
Comments	312	312
Number of countries	38	38
Instruments	25	25
Dummie Country	Yes	Yes
Ar1p	0.0770	0.0973
Ar2p	0.857	0.781
Sargan probability	0.0301	0.0103
Hansen probability	0.726	0.683
Wald statistics	416.7***	355.5***

Notes : Numbers in parentheses represent standard deviations. ***, **, * represent the 1%, 5% and 10% significance levels, respectively. The operator L. symbolizes that we are using a variable delayed to order 1.
Source: author

Table 1 groups together two specifications. In column 1 we estimate the effect of inflation dynamics on the rate of new business registration. In column 2 we estimate the effect of inflation dynamics on the number of new business registrations. We note that the coefficient associated with the inflation variable in columns 1 and 2 is negative and significant at the 1% level. This shows that inflation has a negative influence on entrepreneurship in Africa. In other words, a 1% increase in the inflation rate leads to a 6.7% decrease in the entrepreneurship rate. This is an important finding as it highlights the need for policymakers to focus on developing strategies to reduce inflation in order to increase entrepreneurship in Africa. This could be done by reducing public spending, increasing taxation or introducing tighter monetary policies. High levels of inflation can cause a decline in consumer confidence, which can lead to a decrease in demand for goods and services. This can reduce the need for entrepreneurs to enter the market, thereby decreasing the rate of entrepreneurship. Additionally, high levels of inflation can also lead to higher costs for businesses, leading them to reduce production and making it more difficult for new entrepreneurs to enter the market. Similarly, a 1% increase in the inflation rate leads to a 7% decline in the number of new business registrations. This can lead to a reduction in economic growth and development. It can also have a negative effect on the job market in general, as fewer businesses mean fewer jobs. This is because businesses need capital to get started, and when the costs of goods and services increase, the capital needed to start a business becomes more difficult to acquire. This reduces the number of people willing and able to start their own businesses, which can lead to lower economic growth and employment opportunities. Turning to the control variables, our results show that foreign direct investment (FDI) flows reduce entrepreneurial opportunities in Africa. Indeed, in columns 1 and 2, the coefficients of the FDI variable are negative and significant at the 1% level. A 1% increase in FDI inflows leads to a 1.1% decline in the business creation rate and a 1.2% decline in the new business registration rate. These results are consistent with those of Awoa et al (2022). They suggest that inward FDI flows may pose a barrier to entrepreneurship in African countries. Policymakers should be aware of this effect when implementing FDI-based development strategies. This phenomenon can be explained by the fact that FDI often competes with local companies and can lead to the crowding out of local companies due to the influx of foreign competition. As a result, the creation and registration of new businesses is negatively affected. Policymakers should therefore be wary of the potential downsides of FDI and take steps to mitigate them, for example by supporting local businesses or encouraging foreign investors to partner with local entrepreneurs. In India, for example, the government launched a program of mentoring, business advice and other support for local businesses to help them compete with foreign companies. In the case of business creations, the coefficient is only significant for new business registrations (column 2). Indeed, a 1% increase in the degree of trade openness leads to a 25.3% reduction in new business registrations. This result is in line with the same logic as that obtained with incoming foreign direct investments.

PRICE DYNAMICS AND ENTREPRENEURSHIP: TAKING INTO ACCOUNT ALTERNATIVE MEASURES OF THE COMMODITY PRICE INDEX

In this section, we examine the effects of alternative measures of price dynamics on entrepreneurship. In Table 2 two price indices are used. These are the energy product price index and the non-energy product price index. The statistics obtained at the end of the estimation of the different estimates show that these four validation tests of the technique are conclusive. Our results show that the commodity price index increases entrepreneurship in Africa. Indeed, the two variants of the raw material price index present positive and significant coefficients at the 1 and 5%

thresholds. Thus, an increase in the energy raw materials price index of 1% leads to an increase in entrepreneurship of 14.2 and 12.1% respectively (column 1 and 3). While an increase in the non-energy commodity price index leads to an increase in entrepreneurship by 41.1 and 44.3% in Africa (column 2 and 4). This indicates that an increase in commodity prices can have a positive effect on entrepreneurship in Africa. Furthermore, the increase in the price of non-energy commodities has a greater effect on entrepreneurship than the increase in the price of energy commodities. This suggests that better access to non-energy commodities, such as agricultural products, can lead to higher levels of entrepreneurship in Africa. This can be attributed to the fact that these products are relatively cheaper to produce and therefore can be used to create more profitable businesses. Furthermore, the increased availability of these commodities can also lead to increased economic activity and investments in the region. For example, the increased availability of maize in East Africa has led to the emergence of small-scale milling businesses, which provide an important source of income for local populations.

Table 2. Effect of alternative price measures on entrepreneurship in Africa

	(1)	*(2)*	*(3)*	*(4)*
Variables	*Entrepreneurship rate*		*Number of records*	
L.Entrepreneurship rate	*0.697****	*0.745****		
	(0.067)	*(0.051)*		
L. Number of records			*0.771****	*0.803****
			(0.049)	*(0.039)*
Energy	***0.142*****		***0.121*****	
	(0.060)		***(0.052)***	
No Energy		***0.411******		***0.443******
		(0.136)		***(0.160)***
IDE	*0.013***	*0.007*	*0.020***	*0.013**
	(0.006)	*(0.005)*	*(0.008)*	*(0.008)*
GDP	*0.174**	*0.109**	*0.150**	*0.082*
	(0.088)	*(0.064)*	*(0.089)*	*(0.073)*
Commercial opening	*0.091*	*0.004*	*-0.420****	*-0.387****
	(0.082)	*(0.094)*	*(0.118)*	*(0.117)*
Natural resources annuity	*-0.083****	*-0.093****	*-0.011*	*-0.032*
	(0.027)	*(0.023)*	*(0.043)*	*(0.036)*
Constant	*-2.276****	*-2,562****	*2,064****	*0.784*
	(0.773)	*(0.701)*	*(0.566)*	*(0.746)*

continued on following page

Table 2. Continued

	(1)	(2)	(3)	(4)
Comments	317	317	317	317
Number of countries	38	38	38	38
Instruments	25	25	25	25
Dummie Country	Yes	Yes	Yes	Yes
Ar1p	0.0696	0.0655	0.0668	0.0670
Ar2p	0.893	0.978	0.791	0.872
Sargan p	0.00264	0.00444	0.00354	0.00463
Hansen	0.294	0.318	0.305	0.367
Wald statistics	124.5***	218.3***	108.3***	132.8***

Notes : Numbers in parentheses represent standard deviations. ***, **, * represent the 1%, 5% and 10% significance levels, respectively. The operator L. symbolizes that we are using a variable delayed to order 1.
Source: author

In terms of control variables, inward FDI increases entrepreneurial opportunities (column 1, 3 and 4) as much as gross domestic product (column 1 to 4) in Africa. The coefficients of the two variables are positive and significant at the 5 and 10% thresholds. The increased availability of maize and the presence of FDI have both contributed to the growth of small businesses in East Africa. These businesses have created jobs and are helping to reduce poverty levels in the region. In addition, they help stimulate the local economy. Inward FDI enabled the development of infrastructure and technology that helped increase the efficiency of local businesses. This allowed them to produce more goods and services, which translated into increased employment opportunities and income. Furthermore, the presence of inward FDI has also provided local entrepreneurs with access to capital, enabling them to expand their businesses and create more jobs. All of these factors have contributed to the growth of small businesses in East Africa, which is helping to reduce poverty levels in the region. However, trade openness and natural resource rents are reducing entrepreneurial opportunities in Africa. The coefficients of these variables are negative and significant at the 1% level, such that a percentage increase in the degree of trade openness and natural resource rents leads to a percentage reduction in entrepreneurship in Africa. This suggests that Africa needs to diversify its sources of economic development, particularly by developing the services sector. Policymakers can also promote entrepreneurship by implementing policies to support small and medium-sized businesses. Additionally, access to finance needs to be improved. This would create more job opportunities for the workforce and allow more people to access the capital they need to start their own businesses. Additionally, diversifying sources of economic development will help reduce the risk of relying too heavily on a single industry, such as the oil industry.

Analysis of the Robustness of the Results

This analysis consists of integrating into our different specifications the sub-components of the price index of non-energy basic products. According to the World Bank, this index, unlike that of energy commodities, is fragmented into several sub-indexes. Among them, we distinguish: prices of agricultural products, prices of dairy products, prices of fertilizers, prices of food products, prices of raw materials and prices of other food products. These different sub-indexes contribute unequally to the construction of the overall price index of non-energy basic products. We sequentially examine these prices across different measures of entrepreneurship. In tables 3 and 4, an approval of the results requires validation of the instruments used at the end of our estimation. It is carried out jointly by the autocorrelation tests of Arellano and Bond (1991) and the tests of Sargan and Hansen. The statistics obtained at the end of the estimation of the different estimates described by relation 1 show that these four tests are conclusive. The number of instruments is less than the number of countries and the Sargan and Hansen statistics are all above the 10% threshold, which allows us not to reject the hypothesis of validity of lagged variables in level and difference as instruments.

Table 3. Effect of sub-dimensions of the non-energy commodity price index on the entrepreneurship rate in Africa

	(1)	(2)	(3)	(4)	(5)	(6)
Variables	**Entrepreneurship rate**					
L.Entrepreneurship rate	0.755***	0.716***	0.737***	0.699***	0.801***	0.713***
	(0.056)	(0.062)	(0.101)	(0.066)	(0.047)	(0.077)
Agriculture	**0.364***					
	(0.199)					
Fertilizer		**0.144*****				
		(0.052)				
Drinks			**-0.372*****			
			(0.115)			
Foodstuffs				**0.429****		
				(0.200)		
Raw materials					**0.228***	
					(0.114)	
Other food products						**-0.594*****
						(0.194)

continued on following page

Table 3. Continued

	(1)	(2)	(3)	(4)	(5)	(6)
IDE	0.009*	0.002	-0.010***	0.008*	0.005	0.006
	(0.005)	(0.003)	(0.002)	(0.004)	(0.005)	(0.008)
GDP	0.090	0.166*	0.623***	0.138**	0.029	0.231**
	(0.062)	(0.083)	(0.196)	(0.066)	(0.063)	(0.102)
Commercial opening	0.028	0.018	-0.366**	0.015	0.017	0.068
	(0.098)	(0.091)	(0.170)	(0.099)	(0.090)	(0.096)
Natural resources annuity	-0.091***	-0.089***	0.044	-0.102***	-0.093***	-0.080**
	(0.022)	(0.017)	(0.059)	(0.024)	(0.028)	(0.032)
Constant	-2.294***	-1,869**	-1.666	-2,928***	-1.133*	0.733
	(0.798)	(0.723)	(1.001)	(0.988)	(0.566)	(0.858)
Comments	317	317	317	317	317	317
Number of countries	38	38	38	38	38	38
Instruments	25	25	25	25	25	25
Dummie Country	Yes	Yes	Yes	Yes	Yes	Yes
Ar1p	0.0690	0.0744	0.0726	0.0786	0.0590	0.0638
Ar2p	0.986	0.903	0.793	0.926	0.954	0.744
Sargan	0.00132	0.00242	0.100	0.00151	0.00158	0.00340
Hansen	0.284	0.382	0.820	0.330	0.198	0.180
Wald statistics	128.2***	285.9***	114.1***	151.3***	195.8***	236.9***

Notes : Numbers in parentheses represent standard deviations. ***, **, * represent the 1%, 5% and 10% significance levels, respectively. The operator L. symbolizes that we are using a variable delayed to order 1.
Source: author

Considering the results obtained in Table 3, two trends emerge. It can be distinguished that the sub-dimensions of the non-energy commodity price index can lead to positive and negative effects on the rate of entrepreneurship in Africa. Prices of agricultural products, fertilizers, foodstuffs and raw materials improve the rate of entrepreneurship in Africa (column 1, 2, 4 and 5). The effect varies between 14.4% and 42.9%. This result is similar to that obtained under the overall energy and non-energy commodity price indices obtained in Table 2. This indicates that rising prices of non-energy commodities can have a positive impact on the entrepreneurship in Africa. Indeed, better access to non-energy commodities such as agricultural products can increase levels of entrepreneurship in Africa. This helps create more jobs and reduce poverty. Diversification also helps spread the wealth generated by different industries and reduces instability if a particular industry slows down. By investing in a wide range of sectors, African countries can achieve sustainable economic development, reduce poverty and create more jobs. However, the price of drinks and other food products have a negative impact on the rate of entrepreneurship in Africa (column 3 and 6). This result is in line with that obtained in Table 1 for the case of inflation. An increase in these price indices by 1% leads to an increase of 37.2% and 59.4% in the entrepreneurship rate in Africa. A plausible explanation for this result can be formulated as follows. This is because small businesses find it difficult to compete with large corporations due to the high cost of goods. As a result, it is difficult for small businesses to remain profitable and viable, preventing entrepreneurs from starting their business and becoming successful Tchouassi, G., & Tchougon, EFJ (2022). High food and drink prices lead to increased costs for small businesses, making it harder for them to be cheaper than larger businesses. This results in less competition and increased prices, which can make goods more difficult for consumers to purchase, further reducing demand for small businesses. Additionally, rising food and beverage prices may also make it difficult for entrepreneurs to obtain capital to start their businesses, as potential investors may be hesitant to invest in a struggling sector. As a result, small businesses find themselves in a precarious situation, with lower demand and fewer resources to fill the gap.

Table 4. Effect of sub-dimensions of the non-energy commodity price index on the number of new business registrations in Africa

	(1)	(2)	(3)	(4)	(5)	(6)
VARIABLES	**Number of records**					
L. Number of records	0.808***	0.795***	0.851***	0.774***	0.875***	0.832***
	(0.044)	(0.048)	(0.063)	(0.050)	(0.043)	(0.052)
Agriculture	**0.394***					
	(0.203)					
Fertilizer		**0.137*****				
		(0.048)				
Drinks			**-0.323*****			
			(0.109)			
Foodstuffs				**0.375****		
				(0.172)		
Raw materials					**0.299****	
					(0.141)	
Other food products						**-0.555*****
						(0.147)
IDE	0.015**	0.003	-0.010***	0.015**	-0.003	0.013
	(0.007)	(0.004)	(0.002)	(0.007)	(0.006)	(0.010)

continued on following page

Table 4. Continued

	(1)	(2)	(3)	(4)	(5)	(6)
GDP	0.089	0.119	0.362**	0.141*	-0.033	0.149
	(0.077)	(0.072)	(0.158)	(0.078)	(0.048)	(0.090)
Commercial opening	-0.355***	-0.413***	-0.470**	-0.448***	-0.384***	-0.382***
	(0.121)	(0.100)	(0.188)	(0.135)	(0.111)	(0.103)
Natural resources annuity	-0.027	-0.026	0.042	-0.018	-0.031	0.003
	(0.040)	(0.024)	(0.064)	(0.039)	(0.026)	(0.043)
Constant	0.781	2,040***	1,894*	1,098	1,805*	4,451***
	(0.841)	(0.588)	(1.018)	(0.689)	(0.904)	(0.911)
Comments	317	317	317	317	317	317
Number of countries	38	38	38	38	38	38
Instruments	25	25	25	25	25	25
Dummie Country	Yes	Yes	Yes	Yes	Yes	Yes
Ar1p	0.0689	0.0767	0.0635	0.0754	0.0663	0.0644
Ar2p	0.878	0.988	0.796	0.783	0.966	0.884
Sargan	0.00150	0.00222	0.0272	0.00171	0.0195	0.000748
Hansen	0.347	0.519	0.566	0.355	0.260	0.292
Wald statistics	123.2	115.8	46.85	118.2	81.14	218.1

Notes: Numbers in parentheses represent standard deviations. ***, **, * represent the 1%, 5% and 10% significance levels, respectively. The operator L. symbolizes that we are using a variable delayed to order 1.
Source: author

The same analysis can be done in Table 4. In this table, we also observe the effects of price indices in two categories. Prices of agricultural products, fertilizers, food and raw materials improve the number of new business registrations in Africa (columns 1, 2, 4 and 5). The effect varies from 13.7% to 39.4%. While the price of drinks and other food products has a negative impact on the number of new business registrations in Africa (columns 3 and 6). These results suggest that prices of agricultural products, fertilizers, food and raw materials have a positive impact on the economics of new business registrations in Africa. This indicates that a reduction in the price of these products can lead to a reduction in the number of new businesses registered in Africa. This could potentially lead to a more stable and prosperous economy in the region. This relationship is similar to that of two cogs in a machine: if the price of one falls, more businesses will be registered, allowing the "machine" of the economy to run more smoothly and more efficiently.

DISCUSSION

Entrepreneurship is today a major theme with an ideological content marked by the "enterprise" of the world and which belongs to the current of institutionalization of the organization, but which does not necessarily constitute an institution. To this end, it is considered a social activity occupying a major place in contemporary societies. Several empirical research studies have been the subject of the dichotomy of the relationships between price dynamics and the entrepreneurial ecosystem due to several methodological and even epistemological aspects. Indeed, some authors argue that inflation is a demotivating factor for entrepreneurship. While others believe that price dynamics are a stimulus to entrepreneurship in Africa. The empirical literature examining the impact of price fluctuations (exchange rates and market prices) on international trade is divided into three groups: some authors provide evidence of a negative effect while others support the Although there is a positive influence, another group of researchers suggests a mixed effect. Bedard M. (2016) notes a correlation between economic freedom and entrepreneurship in the provinces of Canada, inflation reduces economic freedom and in turn entrepreneurship since it makes long-term economic calculation more difficult. Also, Khyared Mohammadi M. and Rostami N., (2021) show the negative effects of tax rates, FDI, inflation on the costs of business creation as well as the positive effects of unemployment and access to financing entrepreneurial activities in countries focused on short and long term efficiency. Also, the negative effects of tax rates, the unemployment rate on business start-up costs and the positive effects of inflation and access to financing and the absence of FDI in countries in the short and long term.

The results of our research reinforce the conclusions of Bedard and Khyared Mohammadi M. and Rostami in Africa. This shows that inflation has a negative influence on entrepreneurship in Africa. In other words, a 1% increase in the inflation rate leads to a 6.7% decrease in the entrepreneurship rate. This is an important finding as it highlights the need for policymakers to focus on developing strategies to reduce inflation in order to increase entrepreneurship in Africa. High levels of inflation can cause a decline in consumer confidence, which can lead to a decrease in demand for goods and services. This can reduce the need for entrepreneurs to enter the market, thereby decreasing the rate of entrepreneurship. Additionally, high levels of inflation can also lead to higher costs for businesses, leading them to reduce production and making it more difficult for new entrepreneurs to enter the market. Similarly, a 1% increase in the inflation rate leads to a 7% decline in the number of new business registrations. This can lead to reduced economic growth and development. It can also have a negative effect on the job market in general, as fewer businesses mean fewer jobs. This is because businesses need capital to get started, and when the costs of goods and services increase, the capital needed to start a business becomes more difficult to acquire. This reduces the number of people willing and able to start their own businesses, which can lead to lower economic growth and employment opportunities. However, Orji Olo J., and Opualla -Charles S., (2022) demonstrate that there is a statistically significant positive relationship between the unemployment rate and private sector productivity while the inflation rate was consistent with expected signs but statistically insufficient to explain business development in Nigeria. Our results are the same as those of previously mentioned work and show that the commodity price index increases entrepreneurship in Africa. Indeed, the two variants of the raw material price index present positive and significant coefficients at the 1 and 5% thresholds. Thus, an increase in the energy raw materials price index of 1% leads to an increase in entrepreneurship of 14.2 and 12.1% respectively (column 1 and 3). While an increase in the non-energy commodity price index leads to an increase in entrepreneurship by 41.1 and 44.3% in Africa (column 2 and 4). This indicates that an increase in commodity prices can have a positive effect on entrepreneurship in Africa. Furthermore, the increase in the price of non-energy commodities has a greater effect on entrepreneurship than the increase in the price of energy commodities. Oumari L. and Adamou Illou M, (2022) show that inflation has no impact on growth and indirectly on entrepreneurship in Morocco whether in the long term or in the short term. Our results differ from these in the sense that Morocco taken in isolation shows that inflation does not influence entrepreneurship and contrary to our analyses, we found negative effects at the level of the whole of Africa by the CPI and positive by dividing the index into prices of energy and non-energy products. Intercountry effects are more robust than those taken in isolation.

CONCLUSION AND IMPLICATIONS IN TERMS OF ECONOMIC POLICIES

The level of entrepreneurship in Africa remains the lowest in the world compared to developed and developing countries. Throughout the world, Africa is characterized by high inflation rates. The hypothesis of this study assumes that price dynamics would have positive and negative effects on entrepreneurship in African countries. This chapter questions the influence of price dynamics on entrepreneurship in Africa.

The results of this chapter show that price dynamics exert nuanced effects on entrepreneurship in Africa depending on the model and robustness applied. The CPI negatively influences entrepreneurship in Africa while the prices of energetic and non-energetic products have positive effects on entrepreneurship. The robustness analysis demonstrates that the sub-dimensions of the non-energy commodity price index lead to positive and negative effects on entrepreneurship. Policymakers should develop strategies to reduce inflation by reducing public spending, raising taxes and introducing tight monetary policies, promoting better access to non-energy commodities by regulating the beverage sector, implementing policies to support SMEs, boosting access to financing from popular banks and requiring FDI to partner with local entrepreneurs, business facilitation policies thus improving the business climate through revitalization of One-Stop Shops, strengthening the SME mentoring program through FDI. That African governments implement the strengthening of programs for the creation of incubators and subsidies for entrepreneurs through the creation of common support funds for entrepreneurs.

On the macroeconomic level, policies for resilience to global shocks are possible, in particular interest rate policy, exchange rate policy, income policy, counter-cyclical budgetary policies and targeted monetary policy. The policies of setting and monitoring the prices of certain products through the creation of a Price Surveillance and Regulation Authority (ASRP) in all African countries. Public authorities therefore have important work to do before them to raise the level of competitiveness and strengthen the entrepreneurial ecosystem through university education internalizing the entrepreneurial ecosystem. This involves modernizing existing infrastructures in order to align them with global standards. Pursue the policy of liberalization and opening of African economies to stimulate innovation and the creation of new wealth. Finally, decision-makers should consider encouraging investments in formal entrepreneurship.

The findings drawn from this chapter make important contributions to the academic discourse and practical applications of entrepreneurship in economics. From an academic point of view, this study enriches the understanding of the economic policies applied by States around their entrepreneurial ecosystem. Future research can therefore study and evaluate whether price dynamics influence entrepreneurship by categories of male, female and youth actors in Africa.

REFERENCES

Abdallah, R., Juaidi, A., Savaş, M. A., Çamur, H., Albatayneh, A., Abdala, S., & Manzano-Agugliaro, F. (2021). A critical review on recycling composite waste using pyrolysis for sustainable development. *Energies*, 14(18), 5748. DOI: 10.3390/en14185748

Addisu, T. (2020). Price volatility and food insecurity the case of Ethiopia [PhD Thesis]. Ph.D. Thesis, Wageningen University and Research Center.

Afonso, A., & Blanco-Arana, M. C. (2022). Financial and economic development in the context of the global 2008-09 financial crisis. *Inter Economics*, 169, 30–42. DOI: 10.1016/j.inteco.2021.11.006

Allard, C. Kriljenko, MJIC, Gonzalez-Garcia, MJR, Kitsios, E., Trevino, MJP, & Chen, MW (2016). Trade integration and global value chains in sub-Saharan Africa: In pursuit of the missing link. International Monetary Fund.

AMAMEUR, L. (2022). Social Entrepreneurship, a theory under construction and an opportunity for the unemployed to become entrepreneurs. *International Review of Management Sciences*, 5(1).

Anderson, T. W., & Hsiao, C. (1982). Formulation and estimation of dynamic models using panel data. *Journal of Econometrics*, 18(1), 47–82. DOI: 10.1016/0304-4076(82)90095-1

Andrews, D., & Cingano, F. (2014). Public policy and resource allocation: Evidence from firms in OECD countries. *Economic Policy*, 29(78), 253–296. DOI: 10.1111/1468-0327.12028

Andrews, D., Gal, P., & Witheridge, W. (2018). A genius in a bottle?: Globalization, competition and inflation. OECD Economics Department Working Papers 1462, OECD Publishing.

ANDRIANADY. J., & Njakanasandratra, R. (2023). Monetary Inflation Relationship in Madagascar: A DSGE Model Analysis. Available at SSRN 4453195.

Andrianady, JR, & Rajaonarison, NR (2023). Effect of a monetary shock on inflation: An approach using a DSGE model.

Arellano, M., & Bond, S. (1991). Some tests of specification for panel data: Monte Carlo evidence and an application to employment equations. *The Review of Economic Studies*, 58(2), 277–297. DOI: 10.2307/2297968

Arnold, J. M., & Flach, L. (2017). *Who Gains from Better Access to Credit?* Credit Reform and Reallocation of Resources.

Auty, R. M. (1994). Industrial policy reform in six large newly industrializing countries: The resource curse thesis. World Development, 22(1), 11–26.

Avis, R. (2022). Social Impacts of China's Approach to Development

Awoa, P. A., Efogo, F. O., & Ondoa, H. A. (2023). Oil dependence and entrepreneurship: Non-linear evidence. *Economic Systems*, 47(1), 101059. DOI: 10.1016/j.ecosys.2022.101059

Azariadis, C. (1996). The economics of poverty traps part one: Complete markets. *Journal of Economic Growth*, 1(4), 449–486. DOI: 10.1007/BF00150197

Baldwin, R., & Venables, A. J. (2013). Spiders and snakes: Offshoring and agglomeration in the global economy. *Journal of International Economics*, 90(2), 245–254. DOI: 10.1016/j.jinteco.2013.02.005

Bédard, M. (2016a). Entrepreneurship and economic freedom: An analysis of empirical studies. Institute economy of Montreal.

Bédard, M. (2016b). *Entrepreneurship and Economic Freedom an Analysis of Empirical Studies*. Montreal Economic Institute.

Ben Abdallah, M., Fekete-Farkas, M., & Lakner, Z. (2021). Exploring the link between food security and food price dynamics: A bibliometric analysis. *Agriculture*, 11(3), 263. DOI: 10.3390/agriculture11030263

Bergman, U. M., & Hutchison, M. (2020). Fiscal procyclicality in emerging markets: The role of institutions and economic conditions. *International Finance*, 23(2), 196–214. DOI: 10.1111/infi.12375

Bittencourt, M. (2012). Financial development and economic growth in Latin America: Is Schumpeter right? *Journal of Policy Modeling*, 34(3), 341–355. DOI: 10.1016/j.jpolmod.2012.01.012

Blundell, R., & Bond, S. (2000). GMM Estimation with persistent panel data: An application to production functions. *Econometric Reviews*, 19(3), 321–340. DOI: 10.1080/07474930008800475

Boutillier, S. (2008). The social entrepreneur, an entrepreneur socialized in an entrepreneurial society? *Humanism and Business*, 5, 41–60.

Boutillier, S., & Uzunidis, D. (2017). *The Entrepreneur: The Economic Function of Free Enterprise* (Vol. 8). ISTE Group.

Buera, F. J., Kaboski, J. P., & Shin, Y. (2011). Finance and development: A tale of two sectors. *The American Economic Review*, 101(5), 1964–2002. DOI: 10.1257/aer.101.5.1964

Cattanéo, F., Guillard, J., Diouf, S., O'Rourke, J., & Grimardias, D. (2021). Mitigation of ecological impacts on fish of large sediment reservoir management through controlled flushing–The case of the Verbois dam (Rhône River, Switzerland). *The Science of the Total Environment*, 756, 144053. DOI: 10.1016/j.scitotenv.2020.144053 PMID: 33279192

Cattaneo, O., Gereffi, G., Miroudot, S., & Taglioni, D. (2013). Joining, upgrading and being competitive in global value chains: A strategic framework. World Bank Policy Research Working Paper, 6406.

Cypher, J. M., & Dietz, J. L. (2008). *The process of economic development*. Routledge. DOI: 10.4324/9780203895061

Danil, L., & Fordian, D. (2022). Does Rural Entrepreneurship Performance Support Sustainable Development Goals (SDGs) and Sustainable Entrepreneurship? *Review of Integrative Business and Economics Research*, 11, 145–165.

De Meo, E. (2013). Are Commodity Prices Driven by Fundamentals? *Economic Notes*, 42(1), 19–46. DOI: 10.1111/ecno.12001

De Soyres, F., & Franco, S. (2019). Inflation dynamics and global value chains. World Bank Policy Research Working Paper, 9090.

Dimitropoulou, A. (2021). *World's Most Entrepreneurial Countries*. World's Most Entrepreneurial Countries.

Djankov, S., Ganser, T., McLiesh, C., Ramalho, R., & Shleifer, A. (2010). The effect of corporate taxes on investment and entrepreneurship. *American Economic Journal. Macroeconomics*, 2(3), 31–64. DOI: 10.1257/mac.2.3.31

Doubogan Unibon Y. & Aliha G. (2020), the growing use of PPPs in French-speaking Africa: what opportunities for entrepreneurship? Doumbouya ML (2011), entrepreneurial monitoring in Africa: the cases of Guinean companies.

Dzaka-Kikouta, T., Kamavuako-Diwavova, J., & Bitemo-Ndiwulu, X. Makiese- Ndoma, F., Manika Manzongani, JP, & Masamba-Lulendo, V. (2020). Entrepreneurship of Young Francophone Africans in the Republic of Congo and the Democratic Republic of Congo: Challenges and Perspectives. OFE-RP Project Report, 3.

Engel, C., Mark, N. C., West, K. D., Rogoff, K., & Rossi, B. (2007). Exchange rate models are not as bad as you think [with comments and discussion]. *NBER Macroeconomics Annual*, 22, 381–473. DOI: 10.1086/ma.22.25554969

Ephrem, AN, & Murimbika, M. (2023a). Development and validation of an individual entrepreneurial potential new measurement scale. Journal of Research in Marketing and Entrepreneurship.

Ephrem, A. N., & Murimbika, M. (2023b). I wish I had a paid job or a business: A moderated effect of entrepreneurial potential on career choice regret. *Career Development International*, 28(5), 518–535. DOI: 10.1108/CDI-09-2022-0249

Ephrem, A. N., Nguezet, P. M. D., Charmant, I. K., Murimbika, M., Awotide, B. A., Tahirou, A., Lydie, M. N., & Manyong, V. (2021). Entrepreneurial motivation, psychological capital, and business success of young entrepreneurs in the drc. *Sustainability (Basel)*, 13(8), 4087. DOI: 10.3390/su13084087

Farahani, S. S., Raman, V., & Murray, R. M. (2015). Robust model predictive control for signal temporal logic synthesis. *IFAC-PapersOnLine*, 48(27), 323–328. DOI: 10.1016/j.ifacol.2015.11.195

Fayolle, A., Ben Salah, A., Ben Salah, I., & Belkacem, L. (2010). Effectiveness of incubators in the creation of innovative businesses: Case of Tunisia 1. *Innovations*, 3, 157–179. DOI: 10.3917/inno.033.0157

Fernandez-Stark, K., & Gereffi, G. (2019). Global value chain analysis: A primer. In *Handbook on global value chains* (pp. 54–76). Edward Elgar Publishing. DOI: 10.4337/9781788113779.00008

Foremny, D. (2014). Sub-national deficits in European countries: The impact of fiscal rules and tax autonomy. *European Journal of Political Economy*, 34, 86–110. DOI: 10.1016/j.ejpoleco.2014.01.003

Fouda, CNFB (2014). Entrepreneurial dynamism of Cameroonian women: Case studies of business development.

Gérard, T., & Thomas, G. N. (2023). The Past and the Future Effects of Russian-Ukrainian Conflict on the Democratic Republic of Congo Economic Policy. *Futurity Economics&Law*, 3(3), 201–218.

Ghanem, Y., & Achouche, M. (2015). Impact of financial development on the dynamics of business creation: Evidence from panel data on MENA countries. https://mpra.ub.uni-muenchen.de/id/eprint/68125

GUEYE, TN. (2022). Role of social capital on entrepreneurial effects on economic growth in developing countries: An empirical analysis. *American Scientific Journal*, 3(15), 112–141.

GUEYE, TN. (2023). Impact of entrepreneurial dynamics on economic growth: Mediating role of social capital. *Economic Managerial Alternatives*, 5(1), 260–280.

Gupta, P., Chauhan, S., Paul, J., & Jaiswal, M. P. (2020). Social entrepreneurship research: A review and future research agenda. *Journal of Business Research*, 113, 209–229. DOI: 10.1016/j.jbusres.2020.03.032

Gupta, V., MacMillan, I. C., & Surie, G. (2004). Entrepreneurial leadership: Developing and measuring a cross-cultural construct. *Journal of Business Venturing*, 19(2), 241–260. DOI: 10.1016/S0883-9026(03)00040-5

Hansen, L. P. (1982). Large sample properties of generalized method of moments estimators. *Econometrica*, 50(4), 1029–1054. DOI: 10.2307/1912775

Harris, P. A., Taylor, R., Thielke, R., Payne, J., Gonzalez, N., & Conde, J. G. (2009). Research electronic data capture (REDCap)—A metadata-driven methodology and workflow process for providing translational research informatics support. *Journal of Biomedical Informatics*, 42(2), 377–381. DOI: 10.1016/j.jbi.2008.08.010 PMID: 18929686

Heather, M. C. (2019). OECD SME and Entrepreneurship Outlook 2019.

Henry, C., Hill, F., & Leitch, C. (2005). Entrepreneurship education and training: Can entrepreneurship be taught? Part I. *Education + Training*, 47(2), 98–111. DOI: 10.1108/00400910510586524

Herkenhoff, K., Phillips, G., & Cohen-Cole, E. (2016). The impact of consumer credit access on employment, earnings and entrepreneurship. National Bureau of Economic Research. https://www.nber.org/papers/w22846

Herron, L., & Robinson, R. B.Jr. (1993). A structural model of the effects of entrepreneurial characteristics on venture performance. *Journal of Business Venturing*, 8(3), 281–294. DOI: 10.1016/0883-9026(93)90032-Z

Holmes, P., & McGowan, F. (1998). Public service reform in the United Kingdom. Privatization, regulation and liberalization. *Science and Society*, 43(1), 93–109.

Huybens, E., & Smith, B. D. (1999). Inflation, financial markets and long-run real activity. *Journal of Monetary Economics*, 43(2), 283–315. DOI: 10.1016/S0304-3932(98)00060-9

Hwang, D.-W., Lee, Y.-W., & Kim, G. (2005). Large submarine groundwater discharge and benthic eutrophication in Bangdu Bay on volcanic Jeju Island, Korea. *Limnology and Oceanography*, 50(5), 1393–1403. DOI: 10.4319/lo.2005.50.5.1393

Isenberg, D. (2011). *The Entrepreneurship Ecosystem Strategy as a New Paradigm for Economic Policy: Principles for Cultivating Entrepreneurship*. The Babson Entrepreneurship Ecosystem Project.

Jegourel, Y., & Chalmin, P. (2017). The Dynamics of the Price of Raw Materials and Industrial Strategies in African Producer Countries: What are the Challenges? International Development Policy| International Journal of Development Policy, 8.1.

Karl, T. L. (1998). The Paradox of Plenty: Oil booms and petro -states. Journal of energy literature, 4, 65–65.

Kerr, W., & Nanda, R. (2009). *Financing constraints and entrepreneurship*. National Bureau of Economic Research. DOI: 10.3386/w15498

Kim, D.-H., Lin, S.-C., & Suen, Y.-B. (2010). Dynamic effects of trade openness on financial development. *Economic Modelling*, 27(1), 254–261. DOI: 10.1016/j.econmod.2009.09.005

Kuratko, D. F., Fisher, G., Bloodgood, J. M., & Hornsby, J. S. (2017). The paradox of new venture legitimation within an entrepreneurial ecosystem. *Small Business Economics*, 49(1), 119–140. DOI: 10.1007/s11187-017-9870-x

Levy- Tadjine, T. (2006). Immigrant entrepreneurship and its support in France. *Life & Economic Sciences*, 4, 31–45.

Lin, X. (2010). The diaspora solution to innovation capacity development: Immigrant entrepreneurs in the contemporary world. *Thunderbird International Business Review*, 52(2), 123–136. DOI: 10.1002/tie.20319

Lopes Valadares, J., Emmendoerfer, L., Christina Resende, T., Morais, A., & Cerqueira, M. (2023). Leis Delegadas E Empreendedorismo Publico no Brasil: Analise À Luz DO Modelo DE Skowronek . Revista Jurídica (0103-3506), 2(74).

López-Núñez, M. I., Rubio-Valdehita, S., Aparicio-García, M. E., & Díaz-Ramiro, E. M. (2020). Are entrepreneurs born or made? The influence of personality. *Personality and Individual Differences*, 154, 109699. DOI: 10.1016/j.paid.2019.109699

Maltritz, D., & Wüste, S. (2015). Determinants of budget deficits in Europe: The role and relations of fiscal rules, fiscal councils, creative accounting and the Euro. *Economic Modelling*, 48, 222–236. DOI: 10.1016/j.econmod.2014.12.001

Marcolin, L., Miroudot, S., & Squicciarini, M. (2016). Routine jobs, employment and technological innovation in global value chains.

Mason, C., & Brown, R. (2014). "Entrepreneurial Ecosystems and Growth Oriented Entrepreneurship." Background paper prepared for the workshop organized by the OECD LEED Program and the Dutch Ministry of Economic Affairs on Entrepreneurial Ecosystems and Growth Oriented Entrepreneurship, The Hague, Netherlands, 7th November 2013. Final Version: January 2014, 38 p. Available on: https://www.oecd.org/cfe/leed/entrepreneurial-ecosystems.pdf

Mishkin, F. S. (2007). Inflation dynamics. *International Finance*, 10(3), 317–334. DOI: 10.1111/j.1468-2362.2007.00205.x

Mishkin, F. S., & Schmidt-Hebbel, K. (2007). *Does inflation targeting make a difference?* National Bureau of Economic Research Cambridge. DOI: 10.3386/w12876

Mohammadi Khyareh, M., & Rostami, N. (2021). The impact of macroeconomic variables on entrepreneurship: Generalized Method of Moments (GMM). *Macroeconomics Research Letter*, 15(30), 34–61.

Nam, C. W. (2022a). World economic outlook for 2022 and 2023. *CESifo Forum*, 23(03), 50–51.

Nnadi, M., & Soobaroyen, T. (2015). International financial reporting standards and foreign direct investment: The case of Africa. *Advances in Accounting*, 31(2), 228–238. DOI: 10.1016/j.adiac.2015.09.007

Nnadi, M., & Soobaroyen, T. (2015). International financial reporting standards and foreign direct investment: The case of Africa. *Advances in Accounting*, 31(2), 228–238. DOI: 10.1016/j.adiac.2015.09.007

Obiamaka, OS (2011). The impact of human resources management (HRM) practices on organizational performance in Globalcom NIGERIA. Research Journal of Management Practice | ISSN, 2782, 7674.

Okah Efogo, F. (2020b). Does trade in services improve African participation in global value chains? *African Development Review*, 32(4), 758–772. DOI: 10.1111/1467-8268.12476

Okah Efogo, F., Wonyra, K. O., & Osabuohien, E. (2022). Foreign direct investment and participation of developing countries in global value chains: Lessons from the last decade. *International Review of Applied Economics*, 36(2), 264–284. DOI: 10.1080/02692171.2021.1962255

Orji, JO, & Opualla -Charles, S. (2022). The Unemployment–Inflation Dynamics: The role of Entrepreneurship Development in Nigeria. https://www.researchsquare.com/article/rs-1820633/latest

Papcunová, V., Dvořák, M., Vavrek, R., Mižičková, J., Harasimová, P., Víchová, M., & Váňa, T. (2023). Availability and Quality of School Facilities as a Determinant of Local Economic Development: The Slovak. *Experimental Economics*, 11(2), 35.

Pekarčíková, K., Vaněk, M., & Sousedíková, R. (2022). Determinants of economic growth: Panel data analysis of OPEC. *Resources Policy*, 79, 103129. DOI: 10.1016/j.resourpol.2022.103129

Perkins, D., & Robbins, G. (2011). The contribution to local enterprise development of infrastructure for commodity extraction projects: Tanzania's central corridor and Mozambique's Zambezi Valley. Making Most of Commodities Program (MMCP) Discussion Paper, 9.

Pesqueux, Y. (2022). The tale of entrepreneurship in Africa. *Revue Organizations & Territoires*, 31(1), 1–10. DOI: 10.1522/revueot.v31n1.1442

Qu, M., McCormick, A. D., & Funck, C. (2022). Community resourcefulness and partnerships in rural tourism. *Journal of Sustainable Tourism*, 30(10), 2371–2390. DOI: 10.1080/09669582.2020.1849233

Ramaharo, F., Razanajatovo, Y.H., & Aljaona, E.M. (2023). Macroeconomic models in use in Madagascar.

Roodman, D. (2009). How to do Xtabond2: An Introduction to Difference and System GMM in Stata. *The Stata Journal*, 9(1), 86–136. DOI: 10.1177/1536867X0900900106

Rousseau, P. L., & Wachtel, P. (2002). Inflation thresholds and the finance–growth nexus. *Journal of International Money and Finance*, 21(6), 777–793. DOI: 10.1016/S0261-5606(02)00022-0

Sayek, S. (2009). Foreign Direct Investment and Inflation. *Southern Economic Journal*, 76(2), 419–443. DOI: 10.4284/sej.2009.76.2.419

Sen, A. (2000). A Decade of Human Development. *Journal of Human Development*, 1(1), 17–23. DOI: 10.1080/14649880050008746

Sénicourt, P., & Verstraete, T. (2000). Learn to undertake. Reflections and Perspectives, 39(10).

Severino JM et al. (2021), New entrepreneurial dynamics in Africa.

Smith-Hunter, A. E., & Boyd, R. L. (2004). Applying theories of entrepreneurship to a comparative analysis of white and minority women business owners. *Women in Management Review*, 19(1), 18–28. DOI: 10.1108/09649420410518403

Soffiantini, G. (2020). Food insecurity and political instability during the Arab Spring. *Global Food Security*, 26, 100400. DOI: 10.1016/j.gfs.2020.100400

Soltow, J. H. (1968). The entrepreneur in economic history. *The American Economic Review*, 58(2), 84–92.

St-Pierre, J., Foleu, L., Abdul-Nour, G., & Nomo, S. (2015). the obstacles to the development of Cameroonian SMEs: what do entrepreneurs think? Kaldor, M. (2023). Commentary on Kögler: Analyzing the Ukraine war through a 'new wars' perspective. *European Journal of Social Theory*, •••, 136843102311688.

Taghouti, Y., & Abdelbaki, N. (2023). The determinants of territorial development in developing countries: Literature review. International Journal of Accounting, Finance, Auditing, Management and Economics, 4(1–1), 481–504.

Tchamanbe Djine, L., & Tchouassi, G. (2001). *Strengthening the entrepreneurial capacities of women through training: An analysis of the case of Cameroon.* University of Yaoundé II, Communication at the VII Scientific Days of the AUF Entrepreneurship Network on Entrepreneurship Training.

Tchouassi, G. (2019). The specificity of the African socio-cultural model and the hiring process in Cameroonian companies. *Revue Congolaise de Gestion*, 2, 154–192. DOI: 10.3917/rcg.028.0154

Tchouassi, G., Ngwen, N., Tékam Oumbé, H., & Temfack, S. (2018). Entrepreneurial knowledge of young people and women and economic development. *International Review of Organization Sciences*, 1, 57–79.

Tchouassi, G., & Niyonzima, T. G. (2024). Effet de dynamique des prix et participation des pays Africains aux chaines de valeurs mondiales. *Revue Management Innovation*, 9(1), 165–191. DOI: 10.3917/rmi.209.0165

Tchouassi, G., & Tagne, J. S. (2020). Chapter 11 University incubators for young entrepreneurs. B. Boudarbat & AA Mbaye (Eds.), Economic Development and Employment in Francophone Africa: Entrepreneurship as a Means of Realization. University of Montreal Press.

Tchouassi, G., & Tchougon, EFJ (2022). Entrepreneurial education in higher education in Cameroon. The Education System in Francophone Africa: Challenges and Opportunities, 238.

Tian, N., Poudyal, N. C., Augé, R. M., Hodges, D. G., & Young, T. M. (2017). Meta-analysis of Price responsiveness of timber supply. *Forest Products Journal*, 67(3–4), 152–163. DOI: 10.13073/FPJ-D-16-00017

Upadhyaya, R., & McCormick, D. (2020). Entrepreneurial capabilities of successful firms: A study of small and medium-scale equipment manufacturers in Nairobi, Kenya. International Journal of Technological Learning. *Innovation and Development*, 12(3), 169. DOI: 10.1504/IJTLID.2020.112226

Van Praag, C. M. (1999).. . *De Economist*, 147(3), 311–335. DOI: 10.1023/A:1003749128457

Verstraete, T. (2000). *History of entrepreneurship: The realities of entrepreneurship*. EMS Editions.

Vogel, P. (2013). "Building and assessing entrepreneurial ecosystems", Presentation to OECD LEED Program Workshop on Entrepreneurial ecosystems and Growth-oriented entrepreneurship, The Hague, 7 November 2013. Available on: https://fr.slideshare.net/OECDLEED/6-vogel-building-and-assessin

Voigt, F. (2019). Regional development and the transport system. Regional Development and Economic Sectors: Results of European Comparative Research on. *Lagging Regions of Industrialized Countries*, 8, 105.

Wales, W. J., Gupta, V. K., & Mousa, F.-T. (2013). Empirical research on entrepreneurial orientation: An assessment and suggestions for future research. *International Small Business Journal*, 31(4), 357–383. DOI: 10.1177/0266242611418261

World Bank. (2020). World Development Report 2020: Trade for Development in an Era of Value Chain Globalization. In *Abridged*. World Bank.

Zhang, F., & Wang, C. (2018). Dynamic pricing strategy and coordination in a dual-channel supply chain considering service value. *Applied Mathematical Modelling*, 54, 722–742. DOI: 10.1016/j.apm.2017.10.006

Chapter 9
Integrating Crowdfunding and Financial Planning for Entrepreneur Success

Krishna Murthy
https://orcid.org/0000-0001-8989-8862
Department of Business Studies, College of Economics and Business Administration, University of Technology and Applied Sciences, Oman

Hassan Sanadi
Department of Business Studies, College of Economics and Business Administration, University of Technology and Applied Sciences, Oman

Sameena Begum
College of Economics and Business Administration, University of Technology and Applied Sciences, Oman

Smriti Sethi
https://orcid.org/0000-0002-6273-9607
Amity Institute of Psychology and Allied Sciences, Amity University, Noida, India

P. Karthikeyan
Department of Management Studies, Kongu Engineering College, Erode, India

ABSTRACT

The chapter elaborates on how crowdfunding can become a powerful tool for financial growth and stability for solopreneurs. It covers strategies concerning the creation of compelling crowdfunding campaigns and therefore highlights that, before doing so, fundraising goals should align explicitly with long-term financial planning. It further shared some tips on how to assess whether there is a real need

DOI: 10.4018/979-8-3693-9486-1.ch009

for finance, how to set realistic funding targets, and how to craft persuasive pitches that charm potential backers. It also deals with important areas of post-campaign financial management, such as budgeting, expense tracking, and how to reinvest. Integrating effective crowdfunding techniques with robust financial planning allows solopreneurs not only to raise the capital needed for the launch and scaling of ventures but also to maintain business practices and achieve long-term success. This comprehensive approach provides a solopreneur with the necessary tools and insights to turn financial challenges into growth opportunities.

INTRODUCTION

Crowdfunding has turned out to be one key game-changing funding mechanism in its ability to democratize access to capital and help entrepreneurs raise funds from a large number of people, mostly through online platforms. There are numerous advantages to this approach over more traditional funding sources like bank loans or venture capital. It gives the solopreneur an ability to reach a large audience, collect feedback, and build a community around their ideas. Successful crowdfunding campaigns can often work as influential marketing devices for creating buzz and drawing early adopters. However, the actual process of launching a crowdfunding campaign and managing it involves much more than getting the number of pledged results. It requires proper insight into the principles of financial planning so that money raised is appropriately utilized(Jenik et al., 2017a).

Of all the available tools in this fast-changing entrepreneurship field today, solopreneurs have different challenges and opportunities. Of these, one of the most compelling is crowdfunding. It's not only going to provide the entrance to capital, but also business idea validation and building a community of supporters. To successfully harness the power of crowdfunding requires more than just a great pitch, however. It requires rigorous financial planning and strategic management so that money raised successfully transudes into sustainable business growth. This chapter will explore ways in which solopreneurs can effectively integrate crowdfunding with financial planning in securing long-term success(De Luca et al., 2019).

The most critical part of this equation is financial planning. Careful budgeting and financial management become extremely important in turning a vision into reality when resources and capacity are restricted. Effective financial planning would include setting realistic funding targets, creating a line-item budget, and estimating the future funding requirements. It also entails rigorous expense management and strategic decisions regarding how to reinvest funds for supporting growth. coupling these financial concepts with an effective crowdfunding campaign could be the difference-maker between failure and success for a solopreneur. In order to effectively incorporate this with financial planning, one must know the various types of crowdfunding. Of these, donation-, reward-, equity-, and debt-based crowdfunding all hold different implications for financial planning and campaign management(Kukurba et al., 2021). Solopreneurs need to be involved in picking the crowdfunding model that best aligns with their business goals and financial needs. For instance, if a product-based business intends to presell its products, then reward-based crowdfunding would be most suitable. On the other hand, equity-based crowdfunding would work well when raising capital by giving ownership stakes in the business.

After choosing an appropriate model of crowdfunding, there is a need to build an impressionable campaign. This will be done by defining objectives, coming up with a well-framed pitch, and building an online presence. The success of the campaign depends on the resonance with potential backers and how effective it is in communicating the value proposition. Solopreneurs must develop a great pitch that includes the peculiarity of the business and shows how the funds will be channeled towards achieving well-defined milestones. The process thus calls for effective financial planning, by this time the solo entrepreneur is supposed to come up with a well-rounded budget detailing where all the funds will be allocated(Meoli et al., 2022). The budget in such a case would thus give product development costs, marketing costs, and all other operational expenses. Moreover, goals set in terms of funding for solopreneurs have to be realistic and be based on the results from a critical financial needs assessment and all the potential expenses. The goals should be considered attainable and in coherence with the general strategy of the business.

This is another critical aspect of financial planning: managing the funds post-campaign. Fundraising through crowdfunding may feel like a victory in itself, but that's just half the battle; the hard work lies in deploying the capital effectively. Solopreneurs need to establish good systems for keeping track of expenses and keep reviewing their financial performance regularly in order to make sure that the funds are put to proper use—track cash flow, vigilantly manage expenditure, and make prudent decisions about re-investment. Scaling of business and long-term growth will be seen only through strategic reinvestment(Deng et al., 2022). An integrated approach toward crowdfunding and financial planning also calls for a proactive management of risk. There should be a need to anticipate problems and have a Plan B to mitigate challenges as they come, as Goodspeak elaborates. This includes preparing for contingencies such as product development delays, funding flux, or other miscellaneous expenses. In this way, solopreneurs can reduce their chances of risks and maintain stability in their finances.

This, therefore, happens to be the intersection of crowdfunding and financial planning, which creates a powerhouse for entrepreneurial success by solopreneurs. This is where the knowledge of the dynamics associated with crowdfunding, having set clear financial goals, and managing the money will help solopreneurs to turn their ideas into flourishing endeavors. This chapter will then inform and strategize on how solopreneurs can effectively integrate this in ensuring that their efforts in crowdfunding do lead to long-lasting growth and, thereby, long-term success(Goodspeed, 2019a). Crowdfunding is democratizing, for entrepreneurs and solopreneurs alike, access to capital through the power of the crowd—people who want to participate by giving small quantities of money in anticipation of receiving something in return, be it a good or service, equity, or debt. This novel way of funding a business allows businesses to cross over the traditional financial institutions of banks and venture capitalists and be able to relate directly to many of these potential supporters or customers. Crowdfunding sites like Kickstarter, Indiegogo, and GoFundMe have made it easy for solopreneurs to pitch their ideas, acquire maximum publicity, and get funds to develop an idea into a real business. In its pure form, crowdfunding works on the basis of collective effort(Dushnitsky & Zunino, 2019).

Entrepreneurs present their projects or business ideas on a crowdfunding platform, where they can reach a global audience of potential backers. These backers are often motivated by the prospect of supporting a promising idea, receiving early access to products, or earning a return on their investment. Depending on the type of crowdfunding—donation-based, reward-based, equity-based, or debt-based—solopreneurs offer different incentives or benefits to attract contributions. This direct engagement not only helps in raising capital but also serves as a valuable marketing tool, building a community of early adopters and brand advocates(Dushnitsky & Zunino, 2019).

A good idea or product does not amount to the guarantee of success in crowdfunding. Rather, it calls for the proper plan, communication, and management to realize what is written on paper. The first important element is financial planning. This is a strategy containing sources, allocation, and management of funds for the entire project life cycle. This involves planning a budget, forecasting, and cash flow management, so that the money received from crowdfunding is spent effectively and it helps achieve the business's long-term goals(Thaker et al., 2019). A detailed budget is one of the major facets within any financial plan when putting a campaign forward for crowdfunding. This budget has to regard any type of expense that may arise: production, marketing, shipping, and platform fees. That is, making realistic funding targets requires a solopreneur to be very clear about their financial requirements—since, probably otherwise, overestimation of the amount raised or underestimation of costs gets set up. An effective budget makes one avoid some common pitfalls that include overpromising on rewards and mismanaging the funds raised, which might jeopardize the success of the campaign and even the financial health of the business.

M-Measurable. Make sure all identified goals are measurable. A-Achievable. Are the goals relevant to your business or not? Meaning, all the money that solopreneurs request as funding should come in alignment with their business strategy. An example of this could be a new product; a financial plan can detail the costs of development and how much it will cost to market and distribute the new product(Kaminski et al., 2019). Clear definition in goals keeps the campaign on track, ensuring along the way that monies are spent in such a way as to maximize the odds of success. Post-campaign financial management helps in the effective integration of crowdfunding and financial planning. Once the capital is secured, solopreneurs should institute a system to track and manage spending to ensure that their funding improves business operations. This includes cash flow monitoring, effective budget management, and making data-driven decisions on reinvestments and growth. The above helps a lot to eliminate wastage in other areas and ensures that the business can be sustainable into the future.

Besides, solopreneurs need to be prepared for potential financial challenges and risks. Crowdfunding campaigns may suffer from unanticipated issues related to delays in product development, changes in market conditions, or unexpected costs. To offset such challenges and stay financially afloat, solopreneurs can develop contingency and risk management strategies. Proactive financial planning helps in not only maneuvering through financial uncertainties but also in overall business resiliencies. These will be proactive in financial planning and cushion not only to maneuver through financial uncertainties but to overall business resiliencies(Jelinčić & Šveb, 2021).

Hence, financial planning and crowdfunding are two intertwined components that would make a solopreneur successful. Crowdfunding gives the opportunity to raise funds and create a community, while financial planning is done to make sure that such raised money will be put into the proper use of reaching such business goals. Dynamic use in application of professional financial planning practices will put the solopreneur far much better positioned to succeed, to grow in a sustained manner, and to convert those innovative ideas into assured businesses(Jelinčić & Šveb, 2021).

Scope

This chapter is on crowdfunding and financial planning, especially for solopreneurs. It starts by detailing crowdfunding as a source of funds, including the campaign strategies in setting goals and developing the pitch. The scope extends to detailed financial planning around how to align crowdfunding efforts with broader business goals. It includes practical advice on budgeting, managing expenses, and making informed financial decisions after securing funds. The chapter goes on to elicit case studies and real-life examples that point out successful integration of crowdfunding with financial planning. This will further be used to ensure actionable insight toward sustainable solopreneur success.

Objectives

This chapter is designed to equip solopreneurs with appropriate knowledge and skills in order to infuse crowdfunding with finance and planning in the right way. First, it guides solopreneurs on how to make effective crowdfunding campaigns by harmonizing their financial goals with the business vision. This brings out the need to put transparent funding targets over designing compelling pitches to allure potential backers. The next chapter will, therefore, focus on post-campaign financial management that will include budgeting, tracking expenses, and reinvestment strategies. It is, therefore, the intention of the chapter to enable solopreneurs in fostering sustainable business growth and stability in the management of financial resources.

Figure 1. Essential elements of crowdfunding

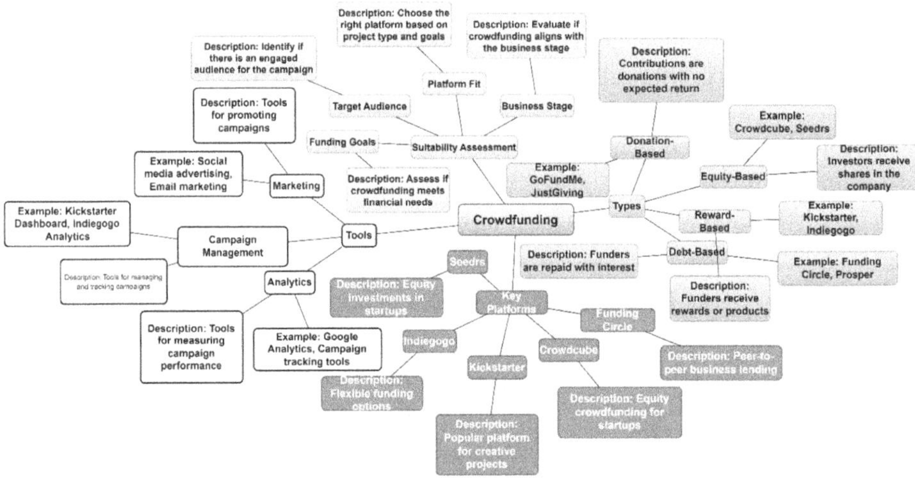

CROWDFUNDING

Crowdfunding is new in this regard, a transformational approach to the way capital raising can be accomplished through the pooled effort of both people and organizations. Typically, this occurs somewhere on the Internet, and it gives entrepreneurs, startups, and solopreneurs an opportunity to tap into potential backers otherwise not available through traditional sources of funding. To understand crowdfunding most effectively, you should be learning the different types available, coupled with the key platforms and the major tools, and then conclude whether it suits your kind of needs(Jenik et al., 2017b).

Figure 1 outlines the key elements of crowdfunding, including its types, popular platforms, useful tools, and factors to consider when evaluating its suitability for a project.

Types of Crowdfunding

- **Donation-Based Crowdfunding:** In this model of crowdfunding, people fund causes and projects without financial return. This manner is often applied in charity-based causes, community projects, or even social enterprise. The model works on feeling altruistic and being inclined to support worthy projects displayed by the donors. Good examples include platforms such as GoFundMe and JustGiving. This model is non-repayable and does not demand equity but is very dependent on the ability of the project to appeal emotionally to potential contributors(Dushnitsky & Zunino, 2019).
- **Reward-Based Crowdfunding:** Here, the backers get non-financial returns or some other incentive in exchange. It can be in the form of early access to products, branded merchandise, or exclusive experiences. This model is often used when launching new products or creative projects because the backers are interested in a tangible benefit or being part of the project journey. The two leading platforms in this category are Kickstarter and Indiegogo. The attractiveness and meaningfulness of the rewards decide the success of reward-based crowdfunding.
- **Equity-Based Crowdfunding:** Equity-based crowdfunding allows people to invest in a business in exchange for the business's securities. It is quite the model for a startup, a growing business in search of capital for expansion, and in return, offer a share to the investors in the company's future profits and potential exit gains. Some of the platforms used in equity-based crowdfunding include SeedInvest and Crowdcube. More legal and regulatory scrutiny is involved in this approach because the investors become the oblique owners of the business.
- **Peer-to-Peer Debt-Based Crowdfunding (Lending):** This form of crowdfunding is essentially peer-to-peer lending, in which several individuals extend loans to a business or individual, with expectations of repayment with interest. This is much the same as loans, but the finance is acquired directly from the lenders. Examples include LendingClub, Funding Circle, and several others. Business that is looking for debt-based crowdfunding—it should

have a good plan for repaying the debt and be able to present the creditworthy venture to get more lenders.

Key Platforms and Tools

Kickstarter: Kickstarter belongs to the type of reward-based crowdfunding platforms and is among the most popularly known. It is heavily utilized in creative projects, technology innovations, and product launches. Kickstarter has an all-or-nothing funding model where funders only get into projects if the fundraising goals set are met. It offers detailed resources and campaigning support to creators, including marketing tools and community engagement features(Green et al., 2022).

Indiegogo: Indiegogo does both reward-based and equity-based crowdfunding. It has flexible funding options where your money is yours to keep, even if it doesn't reach the goal. Indiegogo hosts a vast array of projects—tech innovations to social causes—putting into action varied campaign tools like analytics and promotional features.

GoFundMe: GoFundMe is a donation-based crowdfunding site, principally used for personal causes, covering medical expenses, and funding charitable initiatives. It allows users to raise money for a cause with no return of reward or equity. This platform supports the tools for easy fund-raising and options for social sharing so as to reach the goals set by campaigns.

SeedInvest: SeedInvest is an equity-based crowdfunding platform that connects startups with accredited investors. Not only does it implement an in-depth vetting process but also ensures legal support to protect both the investor and the entrepreneur, plus tools for managing investments and monitoring company performance.

LendingClub: One of the prime platforms for debt-based crowdfunding, LendingClub allows both personal and business loans. Basically, it bridges the gap between those needing a loan and the people who provide them with money against an agreed interest rate. Again, the platform provides the tools for loan management and communication between borrowers and lenders.

Assessing Crowdfunding Suitability

It is the process of evaluating all the below-mentioned key factors if crowdfunding is a good approach for your project or business(Goodspeed, 2019b).

Type of Project or Business: Check the nature of your project and whether it falls under the table of any model of crowdfunding. The reward-based is for launches of products and creative initiatives, and the equity-based is ideally for start-ups requiring funds in exchange for a share, whereas donation-based crowdfunding is suitable for people forwarded for charitable or personal causes.

Funding Needs: Determine how much capital is required and if crowdfunding is sufficient to meet this need. Crowdfunding is suitable for medium fundraising, not for big fundraising requirements unless it has done huge preparations along with marketing.

Engagement: Determine your capabilities to engage the target audience and set up a community around your idea. Crowdfunding requires a strong marketing campaign and social media to be successful.

Regulatory Issues: Check the legal and regulatory application of the chosen crowdfunding model. Equity-based and debt-based models do involve compliances with some of the financial regulations and securities laws, which may require the need of legal advice and for proper documentation to meet them.

Marketing and Promotion: Establish if your crowdfunding campaign would be supported by effective marketing. Making the crowdfunding campaign more visible and promoting it by all possible means to the target audience is an absolute must-to-do to reach out and achieve the funding target.

This diversity in raising capital comes with its advantages and requirements. Knowledge about types of crowdfunding, key platforms and tools in use, and assessment of suitability of crowdfunding for your specified needs will enable you exploit this new and innovative source of funding so laudably, towards achievement of financial and business goals.

CRAFTING A COMPELLING CAMPAIGN

Establishing a successful crowdfunding initiative is much more than having an exceptional concept; rather, it requires deep planning and implementation. An appealing campaign stipulates the establishment of precise objectives and aims, creating an influential pitch, and cultivating and involving one's audience. All these elements come into play in attaining donors and financing your goals(Meoli et al., 2022).

A crowdfunding campaign is organized by planning, pitching, engagement of the audience, launch, monitoring, adjusting, and completion. The objectives have to be defined for the campaign, and a pitch has to be created. Launching of the campaign is done by tracking its performance and making adjustments wherever necessary. The process of creating a compelling crowdfunding campaign is illustrated in Figure 2.

Figure 2. Process of crafting a compelling crowdfunding campaign

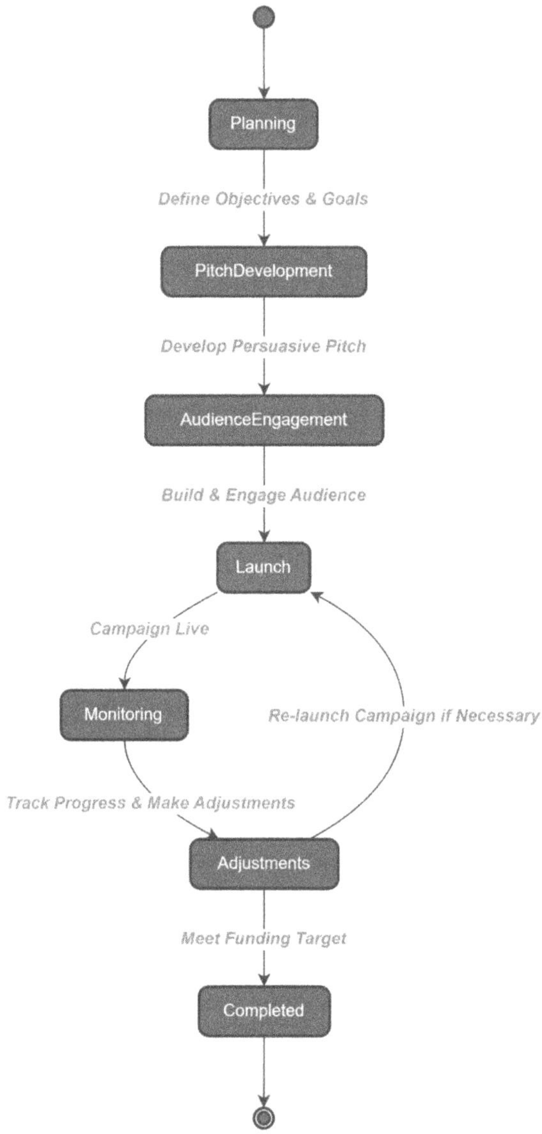

Setting Clear Objectives and Goals

The foundation of a successful crowdfunding campaign is well-defined objectives and goals. Start by clearly articulating what you aim to achieve with the campaign. This involves setting specific, measurable, achievable, relevant, and time-bound

(SMART) goals. These objectives will guide your campaign's strategy and provide a benchmark for measuring success(Ogwu et al., 2022).

Set Your Funding Goal: Ensure that your funding goal represents the actual cost to bring the project to life. This includes production and marketing expenses, platform fees, and other things incurred in the process. Also, make sure your goal is achievable and reasonable; this will retain potential backers. Avoid an overall too high target since this will scare potential contributors away because they may feel that your goal is not realistic.
Set Milestones: Break down your main purpose into smaller, practical milestones. These may include raising certain funding levels, completion of important stages of the project, or levels of production reached. Milestones help to let donors know how your project is progressing and can show a feeling of accomplishment as each one is completed.
Conform to Your Vision: It is important that your objectives conform to the broader vision of your organization or project. Clearly explain the way the finances will be used to advance your work and reach your long-term goals. Such coherence breeds trust and assurance in potential funders—who are now looking to indeed see a quantifiable impact for any investment made in a cause.

Developing a Persuasive Pitch

An effective pitch is one that will catch and hold the attention of possible supporters. Your pitch needs to be well-phrased with messages that demonstrate a value proposition to the audience, establish an emotional bond, and give a clear call to action(Deng et al., 2022).

Build a Persuasive Story: Start with an interesting story that summarizes the core essence of your project. Explain what problem you are trying to solve, what solution you are providing, and what impact your project is going to make. Use appealing graphics, testimonials, and real-life scenarios to explain your points and give your story a more personal touch.
Bring Out the USP: Clearly tell what differentiates your project from others. Emphasize any unique features, innovations, or benefits that make your project special. Differentiation is very important when explaining to potential backers why they should fund your campaign and not others.
Establish a Strong Call to Action: Your pitch really needs to include an obvious and compelling call to action. You should encourage potential backers to contribute, share news about the campaign, or help in another capacity.

Make their next steps easy; supply explicit instructions and links to make contributions or pledges.

Use High-Quality Visuals: Attractive videos, images, and infographics can add immense value to your pitch. A well-made video has the potential to effectively communicate your message or even showcase your product and evoke emotions. Your visuals need to be professional in appeal and must align strictly with the campaign brand and message.

Building and Engaging Your Audience

Active involvement of the audience is one of the success factors of crowdfunding. Proper cultivation and nurturing of a close relationship with contributors may boost support, foster loyalty, and prompt recommendations by word-of-mouth(Thaker et al., 2019).

Leverage Social Media: Use social media platforms to promote your campaign, share updates, and engage with your audience. Regularly post content that highlights your progress, shares behind-the-scenes insights, and acknowledges backers. Social media is a powerful tool for expanding your reach and generating buzz around your campaign.

Create an Email List: Build a mailing list of your potential donors and supporters. Use email marketing techniques to send out updates, share news of progress on the campaign, and offer special content or offers. Targeted emails can help keep in touch long-term and encourage continued support throughout the campaign.

Engage with Your Backers: The key here is to actively engage with your backers by responding to their comments, answering questions, and acknowledging contributions. Be grateful for their support and transparent about project progress. This level of engagement will build trust and foster a community around your project.

Offer Incentives and Rewards: Provide meaningful incentives and rewards to backers in order to encourage contributions. Tailor rewards according to different levels of pledges and ensure they offer value for money to your supporters. This can include special access, early-bird discounts, or limited special editions that will spur the backers to contribute and share your campaign forward.

This means that a good crowdfunding campaign requires clear goals, the development of a compelling pitch, and active engagement with your potential target or audience. By thinking carefully about all the above elements and then proceeding in their execution, one can create a campaign that gets funded and builds an audience committed to seeing this project through.

FINANCIAL PLANNING FUNDAMENTALS

Effective financial planning is essential in undertaking a crowdfunding campaign. This will, in most cases, incorporate budgeting, setting targets in terms of funding that is realistic, and inferring financial results. Having the basics of this will ensure that the campaign is organized and aligned to the financial needs, thereby being in a position to realize its goals(Goodspeed, 2019a). Figure 3 illustrates the essential aspects of effective financial planning for a crowdfunding campaign.

Figure 3. Effective financial planning for a crowdfunding campaign

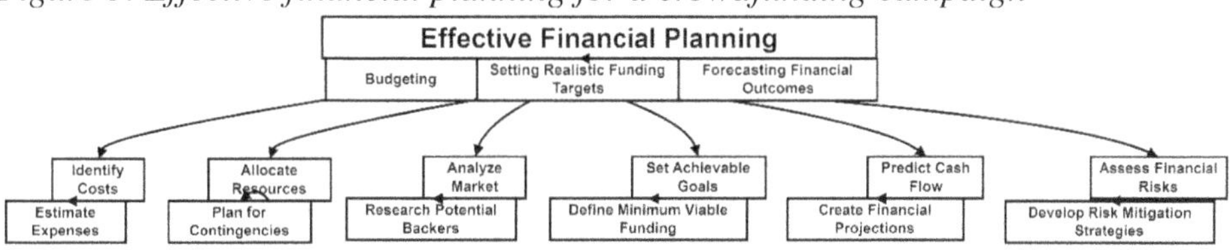

Budgeting for Your Campaign

Budgeting is the process of estimating and allocating the funds required to run your crowdfunding campaign. A comprehensive budget helps in managing resources efficiently and avoiding unexpected financial shortfalls. Here's how to approach budgeting for your campaign:

i. **List Every Possible Cost:** Write down all possible costs that might be incurred when running your campaign. This should include costs of production (manufacturing, materials), platform fees (fees from transactions and listing), marketing costs (advertisements and promotions), costs of distributing the reward (shipping, packaging), and all other overheads (legal fees, contingencies). This detailed listing ensures that nothing is left out.
ii. For each cost, make a reasonable estimate using quotations, historical data, or market research. Again, overestimation and under-estimation of the costs could be of serious consequence to the economics of your campaign. The conservatism will err on the side by adding a contingency to account for unknown costs(N. et al., 2024; Pasumarthy et al., 2024; Vijaya Lakshmi et al., 2024).

iii. **Allocate Money Appropriately:** Budget regarding priorities. For example, enough funds should be allotted for use in product development and in rewards redemption that will assure results. Ensure that the budget allocation for advertising and promotion is enough to get exposure and plenty of it.
iv. **Monitor and Adjust:** During the campaign, inch by inch, constantly monitor your budget against the actual expenditure. Make adjustments as required to accommodate financial deviations or other miscellaneous expenses that may come up. This proactive approach helps stay within budget and maintain financial control.

Setting Realistic Funding Targets

Setting realistic financial goals is the most important thing for the success of your campaign. Your amount should reflect the actual monetary needs of your project after considering possible contributions from the audience.

i. **Calculate Overall Capital Requirements:** Add up all of the budgeted expenses to get the amount of capital to be raised. By definition, such an amount must be more than the coverage of the major expenses and a bit more for the unexpected ones.
ii. **Campaign Viability:** It is the guestimate of your target audience size, crowdfunding model in use, and usual funds raised by like-minded campaigns. Any analysis of this kind makes setting a goal challenging yet realistic.
iii. **Setting Stretch Goals:** Other than a primary funding target, set stretch goals that include what else you can provide if you can reach more than your goal. Stretch goals will help inspire the backers to give more and sometimes help increase overall funding.
iv. **Clearly Communicate:** Mention the exact purpose of your funding and how the money is going to be spent. It means that transparency can induce trust in potential donors and increase their understanding towards the contribution they are making.

Financial Forecasting and Projections

The financial forecasting and projection estimations result mainly from your campaign performance and financial planning. This helps to plan for some financial scenarios, allowing one to make informed decisions(Babu et al., 2022; Dhanya et al., 2023; Mohanty et al., 2023; Venkateswaran et al., 2023).

- **Financial Projections:** Projections for key financial measures, including income, expenses, and liquidity, will be prepared. Since the information is taken from historical data, market research, and assumptions about campaign effectiveness, financial projections will be made based on it. Build base best-case and worst-case scenarios to include in some kind of contingency plan.
- **Track Performance Metrics:** Record the performance metrics, namely, the amount of funds raised, total number of backers, and average amount pledged. Compare these noted indicators against your early projections to identify whether you're on course toward meeting your funding objective.
- **Revise Forecasts as Needed:** Keep updating your forecasts frequently, more so to adapt to actual campaign performance and new information. Revisit all of your financial strategies and plans to discover the variances from your projection.
- **Post-Campaign Financial Planning:** It should consider the disposition of funds after the campaign. This touches on the disbursal of funds, cash flow management, and financial obligation or commitment incurred by the campaign.

A well-planned crowdfunding project requires careful budgeting, setting realistic funding targets, and financial projections. Having all of that at your fingertips, the well-adjusted and well-executed financial elements set the success rate of your campaign and the chances that funds are going to be used efficiently for achieving the ends of your initiative.

INTEGRATING CROWDFUNDING WITH FINANCIAL PLANNING

Crowdfunding and financial planning must go hand in hand to maximize campaign benefits and ensure sustainable growth. This includes setting campaign goals that align with overall business objectives, effective management of funds post-campaign, a robust expense tracker, and reinvestment strategy that ensures a strategic approach toward long-term success.(Jenik et al., 2017b).

Figure 4. Integrating crowdfunding with financial planning

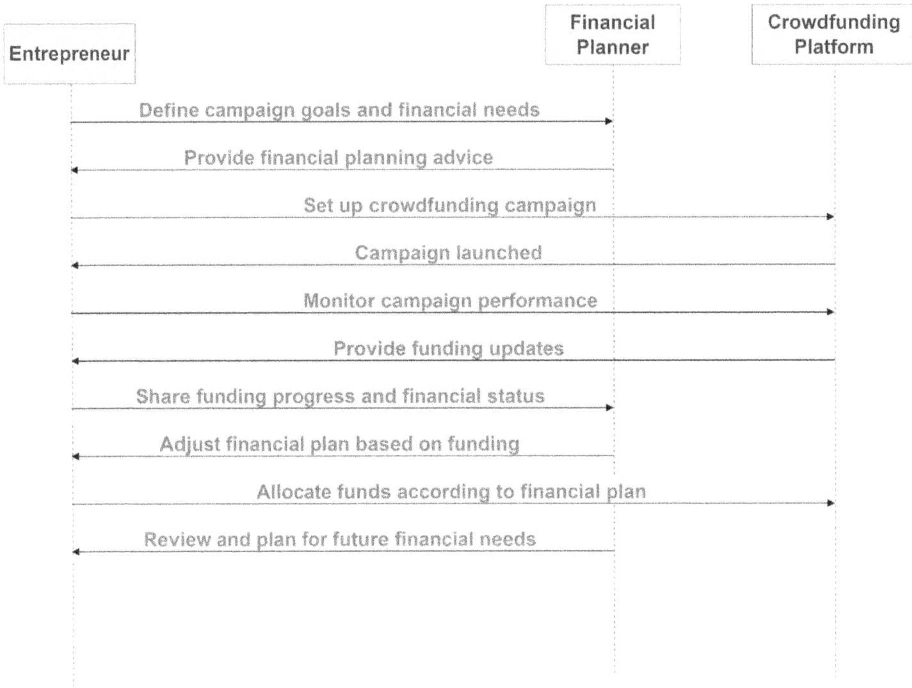

Basically, the process is one of defining campaign goals and financial needs, offering advice on financial planning, setting up the campaign on a crowdfunding platform, monitoring campaign performance, updating funding progress, and sharing it with the financial planner for updating the financial plan with respect to the received funding. After that, funds are allocated according to the updated plan. Review and plan future financial needs to achieve both campaign and financial goals. Figure 4 illustrates crowdfunding collaboration with financial planning in the course of a campaign. The financial planner guides the entrepreneur in planning for future financial needs while ensuring the success of the campaigns towards set objectives (Ogwu et al., 2022).

Aligning Campaign Goals with Business Objectives

Define Business Objectives: Clearly define the overall business goals and the role that this crowdfunding campaign will play in them. That is, launch a new product, expand market reach, fund research and development—the campaign must ensure its goals support your vision and strategic plan(Boopathi, 2024; Boopathi et al., 2023; Ravisankar et al., 2024).

Integrate Campaign and Business Strategies: Design a campaign strategy in line with your business plan. For example, if the business goal is brand awareness, design a campaign strategy that will focus on storytelling and brand values. In the case of new product development, make sure the campaign highlights features and benefits.
Measure Success Against Objectives: Establish KPIs for the success of your campaign relative to the business objectives. One can measure how many new customers have been acquired, how high or low the engagement levels are, and how much your sales have grown. Use such insights to appraise whether the campaign has impacted your overall business goals.
Success in Campaigns on Business Growth: Leverage a successful campaign to drive business growth by using the gained momentum and visibility. Use positive media coverage, customer feedback, backer testimonials to build credibility in attracting more customers or investors.

Managing Funds Post-Campaign

- **Allocate According to Campaign Budget:** After your campaign is finished, allocate funds based on what you have campaigned for. Make sure these funds are used in very important areas like production, fulfillment of rewards, and marketing. Make sure funds are disbursed correctly in order to leverage the campaign's promise.
- **Financial Management System:** Establish a sound system for financial management that will enable the tracking and management of campaign funds. This will entail keeping records of every expenditure, ensuring a cash flow system is in place, and deploying money as per the budget.
- **Keep Your Backers in the Loop:** Update your backers on what your donations are currently being used for. At a minimum, update them on project development, fiscal monitoring, and any deviations that are made from the original plan. Transparent communication is a good way to maintain their trust and good standing with their supporters.
- **Be Prepared for Tax Implications:** Be conversant with the tax implication that the funds raised through crowdfunding will have on the venture. Make sure to consult a tax professional so as to be well informed on tax compliance regulation, and the handling and maintenance of tax liabilities.

Expense Tracking and Reinvestment Strategies

Keep a Detailed Record of Expenditure The company or campaign should install a proper system for keeping records of expenditure. The company needs to record all the money spent on the campaign execution and project in general. The management can then categorize these expenditures in order to trace money used against the budget and notice any deviations or unforeseen costs. Spotting deviations in time will enable corrective action in case the actual expenditure is against forecasts. Regular Expenses Data Analysis Regularly scrutinize data on expenditure and find the pattern or any other area where proper costs can be reallocated. Find a place where cost-cutting opportunities exist or better deals can be negotiated with vendors and service providers for better terms(Fortezza et al., 2021; Jelinčić & Šveb, 2021; Ogwu et al., 2022).

- **Reinvestment Strategy:** Develop a reinvestment strategy with the remaining funds or profits anticipated from the campaign. Reinvestment strategies can be considered for scaling up production, expanding marketing efforts, or product development. The reinvestment business objective should shine through when identifying and then dealing with that investment with the most potential return.
- **Monitor Financial Performance:** Monitor the financial functioning at regular periods so as to know whether the investments are generating the expected return. Change reinvestment strategies according to the data related to function and associated changes in business needs.
- **Plan Future Campaigns:** Following the lessons learned during the current campaign, plan future crowdfunding efforts by paying attention to what seems to be working and what needs to be improved upon. Apply lessons from the campaign to your future campaign in an effort to make it more effective and more appropriate for reaching business goals.

Integrate crowdfunding with your planning process by establishing campaign goals that are in alignment with your business goals, considerations of fund management post-campaign, and finally, the availability of mechanisms to record spending for re-investing into the business. You need to ensure that the following three elements are properly considered and executed for you to realize the maximum benefits that accrue from your crowdfunding effort—with overall sustainability and long-term success.

CASE STUDIES AND REAL-WORLD EXAMPLES

Case studies and real-life examples could also be explored to understand better the dynamics behind a successful crowdfunding campaign and the practical application of crowdfunding strategies. One can draw knowledge from the best practices and effective approaches applied in myriad campaigns from varied industries(Goodspeed, 2019a).

Pebble Technology

One large example of successful crowdfunding is Pebble Technology's campaign. Pebble launched a campaign on Kickstarter in the year 2012 to fund the development of a smart wristwatch compatible with iOS and Android devices. This achieved a modest funding goal of $100,000 but ultimately raised over $10 million from more than 68,000 backers. The strength of Pebble lay in a few aspects: the exciting vision of the product created, making use of early prototypes, and a good promotional strategy. Pebble effectively made use of a well-produced promotional video that allowed potential backers to see the product features and their benefits in action, therefore insightfully understanding its worth proposition. It also means the project kept talking to the backers by updating them and meeting the high level of transparency in the campaign. Pebble was able to create massive buzz around its newfangled innovation and amass a huge base of followers, which was central to Pebble's success in raising funds.

Exploding Kittens

"Exploding Kittens" card game, designed by Elan Lee and Matthew Inman, is an example of how a very cool idea paired with good marketing can create unbelievable crowdfunding success. The Kickstarter campaign was started in 2015 for the same reason, and while the desired target was to raise $10,000, it actually raised over $8.7 million from upwards of 200,000 backers. A number of very important factors served as a root for this campaign. First, there was an extremely unique and funny concept product-wise. Second, it has an engaging promotional strategy. Third, a well-defined reward structure rounds out the campaign. There was an included video with some humor furnishing the whole concept about the game and its appeal. Stretch goals and limited-time offers were also used to spur interest and increase pledges. The value of community engagement and so-called viral marketing, combined with the attractiveness of the product, made the project a real blockbuster.

Oculus Rift

The Oculus Rift crowdfunding campaign is a great example of how crowdfunding can be used to raise serious money and hit major milestones in product development. The campaign on Kickstarter for raising funds to develop a virtual reality headset was started in 2012. It had a target of $250,000 but raised almost $2.5 million from over 10,000 backers. The innovative technology of Oculus Rift, coupled with the ability to spark the interest of the gaming community, drove it to success. It was this well-presented campaign, complete with technical details and testimonials from developers, that really built credibility and gave it a great deal of attention from backers. Its success on Kickstarter not only provided critical funds but also proved market demand for virtual reality technology, hence winning further investments from giant technology corporations like Facebook.

The Coolest Cooler

One high-tech cooler, The Coolest Cooler, included the features of a blender, Bluetooth speakers, and a USB charging port. It's a case study in managing expectations and the challenges of fulfillment. Launched on Kickstarter in 2014, the campaign raised over $13 million, far above its goal of $50,000. Despite these impressive fundraising results, there were extensive challenges during production and trying to fulfill the campaign. The case focuses on the most prominent issues of setting practical goals, efficient management of the project, and keeping the backers updated. This initial great success was soon followed by important dissatisfactions with the product because of delays in delivery and production problems. This case illustrates that it requires not only detailed planning but also execution if the promises given in a campaign are to be fulfilled and the satisfaction of backers ensured.

The three case studies identify various factors that contribute to successful crowdfunding. Among them are the clarity of vision, creative marketing strategies, innovative products, and overcoming fulfillment challenges. Future campaigners can learn from these concrete examples of key insights into effective practices and strategies for successful crowdfunding campaigns.

CHALLENGES AND FUTURE TRENDS

With opportunities and challenges the crowdfunding environment may change. Understanding challenges and being prepared for future trends can help campaigners through the complexities of crowdfunding, identify opportunities, and attain success (Green et al., 2022).

Figure 5. Crowdfunding challenges and emerging opportunities

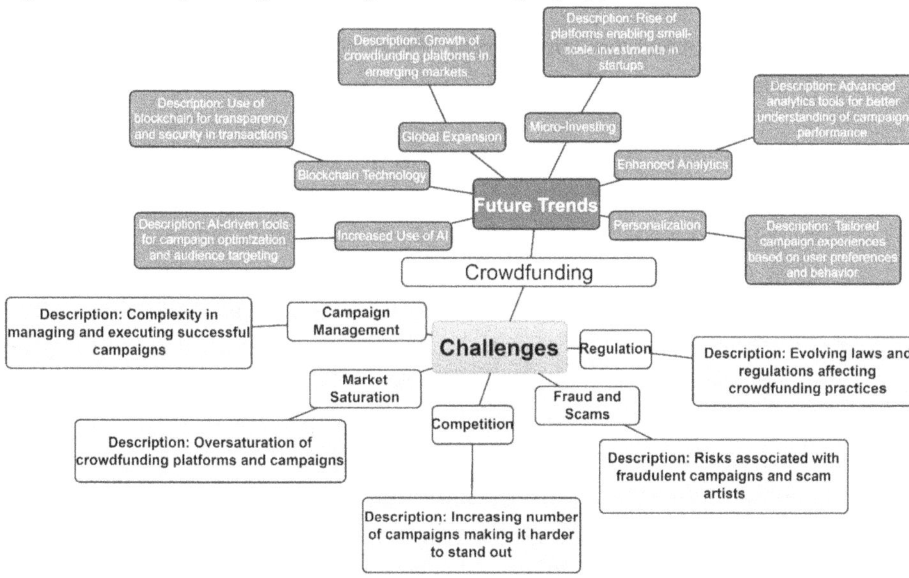

With the increase in campaigns comes challenges in terms of competition, regulation, fraud, market saturation, and campaign management. Other future trends will be the use of AI and blockchain technology to change the campaign landscape, emergent investment trends like micro-investing, globalizing campaigns, better analytics, and the creation of personalized campaigns. Notable among the challenges are the issues of competition, regulation, fraud, market saturation, and cumbersome campaign management. Figure 5 depicts the challenges and opportunities of crowdfunding.

Challenges in Crowdfunding

Market Saturation and Competition: Crowdfunding's popularity has resulted in a saturated market where this heightened competition makes it hard to be conspicuous among the thousands of campaigns. Crowdfunding requires one to tell an interesting story, building new innovative marketing strategies to engage with audiences and arouse attention in a jammed marketplace(Jenik et al., 2017b).

Campaign Visibility and Reach: Getting noticed in crowdfunding is difficult. Even the most thought-out campaigns miss their target audiences, whether through platform algorithms, limited organic reach, or ineffective promotional strategies. To beat this, you need to engage in proactive activities that will increase your campaign's visibility: social media, influencer partnerships, and targeted advertising.

Funding Risks and Uncertainty: One of the inherent factors in crowdfunding is financial uncertainty. There can never be any sort of guarantee that money will be raised for a campaign, and further, even if it does, there are huge risks involved with managing those funds and ultimately delivering on the promises made. Campaigners need to plan extremely carefully, set realistic goals, and implement sound financial management strategies to mitigate such risks and ensure successful execution.

Legal/Regulatory Compliance: This remains another big challenge, as there are different regulations on crowdfunding, intellectual property, and financial transactions across different regions. None of these can be infringed, lest the campaigners face resultant lawsuits, fines, or suspension of their campaigns. The changing laws have to be kept updated, and legal advice has to be sought by campaigners(Vennila et al., 2022).

Fulfillment and Delivery: Delivering rewards and fulfilling promises in campaigns with a huge number of backers can be very challenging. Delays in production, shipping problems, and quality control affect the success of a campaign and satisfaction from the backers. Efficient fulfillment processes and clear communication with the backers, in such respect, are able to deal with these challenges effectively.

Future Trends in Crowdfunding

Blockchain Technology Integration: Blockchain technology is about to disrupt the crowdfunding process with improved transparency, security, and efficiency. Through smart contracts, blockchain platforms can execute automated transactions, contractual agreements, reduce the likelihood of fraud, and then increase trust. In addition, blockchain can offer records of transactions that are immutable and logs of backer contributions that increase accountability(Green et al., 2022).

Rise of Equity Crowdfunding: Increased popularity is noted in equity crowdfunding, where investors are given shares in return for their contributions. This trend is reflected in the growing interest to offer backers a stake in the project's successful outcome rather than only rewards. Equity crowdfunding will attract more substantial investments and align the interests of the backers with the long-term success of the project.

Higher AI and Data Analytics: With an increased role in crowdfunding, AI and data analytics have been assisting more often. AI can further support campaign personalization, predict backer behavior, and optimize marketing strategies. Data analytics, on the other hand, retrieved insights into campaign performance, preferences of the backer, and market trends that would allow campaigns to make data-driven decisions and fine-tune strategies.

Emphasis on Social Impact and Sustainability: There is an increasing push for crowdfunding campaigns to be centered around social impact and sustainability. More and more investors are motivated by projects inspired by environmental, social, and ethical causes. Consequently, campaigns that emphasize a positive impact on the environment or society are going to be better supported and funded.

Crowdfunding platforms and models are also proliferating in order to attend to myriad specific needs. This has led to the formation of several niche platforms focused only on particular industries or types of projects to serve particular needs with unique features and targeted audiences. Hybrid models of fundraising, among which some traditional crowdfunding elements are combined with others, have continued to grow in popularity; this growth allows for some flexibility and more options for campaigners.

Enhanced Engagement and Experience for the Backers: Most campaigns on crowdfunding are going to focus on personal backer engagement as well as experience. These would include personalized one-on-one communication, interactive content, and exclusive updates. An enhanced backer experience may help build stronger relationships, more loyalty, and repeat support in the case of future campaigns.

In this way, crowdfunding presents huge challenges for the future and puts impressive trends into play. Addressing the challenges of market saturation, funding-related risks, and regulatory compliance and leveraging the emerging trends of blockchain technology, equity crowdfunding, and AI could enhance the chances for success for campaigners. The crux of sailing through this evolving crowdfunding landscape and seizing new opportunities to grow and make an increased impact is being aware of these developments and developing strategies accordingly.

CONCLUSION

Crowdfunding platforms have developed into solid enablers for solopreneurs to validate ideas, source capital, and build communities of supporters around their ideas. And in this changing landscape, a grasp of what lies ahead and what changes that means in getting crowdfunding success very much sits at the center. But effective campaigns are not just about strong fundraising strategies; they entail meticulous planning, good storytelling, and great financial management.

There is an integrative aspect of crowdfunding when relating it to financial planning. Clear objectives, good campaign design, and perfect fund-flowing mechanism are the key elements of a successful crowdfunding campaign. Aligning campaign goals with business objectives and using strong financial forecasting can add to the ability of solopreneurs to meet funding objectives for the long term.

This includes navigating challenges like market saturation, visibility issues, and legal compliance. Some best practices include contact with the backers, some attractive rewards for the backers, and the use of data analytics along with other tools. Further, staying on top of new trends in this market—such as the use of blockchain technology and the rise of equity crowdfunding—provides some of the best competitive advantages.

In conclusion, crowdfunding can provide solopreneurs with an opportunity to manifest their imaginations before a very receptive audience. The proper understanding and use of effective strategies built from real-life cases and the readiness to be part of future trends will give solopreneurs the possibility of doing the greatest good in that campaign and achieving their vision in finance and business. The domain is ever-changing, hence calling for continuous change and innovation at the crossroads of crowdfunding and financial planning. These will enable solopreneurs to overcome the complexities associated with crowdfunding and set them up for long-term success in this rapidly changing environment.

REFRENCES

Babu, B. S., Kamalakannan, J., Meenatchi, N., Karthik, S., & Boopathi, S. (2022). Economic impacts and reliability evaluation of battery by adopting Electric Vehicle. *IEEE Explore*, 1–6.

Boopathi, S. (2024). Digital HR Implementation for Business Growth in Industrial 5.0. In *Convergence of Human Resources Technologies and Industry 5.0* (pp. 1–22). IGI Global. DOI: 10.4018/979-8-3693-1343-5.ch001

Boopathi, S., Kumar, P. K. S., Meena, R. S., Sudhakar, M., & Associates. (2023). Sustainable Developments of Modern Soil-Less Agro-Cultivation Systems: Aquaponic Culture. In *Human Agro-Energy Optimization for Business and Industry* (pp. 69–87). IGI Global.

De Luca, V. V., Margherita, A., & Passiante, G. (2019). Crowdfunding: A systemic framework of benefits. *International Journal of Entrepreneurial Behaviour & Research*, 25(6), 1321–1339. DOI: 10.1108/IJEBR-11-2018-0755

Deng, L., Ye, Q., Xu, D., Sun, W., & Jiang, G. (2022). A literature review and integrated framework for the determinants of crowdfunding success. *Financial Innovation*, 8(1), 41. DOI: 10.1186/s40854-022-00345-6

Dhanya, D., Kumar, S. S., Thilagavathy, A., Prasad, D., & Boopathi, S. (2023). Data Analytics and Artificial Intelligence in the Circular Economy: Case Studies. In *Intelligent Engineering Applications and Applied Sciences for Sustainability* (pp. 40–58). IGI Global.

Dushnitsky, G., & Zunino, D. (2019). The role of crowdfunding in entrepreneurial finance. In *Handbook of research on crowdfunding* (pp. 46–92). Edward Elgar Publishing. DOI: 10.4337/9781788117210.00008

Fortezza, F., Pagano, A., & Bocconcelli, R. (2021). Serial crowdfunding in start-up development: A business network view. *Journal of Business and Industrial Marketing*, 36(13), 250–262. DOI: 10.1108/JBIM-05-2020-0243

Goodspeed, R. (2019a). Participatory e-Planning with civic crowdfunding: Donor background, involvement, and social capital outcomes. [IJEPR]. *International Journal of E-Planning Research*, 8(2), 68–87. DOI: 10.4018/IJEPR.2019040104

Goodspeed, R. (2019b). Participatory e-Planning with civic crowdfunding: Donor background, involvement, and social capital outcomes. [IJEPR]. *International Journal of E-Planning Research*, 8(2), 68–87. DOI: 10.4018/IJEPR.2019040104

Green, E., Sukumar, A., Jafari-Sadeghi, V., Pandya, K., & Khavarinezhad, S. (2022). Analysis of factors impeding access to finance in internet enabled crowdfunding: A systematic literature review. *International Journal of Technology Transfer and Commercialisation*, 19(2), 249–269. DOI: 10.1504/IJTTC.2022.124342

Jelinčić, D. A., & Šveb, M. (2021). Financial sustainability of cultural heritage: A review of crowdfunding in Europe. *Journal of Risk and Financial Management*, 14(3), 101. DOI: 10.3390/jrfm14030101

Jenik, I., Lyman, T., & Nava, A. (2017a). Crowdfunding and financial inclusion. *CGAP (Consultative Group to Assist the Poor) Working Paper, 41*.

Jenik, I., Lyman, T., & Nava, A. (2017b). Crowdfunding and financial inclusion. *CGAP (Consultative Group to Assist the Poor) Working Paper, 41*.

Kaminski, J., Hopp, C., & Tykvova, T. (2019). New technology assessment in entrepreneurial financing–Does crowdfunding predict venture capital investments? *Technological Forecasting and Social Change*, 139, 287–302. DOI: 10.1016/j.techfore.2018.11.015

Kukurba, M., Waszkiewicz, A. E., Salwin, M., & Kraslawski, A. (2021). Co-created values in crowdfunding for sustainable development of enterprises. *Sustainability (Basel)*, 13(16), 8767. DOI: 10.3390/su13168767

Meoli, M., Rossi, A., & Vismara, S. (2022). Financial literacy and security-based crowdfunding. *Corporate Governance*, 30(1), 27–54. DOI: 10.1111/corg.12355

Mohanty, A., Venkateswaran, N., Ranjit, P., Tripathi, M. A., & Boopathi, S. (2023). Innovative Strategy for Profitable Automobile Industries: Working Capital Management. In *Handbook of Research on Designing Sustainable Supply Chains to Achieve a Circular Economy* (pp. 412–428). IGI Global.

N., S. P., Goritiyal, C., Ramana, N. V., Matcha, A., Sukania, P., & Boopathi, S. (2024). Economic Growth Study and Inferences From Developments in E-Mobility. In *Advances in Mechatronics and Mechanical Engineering* (pp. 178–199). IGI Global. DOI: 10.4018/979-8-3693-5247-2.ch010

Ogwu, K., Hickey, P., Okeke, O. J.-P., Haque, A., Pimenidis, E., & Kozlovski, E. (2022). An integrated online/offline social network-based model for crowdfunding support in developing countries: The case of Nigeria. *Sustainability (Basel)*, 14(15), 9333. DOI: 10.3390/su14159333

Pasumarthy, R., Mohammed, S., Laxman, V., Krishnamoorthy, V., Durga, S., & Boopathi, S. (2024). Digital Transformation in Developing Economies: Forecasting Trends, Impact, and Challenges in Industry 5.0. In *Convergence of Human Resources Technologies and Industry 5.0* (pp. 47–68). IGI Global. DOI: 10.4018/979-8-3693-1343-5.ch003

Ravisankar, A., Shanthi, A., Lavanya, S., Ramaratnam, M., Krishnamoorthy, V., & Boopathi, S. (2024). Harnessing 6G for Consumer-Centric Business Strategies Across Electronic Industries. In *AI Impacts in Digital Consumer Behavior* (pp. 241–270). IGI Global.

Thaker, M., Thaker, H. B. M. T., Pitchay, A. B. A., & Khaliq, A. B. (2019). A proposed integrated Zakat-Crowdfunding Model (IZCM) for effective collection and distribution of Zakat fund in Malaysia. *Journal Website: Journal. Zakatkedah. Com. My*, 1(2), 1–12.

Venkateswaran, N., Vidhya, K., Ayyannan, M., Chavan, S. M., Sekar, K., & Boopathi, S. (2023). A Study on Smart Energy Management Framework Using Cloud Computing. In *5G, Artificial Intelligence, and Next Generation Internet of Things: Digital Innovation for Green and Sustainable Economies* (pp. 189–212). IGI Global. DOI: 10.4018/978-1-6684-8634-4.ch009

Vennila, T., Karuna, M., Srivastava, B. K., Venugopal, J., Surakasi, R., & Sampath, B. (2022). New Strategies in Treatment and Enzymatic Processes: Ethanol Production From Sugarcane Bagasse. In *Human Agro-Energy Optimization for Business and Industry* (pp. 219–240). IGI Global.

Vijaya Lakshmi, V., Mishra, M., Kushwah, J. S., Shajahan, U. S., Mohanasundari, M., & Boopathi, S. (2024). Circular Economy Digital Practices for Ethical Dimensions and Policies for Digital Waste Management. In *Harnessing High-Performance Computing and AI for Environmental Sustainability* (pp. 166–193). IGI Global., DOI: 10.4018/979-8-3693-1794-5.ch008

KEY TERMS AND DEFINITIONS

AI: Artificial Intelligence
KPI: Key Performance Indicator
OS: Operating System
SMART: Specific, Measurable, Achievable, Relevant, Time-bound
USB: Universal Serial Bus

Chapter 10
Balanced Scorecard Promotes the Strategic Alignment

Jorge Vareda Gomes
https://orcid.org/0000-0003-0656-9284
Universidade Lusófona, Portugal

Mário Romão
https://orcid.org/0000-0003-4564-1883
ISEG, Universidade de Lisboa, Portugal

ABSTRACT

Strategic alignment has become a key focus due to its significant impact on organizational performance and competitive advantage. Organizations seek alignment to enhance performance and gain a competitive edge by effectively interpreting and responding to their external business environment. In today's dynamic markets, it's crucial for organizations to leverage their strengths, address weaknesses, and seize opportunities. The Balanced Scorecard (BSC) addresses the limitations of traditional financial metrics by incorporating both financial and non-financial measures. It translates an organization's mission and strategy into a comprehensive set of performance measures, using a cause-and-effect logic across four perspectives: financial, customer, internal processes, and learning and growth. By aligning these perspectives with strategic objectives, the BSC helps ensure that all levels of the organization work towards shared goals, facilitating effective strategy implementation and performance management.

DOI: 10.4018/979-8-3693-9486-1.ch010

INTRODUCTION

Historically, IS/IT literature has emphasized the general importance of these technologies and their transformative potential concerning strategic and industry structure variables. Early works by Porter (1985) and Clemons (1986) laid the foundation by exploring how IS/IT could alter competitive dynamics and industry structures. These studies highlighted the revolutionary potential of technology to redefine strategic landscapes and create competitive advantages.

In recent years, however, the focus has shifted from a broad examination of IS/IT's potential to a more detailed analysis of its relationship with specific strategic components of firms. Contemporary research delves into how IS/IT interacts with various aspects of firm strategy, including:

- Business Environment: Maier et al. (1997) explored how IS/IT can enhance an organization's responsiveness to its business environment, facilitating better adaptation to external changes.
- Competitive Advantage: Mata et al. (1995) investigated how IS/IT contributes to competitive advantage by enabling differentiation and operational efficiencies.
- Organizational Performance: Powell and Dent-Micallef (1997) and Bharadwaj (2000) examined the impact of IS/IT on overall organizational performance, emphasizing its role in improving efficiency and effectiveness.
- Knowledge Accumulation: Grant (1996) focused on how IS/IT supports knowledge management and accumulation, crucial for innovation and organizational learning.

The concept of strategic alignment, initially introduced by Venkatraman (1989), has become central in understanding how the integration of business strategy and IT infrastructure can create value and enhance competitive advantage. According to Henderson and Venkatraman (1993), a critical issue for many organizations is the inability to realize value from IS/IT investments, which is often attributed to a misalignment between business strategies and IS/IT strategies. This alignment has become a major focus of both researchers and practitioners for over two decades. Despite the evolution of IS/IT from a traditional administrative support role to a strategic asset, there remains a notable gap in frameworks that fully leverage its potential and inform new business strategies (Gerow et al., 2014; Tallon & Pinsonneault, 2011; Wu, Straub, & Liang, 2015).

Recent studies underscore that managers continue to face fundamental concerns about strategic alignment in relation to IS/IT investments (Kappelman et al., 2020). From the IS/IT perspective, a lack of alignment often results in a reactive approach, treating IS/IT as a cost center rather than a strategic partner. Conversely, from the business perspective, misalignment can lead to diminished returns on IS/IT investments and reduced competitive capabilities (Karpovsky & Galliers, 2015; Tallon et al., 2016; Tarafdar & Tanriverdi, 2018).

Research highlights several challenges in capturing the business value of IS/IT investments. Traditional financial measures often fail to account for non-financial benefits such as customer satisfaction and employee training. Various methods and frameworks have been explored to address these challenges, including those aimed at capturing value that extends beyond direct financial metrics (Chen et al., 2010; Dehning et al., 2013; Mithas et al., 2012).

One notable tool in this context is the Balanced Scorecard (BSC), developed by Kaplan and Norton (1992). The BSC has emerged as a prominent management framework designed to address the limitations of traditional management systems, which typically rely on financial measures that reflect lagging indicators. By integrating financial and non-financial measures into a unified report, the BSC provides managers with a comprehensive view of organizational performance, enhancing their ability to manage activities effectively (Kaplan & Norton, 1996; Oliveira & Ferreira Oliveira, M., & Ferreira, 2019; Lueg & Vu, 2015). This framework offers a structured approach to measuring critical success factors, thus improving the understanding of business dynamics and supporting more effective decision-making processes (Mooraj et al., 1999).

The BSC has found widespread application across various sectors, demonstrating its utility in aligning business activities with organizational vision and strategy (Gomes & Romão, 2015; Hoque, 2014; Nørreklit et al., 2016). It effectively bridges the gap between strategic objectives and operational execution, ensuring that all organizational levels work cohesively towards shared goals. As organizations continue to navigate the complexities of modern business environments, the BSC remains a valuable tool for achieving strategic alignment and enhancing overall performance.

IS/IT STRATEGIC ALIGNMENT

The primary objective of any business activity is to create value. If an activity destroys value, it should not be pursued. In today's rapidly changing technological landscape, the importance of Information Systems (IS) and Information Technology (IT) in creating business value has never been more critical. However, there is no universally agreed definition of IS/IT business value. Cronk and Fitzgerald (1999) define IS/IT business value as the sustainable value added to a business by IS/IT investments, while Banker and Kauffman (1991) emphasize IS/IT's contribution to the management goal of profit maximization.

The Evolving Role of IS/IT in Business

With the continuous advancements in technology, organizations are increasingly leveraging IS/IT to gain a competitive advantage. Technologies such as artificial intelligence (AI), machine learning (ML), cloud computing, and big data analytics are transforming the business landscape (Brynjolfsson & McAfee, 2014). These technologies enable organizations to optimize operations, enhance customer experiences, and create new business models (Porter & Heppelmann, 2015). The strategic application of IS/IT allows businesses to not only streamline operations but also to innovate and respond swiftly to market changes. This requires aligning IS/IT strategies with broader business goals to ensure that technology investments drive tangible business outcomes (Bharadwaj et al., 2013).

Strategic Alignment of IS/IT and Business Strategies

The effective and efficient use of IS/IT necessitates alignment between IS/IT strategies and business strategies. This alignment is crucial for enhancing competitiveness and productivity by improving core business processes and leveraging technology to redesign these processes (Luftman, 2000). An IS/IT strategy should contribute to business value creation. IS/IT managers must understand the external environment's impact on the organization and adapt strategies accordingly (Ward & Peppard, 2002). In recent years, the concept of digital transformation has gained prominence, emphasizing the need for organizations to integrate digital technologies into all areas of business (Westerman et al., 2014). This transformation requires a holistic approach to aligning technology with business strategy to achieve sustainable growth and competitive advantage.

Key Aspects of Strategic Alignment

Over the last two decades, research on strategic alignment has highlighted several key aspects:

- Strategic Fit and Functional Integration: Henderson and Venkatraman (1993) discuss the integration between business strategy, IS/IT strategy, business infrastructure, and IS/IT infrastructure. The alignment ensures that technology investments support business objectives and enable seamless operations.
- Strategic Information Systems: Lederer and Salmela (1996) emphasize the degree to which planning processes result in strategic information systems. Effective planning ensures that technology initiatives align with business goals and drive value creation.

- Mission, Objectives, and Plans: Reich and Benbasat (1996, 2000) focus on the alignment of IS/IT missions and objectives with business goals. This alignment ensures that technology initiatives are strategically focused and contribute to overall business success.
- Timely Application of IS/IT: Luftman (2000) refers to applying IS/IT appropriately and timely in harmony with business strategies, enhancing business performance by aligning organizational and technological infrastructures (Croteau et al., 2001). This timely application of technology is critical for maintaining competitive advantage.

The Importance of Managing IS/IT Strategically

To remain competitive, organizations must manage IS/IT strategically. The strategic use of IS/IT is vital for creating business value (Henderson & Venkatraman, 1993; Luftman et al., 1993). A critical business issue is aligning business strategy with IS/IT deployment choices (Silvius, 2007; Kefi & Kalika, 2005; Ward & Peppard, 2002). IS/IT alignment consistently ranks as a top concern for researchers and executives (Luftman et al., 2005). Studies demonstrate the performance implications of alignment, leading to a more focused and strategic IS/IT use, which enhances performance (Chan et al., 2006). Misalignment often results in IS/IT investments failing to support business objectives, duplicating efforts, poor information management, and missed opportunities (Ward & Peppard, 2002). The consequences of misalignment are evident in wasted resources, inefficiencies, and missed opportunities for innovation and growth (Chen, Mocker, Preston, & Teubner, 2010).

Balanced Scorecard and Strategic Alignment

Kaplan and Norton (2001) note that the Balanced Scorecard (BSC) facilitates strategy communication throughout an organization, aligning personal and departmental goals. As part of this strategic process, long-term initiatives are identified and aligned with reduced emphasis on short-term financial measures and a focus on long-term success drivers. Organizational alignment involves evaluating structures, reporting lines, policies, and procedures to ensure consistency with strategy, including realigning business units or redefining support roles to best support the strategy (Kaplan & Norton, 2001). Kaplan and Norton (2001) describe strategic alignment with key components:

- Strategic Fit: Internal consistency in activities that implement unique strategy aspects. Achieving strategic fit ensures that all organizational activities are aligned and contribute to strategic goals.

- Organizational Alignment: Synchronization of company parts to create integration and synergy. Organizational alignment enhances coordination and cooperation across departments, enabling seamless operations and innovation.
- Human Capital Alignment: Aligning employees' goals and incentives with the strategy. Human capital alignment ensures that employees are motivated and equipped to contribute to strategic objectives.
- Alignment of Planning and Control Systems: Linking management systems for planning, operations, and control to strategy. Alignment of planning and control systems ensures that management processes are focused on strategic priorities.

Through various organizational experiences, Kaplan and Norton (2001) demonstrate successful strategy execution, showing how success relies on aligning strategy, organization, employees, and management systems (Schlosser et al., 2015; Gerow et al., 2014). Recent studies reinforce the importance of strategic alignment, highlighting its role in driving digital transformation and enabling organizations to navigate complex and dynamic environments (Kappelman et al., 2020).

THE BALANCED SCORECARD

Research has consistently highlighted the challenges private sector organizations face in effectively implementing their strategic objectives. Niven (2003) reported that an alarming 98% of private sector clients struggled to integrate their strategic goals into everyday operations. Kaplan and Norton (2001) further estimated that nine out of ten organizations fail to execute their strategies successfully. These findings underscore the critical need for effective tools and frameworks capable of accurately measuring the impact and leverage of organizational activities and long-term goals.

In response to these challenges, Luftman and Brier (1999) identified that organizations which achieve alignment between their strategy and operations can build a sustainable competitive advantage. This alignment facilitates greater visibility, efficiency, and profitability, enhancing a firm's ability to adapt to and respond to rapid market changes. Effective strategic alignment ensures that organizations can better manage their resources and operations in accordance with their strategic objectives.

The Balanced Scorecard (BSC), developed by Kaplan and Norton (1992), emerges as a pivotal framework designed to address these implementation challenges. The BSC integrates both financial and non-financial performance measures into a comprehensive system that aligns strategy with business operations and improves communication across organizational levels. This holistic approach bridges the gap between strategic objectives and daily operations, providing a robust tool for managing performance and driving long-term success (Kaplan & Norton, 1996). By incorporating a balanced set of metrics, the BSC enables organizations to monitor financial outcomes and assess factors such as customer satisfaction, internal processes, and learning and growth.

Recent research reaffirms the relevance and effectiveness of the BSC. Gomes and Romão (2015) and Hoque (2014) highlight that the BSC is widely utilized across various sectors to align business activities with organizational vision and strategy. These studies demonstrate that the BSC framework offers a structured approach to measuring critical success factors, leading to a deeper understanding of business dynamics and more informed decision-making (Mooraj et al., 1999; Nørreklit et al., 2016). By providing a comprehensive view of performance, the BSC supports organizations in translating strategic objectives into actionable plans and measurable outcomes.

Recent studies have continued to explore and refine the BSC framework. For example, Nair and Tschang (2022) examine how the BSC can be adapted to incorporate digital transformation initiatives, reflecting the need for agility in modern business environments. Similarly, Monecke and Bredereck (2021) discuss the role of the BSC in aligning with sustainability goals, demonstrating its adaptability to contemporary strategic challenges. These studies underscore the BSC's ongoing relevance and its capacity to evolve in response to emerging trends and organizational needs.

However, the BSC is not without its limitations and criticisms. Some scholars argue that while the BSC integrates financial and non-financial measures effectively, it may fall short in addressing dynamic external environments and the rapid pace of technological change (Voelpel, 2005; Gomes & Romão, 2012). These criticisms suggest that the BSC's static framework may struggle to adapt quickly to evolving market conditions and emerging technologies. Additionally, concerns have been raised regarding the BSC's ability to fully account for stakeholder contributions and navigate the complexity of modern business processes (Reilly & Reilly, 2000; Kennerley & Neely, 2003). These critiques highlight the need for continuous refinement of the BSC to enhance its applicability and effectiveness in diverse and rapidly changing environments.

Despite these criticisms, the BSC remains a valuable framework for organizations aiming to align their strategic objectives with operational activities and achieve sustained performance improvement. Its ability to integrate various performance measures into a cohesive strategy makes it an enduring tool for managing organizational performance and achieving strategic goals.

The Balanced Scorecard Framework

The Balanced Scorecard (BSC) is a comprehensive management tool developed to integrate traditional financial metrics with other crucial performance indicators, thereby providing a well-rounded view of organizational performance. This multifaceted approach ensures that organizations can effectively balance financial results with other critical aspects that drive long-term success. The BSC encompasses four main perspectives, each offering valuable insights into different dimensions of performance:

- Financial Perspective: This dimension focuses on the economic outcomes of past actions and serves as a key indicator of the financial health and profitability of an organization. It includes metrics such as revenue growth, cost management, and profitability ratios. These financial measures reflect the results of strategic decisions and operational effectiveness, providing stakeholders with an understanding of the organization's financial performance (Kaplan & Norton, 1992).
- Customer Perspective: The customer perspective evaluates how well the organization meets the needs and expectations of its target customer segments. It assesses performance through metrics such as customer satisfaction, retention rates, and market share. By focusing on this perspective, organizations can gain insights into customer perceptions and loyalty, which are critical for sustaining competitive advantage and driving revenue growth (Kaplan & Norton, 1996).
- Internal Process Perspective: This perspective examines the efficiency and effectiveness of key internal processes that drive organizational performance. It emphasizes process improvement, innovation, and quality management. Metrics in this area might include process cycle times, defect rates, and innovation rates. By optimizing internal processes, organizations can enhance operational efficiency, reduce costs, and improve overall product and service quality (Kaplan & Norton, 1996).
- Learning and Growth Perspective: This dimension measures the organization's capacity for innovation and improvement. It focuses on employee skills, organizational culture, and the technological infrastructure necessary for long-term success. Metrics might include employee engagement levels, training and development programs, and investments in new technologies. This perspective highlights the importance of fostering a culture of continuous learning and adaptation to support future growth and competitiveness (Kaplan & Norton, 1996).

Recent advancements and studies have further refined the application of the BSC. For example, recent research has examined how the BSC framework can be adapted to integrate sustainability goals and digital transformation initiatives (Nair & Tschang, 2022; Gomes & Romão, 2015). These updates ensure that the BSC remains relevant in addressing contemporary challenges and leveraging emerging opportunities.

Implementing the Balanced Scorecard

The Balanced Scorecard (BSC) transcends its role as a mere performance measurement tool to become a comprehensive strategic management system. It plays a crucial role in translating an organization's vision and strategy into actionable objectives and measurable outcomes. By integrating performance management across all levels of the organization, the BSC ensures that strategic objectives are aligned with business units and individual goals, fostering a cohesive approach to achieving strategic success (Kaplan & Norton, 1992). The key elements of successful BSC implementation are:

- **Communication**: Effective communication is a cornerstone of successful BSC implementation. The BSC framework facilitates the dissemination of strategic objectives throughout the organization, ensuring that every employee understands their role and contribution towards achieving the overarching strategy. This alignment is crucial for fostering a shared vision and driving collective efforts towards common goals (Kaplan & Norton, 2001). Recent studies have emphasized the importance of clear communication channels in enhancing organizational performance and strategic coherence (Roh, 2021).
- **Feedback and Learning**: The BSC is designed to provide continuous feedback on performance, which is vital for organizational learning and adaptation. Regular performance reviews enable organizations to assess their progress towards strategic objectives, learn from successes and setbacks, and make necessary adjustments to strategies. This iterative process helps organizations remain agile and responsive to changing conditions, thereby improving long-term strategic execution (De Geuser, Mooraj, & Oyon, 2009). Contemporary research highlights the role of feedback mechanisms in enhancing dynamic capabilities and fostering a culture of continuous improvement (Drew & Kuehl, 2021).
- **Alignment of Initiatives**: A key feature of the BSC is its ability to align strategic initiatives with business challenges. By ensuring that all initiatives are directly linked to strategic objectives, the BSC helps organizations focus their efforts and resources on activities that drive the achievement of

overarching goals. This alignment not only enhances operational efficiency but also ensures that strategic initiatives are effectively integrated into daily operations and decision-making processes (Kaplan & Norton, 1996). Recent advancements in BSC research have explored how to better align strategic initiatives with emerging business trends and technological advancements (Pérez & Martínez, 2022).

Figure 1. Strategic perspectives

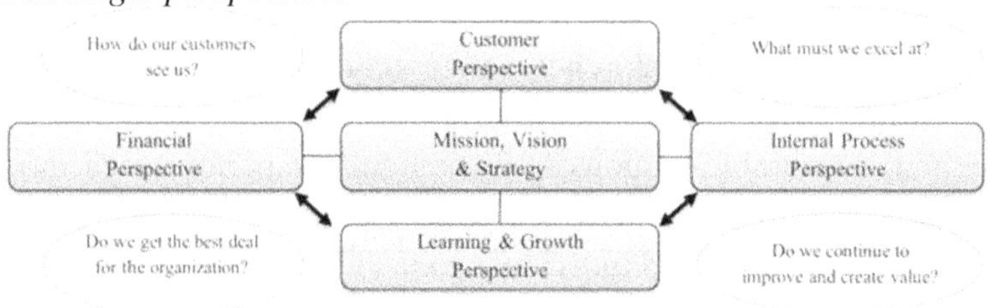

(adapted from Kaplan & Norton, 1996)

Recent research highlights the importance of the BSC in navigating complex and rapidly changing business environments. For instance, digital transformation initiatives require aligning technological investments with business objectives, a process that the BSC can facilitate by ensuring strategic alignment across various dimensions of the organization (Davenport & Westerman, 2018). The Balanced Scorecard has evolved to address contemporary business challenges, such as sustainability and corporate social responsibility (CSR). Modern adaptations of the BSC incorporate environmental, social, and governance (ESG) metrics, providing a more comprehensive view of organizational performance and accountability (Hristov, Chirico, & Appolloni, 2019). Moreover, advancements in data analytics and digital technologies have enhanced the BSC's capabilities, enabling organizations to track and analyze performance metrics in real-time. This real-time feedback allows for more agile and responsive decision-making, crucial for maintaining competitive advantage in fast-paced markets (Rikhardsson & Yigitbasioglu, 2018).

The Balanced Scorecard (BSC) framework uses the language of measurement to define strategic concepts such as quality, customer satisfaction, innovation, and learning and growth with greater clarity. By translating these concepts into measurable outcomes, the BSC enables organizations to track progress and align their activities with strategic goals effectively. A well-constructed scorecard that accurately reflects the strategy serves as an organizing framework for the management system, facilitating the alignment of various organizational elements with the overall strategic vision.

Key Elements of the Balanced Scorecard Approach

The Balanced Scorecard (BSC) approach stands out due to its distinctive elements that set it apart from other strategic management and learning frameworks. These elements, as articulated by Kaplan and Norton (2001), include:

- Translation of strategy into operational terms: The BSC excels in translating abstract strategic goals into concrete, actionable objectives and metrics. This transformation is crucial for operationalizing strategy, making it accessible and understandable across all levels of the organization. By clarifying strategic priorities, the BSC fosters a shared understanding among employees, which encourages alignment with the organization's strategic goals (Kaplan & Norton, 2001; Niven, 2003). This clear communication of strategy helps ensure that every team and individual knows their role in achieving the broader organizational objectives (Hendricks, 2018).
- Organizational alignment with strategy: The BSC emphasizes the importance of aligning organizational structures, processes, and resources with the strategic vision. This alignment is vital for ensuring that all parts of the organization are working towards a unified goal, which eliminates conflicting objectives and fosters synergy. By using the BSC framework, organizations can streamline their efforts, enhancing the impact of strategic initiatives and improving overall efficiency (Kaplan & Norton, 1996; Hiebl, 2015). Recent research also highlights how this alignment can lead to improved organizational performance and strategic coherence (Chung et al., 2020).
- Alignment of daily tasks with strategy: One of the BSC's key strengths is its ability to communicate strategy effectively at all organizational levels. By aligning daily tasks and activities with strategic objectives, the BSC ensures that employees understand how their individual contributions support the organization's broader goals. This alignment enhances motivation and engagement, as employees can see the direct impact of their work on organizational success (Kaplan & Norton, 2001; Papageorgiou & Papageorgiou, 2021). This connection between daily activities and strategic goals helps maintain focus and drive performance throughout the organization.
- Linking strategy to the budgeting process: The BSC integrates strategy into the budgeting process, reinforcing the idea that strategy is an ongoing commitment rather than a one-time event. By aligning strategic objectives with budgeting decisions, organizations can allocate resources more effectively, ensuring that financial investments support strategic priorities. This approach fosters a long-term perspective and encourages sustained attention to strategic goals, integrating financial planning with strategic execution (Kaplan

& Norton, 1996; Kaplan et al., 2017). Recent studies also underscore the benefits of this integration in enhancing financial performance and strategic alignment (Feng et al., 2020).

Influence of Top Management

Executive leadership is pivotal to the successful implementation and sustained effectiveness of the Balanced Scorecard (BSC) framework. The role of top management extends beyond mere endorsement; it involves actively driving the change and strategic alignment necessary for BSC to thrive. Leaders must champion the strategic vision and demonstrate a commitment to its integration across the organization. Their active engagement helps inspire confidence among employees, cultivates a culture of continuous improvement, and ensures that strategic objectives are consistently aligned with operational activities.

Recent research underscores the impact of executive leadership on the successful deployment of the BSC. For instance, Bhagwat and Sharma (2007) illustrate how the BSC can significantly enhance supply chain performance by aligning logistics activities with broader strategic goals. This alignment not only streamlines processes but also improves overall efficiency and effectiveness within the supply chain, showcasing the BSC's adaptability to different operational contexts.

Similarly, Bento, Bento, and White (2014) demonstrate the BSC's role in fostering organizational learning and innovation. The BSC provides a structured framework for measuring and tracking progress in these critical areas, facilitating a more systematic approach to learning and development. This structured approach aids organizations in developing innovative strategies and improving their competitive edge.

The integration of digital technologies and data analytics has further amplified the capabilities of the BSC. As Rikhardsson and Yigitbasioglu (2018) note, the use of real-time data and advanced analytics allows organizations to gain deeper insights into their performance metrics. This enhanced visibility enables more agile and informed decision-making, helping organizations to adapt to changing market conditions and capitalize on emerging opportunities. The integration of these technologies reinforces the BSC's role as a dynamic and valuable strategic management tool.

Overall, the effectiveness of the BSC is greatly influenced by the active involvement of executive leadership. Their commitment to aligning initiatives with strategic objectives and fostering a culture of continuous improvement is essential for leveraging the BSC's full potential. The framework's adaptability to various contexts and its enhancement through digital tools further underscore its value in driving organizational performance and strategic success.

Figure 2. Linking strategies to balanced scorecard measures

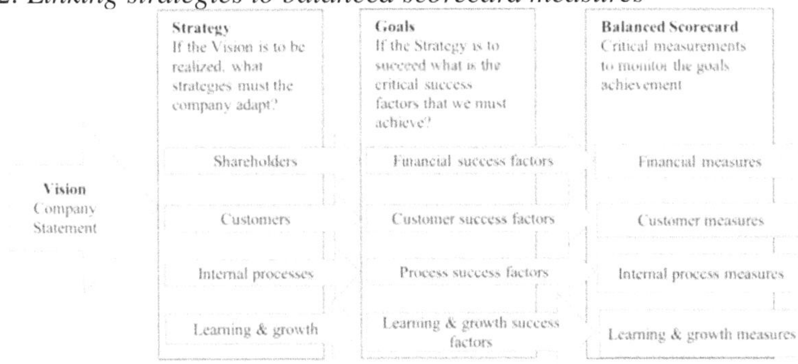

(adapted from Kaplan & Norton, 1993)

The introduction of the Balanced Scorecard (BSC) in organizations offers several advantages that support strategic alignment and performance management. According to Pandey (2005), these benefits include:

- Comprehensive Understanding of Customer Expectations: The BSC is a tool that facilitates the identification and understanding of customers' needs and expectations. By incorporating customer-focused metrics, organizations can better align their strategies with market demands and enhance customer satisfaction.
- Emphasis on Intangible and Intellectual Capital: The BSC framework prioritizes non-financial initiatives that contribute to the development of intangible assets, such as intellectual capital and organizational culture. This focus on intangible assets helps align strategic growth objectives with business requirements, fostering innovation and long-term value creation (Kaplan & Norton, 2004).
- Strategic Alignment of Employee Activities: One of the BSC's core strengths is its ability to link strategic objectives with daily operations. By clearly communicating strategic goals to employees, the BSC enables individuals to understand how their work contributes to the organization's overall strategy, enhancing motivation and engagement.
- Systematic Performance Review and Feedback: The BSC provides a structured approach to performance measurement, allowing organizations to conduct regular performance reviews and provide feedback. This systematic process helps identify areas for improvement and ensures that strategic objectives are being met.

Strategy Mapping and Performance Alignment

Mapping a strategy is crucial for visualizing and aligning an organization's perspectives, objectives, and measures, and for understanding the causal linkages between them. Strategy Maps, as introduced by Kaplan and Norton (2000), are instrumental in this process. They offer a visual representation of how performance measures are connected to the organization's strategic objectives, facilitating clearer communication and alignment throughout the organization.

Strategy Maps help in clarifying the relationship between strategic objectives and performance measures by outlining the cause-and-effect relationships among various elements of the strategy. This visual tool allows managers to identify key strategic objectives within each of the Balanced Scorecard perspectives—financial, customer, internal processes, and learning and growth—and to link these objectives through a hierarchical model.

In developing a Strategy Map, managers first select critical strategic objectives for each perspective. For instance, in the learning and growth perspective, objectives might include improving employee training and development. These objectives are then linked to other perspectives in the Strategy Map. For example, enhanced employee training and development can lead to greater efficiency in internal processes. Improved process efficiency might then enhance customer satisfaction, which ultimately contributes to increased profitability in the financial perspective.

The hierarchical model embedded in Strategy Maps illustrates how improvements in one area can positively influence other areas, thereby generating shareholder value. This model provides a structured approach to understanding how various performance measures and strategic objectives are interrelated. By making these linkages explicit, Strategy Maps enable organizations to better communicate their strategy, align departmental and individual goals with overarching strategic objectives, and ultimately drive more effective execution and performance.

Cause-and-Effect Relationships in the BSC

Kaplan and Norton (2001) argue that the Balanced Scorecard (BSC) framework effectively illustrates cause-and-effect relationships among its four perspectives: financial, customer, internal processes, and learning and growth. These relationships are crucial for understanding how improvements in lower-level perspectives—such as internal processes or employee learning and growth—can predict and drive higher-level financial outcomes. By making these connections explicit, organizations can better comprehend how non-financial initiatives impact financial performance.

For instance, enhancements in the learning and growth perspective, which may include investments in employee training or technological upgrades, can lead to more efficient internal processes. Improved internal processes, in turn, can enhance customer satisfaction and retention, ultimately contributing to stronger financial performance, such as increased revenue or profitability. This cascade of improvements underscores how non-financial measures and strategic objectives are interlinked with financial results.

Kaplan and Norton's (2006) approach emphasize the derivation of a Balanced Scorecard from strategic objectives, allowing organizations to align their long-term strategic initiatives with their performance measurement systems. This alignment is essential for shifting focus from short-term financial metrics to long-term drivers of success. By focusing on these drivers, organizations ensure that their strategic goals are pursued in a consistent and integrated manner. This strategic alignment helps organizations to achieve sustained success by addressing both financial and non-financial aspects of performance.

Organizational Alignment through the BSC

Kaplan and Norton (2006) propose that achieving organizational alignment through the Balanced Scorecard (BSC) requires the development of scorecards at all organizational levels. This multi-tiered approach ensures that every level of the organization, from top executives to front-line employees, is working towards goals that are consistent with the overarching organizational strategy.

By cascading the BSC throughout the organization, individual and departmental objectives can be directly linked to the strategic vision. This alignment helps ensure that all efforts are directed towards achieving the organization's long-term goals. The process involves translating high-level strategic objectives into actionable targets at lower levels, thereby creating a clear line of sight between daily activities and strategic outcomes.

This alignment fosters a cohesive approach to performance management, where all employees understand how their roles contribute to broader organizational goals. As a result, the BSC enhances organizational effectiveness by promoting consistency in goal setting and performance evaluation across different levels of the organization. This alignment not only improves individual and team performance but also strengthens the overall execution of the organization's strategy, leading to greater success and sustainability.

Recent Developments and Applications

The Balanced Scorecard (BSC) has indeed undergone significant evolution in recent years to address the growing complexity of modern organizational environments. This evolution reflects the need to integrate emerging technologies, data analytics, and broader considerations of sustainability and corporate social responsibility (CSR) into strategic management frameworks.

Recent advancements in technology and data analytics have enabled organizations to enhance their performance tracking and analysis capabilities. According to Rikhardsson and Yigitbasioglu (2018), these technologies provide real-time insights into strategic progress, allowing organizations to make more informed and agile decisions. The integration of advanced data analytics into the BSC framework has transformed it from a static measurement tool into a dynamic system that can adapt to rapidly changing business environments and provide actionable insights that drive strategic initiatives.

The BSC framework has also evolved to incorporate sustainability and CSR metrics, reflecting the increasing importance of environmental and social factors in organizational strategy. Figge et al. (2002) discuss how the integration of these metrics into the BSC aligns organizational performance with broader societal goals, such as reducing environmental impact and enhancing social responsibility. This integration helps organizations address stakeholder expectations and regulatory requirements, while also contributing to long-term strategic success by fostering a more sustainable and socially responsible approach to business.

Originally introduced to balance financial and non-financial performance measures, the BSC has expanded its role to become a comprehensive framework for strategic change and managing intangible value drivers. Kaplan and Norton (2001) highlight how the BSC now supports the assessment of intangible assets such as employee knowledge, customer relationships, and innovation capabilities. Ittner and Larcker (2003) further emphasize that this evolution reflects a broader understanding of value creation, moving beyond traditional financial metrics to encompass a more holistic view of organizational performance

Figure 3. Balanced scorecard strategy map

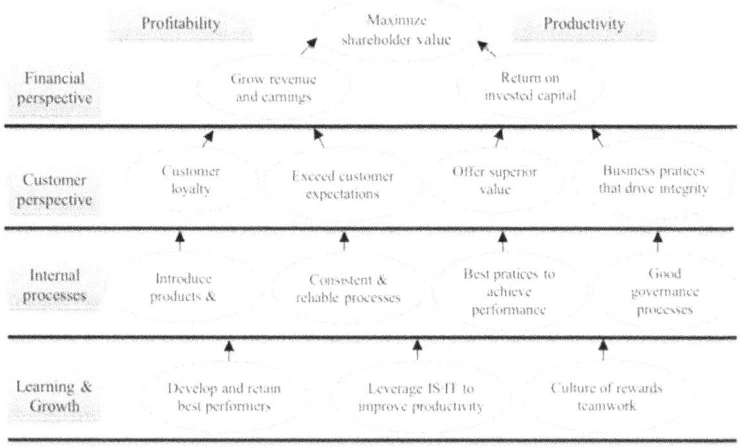

(adapted from Kaplan & Norton, 2000)

One of the core strengths of the BSC is its ability to compel management teams to scrutinize the underlying beliefs and assumptions of their strategies. By integrating various perspectives—financial, customer, internal processes, and learning and growth—the BSC forces organizations to articulate and examine their strategic hypotheses. This introspective approach ensures that strategies are not only well-formulated but also robust against evolving business challenges (Kaplan & Norton, 2004). For the BSC to be effective, it must be driven from the top of the organization. Senior leadership plays a pivotal role in setting the vision, allocating resources, and demonstrating commitment to the BSC framework. Successful implementation depends on a well-developed organizational structure that supports strategic goals and integrates BSC metrics into everyday operations (Kaplan & Norton, 2006; Malina & Selto, 2001). Ownership of the BSC should extend beyond top management to include middle management as well. Engaging both levels ensures that strategic objectives are translated into actionable plans and operational tasks, fostering a culture of accountability and alignment throughout the organization (Kaplan & Norton, 2004; Al-Mashari et al., 2017). What distinguishes the BSC from other strategic measurement tools is its incorporation of outcome measures and the linkage of performance drivers through cause-and-effect relationships. The BSC is not just a retrospective evaluation tool but functions as a feed-forward control system, helping organizations anticipate and influence future performance outcomes. This dynamic approach enables organizations to proactively address potential issues and align their strategies with long-term objectives (Kaplan & Norton, 2001; Neely et al., 2017). Despite its advantages, the BSC is not without challenges. Its successful implementation requires a deep commitment to aligning strategic objectives with day-to-day operations, and a comprehensive understanding of customer needs and organizational capabilities. Furthermore, while the BSC provides a structured framework for performance measurement and strategic alignment, its effectiveness is contingent upon full integration and adoption within the organization (Niven, 2003; Rompho, 2011). The BSC remains a powerful tool for internal communication, facilitating clarity and alignment of strategic goals across various levels of the organization. When fully integrated and embraced, the Balanced Scorecard (BSC) can significantly enhance organizational performance and strategic coherence. Research supports the notion that effective implementation of the BSC aligns organizational activities with strategic objectives, leading to improved overall performance. For instance, Ahn (2001) demonstrates that the BSC, when thoroughly integrated, can drive enhanced organizational effectiveness by ensuring that strategic goals are clearly communicated and executed across all levels. This alignment fosters a unified approach to achieving long-term objectives, thereby optimizing performance outcomes. Similarly, Lueg and Radlach (2016) highlight that the BSC's ability to integrate financial and non-financial measures creates a more comprehensive performance management system. This integrated approach helps organizations not only track their progress but also adapt to changing conditions and strategic priorities. By bridging the gap between strategy formulation and execution, the BSC supports a cohesive strategic framework that enhances decision-making and organizational agility. The BSC's impact on strategic coherence and performance is evident across various sectors, where it has been instrumental in aligning operational activities with broader business goals. This alignment is crucial for navigating complex and dynamic market environments, as it provides a structured method for translating strategic vision into actionable objectives and measurable results. Therefore, organizations that effectively implement and leverage the BSC are better positioned to achieve sustained competitive advantage and operational excellence.

Recent research and applications have further refined the BSC framework, incorporating advances in technology and data analytics to provide more nuanced insights into performance metrics and strategic alignment. The integration of real-time data and advanced analytics into the BSC system has enabled organizations to track and adjust their strategies more dynamically, ensuring ongoing relevance and effectiveness in a rapidly changing business environment (Rikhardsson & Yigitbasioglu, 2018; Gibbons & Kaplan, 2018). Additionally, the incorporation of sustainability and corporate social responsibility (CSR) metrics into the BSC framework has gained prominence, reflecting the growing importance of environmental and social considerations in strategic planning and performance management (Figge et al., 2002; Azzone & Manzini, 2013).

STRENGTHS AND LIMITATIONS OF THE BALANCED SCORECARD

"Management control systems provide information that is intended to be useful for managers in performing their jobs and for assisting organizations in developing and maintaining viable patterns of behavior" (Otley, 1999, p. 364). Despite the considerable impact of the Balanced Scorecard (BSC) on organizations globally, the framework has attracted various criticisms, particularly from the academic community, who have raised concerns about its empirical nature and practical limitations (Frigo, 2002).

Criticisms of the Balanced Scorecard

The critique of the BSC has focused on several areas, including its methodological design and practical application:

- Incomplete Model: Atkinson et al. (1997) argue that the BSC is an incomplete model as it does not adequately address the contributions of employees, suppliers, or the community. This limitation suggests that the BSC fails to fully capture the external and internal factors that influence a firm's performance.
- Employee Motivation: Smith (1998) contends that the BSC does not adequately account for employee motivation, which is crucial for achieving organizational objectives. The framework's emphasis on performance metrics may overlook the importance of motivating and engaging employees.
- Means versus Ends: The distinction between "means" and "ends" within the BSC has been criticized for lacking clarity. Maltz et al. (2003) highlight the need for additional empirical validation to clarify these concepts and ensure that the BSC provides a comprehensive strategic management tool.
- Balancing Perspectives: Reilly and Reilly (2000) point out that the BSC does not adequately balance the different perspectives, particularly concerning stakeholder contributions. The connections between measurements and perspectives are not always clear, which can undermine the effectiveness of the BSC.
- Focus on Internal Measures: Kennerley and Neely (2003) argue that the BSC's focus on internal measures limits its ability to address external competitive factors. This narrow focus may prevent managers from gaining a complete understanding of market dynamics.
- Cause-and-Effect Relationships: Norreklit questions the validity of the cause-and-effect relationships presumed by the BSC, arguing that these relationships may not always hold true in practice.

- Strategic Control Model: There is debate about whether the BSC should be considered a strategic control model, with some scholars suggesting that it may not fully serve this function.
- Performance Measures: The adequacy of the number of performance measures and their ability to provide a comprehensive view of organizational performance is questioned. The effectiveness of these measures in judging performance remains a topic of discussion.
- Reliability and Effectiveness: Concerns about the reliability and overall effectiveness of the BSC as a management solution persist, with critics questioning whether it delivers on its promises.
- Rigidity of the BSC: Gomes and Romão (2012) and Voelpel (2005) criticize the BSC for its relative rigidity, which can constrain the flexibility needed to adapt to rapid changes and external challenges. The framework's requirement to map indicators into predefined perspectives may limit its responsiveness.
- Measures: The BSC's reliance on a limited number of measures can be both an advantage and a disadvantage. Mohobbot (2004) and Akkermans and Oorschot (2004) point out the importance of integrating measures across different organizational levels to ensure coherence between strategic and operational goals.
- Static Organizations: The BSC has been seen as fostering static organizational structures that may struggle to cope with the dynamic and competitive nature of modern business environments. This static nature can inhibit an organization's ability to innovate and adapt (Gomes & Romão, 2012).
- External Environment: The BSC's focus on internal processes and metrics can lead to a disconnect from external factors such as innovation and connectivity. This limitation highlights the BSC's shortcomings in addressing the broader corporate network environment (Voelpel, 2005).
- Knowledge Generation and Learning: The BSC has been criticized for its limited ability to support knowledge generation and dynamic learning, which are essential for long-term organizational growth (Gomes & Romão, 2012).
- Complex Business Processes: The linear format of the BSC may not adequately capture the complexity of modern business processes, leading to challenges in understanding and managing intricate organizational dynamics (Voelpel, 2005).

Academic Contributions Highlight the Following Aspects of the BSC

Academic contributions to the Balanced Scorecard (BSC) have highlighted several key aspects, emphasizing its role in strategic management, performance measurement, and organizational alignment. These aspects reflect the BSC's adaptability and comprehensive nature, providing valuable insights into its applications and impact on contemporary organizational practices.

- Strategic Alignment and Integration: One of the most significant academic contributions is the BSC's ability to align organizational activities with strategic objectives. Kaplan and Norton (1996) originally emphasized how the BSC integrates financial and non-financial performance measures to align day-to-day operations with strategic goals. This alignment ensures that all organizational levels are working towards common objectives, which enhances coherence and focus across the enterprise.
- Enhanced Performance Measurement: he BSC's approach to measuring performance goes beyond traditional financial metrics to include non-financial indicators that reflect other critical aspects of organizational performance. This includes customer satisfaction, internal process efficiency, and employee learning and growth. By incorporating these dimensions, the BSC provides a more comprehensive view of organizational health and success (Kaplan & Norton, 2001).
- Strategic Communication and Learning: The BSC facilitates strategic communication by translating complex strategic objectives into actionable and understandable terms for employees at all levels. It also supports organizational learning by providing feedback on performance, which helps organizations adjust strategies and improve over time. This feedback loop is essential for continuous improvement and strategic adaptation (De Geuser et al., 2009).
- Cause-and-Effect Relationships: Kaplan and Norton (2001) argue that the BSC illustrates cause-and-effect relationships among its four perspectives: financial, customer, internal processes, and learning and growth. These relationships help organizations understand how improvements in lower-level perspectives can drive higher-level financial outcomes, thereby linking non-financial initiatives to financial performance (Kaplan & Norton, 2001)..
- Adaptation to Emerging Trends: Recent academic work highlights the BSC's adaptability to emerging trends such as digital transformation, sustainability, and corporate social responsibility (CSR). Integrating these contemporary issues into the BSC framework allows organizations to address modern chal-

lenges while maintaining alignment with their strategic goals (Figge et al., 2002; Rikhardsson & Yigitbasioglu, 2018)

- Strategic Management and Change: The BSC has evolved into a strategic management framework that helps organizations manage change and drive strategic initiatives. By linking strategic objectives with performance measures, the BSC supports the management of intangible value drivers such as innovation and organizational culture (Ittner & Larcker, 2003).
- Application Across Sectors: The BSC has demonstrated versatility and applicability across various sectors, from manufacturing to service industries, and has been used to improve performance in diverse organizational contexts. This broad applicability underscores its relevance as a strategic management tool (Gomes & Romão, 2015; Hoque, 2014).

CONCLUSION

IS/IT alignment is achieved when information systems and technology capabilities support the core functions of the business and possess the flexibility to adapt to changes in business strategy. This alignment ensures that IS/IT investments are justified by their ability to deliver tangible benefits and drive transformational change within the organization. Additionally, the principles, policies, standards, and architectures of IS/IT should be guided by and supportive of the overarching business strategies. This alignment guarantees that the IT infrastructure and practices contribute effectively to the achievement of business goals (Luftman & Kempaiah, 2007; Chan et al., 2010; Peppard & Ward, 2016). The future success of a firm increasingly relies on its ability to manage intangible assets effectively. These include customer relationships, which drive future revenue and enhance brand loyalty; internal business processes, which contribute to operational excellence and competitive advantage; and employee learning and development, which ensures that the workforce remains skilled and capable of advancing strategic initiatives. Measuring organizational success and implementing effective strategies for sustainable performance are ongoing challenges for managers, researchers, and practitioners. Financial metrics alone are insufficient for forecasting future performance, necessitating a balanced approach that incorporates both financial and non-financial measures (Kaplan & Norton, 2001; Neely et al., 2005). Although many organizations have begun to adopt non-financial performance measures to assess aspects such as customer loyalty and employee satisfaction, the full potential of these measures remains underutilized. There is often a gap between recognizing the importance of non-financial metrics and effectively integrating them into strategic management practices (Dixon et al., 2000). The Balanced Scorecard (BSC) continues to be a global benchmark for measuring organizational performance, despite some criticisms. It assists organizations in translating their strategies into actionable objectives and aligning various business activities to achieve these objectives. Additionally, BSC facilitates the communication of the organization's vision, mission, and strategic goals across all levels of the organization and ensures that all investment initiatives, including those related to IS/IT, are aligned with the strategic objectives (Kaplan & Norton, 2004; Kaplan & Norton, 2006). BSC has evolved beyond a measurement tool to become a comprehensive strategic management framework. It now plays a crucial role in assessing the readiness of intangible value drivers and supporting long-term strategic change. The framework's ability to integrate outcome measures with performance drivers through cause-and-effect relationships makes it a powerful tool for internal communication and strategic alignment. However, BSC is not without its criticisms. Some critiques highlight the model's relative rigidity and its focus on internal processes, which may limit its ability to respond to rapid external changes and competitive pressures (Gomes & Romão, 2012; Voelpel, 2005). Furthermore, concerns have been raised regarding the model's ability to address knowledge generation and dynamic learning environments, and its limitations in understanding complex business processes (Kennerley & Neely, 2003; Norreklit, 2000, 2003). Despite these criticisms, the Balanced Scorecard remains a valuable framework for organizations seeking to align their strategies and measure performance comprehensively. It is particularly effective when fully integrated and supported by both top and middle management, demonstrating its relevance and adaptability in contemporary strategic management practices (Ittner & Larcker, 2003; Kaplan & Norton, 2004)..

REFERENCES

Ahn, H. (2001). Applying the Balanced Scorecard concept: An empirical study. *International Journal of Productivity and Performance Management*, 50(2), 104–114.

Akkermans, H., & Oorschot, K. (2004). Relevance assumed: A case study of Balanced Scorecard development using System Dynamics. *The Journal of the Operational Research Society*, 56(8), 931–941. DOI: 10.1057/palgrave.jors.2601923

Al-Mashari, M., Al-Mudimigh, A., & Zairi, M. (2017). Enterprise resource planning: A taxonomy of critical factors. *European Journal of Operational Research*, 146(2), 352–366. DOI: 10.1016/S0377-2217(02)00554-4

Atkinson, A. A., Waterhouse, J. H., & Wells, R. B. (1997). A Stakeholder Approach to Strategic Performance Measurement. *Sloan Management Review*, 38, 25–37.

Azzone, G., & Manzini, R. (2013). The integration of environmental and social aspects into the Balanced Scorecard. *Business Strategy and the Environment*, 22(2), 118–131.

Banker, R., & Kauffman, R. (1991). *Quantifying the Business Value of IT: An illustration of the Business Value Linkage Framework*. Sterm School of Business, NewYork, working paper nº IS-91-21.

Bento, R. F., Bento, M. S., & White, K. C. (2014). The Balanced Scorecard as a Strategic Management Tool for Innovation and Learning. *Journal of Business Research*, 67(6), 1140–1148.

Bhagwat, R., & Sharma, M. K. (2007). Performance measurement in supply chains: An overview of the Balanced Scorecard approach. *International Journal of Production Economics*, 106(2), 291–303.

Bharadwaj, A. (2000). A Resource-Based Perspective on Information Technology Capability and Firm Performance: Am Empirical Investigation. *Management Information Systems Quarterly*, 24(1), 169–196. DOI: 10.2307/3250983

Bharadwaj, A., El Sawy, O. A., Pavlou, P. A., & Venkatraman, N. (2013). Digital business strategy: Toward a next generation of insights. *Management Information Systems Quarterly*, 37(2), 471–482. DOI: 10.25300/MISQ/2013/37:2.3

Brynjolfsson, E., & McAfee, A. (2014). *The second machine age: Work, progress, and prosperity in a time of brilliant technologies*. W.W. Norton & Company.

Chan, Y. E., Huff, S. L., Barclay, D. W., & Copeland, D. G. (1997). Business Strategic Orientation, Information Systems Strategic Orientation, and Strategic Alignment. *Information Systems Research*, 8(2), 125–150. DOI: 10.1287/isre.8.2.125

Chan, Y. E., Sabherwal, R., & Thatcher, J. B. (2006). Antecedents and Outcomes of Strategic IS Alignment: An empirical investigation. *IEEE Transactions on Engineering Management*, 51(3), 27–47. DOI: 10.1109/TEM.2005.861804

Chen, D. Q., Mocker, M., Preston, D. S., & Teubner, A. (2010). Information systems strategy: Reconceptualization, measurement, and implications. *Management Information Systems Quarterly*, 34(2), 233–259. DOI: 10.2307/20721426

Chung, C., Lee, D., & Lee, J. (2020). The Impact of Organizational Alignment on Strategic Performance: Evidence from Korean Firms. *International Journal of Strategic Management*, 21(2), 119–137.

Clemons, E. K. (1986). Information systems for sustainable competitive advantage. *Information & Management*, 11(3), 131–136. DOI: 10.1016/0378-7206(86)90010-8

Cobbold, I., & Lawrie, G. (2002). The development of the Balanced Scorecard as a strategic management tool. *International Journal of Business Performance Management*, 4(1), 1–11.

Cragg, P., Tagliavini, M., & Mills, A. (2011). Evaluating the alignment of IT with business processes in SMEs. *Communications of the Association for Information Systems*, 28(1), 1–34.

Cronk, M. C., & Fitzgerald, E. P. (1999). Understanding "IS business value": Derivation of dimension. *Logistics Information Management*, 12(1-2), 40–49. DOI: 10.1108/09576059910256240

Croteau, A. M., Bergeron, F., & Raymond, L. (2001). Business Strategy and Technological Deployment: Fit and Performance. *Information Systems Management*, 6(4).

Davenport, T. H., & Westerman, G. (2018). Why so many high-profile digital transformations fail. *Harvard Business Review*. Retrieved from https://hbr.org

De Geuser, F., Mooraj, S., & Oyon, D. (2009). Does the Balanced Scorecard add value? A differential analysis of the BSC's benefits for different types of firms. *European Accounting Review*, 18(3), 503–536.

de Leede, J., Looise, J. C., & Alders, B. (2002). Innovation, improvement and operations: An exploration of the management of alignment. *International Journal of Technology Management*, 23(4), 353–368. DOI: 10.1504/IJTM.2002.003015

Dixon, J. R., Nanni, A. J., & Vollmann, T. E. (2000). *The New Performance Challenge: Measuring Operations for World-Class Competition*. Wiley.

Drew, S., & Kuehl, D. (2021). Feedback and Learning in Strategic Management: The Role of the Balanced Scorecard. *Strategic Management Journal*, 42(9), 1678–1696.

Feng, M., Li, S., & Zhang, J. (2020). Strategic Alignment and Financial Performance: An Empirical Study of the Balanced Scorecard. *Journal of Financial Management*, 40(3), 543–562.

Figge, F., Hahn, T., Schaltegger, S., & Wagner, M. (2002). The sustainability balanced scorecard–linking sustainability management to business strategy. *Business Strategy and the Environment*, 11(5), 269–284. DOI: 10.1002/bse.339

Frigo, M. (2002). Strategy and the Balance Scorecard. *Strategic Finance*, 84(5), 6–9.

Gerow, J. E., Thatcher, J. B., & Grover, V. (2014). Six types of IT-business strategic alignment: An investigation of the constructs and their measurement. *European Journal of Information Systems*, 23(5), 456–472.

Gibbons, R., & Kaplan, R. S. (2018). The balanced scorecard and strategy management: A framework for improved performance. *Journal of Management Accounting Research*, 30(1), 1–20.

Gomes, J., & Romão, M. (2012). How benefits management helps Balanced Scorecard to deal with business dynamic environments. *Tourism & Management Studies*, 9(1), 129–138.

Gomes, J., & Romão, M. (2015). Achieving project success through alignment with organizational strategy: Balanced Scorecard approach. In Proceeding of 8th IADIS International Conference - Information's Systems 2015, Funchal, Portugal.

Grant, R. M. (1996). Toward a knowledge-based theory of the firm. *Strategic Management Journal*, Summer Special Issue 17, 109–122.

Grembergen, W. V. (2001). *Information Technology Evaluation Methods & Management*. Idea Group Publishing. DOI: 10.4018/978-1-878289-90-2

Henderson, J. C., & Venkatraman, N. (1993). Strategic Alignment: Leveraging Information Technology for Transforming Organisations. *IBM Systems Journal*, 32(1), 4–16. DOI: 10.1147/sj.382.0472

Hendricks, K. B. (2018). The Balanced Scorecard: A Primer for Healthcare Organizations. *Journal of Healthcare Management*, 63(4), 256–263.

Hiebl, M. R. W. (2015). The Influence of Organizational Culture on Balanced Scorecard Usage: Evidence from the German Manufacturing Sector. *Journal of Management Control*, 26(4), 363–387.

Irani, Z. (2002). Information Systems Evaluation: Navigating through the problem domain. *Information & Management*, 40(1), 11–24. DOI: 10.1016/S0378-7206(01)00128-8

Kaplan, R. S., & Norton, D. P. (1992). Using the Balanced Scorecard as a Strategic Management System. *Harvard Business Review*, 74(1), 75–85.

Kaplan, R. S., & Norton, D. P. (1993). *Putting the Balanced Scorecard to Work. Harvard Business Review*. September-October.

Kaplan, R. S., & Norton, D. P. (1996). *The Balanced Scorecard: Translating Strategies into Action*. Harvard Business School Press.

Kaplan, R. S., & Norton, D. P. (2000). *The Strategy-Focused Organisation*. Harvard Business School Press.

Kaplan, R. S., & Norton, D. P. (2001). *The Strategy Focused Organisations: How Balanced Scorecard Companies Thrive in the New Business Environment*. Harvard University Press.

Kaplan, R. S., & Norton, D. P. (2004). *Strategy Maps: Converting Intangible Assets into Tangible Outcomes*. Harvard Business School Press.

Kaplan, R. S., & Norton, D. P. (2006). *Alignment: Using the Balanced Scorecard to Create Corporate Synergies*. Harvard Business School Press.

Kearns, G. S., & Lederer, A. L. (2003). A Resource-Based View of Strategic IT Alignment: How knowledge sharing creates competitive advantage. *Decision Sciences*, 34(1), 1–29. DOI: 10.1111/1540-5915.02289

Keen, P. G. W. (1991). *Shaping the Future*. Harvard Business School Press.

Kefi, H., & Kalika, M. (2005). Survey of Strategic Alignment Impacts on Organisational Performance in International European Companies. *In Proceedings HICSS '05,38th Annual Hawaii International Conference.*

Kennerley, M., & Neely, A. (2003). Measuring performance in a changing business environment. *International Journal of Operations & Production Management*, 23(2), 213–229. DOI: 10.1108/01443570310458465

Konsynski, B. R., & McFarlan, W. F. (1990). Information Partnerships: Shared Data, Shared Scale. *Harvard Business Review*, 68(5), 114–120. PMID: 10107083

Lederer, A., & Salmela, H. (1996). Towrds a theory of strategic information systems planning. *The Journal of Strategic Information Systems*, 4(14), 1–50.

Lueg, R., & Radlach, R. (2016). The Balanced Scorecard: A review of its application in Germany. *European Management Journal*, 34(6), 573–586.

Lueg, R., & Vu, L. (2015). Success factors in balanced scorecard implementations – A literature review. *Management Review*, 26(4), 306–327.

Luftman, J., & Brier, T. (1999). Achieving and Sustaining Business–IT Alignment. *California Management Review*, 42(1), 109–122. DOI: 10.2307/41166021

Luftman, J., Kempaiah, R., & Nash, E. (2005). Key Issues for IT Executives 2005. *MIS Quarterly Executive*, 5(2), 81–101.

Luftman, J. N. (2000). Assessing business IT-alignment maturity. *Communications of the Association for Information Systems*, 4(14).

Luftman, J. N., Lewis, P. R., & Oldach, S. H. (1993). Transforming the Enterprise: The Alignment of Business and Information Technology Strategies. *IBM Systems Journal*, 32(1), 198–221. DOI: 10.1147/sj.321.0198

Maier, J. L., Rainer, R. K.Jr, & Snyder, C. A. (1997). Environmental scanning for information technology: An empirical investigation. *Journal of Management Information Systems*, 14(2), 177–201. DOI: 10.1080/07421222.1997.11518170

Maisel, L. S. (1992). Performance measurement: The balanced scorecard approach. *Journal of Cost Management*, (Summer), 47–52.

Malina, M. A., & Selto, F. H. (2001). Communicating and controlling strategy: An empirical study of the effectiveness of the balanced scorecard. *Journal of Management Accounting Research*, 13(1), 47–73. DOI: 10.2308/jmar.2001.13.1.47

Maltz, A. C., Shenhar, A. J., & Reilley, R. R. (2003). Beyond the balanced Scorecard: Refining the search for organisational success measures. *Long Range Planning*, 36(2), 187–204. DOI: 10.1016/S0024-6301(02)00165-6

Mata, F. J., Fuerst, W. L., & Barney, J. B. (1985). Information technology and sustained competitive advantage: A resource-based-analysis. *MIS Quartely*, (December), 487–504.

Mithas, S., Ramasubbu, N., & Sambamurthy, V. (2012). How information management capability influences firm performance. *Management Information Systems Quarterly*, 36(1), 25–49.

Mohobbot, A. (2004). The Balanced Scorecard (BSC): A critical analysis. *Journal of humanities and social*, 18, 219-232.

Monecke, A., & Bredereck, R. (2021). The Balanced Scorecard and sustainability: Aligning performance measures with environmental goals. *Business Strategy and the Environment*, 30(5), 2425–2440.

Mooraj, S., Oyon, D., & Hostettler, D. (1999). The Balanced Scorecard: A necessary good or an unnecessary evil. *European Management Journal*, 17(5), 481–491. DOI: 10.1016/S0263-2373(99)00034-1

Nair, A., & Tschang, F. T. (2022). Integrating digital transformation into the Balanced Scorecard framework. *Information & Management*, 59(2), 103–115.

Neely, A., Gregory, M., & Platts, K. (2017). Performance measurement system design: A literature review and research agenda. *International Journal of Operations & Production Management*, 37(5), 581–610.

Neely, A., & Kennerley, M. (2003). Measuring Performance in a Changing Business Environment. *International Journal of Operations & Production Management*, 23(2), 213–229. DOI: 10.1108/01443570310458465

Niven, P. (2003). *Balanced Scorecard: Step-by-Step for Government and Nonprofit Agencies*. John Wiley & Sons, Inc.

Norreklit, H. (2000). The Balanced Scorecard: A critical analysis of some assumptions. *Management Accounting Research*, 11(1), 65–88. DOI: 10.1006/mare.1999.0121

Norreklit, H. (2003). The Balanced Scorecard: What is the score? A rhetorical analysis. *Accounting, Organizations and Society*, 28(6), 591–619. DOI: 10.1016/S0361-3682(02)00097-1

Nørreklit, H., Mitchell, F., & O'Regan, N. (2016). The Balanced Scorecard in the public sector: A review. *Public Money & Management*, 36(2), 139–146.

Oliveira, M., & Ferreira, J. J. (2019). Enhancing innovation capability with balanced scorecard approach. *Journal of Business Research*, 101, 706–716.

Oliveira, R., Ramalho, M., & Macedo, L. (2019). Balanced Scorecard and Performance Measurement: A review of the literature. *Journal of Business Research*, 101, 369–379.

Olve, N. G., Roy, J., & Wetter, M. (1999). *Performance Drivers*. John Wiley & Sons.

Otley, D. (1999). Performance Management: A Framework for Management Control Systems Research. *Management Accounting Research*, 10(4), 363–382. DOI: 10.1006/mare.1999.0115

Pandey, I. M. (2005, January-March). Balanced Scorecard: Myth and Reality. *Vikalpa*, 30(1), 51–66. DOI: 10.1177/0256090920050105

Papageorgiou, A., & Papageorgiou, M. (2021). Employee Engagement and Organizational Performance: The Role of Balanced Scorecard. *Business Research Quarterly*, 24(2), 123–137.

Peppard, J., & Ward, J. (2004). Beyond strategic information systems: Towards an IS capability. *The Journal of Strategic Information Systems*, 13(2), 167–194. DOI: 10.1016/j.jsis.2004.02.002

Peppard, J., & Ward, J. (2016). *Managing the Business of IT: What Every Executive Needs to Know*. Wiley.

Pérez, J., & Martínez, E. (2022). Aligning Strategic Initiatives with Technological Advancements: A Balanced Scorecard Approach. *Information Systems Research*, 33(1), 80–95.

Porter, M. E. (1985). *The Competitive Advantage: Creating and Sustaining Superior Performance*. Free Press.

Powell, T. C., & Dent-Micallef, A. (1997). Information technology as competitive advantage: The role of human, business, and technology resources. *Strategic Management Journal*, 18(5), 375–405. DOI: 10.1002/(SICI)1097-0266(199705)18:5<375::AID-SMJ876>3.0.CO;2-7

Reich, B. H., & Benbasat, I. (1996). Measuring the Linkage between Business and Information Technology Objectives. *Management Information Systems Quarterly*, 20(1), 55–81. DOI: 10.2307/249542

Reich, B. H., & Benbasat, I. (2000). Factors that Influence the Social Dimensions of Alignment between Business and Information Technology Objectives. *Management Information Systems Quarterly*, 24(1), 81–113. DOI: 10.2307/3250980

Reilley, G. & Reilley, R. (2000). Using a measure network to understand and delivery value. *Journal of Cost Management,* 5-14.

Rikhardsson, P., & Yigitbasioglu, O. (2018). Business intelligence & analytics in management accounting research: Status and future focus. *International Journal of Accounting Information Systems*, 29, 37–58. DOI: 10.1016/j.accinf.2018.03.001

Roh, H. (2021). Enhancing organizational performance through effective communication strategies: Insights from the Balanced Scorecard. *Journal of Business Communication*, 58(4), 491–514.

Rompho, N. (2011). Why the Balanced Scorecard Fails in SMEs: A Case Study. *International Journal of Business and Management*, 6(11), 39–46. DOI: 10.5539/ijbm.v6n11p39

Schlosser, F., Wagner, H.-T., & Coltman, T. (2015). Reconsidering the dimensions of business-IT alignment. *The Journal of Strategic Information Systems*, 24(2), 98–112.

Silvius, G. A. J. 2007. Business and IT alignment in theory and practice. *In Proceedings of the HICSS '07,40th Annual Hawaii International Conference on System Sciences.*

Smith, M. (1998). *Measuring organisational e effectiveness*. Management Accounting.

Tallon, P. P., Kraemer, K. L., & Gurbaxani, V. (2000). Executives' perceptions of the Business Value of Information Technology: A Process-Oriented Approach. *Journal of Management Information Systems*, 16(4), 145–173. DOI: 10.1080/07421222.2000.11518269

Tallon, P. P., & Pinsonneault, A. (2011). Competing perspectives on the link between strategic information technology alignment and organizational agility: Insights from a mediation model. *Management Information Systems Quarterly*, 35(2), 463–486. DOI: 10.2307/23044052

Tallon, P. P., Queiroz, M., Coltman, T., & Sharma, R. (2016). Business process and information technology alignment: Construct conceptualization, empirical illustration, and directions for future research. *Journal of the Association for Information Systems*, 17(9), 563–589. DOI: 10.17705/1jais.00438

Tarafdar, M., & Tanriverdi, H. (2018). Impact of the information technology–human resource (IT-HR) alignment on performance: A study of IT and HR managers' perceptions. *Journal of Management Information Systems*, 34(2), 375–413.

Voelpel, S. C., Leibold, M., Eckhoff, R. A., & Davenport, T. H. (2005). The Tyranny of Balanced Scorecard in the Innovation Economy. In *Proceedings of 4th International Critical Management Studies Conference-Intellectual Capital Stream*. Cambridge University.

Ward, J., & Peppard, J. (2002). *Strategic Planning for Information Systems* (3rd ed.). John Wiley.

Wu, S. P. J., Straub, D. W., & Liang, T. P. (2015). How information technology governance mechanisms and strategic alignment

Chapter 11
Role of Networking and Partnerships in the Success of Hybrid Entrepreneurs

Sasmita Misra
https://orcid.org/0009-0001-1147-1081
NMIMS, Hyderabad, India

Ashutosh Pandey
https://orcid.org/0000-0002-8255-8459
FORE School of Management, New Delhi, India

Shashank Mittal
O.P. Jindal Global University, India

Shubham Kumar
University of Minnesota, Minneapolis, USA

ABSTRACT

Hybrid entrepreneurship, where individuals balance traditional employment with entrepreneurial ventures, relies heavily on effective networking and partnership building. This paper explores the crucial role of networking and partnerships in the success of hybrid entrepreneurs, highlighting the benefits and challenges associated with these activities. It examines various strategies for leveraging social capital, including online platforms, industry events, and professional organizations. The study also addresses future trends impacting networking, such as digital transformation, remote work models, and ethical business practices. Through case studies

DOI: 10.4018/979-8-3693-9486-1.ch011

and real-world examples, the paper illustrates how hybrid entrepreneurs navigate these dynamics to achieve business growth and professional development. By understanding and utilizing these networking tools and strategies, hybrid entrepreneurs can enhance their chances of success in an evolving business landscape.

INTRODUCTION

In the changing dynamics of entrepreneurship, hybrid entrepreneurship is one of the significant new trends where entrepreneurial activities are mixed with regular employment. There are many people who are termed as hybrid entrepreneurs: individuals who manage a salaried employee status with the start-up of their own business and an aim to become successful in both (Demir et al., 2020) This peculiar manner of engagement has a number of advantages, at that independence in financial matters and mitigation of risks, but it is also posing specific challenges to business planning.

Networking and partnerships are very necessary for hybrid entrepreneurs to prosper; they offer the necessary resources, opportunities, and support. Effective networking will create ways for business opportunities, source knowledge, and create a positive image. Any form of partnerships, be it formal or informal, brings added-value resources, strategic skills, and advantages that are crucial for leveraging the complexities of hybrid entrepreneurship. (Tang et al., 2024)

The following section is going to discuss why networking and partnerships are so important to a hybrid entrepreneur. It aims to make the reader able to comprehend how the given aspects help in growing and sustaining hybrid ventures. The chapter, hence, pursues an understanding of the dynamics of networking, the benefits of strategic partnership, and practical strategies of building, and maintaining the same. In doing that, the chapter will also avail the hybrid entrepreneur with so much insight that is relevant in his practice.

This chapter is going to explain, through relative theories, real-world case studies, and practical examples that clarify the fact that the importance of professional and social networks in building effective partnerships should not be underestimated but should be worked upon with dedication in overcoming the challenges that come with it. To understand how networking and partnerships can be achieved in respect of entrepreneurial success while accomplishing business goals, these are the key areas that will be the crux of what is in the mind of the readers by the end.

UNDERSTANDING HYBRID ENTREPRENEURSHIP

Hybrid entrepreneurship is a dynamic approach in which people engage in traditional employment and entrepreneurial activities at the same time. That is a strategy of dual operation. One gives a person a tested water of viaticum in providing some stability and resources, whereas the other is directed toward innovative ventures. Recognition of this understanding in hybrid entrepreneurship requires understanding the unique challenges and opportunities engendered by the dual operation.

Hybrids frequently begin their entrepreneurial activities while still holding down another job, in order to ensure a steady income and to decrease the risks associated with starting a new business. Hybrid entrepreneurship gives one a chance to research certain entrepreneurial ideas that would otherwise be very hard to experiment with or put into use without a safety net. This instils stability in traditional employment, which enables access to various valued resources—from industry experience and contacts to skills considered critical in sustaining an entrepreneurial initiative. (Timothy et.al., 2009)

However, managing these two concurrently faces different kinds of difficulties. Hybrid entrepreneurs are expected to balance their employer's needs on their time and energy against the demands of their business. This usually requires them to have high time management skills, organizational skills, the ability to set priorities, and establish boundaries to prevent burnout (Jay, J.,2012; Tunio et.al., 2022).

More so, hybrid entrepreneurs have to blend their professional role with the entrepreneurial to optimize both career and business ventures. The integration may include the use of the connections and resources of the main job to support business while these latter do not hamper the obligations of employment. Successful hybrid entrepreneurs manage to reconcile their dual roles through means that help ensure their employment can aid in gathering insights, network establishment, and resources that prove worthwhile to entrepreneurship. (Ferreira et.al., 2019)

It proposes a middle ground strategy that creates repetitive potential for both exploring business opportunities and staying with the job in a safe form of doing work. Hybrid entrepreneurship can only be well comprehended when seen as an interplay between the security that one is paid to work and the pursuit of business opportunities with a great deal of flexibility and dynamic that is needed for the individual to balance and harvest from the two positions.

Role of Networking in Hybrid Entrepreneurship

Hence, it's important networking for the success of hybrid entrepreneurs to address balancing of the two worlds, such as traditional employment and their entrepreneurial ventures; building and maintaining a strong network; accessing resources and gaining insights; and opportunities that would support their dual roles. (Chen et.al., 2024)

Networking provides hybrid entrepreneurs with an extensive range of highly resourceful contacts. Professional connections might provide invaluable advice, industry knowledge, and referrals that are essential to the development of a business. Hybrid entrepreneurs can, therefore, find partners, potential clients, and mentors who will offer the necessary support and guidance with regular participation in industry events, conferences, and seminars. These are the actions that build an active contact base from which help is solicited in business development or problem solving. (Aaboen et al., 2013)

Furthermore, networking helps hybrid entrepreneurs to remain aware of industry trends and possible emerging opportunities. They get in contact with peers and other company drivers to remain up-to-date on the latest developments in markets, technologies, or even best practices. This is important knowledge for making informed decisions and staying competitive in both their main job and entrepreneurial pursuit (Riaz et al., 2024)

Collaboration and partnering are also other main features of networking. From the interactions with other professionals, hybrid entrepreneurs are in a position to find shared projects, joint marketing campaigns, and collaborative work. The collaborations empower them into greater horizons of business, expanding their strengths and synergizing growth opportunities that, for instance, collaborating with industry experts or other entrepreneurs, can direct to innovative solutions and a new business opportunity that one could not reach independently. (Aray et.al.2023)

Besides, it provides two sources of support: emotional and professional. The whole way through, trying to balance a traditional job with "entrepreneurial acts" is quite demanding and lonely. A core network involving peers and mentors who really know what's going on can cheerlead. This support network helps motivate, provides shared experiences, and points out the complexity of what hybrid entrepreneurs will actually face, in terms of playing multiple roles (Reuer, J. J., et.al. 2019).

In other words, networking is a key characteristic of hybrid entrepreneurship that allows acquiring the leverage of resources, insights, and opportunities for balancing conventional employment with entrepreneurship. A devoted network facilitates hybrid entrepreneurs in enhancing the business possibilities and remaining informed about industry trends, searching for opportunities to achieve greater results, and acquiring support for effectively overcoming the issues that are directly or indirectly triggered by their dual role (P. J. Batt & S. Purchase, 2004).

Creating Effective Alliances

Effective partnering is at the core of success by hybrid entrepreneurs, allowing them opportunities for complementary skills, resources and opportunities that will expand the business ventures. In the end, effective partnerships are based on mutual benefit, trust and a clear communication, which comes in handy in dealing with the complexities of managing both the conventional job and entrepreneurial activities. Building a successful partnership begins with setting mutual goals and expectations. Hybrid entrepreneurs should clearly define what they seek to get out of the partnership and understand what the potential partners want. Converging their objectives will give a common vision and hence preclude fights and misunderstandings. All these should be communicated openly with goals and roles and responsibilities of collaboration agreed upon to ensure seamless collaboration (Cacciolatti et.al.2020).

Trust and credibility are key aspects of making a successful partnership. Hybrid entrepreneurs have to instigate and hold the sense of trust in their partners by showing to be reliable, transparent, and to being of high integrity. Building trust means rising to whatever is promised and to be honest on what one can or can't do, but in cases of issues, resolving the issues or answering the concerns should always be on time. Trust results in positive working relationships in which both parties are sure of the partnership.

Communication is an important element in making a relationship efficient. From time to time, there is a need for regular and clear communication in order to allow for the free flow of information that is necessary regarding progress, changes, and problems. Hybrid entrepreneurs need to establish mechanisms through which ongoing dialogue can be held, whether meetings, reports, digital means, all aimed at maximum alignment and addressing any hiccups that may have arisen. Open communication encourages a spirit of collaboration, problem-solving, and sharing of insights and resources.

The potentials of flexibility and adaptability make partnership management effective. Traditional employment and entrepreneurial activities are both very dynamic; hence, thus, circumstances change quite frequently. This makes the hybrid entrepreneur adopt changes in his approach and cooperate with his partner to proceed in this milieu. Flexibility in changing plans, re-negotiating terms and looking for avenues anew goes a long way in housing an active and responsible partnership. (Banal-Estanol et.al.2015)

Finally, the partnership's effectiveness may have some needed adjustments effected through constant appraisal. Every once in a while, reviews of how the partnership is performing, its outcomes, and satisfaction levels could be a good pointer as to what works and what might not. It is through reflective practice that the partnership keeps on track, meeting its goals, and maintaining value from one party to the other.

In conclusion, effective partnership practices have been noted to involve goal alignment, building trust, clear communication, flexibility, and the practice of evaluation. These are the practices enabling hybrid entrepreneurs to exploit the maximum potential from collaborations and attain success in their dual roles. All these dimensions have the potential to empower hybrid entrepreneurs so that they could create and sustain functional collaborations, further advancing their entrepreneurial pursuit and professional development (Weihe, 2006).

Hybrid entrepreneurs will be able to utilize social capital to balance traditional employment with entrepreneurial efforts. In generally, social capital indicates the value accumulated from relations, networks, and social interaction through which access to resources, opportunities, and support is obtained. Proper use of social capital by hybrid entrepreneurs will be found to be of great help in the direction of dual-role management and business success (Humam, M., & Hariadi, 2022).

A primary way of using social capital is in the cultivation and maintenance of a diverse professional network. Building one's relationships with industry peers, mentors, clients, and collaborators will enable the hybrid entrepreneur to access a broad spectrum of expertise and resources. These connections can provide valuable insights, offer guidance, and open doors to new opportunities. Hybrid entrepreneurs would update their venture partnerships actively within their network, be it through social media, industry events, or professional associations, to remain current on the trends, garner referrals, and crystallize potential business venture partners.

Social capital also allows for direct access to resources and even support that can significantly act as tools in the growth of an entrepreneur. Such relationships can avail strategic advice, business development support, and the presence of knowledge in a particular industry. Similarly, professional community linkages can produce funding, collaboration, and partnering to make better the already available capacities and market reach of the business. In this regard, hybrid entrepreneurs may access resources otherwise beyond their grasp.

With bridging social capital, hybrid entrepreneurs link into different groups, further expanding into new spheres of collaboration and innovation. For example, the synergies created between connections of the main occupation with this entrepreneurial network can prove beneficial for all standpoint businesses. It is the bridging capital such that it helps in realizing wider perspectives, skills, and resources in a general way.

Besides, social capital is great for the sake of emotional and professional support. Balancing the traditional employment with entrepreneurship can at times be challenging or even isolating. A strong framework and effective network base of peers, mentors, and advisors who extend their support will encourage the entrepreneur by sharing experiences and practical advice. Such a support system is invaluable in helping an entrepreneur to manage stress and stay motivated to ultimately overcome some dilemmas that juggle up due to dual roles.

In short, using social capital involves developing and maintaining a varied network of business relationships, drawing on resources and reassurance, linking various networks, and looking for emotional and business encouragement. Harnessing such social capital power, hybrid businesspeople will be better placed to balance their two roles and draw on critical resources, which will consequently propel them toward successes. Hybrid entrepreneurs can further optimize and improve their application and accomplishments using entrepreneurial activities for intended business endeavours by taking advantage of the merits from their social capital by strategically involving themselves in their network.

Networking and Partnership Challenges

Being hybrids, the hybrid entrepreneurs are disadvantaged in networking and partnership-building, having to work at two levels: conventional employment and entrepreneurial ventures, with conflicting demands most of the time. All these in turn affect the way they can establish and manage professional relationships and, therefore, the way their ventures will perform. (Noworól, .2013)

The most significant barrier to hybrid entrepreneurs is a **time constraint**. Running a business on a full-time schedule always leaves little time to make the necessary contacts, which are one of the basic characteristics of this type of entrepreneurship. Because of their tight schedules, hybrid entrepreneurs cannot avail themselves of industry events, quality conversations, or follow-ups with potential partners. A lack of time can then result in opportunities going by the wayside to develop crucial relationships and to locate potentially useful partnerships.

Another challenge is that of **conflicting priorities.** The dual roles bring in the aspect of managing a salaried position at the same time as an entrepreneurial venture, causing dual demands of time and energy for the respective individual. A balancing act is required in dual conflicting priorities if the espoused hybrid entrepreneur is to execute their dual functions effectively; hence, in the process of facing difficult times, they will maintain a responsible amount of attention to the aspects of networking. It hinders abilities to develop and maintain relationships that are required for the growing and sustaining of businesses.

For instance, a further challenge arises from the fact that hybrid entrepreneurs must contend with the **limitation of resources.** Since they are engaging in full-time commitment to employment as well as entrepreneurship, experience has shown that hybrid entrepreneurs may experience financial deficiencies, and a relative lack of networking presented by, for instance, conferences, professional associations, or networking events, which normally require substantial financial outlay and personal time. This hinders networking with potential partners and collaborative agencies. (Gielnik et.al., 2020)

Difficulty to build trust can complicate partnership building even more. Building trust and credibility is essential in any profession, but it can be more labour-intensive when one is balancing multiple roles. This follows that the hybrid entrepreneur has a lack of concentration when it comes to making a real difference or succeeding in terms of having a sustainable, long-term relationship. Trust is architected and nurtured with constant communication, consistency, reliability, and follow-up—all those things that are so hard to do if you're holding a full-time job and trying to engage in entrepreneurial activities.

Another issue related to this is that of the **perception about commitment**. Hybrid entrepreneurs are perceived to be less committed and less dedicated by potential partners and contacts in networks. One would think, for example, that the entrepreneur may be dividing his attention and thus not having space to be truly committed to any kind of collaborative effort or business venture. Reliability and clearly communicated intentions can defuse these perceptions. Thus, in a nutshell, effective management of the balancing act of both requires one to be also viewed as committed and capable.

Overcoming these challenges requires strategic steps: focusing on networking activities, finding time management tools that work, and creatively leveraging extant resources. In understanding and dealing with these barriers ahead of time, hybrid entrepreneurs are better positioned to network effectively and form support relations that will ultimately help them to be effective in their dual roles. (Thompson & Bolton, 2024)

Case Studies and Real-World Examples

Looking at applied cases gives a glimpse of how hybrid entrepreneurs seem to leverage networking and partnerships to achieve success. And one good example is **Jane Smith**, one of the hybrid entrepreneurs based in San Francisco, California. A tech consultant in her day job, she decided to be a founder of a startup that develops AI-driven health solutions as her side hustle. She utilized her professional network to source seed money and strategic advice from colleagues within the professional network. She also participated in several tech meetups and conferences, from where she could make her strategic partnership with other tech entrepreneurs for collaboration that could increase her market reach and credibility for her startup.

Another powerful example is **Tom Nguyen,** who is part-time graphic designer and full-time marketing manager based out of Toronto, Canada. Tom used his wide network within the marketing community to create partner relationships with other designers and creative professionals. Through joint marketing campaigns and joint ventures, Tom was able to expand his customer base and really build the new, solid opportunities which otherwise would be merely a dream than an ambition. His proactive approach at industry events and online forums aided him in establishing useful contacts and resource exchange that were quite helpful in developing his freelance business.

Maria Lopez is a hybrid entrepreneur based in Barcelona, Spain; she remains another best example for this. Maria is a project manager within a multinational corporation. However, she also pursues a side business of her own, a boutique event planning firm. She leveraged her own corporate network to great effect to kick-start the entrepreneurial activity by securing new customers, and important word-of-mouth recommendations about the services she offered. By attending events and keeping in touch with her industry contacts, she managed to turn some of these relationships into platforms for her side business, which brought high-profile projects in its direction.

Joint Analysis of the Caselets

The caselets of Jane Smith, Tom Nguyen, and Maria Lopez provide deep insights into how hybrid entrepreneurs leverage networking and partnerships to further their venture-related ends. There are unique approaches and shared strategies in each of these cases that contribute to the success of individuals when trying to manage traditional employment with entrepreneurial pursuits.

The Jane Smith story is an example of how professional networks can be accessed for an initial funding source and strategic advice. Her habit of attending tech meetups or conferences exemplifies how a hybrid entrepreneur can use these kind of industry events to establish relevant connections and seek cooperation. In Jane's case, the integration of insights and resources coming from the primary job into the startup underscores the need for role alignment that permits the maximization of benefits from professional and entrepreneurial roles.

This translates from Tom Nguyen's experience to be a clear call of the importance of a good network in the chosen field of business. With the help of his marketing networks, Tom was able to grow his base of clientele and also identify new opportunities for working in his freelancing business. His proactive approach to engage design professionals and other creative peers asserts that understanding collaborations and joint marketing hones the business capabilities of hybrid entrepreneurs.

The case of Maria Lopez shows the strategic use of corporate connections in boosting her boutique event planning business. The ability of Maria to translate this network of corporates into contacts and high-profile projects speaks to the importance of making partnerships that are relevant to one's professional knowledge. How she has been able to stay involved while playing active roles in her corporate and entrepreneurial capacities is characteristic of how hybrid entrepreneurs can effectively integrate their networks to achieve business growth.

A joint analysis of the caselets brings out several common themes; in a way, all three entrepreneurs are bringing out very clearly the role of networking to access resources, gain referrals, and finally explore collaborative opportunities. They also underline how such targeted engagement with industry-specific networking and events tends to forge relationships that make possible furtherance of the business goals. The caselets also show how effectively playing with this social capital can yield serious dividends in terms of gaining visibility, expanding market reach, or acquiring important business supports.

The caselets overlay the different elements that underline the role of networking and partnerships in the hybrid entrepreneurship domain. Such entrepreneurs effortlessly combine their professional networks with entrepreneurial activities, negotiate the intricacies of dual identities to finally meet with considerable enterprise success. Their cases provided valuable lessons for others in the hybrid entrepreneurship space, with the underlying theme being the strategic networking and collaboration in order to grow a business and, in turn, develop professionally.

Overall, the two cases illustrate different ways hybrid entrepreneurs might leverage their network and partnerships. How an entrepreneur strategically uses their social capital—from raising finance and resources to gaining market traction with referrals—often makes the difference between navigating challenges toward entrepreneurial success. In the cases, entrepreneurs actively network and partner in meaningful ways to show the balance of traditional employment with entrepreneurship as leading to important business growth and professional fulfillment.

Tools and Resources for Networking and Partnerships

Effective networking and partnership building is based upon a set of tools and resources that act to make connections, manage relationships, and enhance collaboration. These tools can be of great help to hybrid entrepreneurs in building professional relationships and effective partnerships.

Online networking sites form an important part of contemporary networking tools. Platforms such **as LinkedIn, Twitter, and even Facebook** can be used to find a place to connect with other professionals within the industry, join related groups, and discuss any issues. In particular, LinkedIn is one great platform for professional networking and for showcasing one's expertise and reaching out for partnership and joint venture opportunities. By actively participating in groups and forums related to the specific business or industry, hybrid entrepreneurs can expand their network and be up-to-date on its overall state, trends, and potential opportunities.

The Events/Conferences in the Industry: conferences and events offer the unmatched, face-to-face freedom of networking. One can attend when there are trade shows, seminars, and workshops in person for potential partners, clients, or mentors. Such events usually have networking sessions and panel discussions facilitating meaningful interactions and new contacts. One can even download the application specific to the event or program, which can help one schedule meetings with the contacts that are received during the time of the event and in maintaining a contact list for future reference.

Professional organizations and associations are structured opportunities for networking and partnership development. The peers, industry resources, and key events for opportunities in the American Marketing Association or Project Management Institute can be pages long. Those organizations often sponsor networking events, additional professional development resources, and forums for collaborating and sharing knowledge.

CRM Software may be looked at as a handy tool toward managing and nurturing professional relationships. With the likes of Salesforce or HubSpot, all the interactions will be tracked and followed by the details put in the record of contact and associated communication trace. This organized approach will get the networks well managed and create a platform where the hybrid entrepreneur will be able to leverage the relationships in growing the business.

Collaboration Tools, such as Slack, Microsoft Teams, and Asana, help with effective communication and project management among other partners and any other team members. They provide real-time communication for easy coordination, file sharing, and task management. As such, project collaboration and productive partnerships are ensured.

Mentorship platforms such as SCORE or MicroMentor provide a view for the entrepreneurial community to connect with experienced mentors who could keep them on track or give just a bit of guidance on their path. It gives the confidence in a structured way to go out there and find somebody who can solve a business challenge and what insights they can give through their experiences.

These tools and resources can be very instrumental in improving a hybrid entrepreneur's networking and partnership-building capacity. Thus, online platforms, industry events, professional organizations, relationship management with CRM software, collaboration tools, and mentorship programs can be used by hybrid entrepreneurs to resolve the multiple challenges they face while balancing their dual roles in running their businesses.

FUTURE TRENDS AND IMPLICATIONS

The state of affairs in networking and partnership building for hybrid entrepreneurs is very dynamic, with changes brought about by technological, working dynamics, and business environment changes. Grasping future trends and their implications can assist hybrid entrepreneurs to be ahead of the game and able to leverage emerging opportunities for success.

Digital transformation is among the main trends that change the landscape of networking and partnerships. Technological improvement, including AI, machine learning, and data analytics, changes the way people network and collaborate. AI-driven tools contribute to making improvements in networking, with top-notch applications to provide personalized recommendations of potential contacts and partnerships through data analytics. Furthermore, other forms being availed are virtual and augmented reality platforms as a new medium for highly immersive experiences in networking, allowing entrepreneurs to reach others in newer ways that go beyond geographical boundaries.

The Remote and Hybrid Work Models are becoming more dominant and in their own right set the paradigms on how networking and partnerships can be developed and sustained. With the rise in remote work, there is more capacity for hybrid entrepreneurs to build relationships with professionals and partners all over their respective nations and the world at large. However, it also presents challenges in maintaining personal connections and managing relationships in a virtual environment. The ability to work effectively within remote networking platforms and tools will be vital to growing and sustaining value-based partnerships associated with this rapidly changing work landscape.

A strong trend will be toward **increased personal branding**. In this rapidly competitive field, it is safest to say that hybrid entrepreneurs have to invest in personal branding to differentiate their efforts amidst the clutter. Good personal branding involves the demonstration of authority and sharing great wisdom, including regular engagement within community channels on industry matters. By having a visible and credible online presence, they translate promising connections and opportunities that could better equip them to establish partnerships that bear fruit.

Collaboration and Innovation Ecosystems are growing to be some of the critical ingredients to business success. The arising innovation hubs, start-up accelerators, and industry-specific ecosystems develop access in hybrid entrepreneurs to resources, mentorship, and collaboration opportunities. More so, these bring forth environments that work in the way of enabling entrepreneurs to contact related personalities, get connected for financing, and engage in undertakings that see a collaborative approach brought on board. Involvement with such ecosystems has immense advantages in issues to do with growth and development.

Partnerships and networking activities are two areas where **ethical and sustainable business practices** are slowly beginning to find their ground and influence approaches. In other words, nowadays, business relationships tend to place more emphasis on ethical practice, social responsibility, and sustainability. Hybrid entrepreneurs are increasingly, therefore viewed as those who must align partners with shared values and commitments in ethical practice. Partnerships built on shared ethical standards help in upholding reputations, are trustworthy, and result in long-term successes.

Conclusively, digital transformation, changing work models, personal branding, collaborative ecosystems, and ethical considerations shape the future trend of hybrid entrepreneurship networking and partnership relations. On the other hand, one may wish to argue that an entrepreneur being well-informed by these trends will only assist in guiding how best to go about the dynamism in the landscape to effectively pilot through the complexities of this dual role and tame new opportunities to achieve sustained success in their entrepreneurial endeavours.

CONCLUSION

In summary, networking and partnership building are imperative questions for success in hybrid entrepreneurship, experiencing a double role: traditional employment and self-employment. Strong networking and the ability to create effective partnerships enable one to access the knowledge, resources, and opportunities required for augmenting immense growth in businesses or career development. Hybrid entrepreneurs can use a plethora of tools and strategies to address all challenges and other difficulties related to time-constraint, conflicting priorities, and scarcity of resources. They can build a good network through an online presence, attendance of events in the industry, or even through membership of professional bodies. Some key benefits include embracing forthcoming trends in digital transformation, remote work models, and other ethical business practices. Hybrid entrepreneurs who will embrace these changes in the networking and partnership-building landscape and can make good and smart strategic usage of their social capital will have the best opportunity to meet their goals and drive their ventures to new height.

REFERENCES

Aaboen, L., Dubois, A., & Lind, F. (2013). Strategizing as networking for new ventures. *Industrial Marketing Management*, 42(7), 1033–1041. DOI: 10.1016/j.indmarman.2013.07.003

Aray, Y. N., Christodoulou, I., Borodin, D. A., Klimova, E. V., Troshneva, S. G., & Paikin, N. M. (2023). Collaboration between social entrepreneurs and large companies: Mutual value creation through different forms of partnership

Banal-Estanol, A., Kretschmer, T., Meloso, D., & Seldeslachts, J. (2015). The Dynamics of Strategic Alliances Theory and Experimental Evidence. Working Paper.

Batt, P. J., & Purchase, S. (2004). Managing Collaboration within Networks and Relationships. *Industrial Marketing Management*, 33(3), 169–174. DOI: 10.1016/j.indmarman.2003.11.004

Cacciolatti, L., Rosli, A., Ruiz-Alba, J. L., & Chang, J. (2020). Strategic alliances and firm performance in startups with a social mission. *Journal of Business Research*, 106, 106–117. DOI: 10.1016/j.jbusres.2019.08.047

Carr, J. C., Marshall, D. R., Michaelis, T. L., Pollack, J. M., & Sheats, L. (2022). The role of work-to-venture role conflict on hybrid entrepreneurs' transition into entrepreneurship. *Journal of Small Business Management*, 61(5), 2302–2325. DOI: 10.1080/00472778.2022.2082455

Chen, X., Ma, Y., & Xie, Y. (2024). The Influence Mechanism of Online Social Network Relationships on Sustainable Entrepreneurial Success. *Sustainability (Basel)*, 16(9), 3755. DOI: 10.3390/su16093755

Demir, C., Werner, A., Kraus, S., & Jones, P. (2020). Hybrid entrepreneurship: A systematic literature review. *Journal of Small Business and Entrepreneurship*, 34(1), 29–52. DOI: 10.1080/08276331.2020.1764738

Ferreira, C. C., Ferguson, S. L., & Pitt, L. F. (2019). Entrepreneurial marketing and hybrid entrepreneurship: The case of JM Reid Bamboo Rods. *Journal of Marketing Management*, 35(9-10), 9–10, 867–885. DOI: 10.1080/0267257X.2019.1637921

Folta, T. B., Delmar, F., & Wennberg, K. (2009). Hybrid Entrepreneurship. *Management Science*, 56(2), 253–269. DOI: 10.1287/mnsc.1090.1094

Gielnik, M. M., Cardon, M. S., & Frese, M. (2020). *The psychology of entrepreneurship*. Routledge. DOI: 10.4324/9781003137573

Humam, M., & Hariadi, M. F. (2022). The Effect Of Social Capital Of Entrepreneurs In Entrepreneurial Process, *Journal of Innovation, Business and Entrepreneurship.*

Jay, J. (2012). Navigating paradox as a mechanism of change and innovation in hybrid organizations. *Academy of Management Journal*, 56(1), 137–168. DOI: 10.5465/amj.2010.0772

McGrath, H., O'Toole, T., & Canning, L. (2019). Coopetition: A fundamental feature of entrepreneurial firms' collaborative dynamics. *Journal of Business and Industrial Marketing*, 34(7), 1555–1569. DOI: 10.1108/JBIM-10-2018-0287

Noworól, A. (2013, May). The role of hybrid partnerships in the management of development. In *NispaCEE Conference* (pp. 1-10).

Reuer, J. J., Matusik, S. F., & Jones, J. (2019). The Interplay of Entrepreneurship and Collaboration. *The Oxford Handbook of Entrepreneurship and Collaboration*, 1-15.

Riaz, S., Yanqing, W., Ishaq, M. I., Raza, A., & Siddiqui, R. A. (2024). Role of social networks and entrepreneurial success: Understanding the dynamics of knowledge acquisition and green entrepreneurial orientation. *Journal of Entrepreneurship & Innovation Management*, 1-23.

Tang, X., Li, G., Lv, L., Wang, P., & Zhu, R. (2024). Relationship between the informal social networks and entrepreneurial intentions of Chinese college students: The mediating role of entrepreneurial learning. *Education + Training*. Advance online publication. DOI: 10.1108/ET-08-2023-0338

Thompson, J., & Bolton, B. (2024). *Entrepreneurs: Talent, Temperament, Opportunity, and Mindset.* Taylor & Francis. DOI: 10.4324/9781003385790

Tunio, M. N., Chaudhry, I. S., Mughal, F., & Shaikh, E. (2022). Marketing Mode and Survival of the Entrepreneurial Activities of Nascent Entrepreneurs. In *Big Data Analytics* (pp. 1–18). Auerbach Publications. DOI: 10.1201/9781003307761-1

Weihe, G. (2006). *Drivers of Collaborative Advantage: On the Operational Dynamics and Social Dimensions of Public-Private Partnerships. Department of Business and Politics.* Copenhagen Business School.

Chapter 12
Influence of University Support on Entrepreneurial Intentions:
Examining the Mediating Effect of Entrepreneurial Climate

Kavita Dahiya
Manipal Jaipur University, India

Sanjay Taneja
https://orcid.org/0000-0002-3632-4053
Graphic Era University, India & Universiti Sultan Zainal Abidin, Malaysia

Anuradha Jain
https://orcid.org/0000-0001-6996-8309
Vivekananda Institute of Professional Studies-TC Delhi, India

Zelhuda Shamsuddin
Universiti Sultan Zainal Abidin, Malaysia

ABSTRACT

This research utilizes the framework of institutional theory to explore the dynamics between student entrepreneurial ambitions and the support mechanisms provided by their educational institutions. The study involves a survey of 420 students from a selection of universities in Haryana, chosen for their diverse entrepreneurial programs. The study employs structural equation modeling to analyze the data and

DOI: 10.4018/979-8-3693-9486-1.ch012

test our theoretical propositions. This research contributes a novel perspective to the discourse on entrepreneurship education by underscoring the significance of the institutional environment, rather than individual entrepreneurial traits, as a determinant of entrepreneurial intent among students.

INTRODUCTION

Entrepreneurial ventures are widely acknowledged as a catalyst for economic growth, employment opportunities, and innovation, particularly in the context of developing countries. This perspective is supported by recent scholarship which highlights the contrast between the robust infrastructures of developed nations and the often volatile and less structured environments of emerging economies. Such conditions can lead to a business landscape fraught with uncertainty (Recent studies, 2020). Moreover, policy shifts in these regions tend to be erratic, impacting the entrepreneurial landscape significantly (Academic discourse, 2000). Despite this, there is ongoing debate regarding the effectiveness of developing countries in nurturing entrepreneurial mindsets and activities (Contemporary analysis, 2014). It is, therefore, crucial for researchers and policymakers to delve into strategies that can bolster entrepreneurial practices within these economies (Recent studies, 2020). The genesis of entrepreneurship is frequently linked to the complex process of forming entrepreneurial intentions. Entrepreneurial intention is posited as a key predictor of entrepreneurial tendencies, which in turn, are essential for stimulating entrepreneurial endeavors (Contemporary entrepreneurship research, 2015). Without this emotional acumen, the likelihood of successful entrepreneurial ventures diminishes. Studies suggest that a person's entrepreneurial intention can be anticipated through individual beliefs, societal expectations, and perceived control over behavior (Contemporary entrepreneurship research, 2015). However, these factors alone may not suffice in explaining entrepreneurial intention comprehensively, as individuals are shaped by diverse sociocultural influences that can alter their entrepreneurial outlook (Cultural entrepreneurship studies, 2011). Therefore, it is vital to consider the impact of both formal and informal educational environments on the development of entrepreneurial intention, especially in the milieu of developing nations where the role of academic institutions is pronounced.

Efforts by educational institutions and policymakers to foster entrepreneurship through academic programs have been a focal point of recent initiatives. However, the impact of such educational programs on students' entrepreneurial intention (EI), a key component of entrepreneurial potential, remains a subject of debate. While some research points to a positive correlation, others suggest a negative or negligible relationship (Educational Impact Studies, 2015). The effectiveness of entrepreneurial education is still under scrutiny, prompting inquiries into how the environment of entrepreneurial universities might influence students' EI (Innovation and Education Research, 2015; Entrepreneurial Academic Studies, 2019). The term "university support for entrepreneurship" encompasses a range of institutional efforts aimed at nurturing entrepreneurial skills beyond traditional educational offerings (Entrepreneurial Support Research, 2015). This support includes a variety of initiatives such as incubation programs, competitions, mentorship opportunities, and networking events, all designed to cultivate students' entrepreneurial capabilities and, consequently, their EI (University Entrepreneurship Report, 2020). Research has indicated that such comprehensive university support can explain a significant portion of students' EI (Entrepreneurial Education Analysis, 2016; Student Development Studies, 2017). However, the varied aspects of university support may have differing impacts on EI, suggesting a need for more nuanced research to dissect these effects (Entrepreneurial Education Analysis, 2016; Academic Support Research, 2020). This is especially pertinent in less developed regions where challenges such as institutional barriers, resource constraints, and limited staff can hinder the provision of robust entrepreneurial support (Emerging Economies Research, 2019). The role of individual attitudes as a mediator between university support and students' EI has been a focus of several studies (Entrepreneurial Attitude Research, 2015; Educational Environment Studies, 2020). Yet, the potential of universities in developing countries to foster an entrepreneurial ethos through formal support mechanisms remains an underexplored area. A study by Educational Culture Research (2020) posits that institutional backing can shape students' entrepreneurial mindsets and contribute to the creation of entrepreneurial cultures within universities. Nonetheless, there is a scarcity of empirical data on how EI develops within the informal entrepreneurial cultures of universities (Entrepreneurial Culture and Education Research, 2020). Organizational climate, as defined by Organizational Studies (1998), encompasses the shared perceptions of organizational members regarding the significance of policies and the acceptability of certain behaviors. Such climates are pivotal for nurturing students' entrepreneurial ambitions and EI (Entrepreneurial Climate Studies, 2018). It is recognized that initiatives aimed at promoting entrepreneurship can lead to the formation of entrepreneurial ecosystems within educational settings, which in turn can enhance students' EI and entrepreneurial traits (Entrepreneurial Ecosystem Research, 2018). Therefore, it is imperative to examine how formal and informal university environments work in tandem to bolster students' EI (Educational Environment Analysis, 2021).

The current investigation underscores the dual influence of both structured and emergent facets of university environments on the enhancement of students' entrepreneurial intention (EI). Bridging the research void on how entrepreneurial settings affect the relationship between EI and institutional support for entrepreneurship

(Educational Dynamics Research, 2015), this study employs the "Foundational Institutional Analysis" (1990) as a theoretical backdrop to assess the intermediary role of entrepreneurial climates. Through the application of partial least squares structural equation modeling (PLS-SEM), the study scrutinizes data from 420 graduate and postgraduate students from three distinct universities in Haryana. The research contributes to scholarly discussions in several ways. It analyzes the effects of diverse forms of academic entrepreneurial support on student EI, referencing studies such as the "Educational Support Dynamics Study" (2021) and the "Entrepreneurial Education Inquiry" (2020). Furthermore, it illuminates the dynamics between entrepreneurial environments and student EI within the context of institutions adhering to the tenets of institutional theory. Finally, the study expands the growing compendium of knowledge on the efficacy of entrepreneurial support mechanisms in universities to fortify student EI, with a particular focus on the milieu of developing economies.

THEORETICAL FRAMEWORK

This investigation explores the premise that behavior and experiences shape intentions aimed at specific goals or actions. Intentions are indicative of the underlying motivations for actions and the level of effort one is prepared to exert to attain a goal (Foundational Intentions Research, 1988). (Behavioral Intentions Theory, 1991). The academic field has seen the development of various models that delve into the interplay between an individual's environment and personal traits in shaping their entrepreneurial journey. These models include the works of scholars from the early 1990s to the mid-1990s, who have contributed to our understanding of entrepreneurial intentions. This research utilizes a situational lens to probe the effects of environmental factors on entrepreneurial intention, as discussed in the "Contextual Dynamics Research" (2011). The study interprets university settings through the "new institutionalism" paradigm, introduced in the "Institutional Analysis Framework" (1983). This viewpoint indicates that the attributes of institutions are frequently shaped by their evolutionary paths or by replication rather than by direct compulsion or the influence of state mechanisms, a concept elaborated in "Organizational Theory" (1987). Departing from the rational-actor models prevalent in traditional economic theories, the neo-institutional framework leans towards understanding social and organizational actions through cognitive and cultural lenses, as established in the "Institutional Analysis Framework" (1983). An institution is described as a sophisticated and stable social construct, consisting of symbolic elements, social activities, and material components, as characterized on page 49 in "Institutional Theory" (2001). It encompasses the conventions, norms, and regulatory elements that constitute an organization. Building on this, the distinction between formal and informal institutions was further refined (Institutional Economics, 1990). Formal institutions are typified by tangible systems like property rights and legal frameworks, characterized by explicit rules. This study operationalizes the notion of academic support for entrepreneurship within these formal constructs. In contrast, informal institutions are the bedrock of the study's conceptualization of entrepreneurial climates, encompassing the norms, traditions, and behaviors that are cultivated, shared, and maintained outside of formally sanctioned frameworks (Institutional Theory, 2001). Both formal and informal institutions govern acceptable behavior, shaping individuals' beliefs and aspirations, which in turn influence their motivation and actions (Organizational Culture Research, 2000).

Contemporary discussions on the influence of context on entrepreneurial intention (EI) underscore the need to differentiate between structured and unstructured environments. This distinction is crucial for comprehending how macro-level contexts can shape micro-level phenomena, such as the development of EI within informal settings (Contextual Influence Research, 2019; Entrepreneurial Context Studies, 2011). The intricate and layered nature of academic environments, which include both structured and unstructured elements, is believed to exert a diverse range of influences on students' EI (Educational Environment Analysis, 2019). Our theory posits that formal academic initiatives designed to foster entrepreneurship reshape the cognitive frameworks of aspiring entrepreneurs. Concurrently, the less structured, community-driven entrepreneurial cultures act as conduits for the propagation of entrepreneurial values and ethics (Entrepreneurial Dynamics Research, 2017). The study argues that the nurturing of an informal entrepreneurial atmosphere, which subsequently enhances students' EI, is fundamentally driven by the structured context, namely, institutional entrepreneurship support. Formal university programs aimed at bolstering EI represent structured interventions that promote entrepreneurial activities (Entrepreneurial Education Study, 2020). As identified in prior research, university entrepreneurship support is multifaceted, encompassing the evaluation of business idea development, educational assistance, and business growth support (Entrepreneurial Support Framework, 2015). It has been observed that students benefiting from such structured support exhibit heightened EI and a propensity towards entrepreneurship (Entrepreneurial Behavior Study, 2014). The impact of entrepreneurial environments on individuals' perception of entrepreneurship as a viable career path has been documented (Vocational Perception Research, 2012). Institutional theory regards culture as a vehicle for the diffusion of normative and cognitive schemas that can foster productive informal settings. Cultural influences shape individuals' worldviews, behaviors, and both conscious and unconscious decision-making processes (Cultural Influence on Behavior Study, 1989). To enhance students' entrepreneurial intention (EI), educational institutions may need to foster an entrepreneurial culture in addition to providing tangible support structures, as suggested by the "Entrepreneurial Culture and Education Study" (2015). This research specifically examines students' perceptions of entrepreneurial climates within universities, distinguishing it from broader corporate culture studies, as noted in the "Organizational Culture Analysis" (2000) Climate is characterized by the specific, culturally informed actions that organizations undertake to direct their members' energies (Organizational Climate Research, 2013). While closely related, culture and climate are distinct concepts. University entrepreneurial climates are defined as the individual student's perception of university elements related to entrepreneurial activities, such as opportunity seeking, idea generation, or other entrepreneurial actions endorsed and facilitated by the institution (Entrepreneurial Climate Framework, 2018). It has been suggested that an organization's ethos and the views of its members about their workplace are reflected in its policies and practices, which in turn define its environment (Organizational Environment Study, 1996). Research indicates that students with an entrepreneurial orientation tend to display higher EI, more behaviors related to commercialization, and entrepreneurial dispositions (Entrepreneurial Orientation and EI Study, 2018; University Commercialization Research, 2005). The study proposes that by nurturing an entrepreneurial atmosphere, structured university support for entrepreneurship (the structured context) can enhance students' EI. Figure 1 presents our conceptual model

Hypothesis Development

The exploration of the role of university support in fostering entrepreneurial competencies among students reveals a multifaceted impact on their acquisition of business strategies, knowledge, and skills, as highlighted by Mustafa et al. (2016). Within this framework, entrepreneurship education emerges as a potential catalyst for the enhancement of entrepreneurial intention (EI), broadening the learner's knowledge and honing critical thinking, as discussed by Donckels (1991). Such education is posited to significantly contribute to the development of students' self-efficacy, a concept deeply rooted in the four foundational pillars identified by Bandura (1992): mastery experiences, observational learning, verbal encouragement, and physiological feedback. The provision of entrepreneurship education that integrates career guidance and practical business engagement opportunities is seen as a key driver in strengthening students' confidence. Despite this, the literature presents a dichotomy in findings regarding the influence of entrepreneurial education on EI. Studies by Saeed et al. (2015) and Wegner et al. (2020) suggest a positive correlation, whereas research by Mustafa et al. (2016) and Rocha et al. (2021) does not establish a significant link, indicating an ongoing scholarly debate.

Figure 1. Conceptual model of proposed relationships

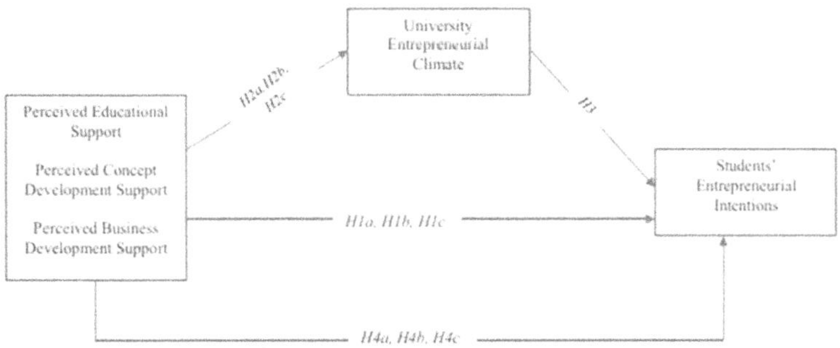

Further research by Choi et al. (2018) underscores the value of concept development assistance in refining business ideas, potentially leading to successful commercialization. Shi et al. (2020) complement this view by suggesting that such guidance enhances students' evaluation of their business concepts' viability, a critical component of EI as per Vuorio et al. (2018). Moreover, business development support extends beyond ideation, offering students capital access, leveraging institutional reputation for venture launching, and facilitating connections with entrepreneurial mentors, thereby creating a robust support ecosystem for aspiring entrepreneurs, as documented by Mustafa et al. (2016) and Shahid et al. (2017). The interplay between entrepreneurship education and entrepreneurial intention is complex and multifaceted. While the debate on the direct impact of such education on EI continues, the broader implications for student self-efficacy and business acumen are evident. The support provided by universities in this regard is not only instrumental in nurturing entrepreneurial skills but also in potentially enhancing the entrepreneurial intention of students, equipping them with a more holistic set of competencies for their future endeavors. The research indicates that academic support for entrepreneurship can cultivate students' entrepreneurial spirit, awareness, and ideation, as well as the cognitive abilities and skills necessary for entrepreneurial success. As a result, the research effort was directed by the following hypothesis:

> **H_{11}.** Students' perceptions of educational, concept development, and business development support from their university are collectively positively related to their entrepreneurial intentions (EI).
> **H_{12}.** University entrepreneurial climates are positively related to students' entrepreneurial intentions (EI).
> **H_{13}.** Students' perceptions of educational, concept development, and business development support offered by their university are each positively related to their perceptions of a university entrepreneurial climate.

H_{14}. An entrepreneurial climate mediates the relationship between students' perceptions of educational, concept development, and business development support from their university and their entrepreneurial intentions (EI).

The research by Zohar and Luria (2005) highlights that social norm, along with organizational policies and procedures, can serve as guides for expected behaviors within specific contexts. In the realm of higher education, the informal aspects of university life can shape the entrepreneurial intention (EI) of individuals by influencing their perception of the institution's support for entrepreneurial endeavors (Bergmann et al., 2018; Entrepreneurial Climate Studies, 2015). Hunter et al. (2011) identify key mechanisms through which universities with an entrepreneurial focus can bolster the EI of their students. One mechanism is through the cultivation of an entrepreneurial culture that not only assists students in recognizing opportunities and formulating ideas but also enhances their ability to effectively commercialize these ideas (Martin et al., 2013). Such a culture can raise students' EI by integrating technology commercialization into the organization's goals and by tracking the success of these endeavors (Innovation and Commercialization Research, 2011). For instance, studies like that of O'Shea et al. (2005) have shown that institutions like the Massachusetts Institute of Technology excel in fostering student-led ventures due to a robust entrepreneurial culture that prioritizes commercialization. Additionally, exposure to faculty and peers engaged in entrepreneurial activities can inspire students and elevate their EI by providing real-world examples of entrepreneurship (Academic Entrepreneurship Study, 2008). Another pathway is through the reinforcement of entrepreneurial self-efficacy. Entrepreneurial climates can empower students by showcasing how ideas can be transformed into marketable products or services, often facilitated by the presence of entrepreneurial role models (Fietze and Boyd, 2017; Walter et al., 2013). Overall, the presence of an entrepreneurial culture within a university can effectively communicate to students that entrepreneurship is a valued and viable career path. Universities with distinctive entrepreneurial cultures are recognized for nurturing unique entrepreneurial spirits within their communities (Innovation in Higher Education Study, 2017; O'Shea et al., 2005). Universities that emphasize entrepreneurship may adopt strategies that encourage students to adopt entrepreneurial behaviors and mindsets (Bergmann et al., 2018). For example, educational support can broaden the entrepreneurial perspectives of students across various disciplines, fostering entrepreneurial attitudes, knowledge, and skills, even among those who may not have initially been inclined towards entrepreneurship (Entrepreneurial Attitude and Education Research, 2013; Turker and Selcuk, 2009). Furthermore, the establishment of entrepreneurship chairs can influence students' perceptions of the educational environment, as these positions promote entrepreneurship through course offerings and mentorship (Entrepreneurship Education Impact Study, 2008).

The research conducted by Meoli et al. (2020) indicates that when students receive support in developing their business concepts, they are more likely to engage in prototype testing, acquire entrepreneurial skills, and establish networks that are essential for generating business ideas. The provision of resources such as networking opportunities and initial funding for startups can enhance the local entrepreneurial ecosystem, contributing to a more favorable perception of the entrepreneurial climate (Geissler et al., 2010; Walter et al., 2013). Investigations into the relationship between university support and students' entrepreneurial intention (EI) suggest an indirect connection (Entrepreneurial Support Studies, 2015; Entrepreneurial Education Research, 2020). Universities are increasingly facilitating entrepreneurial attitudes and behaviors among students by providing greater access to incubators, as well as financial and advisory resources for new venture creation (Innovation and Entrepreneurship Research, 2016; New Business Support Studies, 2015). According to the findings of Lannegrand-Willems and Bosma (2006), students' perceptions of an entrepreneurial environment can motivate them to apply their entrepreneurial knowledge and skills in identifying opportunities, embracing calculated risks, and promoting their ideas, which in turn positively influences their EI. Therefore, the promotion of entrepreneurship by academic institutions can enhance students' views of the entrepreneurial climate, thereby making the pursuit of an entrepreneurial career path more attractive.

Within academic settings, social norms and institutional guidelines provide individuals with a framework for understanding expected behaviors in specific contexts, as noted by Zohar and Luria (2005). Similarly, the informal atmosphere of a university can shapes the entrepreneurial intention (EI) of its members, akin to the way entrepreneurial environments influence perceptions of entrepreneurship, as suggested by Bergmann et al. (2018) and Huyghe and Knockaert (2015). Research by Hunter et al. (2011) indicates that universities with an entrepreneurial ethos can enhance the EI of their students through distinct mechanisms. Firstly, entrepreneurial cultures within universities can augment the capacity of students to not only identify entrepreneurial opportunities but also to effectively communicate and market their innovative ideas, as Martin et al. (2013) have observed. Such cultures, by emphasizing the goal of technology commercialization and monitoring its success, can further develop the EI of students (Hunter et al., 2011). For instance, the Massachusetts Institute of Technology, as identified by O'Shea et al. (2005), has established a robust entrepreneurial culture that fosters commercialization, leading to a high rate of student-led venture creation. Additionally, the presence of entrepreneurial role models within these environments can inspire both faculty and students, enhancing EI by providing exposure to active engagement in entrepreneurship (Bercovitz and Feldman, 2008). Secondly, the opportunity for students to observe the rapid progression of ideas to marketable products through entrepreneurial exemplars can bolster their confidence in their own entrepreneurial capabilities, thereby nurturing entrepreneurial self-efficacy (Fietze and Boyd, 2017; Walter et al., 2013). The entrepreneurial culture prevalent in universities serves as a valuable pedagogical tool, demonstrating to students the societal endorsement of pursuing a career as an independent entrepreneur.

In contemporary higher education, research indicates that universities play a crucial role in developing entrepreneurial ecosystems that are unique to their environments (Erina et al., 2017; O'Shea et al., 2005). These institutions, by emphasizing entrepreneurship, implement diverse strategies that encourage students to embrace entrepreneurial behaviors and mindsets, contributing to the establishment of an entrepreneurial culture within the university setting (Bergmann et al., 2018). Educational support in these institutions is designed to nurture entrepreneurial attitudes, broaden the knowledge base, and enhance skill sets among students. This approach not only benefits those with a pre-existing interest in entrepreneurship but also influences a wider student population to consider entrepreneurial paths, shifting perceptions across various demographics (Martin et al., 2013; Turker and Selcuk, 2009). The educational strategies employed by these universities aim to foster an environment where entrepreneurial thinking is not just for business students but is integrated across disciplines, encouraging a cross-pollination of ideas and innovation. By doing so, they create a fertile ground for entrepreneurial initiatives and mindset development, which is essential in today's rapidly changing economic landscape. The impact of such educational support is profound, potentially altering the career trajectories of students and equipping them with the entrepreneurial acumen necessary to navigate and shape the future of industry and commerce. Additionally, the role of an entrepreneurship chair in an academic setting can alter student perceptions of the learning environment, as these chairs actively promote entrepreneurship through course offerings and mentorship (Schmude et al., 2008). The research by Meoli et al. (2020) suggests that students receiving support in the ideation phase are more likely to engage in prototype testing, thereby enhancing their entrepreneurial skills and forming networks that are essential for the generation of business concepts. The perception of an entrepreneurial-friendly atmosphere is also shaped by the accessibility of resources for local entrepreneurs, including networking opportunities and initial capital for new ventures (Geissler et al., 2010; Walter et al., 2013). Scholarly investigations have revealed that the support systems established by universities for entrepreneurship may have a consequential effect on the entrepreneurial intention (EI) of students, as suggested by Saeed et al. (2015) and Wegner et al. (2020). These institutions are progressively providing resources such as incubators and a range of both financial and advisory services, which are instrumental in cultivating entrepreneurial mindsets and capabilities within the student body. This creates a nurturing backdrop for entrepreneurial ventures (Bergmann et al., 2016; Mas-Verdú et al., 2015; Mustafa et al., 2016; Shi et al., 2020). Lanncgr and-Willems and Bosma (2006) posit that the perception of an entrepreneurial-friendly environment can act as a significant motivator for students, encouraging them to apply their entrepreneurial knowledge and skills in identifying and seizing new opportunities, embracing risks judiciously, and passionately promoting their innovative ideas. This supportive framework provided by universities is not merely about the resources; it is about shaping an ecosystem that is conducive to the growth and development of entrepreneurial competencies. Such an ecosystem can enhance students' ability to navigate the complexities of the business world with greater emotional acuity, thereby enriching their professional and personal development. This engagement is known to have a beneficial impact on their entrepreneurial intention. Hence, the advocacy of entrepreneurship within academic settings can enhance students' perceptions of the entrepreneurial landscape and may serve as an inspiration for others to contemplate entrepreneurial careers.

METHODS

Sample and Data Collection

The objective of the investigation was to assess the influence of entrepreneurial support mechanisms on the entrepreneurial intention (EI) of students within public universities located in Haryana. The research design was carefully crafted to yield thorough and trustworthy outcomes. A cohort of 420 students from a variety of public universities in Haryana, each with its own entrepreneurial program, was assembled. The selection process utilized a random sampling method to achieve a representative cross-section of students from assorted entrepreneurial disciplines/ courses. This strategy aimed to encompass a broad spectrum of student experiences and attitudes towards the entrepreneurial support offered by their institutions. The determination of the sample size was guided by the tenets of reliability and validity to ensure the extrapolation of the findings to the larger student body. A structured questionnaire, incorporating established scales for gauging entrepreneurial intention and the perceived impact of entrepreneurial support, served as the data collection instrument. This questionnaire was meticulously constructed to amalgamate both quantitative and qualitative insights, thereby providing a holistic perspective on the students' encounters. To ascertain the reliability and accuracy of the questionnaire, standard psychometric evaluations were employed, including the computation of Cronbach's alpha to measure reliability and validity for content accuracy. The research was conducted with a stringent adherence to ethical standards. Participants engaged in the study with full knowledge and consent, with all personal information treated with the utmost confidentiality. The study's ethical protocol was designed to mitigate any potential adverse effects and to prioritize participant welfare. The analysis of the data was performed using sophisticated statistical tools. Quantitative data underwent percentage analysis to discern prevalent trends and patterns, while qualitative responses were scrutinized to complement and deepen the understanding gleaned from the numerical data. This dual-faceted approach to data analysis ensured that the research findings were both dependable and significant.

Measures

Mueller (2011) developed a comprehensive set of four evaluations designed to measure entrepreneurial tendencies among students. This assessment includes a specific query regarding the students' aspirations to initiate their own ventures within a five-year timeframe. Responses to each item were captured using a seven-point Likert scale, with options ranging from 1, indicating 'strongly disagree,' to 7, representing 'strongly agree.' The extent of university support for entrepreneurial endeavors (USE) was quantified through a thirteen-item metric derived from the work of Saeed et al. (2015). The original measure by Saeed et al. (2015) encompassed items that assessed perceived support within the students' national context. However, the current study narrowed its focus to the university environment, hence only those items relevant to the university context were considered. The assessment of perceived entrepreneurial support (PES) was conducted using various components, with four items dedicated to measuring perceived curriculum design support (PCDS), and three aimed at gauging perceived behavior development support (PBDS). These items were rated on a five-point Likert scale, where 1 signified 'strongly disagree' and 5 indicated 'strongly agree.'

Table 1. Demographical analysis for the respondents

Demographic Factor	Category	Number of Students	Percentage (%)
Gender	Male	243	57.8
	Female	177	42.2
Age Group	18-20	140	33.3
	21-23	180	42.9
	24-26	100	23.8

continued on following page

Table 1. Continued

Demographic Factor	Category	Number of Students	Percentage (%)
Educational Level	Undergraduate	280	66.7
	Postgraduate	140	33.3
Residence	Urban	252	60
	Rural	168	40
Parents Self-employed	Yes	87	49.2
	No	106	50.8

The demographic analysis of the respondents, as presented in Table No. 1, reveals a diverse group of students with varying backgrounds. Gender distribution among the respondents shows a higher proportion of males (243 students) accounting for 57.8% compared to females (177 students) who make up 42.2%. This indicates a somewhat skewed representation towards male students in the sample. In terms of age groups, most of the respondents fall within the 21-23 age bracket, representing 42.9% with 180 students. This is followed by the 18-20 age group, which includes 140 students and constitutes 33.3% of the sample. The 24-26 age group is the least represented, with 100 students making up 23.8%. This distribution suggests that the sample is predominantly composed of younger individuals who are likely in the early stages of their higher education journey. When examining the educational level of the respondents, undergraduates form the bulk of the sample, with 280 students representing 66.7%. Postgraduates, on the other hand, account for 33.3% with 140 students. This significant difference highlights a greater undergraduate presence in the sample, which may reflect the general population of students at higher education institutions. The analysis of the residence of the respondents indicates a majority living in urban areas, with 252 students making up 60% of the sample, while the remaining 40% or 168 students reside in rural areas. This urban predominance could be indicative of the accessibility and proximity of educational institutions to urban centers. Lastly, the data on whether the respondents' parents are self-employed shows a nearly even split. There are 87 students (49.2%) with self-employed parents, while a slightly higher number of students, 106 (50.8%), have parents who are not self-employed. This balance offers a unique perspective on the economic backgrounds of the students, suggesting a diverse socio-economic composition within the sample. Overall, the demographic analysis provides a snapshot of the student population, revealing a male-dominated sample with a strong representation of younger undergraduates predominantly residing in urban areas and coming from varied economic backgrounds. This diversity within the sample could have implications for the generalizability of any further research conducted with this group.

Data Analysis and Results

The dataset was analyzed using the Partial Least Squares Structural Equation Modeling (PLS-SEM) approach, a methodology originally introduced by Wold (1982). Throughout the analytical process, the study adhered to the established guidelines, protocols, and foundational principles as set forth by Hair et al. (2019). To achieve a model capable of predicting the dependent variable with a significance level of 95% and an effect size of 0.15, the sample size calculation, conducted via G*Power version 3.1.9.4, indicated a requirement for a minimum of 420 participants. This criterion for sample size has been met by current research. Given that the measures employed in this study are well-documented and validated in existing scholarly work, there was no necessity for exploratory factor analysis. Consequently, the research proceeded directly to confirmatory factor analysis, as per the precedent established in the literature (cited by Mumtaz et al., 2017). This step ensures that the constructs used are indeed reflective of the variables they are intended to measure, thereby affirming the reliability and validity of the research instruments.

Model Assessments

The research integrates reflective indicators within each element of the proposed model, as depicted in Figure 1. Data analysis presented in Table 2, which details various constructs and their associated items, provides insights into the reliability and validity of the measured constructs. For the construct of Perceived Ease of Use (PES), factor loadings are observed to fall within the range of 0.754 to 0.823. This range demonstrates a robust association between the items and the construct in question. Furthermore, both the composite reliability and the Rho_A coefficient for PES exceed the 0.8 benchmark, which is indicative of high internal consistency. Additionally, the Average Variance Extracted (AVE) for PES stands at 0.64. This figure surpasses the generally accepted threshold of 0.5, thereby reflecting a satisfactory proportion of variance that the construct extracts from its indicators.

Table 2. Comprehensive analysis of factor loadings and reliability measures

Construct	Item	Factor Loadings	Composite Reliability	Rho_A Coefficient	Average Variance Extracted (AVE)
PES	ES3	0.785	0.813	0.815	0.64
	ES4	0.823			
	ES7	0.818			
	ES8	0.754			
	ES9	0.762			
PCDS	CS5	0.832	0.853	0.858	0.695
	CS6	0.881			
	CS7	0.868			
	CS8	0.749			
	CS9	0.76			
PBDS	BS4	0.812	0.798	0.813	0.705
	BS5	0.871			
	BS6	0.834			
	BS7	0.789			
EC	UC4	0.872	0.848	0.852	0.765
	UC5	0.853			
	UC6	0.892			
	UC7	0.861			
EI	EI5	0.927	0.909	0.913	0.785
	EI6	0.889			
	EI7	0.919			
	EI8	0.808			
	EI9	0.831			

The Perceived Content Difficulty (PCDS) construct shows even higher factor loadings, with items ranging from 0.749 to 0.881, which denotes a very strong relationship with the construct. The composite reliability and Rho_A coefficient for PCDS is 0.853 and 0.858, respectively, both of which are commendably high and denote that the construct is measured reliably. The AVE for PCDS stands at 0.695, which is well above the recommended threshold, suggesting excellent construct validity. For the Perceived Behavioral Difficulty (PBDS) construct, the factor loadings are also robust, ranging from 0.789 to 0.871. The composite reliability is slightly lower than the previous constructs at 0.798, but still within an acceptable range, while the Rho_A coefficient is consistent at 0.813. The AVE for PBDS is 0.705, indicating a high level of variance explained by the construct from its indicators. The Enjoyment Construct (EC) presents factor loadings between 0.853 and 0.892, which are indicative of a very strong association with the construct. The composite reliability and Rho_A coefficient are 0.848 and 0.852, respectively, both of which reflect high reliability. The AVE for EC is 0.765, suggesting that the construct has a strong ability to explain the variance in its items. Lastly, the Entrepreneurial intention (EI) construct exhibits the highest factor loadings among all constructs, with a minimum loading of 0.808 and a maximum of 0.927. This indicates an exceptionally strong relationship between the items and the construct. The composite reliability and Rho_A coefficient are very high at 0.909 and 0.913, respectively, which underscores the reliability of the EI construct. Furthermore, the AVE for EI is 0.785, which is significantly above the acceptable level, confirming that a substantial amount of variance in the items is accounted for by the EI construct. In summary, the data analysis suggests that all constructs are measured with high reliability and validity, as evidenced by strong factor loadings, high composite reliability, Rho_A coefficients, and AVE values. These constructs and their items appear to be well-designed to capture the underlying theoretical concepts they are intended to measure.

Structural Model Assessments

The analysis of the inter-construct correlations presents a nuanced understanding of the relationships between various psychological constructs related to student perceptions and entrepreneurial intention within an educational context. The correlation between Perceived Content Difficulty (PCDS) and Perceived Ease of Use (PES) is notably strong, with a coefficient of 0.872, indicating a substantial positive relationship within the confidence interval of 0.795 to 0.934. This suggests that students who find content difficult also tend to perceive it as less easy to use, or vice versa. The Perceived Behavioral Difficulty (PBDS) construct also shows a significant positive correlation with PES, albeit to a lesser extent, with a coefficient of 0.620 and a confidence interval ranging from 0.462 to 0.719. This indicates that ease of use perceptions is moderately associated with behavioral difficulty perceptions. Furthermore, PBDS has a very strong positive correlation with PCDS, as evidenced by a coefficient of 0.845 within a confidence interval of 0.760 to 0.910, suggesting that content difficulty and behavioral difficulty are closely linked in the minds of students. Enjoyment Construct (EC) correlations follow a similar pattern, with a positive correlation of 0.665 with PES and an even stronger correlation of 0.825 with PCDS, within the respective confidence intervals of 0.530 to 0.770 and 0.740 to 0.898. The correlation between EC and PBDS is also strong, with a coefficient of 0.762. These correlations suggest that students' enjoyment is related to their perceptions of ease of use, content difficulty, and behavioral difficulty, with higher enjoyment associated with more positive perceptions in these areas. Entrepreneurial intention (EI), however, shows a markedly different pattern of correlations. The correlation between EI and PES is relatively weak, with a coefficient of 0.152, and the confidence interval of 0.070 to 0.245 indicates a wide range of possible true correlation values. Similarly, EI's correlation with PCDS and PBDS is also weak, with coefficients of 0.085 and 0.095, respectively. The strongest correlation for EI is with EC, at 0.213, but it still falls within a low range. These weak correlations suggest that entrepreneurial intention, as measured in this context, has a limited direct relationship with perceptions of ease of use, content difficulty, and behavioral difficulty, but may have a slightly more pronounced relationship with enjoyment. The data indicates that while student perceptions regarding ease of use, content difficulty, and behavioral difficulty are interrelated, entrepreneurial intention appears to be a distinct construct with weaker connections to these perceptions. The implications of these findings could be significant for educational strategies that aim to address student perceptions and entrepreneurial intention independently.

Table 3. Correlation analysis of student perceptions, entrepreneurial intention, and enjoyment constructs in an educational setting

Construct	PES	PCDS	PBDS	EC	EI
PES	-	-	-	-	-
PCDS	0.872[0.795;0.934]	-	-	-	-
PBDS	0.620[0.462; 0.719]	0.845[0.760;0.910]	-	-	-
EC	0.665[0.530; 0.770]	0.825[0.740;0.898]	0.762[0.677;0.832]	-	-
EI	0.152[0.070; 0.245]	0.085[0.050;0.102]	0.095[0.042; 0.159]	0.213[0.098;0.334]	-

The analysis of the inter-construct correlations presents a nuanced understanding of the relationships between various psychological constructs related to student perceptions and entrepreneurial intention within an educational context. The correlation between Perceived Content Difficulty (PCDS) and Perceived Ease of Use (PES) is notably strong, with a coefficient of 0.872, indicating a substantial positive relationship within the confidence interval of 0.795 to 0.934. This suggests that students who find content difficult also tend to perceive it as less easy to use, or vice versa. The Perceived Behavioral Difficulty (PBDS) construct also shows a significant positive correlation with PES, albeit to a lesser extent, with a coefficient of 0.620 and a confidence interval ranging from 0.462 to 0.719. This indicates that ease of use perceptions is moderately associated with behavioral difficulty perceptions. Furthermore, PBDS has a very strong positive correlation with PCDS, as evidenced by a coefficient of 0.845 within a confidence interval of 0.760 to 0.910, suggesting that content difficulty and behavioral difficulty are closely linked in the minds of students. Enjoyment Construct (EC) correlations follow a similar pattern, with a positive correlation of 0.665 with PES and an even stronger correlation of 0.825

with PCDS, within the respective confidence intervals of 0.530 to 0.770 and 0.740 to 0.898. The correlation between EC and PBDS is also strong, with a coefficient of 0.762. These correlations suggest that students' enjoyment is related to their perceptions of ease of use, content difficulty, and behavioral difficulty, with higher enjoyment associated with more positive perceptions in these areas. Entrepreneurial intention (EI), however, shows a markedly different pattern of correlations. The correlation between EI and PES is relatively weak, with a coefficient of 0.152, and the confidence interval of 0.070 to 0.245 indicates a wide range of possible true correlation values. Similarly, EI's correlation with PCDS and PBDS is also weak, with coefficients of 0.085 and 0.095, respectively. The strongest correlation for EI is with EC, at 0.213, but it still falls within a low range. These weak correlations suggest that entrepreneurial intention, as measured in this context, has a limited direct relationship with perceptions of ease of use, content difficulty, and behavioral difficulty, but may have a slightly more pronounced relationship with enjoyment. The data indicates that while student perceptions regarding ease of use, content difficulty, and behavioral difficulty are interrelated, entrepreneurial intention appears to be a distinct construct with weaker connections to these perceptions. The implications of these findings could be significant for educational strategies that aim to address student perceptions and entrepreneurial intention independently.

The structural model assessment within the study commenced with a thorough examination of potential collinearity issues, which can significantly impact the validity of the model's conclusions. The variance inflation factor (VIF) values, which serve as indicators of collinearity, ranged from 1.026 to 3.482. These values are comfortably below the commonly accepted threshold of 5, as suggested by Hair et al. (2019), thereby eliminating collinearity as a concern and affirming the integrity of the structural model. After the collinearity check, the study delved into the structural path relationships, employing a robust bootstrapping method with 5,000 subsamples to ensure the reliability of the findings. The direct effects scrutinized within the model revealed that university support for entrepreneurship, as measured by constructs such as PES, PCDS, and PBDS, did not exhibit a significant direct impact on Entrepreneurial intention (EI), leading to the non-support of Hypothesis 1 (H1). Conversely, the entrepreneurial climate within the university setting demonstrated a significant positive influence on EI, thereby lending support to Hypothesis 2 (H2). Further analysis of the direct effects indicated that only PCDS and PBDS had a significant impact on Enjoyment Construct (EC), which aligns with and supports Hypothesis 3 (H3). Additionally, the study explored the mediating role of the entrepreneurial climate and found that it indeed mediated the relationships between PCDS, PBDS, and EI, thus providing support for Hypothesis 4 (H4). To assess the predictive power of the model, the study employed the PLS predict approach, as proposed by Shmueli et al. (2016). This method is designed to evaluate the model's predictive accuracy. The findings indicated that only three of the Q2_predict values were greater than zero, which is less than half of the indicators assessed. Consequently, the study opted to utilize the root mean square error (RMSE) as a more reliable measure for comparing the predictive capabilities of the Partial Least Squares Structural Equation Modeling (PLS-SEM) against those of a basic linear model (LM). The RMSE values for the PLS model were lower than those for the LM, as indicated by the negative signs in the results table. This outcome suggests that the PLS model employed in the study possesses predictive validity, with most of the indicators demonstrating high predictive power. This finding underscores the model's effectiveness in forecasting outcomes based on the constructs measured, thereby confirming the utility of the PLS-SEM approach in this research context.

Table 4. Impact of perceived ease, enjoyment, and content difficulty on entrepreneurial intention in higher education

H	Relationship	Std beta	Std error	t-value	95% confidence intervals	H support?
H1	PES -> EI	0.17	0.121	1.41	[-0.048; 0.352]	No
H2	EC -> EI	0.275	0.108	2.550*	[0.085; 0.440]	Yes
H3	PCDS -> EC	0.435	0.095	4.63**	[0.280; 0.580]	Yes
H4	PCDS -> EC -> EI	0.12	0.056	2.155*	[0.043; 0.227]	Yes

Notes: $^{**}p < 0.01$; $^{*}p < 0.05$

The analysis of the data presented in Table No. 4 focused on the relationships between Perceived Ease (PES), Enjoyment Construct (EC), Perceived Content Difficulty (PCDS), and Entrepreneurial intention (EI) within the context of higher education. The standardized beta coefficients, standard errors, t-values, and confidence intervals were scrutinized to determine the support for the proposed hypotheses. Hypothesis 1 (H1) posited a direct relationship between PES and EI. However, the analysis revealed a standard beta of 0.17 with a t-value of 1.41, which fell short of the conventional threshold for statistical significance. The confidence interval straddling zero further indicated a lack of a reliable effect, leading to the conclusion that H1 is not supported. In contrast, Hypothesis 2 (H2) suggested a positive relationship between the Enjoyment Construct (EC) and EI. The data supported this hypothesis, with a standard beta of 0.275 and a t-value of 2.550, which exceeded the level of significance, and a confidence interval that did not include zero. This finding confirms that EC has a significant positive effect on EI. Hypothesis 3 (H3) examined the relationship between PCDS and EC. The results were quite robust, with a standard beta of 0.435 and a t-value of 4.63, which is well above the significant threshold. The confidence interval ranged from 0.280 to 0.580, indicating a strong and significant positive relationship, thereby supporting H3. Finally, Hypothesis 4

(H4) explored the mediating effect of EC on the relationship between PCDS and EI. The standard beta for this indirect relationship was 0.12 with a t-value of 2.155, suggesting a significant mediating effect and leading to the acceptance of H4. The analysis indicates that while Perceived Ease does not have a direct significant effect on Entrepreneurial intention, both the Enjoyment Construct and Perceived Content Difficulty are significant predictors of Entrepreneurial intention in the higher education context. Moreover, the Enjoyment Construct serves as a significant mediator in the relationship between Perceived Content Difficulty and Entrepreneurial intention. These findings underscore the importance of fostering an enjoyable learning environment and managing content difficulty to enhance students' Entrepreneurial intention, which is a critical factor in their academic and professional success.

DISCUSSION

The study examines the evolving role of universities, which have broadened their scope beyond traditional teaching and research to foster entrepreneurial environments conducive to nurturing student entrepreneurs. This expansion is evidenced by the implementation of a comprehensive array of activities aimed at bolstering not only academic prowess but also intellectual and professional growth among students. The impact of these structured academic settings on the development of students' entrepreneurial intention (EI) remains an area ripe for exploration, particularly within the context of emerging economies where institutional structures and cultural dynamics may deviate from Western paradigms. The research delves into the interplay between the entrepreneurial culture prevalent in universities and the entrepreneurial intention of students. By concentrating on the meso-level elements, namely the formal and informal frameworks within the university setting, the study sheds light on the formation of entrepreneurial intention in the milieu of emerging economies. Through this approach, the research contributes three significant insights to the existing body of knowledge on entrepreneurial intention. These insights enhance the understanding of how entrepreneurial intention is cultivated within university environments that are increasingly geared towards entrepreneurial development, especially in contexts that are not as frequently studied as their Western counterparts.

The research contributes to the discourse on the influence of university support on the entrepreneurial intention (EI) of students, addressing discrepancies found in existing literature. It challenges the notion, as suggested by prior studies, that experiential and practice-based education significantly enhances EI. Recent findings indicate that programs such as Project-Based Education Strategies (PES), Problem-Centered Design Strategies (PCDS), or Practice-Based Design Strategies (PBDS) do not directly augment the EI of students. These insights suggest that targeted university initiatives may not substantially affect the entrepreneurial intentions of students in a developing region like Haryana. The absence of a direct impact from these educational strategies on EI could be attributed to the possibility that certain pedagogical approaches, while intended to motivate and shape students' entrepreneurial aspirations, may inadvertently dissuade them from pursuing entrepreneurship. This aligns with findings from Kassean et al., which posited that exposure to entrepreneurial education and related activities might temper students' initial enthusiasm for entrepreneurship by presenting a more nuanced and realistic understanding of its demands. Furthermore, the findings imply that the broader socio-economic and institutional context of Haryana may play a more significant role in shaping the entrepreneurial intention of individuals. This perspective opens avenues for further investigation into how external environmental factors, beyond university-led initiatives, contribute to the development of EI among students in emerging economies.

Table 5. Comparative analysis of PLS-SEM and LM RMSE in predicting entrepreneurial intention and user control constructs

Items	PLS-SEM RMSE	Q^2_predict	LM RMSE	PLS-SEM – LM RMSE
EI4	1.785	0.003	1.848	-0.063
EI3	1.731	-0.010	1.815	-0.084
EI1	1.719	-0.032	1.792	-0.073
EI2	1.868	0.009	1.942	-0.074
UC3	0.701	0.403	0.708	-0.007
UC1	0.637	0.464	0.641	-0.004
UC2	0.864	0.284	0.894	-0.030

The analysis presented in Table No. 5 provides a detailed comparison between two predictive modeling techniques: Partial Least Squares Structural Equation Modeling (PLS-SEM) and Linear Modeling (LM), as applied to the prediction of Entrepreneurial intention (EI) and User Control (UC) constructs. The comparison is based on the Root Mean Square Error (RMSE) values obtained from both models, alongside the Q2 predictive relevance measure for PLS-SEM. For the Entrepreneurial intention construct items (EI1, EI2, EI3, and EI4), the RMSE values obtained from PLS-SEM were consistently lower than those from LM, as indicated by the negative differences in the PLS-SEM – LM RMSE column. This suggests that PLS-SEM provided a slightly better fit for the data than LM for these items. The Q2_predict values for EI items, which indicate the model's predictive relevance, were close to zero and even negative in some cases. This implies that while PLS-SEM may have an edge over LM in terms of model fit, its predictive power for EI is questionable. In the case of User Control construct items (UC1, UC2, and UC3), the RMSE values were relatively low for both PLS-SEM and LM, with PLS-SEM again showing marginally lower values. The Q2_predict values for UC items were substantially higher than those for EI, particularly for UC1 and UC3, indicating good predictive relevance of the PLS-SEM model for these items. In conclusion, the comparative analysis suggests that PLS-SEM has a slight advantage over LM in terms of fitting the data for both Entrepreneurial intention and User Control constructs. However, the advantage is more pronounced in the User Control construct, where PLS-SEM also demonstrates good predictive relevance. For Entrepreneurial intention, the predictive relevance of PLS-SEM is less clear, and the model's advantage over LM is minimal. These findings highlight the importance of choosing the appropriate modeling technique based on the specific characteristics of the data and the constructs being predicted. It also underscores the need for further investigation into the predictive capabilities of PLS-SEM for Entrepreneurial intention constructs, as the Q2_predict values suggest there may be room for improvement.

The investigation yielded a surprising result: Project-Based Education Strategies (PES) did not have a noticeable direct effect on cultivating an entrepreneurial environment, nor did it indirectly influence students' entrepreneurial intention (EI) through the creation of such a climate. The academic community is currently divided on whether entrepreneurship education enhances or diminishes students' EI, with studies by Bae et al. (2014) and Von Graevenitz et al. (2010) reflecting this dichotomy. Drawing from human capital theory, which posits that entrepreneurship education equips students with the skills to identify, develop, and exploit opportunities, the research by Westhead and Solesvik (2016) supports the notion that such education contributes positively to students' capabilities. However, the debate persists as to whether entrepreneurial education effectively instills skills like entrepreneurial alertness, as discussed by McCaffrey (2014). Moreover, the study by Bae et al. (2014) suggests that contextual factors and cultural differences might influence the interplay between EI and entrepreneurial education. The current research posits that the PES implemented by the institutions involved may have been more theoretical in nature, focusing on imparting entrepreneurial knowledge rather than practical entrepreneurial skills. Additionally, previous studies, including those by Bergmann et al. (2016) and Mas-Verdú et al. (2015), have indicated that entrepreneurial cultures are influenced by various forms of support, such as business competitions, direct financial assistance, and access to mentors and investors. However, the research suggests that the three private institutions studied may not have provided sufficient support to foster entrepreneurial intentions, as there was no direct impact observed on the assistance for idea or business development. This lack of tangible support could have led to a diminished belief among participants in the potential benefits of such support on their EI, as discussed in the work of Dvouletý et al. (2021).

The study presents a novel finding: the entrepreneurial environment serves as the sole mediator in the relationship between Problem-Centered Design Strategies (PCDS), Practice-Based Design Strategies (PBDS), and entrepreneurial intention (EI). This insight extends the understanding of how institutional support for entrepreneurship influences EI among students, building upon prior research that has predominantly concentrated on individual traits as mediators in the nexus between university support and EI. The work of Schmutzler et al. (2019), Boyd and Vozikis (1994), and Shahid et al. (2017) has explored these individual attributes, but this study shifts the focus to the broader institutional context. By examining the mediating role of the entrepreneurial climate, the study responds to the call by Bergmann et al. (2018) for more research into the relationship between students' perceptions of entrepreneurial environments and their EI. It also heeds Welter's (2011) advice to contextualize EI within the interplay of formal and informal institutional settings. Furthermore, the research enriches the limited literature on the entrepreneurial climate in developing countries and the support provided by universities for entrepreneurship within these contexts. While previous studies have employed the theory of planned behavior, as proposed by Ajzen (1991), to explore the determinants of students' EI in developing economies, they have often neglected the unique formal and informal institutional landscapes of emerging economy universities. This study, drawing on Institutional Theory (North, 1990) and the constructs of formal and informal environments, offers a fresh perspective on the factors shaping students' EI. The findings suggest that entrepreneurial education programs may not be as effective in creating an entrepreneurial culture within universities in emerging economies as practical support measures, such as connecting students with established entrepreneurs for idea development or providing access to startup capital. This supports the notion that fostering an entrepreneurial environment on campus may require specific actions underpinned by university policies. Moreover, the proximity of these entrepreneurial settings to students could potentially enhance their EI. Collectively, these insights expand the understanding of how universities in developing countries can support their students in cultivating EI, aligning with the observations made by Mustafa et al. (2016) regarding the role of educational institutions in this developmental process.

Practical Implications

The findings of the study carry significant implications for the strategies and practices of academic institutions in developing countries. It is advised that policymakers and university leaders prioritize the development of an entrepreneurial culture within their institutions, echoing the sentiments of Bergmann et al. (2018). To facilitate this, it is suggested that management and policy frameworks be designed to enable students to engage with the business community, thereby aiding in the refinement of their entrepreneurial projects and the initiation of new ventures, as highlighted by Matlay (2010).Furthermore, the establishment of peer mentorship programs for students interested in entrepreneurship and the creation of informal support mechanisms, such as career centers, can play a pivotal role in promoting entrepreneurship as a viable career path, as supported by the research of Liguori et al. (2020). Additionally, it is proposed that policymakers consider offering fiscal incentives and financial support to educational institutions that demonstrate a commitment to nurturing student entrepreneurs, thereby reinforcing the entrepreneurial ecosystem within the higher education sector. To augment these efforts, university administrations should actively seek to strengthen partnerships with entrepreneurial entities, providing students with access to mentorship and entrepreneurial resources. This could involve the formation of dedicated technology transfer offices and professional teams tasked with guiding students through the intricacies of commercial negotiations, intellectual property rights, business formation, and management. These initiatives are crucial for fostering an environment conducive to entrepreneurial growth and innovation within academic settings.

Limitations and Suggestions for Future Research

The research is subject to certain limitations that must be acknowledged. Primarily, the dataset was derived from final-year business students at three universities in Haryana and was cross-sectional. This necessitates a cautious approach to the extrapolation and interpretation of the findings. Hence, it is recommended that the proposed model be tested in diverse university settings across different economies to validate its applicability and robustness, as suggested by Chan and Mustafa (2020). Additionally, the study concentrated solely on contextual factors, overlooking individual-level characteristics known to affect EI. Future inquiries could benefit from employing multi-level analytical methods to explore the interplay between various aspects of the university environment and individual dispositions in the development of EI, as indicated by Schmutzler et al. (2019). The impact of the COVID-19 pandemic on academic institutions and their ability to support entrepreneurial initiatives is another dimension that warrants attention, as highlighted by Dvouletý et al. (2021). The pandemic's influence on operational capacities could provide valuable insights into the resilience and adaptability of entrepreneurial support mechanisms within universities. Lastly, the study's cross-sectional design focused on intentions rather than actual entrepreneurial behaviors. While the responses captured a snapshot of students' EI, they may not necessarily reflect genuine entrepreneurial actions. Future research could adopt a longitudinal approach to gain a deeper understanding of how contextual factors longitudinally influence the development of EI over time.

CONCLUSION

The study explores the influence of university-provided entrepreneurial support on the entrepreneurial intention (EI) of students, utilizing Institutional Theory (North, 1990) to understand the role of entrepreneurial climates. The findings indicate that it is the presence of an entrepreneurial atmosphere, fostered by official university support, that enhances students' EI, rather than a direct impact on EI itself. Prior research has often emphasized the structured components of university support for EI, such as knowledge transfer mechanisms, incubators, and formal entrepreneurial education programs. However, the significance of less formalized, informal environments, particularly in the context of emerging economies, has not been extensively explored. This study contributes to the understanding of how entrepreneurial universities can encourage and sustain entrepreneurial activities. It posits that policies and procedures designed to support entrepreneurship should actively cultivate a university culture that can serve as a competitive advantage. Therefore, the study suggests that public policymakers and university administrators should place a particular emphasis on the creation and sustenance of entrepreneurial environments within academic institutions to foster an increase in students' EI. This strategic focus on entrepreneurial climate is essential for nurturing the emotional and cognitive competencies that students require to thrive in entrepreneurial endeavors.

REFERENCES

Ahmad, S. Z., & Buchanan, R. F. (2015). Entrepreneurship education in Malaysian universities. *Tertiary Education and Management*, 21(4), 349–366. DOI: 10.1080/13583883.2015.1106577

Ajzen, I. (1991). The theory of planned behavior. *Organizational Behavior and Human Decision Processes*, 50(2), 179–211. DOI: 10.1016/0749-5978(91)90020-T

Bae, T. J., Qian, S., Miao, C., & Fiet, J. O. (2014). The relationship between entrepreneurship education and entrepreneurial intentions: A meta-analytic review. *Entrepreneurship Theory and Practice*, 38(2), 217–254. DOI: 10.1111/etap.12095

Bandura, A. (1992). Exercise of personal agency through the self-efficacy mechanism. In Schwarzer, R. (Ed.), *Self-Efficacy: Thought Control of Action* (pp. 3–38). Hemisphere.

Bercovitz, J., & Feldman, M. (2008). Academic entrepreneurs: Organizational change at the individual level. *Organization Science*, 19(1), 69–89. DOI: 10.1287/orsc.1070.0295

Bergmann, H., Geissler, M., Hundt, C., & Grave, B. (2018). The climate for entrepreneurship at higher education institutions. *Research Policy*, 47(4), 700–716. DOI: 10.1016/j.respol.2018.01.018

Bergmann, H., Hundt, C., & Sternberg, R. (2016). What makes student entrepreneurs? On the relevance (and irrelevance) of the university and the regional context for student start-ups. *Small Business Economics*, 47(1), 53–76. DOI: 10.1007/s11187-016-9700-6

Bird, B. (1988). Implementing entrepreneurial ideas: The case for intention. *Academy of Management Review*, 13(3), 442–453. DOI: 10.2307/258091

Boyd, N. G., & Vozikis, G. S. (1994). The influence of self-efficacy on the development of entrepreneurial intentions and actions. *Entrepreneurship Theory and Practice*, 18(4), 63–77. DOI: 10.1177/104225879401800404

Chan, W. L., & Mustafa, M. J. (2020). Journal of entrepreneurship in emerging economies (JEEE): Reflecting on the past five years while thinking about the future. *Journal of Entrepreneurship in Emerging Economies.*

Choi, K., Park, J., Cho, D., & Chu, H.-Y. (2018). The impact of university support on the creation of student entrepreneurs: Evidence from South Korea. *Entrepreneurship Research Journal*, 8(1), 1–14.

Clark, D. N., Reboud, S., Toutain, O., Ballereau, V., & Mazzarol, T. (2020). Entrepreneurial education: An entrepreneurial ecosystem approach. *Journal of Management & Organization*, , 1–21. DOI: 10.1017/jmo.2020.26

Cox, L., Mueller, S., & Moss, S. (2002). The impact of entrepreneurship education on entrepreneurial self-efficacy. *International Journal of Entrepreneurship Education*, 1(2).

Dalmarco, G., Hulsink, W., & Blois, G. V. (2018). Creating entrepreneurial universities in an emerging economy. *Technological Forecasting and Social Change*, 135(1), 99–111. DOI: 10.1016/j.techfore.2018.04.015

De Long, D. W., & Fahey, L. (2000). Diagnosing cultural barriers to knowledge management. *The Academy of Management Perspectives*, 14(4), 113–127. DOI: 10.5465/ame.2000.3979820

Denison, D. R. (1996). What is the difference between organizational culture and organizational climate? A native's point of view on a decade of paradigm wars. *Academy of Management Review*, 21(3), 619–654. DOI: 10.2307/258997

DiMaggio, P. J., & Powell, W. W. (1983). The iron cage revisited: Institutional isomorphism and collective rationality in organizational fields. *American Sociological Review*, 48(2), 147–160. DOI: 10.2307/2095101

Donckels, R. (1991). Education and entrepreneurship experiences from secondary and university education in Belgium. *Journal of Small Business and Entrepreneurship*, 9(1), 35–42. DOI: 10.1080/08276331.1991.10600389

Dvouletý, O., Fernandez de Arroyabe, J. C., & Mustafa, M. (2021). Guest editorial. *Journal of Entrepreneurship in Emerging Economies*, 13(4), 489–496. DOI: 10.1108/JEEE-09-2021-461

Erina, I., Shatrevich, V., & Gaile-Sarkane, E. (2017). Impact of stakeholder groups on development of a regional entrepreneurial ecosystem. *European Planning Studies*, 25(5), 755–771. DOI: 10.1080/09654313.2017.1282077

Fietze, S., & Boyd, B. (2017). Entrepreneurial intention of Danish students: A correspondence analysis. *International Journal of Entrepreneurial Behaviour & Research*, 23(4), 656–672. DOI: 10.1108/IJEBR-08-2016-0241

Foss, L., & Gibson, D. V. (2015). *The Entrepreneurial University: Context and Institutional Change*. Routledge, 1-17. DOI: 10.4324/9781315737065

Geissler, M., Jahn, S., & Haefner, P. (2010). The entrepreneurial climate at universities: The impact of organizational factors. *The Theory and Practice of Entrepreneurship*, 12-31.

Gianiodis, P. T., & Meek, W. R. (2020). Entrepreneurial education for the entrepreneurial university: A stakeholder perspective. *The Journal of Technology Transfer*, 45(4), 1167–1195. DOI: 10.1007/s10961-019-09742-z

Guerrero, M., Urbano, D., Cunningham, J. A., & Gajon, E. (2017). Determinants of graduates' start-ups creation across a multi-campus entrepreneurial university: The case of Monterrey Institute of Technology and Higher Education. *Journal of Small Business Management*, 56(1), 150–178. DOI: 10.1111/jsbm.12366

Hair, J. F., Risher, J., Sarstedt, M., & Ringle, C. (2019). When to use and how to report the results of PLS-SEM. *European Business Review*, 31(1), 2–24. DOI: 10.1108/EBR-11-2018-0203

Hansen, G. S., & Wernerfelt, B. (1989). Determinants of firm performance: The relative importance of economic and organizational factors. *Strategic Management Journal*, 1(5), 399–411. DOI: 10.1002/smj.4250100502

Hoskisson, R. E., Eden, L., Lau, C. M., & Wright, M. (2000). Strategy in emerging economies. *Academy of Management Journal*, 43(3), 249–267. DOI: 10.2307/1556394

Hunter, E. M., Perry, S. J., & Currall, S. C. (2011). Inside multi-disciplinary science and engineering research centers: The impact of organizational climate on invention disclosures and patents. *Research Policy*, 40(9), 1226–1239. DOI: 10.1016/j.respol.2011.05.024

Huyghe, A., & Knockaert, M. (2015). The influence of organizational culture and climate on entrepreneurial intentions among research scientists. *The Journal of Technology Transfer*, 40(1), 138–160. DOI: 10.1007/s10961-014-9333-3

Jones, P., Huxtable-Thomas, L., Hannon, P., Hamidon, S., & Mohd Tawil, N. (2021). Introduction to entrepreneurial activity in Malaysia: A country-level perspective. In *Entrepreneurial Activity in Malaysia* (pp. 1–10). Palgrave Macmillan. DOI: 10.1007/978-3-030-77753-1_1

Kassean, H., Vanevenhoven, J., Liguori, E., & Winkel, D. E. (2015). Entrepreneurship education: A need for reflection, real-world experience and action. *International Journal of Entrepreneurial Behaviour & Research*, 21(5), 690–708. DOI: 10.1108/IJEBR-07-2014-0123

Kolvereid, L. (1996). Prediction of employment status choice intentions. *Entrepreneurship Theory and Practice*, 21(1), 47–58. DOI: 10.1177/104225879602100104

Lannegrand-Willems, L., & Bosma, H. A. (2006). Identity development-in-context: The school as an important context for identity development. *Identity*, 6(1), 85–113. DOI: 10.1207/s1532706xid0601_6

Liguori, E., Winkler, C., Vanevenhoven, J., Winkel, D., & James, M. (2020). Entrepreneurship as a career choice: Intentions, attitudes, and outcome expectations. *Journal of Small Business and Entrepreneurship*, 32(4), 311–331. DOI: 10.1080/08276331.2019.1600857

Liñán, F., & Fayolle, A. (2015). A systematic literature review on entrepreneurial intentions: Citation, thematic analyses, and research agenda. *The International Entrepreneurship and Management Journal*, 11(4), 907–933. DOI: 10.1007/s11365-015-0356-5

Looi, K. H., & Maritz, A. (2021). Government institutions, entrepreneurship education and entrepreneurship education programmes in Malaysia. *Education + Training*, 63(2), 271–291. DOI: 10.1108/ET-07-2020-0217

Marcotte, C. (2014). Entrepreneurship and innovation in emerging economies: Conceptual, methodological and contextual issues. *International Journal of Entrepreneurial Behaviour & Research*, 20(1), 42–65. DOI: 10.1108/IJEBR-09-2012-0089

Martin, B. C., McNally, J. J., & Kay, M. J. (2013). Examining the formation of human capital in entrepreneurship: A meta-analysis of entrepreneurship education outcomes. *Journal of Business Venturing*, 28(2), 211–224. DOI: 10.1016/j.jbusvent.2012.03.002

Mas-Verdú, F., Ribeiro-Soriano, D., & Roig-Tierno, N. (2015). Firm survival: The role of incubators and business characteristics. *Journal of Business Research*, 68(4), 793–796. DOI: 10.1016/j.jbusres.2014.11.030

Matlay, H. (2010). Introduction: Contemporary perspectives on entrepreneurship education and training. *Journal of Small Business and Enterprise Development*, 17(4). Advance online publication. DOI: 10.1108/jsbed.2010.27117daa.001

Matt, M., & Schaeffer, V. (2018). Building entrepreneurial ecosystems conducive to student entrepreneurship: New challenges for universities. *Journal of Innovation Economics Management*, 1(25), 9–32. DOI: 10.3917/jie.025.0009

McCaffrey, M. (2014). On the theory of entrepreneurial incentives and alertness. *Entrepreneurship Theory and Practice*, 38(4), 891–911. DOI: 10.1111/etap.12013

Meoli, A., Fini, R., Sobrero, M., & Wiklund, J. (2020). How entrepreneurial intentions influence entrepreneurial career choices: The moderating influence of social context. *Journal of Business Venturing*, 35(3), 105–982. DOI: 10.1016/j.jbusvent.2019.105982

Miralles, F., Giones, F., & Gozun, B. (2017). Does direct experience matter? Examining the consequences of current entrepreneurial behavior on entrepreneurial intention. *The International Entrepreneurship and Management Journal*, 13(3), 881–903. DOI: 10.1007/s11365-016-0430-7

Mohamad, N., Lim, H.-E., Yusof, N., & Soon, J.-J. (2015). Estimating the effect of entrepreneur education on graduates' intention to be entrepreneurs. *Education + Training*, 57(8/9), 874–890. DOI: 10.1108/ET-03-2014-0030

Moraes, G. H. S. M., Fischer, B. B., Campos, M. L., & Schaeffer, P. R. (2020). University ecosystems and the commitment of faculty members to support entrepreneurial activity. *BAR - Brazilian Administration Review*, 17(2), 1–26. DOI: 10.1590/1807-7692bar2020190013

Mueller, S. (2011). Increasing entrepreneurial intention: Effective entrepreneurship course characteristics. *International Journal of Entrepreneurship and Small Business*, 13(1), 55–74. DOI: 10.1504/IJESB.2011.040416

Mumtaz, A. M., Ting, H., Ramayah, T., Chuah, F., & Cheah, J. H. (2017). Editorial, 'A review of the methodological misconceptions and guidelines related to the application of structural equation modelling: A Malaysian scenario'. *Journal of Applied Structural Equation Modeling*, 1(1), 1–13.

Mustafa, M. J., Hernandez, E., Mahon, C., & Chee, L. K. (2016). Entrepreneurial intentions of university students in an emerging economy: The influence of university support and proactive personality on students' entrepreneurial intention. *Journal of Entrepreneurship in Emerging Economies*, 8(2), 162–179. DOI: 10.1108/JEEE-10-2015-0058

Narayanan, V. K., & Shin, J. N. (2019). The institutional context of incubation: The case of academic incubators in India. *Management and Organization Review*, 15(3), 563–593. DOI: 10.1017/mor.2018.52

North, D. C. (1990). A transaction cost theory of politics. *Journal of Theoretical Politics*, 2(4), 355–367. DOI: 10.1177/0951692890002004001

Nowiński, W., Haddoud, M. Y., Lančarič, D., Egerová, D., & Czeglédi, C. (2019). The impact of entrepreneurship education, entrepreneurial self-efficacy and gender on entrepreneurial intentions of university students in the Visegrad countries. *Studies in Higher Education*, 44(2), 361–379. DOI: 10.1080/03075079.2017.1365359

O'Shea, R. P., Allen, T. J., Chevalier, A., & Roche, F. (2005). Entrepreneurial orientation, technology transfer and spinoff performance of US universities. *Research Policy*, 34(7), 994–1009. DOI: 10.1016/j.respol.2005.05.011

Politis, D., Winborg, J., & Dahlstrand, Å. L. (2012). Exploring the resource logic of student entrepreneurs. *International Small Business Journal*, 30(6), 659–683. DOI: 10.1177/0266242610383445

Rocha, A. K. L. D., Moraes, G. H. S. M. D., & Fischer, B. (2021). The role of university environment in promoting entrepreneurial behavior: Evidence from heterogeneous regions in Brazil. *Innovation & Management Review*.

Saeed, S., Yousafzai, S. Y., Yani-De-Soriano, M., & Muffatto, M. (2015). The role of perceived university support in the formation of students' entrepreneurial intention. *Journal of Small Business Management*, 53(4), 1127–1145. DOI: 10.1111/jsbm.12090

Schein, E. H. (2000). *Organizational Culture and Leadership* (2nd ed.). John Wiley and Sons.

Schmude, J., Welter, F., & Heumann, S. (2008). Entrepreneurship research in Germany. *Entrepreneurship Theory and Practice*, 32(2), 289–311. DOI: 10.1111/j.1540-6520.2007.00227.x

Schmutzler, J., Andonova, V., & Diaz-Serrano, L. (2019). How context shapes entrepreneurial self-efficacy as a driver of entrepreneurial intentions: A multilevel approach. *Entrepreneurship Theory and Practice*, 43(5), 880–920. DOI: 10.1177/1042258717753142

Schneider, B., Ehrhart, M. G., & Macey, W. H. (2013). Organizational climate and culture. *Annual Review of Psychology*, 64(1), 361–388. DOI: 10.1146/annurev-psych-113011-143809 PMID: 22856467

Schneider, B., White, S. S., & Paul, M. C. (1998). Linking service climate and customer perceptions of service quality: Tests of a causal model. *The Journal of Applied Psychology*, 83(2), 150–163. DOI: 10.1037/0021-9010.83.2.150 PMID: 9577232

Scott, R. W. (2001). *Institutions and Organizations* (2nd ed.). Sage Publications.

Shahid, M. S., Imran, Y., & Shehryar, H. (2017). Determinants of entrepreneurial intentions: An institutional embeddedness perspective. *Journal of Small Business and Entrepreneurship*, 30(2), 139–156. DOI: 10.1080/08276331.2017.1389053

Shapero, A., & Sokol, L. (1982). *The social dimensions of entrepreneurship*. University of Illinois at Urbana-Champaign's Academy for Entrepreneurial Leadership Historical Research Reference in Entrepreneurship.

Shi, L., Yao, X., & Wu, W. (2020). Perceived university support, entrepreneurial self-efficacy, heterogeneous entrepreneurial intentions in entrepreneurship education: The moderating role of the Chinese sense of face. *Journal of Entrepreneurship in Emerging Economies*, 12(2), 205–223. DOI: 10.1108/JEEE-04-2019-0040

Shmueli, G., Ray, S., Estrada, J. M. V., & Chatla, S. B. (2016). The elephant in the room: Predictive performance of PLS models. *Journal of Business Research*, 69(10), 4552–4564. DOI: 10.1016/j.jbusres.2016.03.049

Thornton, P. H., Ribeiro-Soriano, D., & Urbano, D. (2011). Socio-cultural factors and entrepreneurial activity: An overview. *International Small Business Journal*, 29(2), 105–118. DOI: 10.1177/0266242610391930

Turker, D., & Selcuk, S. (2009). Which factors affect entrepreneurial intention of university students? *Journal of European Industrial Training*, 33(2), 142–159. DOI: 10.1108/03090590910939049

Urbano, D., Aparicio, S., & Audretsch, D. (2019). Twenty-five years of research on institutions, entrepreneurship, and economic growth: What has been learned? *Small Business Economics*, 53(1), 21–49. DOI: 10.1007/s11187-018-0038-0

Von Graevenitz, G., Harhoff, D., & Weber, R. (2010). The effects of entrepreneurship education. *Journal of Economic Behavior & Organization*, 76(1), 90–112. DOI: 10.1016/j.jebo.2010.02.015

Vuorio, A. M., Puumalainen, K., & Fellnhofer, K. (2018). Drivers of entrepreneurial intentions in sustainable entrepreneurship. *International Journal of Entrepreneurial Behaviour & Research*, 24(2), 359–381. DOI: 10.1108/IJEBR-03-2016-0097

Walter, S. G., Parboteeah, K. P., & Walter, A. (2013). University departments and self-employment intentions of business students: A cross-level analysis. *Entrepreneurship Theory and Practice*, 37(2), 175–200. DOI: 10.1111/j.1540-6520.2011.00460.x

Wegner, D., Thomas, E., Teixeira, E. K., & Maehler, A. E. (2020). University entrepreneurial push strategy and students' entrepreneurial intention. *International Journal of Entrepreneurial Behaviour & Research*, 26(2), 307–325. DOI: 10.1108/IJEBR-10-2018-0648

Welter, F. (2011). Contextualizing entrepreneurship – conceptual challenges and ways forward. *Entrepreneurship Theory and Practice*, 35(1), 165–184. DOI: 10.1111/j.1540-6520.2010.00427.x

Westhead, P., & Solesvik, M. Z. (2016). Entrepreneurship education and entrepreneurial intention: Do female students benefit? *International Small Business Journal*, 34(8), 979–1003. DOI: 10.1177/0266242615612534

Wold, H. O. A. (1982). Soft modeling: The basic design and some extensions. In Jöreskog, K. G., & Wold, H. O. A. (Eds.), *Systems under Indirect Observations: Part II* (pp. 1–54).

Zhang, Y., Duysters, G., & Cloodt, M. (2014). The role of entrepreneurship education as a predictor of university students' entrepreneurial intention. *The International Entrepreneurship and Management Journal*, 10(3), 623–641. DOI: 10.1007/s11365-012-0246-z

Zohar, D., & Luria, G. (2005). A multilevel model of safety climate: Cross-level relationships between organization and group-level climates. *The Journal of Applied Psychology*, 90(4), 616–628. DOI: 10.1037/0021-9010.90.4.616 PMID: 16060782

Zucker, L. G. (1987). Institutional theories of organization. *Annual Review of Sociology*, 13(1), 443–464. DOI: 10.1146/annurev.so.13.080187.002303

Chapter 13
Innovation Culture and Employee Engagement:
Relationship Between an Organization's Innovation Culture and Employee Engagement and Retention

Ajay Chandel
https://orcid.org/0000-0002-4585-6406
Lovely Professional University, India

Ashutosh Pandey
https://orcid.org/0000-0002-8255-8459
FORE School of Management, India

Mohit Yadav
https://orcid.org/0000-0002-9341-2527
O.P. Jindal Global University, India

Narayanage Jayantha Dewasiri
https://orcid.org/0000-0002-5908-8890
Sabaragamuwa University of Sri Lanka, Sri Lanka

ABSTRACT

This chapter explores the critical relationship between an organization's innovation culture and its impact on employee engagement and retention. An innovation culture fosters an environment that encourages creativity, autonomy, and continuous development, which significantly influences employees' motivation and satisfaction. By examining key metrics such as engagement surveys, retention rates, performance

DOI: 10.4018/979-8-3693-9486-1.ch013

metrics, and innovation outcomes, the chapter highlights how these factors interrelate to enhance organizational performance. Best practices for cultivating a supportive innovation environment, empowering employees, investing in professional development, and maintaining work-life balance are discussed. Additionally, strategies for recognizing and rewarding innovation and fostering collaboration are examined. Understanding these dynamics provides organizations with actionable insights to improve engagement and retention, ultimately driving long-term success and growth.

INTRODUCTION

The fast pace of the changing environment in today's business world is making it important for any organization that seeks to maintain a competitive edge to establish a strong innovation culture. An innovation culture characterizes a value and practice set that encourages creativity, experimentation, and risk-taking, leading to an environment in which new ideas may be harnessed. This culture does not only drive organizational growth and adaptability, it equally involves employee engagement and retention. Employee engagement is the emotional commitment and enthusiasm that employees have toward their work and the organization. It is increasingly being recognized as one of the most important sources of competitive advantage. In return, employees who show a high level of engagement are more motivated, productive, and loyal in their businesses, so the levels of turnover are low with high-performance products (Chang et al., 2013).

The connection between culture of innovation and employee engagement is intricate and multi-layered. First, an innovation-driven culture will contribute to better employee engagement by opening more opportunities for personal and professional development, respect, and having a purpose for work. Second, engaged employees would be the significant drive forces of innovations, as their motivation and commitment often turns into increased creativity and initiative. In this light, this chapter attempts to study the relationship between the innovation culture of an organization and employee engagement by investigating how the development of a culture prematurely prepares the innovation infrastructure which may affect employee satisfaction and retention. Understanding this interdependency will help the chapter put forth specific recommendations on how organizations will be able to strategically use their innovation culture to increase employee engagement as a means to long-term success (Eva et al., 2019).

THE CONCEPT OF INNOVATION CULTURE

Innovation Culture Defined

An innovation culture is the organizational backdrop that provokes and supports the generation, development, and implementation of new ideas and solutions. This is basically defined by a value set, norms, and practices that promote creativity, experimentation, and a willingness to carry out risks. This is most often expressed in openness to ideas, teamwork in problem-solving, and a commitment to ongoing improvement. With such an innovation culture in organizations, workers feel free to question the status quo, search for out-of-the-box solutions, and be stakeholders in the development of new and improved products, services, and processes of their organization (Hooi & Chan, 2023).

Key Drivers of the Innovation Culture

Various drivers will lead to developing and sustaining an innovation culture.

1. **Leadership Commitment:** Good leaders drive an innovation culture. They set the tone by championing different innovations, resourcing toward that effect, and modeling behaviors that tell employees they should take risks with their ideas and experiment. Leadership support also entails creating the vision for innovation and its communication to the rest of the organization.
2. **Organizational Structure:** The structure of an organization may help or hurt innovation. Basically, organizational structures that indicate collaboration, flexibility, and decentralization in decision-making are those that foster innovation. Flatter reporting structures and cross-functional teams can improve communication and collaboration, resulting in more innovative outputs (Iqbal, 2023).
3. **Resources and Support:** This includes the allocation of necessary resources, for instance, time, money, and tools, to 'nourish' innovation. Organizations that invest in R&D, training, and technology are in a better position to facilitate creative efforts and implement new ideas.
4. **Recognition and Rewards**: Maintenance of an innovation culture calls for the proper recognition and rewarding of innovative effort. This can be achieved through celebrating success and acknowledging contributions, with incentives on creativity and solution-finding, to motivate the staff to continue finding innovative solutions (Izzatuddin & Kusumastuti, 2021).

5.Tolerance for Failure: A culture of innovation also requires the tolerance for failure. Realization that not every idea is supposed to pan out and allows experimentation with no fear of failure can lead to employees willing to take calculated risks or think outside the box.

Case Studies

1. Google: Google has a very innovative culture, which is supported by the implementation of the "20% time" policy. Under this, an employee can spend a maximum of 20% of his time at work on any project that he wishes to. Through the application of the policy, there are a number of successful products that have come into being, for example, Gmail and AdSense. It also emphasizes openness, collaboration, and follows a flat organizational structure.
2. 3M: Leveraging innovation as its key marketing strategy, 3M has incorporated innovation through its "Innovation Time Off," by which its employees can spend part of his/her time thinking about, researching, and working with related innovative products. The development of iconic products includes Post-it Notes. By supporting innovations that are driven by employees, 3M is able to instigate a culture of risk-taking and creativity (Kumar & Raghavendran, 2015).

Understanding innovation culture is to understand the interaction of organizational values, leadership, resources, and structures in a manner that allows creativity and experimentation. A study of successful cases provides hints on ways to generate and maintain an innovation culture based on values that radiate business success and simultaneous increase employees' ability to derive dictatorial conclusions on how to act.

Employee Engagement

Engagement of employees is a core driver of success in any organization; it reflects the intensity of employees' commitment and motivation toward the organization. The leading core dimensions to be had within it might be emotional investment, discretionary effort, and alignment with organizational goals. High levels of engagement associate with burning issues, better productivity, good satisfaction in job, and decreased turnover. As such, an engaged employee is bound to take the initiative, present new ideas, and experience a sense of ownership and accountability in his/her work (Park et al., 2013).

Core engagement builders include recognition and reward, providing for an employee's career and supporting a congenial work atmosphere. A well-designed structure of employees' recognition brings the intended positive effects to them, motivating them towards more engaged ways. Important in making employees feel as though they are being developed is an increase in the level of engagement; such factors include opportunities for professional growth, such as training, mentorship, and clear avenues for career progression. A supportive work environment that encourages open communication, collaboration, and work-life balance nurtures an increased level of engagement by ensuring employees feel valued and supported (Rachman et al., 2022).

Organizations that focus on employee engagement reap the benefits of a more committed and enthusiastic workforce. An employee who is fully engaged will most likely have an increase in performance, among other variables in an organization. Engaged employees remain with organizations, thus minimizing staff turnover and associated costs brought about by recruitment and training processes. High engagement leads to rich organ izational culture, uplifted total morale, and high levels of energy, therefore having a vibrant and productive work atmosphere. By investing in engagement-enhancing strategies, businesses can build a diligent, inspired workforce that will drive their long-term success and growth (Setyawasih et al., 2022).

THE RELATIONSHIP BETWEEN INNOVATION CULTURE AND EMPLOYEE ENGAGEMENT

How Innovation Culture Influences Engagement

1. **Empowerment and Autonomy:** An innovation culture will often drive through the reasoning that employees have to be empowered in decision-making and feel a sense of possession in their work. This, to a good extent, boosts employee engagement, whereby they feel trusted and valued by their organization. With freedom provided in an organizational context to explore newer ideas and solutions, this works as a motivation for employees to be channeled towards their respective roles.
2. **Growth Opportunities:** Innovative cultures are also usually strong growth cultures, meant that there will be many possibilities to grow personally and professionally. Whenever employees work in a state of innovation, there will often be chances for training, mentorship as well as career development in their interests and ability, leading to satisfaction and engagement (Shanker et al., 2017).
3. **Recognition and Reward Systems:** Organizations with good innovative cultures regularly institute recognition and reward systems that reward creativity and innovations that become successful. Recognition and rewarding employees for their contributions not only serve as reinforcement for the importance of

innovation but also boost morale and employee engagements. Employees who feel that they are recognized and appreciated are bound to keep their motivation and engagement (Chang et al., 2013).

4. **Collaborative Environment**: Cultures of innovation engage working employees from departments or backgrounds in the generation of problems and ideas. The kind of collaborative environment enhances the engagement of employees, as they feel being part of some community related to the organization. Whenever employees are busy working collaboratively on problems and issues, they remain connected to the organization.
5. **Risk-taking Support:** Supported risk and experimentation should be considered one of the hallmarks of an innovative culture. In such an environment, employees who work with the feeling that they can take some good risks and experiment with new ways of doing things without fear of their failures get tiered higher in terms of engagement and emotional involvement toward their work. This supportive environment provides a sense of protection in jobs, which boosts the overall engagement (Eva et al., 2019).

Engagement as a Driver of Innovation

1. **High Creativity:** Engaged employees are likely to bring out creative ideas with their innovative suggestions. That enthusiasm and commitment at the workplace stimulate such employees to think beyond obvious ideas and venture into new possibilities. Creative energy is quintessential for the development of an innovative culture and an effective idea generation.
2. **Proactive Problem-Solving:** Engaged employees have a proactive attitude toward problem-solving; they look for opportunities to make improvements in processes that will help drive the organization toward success. Such proactive behavior helps to develop and create innovative solutions, which can be adopted and implemented for continuous improvement within the organization.
3. **Alignment to Organizational Goals:** Employees with a high engagement should be keen to ensure that what they want ultimately aligns with the organization's strategic objectives. This way, direction of innovative efforts is channeled towards the vision and goals set up by the organization, increasing the general effectiveness of the innovation culture (Hooi & Chan, 2023).

Synergies and Challenges

1. **Synergies:** Interaction between innovation culture and engagement in the organization sets in place a virtuous circle. An innovation culture improves engagement through a stimulating and supportive working environment, and

engaged employees contribute to and drive the innovation process. In sum, there emerges a more dynamic and adaptive organization fit to respond effectively to changes and challenges.

2. **Challenges:** Though the overall relation between culture and innovation together with employee engagement is positive there are some challenges. An example would be the balance between need for risk-taking with desire for security. Involvement in the innovation culture can demand high engagement levels at the same time; this has to be managed against pressures and demands arising from an innovation-driven environment with much attention being made to the welfare of employees and their work-life balance (Iqbal, (2023).

Case Studies

1. **Apple**: The culture of innovation at Apple is said to be based on creativity, collaboration, and a commitment to excellence, where a fiery build on the feet of many employees is said to be involved. The company's keenness on employee empowerment and the instrumental role that they play in recognizing employees' contributions further motivate the as-is workforce toward ever more innovations (Izzatuddin & Kusumastuti, 2021).
2. **Netflix:** Netflix creates an innovative culture by the management accent at freedom and responsibility. This has made employees take up the responsibility for the work and try out new ideas, resulting in high engagement levels and being motivated to participate in the success of the company

While innovation cultures drive up the levels of employee engagement through providing opportunities for growth, recognition, and autonomy, engaged employees drive the innovation process through creativity and proactive problem solving. Understanding this relationship helps an organization set up a conducive environment where both employee engagement and innovation take place for continued success and growth (Izzatuddin & Kusumastuti, 2021).

THE RELATIONSHIP BETWEEN INNOVATION CULTURE AND EMPLOYEE ENGAGEMENT

There is quite a deep connection between the innovation culture and employee engagement, where a strong innovation culture increases the level of employee engagement massively. An innovation culture creates a dynamic and stimulating work atmosphere in which employees feel encouraged to express ideas and experiment to some extent against standing practices. It is this feeling of being empowered and involved in creative processes that create an attachment to work. When employees feel that their input is valued and they make a meaningful contribution to the organization, it increases motivation and enthusiasm.

That comprises the innovation culture of ownership and pride among the employees that breeds their engagement with the company. In another word: the employees would have a strong sense of attachment to the goals of an entity and be more interested in accomplishing objectives, having participated in the forming of these new products, services, or processes. Such level of engagement is bound to work much more and better in employees when efforts that are made in innovation are recognized and supported, reinforcing this sense of accomplishment and belonging among the employees (Kumar & Raghavendran, 2015).

Majorly, innovation culture comes with learning opportunities within the organization and ensures professional development, which supports the drivers of engagement. Engaged employees are those provided with training, resources, and mentorship that generally make employees feel valued within the organization. Continuous development meets the employees' aspirations and keeps them motivated and engaged.

Basically, making the organization pro-innovation would directly impact the engagement level of employees as it provides an environment that enables free flow of creativity, recognition of contributions, and nurtures professional growth. As such, this symbiosis not only positively affects employees' job satisfaction and motivation but also leads to overall organizational success and productivity (Park et al., 2013).

Measuring the Impact

A range of measures regarding the effectiveness of an innovation culture on engagement and retention is through employee metrics and tools to assess changes in those key areas that innovation initiatives bring about. The principal tool for doing so is an engagement survey, while it also captures job satisfaction, motivation, and commitment from employees. These surveys usually include some aspect of the innovation culture within the firm, such as the opportunities for creative input and the perceived value of the employees' contribution. That can be achieved by administering the surveys regularly—quarterly or annually—to help organizations track changes in engagement over time and identify various ways of improving those scores (Rachman et al., 2022).

Retention metrics are another sensitive indicator for gauging the impact of an innovation culture. Through this, analysis of turnover or exit interviews organizations can present whether dissatisfaction with the innovation culture or non-participative behavior leads to higher employee attrition levels. A feedback effect of innovation programs on talent retention is given by tracking the rate of retention across departments or roles and obtaining the causes for such departures.

Other performance measures include the level of productivity and thc work quality, as well as the success or failure of innovation projects. Comparing the performance data from the past and post-adoption of the innovation programs, therefore, the organizations can gauge whether such innovation initiatives are driving improved employee performance and engagement. Increased productivity and successful innovation outcomes may be taken to be a sign of the innovation culture positively influencing employee effectiveness (Setyawasih et al., 2022).

360-degree feedback furthers information on the interaction an employee has through the engagement channels with the help of colleague, subordinate, and superior feedback, whereby employees contribute and collaborate within the innovation culture and levels of engagement. This feedback provides an interesting level of nuance between those places where the effect on engagement is with strength and where there are developed areas.

Success in innovation and its impetus on the organizational performance and employee engagement can be specifically measured by using innovation metrics. Metrics might include the number of new ideas, innovation organization success rate, and the financial impact of innovations on innovative employees' compensation. Movements in these metrics may indicate that the innovation climate is supportive of innovation and its being tied in effectively to result in employee satisfaction (Shanker et al., 2017).

Such measurement efforts are supplemented by internal benchmarking—the comparison of engagement and retention metrics between the organizational departments or time—thus, helping to understand the best practices currently and those that need improvement. External benchmarking is reckoning the organizational performance against the industry standards or competitors, therefore putting in context the evaluation at hand for effectiveness in an innovation culture. Organizations can participate in industry surveys or reports, that would enable benchmarking the innovation practices for their organizations and highlight areas that may require improvement.

Broadly, a deep approach to measure the influence of the innovation culture would demand a mix of different reports and tools that would measure the extent to which employee involvement and retention are. By aggregating all those measures that come from employee engagement surveys, retention metrics, performance metrics, 360-degree feedback, innovation metrics, internal benchmarking, and external benchmarking, a company may get a real sense of how its innovation culture is really impacting in these matters. It provides organizations a data-driven basis to make an informed decision on innovations, thus enhancing continuous improvement in innovation practices to drive higher levels of employee satisfaction and retention (Chang et al., 2013).

BEST PRACTICES AND RECOMMENDATIONS

Recommendations and Best Practices which organization should do to make use an innovation culture in enhancing the employee engagement and employee retention: Create a supportive environment that fosters creativity and recognizes contributions aligning with employee needs.

1. **Cultivate a Supportive Innovation Environment**: Be an active supporter and encourager of innovation by employees. This will ensure an open and inclusive environment, thereby enabling all people to bring on board their ideas and experiments, without the fear of failure. Some of the ways include opening platforms deemed fit for the generation of ideas, like brainstorming, innovation labs, or suggestion boxes, while the taken ideas remain serious to ensure engagement and commitment from employees, in some cases (Eva et al., 2019).
2. **Empower Employees with Autonomy:** When employees are given independence to take decisions and own the project, they feel empowered and engaged, as it allows the employees to be more associated with their work and, in turn, the organization. When employees are autonomous in exploring new ideas and creation of solutions, they feel more strengthened in their roles and organizational success. Giving employees chances to lead projects, participate in cross-functional teams, and influence decisions improves the feelings of responsibility and connection with the organization (Hooi & Chan, 2023).
3. **Invest in Professional Development:** Continuous learning and development opportunities will keep the workforce engaged and retained. Organizations should invest in training programs, workshops, and mentoring initiatives in tune with employees' career goals and interests. Skill development resources will support, encourage, and give their workers the ability to grow their skills professionally by having a sense of allegiance to their organizations. By investing in employee development, the organization shows that it values its contribution and is interested in the long-term success of its partakers (Izzatuddin & Kusumastuti, 2021).
4. **Implement Recognition and Reward Programs**: Recognizing and rewarding employees for their innovative contributions is a powerful way in raising their engagement and thus retention. Design intensive organizational recognition programs taking into account the achievements and the milestones an organization has achieved through new innovations. This could be from giving formal awards to public recognition and the issuing of performance bonuses among a host of others, as recognition that offers incentive value to employees. A constant acknowledgment keeps confirming to the employees of the value of their work

and they will want to keep contributing persistently to organizational innovative efforts (Suifan et al., 2018).

5. **Promote Work-Life Balance**: A healthy balance between job and personal life on the part of employees is highly important for maintaining engagement and increasing their period of stay in a company. Work flexibility, like work-from-home and flexi-timings, is something employees must be provided by organizations to be able to balance personal and professional responsibilities in their lives. This support in balancing work life with personal life reduces the probability of burnout from one's job and thus contributes more toward the retention of employees in the organization and job satisfaction—such reasons as engagement are developed on the job (Kumar & Raghavendran, 2015).
6. **Foster Collaboration and Communication**: The fact that one has to work together and communicate within the organization gives rise to an innovative culture and teamwork among the employees. Having an opportunity to work with colleagues on joint projects, to share ideas, and obtain feedback brings the sense of community and belonging. Informal team meetings, collaborative platforms, and an open-door policy help in facilitating communication to enhance the quality of relationships between employees. Excellence in collaboration allows a formation of innovation based on a difference in perspective and skills, hence fusing a creative view and higher engagement (Park et al., 2013).
7. **Continuously Assess and Improve:** Evaluation of the effectiveness of innovation initiatives and their effect on engagement and retention is part and parcel of continuous improvement. There exists a necessity for individuals and organizations to have a measurable employee engagement score, retention data, and performance reviews to indicate the levels and areas of success of 'innovation culture,' and gauge areas of improvements. Through soliciting the feedback of employees and analyzing data, the organization will be better placed to make informed changes to the strategies and practices of innovation to suit the current and emerging needs of the workforce (Park et al., 2013).

In summary, through embracing all the best practices above—providing a supportive innovation environment, enabling and empowering innovators, investing in more development, recognizing and rewarding, striking a work-life balance with manageable workloads while intensifying teamwork and relationships, and constantly gauging and improving—employee engagement and retention will be positively influenced. An organization can cultivate a workforce that is motivated and engaged, one that is ready to support the values and goals set in the development of the culture that supports and values innovation (Rachman et al., 2022).

IMPLICATIONS

Practical Implications

These have major important practical implications for organizational application in enhancing employee engagement and retention: organizations must put in place structures and processes that support and are rewarded by innovation. This includes the development of programs for idea generation, provision of resource and time for experimentation, and being clear regarding channels in which employees share their contribution. Organizations should further strive to create environments that permit employees to take risks and fail without punitive consequences to them. With such mechanisms, an organization is bound to increase employee motivation, productivity, and satisfaction, resulting in improved performance of the employees and reduced turnover (Izzatuddin & Kusumastuti, 2021).

Societal Implications

In a societal context, fostering an innovation culture can generate broader economic and social dividends. When organizations create climates that foster creativity and innovation at all levels, then advances in technology, services, and products improve and positively affect society. Often, innovation is what brings about improvements in quality of life, economic growth, and in resolving problems in the social sphere. This way, employees in innovative organizations able to feel a healthier workface, better engaged and developed, and are involved in the overall health and wellness of life. This may boost social productivity and job satisfaction, and, therefore, to a more active and robust economy (Rachman et al., 2022).

Theoretical Implications

From a theoretical perspective, the link between the innovation culture and the engagement of employees contributes to the theoretical development of current studies in organizational behavior and management. It is congruent with and builds on theories and practices that derive from motivation, such as Self-Determination Theory, and Job Characteristics Theory, by accounting for the role of autonomy, recognition, and meaningful work in increasing engagement. The results build on further theoretical considerations about the manner in which organizational culture impacts on employee outcomes and build a schema so that the interplay of innovation and engagement can be considered. This would lead further research in exploring the manner in which various aspects of organizational culture have an impression on several employee centric measures (Azevedo et al., 2020).

Managerial Implications

The managerial implication is widespread. Managers are expected to concentrate on practices that will create and support the view of an innovative atmosphere. Accordingly, they must lead, encourage creative thinking, and make the recognition and reward systems in support of innovation very inculcative. The second focus will be to provide professionalism development opportunities that allow employees to get a culture of learning continuously. Thereby, the process of their implementation will assist in raising employee engagement, leading to lower employee turnover and increased organizational effectiveness. Further, understanding the linkage between innovation culture and employee engagement, managers' could put their entire strategies even into a relevant perspective of organizational goals, ensuring innovation to be value-added for the sustainability and success of the company towards its long-term survival (Rachman et al., 2022).

LIMITATIONS AND FUTURE RESEARCH SCOPE

Although the future scope for management because of this research can be indicated, and the peripheries of research limits could be deduced into the sample of how innovation culture varies and gets implemented in each organization. However, the specific practices and outcomes of the culture of innovation may be applicable across industries and organizational sizes, and that is very much expected to impact the generalizability of the results. Furthermore, the evaluation of innovation culture and its points of relevance with engagement could be problematic because the measures of such an assessment can be subjective and be different due to the applied methodologies and the perspective of employees and management (Setyawasih et al., 2022).

A further shortcoming is that self-report data from surveys and feedback given by employees always have the potential for bias. Employees might give socially desirable answers instead of honest evaluations, which might bias the results and influence the accuracy of the findings. Furthermore, although it is examined in the relationship with the innovation culture and engagement, the impact on other employee outcomes, such as job performance and organizational citizenship behavior, should be further studied (Shanker et al., 2017).

Other research questions which are required to check out these days related with the present one are longitudinal in nature, examining the relationship between innovation culture and employee engagement at different organizational contexts, and industries in general to gain a high degree of generalizability on these findings. Longitudinal studies may provide even more insight into such aspects of how innovation culture influences engagement over a period and how these effects might evolve. Alternatively, future research might study the differential effect of specific innovation practices, either separately or in combination, on various employee outcomes and how individual differences—such as personality traits and career aspiration—interact with an innovation culture in their effect on engagement and retention. With greater breadth of scope and methodologies, researchers might build a complete knowledge on the effects of innovation culture on employee engagement, hence influencing and implementing organizational practices more effectively (Suifan et al., 2018).

CONCLUSION

In other words, this is a very deep and mutually enhancing relationship pertaining to the innovation culture of organizations toward employee engagement and retention. A strong culture of innovation belongs to the organization in which employees are empowered to give meaningfully creative contributions by personally taking responsibility for work and ultimately growing. Such a supportive atmosphere does not only increase job satisfaction but also brings a sense of purpose and commitment, leading toward higher levels of engagement. Besides, their involvement in the innovative processes of creating and effectively implementing innovations itself and valued contribution increases motivation and commitment to the company and thus reduces labor turnover and increases staff's long-term involvement.

To extract the maximum from the culture of innovation some principally efficient methods are to provide employees with proper working conditions and atmosphere as well as autonomy and possibilities for development and training and a possibility of maintaining work and life balance. Understanding and rewarding the innovative contributions of employees, along with fostering open communication and collaboration, further strengthen the link between an innovation culture and employee engagement. The continuous testing of innovation strategies for effectiveness and change based on feedback and data help organizations ensure their culture is dynamic and responsive to the needs of workers.

In the end, innovation-infused organizational culture will drive a motivated, engaged, and loyal workforce, leading to increased organizational innovation and, in turn, success and growth. Those practices embraced likewise help to build a resilient, thriving workforce that will accomplish high-level sustainable success in a competitive, changing business environment.

REFERENCES

Azevedo, M., Schlosser, F., & McPhee, D. (2020). Building organizational innovation through HRM, employee voice and engagement. *Personnel Review*, 50(2), 751–769. DOI: 10.1108/PR-12-2019-0687

Chang, H., Hsu, H., Liou, J., & Tsai, C. (2013). Psychological contracts and innovative behavior: A moderated path analysis of work engagement and job resources. *Journal of Applied Social Psychology*, 43(10), 2120–2135. DOI: 10.1111/jasp.12165

Eva, N., Meacham, H., Newman, A., Schwarz, G., & Tham, T. (2019). Is coworker feedback more important than supervisor feedback for increasing innovative behavior? *Human Resource Management*, 58(4), 383–396. DOI: 10.1002/hrm.21960

Hooi, L., & Chan, A. (2023). Does workplace digitalization matter in linking transformational leadership and innovative culture to employee engagement? *Journal of Organizational Change Management*, 36(2), 197–216. DOI: 10.1108/JOCM-06-2022-0184

Hu, N., Wu, J., & Gu, J. (2017). Cultural intelligence and employees' creative performance: The moderating role of team conflict in interorganizational teams. *Journal of Management & Organization*, 25(1), 96–116. DOI: 10.1017/jmo.2016.64

Iqbal, M., Warraich, I. A., & Haq, S. U. (2023). Impact of employee resilience and job engagement on project success: Mediating role of innovative work behavior. *Research Journal for Societal Issues*, 5(3), 234–257. DOI: 10.56976/rjsi.v5i3.144

Izzatuddin, S., & Kusumastuti, R. (2021). Relationship between employee engagement and innovative behavior: Empirical study of pt bank bri syariah tbk in dki jakarta, west java, and banten. *Jurnal Administrasi Bisnis*, 10(2), 87–98. DOI: 10.14710/jab.v0i0.36684

Kumar, H., & Raghavendran, S. (2015). Gamification, the finer art: Fostering creativity and employee engagement. *The Journal of Business Strategy*, 36(6), 3–12. DOI: 10.1108/JBS-10-2014-0119

Letchmiah, L., & Thomas, A. (2017). Retention of high-potential employees in a development finance company. *SA Journal of Human Resource Management*, 1(2). Advance online publication. DOI: 10.4102/sajhrm.v15i0.924

Park, Y., Song, J., Yoon, S., & Kim, J. (2013). Learning organization and innovative behavior. *European Journal of Training and Development*, 38(1/2), 75–94. DOI: 10.1108/EJTD-04-2013-0040

Rachman, T., Anindita, R., Izmi, N., Ewaldo, C., Rezki, F., & Andini, E. (2022). Fostering innovative work behavior of employees in the tourism industry: Strategies for successful remote tourism during the covid-19 pandemic. *Jurnal Manajemen Dan Pemasaran Jasa*, 15(2), 227–240. DOI: 10.25105/jmpj.v15i2.13573

Setyawasih, R., & Buchdadi, A. (2022). Organizational culture and innovative work behavior in manufacturing company: The role of employee engagement as a mediator. *International Journal of Research and Review*, 9(1), 360–371. DOI: 10.52403/ijrr.20220143

Shanker, R., Bhanugopan, R., Heijden, B., & Farrell, M. (2017). Organizational climate for innovation and organizational performance: The mediating effect of innovative work behavior. *Journal of Vocational Behavior*, 100, 67–77. DOI: 10.1016/j.jvb.2017.02.004

Suifan, T., Abdallah, A., & Janini, M. (2018). The impact of transformational leadership on employees' creativity. *Management Research Review*, 41(1), 113–132. DOI: 10.1108/MRR-02-2017-0032

Chapter 14
Blurring the Boundaries Between Employment and Entrepreneurship:
Role of Employee Ownership and Profit-Sharing

Deepak Kumar Sahoo
Biju Patnaik University of Technology, Rourkela, India

Saroj Kanta Biswal
Siksha O Anusandhan, India

Thi Trang Dang
Vietnam National University, Hanoi, Vietnam

Anish Kumar
https://orcid.org/0000-0002-8047-4227
O.P. Jindal Global University, India

Ajay Chandel
https://orcid.org/0000-0002-4585-6406
Lovely Professional University, India

ABSTRACT

This chapter explores how employee ownership and profit-sharing arrangements blur the traditional boundaries between employment and entrepreneurship. It examines the historical evolution and various models of employee ownership, including stock options, ESOPs, and profit-sharing plans. By analyzing the entrepreneurial mindset fostered through these models, the chapter highlights their impact on organizational

DOI: 10.4018/979-8-3693-9486-1.ch014

culture, employee engagement, and business performance. The discussion also covers the benefits, challenges, and limitations of implementing such models, supported by case studies from notable companies like John Lewis Partnership and Mondragon Corporation. Looking ahead, the chapter identifies key trends and implications for the future, including technological advancements, inclusivity, and regulatory developments. The findings underscore the potential of these models to transform work environments, enhance employee motivation, and drive organizational success.

INTRODUCTION

Introduction Employee ownership and profit-sharing have been the new structural models receiving the most attention in the recent past. These models—having employees either own shares in the organization or become participants in profit-sharing schemes—are viewed as having the capacity to align employees' interests with those of the company. Unlike the traditional employment arrangement, where the basic relationship is that of employer-employee, employee ownership and profit-sharing blur the distinction by instilling in workers the sense of ownership, with its attendant responsibilities (Aerts et al., 2013). The purpose of this chapter is to explore more deeply the concept of employee ownership and profit-sharing and how models of employee ownership can foster an environment in which employees act more as entrepreneurs, contributing to their own success and to the enterprise. Understanding the evolution, benefits, challenges, and future trends of these models better enables individuals to appreciate the potential for the workplace to become more collaborative and innovative. Vested models of organizations are very timely to study today when the economic world is on a fast development pace and companies are urging to look for new, innovative ways to engage their workforce and drive sustainable growth. In this chapter, several varieties of employee ownership and profit-sharing schemes will be canvassed in an attempt to cast some light on how the transference of ownership capital is redrawing the boundaries of what constitutes work and enterprise (Azfar & Danninger, 2001).

Historical Context and Evolution

There is a long history associated with employee ownership and profit-sharing, which emanates from an earlier cooperative and profit-sharing enterprise. Such models could trace their roots back to the 19th century, when the industrial revolution was really changing the working environment and giving birth to new economic problems and opportunities. Early pioneers like social reformer Robert Owen experimented with cooperative societies where the profits would be distributed among the workers and the employees had a say in running the enterprise. These early efforts laid the groundwork for the development of more formalized models of employee ownership. In the early 20th century (Braam, 2024), the concept of employee ownership gained prominence as part of dual-pronged reactions in the United States and Europe to spreading labor unrest and to bringing about more equitable and sustainable business practices. A good example of this dates back to 1956 when Louis Kelso introduced an ESOP where employees could buy shares of stock from the company in which they worked, creating ownership and aligning workers' interests with management. ESOPs gained popularity in the second part of the 20th century, particularly in America, for being considered a form of resistance to a hostile acquisition, as well as for enhancing employee loyalty and, in consequence, company performance (D'Art & Turner, 2004).

Simultaneously with the onset when worker cooperatives have recently gained importance as a determinant factor in the economies of various European countries, the ESOPs began to gain increased significance. These cooperatives were particularly well represented in regions with very well-developed mutual help and community solidarity traditions among workers. For instance, the Mondragon Corporation, established in 1956, is the most highly publicized worker-owned cooperative in history and turned out to be the functionality of this model at a larger scale (Fakhfakh & FitzRoy, 2018). The success of Mondragon made clear the strength of worker ownership in building resilient, socially responsible businesses, capable of competing worldwide. Those elements of employee ownership and profit sharing have continued to build models into the second half of the 20th century and into the 21st. Following the lead of Silicon Valley and the high technology industry, new equity compensation models emerged in the form of stock options and restricted stock units (RSUs) that have become very common in the startup culture. These forms provide workers with an interest in the future success of their companies and, accordingly, provide a powerful impetus for innovation and secure long-term commitment to the goals of the company (Fibírová & Petera, 2013).

These models have evolved over time, impinging on a variety of economic, social, and political factors, such as changes in labor laws, tax incentives, and shifts in corporate governance practices. For example, in 2013, the United Kingdom devised Employee Shareholder Status, in which employees could take up company shares in return for sacrificing some employment rights. It was meant to achieve entrepreneurship in already established companies, reflecting a larger trend blending traditional employment with entrepreneurial opportunities (FitzRoy & Nolan, 2021).

In general, the development of the historical perspective of employee ownership and profit sharing was an evolving process from early experiments in cooperation towards more complex and differentiated models. They have adapted to economic condition changes and continue to be of prime importance for the contemporary business environment. One can learn from getting to know the history and the development of such schemes that this can again shed light into how will these schemes changes the ways of work in the future to have an economy that is more inclusive, innovative, and resilient.

TYPES OF EMPLOYEE OWNERSHIP AND PROFIT-SHARING MODEL

The rise of employee ownership and profit-sharing models has produced a host of rather different structures devised to grant ownership and participation to employees within the firm. The difference in their legal structure and the level of control employees hold with the firm range, from least complex to most complex (Green & Heywood, 2010). A primary understanding of the different types of employee ownership and profit-sharing models makes it easier to explain how these methods are capable of blurring the distinctions between traditional employment and entrepreneurship.

1. Employee Stock Ownership Plans

Probably the best-known and most widely used form of employee ownership in the United States is the Employee Stock Ownership Plan (ESOP). A qualified retirement plan, it is mainly invested in the stock of the sponsoring employer. In an ESOP, companies create a trust fund to which they contribute new shares of their own stock or cash to buy existing shares. The shares in the trust are then allocated to individual employee accounts according to a generally predetermined formula, usually a function of seniority and/or salary. Employees accrue rights to the shares through vesting and receive the value of their accounts when they terminate from the company for any reason, including retirement (Handel & Levine, 2003). ESOPs are enormously popular because they enjoy an extraordinary range of tax benefits not available to other forms of broadbased ownership. They generally act as an instrument of business succession planning enabling the owner to move out, with a source of securing the firm's legacy, and inspiring the workforce.

2. Worker Cooperatives

Worker cooperatives are firms which are owned and controlled democratically by their workers. In a worker cooperative, each employee owns a share of the business and casts an equal vote in decision-making, regardless of the nature, level or tenure of the position/ job. Workers to these companies are intervened to in order to pay them dividends which are paid in just a matter of hours stipulated by them or an equivalent model. Since these have the workers as partial owners and managers (Kraft & Lang, 2012), the level of engagement and commitment to work is very high since they benefit directly from the success of the company. Worker cooperatives are particularly common in contemporary shared-expertise and teamwork-orientated manufacturing, retailing, and agricultural industries. The cooperative model, which is based on the principles of mutual aid as well as solidarity, mainly suits workers who have altruist beliefs and tend to give importance to democratic governance and shared responsibility.

3. Profit-Sharing Plans

Profit-sharing plans primarily refer to any type of employee benefit plan that companies spread a given part of their profits among the employees. These plans are typically bonus plans under which cash bonuses or deferred compensation are paid to employees according to the financial success of the company for a certain period. The amount of money, which is worked out to be distributed to employees, may be calculated by a variety of methods, including individual or group performance measures (Kruse et al., 2010). Unlike ESOPs, the profit-sharing plan does not offer equity in the company to the employees, but it creates a feeling of ownership and a direct relationship between the workers' effort and the firm's success. The profit-sharing plans can be particularly effective to motivate employees, enhance productivity, and foster an atmosphere of cooperation and shared goals.

4. Stock Options and Restricted Stock Units (RSUs)

Equity compensation tools that are frequently utilized by startups and technology companies to attract and retain outstanding talent include options and restricted stock units. Stock options allow an employee to purchase a designated number of shares at a specified price—otherwise called an exercise price—after a vesting period has passed. In the event that the company's share prices rise above the exercise price, employees get to purchase shares at a lower price and, therefore, benefit from the growth of the company (Tseo et al., 2004). RSUs are more of a promise to issue shares or cash equivalent when certain conditions, such as continuous employment or attaining performance milestones, in the award agreement are achieved. Both stock options and RSUs align the employee's financial interests with the shareholder's interest and instil an entrepreneurial attitude, thus inculcating a long-term relationship toward the welfare of the company (Long & Fang, 2012).

5. Phantom Stock and Stock Appreciation Rights

Phantom stock and SARs are ways to reward employees identically as if they carried an actual ownership in the company but without actually endowing them with voting rights or equity in the company. Phantom stock is the issuance of a cash award to the employee upon the value of a certain number of shares, normally issued after the completion of an agreed period or after attaining some predetermined set of performance parameters. SARs work by granting workers the right to appreciation in the price of the firm's shares over some predetermined period in cash or through shares. These models are particularly attractive to companies that would like to provide incentives tied to equity values without giving out further shares or requiring employees to have an out-of-pocket investment (Poernamasari, 2023).

6. Employee Stock Purchase Plans (ESPPs)

Employee Stock Purchase Plans provide a program through which employees can purchase company shares, usually at a discount, through payroll deductions over a period. ESPPs are designed to encourage employee ownership and better align employee interests with the company's goals. In the case of ESPPs, the employees can benefit from an increase in stock prices and develop a sense of ownership. Most of the time, direct involvement in the decision-making process is not as intensive as in the case of ESOPs or worker cooperatives. ESPPs are taken to mean devices for loyalty and a sense of belonging while providing workers with an actual interest in the future of the company (Zhao et al., 2010).

Each of the models outlined demonstrates a unique approach in terms of involving employees as owners and holders of some success within a company. It is through these different levels of ownership, financial incentives, and decision-making powers that models allow companies to create a more entrepreneurial environment, guiding employees to think and act as owners. A blurring of the edges between employment and entrepreneurship eases innovation and enhances productivity, possibly resulting in more sustainable business practices and long-term growth (Aerts et al., 2013).

THE ENTREPRENEURIAL MINDSET IN EMPLOYEE OWNERSHIP

The entrepreneurial mindset is one that is proactive, innovative, and takes the opportunity to lead in taking ownership of their work and creatively contributing toward organizational goals. In traditional employment settings, the role definition by its very nature tends to be limited, with clear and defined lines of authority and a clear hierarchy that dictates decision-making. However, in an organization with forms of employee ownership, such as an ESOP or worker cooperative, something basically changes about the way employees view their role and the organization at large (Azfar & Danninger, 2001). The entrepreneurial mindset of workers is fostered in these models as one gains a sense of responsibility, innovation, and collaboration as a foundation required for increased business performance and personal growth.

This is one of the major ways in which employee ownership supports an entrepreneurial attitude: it connects the interests of employees with those of the company. If workers own shares or have a piece of the action regarding company success because they get a share of the profits, they will be more likely to think and act like owners. This creates employer mentality and drives staff to go above and beyond the call of duty in considering new opportunities for growth, inefficiencies, and initiative in problem-solving. For instance, a worker-owner in a cooperative might lead a new project or even propose a new product line when she realizes that the work done is related to the company's financial status and personal financial well-being (Braam, 2024).

Employee ownership also encourages innovation and continuous improvement. In line with the desire to enhance company performance, employee-owners take an interest in providing the company with ideas and proposals that could bring out innovation. Unlike the situation in a non-employee-owned situation, where very few of the top executives make decisions, an employee-owned company must make most of its decisions in a more engaging and democratic manner (D'Art & Turner, 2004). Such inclusiveness tends to make all levels of employees feel empowered to share their opinions and insights, opening up further diversity in ideas and solutions. Employee ownership generally creates an environment with open channels of interaction and collaboration with excellent platforms for entrepreneurial thinking and experimentation. If they feel valued and recognized as essential members of the organization, the employees are more likely to be engaged in work and committed to its success. It means that because of this increased level of engagement, they are willing to take risks, invest time in learning new skills, and make contributions to long-term strategic initiatives. For example, an employee shareholder may be more motivated to participate in training, cross-function teams or innovation workshops because he or she understands that all aspects of learning contribute value to the growth and competitiveness of the firm (Fakhfakh & FitzRoy, 2018).

The employee "entrepreneurial" propensity in the owned firm is further demonstrated in the risk behavior and orientation in dealing with uncertainty. Traditional employees are risk averse and would possibly avoid such activities that put their jobs or status within the company in question. On the contrary, interventionalists, aware that greater risk-taking activity translates into a greater potential payoff, are more willing to embrace the unknown and proceed with innovative strategy. It is this wilful acceptance of calculated risk that defines much of entrepreneurial behavior and is often the driver for successful adaptation to new business conditions and market realities. This means that employee ownership models have the most unique dynamic of sharing risk with all, and hence it is pretty convenient to support each other and resilient at the same time (Fibírová & Petera, 2013). The second additional benefit for employee ownership is the fact that it can help in thinking long-term and hence sustainability. The focus in most of the public companies is on the short term profit whose consideration is based on the quarterly, a fact that may make most of its decisions rely on the short term and hence a compromise on sustainability. On the other hand, employee-owned firms are most likely to plan in the long term and care about whether growth is sustainable for the future: more long-term planning can be afforded. Such a long-term orientation has a good minimum compatibility with the entrepreneurial mindset which believes that innovation, adaptability, and resilience are the core drivers of success. Employee-owners likely will be more willing to accept choices made that will be in the best interest of the company overall, securing its long-term viability and prosperity in favor of short-term profits (FitzRoy & Nolan, 2021).

Another method by which employee ownership democratizes entrepreneurship is through reducing its barriers to entry. Real entrepreneurship often is very expensive and involves access to capital—often the largest barrier (Green & Heywood, 2010). Employee ownership models, on the other hand, provide a way through which employees can benefit from the positive aspects of entrepreneurship—through equity ownership, profit-sharing, and pools, and authority in terms of decision-making—with fewer requirements of necessary, huge quantities of personal financial risk. In this way, the democratization of entrepreneurship also allows more diversity in the development of entrepreneurial skills and frames of mind amongst a broader range of people, hence making it feasible for a more inclusive and diverse entrepreneurship landscape (Handel & Levine, 2003).

Altogether, such an entrepreneurial state of mind that is created by employee ownership models is the one that is transforming the classical relationship between an employer and employee; it becomes a partnership, with employees as a well-fledged value co-creator. By encouraging proactive behavior, innovation, taking of risks, and long-term thinking, these models blur the employment-entrepreneurship border and create a dynamic, collaborative work environment capable of driving individual as well as organizational effectiveness. As businesses have to constantly be innovative in an ever complex and competitive environment, inculcating an entrepreneurial mindset by employees has become the key to sustainability in growth and innovation (Kraft & Lang, 2012).

BLURRING THE BOUNDARIES BETWEEN EMPLOYMENT AND ENTREPRENEURSHIP

The whole critiquing ethos of employee ownership and profit-sharing models is based on the fact that they deviate from the norm in actually trying to mesh the two paradigms of employment and entrepreneurship. Traditionally speaking, employment is characterized by a clear division between the employer and the employee; the worker agrees to do specific duties in exchange for a salary at the end of each day (Kruse et al., 2010). They have little involvement in decisions or the financial well-being of the company, other than in how it affects their own pocketbook. Meanwhile, entrepreneurship deals with risking one's own self in an effort to establish, operate, and expand a business with the return at all times being high uncertainty and equally high personal investment in entrepreneurship. Models of employee ownership and profit sharing actually bum the midnight oil on the traditional definition of employment and entrepreneurship, introducing elements of both to produce some hybrid model where employees have a stake in the success of the business and also are more involved in its running process (Long & Fang, 2012).

One major point that differentiates these models from a purely traditional definition of employment or entrepreneurship is the concept of shared ownership and risk. In the traditional employment relationship, workers do not usually share in the business's performance-related risks; if the firm goes underperforming, they still get their salary. However, in the employee-ownership models through ESOPs or worker cooperatives, there is some little level of sharing in the risks since the employees are considered partial owners as they hold some equity in the company. This means, therefore, that the financial results of the company materially affect the employees: when the company prospers, they mutually benefit by an increase of share value or the distribution of profits; when it fails, the value they have may suffer. There is a mutual investment from common risks that aligns the interests of employees to those of the traditional entrepreneurs to produce a collective entrepreneurial spirit (Poernamasari, 2023).

Another huge factor that blurs these lines is employee empowerment into the decision-making process. In most employee-owned firms, workers have a say in most major business decisions, such as strategic planning, investment, and even hiring. This is very sharp, compared to traditional models of employment where decision-making is centralized among the senior executives and shareholders (Tseo et al., 2004). The latter relate to governance mechanisms that make employees more acquainted with the business, endow entrepreneurial reflections, and a feeling of responsibility for the company's success. Employees are not mere workers but are more involved in shaping the future of the organization, like entrepreneurs in their ventures.

Employee ownership and profit-sharing models enkindle attitudes towards innovation and proactive problem solving in organizations, the very entrepreneurial traits. This means that when employees are motivated through ownership or profit sharing, they think more desperately about ways through which they can better the products, services, or processes. This innovation-driven environment impels employees to act like entrepreneurs of the company, always on the lookout for fresh opportunities and resolute with new solutions for the betterment of business competitiveness and profitability. For example, worker cooperatives allow the pooling of insights and skills among employees in the development of a new line of products or entry into a new market. This is typical of entrepreneurial activity in the sense that the demarcation line between being an employee and entrepreneur blurs (Zhao et al., 2010).

Besides innovation inculcation, these models also inculcate a long-term perspective upon the employee. Traditional employees find themselves more interested in short-term performance goals or annual reviews, while employee-owners usually become motivated by the long-term success of the company (Aerts et al., 2013). That is tantamount to thinking like an entrepreneur, in the position of being strategic about the future for sustainable growth over time. Employee-owners become more inclined to argue for strategies that build value over the long term, rather than always chasing short-range gains, if for no other reason because their financial well-being is tied up in the company's condition (Afshan et al., 2021). This once again closes the natural gap between employment and entrepreneurship because, serving the interests of both parties, the prolonged prosperity of the enterprise is sought (Azfar & Danninger, 2001).

Even more, employee ownership and profit-sharing models democratize the entrepreneurial experience, making it accessible to significantly more people who would not start a business without resources and fearing the risks. Such models make it possible for employees to have the opportunity to own, participate in profits, and influence decisions without making a big personal investment or paying the full penalty of entrepreneurial failure (D'Art & Turner, 2004). This democratization contributes to a pathway in which employees are able to develop entrepreneurial skills and mindsets, which in turn contribute to their professional growth and the innovative capacity of the company. In a nutshell, these models provide a really crucial bridge between the security of being an employee and all the opportunities that entrepreneurship offers: more and more people take up entrepreneurship in a structured and supportive environment (Braam, 2024).

In a similar vein, the blending of employment and entrepreneurship via these models carries with it powerful implications in terms of organizational culture and employee engagement. Employee-owned companies very much thrive on the basis of trust, collaboration, and a shared sense of corporate purpose among the workers (Fibírová & Petera, 2013). This breeds a type of corporate culture wherein employees are motivated by more than just money but by the ownership, pride, and sense of shared destiny that emanates from such an environment. This cultural shift translates to high levels of worker engagement and satisfaction, reduced rate of staff attrition while, maximizing organization performance at large. By creating an atmosphere under which employees felt as if they were key stakeholders, these models combine the underlying stability of being in work with the freedom and motivation to the entrepreneurship associated with it (Fakhfakh & FitzRoy, 2018).

The hybrid nature of these models finally displaces it from the traditional notions of the career and professional identity. Employees are said to often develop a dual identity while in forms of ownership and profit-sharing arrangements: that of being an employee and the other of being an entrepreneur. This becomes a ground reality fact that enables them to transit between the structured employment world and the dynamic, opportunity-driven world of entrepreneurship. This provides a platform of continuous growth in learning as the employees gain new skills and experiences that increase their versatility and adaptability. This blurring of roles is in fact part of a much wider pattern for workers in the present day, where career paths are fluid by necessity and the line between worker and entrepreneur ever-more blurred (FitzRoy & Nolan, 2021).

In conclusion, employee ownership and profit-sharing fundamentally redirect the calculus of both employment and entrepreneurship toward greater reciprocity. In achieving ownership sharing, such models blur the usual lines of distinction between employee and entrepreneur and further strengthen the case for giving employees a real say in decision-making, inspiring new innovations, thinking in the long run, democratizing the entrepreneurial experience, and defining a distinctive organizational culture (Tunio et al., 2021). With businesses continuously changing and searching for new ways to motivate the manpower, the hybrid forms provide a future vision where the employees evolve into something else besides workers: co-creators of value and innovators (Green & Heywood, 2010).

BENEFITS OF EMPLOYEE OWNERSHIP AND PROFIT-SHARING

Employee ownership and profit-sharing modalities offer ranges of benefits that are much broader than those obtained through the conventional advantages accredited to the standard employment practices. Such benefits do not only accrue to the employee but also to the organization running such models, fostering a culture of engagement, innovation, and sustainability. Blurring the lines between employment and entrepreneurship, they create much more dynamic and inclusive workplaces driving greater levels of individual and organizational success (Handel & Levine, 2003).

1. Improving Employee Motivation and Engagement

Employee motivation and engagement are among the most sustainable impacts of both employee ownership and profit-sharing. Having a financial stake in the organization's success fosters a sense of commitment because employees are more committed when they have a financial stake of their own (Kruse et al., 2010). The sense of ownership nurtures a deeper emotional attachment to the company, which relates them with a higher level of engagement and job satisfaction. If the employees feel that they are working for themselves and not only for the company, they become more motivated toward making a contributing factor to the success of it. That heightened engagement often translates to increased productivity, reduced absenteeism, and an improved culture at work (Kraft & Lang, 2012).

2. Better Financial Performance

Companies that implement models of employee ownership and profit sharing normally have improved financial performance. Employees having a direct stake in the profits of the company would act in ways to support cost efficiency, an increase in quality, and customer satisfaction on that basis. Studies portray that employee ownership companies outperform their non-employee-ownership counterparts in terms of revenue and profitability as well as the overall financial stability. This improved performance is due to the fact that as a result of the synergy of the employees' interests with that of the company, rigorous financial management is executed, and focus is shifted more towards long-term stability rather than short-run profit making (Long & Fang, 2012).

3. Innovation and Creativity

Both the employee ownership and profit-sharing programs inculcate a culture of innovation and creativity. Because the motivated nature of people considered co-owners shows up differently, their ideas and solutions become drivers for developing business growth and differentiation (Tseo et al., 2004). The pathway to this culture of innovation in employee-owned companies is fortified all the more when decisions taken at the firm are made inclusive in their approach, thereby encouraging the participation of employees in the formation of the strategic direction of the company. Through that, such models will empower the workers, promote open and more innovative products, services, and processes that can bolster the competitive advantage of the company (Poernamasari, 2023).

4. Higher Employee Retention and Reduced Turnover

Employee ownership and sharing of profits are very important in keeping the employees in a company and reducing the employee turnover of a company. The reason the employees will most likely stay longer in the organization is when they feel a sense of ownership, or are financially into the organization's success (Aerts et al., 2013). Some values elicited include personal growth and the desire for one to be part of a company to which they feel connected to contribute to its success. Besides the saving on recruitment and training expenses, reduction in turnover enables the holding of organization knowledge, and stability which are two major factors towards business success in the long term. There is lesser rate of turnover, which will bring the workforce together, and the team will be more experienced in the same. In the long run, better teamwork and productivity will be evident (Zhao et al., 2010).

5. Better Organizational Culture and Morale

The introduction of employee-ownership and profit-sharing models often leads to a less hostile organizational culture and improved morale of the employees themselves. This model instills fairness and equity among employees as they believe that indeed, after the toil of the company's success has been based on their effort, they should be compensated (Braam, 2024). This common sense of purpose and responsibility creates a supportive and inclusive workplace environment where employees are likely to work together and support each other and share pride in their work. A strong organizational culture not only helps employees to be satisfied, but it also improves and develops the company's image as a top employer of choice to make it easier to recruit top talent (Azfar & Danninger, 2001).

6. Alignment of Interests Between Employees and Management

Employee ownership and profit-sharing align the interests of the employees and management; hence, they reduce the potential of conflicts and foster a more amicable working environment. The employee co-owners share the same goals as the management; that is, to improve profitability and sustainability. This alignment motivates employees to try making decisions that are in the best interest of the firm in general, rather than those driven purely by self-interested job-related motives. Such models foster a shared vision and common goals for employees and management, making it possible for employees to work more harmoniously and mutually for success (D'Art & Turner, 2004).

7. Improved Employee Wealth and Financial Security

The implementation of employee ownership and profit-sharing is considered one of the ways through which the financial status of employees is tremendously improved through increasing long-term wealth and financial security for employees. In such a format, employees accumulate huge volumes of financial assets over time either through stock ownership, profit distributions, or any other aspect of equity compensation. This wealth accumulation can serve in the construct their base and, hence, avail the employees and their families with more economic security and safety, that translated to less financial stress and better health. Many times, worker ownership has enabled workers to save to have significant retirement savings, to pay for the education of their children, or to have another chance to enhance the quality of their lives (Fakhfakh & FitzRoy, 2018).

8. Support for Business Succession and Continuity

More often, employee ownership is largely an answer to business succession and continuity for many business owners. As time comes when the owners should retire or move on from their business, employee ownership serves as a way of passing business legacy and value within that model created (FitzRoy & Nolan, 2021). It would see to it that there is a smooth change with minimal disturbances and operations continuing in the business. The employee ownership models, such as ESOPs, are most useful when the practice seems to apply in family businesses or closely held companies. Such companies aim at safeguarding the culture and identity of their company. Through business ownership by employees, there is always a smooth transition that will always guarantee the maintenance of the company and its viability in the long term (Fibírová & Petera, 2013).

9. Community and Social Impact

Employee-owned companies have often made a great positive impact on the society within the environment where the companies are based. It is arguable that the aspects provided by such organizations range from stable employment to fostering economic growth and even encouraging business practices that are inclusive in nature. Models of employee ownership, such as profit-sharing provisions, promote social and environmental responsibility since workers who have a stake in the success of a business tend to act in ways that promote sustainability and community involvement. This social impact commitment boosts the company's reputation (Green & Heywood, 2010).

10. Economic Resilience

The firms that are owned and controlled by its employees are significantly stronger economically than firms not owned by its employees in economic downturn times. The equality shared ownership and equality in shared responsibility in such setups has been seen as generating a working synergy amidst the employees. Employee-owned enterprises are far more ready than others to embrace shared sacrifice, as through temporary wage reductions or flexibility in working hours, in the common interest of preserving jobs and company viability. This resilience enables recovery from economic setbacks in a more time-efficient way and places employee-owned firms in a favorable position for long-term success (Handel & Levine, 2003).

On the whole, employee ownership and profit-sharing result in the improvement of both individual and organizational performance. These models give a sense of ownership, alignment of interests, promotion of innovation, and support for financial security, hence ensure a more engaged, motivated, and resilient workforce (Kraft & Lang, 2012). As businesses continue to face more complex competitive landscapes, the adoption of employee ownership and profit-sharing models has offered an essential strategy in driving sustained growth and success in the business world.

CHALLENGES AND LIMITATIONS

These two affiliation approaches such as employee ownership and profit sharing include challenges and constraints related to opportunity, so this normally means an organization should be careful. These are short of properly managed and can prove to be actual setbacks for these models and can reduce performance in general (Kruse et al., 2010). Therefore, the performance of the business in total should be changed to avoid some challenges of these models that are experienced. Similarly, both approaches, employee ownership and profit sharing, create challenges and constraints that are dangerous and not effective to the business. These, therefore, the organisation should have a proper understanding and address this so as to implement or continue a relationship in the organisation (Long & Fang, 2012).

1. Complexity of implementation and Administration

Among the very first and one of the prime difficulties associated with the model of employee ownership and profit sharing is its complexity in the implementation measures and the following administration. The formation of Employee Stock Ownership Program or, for that matter, a worker cooperative, or any other profit-sharing arrangement this needs to be done with a lot of legal, financial, and administrative investment. Companies create a complex nexus of regulations, implications for tax, and legal requirements, operating differently in different countries and regions (Poernamasari, 2023). Furthermore, the setup of devices like these is usually associated with significant initial costs, including advisory and legal fees and the structuring of trust funds or other financial arrangements. Even after the initiation, these programs need regular administration, keeping the record uptight and correct, compliance to the legal standards, and frequent information to the employees about their rights and benefits. This act can put many companies, especially SMEs with limited resources and expertise, at a disadvantage (Tseo et al., 2004).

2. Chance of Exposure to Risks to Employees' Wealth

Although employee ownership offers greater financial protection to the employees, it also carries some number of financial risks. Workers who are vested in company stock or profit-sharing plans have a direct personal stake in the outcome of the firm, particularly in its financial performance. If the organization got into financial trouble or went bankrupt, the workers could lose a large portion of what their shares are actually valued at, or they could lose what they had expected to receive (Aerts et al., 2013). In worst-case scenarios, employees can lose every dime in their entire investment, which can have devastating personal financial consequences, especially if a substantial portion of one's retirement savings or personal wealth is tied up in the company. This financial risk can be particularly pronounced in companies that are not well-diversified or that operate in volatile industries. But to enjoy the advantages of ownership, the employees need to agree and must have the ability to confront the risks involved, which can be extremely demanding for the undereducated section at least from the perspective of financial consciousness (Zhao et al., 2010).

3. Managing Employee and Management Interests

However, theories and existing evidence reveals that there it can turn out to be a daunting task for the interest of all employee-owners to be coordinated and balanced, and this interest when compared to the management and shareholders' interest cannot be equal. But still, although this model is for aligning the interest among the employees and the management, conflicts can come up with regard to some decision-making processes or financial priorities. For example, employee-owners might have more value for job security and continual income, while management may base its considerations on cost-cutting or strategic investments that have no immediate benefits to the employees. Besides, there is the possibility that when a company has a high level of employee ownership the decision-making process become complex and may tend to be time-consuming. This is since there will be more exposure and consultation of shareholders together with the different perspectives put into consideration besides others. That can slow the pace of reaching a consensus and may even further on fail to reach a decision, especially in big companies or those with considerable diversity (Azfar & Danninger, 2001).

4. Potential for Reduced Entrepreneurial Agility

While employee ownership may instill an entrepreneurial mindset in all employees, it may also potentially get a company lost in the glut and may negatively affect a company's agility and responsiveness to the market. In entrepreneurial ventures, the process of decision-making is pretty swift and taken by a few founders or executives. On the other hand, the decision-making process can be very slow and lengthy in an employee-owned business due to a lot of consultation and agreeing on a consensus over it before a decision is taken (Fakhfakh & FitzRoy, 2018). This can make it difficult for the company to respond quickly to new opportunities or competitive threats, which may stunt growth and innovation. Additionally, employee-owners might have less risk appetite than classic entrepreneurs, and might be primary enjoyers of the security and stability of employment rather than making bold strategic moves and thus not position the company advantageously in an ever-changing market environment (D'Art & Turner, 2004).

5. Cultural and Organizational Challenges

This has enormous cultural and organizational obstacles to employee ownership or profit-sharing implementation. It requires a change in mindset from traditional hierarchical management to governance that is more inclusive and participative. This may be hard to effect in some organizations, particularly if resistance comes from within the management, or employees are simply not used to having their say in decision-making. Further, instilling a culture where employees feel ownership and accountability is often difficult, especially for the companies with a history of professional hierarchy. The element of trust and shared ideology takes a lot of efforts and time, and it is not possible to indulge all the employees in business decision making processes, especially in big companies where the distance between all employees at different functioning levels creates a communication gap (Fibírová & Petera, 2013).

6. Issues in Communication and Transparency

But at the same time, communication and transparency in communicating these models, known to breed success of employee ownership and profit sharing, more often than not turn out to be deficient. Employees have to know how these models work, what the rights and responsibilities of these employees under that model would be, and how their actions would impact the company's performance and consequentially their financial outcomes (FitzRoy & Nolan, 2021). This has to go hand in hand with frequent, clear, and candid communication with and training of employees. Although this is possible, in an organization where number of employees are vast or when the business is geographically spread out, it might be tough to ensure this communication. Also, many a times sharing of financial performance and decision making is not as transparent as expected. This might be because the managers feel it is confidential or are just not willing to share; it will eventually lead to mistrust and disengagement from the employees, which defeats the purpose of the model (Green & Heywood, 2010).

7. Challenges with Scaling and Growth

Scaling and growing a business can be more complicated within companies that share their ownership with their employees or that follow profit-sharing models. With business growth, the situation may get tougher to maintain the culture of ownership and participation, especially when the new employees do not exhibit similar commitment to the vision and values of the company (Handel & Levine, 2003). The other problem is that, with more employee-owners, the burden involved in managing the ownership structure and plotting how the profits are to be distributed increases. Companies may experience difficulty attracting external capital as investors fear investing in companies with a complex set of ownership structures or where decision-making lies with too many members of the firm's employee group. The amount of external capital may not be obtainable. Therefore, companies would not be able to attract the capital they need to grow and expand their operations, leading to a possible failure of long-term success (Kraft & Lang, 2012).

8. Statutory and Regulatory Compliance

A large challenge to companies may be found in navigating the legal and regulatory landscape related to employee ownership and profit-sharing schemes. In various countries and regions, there are different laws and regulations regarding employee ownership, stock allocations, profit-sharing, or any other form of equity compensation. Companies will have to ensure they are compliant with the laws and regulations applicable to them. This is, however, complex and time-consuming. Failure to adhere to such regulations means that the business might be sued, penalties imposed on it, and business reputation damage. Also, changes in laws and regulations might bring about ambiguity and the requirement for companies to change their structures or remuneration plans and therefore be cumbersome to manage (Kruse et al., 2010).

9. Change Challenges and Status Quo Bias

It is a common problematic area to implement employee stock ownership and profit-sharing models due to status quo bias. Employees and management may feel associated with the hierarchical structures of a classical type and are reluctant to adopt more employee-centered and participating models. Ignorance of the benefits of employee ownership or out of fear of losing power may cause the resistance (Long & Fang, 2012). It may also be due to the increase in responsibility and accountability. Effective management means going further to handle the resistance using strategies of change management. Companies also have to be prepared to allay the fears of people who may not be open to the new model and thus make each of them feel appreciated in the process.

10. Potential for Unfairness and Perceived Inequity

Employee ownership and profit-sharing schemes are, by nature, designed for fairness and shared prosperity; however, they can also lead to perceptions of unfairness and inequity on the part of workers. For example, disparities in the ownership of shares or profit-sharing allocations breed divergent financial outcomes among employees, hence a feeling of being wronged or discontented (Poernamasari, 2023). Besides, the newcomers who join the business after the establishment of an ownership model may feel that their ownership status is inferior to others who were there from the beginning, especially since it is commonplace to have fewer shares or receive miniature profit distributions. Companies should design ownership and profit-sharing schemes in such a way that would be perceived as fair to every employee based on these factors.

Though there are many, the benefits from employee ownership and profit-sharing models are not challenge-free and have limitations. These challenges should be considered at both design and implementation levels, and the necessary resources, expertise, and commitment should be availed to make it work. Proactively and openly addressing these challenges can enable companies to maximize such benefits that accrue from employee ownership and profit-sharing, hence creating an engaged, motivated, resilient workforce that sustains long-term success (Tseo et al., 2004).

CASE STUDIES AND EXAMPLES

Employee ownership and profit-sharing models have been adopted across a range of industries and regions, establishing the flexibility and advantages of these models within diverse business contexts. The following case studies and examples make it clear how organizations were able to establish employee ownership and profit-sharing arrangements that were successful and, together with the problems they faced, the results of those systems (Zhao et al., 2010). These are a few cases that explain dimensions of the potential that these models offer in terms of organizational culture change, performance improvement, and shared ownership and responsibility by employees.

1. The John Lewis Partnership (United Kingdom)

The most popular case of employee ownership in the retail industry in the United Kingdom is that of The John Lewis Partnership, formed in 1864 that is based in London. It operates department stores under the name of John Lewis and a chain of supermarkets named Waitrose, with a staff force of over 80,000 employees. In 1929 his son, John Spedan Lewis, founded the company as a business with employees as its owners and transferred its ownership into a trust on behalf of all employees, known as "partners," with this trust sharing all profits with them. Under this unusual ownership structure, the bonus for partners is paid on financial performance of the company annually (Azfar & Danninger, 2001). The inclusive culture of shared responsibility and high employee engagement has enabled John Lewis Partnership to retain its competitive advantage for several years in a hard retail market. It has also helped to recruit talent for the organization and cultivate it because of low rates of turnover and high commitment among partners (Aerts et al., 2013).

2. Mondragon Corporation (Spain)

The Mondragon Corporation is a workers' cooperative, perhaps one of the world's largest, based in the Basque region of Spain. It involves over 90 coops working in industries like manufacturing, finance, retail, and education. Ten young entrepreneurs formed this corporation in 1956. At present, Mondragon has over 80,000 employees and runs under a very different style of governance that emphasizes democratic decision-making authority and shared ownership. Each of the cooperatives that together form the Mondragon Corporation are owned by its employees and managed by them (D'Art & Turner, 2004). This has been able to sustain high-level interaction, innovation, and adaptiveness among employees in Mondragon, even during hard economic times. The corporative structure itself also fosters social responsibility and community development, echoing the corporation's promise to sustainable and fair growth. Mondragon's success has made it a global reference for cooperative enterprise and an example of how employee ownership can drive both business and social success (Braam, 2024).

3. WinCo Foods (United States)

WinCo Foods is a supermarket chain located in Boise, Idaho in the United States. It is one of the striking examples in the retail field that has grown to new heights in the competitive market, solely based on the ownership by its employees. WinCo Foods was established in 1967 and took on the ESOP model in 1985, where employees were given sufficient ownership in the company. To date, WinCo Foods is entirely owned by the employees, holding over 20,000 members in the ESOP (Fakhfakh & FitzRoy, 2018). This leadership model has created an extremely committed workforce; one that is highly interested in cost effectiveness, customer service, and operational excellence toward the highest standards. In this regard, WinCo Foods has effectively staked out its own business model against large national chains through price-cutting while retaining customers. The phenomenal success of the company demonstrates that employee ownership encourages shared responsibility and, thus, can successfully thrive in a competitive business environment to grow in the long term (Fibírová & Petera, 2013).

4. Recology (United States)

Recology is a leading employee-owned company in San Francisco, California, USA, involved in the business of waste management while practicing recycling. The company was established in the year 1921 and became fully owned by its employees in the year 1986. Currently, more than 60% of the company is owned by its employees under an ESOP. Indeed, it has been this pattern of ownership that has driven success within the firm and underpinned a culture of innovation with regards to the environment and community. Recology's employees share a deep commitment to the company's mission to work for a sustainable future; hence, the commitment resonates in the industry-leading recycling rates and other innovative waste management solutions the company has conjured up (FitzRoy & Nolan, 2021). This model has led to high job satisfaction and high retention, with long employee service—a majority of them starting their career and retiring with Recology. This is a best-practice example of how business objectives can be harmonised with social and environmental goals to create value for employees, customers, and society at large.

5. Hypertherm, United States

Hypertherm is headquartered in Hanover, New Hampshire, USA and is an industrial cutting systems and software manufacturing world- class leader. Founded in 1968, Hypertherm adopted an ESOP in 2001 and became a fully employee-owned company by 2014. All of these investments and more, in totally fantastic employees, have created for the company an environment of continuous improvement, innovation, and shared responsibility. Its employees are vested in the future, participative in the decision process, and owners of their way forward (Green & Heywood, 2010). It is because of this that empowerment and collaboration have allowed Hypertherm to remain extremely competitive in the global marketplace and yet continue to enjoy a solid reputation of being a provider of good quality products, as well as world-class customer service provider. It has helped to put Hypertherm on the map as an employer of choice that many would like to work with, in addition to assuring low rates of staff turnover.

FUTURE TRENDS AND IMPLICATIONS

The future trends and developments that take part in employee ownership and profit-sharing models, in all likelihood, will be tremendous as the business landscape continues to evolve. The impact of the trends on the future could also affect how organizations go about the very process of applying these business models, their influence on employee engagement and, hence, organizational performance, and finally, the far-reaching effects on labor markets and the economy in general (Handel & Levine, 2003). These trends can help set businesses and policymakers for the evolving role that employee ownership will play in the future shaping of work and business.

1. Technology-Driven Models Will be Adopted at a Larger Scale

Employee ownership and profit-sharing innovations will see more infusion of technology. Digital platforms, blockchain, and data analytics open new avenues for management and administration, much the same as these innovations have enhanced many other aspects of business over the past years. For example, blockchain technology has the potential for increasing transparency and security in tracking ownership shares and profit distributions, while digital platforms can smoothen the administration of employee stock options and profit-sharing plans (Kraft & Lang, 2012). Technology-based designs will also enhance participation and involvement by increasing workers' access to live information regarding their ownership rights, performance measurements, and financial information. As technology continues to evolve, many organizations will increasingly make use of such tool-based techniques that facilitate the optimum exercise of their employee ownership and sharing schemes and thus be more effective and user-friendly (Kruse et al., 2010).

2. Describing Employee Ownership Expansion into Emerging Economies

Employee ownership and profit sharing are work models that are catching up with globalization in newly emerging markets, whereby most businesses strive to adopt these models to promote employee engagement, talent attraction, and growth. In fact, in countries with very rapidly growing economies and expanding middle-class categories, employee ownership does give it a competitive edge over others since worker interest is now in tandem with the organizational objectives and a feeling of shared purpose (Poernamasari, 2023). Besides, emerging markets further open up new ways of innovation and experimentation inside diverse systems of ownership, e.g. worker cooperatives and employee stock ownership plans. With the growth of these markets, employee ownership models are likely to increase their share and be part of a more equitable and sustainable economic development (Long & Fang, 2012).

3. Integration Into Corporate Social Responsibility and Sustainability

The provision of and alignment of employee ownership and profit-sharing models with corporate social responsibility and sustainability goals will become more widespread. The role of employee ownership in integrating social and environmental considerations into the business strategies of companies is growing and increasingly in the driving seat. For involving employees in proper decision-making regarding CSR and sustainability, the company can further its commitment to ethicality, environmental responsibility, and community participation. The MPs relating to employee ownership that focus on the social impact and sustainability also help to gather more socially responsible investors and customers, driving in the company's reputation and competitive edge (Tseo et al., 2004).

4. Increased Attention to Inclusion and Equity

Inclusivity and Equity will count as the trends of the future for employee ownership and profit sharing. Companies are increasingly being made to realize the need for sorting out disparities in wealth and opportunity, where employee ownership can be a strong tool for greater economic equity. Efforts will be made to ensure that employee ownership models are accessible to a wide variety of workers, including those in lower-wage and part-time positions (Zhao et al., 2010). This allusion to inclusivity shall have them be structured in a manner that is fair and representative of the contributions of all employees, and as well train and avail support to employees for a detailed understanding of how they can best add value to their ownership stakes. These move toward more equity also allows companies to get better engagement from their employees, reduce their turnover and have a work setting that is more supportive and inclusive.

5. Emergence of Hybrid Ownership Models

Hybrid models, then, combining traditional ownership structures with innovative approaches, are not discounted to become progressively popular. Some rather vague features of the employee-ownership model and profit-sharing might therefore be combined, along with venture capital and other financial arrangements for making it flexible and adaptive. For example, some companies would consider entering into a hybrid model that integrates employee stock ownership with external investment for financing growth and expansion while employees are still maintained for involvement in the decision-making process (Aerts et al., 2013). Hybrid models are more flexible in meeting the requirements imposed by diverse parties and changing business conditions; hence, these are the best selection of business models that companies should go for to balance multiple interests and objectives.

6. More Emphasis on Employee Well-Being and Balancing Work and Life

As employee-owned and profit-sharing models develop, more emphasis shall be put on employee well-being and balancing work with life. Businesses are becoming more and more aware of the great importance of supporting employees' all-round health and quality of life, and employee ownership can turn out to be a major constituent of this support. By offering workers a financial stake in the company's good results, businesses can strengthen job satisfaction, reduce financial stress, and improve financial well-being (Azfar & Danninger, 2001). Moreover, as the pattern of the employee ownership model unfolds, organizations might seek an increase in administrative supports including, for example, in flexible working, wellness, and professional development support for their well-being and work-life balance. The more the company effects the supportive, engaging, and rewardable workplace, the importance of the employee ownership will become a staple and the essential ingredient of developing a healthy and accomplished workplace culture (Braam, 2024)

7. Employee Ownership Model as Succession Planning for Business

Employee ownership is destined to play an increased role, one that can even be described as important in business succession planning for family-owned and closely held businesses. For business owners planning for retirement or to transition their companies, viable succession solutions include employee ownership models for business continuation and preservation (Fakhfakh & FitzRoy, 2018). This can allow the business owners to still maintain the business's legacy and values, offering employees a chance to show their interest in higher responsibilities and leadership in the future. This approach can also help to mitigate the challenges that companies face in finding buyers or investors, offering a smoother and controlled transition. With businesses more and more facing difficulties around the effects of succession planning, employee ownership is the logical option that would guarantee the future success and survival of most businesses (D'Art & Turner, 2004).

8. Regulatory and Policy Developments

There are also set to be some regulatory changes as well as the policy developments on employee ownership and profit-sharing models, which would impact how such schemes function and are managed. The adoption of employee ownership may further be promoted by new incentives or support mechanisms established by the government and policy makers in tax benefits—be it grants or funding programs. There may also be an emphasis on transparency, fairness, and legislation in employee ownership arrangements, probably supported by updating legal and regulatory standards. This will make it necessary for companies to be aware of such changes and subsequently change their ways to be within the law and to benefit from the employee ownership models (Fibírová & Petera, 2013).

9. Impact of Demographic Changes

Demographic changes ensured by aging populations as well as changing workforce composition: pose a certain impact on the future of the employee ownership and profit-sharing models. With the old retiring, the young people will be absorbed into employment, and companies have to enforce facilities in accordance with the changing needs and expectations among the different categories of employees (Fakhfakh & FitzRoy, 2018). Among an aging working population, employee ownership models that appeal to younger workers are likely gaining prominence. This will make companies question how their demographic shifts change their plans for transfer of company ownership and how to best manage their talent so that their employee ownership models can sustain the needs of their diverse workforce (D'Art & Turner, 2004).

10. Globalization and Cross-Border Employee Ownership

Globalization of business enterprises and decision to shift the workforce would imply advance implications for the future of employee ownerships and profit-sharing organizations. The firms operating internationally have to face challenges in setting up consistent plans of employee ownership across different countries and regions varying in legal, cultural, and economic settings (FitzRoy & Nolan, 2021). This calls for innovative approaches to design and administer employee ownership models so they take a balanced approach across the diversity of its regulatory regimes and culture. The future will see the growth of cross-border employee ownership arrangements in global business practice, whereby companies engaged in this practice are bound to have to manage complex international frameworks and ensure the fair treatment of staff across different countries (Fibírová & Petera, 2013).

In short, while technological changes, demographics, changes in the regulatory environments, and changing expectations about the workforce will be the determinants, the future of employee ownership and profit-sharing models will evolve. Companies will, therefore, alter their practices and change the principles to conform to these trends by trying to tap into the abilities of employee ownership in driving innovativeness and engagement and ultimately achieve success in the long run. These models will be evolved into more inclusive, equitable, and sustainable business forms shaping the future of work (Green & Heywood, 2010).

CONCLUSION

Employee ownership and profit-sharing models serve as very potent tools in eliciting the alignment of employees' interests toward the success of their employer organizations. Such initiatives allow for the promotion of a culture of shared responsibility, engagement, and long-run commitment in a unique manner. When an organization vests its employees in the financial outcomes of that company, motivation goes up, turnover goes down, and innovation is optimized. Employee ownership has been shown through case studies from very diverse industries and regions to bring improvements in organizational performance, increased employee satisfaction, and a greater sense of community in the workplace.

However, implementation and management of these models entail its own challenges: Administration is such a complex issue; financial risks come into play, as well as the need for balance in divergent interests. Such challenges will require careful planning, clear communication, and a genuine intent to be inclusive and fair in going through with the project. Employee ownership raises both opportunities and challenges in such a dynamic environment of changing business landscapes, driven by technological advancement, demographic changes, and evolving expectations of the workforce. Future trends would seem to indicate that technology will streamline these models significantly and that a focus on inclusivity and sustainability will increase their impact.

In the end, employee-owned and shared-profit models will continue to evolve and contribute to making the business world ever more resilient and just. As companies and policymakers wade their way through these shifts, lessons learned from in-practice models will prove to be of considerable importance in establishing environments where employees could be more than just workers but real partners in their company's success. By embracing these models, businesses can create more engaged, motivated, and innovative workforces, driving both organizational success and broader societal benefits.

REFERENCES

Aerts, K., Kraft, K., & Lang, J. (2013). *Profit-sharing and innovation*. SSRN Electronic Journal. DOI: 10.2139/ssrn.2379462

Afshan, G., Shahid, S., & Tunio, M. N. (2021). Learning experiences of women entrepreneurs amidst COVID-19. *International Journal of Gender and Entrepreneurship*, 13(2), 162–186. DOI: 10.1108/IJGE-09-2020-0153

Azfar, O., & Danninger, S. (2001). Profit-sharing, employment stability, and wage growth. *Industrial & Labor Relations Review*, 54(3), 619–630. DOI: 10.1177/001979390105400305

Braam, G., Poutsma, E., Schouteten, R., & Heijden, B. (2024). Employee financial participation and corporate social and environmental performance: Evidence from european panel data. *British Journal of Industrial Relations*, 62(2), 381–409. DOI: 10.1111/bjir.12784

D'Art, D., & Turner, T. (2004). Profit sharing, firm performance and union influence in selected european countries. *Personnel Review*, 33(3), 335–350. DOI: 10.1108/00483480410528869

Fakhfakh, F., & FitzRoy, F. (2018). Is profit sharing good for the environment? positive evidence from french firms. *Journal of Participation and Employee Ownership*, 1(2/3), 128–143. DOI: 10.1108/JPEO-12-2017-0012

Fibírová, J., & Petera, P. (2013). Profit-sharing – a tool for improving productivity, profitability and competitiveness of firms? *Journal of Competitiveness*, 5(4), 3–25. DOI: 10.7441/joc.2013.04.01

FitzRoy, F., & Nolan, M. (2021). Employee participation, job quality, and inequality. *Journal of Participation and Employee Ownership*, 5(1), 1–13. DOI: 10.1108/JPEO-05-2020-0014

Green, C., & Heywood, J. (2010). P*rofit sharing, separation and training*. *British Journal of Industrial Relations*, 49(4), 623–642. DOI: 10.1111/j.1467-8543.2010.00805.x

Handel, M., & Levine, D. (2003). Editors' introduction: The effects of new work practices on workers. *Industrial Relations*, 43(1), 1–43. DOI: 10.1111/j.0019-8676.2004.00317.x

Kraft, K., & Lang, J. (2012). Profit sharing and training*. *Oxford Bulletin of Economics and Statistics*, 75(6), 940–961. DOI: 10.1111/j.1468-0084.2012.00714.x

Kruse, D., Freeman, R., & Blasi, J. (2010). *Do workers gain by sharing? employee outcomes under employee ownership, profit sharing, and broad-based stock options.*, 257-290. DOI: 10.7208/chicago/9780226056968.003.0009

Long, R., & Fang, T. (2012). Do employees profit from profit sharing? evidence from canadian panel data. *Industrial & Labor Relations Review*, 65(4), 899–927. DOI: 10.1177/001979391206500406

Poernamasari, D.Dhonna Widya Poernamasari. (2023). The effect of profit-sharing on productivity of micro, small, and medium enterprises (msme) in indonesia. *Airlangga Journal of Innovation Management*, 4(2), 198–207. DOI: 10.20473/ajim.v4i2.48385

Tseo, G., Sheng, H., Zhang, P., & Zhang, L. (2004). Employee ownership and profit sharing as positive factors in the reform of chinese state-owned enterprises. *Economic and Industrial Democracy*, 25(1), 147–177. DOI: 10.1177/0143831X04040105

Tunio, M. N., Chaudhry, I. S., Shaikh, S., Jariko, M. A., & Brahmi, M. (2021). Determinants of the sustainable entrepreneurial engagement of youth in developing country—An empirical evidence from Pakistan. *Sustainability (Basel)*, 13(14), 7764. DOI: 10.3390/su13147764

Zhao, L., Trenberth, L., & Kelly, J. (2010). The development and implications of china's employee benefit systems. *Asia Pacific Journal of Human Resources*, 48(3), 287–301. DOI: 10.1177/1038411110378958

Chapter 15

Work-Life Balance of Hybrid Entrepreneurs: Balancing Demands of Personal and Professional Lives

Deepak Kumar Sahoo
Biju Patnaik University of Technology, Rourkela, India

Ashutosh Pandey
https://orcid.org/0000-0002-8255-8459
FORE School of Management, New Delhi, India

Shashank Mittal
O.P. Jindal Global University, India

Thi Minh Ngoc Luu
https://orcid.org/0000-0002-5972-7752
International School, Vietnam National University, Hanoi, Vietnam

ABSTRACT

Hybrid entrepreneurship, where individuals manage both full-time employment and entrepreneurial ventures, presents unique challenges and opportunities for achieving work-life balance. This paper examines the strategies and tools hybrid entrepreneurs use to manage their dual roles effectively. It explores the impact of technology, including project management software and scheduling apps, on balancing personal and professional responsibilities. The study also addresses common challenges such as time constraints, role conflict, and boundary issues, while highlighting future trends like advancements in technology and evolving work environments. By understanding these dynamics, hybrid entrepreneurs can enhance productivity,

DOI: 10.4018/979-8-3693-9486-1.ch015

foster innovation, and maintain well-being. The findings offer insights into creating sustainable practices that support both personal and professional success.

INTRODUCTION

Lately, hybrid entrepreneurship has been a part of this trend, whereby people balance roles in the traditional job and entrepreneurial venture sphere in a fast dynamism and change of economic times. Hybrid entrepreneurs, managing a primary and a secondary business at the same time, redefine the work-life balance. This phenomenon gives quite another view on how, in this growingly integrated world, people manage the complexities of personal and professional demands (Solesvik, 2017).

Work-life balance, a concept at the center of today's wellbeing and productivity discussions, is the balance struck between personal life and professional responsibilities. Estimation of this in one's life is of tremendous importance and helps maintain mental health and develop an overall quality of life. For hybrid entrepreneurs, struggling with balancing these is much pronounced due to the dual pulls experienced between the increased primary job demands and the need to nurture and grow a side business.

In a more general approach, this is the importance of studying work-life balance for hybrid entrepreneurs: the understanding of what enables them to cope with such competing demands and pressures. From the strategies and practices these individuals use in conjoining their personal and work lives, we can deduce extended lessons to pass such experiences relating to hybrid entrepreneurship. While these academic papers might fuel discussion at scientific conferences, the endeavor of this body of research was to also provide practical insights for emerging hybrid entrepreneurs and the organizations that support them (Emslie & Hunt, 2008).

This is a chapter in which we are going to really take a closer look at the balance between work and personal life among hybrid entrepreneurs, examining their unique challenges and the strategies adopted in order to produce a harmonious balance. Based on the above, we will further investigate the role played by effective balance in either enhancing or reducing business performance and the general well-being of the hybrid entrepreneur, providing outrightly how the demands of such a multifaceted role are met. This review is therefore intended to ultimately bring out the need for work-life balance in the purest form by the hybrid entrepreneur, bringing it to the attention of both the individual and the corporate (Shevchuk et al., 2022).

UNDERSTANDING HYBRID ENTREPRENEURSHIP

Hybrid entrepreneurship is a very new and developing way of professional engagement in which individuals simultaneously manage traditional employment with entrepreneurial pursuits. This section introduces hybrid entrepreneurship, defines what it is, what its characteristics are, who hybrid entrepreneurs are, and explains how hybrid entrepreneurship plays out in the contemporary gig economy (Raffiee & Feng, 2014).

Definition and Characteristics of Hybrid Entrepreneurs

They have one foot in traditional employment and one foot in entrepreneurial activities, typically working full-time but having their own side business or freelancing. In doing so, they maintain a safety net that comes from holding down regular employment, while they try to open up opportunities for entrepreneurship that could potentially end up being a full-time endeavour. Some of the characteristics that define hybrid entrepreneurs are:

- Dual Engagement: They handle activities in the primary employments and entrepreneurial ventures. This requires effective time management and organizational skills.
- Risk Mitigation: The hybrid entrepreneur minimizes his financial risks of getting into a new business because his main job gives him a cushion from which to test and nourish his entrepreneurial ideas.

Flexibility and Adaptability: It is most important for an alternate role-playing would-be entrepreneur since hybrid entrepreneurs have to deal with two different worlds. So, they have to operate perfectly in different logics and cultures of job market and business environment. Figure 1 represents the Work-life Balance of Hybrid Entrepreneurs.

Figure 1. Work-life balance of hybrid entrepreneurs

Types of Hybrid Entrepreneurs

Hybrid entrepreneurship can be found in various dimensions depending upon the intensity and span of the primary job and entrepreneurial activity. A few commonly found types are:

- Side-Hustlers: Those with a day job may also be running a small business or freelancing. Most times, entrepreneurial activities are merely a source of creativity or supplementary income. • Freelancer-Entrepreneurs: Professionals

of today are doing freelancing gigs and, at the same time, doing entrepreneurship work to start up or come up with new products.
- Corporate Innovators: Those who are professionals in a company but are also involved in entrepreneurial activities to some extent, either in the scope of their profession or even completely different. They might have been kindled due to their experience of working at a company.

Role of Hybrid Entrepreneurship in the Gig Economy

Described as a short-term, flexible, and freelance type of job system, the gig economy provides increased scope and room for hybrid entrepreneurial activities. The key drivers or the constituents of this relationship are:

- Increased Opportunities: The gig economy provides a sea of platforms and tools that offer everything with an ease for starting and managing one's side businesses. It may include online marketplaces, freelance job boards, and social media channels (Barrios et al., 2020).
- Flexibility and Autonomy: The potential flexibility under gig work allows individuals to balance between main employment and entrepreneurial time use—easy business idea testing without compromise of financial stability.
- Innovation and Disruption: Hybrid entrepreneurs are hallmarks of innovation by combining new technologies and business models in this entrepreneurial career. This, in turn, helps to explain its dynamic underpinning within the gig economy.

Hybrid entrepreneurship requires one to understand its forms and how it interacts with wider economic trends. In treading the two paths availed of them, hybrid entrepreneurs express the new way of balancing professional and personal ambitions and give invaluable insight into how work and entrepreneurship in the contemporary scene are changing.

THE CONCEPT OF WORK-LIFE BALANCE

Work-life balance is a very important aspect of general well-being and productivity that encompasses the appropriate relationship between work responsibilities and personal life. The section reviews theoretical frameworks and models in discussing work-life balance, challenges, and stressors in accomplishing it, and the ways it impacts individuals, especially hybrid entrepreneurs.

Theoretical Frameworks and Models of Work–Life Balance

There are several theoretical frameworks that offer insight into work-life balance, and each of these perspectives provides an account of how individuals can achieve harmony between work and personal life. The important models are as follows:

- Spillover Model: The model argues that the experiences and feelings in one domain will spill over to other domains. Negative as well as positive events at work or in personal life can affect personal life or work life in the same manner. Spillover for hybrid entrepreneurs refers to the creation of boundaries and strategies as a means of managing it so that negative impacts are minimized (Clarke, 2004).
- The Segmentation Model: This approach would suggest that work and one's personal life need to be kept entirely separate with some clear boundaries set between work and one's personal life. Hybrid entrepreneurs, on the other hand, may simply deal with segmentation because their work roles overlap and, thus, practices that would help in one to compartmentalize their time between work and personal life have to be controlled.
- The Compensation Model: This model sees the individual lead a balanced work–life scale, leading to the compensation for the deficiency in one hand and fulfillment in the other. For example, hybrid entrepreneurs might feel satisfied in their sideline business to compensate for dissatisfaction with their job or vice versa.
- The Work-Family Border Theory: This theory points out that one has to create a border in situations relating to working and not working and, even in companies that one is the owner, how individuals handle these borders to achieve work life balance. It identifies strategies such as setting specific work hours and creating dedicated spaces for work and relaxation (Rehman & Roomi, 2012).

Key Challenges and Stressors

Among other things, achieving work-life balance, especially in hybrid entrepreneurship, requires navigating a number of challenges and stressors, including:

- Time management - Playing multiple roles requires the hybrid entrepreneur to be time –efficient for this reason they have to blend time between the primary job and the entrepreneurial activities making sure there is a time for personal and family time.

- Role conflict – The twin pressures of work and entrepreneurial responsibilities can trigger stress and reduced productivity. Hybrid entrepreneurs may experience role conflict when expectations from the primary job are not in tandem with their entrepreneurial or vice versa (Chiang et al., 2010).
- Burnout and Fatigue: The ability to handle the professional and personal tasks can end up in burnouts and inside fatigue. Hybrid entrepreneurs are at very high risks of overworking their capabilities, both physically and emotionally.
- Boundary Management: Wherever there will be blurred lines amidst work and life, it will be problematic to keep the circumstances regarding work and life separate. Clearly, hybrid entrepreneurs demand ways to deal with managing these boundaries for not letting work bleed into their private time.

Impact of Work-Life Balance on Well-Being and Productivity

Moderating a healthy work-life balance positively contributes to individual well-being and productivity in the following ways:

- Mental and Physical Health: A good work-life combination impacts one's mind and body in such a way that it is less stressful and anxious; hence, it leads to a smaller risk of burnout. Their maintenance means everything for hybrid entrepreneurs' health and productivity over the long term.
- Job Satisfaction and Engagement: Balancing work life against personal life can bring forth job satisfaction and, by extension, job engagement. Hybrid entrepreneurs who balance their different roles are likely to be motivated and satisfied in a greater proportion (Santillan, 2023).
- Quality of Relationships: A right balance between work and personal life has a positive status for relationships with family and friends. Hybrid entrepreneurs who achieve a successful balance between their work and life offer quality time towards their close relationships, making their quality of life better.
- Business Performance: The dimension of work-life balance also impacts business performance. Entrepreneurs who can manage their time and stress properly would be more productive and innovative. These, in turn, outline better business performance (Arfandi, 2023).

Given the above nature of the work-life balance issue, it is not straightforward, but it is highly theoretical with several models and challenging in the practical sense. In the hybrid entrepreneurship context, balance needs to be maintained for ensuring both the well-being and success of professional and personal life at the same time.

Knowledge and appreciation of these areas will help one manoeuvre around the complex dual roles toward a more harmonious and rewarding lifestyle.

BALANCING PERSONAL AND PROFESSIONAL DEMANDS

Balancing personal and professional demands is quite complex, especially by hybrid entrepreneurs who have to play the roles in the primary employment and entrepreneurial venture. This section tries to look into how hybrid entrepreneurs manage their two roles using various strategies and practices in time management, boundary-setting practices, together with real-life examples.

Time Management Strategies

Hybrid entrepreneurs need to have effective ways of time management to have the capability to balance their personal and professional demands. Some of the major strategies include:

- Prioritizing: Hybrid entrepreneurs must be able to sort their tasks based on urgency and importance. One such tool is the Eisenhower Matrix, and another is the ABC method of categorizing tasks to focus on some high-priority tasks.
- Scheduling: A detailed schedule containing definite timings for work, entrepreneurial activity, and personal commitments will help in the practice of multiple roles. Techniques such as time blocking, where certain blocks of time in one's schedule are set aside for a particular activity, go a long way in improving productivity and avoiding overlap.
- Task Delegation - One of the most important tools in workload management is task delegation. It is handy that a hybrid entrepreneur can delegate some amount of work between their main job and entrepreneurial venture in order not to overburden themselves with work. • Productivity Tools: Use productivity tools and apps like project management software, calendar applications, and time-tracking tools, among others, that could keep one organized and on track. Such tools enable one to keep a record of different tasks while setting reminders and indicating the progress.

Setting Boundaries

Clear demarcation between profession and personal life is key to balancing your act. Here are some ways to implement good boundary-setting:

- Establish Work Timing: It can be helpful to work during the "work time" of both main employment and entrepreneur work to structure your work and not let it rob your personal and family time. Setting work-start and work-end time are very useful for precluding unnecessary and depletion of personal time and energy.
- Dedicated Workspaces: Creating different spaces for different roles can assist in not blurring the line between work and personal life. An office/workplace separate from the house for entrepreneurial activities could make one be more focused on work. It could improve productivity. One will conduct more business, bringing in more revenue.
- Communication Boundaries: It is important to communicate these boundaries to employers, clients, and members of the family. A hybrid entrepreneur should indicate their availability and make sure people know their limitations so as to manage and respect the kind of expectations they put on them.
- Technology-Free Times: There should be an introduction of technology-free times without any electronic gadgets and work-related communication. It provides the individual with unhampered personal time. This diminishes the work pressure or stress, and relaxation is provided to the mind.

Caselets and Joint Analysis

Caselet 1: Emma, the Full-Time IT Manager and Weekend Artisan

Emma is an IT manager in a technology firm working full time. During weekends, she sells handmade craft from her online store. To balance her demanding job with crafting, Emma works on a meticulous scheduling plan. And on weekdays, she saves hours for corporate responsibilities with no work overlap. In this respect, certain hours for this artisan business have been scheduled for the weekends insofar as production, marketing, and customer service are concerned. Separating her crafting work from the main workspace by creating an extra area for it keeps her away from blending her work with life and living. This gives her the leverage to be well organised and to balance her two roles without compromising on the quality of her professional and/or personal pursuits.

Caselet 2: David, the Corporate Sales Executive and Evening Fitness Coach

David, in the day, plays the corporate sales executive but surprisingly turns out to be an evening fitness coach. To manage his task diversity, David looks up to task prioritisation and time-blocking techniques. David chunks his work time into selling hours and delivers his client's coaching classes during evenings. For this, David has set specific boundaries where he informs his clients about his coaching hours and that they are not clashing with his corporate work. This is also checked in his digital calendar to mark his selling time and coaching time. This way, he can still use his personal hours and not wear himself out to death. David, being structured, will always want to ensure the balance between his roles and this is why he is never compromised for his lifestyle.

Caselet 3: Laura the School Teacher cum Freelancer writer

Laura is a high school teacher engaged in full-time employment, and at the same time she takes up writing assignments as a freelancer. She manages her dual roles by giving a sure shot commitment to strict schedules and adoption of task management software. Weekdays are spent on school going classes, and evenings and weekends are exclusively dedicated to her writing assignments. She sets writing project goals and uses a project management tool to maintain checkpoints for project progress. Laura maintains work-life balance by not opening work emails during personal hours and also making sure that her writing activities never hamper her teaching duties. She ultimate manages her time appropriately and delivers in both of her career fields without infringed on her personal time (Eddleston & Powell, 2012).

Caselet 4: Tom, the Software Developer and Startup Co-Founder

Tom is a software engineer at some tech firm and, today, he co-founded a new start-up focused on innovative tech solutions. To keep a balance between the full-time job and the responsibilities in a start-up, Tom adheres to task delegation and time flexibility. Routine tasks are delegated to his team in the start-up in order to save time for major strategic planning and strategic planning and development issues. Tom carefully schedules set hours in the evenings and weekends to work on his startup activities, ensuring they are not in conflict with his full-time job. Tom uses collaboration tools to manage his startup projects and is in constant communication with his team. In this example, Tom must therefore balance his commitments by effective delegation of tasks and efficient time management such that the responsibilities that come along with each duty, as he grows his startup, are met.

Caselet 5: Olivia, the Marketing Executive and Weekend Event Organizer

For a professional marketer, Olivia is practicing the idea of an event organizer on weekends. Olivia takes advantage of time management by using tools of prioritization and boundary setting. She reserves weekdays to pack in marketing and weekend wholly for event organization. Olivia is able to draw neat lines between her professional and personal activities. She uses different devices and even spaces for working and event planning. Also, Olivia informed her colleagues and event participants about her availability. That all together made it impossible for Olivia to meet the situation of overlapping works and engagements. And her well-being was in place, and she was productive in both areas.

Joint Analysis

The caselets bring out a panorama of strategies used by a hybrid entrepreneur to juggle professional-personal demands. Common aspects cut across all of them, such as effective use of scheduling, setting boundaries, and task management runs like a common thread in all cases. Every individual has certain dedicated techniques that would suit their peculiar roles—setting up in priorities and delegation to balance the two-pronged attack efficiently.

Emma and Laura serve as an example of the need for well-set scheduling and clear distinction of workspaces in attaining the balance. Their practice of clear timelines within settings of activities in place helps in attaining enhanced focus and efficiency both at work places and home-based jobs. David and Tom help in bringing to the fore the importance of setting the boundaries and delegation: from the clear communication that David has put forward about his coaching hours to his wife Tom delegating her routine work at home, both can practice their assigned duties friction-free.

Olivia's case is a highlight that shows the creation of boundaries and expectations that prevent a possible overlap. She maintains the difference by using another gadget and indicates when her time will be fully available for balancing the marketing career with event planning. All these caselets give a proper insight that the hybrid entrepreneurs successfully maintained their dual role by using customized strategies to respond to the inherent challenges and weaknesses to help them leverage their strengths to keep both sides of their life in harmony.

Tools and Techniques for Attaining Balance

There are just as many tools and techniques for attaining balance between personal and professional lives. The implementation of these tools enhances time management skills, improves boundary setting, and increases productivity by hybrid entrepreneurs. Important tools and techniques for ensuring an effective balance include technology solutions, organizational tools, and support mechanisms. Technology and Tools

- Project Management Software: Asana, Trello, Monday.com, and the traditionally in-house Microsoft Project are some of the tools used to structure tasks, mark out deadlines, and monitor progress for hybrid entrepreneurs. These platforms let one create intricate project plans, task assignment, and project status monitoring that enables one to better manage multiple roles and responsibilities.
- Scheduling Apps: scheduling apps, including Google Calendar, Microsoft Outlook, and Calendly, which help a hybrid entrepreneur craft out schedules and keep dates around appointments, deadlines, and personal commitments. Such apps enable the entrepreneur to prepare his time and avoid overcommitting through reminders and blocks of time for work and personal activities.
- Time-Tracking Tools: Tools such as Toggl, Clockify, and RescueTime help in tracking time spent on various different activities. These applications therefore show where time is going—on what activity—and it is then possible for business people to identify those areas where they may need to recalibrate to reclaim their balance.
- Productivity Apps: Apps such as Todoist, Evernote, and Notion help in the management of tasks, notes, and input of information. They help a lot in ensuring that an entrepreneur knows what he has to do daily, in putting down all small ideas that come into the mind, and effectively handling the workflows so that these ideas can be put into practical use.

Strategies for Prioritizing Tasks and Managing Workloads

- Time-Blocking: Time blocking is when you schedule out your day into different blocks of time for a particular task. The focused periods of time will allow hybrid entrepreneurs to work on an area that will need the most time without taking time away from another area.
- Eisenhower Matrix: This helps in assignments prioritization. The urgency and importance categorization of tasks in the matrix are depicted into four parts: "important and urgent," "important but not urgent," "urgent but not important," and "not urgent and not important." The hybrid entrepreneur, by

this method, can put more focus on the most prioritized, high-importance activities and decrease time and energy spent on those that are neither here nor there.

- Pomodoro Technique: Here, one works in concentrated intervals. The interval is usually 25 minutes, after which one goes for a few minutes for a break. The Pomodoro Technique maintains productivity and focus, avoiding burnout, by the provision of little but punctuated break periods.
- Delegation: This is an act of giving out duties to others to help in managing work. Hybrid entrepreneurs may delegate tasks from other people within their businesses, or even look for colleague or freelance help to free up their load and balance their efforts.

Support Systems and Resources

- Mentorship and Networking: Interlocking with mentors and peers facing the same situation provides them with support and guidance. Some of the support that can be received from mentors includes advice on juggling different roles, while networking with other hybrid entrepreneurs allows for insight and the sharing of best practices into the situation at hand.
- Professional Development: Workshops, courses, or seminars on the effective ways of managing time, increasing productivity, and balancing work and life improve the skills of the hybrid entrepreneur with new strategies on how to manage dual roles.
- Health and Wellness Resources: Health and wellness needs to be taken care of by regular exercise, mindfulness, and rest to maintain balance. Hybrid entrepreneurs need resources on the front of apps for wellness, meditation activities, and workout plans to enhance their general well-being.
- Family and Personal Support: A support system within the family or personal network may help in shouldering various responsibilities and conflicts. Sharing the needs and expectations with a family member and enlisting their support can help offset many of the challenges of work–life balance.

In other words, balance to the hybrid entrepreneur is wrought when a melee of technology tools, strategies, and support systems works for him or her. The use of project management software, scheduling apps, and time-tracking tools will enable an entrepreneur to be more organized and focused on tasks and time. Time management strategies, like time-blocking and delegation, with the backing of mentors and wellness resources, do create a harmonious balance between professional and personal demands.

WORK-LIFE AND ITS IMPACT ON BUSINESS PERFORMANCE

Work-life balance is the only way of well-being on the personal part and an enormous way to business performance. Hybrid entrepreneurs can ensure the productivity of the main employment, and at the same time, entrepreneurial activities are well-balanced. The following discusses how successful work-life balance increases the performance of the business through the enhancement of productivity, innovativeness, workers' engagement, and general success of a business.

Enhanced Productivity

Work-life balance is working toward acquiring more productive results in one's personal and professional life. Hybrid entrepreneurships properly managing their time and responsibilities are expected to result in more efficiency in conducting business. Important factors include the following:

- Reduced Burnout: Work-life balancing ensures that the hybrid entrepreneur avoids burnout and fatigue that at times results from overworking. A well-rested and energized individual can carry out tasks faster and with proper efficiency; hence, a maintained good level of productivity.
- Maximized Work Hours: With good time management, an entrepreneur is able to maximize the working hours. Free from distractions and hustle/bustle, they are able to do much more work within the set time.

Increased Innovation

Creativity and innovation can only exist where the mind has a set environment. Hybrid entrepreneurs practicing such a measure are better placed for bringing about innovation in their businesses. These are due to the following reasons:

- Creative Recharge: Time off and out of work offer a great deal of relaxation and a way of thinking up new creations. Hybrid entrepreneurs definitely return to the business full of energy and new insights when they spend their time engaging in hobbies, exercise, or even pure social activities.
- Diverse Experiences: Creation of balance between various roles exposes entrepreneurs to various experiences and enlightenment. These encounters may potentially create new ideas and ways of doing things, thus fuelling innovative solutions and business practice.

- Reduced Stress: With this new balance in life, one can reduce the level of stress and hence improve cognitive functioning and enhance problem-solving ability, resulting in better brainstorming and idea generation.

Improved Employee Engagement

Work-life balance, for those hybrid entrepreneurs who either manage people or engage with others to accomplish their goals and objectives, impacts employee engagement and satisfaction:

- Positive Work Environment: Entrepreneurs who model work-life balance contribute to the development of a positive work environment, increasing the morale and engagement of those working there. When employees observe that their top management has a good work-life balance, they start to tread the same footsteps.
- More Loyalty: Workers exposed to a good working culture that appreciates work-life balance increasingly become loyal to the company. This reduces the turnover costs related to the recruitment and training process.
- Improved Performance: Motivated workers who perceive that the management of the company is supportive of work-life balance generally cultivate a harder-working and more dedicated attitude toward job performance. This affects the business as a whole in terms of performance and how successful it is in the long run.

Long-Term Success and Growth

Work-life balance can continually be a key attribute for business long-term survival and growth:

- Sustainable Practices: Hybrid entrepreneurs who know how to draw the boundary line between professional and personal life are more inclined towards practicing sustainable business by showing gradual growth, being resourceful, and keeping away from burnouts.
- Reputation and Brand: A good reputation among the business community for work–life balance would add feathers to the cap of business. Companies known to take care of their employees' interest build better and solid relationships with clients and users and attract top talent.
- Strategic Focus: Entrepreneurs who maintain balance can focus on long-term strategic planning and growth rather than being consumed by the day-to-day

stressors. This is a forward-thinking approach that makes room for business development and innovation.

To summarize, work-life balance has a strong impact on the performance of a business, particularly in terms of productivity, innovation, employee engagement, and long-term success. Hybrid entrepreneurs who carry out effective balancing of the business and family responsibilities find themselves endowed with increased productivity, an environment that nurtures creativity, and a positive contribution to work atmosphere, leading to the growth and sustainability of their businesses. Hence, with more focus on work-life balance, entrepreneurs can be better assured of business success and a resilient and thriving enterprise.

CHALLENGES AND BARRIERS

Despite the fact that work-life balance has its own benefits, hybrid entrepreneurs typically encounter a few challenges and obstacles that intervene in their status on how they balance both professional and personal duties. One needs to apprehend the nature of these challenges in order to be able to design ways of facing up to them and to live both lives in a balanced manner. In the following section, a few significant challenges encountered by hybrid entrepreneurs are discussed, such as scarcity of time, conflict in role, vague boundaries, and limitations in resources.

Time Constraints

- Overlapping Responsibilities: One of the crucial challenges that face hybrid entrepreneurs is managing the overlapping responsibilities. Meeting the demands fully from full-time job and entrepreneurial activities is most likely time-consuming, and very few hours can be allotted to attend either sufficiently enough not to neglect personal responsibilities (Abdulla, 2023).
- Extended Work Hours: Playing multiple roles can mean extended working hours, which translate into a deficit of rest and personal time. Sometimes entrepreneurs are compelled to work late into the night or during weekends, hence impacting productivity due to fatigue.
- The Resultant Demands: Predictable demands tend to be experienced in both the primary employment and entrepreneurial ventures. For example, unexpected work emergencies or unexpected business issues can interfere with one's schedule, leading to the loss of set balance and planning of the private activities.

Role Conflict

- Competing Priorities: Hybrid entrepreneurs may experience the role conflict when two salient roles exhibit competing priorities—the primary job and entrepreneurial activities. This tends to contribute to stress and trouble accomplishing tasks on time or delivering on responsibilities in either area.
- Inconsistent Expectations: Conflicting expectations between the employer and clients or customers create conflicts at different times. For example, an employee may have very specific requirements from an employer, which might immediately conflict with the needs of an entrepreneurial project, causing tension and difficulties in balancing the requirements of both worlds (Therthani et al., 2022).
- Performance Pressure: Agreed, the demand to perform good in both becomes colossal. For one hybrid entrepreneur, it becomes essential to over-perform in his primary job and at the same time try to achieve that feat in his entrepreneurial venture. Thereby, these pressures culminate in performance pressure, which leads to anxiety and stress.

Boundary Issues

- Blurred Boundaries: One of the major challenges associated with work-life balance is blurred boundaries between work and personal life. Hybrid entrepreneurs may not separate what belongs to work and what belongs to personal life, hence work will eat into family, recreation, or personal recharge time.
- Difficulty to Disconnect: Technology allows constant connectivity and makes it pretty hard for one to disconnect from work. This sees entrepreneurs checking their emails or handling work-related tasks during personal time, which greatly interferes with their relaxation and the ability to fully recharge (Ezzedeen & Zikic, 2015).
- Interruption Management: Regardless of working at home or managing different roles in the workplace, one can expect very frequent interruptions through family members or some other tasks to be done at work. This is going to break focus and productivity in ways that make boundaries hard to sustain.

Resource Limitations

- Financial Constraints: Sometimes, hybrid entrepreneurs might have to face financial constraints that can affect their acquisition of resources or systems of support. If the budget is tight, then access to several apt tools, services, or personnel helpful in managing both roles may be restricted (Reiner et al., 2019).

- Lack of Support: insufficient support from family, colleagues, or the employer prevents a work-life balance from being achieved. Failure of anyone around them to understand and support them may lead a hybrid entrepreneur to being overly responsible and missing the boat on personal well-being (Kalliath & Brough, 2008).
- Poor Infrastructure or Work Resources: such as a dedicated workspace or technological tools—can have a negative effect on work output and balance. Without it, entrepreneurs will have a hard time separating personal from professional activities, leading to inefficiency and stress.

All in all, hybrid entrepreneurs have to tackle a number of hurdles in their road to work–life balance, which may include time, role, boundary, and resource issues; hence, the strategic planning, effective boundary-setting, and seeking support when difficulty arises within the multiple roles that they have. Recognition and addressing of these hurdles will then move hybrid entrepreneurs toward a more balanced and sustainable approach to their professional–personal work–life role (Meliou & Özbilgin, 2023).

TRENDS AND FUTURE IMPLICATIONS

Ever since hybrid entrepreneurship entered an ever-changing scene of work, there also has to be heavy variation. The future trends in both work-life balance and hybrid entrepreneurship will define how individuals can manage these dual roles, and certainly will impact personal well-being and business performance. This section discusses the new trends and their potential implications on business that are associated with improving technology, changing work environments, evolving workforce expectations, and increased emphasis on mental health and well-being.

Advancement of Technology

- **Increased Automation and AI**: The growth in automation and artificial intelligence seems to put into overdrive much about work—potentially contributing to the contraction of time and energy required to conduct more repetitive work. This would mean that, using AI-driven project management, time tracking, and communication tools, hybrid entrepreneurs could focus so much more on driving strategy and creativity for their ventures.

- Enhanced Remote Work Solutions: Advanced remote work solutions: improved technology around tools for virtual collaboration and digital workplaces should continue to increase the potential for effectively managing disparate roles, by and large, from any chosen locus. Advancements in AR and VR that reach further could enable remote collaboration and productivity capabilities, thereby making it easier to better integrate work with personal life (Mouazen & Hernández-Lara, 2023).
- Data-Driven Insights: Increasing access to data and analytics tools will enable hybrid entrepreneurs to gain insights into their work patterns, productivity, and well-being. The insights could provide better decisions on strategies of time management for optimal work-life balance, leading to maximally improved business performances.

Changing Work Environments

- Flexible Work Arrangements: The direction of flexible work arrangements, hybrid and remote working included, is likely to continue. This is more flexible and better integrates the entrepreneur's professional and personal lives, thereby reducing commuting stress and making work scheduling more customized (Mäkinen & Esko, 2022).
- Blended Workspaces: Combining a traditional working environment at the office with remote workspaces and co-working spaces allows for more flexibility on the part of the entrepreneurial hybrid in the development of a bespoke work culture that complements personal interest and environment.
- Sustainable Work Practices: Nowadays, the appetite is on a high peak for everything which is sustainable, and both organizations and entrepreneurs are considering sustainable work practices. Hybrid entrepreneurs involve sustainable practices as part of their business operations and contribute to the environment. This helps them in balancing the dual roles.

Evolving Workforce Expectations

- Work-Life Integration: The concept of work-life balance is traditional and is already evoking change as it integrates work and life into a seamless professional and personal activity that is going on throughout. Hybrid entrepreneurs will have to prepare for this eventuality by ensuring flexible and adaptive schedules to include work and the personal life of an entrepreneur.
- Demand for Well-Being Initiatives: Well-being initiatives are increasingly on demand; employers and business leaders are demanding them. Hybrid entrepreneurs may be out of choice but shall have to position mental health and

well-being initiatives first; therefore, they shall have to provide such resources as counseling services, wellness workshops, or stress management tools.

- Rise of the Gig Economy: The Gig Economy is on the rise; more and more people are engaging in freelance and entrepreneurial activities while simultaneously being part and parcel of other jobs. Hybrid entrepreneurs will straddle this evolving landscape: definitely the demands of gig work need to be balanced with the major job's responsibilities (Lester, 2015).

Emphasis on Mental Health and Wellbeing

- Growing Awareness: There is growing awareness on mental well-being and work performance; hybrid entrepreneurs shall be compelled to proactively win over mental health issues, which include approaches of mindfulness, regular breaks, practices on stress management being made part and parcel of routine (Marques & Berry, 2021).
- Supportive Work Cultures: The increasing development of supportive work cultures that prioritize employee well-being. Hybrid entrepreneurs have a good opportunity to build such cultures within their businesses, creating a healthy and balanced work environment for themselves and their team.
- Innovation of Well-Being Solutions: With the advent of innovative well-being solutions, including mental health apps, virtual therapy, and wellness coaching, hybrid entrepreneurs will be armed with added tools they can use for well-being management. These aids will better balance life and ensure a higher productivity rate.

There are increasing technological innovations, changing work environments, changing personal policies of the workforce, and an increased focus on mental health as well as well-being. Embracing these trends and mastering the implications that arise will equip hybrid entrepreneurs to embrace the intricacies of successfully balancing multiple roles and to secure sustained success both in their personal and work lives.

CONCLUSION

Hybrid entrepreneurship— juggling full-time employment at the same time as entrepreneurial ventures—proves to be challenging but also a worthwhile and rewarding journey. Sustainable work-life balance ensures personal well-being, professional success, and the growth of entrepreneurial activities.

A close examination throughout revealed that the dexterous harmony between work and personal life is not some element of time management; it strategically deals with tools, techniques, and support systems to manage the multiplicity of roles. Use technology for incorporating project management software, scheduling apps, and productivity software. Such strategies further include time-based interception blocking, delegation, the use of productivity applications, and many more.

The significant challenges for hybrid entrepreneurs are the time limitations, boundary issues, role conflict, and resource constraints that must be dealt with through proactivity, clear setting of boundaries, management of tasks, and support by mentors, family, and professional networks.

In the future, hybrid entrepreneurship will be defined by further advances in technology, changing work environments, and a new focus on mental health and well-being. It will be important to embrace these trends and adapt to the implications to keep balance and pointedly do work in a way that is productive.

In sum, hybrid entrepreneurs have concurrent productivity, innovation, and the creation of enabling work environments when they can steer across the usually stormy balancing act of personal and professional demands. At any time and in any place, the appropriate tools, strategic practices, and up-to-date trends can be adopted by hybrid entrepreneurs to create a perfect balance helpful in many ways to support their long-term personal well-being for their ventures.

REFERENCES

Abdulla, F., & Ahmad, A. (2023). Challenges faced by women entrepreneurs of 21st century. *Journal of Management & Science*, 21(1), 16. DOI: 10.57002/jms.v21i1.368

Barrios, J., Hochberg, Y., & Yi, H. (2020). Launching with a parachute: the gig economy and entrepreneurial entry. SSRN Electronic Journal. DOI: 10.2139/ssrn.3603813

Chiang, F., Birtch, T., & Kwan, H. (2010). The moderating roles of job control and work-life balance practices on employee stress in the hotel and catering industry. *International Journal of Hospitality Management*, 29(1), 25–32. DOI: 10.1016/j.ijhm.2009.04.005

Clarke, M., Koch, L. C., & Hill, E. J. (2004). The work-family interface: Differentiating balance and fit. *Family and Consumer Sciences Research Journal*, 33(2), 121–140. DOI: 10.1177/1077727X04269610

Eddleston, K., & Powell, G. (2012). Nurturing entrepreneurs' work–family balance: A gendered perspective. *Entrepreneurship Theory and Practice*, 36(3), 513–541. DOI: 10.1111/j.1540-6520.2012.00506.x

Emslie, C., & Hunt, K. (2008). 'live to work' or 'work to live'? a qualitative study of gender and work–life balance among men and women in mid-life. *Gender, Work and Organization*, 16(1), 151–172. DOI: 10.1111/j.1468-0432.2008.00434.x

Ezzedeen, S., & Zikic, J. (2015). Finding balance amid boundarylessness: An interpretive study of entrepreneurial work–life balance and boundary management. *Journal of Family Issues*, 38(11), 1546–1576. DOI: 10.1177/0192513X15600731

Kalliath, T., & Brough, P. (2008). Work–life balance: A review of the meaning of the balance construct. *Journal of Management & Organization*, 14(3), 323–327. DOI: 10.5172/jmo.837.14.3.323

Lester, J. (2015). Cultures of work–life balance in higher education: A case of fragmentation. *Journal of Diversity in Higher Education*, 8(3), 139–156. DOI: 10.1037/a0039377

Mäkinen, E., & Esko, T. (2022). Nascent academic entrepreneurs and identity work at the boundaries of professional domains. *International Journal of Entrepreneurship and Innovation*, 24(3), 167–177. DOI: 10.1177/14657503211063896

Marques, V., & Berry, G. (2021). Enhancing work-life balance using a resilience framework. [Among Hybrid Entrepreneurs: A Comprehensive Review**]. *Business and Society Review*, 126(3), 263–281. DOI: 10.1111/basr.12237

Meliou, E., & Özbilgin, M. (2023). How is the illusio of gender equality in entrepreneurship sustained? a bourdieusian perspective. *Journal of Management Studies*, 61(4), 1536–1561. DOI: 10.1111/joms.12930

Mouazen, A., & Hernández-Lara, A. (2023). Entrepreneurial ecosystem, gig economy practices and women's entrepreneurship: The case of lebanon. *International Journal of Gender and Entrepreneurship*, 15(3), 249–274. DOI: 10.1108/IJGE-07-2022-0116

Raffiee, J., & Feng, J. (2014). Should i quit my day job?: A hybrid path to entrepreneurship. *Academy of Management Journal*, 57(4), 936–963. DOI: 10.5465/amj.2012.0522

Rehman, S., & Roomi, M. (2012). Gender and work-life balance: A phenomenological study of women entrepreneurs in pakistan. *Journal of Small Business and Enterprise Development*, 19(2), 209–228. DOI: 10.1108/14626001211223865

Reiner, S., Balkin, R., Gotham, K., Hunter, Q., Juhnke, G., & Davis, R. (2019). Assessing life balance and work addiction in high-pressure, high-demand careers. *Journal of Counseling and Development*, 97(4), 409–416. DOI: 10.1002/jcad.12289

Santillan, E., Santillan, E. T., Doringo, J. B., Pigao, K. J. F., & Mesina, V. F. C. (2023). Assessing the impact of a hybrid work model on job execution, work-life balance, and employee satisfaction in a technology company. *Journal of Business and Management Studies*, 5(6), 13–38. DOI: 10.32996/jbms.2023.5.6.2

Shevchuk, A., Strebkov, D., & Bögenhold, D. (2022). Work values and hybrid careers in the gig economy: The evidence from an online labor market. *Economic and Industrial Democracy*, 45(1), 138–163. DOI: 10.1177/0143831X221140153

Solesvik, M. (2017). Hybrid entrepreneurship: How and why entrepreneurs combine employment with self-employment. *Technology Innovation Management Review*, 7(3), 33–41. DOI: 10.22215/timreview/1063

Therthani, S., Balkin, R., Perepiczka, M., Silva, S., Hunter, Q., & Juhnke, G. (2022). Assessing personality traits, life balance domains, and work addiction among entrepreneurs. *The Career Development Quarterly*, 70(3), 190–201. DOI: 10.1002/cdq.12296

Compilation of References

Aaboen, L., Dubois, A., & Lind, F. (2013). Strategizing as networking for new ventures. *Industrial Marketing Management*, 42(7), 1033–1041. DOI: 10.1016/j.indmarman.2013.07.003

Abdallah, R., Juaidi, A., Savaş, M. A., Çamur, H., Albatayneh, A., Abdala, S., & Manzano-Agugliaro, F. (2021). A critical review on recycling composite waste using pyrolysis for sustainable development. *Energies*, 14(18), 5748. DOI: 10.3390/en14185748

Abdulla, F., & Ahmad, A. (2023). Challenges faced by women entrepreneurs of 21st century. *Journal of Management & Science*, 21(1), 16. DOI: 10.57002/jms.v21i1.368

Abreu, M., & Grinevich, V. (2013). The nature of academic entrepreneurship in the UK: Widening the focus on entrepreneurial activities. *Research Policy*, 42(2), 408–422. DOI: 10.1016/j.respol.2012.10.005

Acs, Z., Szekeres, L., & Autio, E. (2013). *The role of entrepreneurship in economic development.*. DOI: 10.4337/9781782540427.00010

Acs, Z. J., Stam, E., Audretsch, D., & O'Connor, A. (2017). The lineages of the entrepreneurial ecosystem approach. *Small Business Economics*, 49(1), 1–10. DOI: 10.1007/s11187-017-9864-8

Addisu, T. (2020). Price volatility and food insecurity the case of Ethiopia [PhD Thesis]. Ph.D. Thesis, Wageningen University and Research Center.

Adelino, M., Ma, S., & Robinson, D. (2017). Firm age, investment opportunities, and job creation. *The Journal of Finance*, 72(3), 999–1038. DOI: 10.1111/jofi.12495

Ademilua, V., Lasisi, T., Ogunmokun, O., & Ikhide, J. (2020). Accounting for the effects of entrepreneurial orientation on smes' job creation capabilities: A social capital and self-determination perspective. *Journal of Public Affairs*. Advance online publication. DOI: 10.1002/pa.2413

Adenfelt, M., & Lagerström, K. (2006). Organizational rejuvenation for knowledge exploitation: Exploring corporate entrepreneurship in an MNE. *Journal of International Entrepreneurship*, 4(2), 83–98.

Adner, R. (2017). Ecosystem as structure: An actionable construct for strategy. *Journal of Management*, 43(1), 39–58. DOI: 10.1177/0149206316678451

Adner, R., & Kapoor, R. (2010). Value creation in innovation ecosystems: How the structure of technological interdependence affects firm performance in new technology generations. *Strategic Management Journal*, 31(3), 306–333. DOI: 10.1002/smj.821

Afonso, A., & Blanco-Arana, M. C. (2022). Financial and economic development in the context of the global 2008-09 financial crisis. *Inter Economics*, 169, 30–42. DOI: 10.1016/j.inteco.2021.11.006

Afshan, G., Shahid, S., & Tunio, M. N. (2021). Learning experiences of women entrepreneurs amidst COVID-19. *International Journal of Gender and Entrepreneurship*, 13(2), 162–186. DOI: 10.1108/IJGE-09-2020-0153

Ahmad, K. (2019, September 22). Telltale Signs of Fascism in Modi's India. Retrieved July 23, 2020, from https://cscr.pk/explore/themes/politics-governance/telltale-signs-of-fascism-in-modis-india/

Ahmad, S. Z., & Buchanan, R. F. (2015). Entrepreneurship education in Malaysian universities. *Tertiary Education and Management*, 21(4), 349–366. DOI: 10.1080/13583883.2015.1106577

Ahmed, H. (2014). What is BJP's ideology? Retrieved 9 July 2020, from https://www.epw.in/blog/hilal-ahmed/what-bjps-ideology.html

Ahmed, E. (2022). The influence of entrepreneurial activity's innovation on job creation. *International Journal of Information Management*, 14(1), 506–514. DOI: 10.15282/ijim.14.1.2022.7247

Ahn, H. (2001). Applying the Balanced Scorecard concept: An empirical study. *International Journal of Productivity and Performance Management*, 50(2), 104–114.

Ajj Tak. (2020). *Sangham: Birth and growth of Rashtriya Swayamsevak Sangh (RSS)* [Video]. Retrieved from https://www.youtube.com/watch?v=Cxz-lBqfVXc

Ajzen, I. (1991). The theory of planned behavior. *Organizational Behavior and Human Decision Processes*, 50(2), 179–211. DOI: 10.1016/0749-5978(91)90020-T

Akbar, S. Z., Kukreti, D., Sagarika, S., & Pal, J. (2020, April 16). Temporal Patterns in COVID-19 misinformation in India. Retrieved July 17, 2020, from http://joyojeet.people.si.umich.edu/temporal-patterns-in-covid-19-misinformation-in-india/

Akinwale, Y. O., Ababtain, A. K., & Alaraifi, A. A. (2019). Structural equation model analysis of factors influencing entrepreneurial interest among university students in Saudi Arabia. *Journal of Entrepreneurship Education*, 22(4), 1–14.

Akkermans, H., & Oorschot, K. (2004). Relevance assumed: A case study of Balanced Scorecard development using System Dynamics. *The Journal of the Operational Research Society*, 56(8), 931–941. DOI: 10.1057/palgrave.jors.2601923

Alammari, A., Khalif, A. A., & DarougI, A. A. (2019). Restructuring the Libyan economy with available and unexploited resources of the tourism sector. *Volume II*, 398.

Alberti, F. G., & Varon Garrido, M. A. (2017). Can profit and sustainability goals co-exist? New business models for hybrid firms. *The Journal of Business Strategy*, 38(1), 3–13. DOI: 10.1108/JBS-12-2015-0124

Alder, K. (2020). The Origins of Today's Hindu Nationalism. Retrieved 9 July 2020, from https://www.usnews.com/news/best-countries/articles/2016-03-02/the-origins-of-todays-hindu-nationalism

Aldrich, H. E., & Ruef, M. (2018). Unicorns, gazelles, and other distractions on the way to understanding real entrepreneurship in the United States. *The Academy of Management Perspectives*, 32(4), 458–472. DOI: 10.5465/amp.2017.0123

Ali, A., Iftikhar, S., & Butt, S. (2022). Is innovation in pakistan driven by specialisation or diversity? *Pakistan Development Review*, , 705–714. DOI: 10.30541/v55i4I-IIpp.705-714

Allard, C. Kriljenko, MJIC, Gonzalez-Garcia, MJR, Kitsios, E., Trevino, MJP, & Chen, MW (2016). Trade integration and global value chains in sub-Saharan Africa: In pursuit of the missing link. International Monetary Fund.

Allon, G., Cohen, M. C., & Sinchaisri, W. P. (2023). The impact of behavioral and economic drivers on gig economy workers. *Manufacturing & Service Operations Management*, 25(4), 1376–1393. DOI: 10.1287/msom.2023.1191

Al-Mashari, M., Al-Mudimigh, A., & Zairi, M. (2017). Enterprise resource planning: A taxonomy of critical factors. *European Journal of Operational Research*, 146(2), 352–366. DOI: 10.1016/S0377-2217(02)00554-4

Almeida, P., & Kogut, B. (1997). The exploration of technological diversity and geographic localization in innovation: Start-up firms in the semiconductor industry. *Small Business Economics*, 9(1), 21–31. DOI: 10.1023/A:1007995512597

Alstete, J. (2003). On becoming an entrepreneur: An evolving typology. *International Journal of Entrepreneurial Behaviour & Research*, 8(4), 222–234. DOI: 10.1108/13552550210436521

Alur, R., Bodik, R., Juniwal, G., Martin, M. M. K., Raghothaman, A., Seshia, S. A., & Udupa, A. (2010). Syntax-guided synthesis. In *Proceedings of the 37th annual ACM SIGPLAN-SIGACT symposium on principles of programming languages* (pp. 637–650).

Alves, A., Fischer, B., Schaeffer, P., & Queiroz, S. (2019). Determinants of student entrepreneurship: An assessment on higher education institutions in Brazil. *Innovation & Management Review*, 16(2), 96–117. DOI: 10.1108/INMR-02-2018-0002

AMAMEUR, L. (2022). Social Entrepreneurship, a theory under construction and an opportunity for the unemployed to become entrepreneurs. *International Review of Management Sciences*, 5(1).

Amaral, A. M., Baptista, R., & Lima, F. (2011). Serial entrepreneurship: Impact of human capital on time to re-entry. *Small Business Economics*, 37(1), 1–21. DOI: 10.1007/s11187-009-9232-4

Amit, R., MacCrimmon, K. R., Zietsma, C., & Oesch, J. M. (2001). Does money matter?: Wealth attainment as the motive for initiating growth-oriented technology ventures. *Journal of Business Venturing*, 16(2), 119–143. DOI: 10.1016/S0883-9026(99)00044-0

Anderson, T. W., & Hsiao, C. (1982). Formulation and estimation of dynamic models using panel data. *Journal of Econometrics*, 18(1), 47–82. DOI: 10.1016/0304-4076(82)90095-1

Andrews, D., Gal, P., & Witheridge, W. (2018). A genius in a bottle?: Globalization, competition and inflation. OECD Economics Department Working Papers 1462, OECD Publishing.

Andrews, D., & Cingano, F. (2014). Public policy and resource allocation: Evidence from firms in OECD countries. *Economic Policy*, 29(78), 253–296. DOI: 10.1111/1468-0327.12028

Andrianady, JR, & Rajaonarison, NR (2023). Effect of a monetary shock on inflation: An approach using a DSGE model.

ANDRIANADY. J., & Njakanasandratra, R. (2023). Monetary Inflation Relationship in Madagascar: A DSGE Model Analysis. Available at SSRN 4453195.

Angevine, C., Cator, K., Roschelle, J., Thomas, S. A., Waite, C., & Weisgrau, J. (2017). *Computational thinking for a computational world.*

Ang, L. (2023). The Legal Classification of Human Capital in 'Markets, Hybrids and Hierarchies'. *The Chinese Journal of Comparative Law*, 11(3), cxae003. DOI: 10.1093/cjcl/cxae003

Anjum, T., Farrukh, M., Heidler, P., & Díaz Tautiva, J. A. (2020). Entrepreneurial intention: Creativity, entrepreneurship, and university support. *Journal of Open Innovation*, 7(1), 11. DOI: 10.3390/joitmc7010011

Ansari, B. (2020, May 13). India's Warmongering Attitude despite Global Pandemic. Retrieved July 17, 2020, from https://moderndiplomacy.eu/2020/05/14/indias-warmongering-attitude-despite-global-pandemic/

Antliff, M. (2012). Fascism and Art History: A Paradigm Shift. Retrieved 10 17, 2019, from https://brill.com/view/journals/fasc/1/1/article-p53_3.xml?lang=en

Antonietti, R., & Gambarotto, F. (2020). The role of industry variety in the creation of innovative start-ups in Italy. *Small Business Economics*, 54(2), 561–573. DOI: 10.1007/s11187-018-0034-4

Anyadike-Danes, M., Hart, M., & Du, J. (2015). Firm dynamics and job creation in the united kingdom: 1998–2013. *International Small Business Journal*, 33(1), 12–27. DOI: 10.1177/0266242614552334

Arabiyat, T., Mdanat, M., Haffar, M., Ghoneim, A., & Arabiyat, O. (2019). The influence of institutional and conductive aspects on entrepreneurial innovation. *Journal of Enterprise Information Management*, 32(3), 366–389. DOI: 10.1108/JEIM-07-2018-0165

Aray, Y. N., Christodoulou, I., Borodin, D. A., Klimova, E. V., Troshneva, S. G., & Paikin, N. M. (2023). Collaboration between social entrepreneurs and large companies: Mutual value creation through different forms of partnership

Arellano, M., & Bond, S. (1991). Some tests of specification for panel data: Monte Carlo evidence and an application to employment equations. *The Review of Economic Studies*, 58(2), 277–297. DOI: 10.2307/2297968

Arnold, J. M., & Flach, L. (2017). *Who Gains from Better Access to Credit?* Credit Reform and Reallocation of Resources.

Asem, A. (2024). *Navigating digital transformation in alignment with vision 2030: a review of organizational strategies, innovations, and implications in saudi arabia.* Journal of Knowledge Learning and Science Technology Issn 2959-6386 (Online), 3(2), 21-29. DOI: 10.60087/jklst.vol3.n2.p29

Athalage, K. C. (2024). THE IMPACT OF HYBRID WORKING ON EMPLOYEE WAY OF LIFE AND THE NEED TO RESHAPE THE EMPLOYEE VALUE PROPOSITION.

Atkinson, A. A., Waterhouse, J. H., & Wells, R. B. (1997). A Stakeholder Approach to Strategic Performance Measurement. *Sloan Management Review*, 38, 25–37.

Audretsch, D. B., Belitski, M., Caiazza, R., & Siegel, D. (2023). Effects of open innovation in startups: Theory and evidence. *Technological Forecasting and Social Change*, 194, 122694. DOI: 10.1016/j.techfore.2023.122694

Auerswald, P., & Dani, L. (2017). Economic ecosystems. In Clarke, G., Feldman, M., Gertler, M., & Wojcik, D. (Eds.), *New Oxford Handbook of Economic Geography*. Oxford University Press.

Ausiku, M., & Matthee, M. (2021). Preparing primary school teachers for teaching computational thinking: A systematic review. In *Learning Technologies and Systems: 19th International Conference on Web-Based Learning, ICWL 2020, and 5th International Symposium on Emerging Technologies for Education, SETE 2020, Ningbo, China, October 22–24, 2020* [Springer International Publishing.]. *Proceedings*, 5, 202–213.

Autio, E. (1997). New, technology-based firms in innovation networks symplectic and generative impacts. *Research Policy*, 26(3), 263–281. 00906-7DOI: <ALIGNMENT.qj></ALIGNMENT>10. 1016/ S0048-7333(96)

Autio, E., Nambisan, S., Thomas, L. D. W., & Wright, M. (2018). Digital affordances, spatial affordances, and the genesis of entrepreneurial ecosystems. *Strategic Entrepreneurship Journal*, 12(1), 72–95. DOI: 10.1002/sej.1266

Autio, E., & Thomas, L. D. W. (2014). Innovation ecosystems: Implications for innovation management. In Dodgson, M., Gann, D. M., & Phillips, N. (Eds.), *The oxford handbook of innovation management*. Oxford University Press.

Autodesk. (2021). *TinkerCAD*. https://www.tinkercad.com/

Auty, R. M. (1994). Industrial policy reform in six large newly industrializing countries: The resource curse thesis. World Development, 22(1), 11–26.

Avis, R. (2022). Social Impacts of China's Approach to Development

Avnimelech, G., & Feldman, M. (2010). Regional Corporate Spawning and the Role of Homegrown Companies. *The Review of Policy Research*, 27(4), 475–489. DOI: 10.1111/j.1541-1338.2010.00452.x

Awoa, P. A., Efogo, F. O., & Ondoa, H. A. (2023). Oil dependence and entrepreneurship: Non-linear evidence. *Economic Systems*, 47(1), 101059. DOI: 10.1016/j.ecosys.2022.101059

Ayyub, R. (2020, January 08). What Happened at JNU During the Attack. Retrieved July 22, 2020, from https://time.com/5760597/what-happened-during-jnu-attack-india/

Azariadis, C. (1996). The economics of poverty traps part one: Complete markets. *Journal of Economic Growth*, 1(4), 449–486. DOI: 10.1007/BF00150197

Azevedo, M., Schlosser, F., & McPhee, D. (2020). Building organizational innovation through HRM, employee voice and engagement. *Personnel Review*, 50(2), 751–769. DOI: 10.1108/PR-12-2019-0687

Azfar, O., & Danninger, S. (2001). Profit-sharing, employment stability, and wage growth. *Industrial & Labor Relations Review*, 54(3), 619–630. DOI: 10.1177/001979390105400305

Azzone, G., & Manzini, R. (2013). The integration of environmental and social aspects into the Balanced Scorecard. *Business Strategy and the Environment*, 22(2), 118–131.

Babu, B. S., Kamalakannan, J., Meenatchi, N., Karthik, S., & Boopathi, S. (2022). Economic impacts and reliability evaluation of battery by adopting Electric Vehicle. *IEEE Explore*, 1–6.

Babu, B. S., Kamalakannan, J., Meenatchi, N., Karthik, S., & Boopathi, S. (2022, December). Economic impacts and reliability evaluation of battery by adopting Electric Vehicle. In *2022 International Conference on Power, Energy, Control and Transmission Systems (ICPECTS)* (pp. 1-6). IEEE.

Bae, T. J., Qian, S., Miao, C., & Fiet, J. O. (2014). The relationship between entrepreneurship education and entrepreneurial intentions: A meta-analytic review. *Entrepreneurship Theory and Practice*, 38(2), 217–254. DOI: 10.1111/etap.12095

Bakar, R., Islam, M. A., & Lee, J. (2015). Entrepreneurship education: Experiences in selected countries. *International Education Studies*, 8(1), 88–99.

Baldwin, R., & Venables, A. J. (2013). Spiders and snakes: Offshoring and agglomeration in the global economy. *Journal of International Economics*, 90(2), 245–254. DOI: 10.1016/j.jinteco.2013.02.005

Banaji, J. (2013). Trajectories of Fascism: Extreme-Right Movements in India and Elsewhere. Retrieved 10 17, 2019, from http://eprints.soas.ac.uk/16825/1/jamia lecture (fascism).pdf

Banaji, S. (2018). Vigilante Publics: Orientalism, Modernity and Hindutva Fascism in India. Javnost-the Public, 25(4), 333-350. Retrieved 10 17, 2019, from https://tandfonline.com/doi/full/10.1080/13183222.2018.1463349

Banal-Estanol, A., Kretschmer, T., Meloso, D., & Seldeslachts, J. (2015). The Dynamics of Strategic Alliances Theory and Experimental Evidence. Working Paper.

Bandura, A. (1992). Exercise of personal agency through the self-efficacy mechanism. In Schwarzer, R. (Ed.), *Self-Efficacy: Thought Control of Action* (pp. 3–38). Hemisphere.

Bangladesh: Close to India but expecting benefits from China. (n.d.). Global Affairs and Strategic Studies. https://www.unav.edu/web/global-affairs/bangladesh-close-to-india-but-expecting-benefits-from-china

Bangladesh's accidental revolutionaries Topple Sheikh Hasina — What's next? (n.d.). United States Institute of Peace. https://www.usip.org/publications/2024/08/bangladeshs-accidental-revolutionaries-topple-sheikh-hasina-whats-next

Bangladesh-India Diplomatic Relations (1975-1996): Transitions, bilateral disputes and Legacies | Global Journal of Human-Social Science. (n.d.). https://socialscienceresearch.org/index.php/GJHSS/article/view/3366/2-Bangladesh-India-Diplomatic_TEI_xml_zip

Banik, N., & Padalkar, M. (2021). The spread of gig economy: Trends and effects. *Форсайт*, 15(1, 1 (eng)), 19–29. DOI: 10.17323/2500-2597.2021.1.19.29

Banker, R., & Kauffman, R. (1991). *Quantifying the Business Value of IT: An illustration of the Business Value Linkage Framework*. Sterm School of Business, NewYork, working paper n° IS-91-21.

Barakat, S., Boddington, M., & Vyakarnam, S. (2014). Measuring entrepreneurial self-efficacy to understand the impact of creative activities for learning innovation. *International Journal of Management Education*, 12(3), 456–468. DOI: 10.1016/j.ijme.2014.05.007

Barboza, G., & Capocchi, A. (2020). Innovative startups in Italy. Managerial challenges of knowledge spillovers effects on employment generation. *Journal of Knowledge Management*, 24(10), 2573–2596. DOI: 10.1108/JKM-08-2019-0436

Barnir, A. (2014). Gender differentials in antecedents of habitual entrepreneurship: Impetus factors and human capital. *Journal of Developmental Entrepreneurship*, 19(1), 1–18. DOI: 10.1142/S1084946714500010

Barrios, J., Hochberg, Y., & Yi, H. (2020). Launching with a parachute: the gig economy and entrepreneurial entry. SSRN Electronic Journal. DOI: 10.2139/ssrn.3603813

Battilana, J., Sengul, M., Pache, A. C., & Model, J. (2015). Harnessing productive tensions in hybrid organizations: The case of work integration social enterprises. *Academy of Management Journal*, 58(6), 1658–1685. DOI: 10.5465/amj.2013.0903

Batt, P. J., & Purchase, S. (2004). Managing Collaboration within Networks and Relationships. *Industrial Marketing Management*, 33(3), 169–174. DOI: 10.1016/j.indmarman.2003.11.004

Baù, M., Sieger, P., Eddleston, K. A., & Chirico, F. (2017). Fail but try again? The effects of age, gender, and multiple–owner experience on failed entrepreneurs' re-entry. *Entrepreneurship Theory and Practice*, 41(6), 909–941. DOI: 10.1111/etap.12233

Baumol, W. J. (1996). Entrepreneurship: Productive, unproductive, and destructive. *Journal of Business Venturing*, 11(1), 3–22. DOI: 10.1016/0883-9026(94)00014-X

Bédard, M. (2016a). Entrepreneurship and economic freedom: An analysis of empirical studies. Institute economy of Montreal.

Bédard, M. (2016b). *Entrepreneurship and Economic Freedom an Analysis of Empirical Studies*. Montreal Economic Institute.

Bellò, B., Mattana, V., & Loi, M. (2018). The power of peers: A new look at the impact of creativity, social context and self-efficacy on entrepreneurial intentions. *International Journal of Entrepreneurial Behaviour & Research*, 24(1), 214–233. DOI: 10.1108/IJEBR-07-2016-0205

Ben Abdallah, M., Fekete-Farkas, M., & Lakner, Z. (2021). Exploring the link between food security and food price dynamics: A bibliometric analysis. *Agriculture*, 11(3), 263. DOI: 10.3390/agriculture11030263

Bento, R. F., Bento, M. S., & White, K. C. (2014). The Balanced Scorecard as a Strategic Management Tool for Innovation and Learning. *Journal of Business Research*, 67(6), 1140–1148.

Bercovitz, J., & Feldman, M. (2008). Academic entrepreneurs: Organizational change at the individual level. *Organization Science*, 19(1), 69–89. DOI: 10.1287/orsc.1070.0295

Bergmann, H., Geissler, M., Hundt, C., & Grave, B. (2018). The climate for entrepreneurship at higher education institutions. *Research Policy*, 47(4), 700–716. DOI: 10.1016/j.respol.2018.01.018

Bergmann, H., Hundt, C., & Sternberg, R. (2016). What makes student entrepreneurs? On the relevance (and irrelevance) of the university and the regional context for student start-ups. *Small Business Economics*, 47(1), 53–76. DOI: 10.1007/s11187-016-9700-6

Bergman, U. M., & Hutchison, M. (2020). Fiscal procyclicality in emerging markets: The role of institutions and economic conditions. *International Finance*, 23(2), 196–214. DOI: 10.1111/infi.12375

Bhagwat, R., & Sharma, M. K. (2007). Performance measurement in supply chains: An overview of the Balanced Scorecard approach. *International Journal of Production Economics*, 106(2), 291–303.

Bharadwaj, A. (2000). A Resource-Based Perspective on Information Technology Capability and Firm Performance: Am Empirical Investigation. *Management Information Systems Quarterly*, 24(1), 169–196. DOI: 10.2307/3250983

Bharadwaj, A., El Sawy, O. A., Pavlou, P. A., & Venkatraman, N. (2013). Digital business strategy: Toward a next generation of insights. *Management Information Systems Quarterly*, 37(2), 471–482. DOI: 10.25300/MISQ/2013/37:2.3

Bhattacharjee, S. (2024, August 15). *Our intelligence failed to predict Bangladesh crisis, say experts*. The Hindu. https://www.thehindu.com/news/cities/Visakhapatnam/our-intelligence-failed-to-predict-bangladesh-crisis-say-experts/article68528761.ece

Bianchini, S., & Pellegrino, G. (2017). *Innovation persistence and employment dynamics.* SSRN Electronic Journal. DOI: 10.2139/ssrn.2919290

Biemer, J. R. (2021). *Our Environmental Handprints: Recover the Land, Reverse Global Warming, Reclaim the Future*. Rowman & Littlefield Publishers. DOI: 10.5771/9781538140666

Bird, B. (1988). Implementing entrepreneurial ideas: The case for intention. *Academy of Management Review*, 13(3), 442–453. DOI: 10.2307/258091

Birdthistle, N., Hynes, B., & Fleming, P. (2007). Enterprise education programmes in secondary schools in Ireland: A multi-stakeholder perspective. *Education + Learning*, 49(4), 265-276. https://doi.org/DOI: 10.1108/00400910710754426

Bischoff, K. (2021). A study on the perceived strength of sustainable entrepreneurial ecosystems on the dimensions of stakeholder theory and culture. *Small Business Economics*, 56(3), 1121–1140. DOI: 10.1007/s11187-019-00257-3

Biswas, S. (2024, August 5). *Bangladesh: Can India help its special ally defuse the crisis?*https://www.bbc.com/news/articles/c39kkkdjkzwo

Bittencourt, M. (2012). Financial development and economic growth in Latin America: Is Schumpeter right? *Journal of Policy Modeling*, 34(3), 341–355. DOI: 10.1016/j.jpolmod.2012.01.012

Blaising, A., Kotturi, Y., Kulkarni, C., & Dabbish, L. (2021). Making it work, or not: A longitudinal study of career trajectories among online freelancers. *Proceedings of the ACM on Human-Computer Interaction, 4*(CSCW3), 1-29. DOI: 10.1145/3432925

Blank, S. (2013). Why the Lean Startup changes everything. *Harvard Business Review*, 91(5), 63–72.

Blundell, R., & Bond, S. (2000). GMM Estimation with persistent panel data: An application to production functions. *Econometric Reviews*, 19(3), 321–340. DOI: 10.1080/07474930008800475

Bögenhold, D., & Klinglmair, A. (2016). Entrepreneurship and hybrid self-employment. *Contemporary entrepreneurship: multidisciplinary perspectives on innovation and growth*, 127-140.

Bögenhold, D. (2019). From hybrid entrepreneurs to entrepreneurial billionaires: Observations on the socioeconomic heterogeneity of self-employment. *The American Behavioral Scientist*, 63(2), 129–146. DOI: 10.1177/0002764218794231

Bögenhold, D., Klinglmair, R., & Kandutsch, F. (2017). Solo-Self-Employment, human capital and hybrid labour in the gig economy. *Форсайт*, 11(4, 4 (eng)), 23–32. DOI: 10.17323/2500-2597.2017.4.23.32

BonikBarta. (n.d.). *Abdur Rouf Talukder: The first Governor to flee in Bangladesh*. Abdur Rouf Talukder: The First Governor to Flee in Bangladesh. https://bonikbarta.net/home/news_description/394649/Abdur-Rouf-Talukder:-The-first-Governor-to-flee-in-Bangladesh

Boopathi, S. (2024). Digital HR Implementation for Business Growth in Industrial 5.0. In *Convergence of Human Resources Technologies and Industry 5.0* (pp. 1–22). IGI Global. DOI: 10.4018/979-8-3693-1343-5.ch001

Boopathi, S., Kumar, P. K. S., Meena, R. S., Sudhakar, M., & Associates. (2023). Sustainable Developments of Modern Soil-Less Agro-Cultivation Systems: Aquaponic Culture. In *Human Agro-Energy Optimization for Business and Industry* (pp. 69–87). IGI Global.

Boopathi, S., & Khang, A. (2023). AI-Integrated Technology for a Secure and Ethical Healthcare Ecosystem. In *AI and IoT-Based Technologies for Precision Medicine* (pp. 36–59). IGI Global. DOI: 10.4018/979-8-3693-0876-9.ch003

Boschma, R., Coenen, L., Frenken, K., & Truffer, B. (2017). Towards a theory of regional diversification: Combining insights from evolutionary economic geography and transition studies. *Regional Studies*, 51(1), 31–45. DOI: 10.1080/00343404.2016.1258460

Bosma, N., Stam, E., & Schutjens, V. (2011). Creative destruction and regional productivity growth: Evidence from the Dutch manufacturing and services industries. *Small Business Economics*, 36(4), 401–418. DOI: 10.1007/s11187-009-9257-8

Boutillier, S. (2008). The social entrepreneur, an entrepreneur socialized in an entrepreneurial society? *Humanism and Business*, 5, 41–60.

Boutillier, S., & Uzunidis, D. (2017). *The Entrepreneur: The Economic Function of Free Enterprise* (Vol. 8). ISTE Group.

Boyd, N. G., & Vozikis, G. S. (1994). The influence of self-efficacy on the development of entrepreneurial intentions and actions. *Entrepreneurship Theory and Practice*, 18(4), 63–77. DOI: 10.1177/104225879401800404

Braam, G., Poutsma, E., Schouteten, R., & Heijden, B. (2024). Employee financial participation and corporate social and environmental performance: Evidence from european panel data. *British Journal of Industrial Relations*, 62(2), 381–409. DOI: 10.1111/bjir.12784

Brixy, U., Brunow, S., & D'Ambrosio, A. (2017). *Ethnic diversity in start-ups and its impact on innovation*. IAB-Discussion Paper.

Bröckling, U. (2015). The entrepreneurial self: Fabricating a new type of subject.

Brown, R., Gregson, G., & Mason, C. (2016). A post-mortem of regional innovation policy failure: Scotland's intermediate technology initiative (ITI). *Regional Studies,* 50(7), 1260–1272. https://doi.org/. 2014. 985644DOI: 10. 1080/ 00343404

Brown, R., Mason, C., & Mawson, S. (2014) *Increasing the Vital 6%: Designing Effective Public Policy to Support High Growth Firms*, National Endowment for Science Technology &Arts (NESTA), London. Download from: https://www.nesta.org.uk/sites/default/files/working_paper_increasing_the_vital_6_percent.pdf

Brynjolfsson, E., & McAfee, A. (2014). *The second machine age: Work, progress, and prosperity in a time of brilliant technologies*. W.W. Norton & Company.

Buera, F. J., Kaboski, J. P., & Shin, Y. (2011). Finance and development: A tale of two sectors. *The American Economic Review*, 101(5), 1964–2002. DOI: 10.1257/aer.101.5.1964

Cacciolatti, L., Rosli, A., Ruiz-Alba, J. L., & Chang, J. (2020). Strategic alliances and firm performance in startups with a social mission. *Journal of Business Research*, 106, 106–117. DOI: 10.1016/j.jbusres.2019.08.047

Cansu, F. K., & Cansu, S. K. (2019). An overview of computational thinking. *International Journal of Computer Science Education in Schools*, 3(1), 17–30. DOI: 10.21585/ijcses.v3i1.53

Cantner, U., Dettmann, E., Giebler, A., Guenther, J., & Kristalova, M. (2019). The impact of innovation and innovation subsidies on economic development in german regions. *Regional Studies*, 53(9), 1284–1295. DOI: 10.1080/00343404.2019.1639656

Carayannis, E. G. (2020). *Encyclopedia of creativity, invention, innovation and entrepreneurship*. Springer. DOI: 10.1007/978-3-319-15347-6

Carr, J. C., Marshall, D. R., Michaelis, T. L., Pollack, J. M., & Sheats, L. (2022). The role of work-to-venture role conflict on hybrid entrepreneurs' transition into entrepreneurship. *Journal of Small Business Management*, 61(5), 2302–2325. DOI: 10.1080/00472778.2022.2082455

Cattaneo, O., Gereffi, G., Miroudot, S., & Taglioni, D. (2013). Joining, upgrading and being competitive in global value chains: A strategic framework. World Bank Policy Research Working Paper, 6406.

Cattanéo, F., Guillard, J., Diouf, S., O'Rourke, J., & Grimardias, D. (2021). Mitigation of ecological impacts on fish of large sediment reservoir management through controlled flushing–The case of the Verbois dam (Rhône River, Switzerland). *The Science of the Total Environment*, 756, 144053. DOI: 10.1016/j.scitotenv.2020.144053 PMID: 33279192

Center, A. R. I. (2024, February 1). *Asia Regional Integration Center*. Copyright 2024. All Rights Reserved. https://aric.adb.org/initiative/bangladesh-bhutan-india-and-nepal-motor-vehicles-agreement

Chan, W. L., & Mustafa, M. J. (2020). Journal of entrepreneurship in emerging economies (JEEE): Reflecting on the past five years while thinking about the future. *Journal of Entrepreneurship in Emerging Economies.*

Chang, H., Hsu, H., Liou, J., & Tsai, C. (2013). Psychological contracts and innovative behavior: A moderated path analysis of work engagement and job resources. *Journal of Applied Social Psychology*, 43(10), 2120–2135. DOI: 10.1111/jasp.12165

Chan, Y. E., Huff, S. L., Barclay, D. W., & Copeland, D. G. (1997). Business Strategic Orientation, Information Systems Strategic Orientation, and Strategic Alignment. *Information Systems Research*, 8(2), 125–150. DOI: 10.1287/isre.8.2.125

Chan, Y. E., Sabherwal, R., & Thatcher, J. B. (2006). Antecedents and Outcomes of Strategic IS Alignment: An empirical investigation. *IEEE Transactions on Engineering Management*, 51(3), 27–47. DOI: 10.1109/TEM.2005.861804

Chappa, C., Varghese, M., & Chandler, K. (2017). Shaping the gig economy. *Proceedings of the Northeast Business& Economics Association*, 70-73.

Chattopadhyay, K. (2009). India, Hindutva, and Fascist Mobilizations, 1989-2002. The International Encyclopedia of Revolution and Protest, 1-4. DOI: 10.1002/9781405198073.wbierp0744

Chen, D. Q., Mocker, M., Preston, D. S., & Teubner, A. (2010). Information systems strategy: Reconceptualization, measurement, and implications. *Management Information Systems Quarterly*, 34(2), 233–259. DOI: 10.2307/20721426

Cheng, F., Ji, S., & Chen, Y. (2023). The contract design of employee stock ownership plan and enterprise innovation investment: Evidence from china. *Sustainability (Basel)*, 15(3), 2601. DOI: 10.3390/su15032601

Chen, X., Ma, Y., & Xie, Y. (2024). The Influence Mechanism of Online Social Network Relationships on Sustainable Entrepreneurial Success. *Sustainability (Basel)*, 16(9), 3755. DOI: 10.3390/su16093755

Cherry, M. A., & Aloisi, A. (2016). Dependent contractors in the gig economy: A comparative approach. *SSRN*, 66, 635. DOI: 10.2139/ssrn.2847869

Chiang, F., Birtch, T., & Kwan, H. (2010). The moderating roles of job control and work-life balance practices on employee stress in the hotel and catering industry. *International Journal of Hospitality Management*, 29(1), 25–32. DOI: 10.1016/j.ijhm.2009.04.005

Chiles, T. H., Bluedorn, A. C., & Gupta, V. K. (2007). Beyond creative destruction and entrepreneurial discovery: A radical Austrian approach to entrepreneurship. *Organization Studies*, 28(4), 467–493. DOI: 10.1177/0170840606067996

Choi, K., Park, J., Cho, D., & Chu, H.-Y. (2018). The impact of university support on the creation of student entrepreneurs: Evidence from South Korea. *Entrepreneurship Research Journal*, 8(1), 1–14.

Choudhury, S. D. (2024, August 7). *Bangladesh's uprising creates political vacuum, impacts for broader region*. Asia Pacific Foundation of Canada. https://www.asiapacific.ca/publication/explainer-bangladeshs-popular-uprising-creates-political-uncertainty

Chung, C., Lee, D., & Lee, J. (2020). The Impact of Organizational Alignment on Strategic Performance: Evidence from Korean Firms. *International Journal of Strategic Management*, 21(2), 119–137.

Ciasullo, M. V., Troisi, O., Grimaldi, M., & Leone, D. (2020). Multi-level governance for sustainable innovation in smart communities: An ecosystems approach. *The International Entrepreneurship and Management Journal*, 16(4), 1167–1195. DOI: 10.1007/s11365-020-00641-6

Clark, B. R. (1998). *Creating entrepreneurial universities: Organisational pathways to transformation*. Pergamon Press.

Clark, D. N., Reboud, S., Toutain, O., Ballereau, V., & Mazzarol, T. (2020). Entrepreneurial education: An entrepreneurial ecosystem approach. *Journal of Management & Organization*, , 1–21. DOI: 10.1017/jmo.2020.26

Clarke, M., Koch, L. C., & Hill, E. J. (2004). The work-family interface: Differentiating balance and fit. *Family and Consumer Sciences Research Journal*, 33(2), 121–140. DOI: 10.1177/1077727X04269610

Clemons, E. K. (1986). Information systems for sustainable competitive advantage. *Information & Management*, 11(3), 131–136. DOI: 10.1016/0378-7206(86)90010-8

Cobbold, I., & Lawrie, G. (2002). The development of the Balanced Scorecard as a strategic management tool. *International Journal of Business Performance Management*, 4(1), 1–11.

Cockburn, P. (2020, February 28). Opinion: While Muslims are being murdered in India, the rest of the world is too slow to condemn. Retrieved July 22, 2020, from https://www.independent.co.uk/voices/delhi-riots-news-narendra-Modi-muslims-hindus-jammu-kashmir-trump-a9365376.html

Cornforth, C. (2020). The governance of hybrid organisations. In *Handbook on hybrid organisations* (pp. 220–236). Edward Elgar Publishing. DOI: 10.4337/9781785366116.00022

Corradini, C., & Propris, L. (2015). Technological diversification and new innovators in european regions: Evidence from patent data. *Environment & Planning A*, 47(10), 2170–2186. DOI: 10.1177/0308518X15599285

Cox, L., Mueller, S., & Moss, S. (2002). The impact of entrepreneurship education on entrepreneurial self-efficacy. *International Journal of Entrepreneurship Education*, 1(2).

Cragg, P., Tagliavini, M., & Mills, A. (2011). Evaluating the alignment of IT with business processes in SMEs. *Communications of the Association for Information Systems*, 28(1), 1–34.

Cronk, M. C., & Fitzgerald, E. P. (1999). Understanding "IS business value": Derivation of dimension. *Logistics Information Management*, 12(1-2), 40–49. DOI: 10.1108/09576059910256240

Croteau, A. M., Bergeron, F., & Raymond, L. (2001). Business Strategy and Technological Deployment: Fit and Performance. *Information Systems Management*, 6(4).

Curran, N. M. (2023). "More like a friend than a teacher": Ideal teachers and the gig economy for online language learning. *Computer Assisted Language Learning*, 36(7), 1288–1308. DOI: 10.1080/09588221.2021.1976801

Cypher, J. M., & Dietz, J. L. (2008). *The process of economic development*. Routledge. DOI: 10.4324/9780203895061

D'Art, D., & Turner, T. (2004). Profit sharing, firm performance and union influence in selected european countries. *Personnel Review*, 33(3), 335–350. DOI: 10.1108/00483480410528869

Dabić, M., Vlačić, B., Paul, J., Dana, L. P., Sahasranamam, S., & Glinka, B. (2020). Immigrant entrepreneurship: A review and research agenda. *Journal of Business Research*, 113, 25–38. DOI: 10.1016/j.jbusres.2020.03.013

Dagienė, V., Jevsikova, T., Stupurienė, G., & Juškevičienė, A. (2022). Teaching computational thinking in primary schools: Worldwide trends and teachers' attitudes. *Computer Science and Information Systems*, 19(1), 1–24. DOI: 10.2298/CSIS201215033D

Dalmarco, G., Hulsink, W., & Blois, G. V. (2018). Creating entrepreneurial universities in an emerging economy. *Technological Forecasting and Social Change*, 135(1), 99–111. DOI: 10.1016/j.techfore.2018.04.015

Damoah, O. (2020). Strategic factors predicting the likelihood of youth entrepreneurship in ghana: A logistic regression analysis. *World Journal of Entrepreneurship, Management and Sustainable Development*, 16(4), 389–401. DOI: 10.1108/WJEMSD-06-2018-0057

Dana, L.-P., Salamzadeh, A., Hadizadeh, M., Heydari, G., & Shamsoddin, S. (2022). Urban entrepreneurship and sustainable businesses in smart cities: Exploring the role of digital technologies. *Sustainable Technology and Entrepreneurship*, 1(2), 100016. DOI: 10.1016/j.stae.2022.100016

Danil, L., & Fordian, D. (2022). Does Rural Entrepreneurship Performance Support Sustainable Development Goals (SDGs) and Sustainable Entrepreneurship? *Review of Integrative Business and Economics Research*, 11, 145–165.

Davenport, T. H., & Westerman, G. (2018). Why so many high-profile digital transformations fail. *Harvard Business Review*. Retrieved from https://hbr.org

Davidsson, P. (1991). Continued entrepreneurship: Ability, need, and opportunity as determinants of small firm growth [November.]. *Journal of Business Venturing*, 6(6), 405–429. DOI: 10.1016/0883-9026(91)90028-C

Davies, I. A., & Doherty, B. (2019). Balancing a hybrid business model: The search for equilibrium at Cafédirect. *Journal of Business Ethics*, 157(4), 1043–1066. DOI: 10.1007/s10551-018-3960-9

Dawn.com. (2019, August 11). *'RSS ideology of Hindu supremacy will lead to suppression of Muslims in India and to targeting of Pakistan'*. DAWN.COM. https://www.dawn.com/news/1499293

De Geuser, F., Mooraj, S., & Oyon, D. (2009). Does the Balanced Scorecard add value? A differential analysis of the BSC's benefits for different types of firms. *European Accounting Review*, 18(3), 503–536.

De la Vega, J. C. A. (2020, July). Making the Gig Economy Work for Workers: An Exploration of Freelancing Platforms. In *Proceedings of the 33rd International BCS Human Computer Interaction Conference* (pp. 55-57). BCS Learning & Development. DOI: 10.14236/ewic/HCI20DC.13

de Leede, J., Looise, J. C., & Alders, B. (2002). Innovation, improvement and operations: An exploration of the management of alignment. *International Journal of Technology Management*, 23(4), 353–368. DOI: 10.1504/IJTM.2002.003015

De Long, D. W., & Fahey, L. (2000). Diagnosing cultural barriers to knowledge management. *The Academy of Management Perspectives*, 14(4), 113–127. DOI: 10.5465/ame.2000.3979820

De Luca, V. V., Margherita, A., & Passiante, G. (2019). Crowdfunding: A systemic framework of benefits. *International Journal of Entrepreneurial Behaviour & Research*, 25(6), 1321–1339. DOI: 10.1108/IJEBR-11-2018-0755

De Meo, E. (2013). Are Commodity Prices Driven by Fundamentals? *Economic Notes*, 42(1), 19–46. DOI: 10.1111/ecno.12001

De Soyres, F., & Franco, S. (2019). Inflation dynamics and global value chains. World Bank Policy Research Working Paper, 9090.

Deakins, D., Glancey, K., Menter, I., & Wyper, J. (2005). Enterprise education: The role of head teachers. *The International Entrepreneurship and Management Journal*, 1(2), 241–263. DOI: 10.1007/s11365-005-1131-9

Dealroom, (2020). *European unicorns* [WWW Document]. URL https://app.dealroom .co/li sts/15129 (accessed 06.12.20) </Dataset>.

Demir, C., Werner, A., Kraus, S., & Jones, P. (2020). Hybrid entrepreneurship: A systematic literature review. *Journal of Small Business and Entrepreneurship*, 34(1), 29–52. DOI: 10.1080/08276331.2020.1764738

Deng, L., Ye, Q., Xu, D., Sun, W., & Jiang, G. (2022). A literature review and integrated framework for the determinants of crowdfunding success. *Financial Innovation*, 8(1), 41. DOI: 10.1186/s40854-022-00345-6

Denison, D. R. (1996). What is the difference between organizational culture and organizational climate? A native's point of view on a decade of paradigm wars. *Academy of Management Review*, 21(3), 619–654. DOI: 10.2307/258997

Desai, R. (2016). Hindutva and Fascism. Retrieved 9 July 2020, from https://www .academia.edu/30813538/Hindutva_and_Fascism

Desai, R. (n.d.). A latter day fascism. Economic and Political Weekly, 49(35), 48–58. Retrieved 10 17, 2019, from http://www.epw.in/journal/2014/35/special-articles/ latter-day-fascism.html

Desk, I. (2019, August 29). BJP inducts 7 crore new members, creates membership drive record. Retrieved July 16, 2020, from https://www.indiatoday.in/india/story/ bjp-inducts-7-crore-new-members-creates-membership-drive-record-1593164-2019 -08-29

Desk, I. (2024, August 16). *The downfall of Sheikh Hasina and its impact on South Asia - IMPRI Impact and Policy Research Institute*. IMPRI Impact and Policy Research Institute. https://www.impriindia.com/insights/downfall-of-sheikh-hasina-impact-asia/

Dhanya, D., Kumar, S. S., Thilagavathy, A., Prasad, D., & Boopathi, S. (2023). Data Analytics and Artificial Intelligence in the Circular Economy: Case Studies. In *Intelligent Engineering Applications and Applied Sciences for Sustainability* (pp. 40–58). IGI Global.

Diegoli, R. B., Gutierrez, H. S. M., & Salmones, M. M. G. (2018). Teachers as entrepreneurial role models: The impact of teacher's entrepreneurial experience and student learning styles in entrepreneurial intentions. *Journal of Entrepreneurship Education*, 21(1), 1–11. https://www.abacademies.org/articles/Teachers-as-entrepreneurial-role-models-1528-2651-21-1-138.pdf

Dieterich, C., & Landrin, S. (2024, August 15). Sheikh Hasina, India's cumbersome guest. *Le Monde.fr*. https://www.lemonde.fr/en/international/article/2024/08/15/sheikh-hasina-india-s-cumbersome-guest_6716062_4.html

DiMaggio, P. J., & Powell, W. W. (1983). The iron cage revisited: Institutional isomorphism and collective rationality in organizational fields. *American Sociological Review*, 48(2), 147–160. DOI: 10.2307/2095101

Dimitratos, P., & Plakoyiannaki, E. (2003). Theoretical foundations of an international entrepreneurial culture. *Journal of International Entrepreneurship*, 1(2), 187–215. DOI: 10.1023/A:1023804318244

Dimitropoulou, A. (2021). *World's Most Entrepreneurial Countries*. World's Most Entrepreneurial Countries.

Dixon, J. R., Nanni, A. J., & Vollmann, T. E. (2000). *The New Performance Challenge: Measuring Operations for World-Class Competition*. Wiley.

Djankov, S., Ganser, T., McLiesh, C., Ramalho, R., & Shleifer, A. (2010). The effect of corporate taxes on investment and entrepreneurship. *American Economic Journal. Macroeconomics*, 2(3), 31–64. DOI: 10.1257/mac.2.3.31

Donckels, R. (1991). Education and entrepreneurship experiences from secondary and university education in Belgium. *Journal of Small Business and Entrepreneurship*, 9(1), 35–42. DOI: 10.1080/08276331.1991.10600389

Doran, J., McCarthy, N., & O'Connor, M. (2016). Entrepreneurship and employment growth across european regions. *Regional Studies, Regional Science*, 3(1), 121–128. DOI: 10.1080/21681376.2015.1135406

Doubogan Unibon Y. & Aliha G. (2020), the growing use of PPPs in French-speaking Africa: what opportunities for entrepreneurship? Doumbouya ML (2011), entrepreneurial monitoring in Africa: the cases of Guinean companies.

Douglas, E. J., & Shepherd, D. A. (2002). Self- employment as a career choice: Attitudes, entrepreneurial intentions, and utility maximization. *Entrepreneurship Theory and Practice*, 26(3), 81–90. DOI: 10.1177/104225870202600305

Drew, S., & Kuehl, D. (2021). Feedback and Learning in Strategic Management: The Role of the Balanced Scorecard. *Strategic Management Journal*, 42(9), 1678–1696.

Duarte, T., & Ruiz Tibana, M. (2009). Emprendimiento, una opción para el desarrollo. *Scientia Et Technica*, 15(43), 326–331.

Duru, I., & Anyanwu, S. (2019). Entrepreneurship in small and medium enterprises: A catalyst for capacity building and sustainable youths' employment generation in the federal capital territory, Abuja, Nigeria. *International Journal of Social and Administrative Sciences*, 4(2), 277–296. DOI: 10.18488/journal.136.2019.42.277.296

Dushnitsky, G., & Zunino, D. (2019). The role of crowdfunding in entrepreneurial finance. In *Handbook of research on crowdfunding* (pp. 46–92). Edward Elgar Publishing. DOI: 10.4337/9781788117210.00008

Duvvuru, K. (2019, July 30). Is India displaying signs of neo-fascism? Retrieved July 22, 2020, from https://mronline.org/2019/07/31/is-india-displaying-signs-of-neo-fascism/

Dvouletý, O., Fernandez de Arroyabe, J. C., & Mustafa, M. (2021). Guest editorial. *Journal of Entrepreneurship in Emerging Economies*, 13(4), 489–496. DOI: 10.1108/JEEE-09-2021-461

Dzaka-Kikouta, T., Kamavuako-Diwavova, J., & Bitemo-Ndiwulu, X. Makiese- Ndoma, F., Manika Manzongani, JP, & Masamba-Lulendo, V. (2020). Entrepreneurship of Young Francophone Africans in the Republic of Congo and the Democratic Republic of Congo: Challenges and Perspectives. OFE-RP Project Report, 3.

Eatwell, R. (2003). Reflections on Fascism and Religion. Totalitarian Movements and Political Religions, 4(3), 145-166. Retrieved 10 17, 2019, from https://tandfonline.com/doi/full/10.1080/1469076041 2331329991

Economist (2019). *The trouble with tech unicorns - Tech's new stars have it all—except a path to high profits* [WWW Document]. URL https://www.economist.com/leaders 56.

Eddleston, K., & Powell, G. (2012). Nurturing entrepreneurs' work–family balance: A gendered perspective. *Entrepreneurship Theory and Practice*, 36(3), 513–541. DOI: 10.1111/j.1540-6520.2012.00506.x

Edpuzzle. (2021). *Edpuzzle*. https://edpuzzle.com/

Elia, G., Margherita, A., & Passiante, G. (2020). Digital entrepreneurship ecosystem: How digital technologies and collective intelligence are reshaping the entrepreneurial process. *Technological Forecasting and Social Change*, 150, 119791. DOI: 10.1016/j.techfore.2019.119791

Emslie, C., & Hunt, K. (2008). 'live to work' or 'work to live'? a qualitative study of gender and work–life balance among men and women in mid-life. *Gender, Work and Organization*, 16(1), 151–172. DOI: 10.1111/j.1468-0432.2008.00434.x

Engel, C., Mark, N. C., West, K. D., Rogoff, K., & Rossi, B. (2007). Exchange rate models are not as bad as you think [with comments and discussion]. *NBER Macroeconomics Annual*, 22, 381–473. DOI: 10.1086/ma.22.25554969

Ephrem, AN, & Murimbika, M. (2023a). Development and validation of an individual entrepreneurial potential new measurement scale. Journal of Research in Marketing and Entrepreneurship.

Ephrem, A. N., & Murimbika, M. (2023b). I wish I had a paid job or a business: A moderated effect of entrepreneurial potential on career choice regret. *Career Development International*, 28(5), 518–535. DOI: 10.1108/CDI-09-2022-0249

Ephrem, A. N., Nguezet, P. M. D., Charmant, I. K., Murimbika, M., Awotide, B. A., Tahirou, A., Lydie, M. N., & Manyong, V. (2021). Entrepreneurial motivation, psychological capital, and business success of young entrepreneurs in the drc. *Sustainability (Basel)*, 13(8), 4087. DOI: 10.3390/su13084087

Erina, I., Shatrevich, V., & Gaile-Sarkane, E. (2017). Impact of stakeholder groups on development of a regional entrepreneurial ecosystem. *European Planning Studies*, 25(5), 755–771. DOI: 10.1080/09654313.2017.1282077

Eva, N., Meacham, H., Newman, A., Schwarz, G., & Tham, T. (2019). Is coworker feedback more important than supervisor feedback for increasing innovative behavior? *Human Resource Management*, 58(4), 383–396. DOI: 10.1002/hrm.21960

Explainers, F. (2024, August 6). 1975 and 2024: The story of Sheikh Hasina's two stays in India. *Firstpost*. https://www.firstpost.com/explainers/bangladesh-sheikh-hasina-india-exile-1975-13801627.html

Ezzedeen, S., & Zikic, J. (2015). Finding balance amid boundarylessness: An interpretive study of entrepreneurial work–life balance and boundary management. *Journal of Family Issues*, 38(11), 1546–1576. DOI: 10.1177/0192513X15600731

Fakhfakh, F., & FitzRoy, F. (2018). Is profit sharing good for the environment? positive evidence from french firms. *Journal of Participation and Employee Ownership*, 1(2/3), 128–143. DOI: 10.1108/JPEO-12-2017-0012

Farahani, S. S., Raman, V., & Murray, R. M. (2015). Robust model predictive control for signal temporal logic synthesis. *IFAC-PapersOnLine*, 48(27), 323–328. DOI: 10.1016/j.ifacol.2015.11.195

Farooq, G. (2018). Politics of Fake News: How WhatsApp Became a Potent Propaganda Tool in India. *Media Watch*, 9(1), 106–117. DOI: 10.15655/mw/2018/v9i1/49279

Fayolle, A., Ben Salah, A., Ben Salah, I., & Belkacem, L. (2010). Effectiveness of incubators in the creation of innovative businesses: Case of Tunisia 1. *Innovations*, 3, 157–179. DOI: 10.3917/inno.033.0157

Feld, B. (2012). *Startup Communities: building an entrepreneurial ecosystem in your city*. Wiley. DOI: 10.1002/9781119204459

Feldman, D. C., & Bolino, M. (2000). Career patterns of the self- employed: Career motivations and career out-comes. *Journal of Small Business Management*, 38(3), 53–67.

Feng, M., Li, S., & Zhang, J. (2020). Strategic Alignment and Financial Performance: An Empirical Study of the Balanced Scorecard. *Journal of Financial Management*, 40(3), 543–562.

Fernandez-Stark, K., & Gereffi, G. (2019). Global value chain analysis: A primer. In *Handbook on global value chains* (pp. 54–76). Edward Elgar Publishing. DOI: 10.4337/9781788113779.00008

Ferreira, C. C., Ferguson, S. L., & Pitt, L. F. (2019). Entrepreneurial marketing and hybrid entrepreneurship: The case of JM Reid Bamboo Rods. *Journal of Marketing Management*, 35(9-10), 9–10, 867–885. DOI: 10.1080/0267257X.2019.1637921

Fibírová, J., & Petera, P. (2013). Profit-sharing – a tool for improving productivity, profitability and competitiveness of firms? *Journal of Competitiveness*, 5(4), 3–25. DOI: 10.7441/joc.2013.04.01

Fietze, S., & Boyd, B. (2017). Entrepreneurial intention of Danish students: A correspondence analysis. *International Journal of Entrepreneurial Behaviour & Research*, 23(4), 656–672. DOI: 10.1108/IJEBR-08-2016-0241

Figge, F., Hahn, T., Schaltegger, S., & Wagner, M. (2002). The sustainability balanced scorecard–linking sustainability management to business strategy. *Business Strategy and the Environment*, 11(5), 269–284. DOI: 10.1002/bse.339

Fitri, S., & Pertiwi, A. (2019). Innovation Mindset Model at the Early Stage Startup With Berkeley Innovation Index Approached. *Technology Management*, 4(13), 57–70.

FitzRoy, F., & Nolan, M. (2021). Employee participation, job quality, and inequality. *Journal of Participation and Employee Ownership*, 5(1), 1–13. DOI: 10.1108/JPEO-05-2020-0014

Folta, T. B., Delmar, F., & Wennberg, K. (2009). Hybrid Entrepreneurship. *Management Science*, 56(2), 253–269. DOI: 10.1287/mnsc.1090.1094

Foremny, D. (2014). Sub-national deficits in European countries: The impact of fiscal rules and tax autonomy. *European Journal of Political Economy*, 34, 86–110. DOI: 10.1016/j.ejpoleco.2014.01.003

Fortezza, F., Pagano, A., & Bocconcelli, R. (2021). Serial crowdfunding in start-up development: A business network view. *Journal of Business and Industrial Marketing*, 36(13), 250–262. DOI: 10.1108/JBIM-05-2020-0243

Fos, V., Hamdi, N., Kalda, A., & Nickerson, J. (2019). Gig-labor: Trading safety nets for steering wheels.

Foss, L., & Gibson, D. V. (2015). *The Entrepreneurial University: Context and Institutional Change.* Routledge, 1-17. DOI: 10.4324/9781315737065

Fouda, CNFB (2014). Entrepreneurial dynamism of Cameroonian women: Case studies of business development.

Franck, L. R. (1935). FASCISM AND THE CORPORATE STATE. The Political Quarterly, 6(3), 355-368. Retrieved 10 17, 2019, from https://onlinelibrary.wiley.com/doi/10.1111/j.1467-923x.1935.tb01262.x/abstract

Frank, H., Lueger, M., & Korunka, C. (2007). The significance of personality in business start-up intentions, start-up realization and business success. *Entrepreneurship and Regional Development*, 19(3), 227–251. DOI: 10.1080/08985620701218387

Friedman, G. (2017). Nationalism Is Rising, Not Fascism. Retrieved 9 July 2020, from https://www.huffpost.com/entry/nationalism-is-rising-not_b_10281138

Frigo, M. (2002). Strategy and the Balance Scorecard. *Strategic Finance*, 84(5), 6–9.

Frontier Post, T. (2019, August 14). Implementing RSS evil ideology. Retrieved July 22, 2020, from https://thefrontierpost.com/implementing-rss-evil-ideology/

Fundamentalism - Sikh fundamentalism. (2020). Retrieved 9 July 2020, from https://www.britannica.com/topic/fundamentalism/Sikh-fundamentalism#ref252670

Gaglio, C. M., & Katz, J. A. (2001). The psychological basis of opportunity identification: Entrepreneurial alertness. *Small Business Economics*, 16(2), 95–111. DOI: 10.1023/A:1011132102464

Gatewood, E. J., Shaver, K. G., & Gartner, W. (1995). A longitudinal study of cognitive factors influencing start- up behaviours and success at venture creation. *Journal of Business Venturing*, 10(5), 371–391. DOI: 10.1016/0883-9026(95)00035-7

Geissler, M., Jahn, S., & Haefner, P. (2010). The entrepreneurial climate at universities: The impact of organizational factors. *The Theory and Practice of Entrepreneurship*, 12-31.

GEM (2021) *Global Entrepreneurship Monitor*. Available at: https://www.gemconsortium.org/data/key-nes (accessed May 26, 2021).

Gérard, T., & Thomas, G. N. (2023). The Past and the Future Effects of Russian-Ukrainian Conflict on the Democratic Republic of Congo Economic Policy. *Futurity Economics&Law*, 3(3), 201–218.

Gerow, J. E., Thatcher, J. B., & Grover, V. (2014). Six types of IT-business strategic alignment: An investigation of the constructs and their measurement. *European Journal of Information Systems*, 23(5), 456–472.

Ghanem, Y., & Achouche, M. (2015). Impact of financial development on the dynamics of business creation: Evidence from panel data on MENA countries. https://mpra.ub.uni-muenchen.de/id/eprint/68125

Ghosh, J. (2024, August 16). *Lessons from Bangladesh's Uprising*. Project Syndicate. https://www.project-syndicate.org/commentary/india-and-imf-should-heed-the-lessons-of-sheikh-hasina-downfall-by-jayati-ghosh-2024-08

Gianiodis, P. T., & Meek, W. R. (2020). Entrepreneurial education for the entrepreneurial university: A stakeholder perspective. *The Journal of Technology Transfer*, 45(4), 1167–1195. DOI: 10.1007/s10961-019-09742-z

Gibbons, R., & Kaplan, R. S. (2018). The balanced scorecard and strategy management: A framework for improved performance. *Journal of Management Accounting Research*, 30(1), 1–20.

Gielnik, M. M., Cardon, M. S., & Frese, M. (2020). *The psychology of entrepreneurship*. Routledge. DOI: 10.4324/9781003137573

Gift, M. D. M., Senthil, T. S., Hasan, D. S., Alagarraja, K., Jayaseelan, P., & Boopathi, S. (2024). Additive Manufacturing and 3D Printing Innovations: Revolutionizing Industry 5.0. In *Technological Advancements in Data Processing for Next Generation Intelligent Systems* (pp. 255–287). IGI Global. DOI: 10.4018/979-8-3693-0968-1.ch010

Gilal, F. G., Gilal, N. G., Channa, N. A., Gilal, R. G., Gilal, R. G., & Tunio, M. N. (2020). Towards an integrated model for the transference of environmental responsibility. *Business Strategy and the Environment*, 29(6), 2614–2623. DOI: 10.1002/bse.2524

Gimenez-Fernandez, E. M., Bogers, M., & Sandulli, F. (2019). How the diversity of cooperation partners affects startups' innovation performance: An analysis of the role of cooperation breadth in open innovation. *Open Innovation and Entrepreneurship: Impetus of Growth and Competitive Advantages*, 9–35.

Gittell, R., Sohl, J., & Tebaldi, E. (2014). Do entrepreneurship and high-tech concentration create jobs? exploring the growth in employment in US metropolitan areas from 1991 to 2007. *Economic Development Quarterly*, 28(3), 244–253. DOI: 10.1177/0891242414530467

Golwalkar, M. S. (1947). *We or Our Nationhood Defined*. Kale.

Gomes, J., & Romão, M. (2015). Achieving project success through alignment with organizational strategy: Balanced Scorecard approach. In Proceeding of 8th IADIS International Conference - Information's Systems 2015, Funchal, Portugal.

Gomes, J., & Romão, M. (2012). How benefits management helps Balanced Scorecard to deal with business dynamic environments. *Tourism & Management Studies*, 9(1), 129–138.

Gompers, P. A., & Wang, S. Q. (2017). *Diversity in innovation*. National Bureau of Economic Research. DOI: 10.3386/w23082

Goodfellow, S. H. (2013). Fascism as a Transnational Movement: The Case of Inter-War Alsace. Contemporary European History, 22(01), 87-106. Retrieved 10 17, 2019, from https://cambridge.org/core/journals/contemporary-european-history/article/fascism-as-a-transnational-movement-the-case-of-interwar-alsace/ac8b472b62511cc03a346a5aed2c344e

Goodspeed, R. (2019a). Participatory e-Planning with civic crowdfunding: Donor background, involvement, and social capital outcomes. [IJEPR]. *International Journal of E-Planning Research*, 8(2), 68–87. DOI: 10.4018/IJEPR.2019040104

Google. (n.d.). *Blockly*. https://developers.google.com/blockly

Gopal, M., Lurdhumary, J., Bathrinath, S., Priya, A. P., Sarojwal, A., & Boopathi, S. (2024). Energy Harvesting and Smart Highways for Sustainable Transportation Infrastructure: Revolutionizing Roads Using Nanotechnology. In *Principles and Applications in Speed Sensing and Energy Harvesting for Smart Roads* (pp. 136–165). IGI Global. DOI: 10.4018/978-1-6684-9214-7.ch005

Gorissen, S. (2024). Content creation and gig-work in the platform economy: What contemporary sex work can teach us about the futures of digital labor. *The Information Society*, •••, 1–20. DOI: 10.1080/01972243.2024.2381481

Goswami, K., Mitchell, J. R., & Bhagavatula, S. (2018). Accelerator expertise: Understanding the intermediary role of accelerators in the development of the Bangalore entrepreneurial ecosystem. *Strategic Entrepreneurship Journal*, 12(1), 117–150. DOI: 10.1002/sej.1281

Goswami, S., & Underwood, Q. (2022). *The Young Entrepreneur: How to Start A Business While You're Still a Student*. Kogan Page Publishers.

Grant, R. M. (1996). Toward a knowledge-based theory of the firm. *Strategic Management Journal*, Summer Special Issue 17, 109–122.

Grant, B. A. (2023). Unleashing Corporate Entrepreneurship. *Brook. L. Rev.*, 89, 1031.

Grare, F. (2024, August 12). *Hasina's downfall may create new opportunities in Bangladesh for China | The Strategist*. The Strategist. https://www.aspistrategist.org.au/hasinas-downfall-may-create-new-opportunities-in-bangladesh-for-china/

Green, C., & Heywood, J. (2010). P*rofit sharing, separation and training.British Journal of Industrial Relations*, 49(4), 623–642. DOI: 10.1111/j.1467-8543.2010.00805.x

Green, E., Sukumar, A., Jafari-Sadeghi, V., Pandya, K., & Khavarinezhad, S. (2022). Analysis of factors impeding access to finance in internet enabled crowdfunding: A systematic literature review. *International Journal of Technology Transfer and Commercialisation*, 19(2), 249–269. DOI: 10.1504/IJTTC.2022.124342

Gregor, A. J., & Chang, M. H. (1979). Nazionalfascismo and the Revolutionary Nationalism of Sun Yat-sen. The Journal of Asian Studies, 39(01), 21-37. Retrieved 10 17, 2019, from https://cambridge.org/core/journals/journal-of-asian-studies/article/nazionalfascismo-and-the-revolutionary-nationalism-of-sun-yatsen/ca75402abf3b43c8005eae9291080e8b

Gregori, P., & Holzmann, P. (2020). Digital sustainable entrepreneurship: A business model perspective on embedding digital technologies for social and environmental value creation. *Journal of Cleaner Production*, 272, 122817. DOI: 10.1016/j.jclepro.2020.122817

Grembergen, W. V. (2001). *Information Technology Evaluation Methods & Management*. Idea Group Publishing. DOI: 10.4018/978-1-878289-90-2

Griffin, R. (1995). Fascism. Oxford University Press. Retrieved 10 17, 2019, from https://books.google.com/books?id=3ssUAQAAIAAJ

Grillitsch, M., & Asheim, B. (2018). Place-based innovation policy for industrial diversification in regions. *European Planning Studies*, 26(8), 1638–1662. DOI: 10.1080/09654313.2018.1484892

Grover, S., & Pea, R. (2013). Computational thinking in K–12: A review of the state of the field. *Educational Researcher*, 42(1), 38–43. DOI: 10.3102/0013189X12463051

Guckenbiehl, P., de Zubielqui, G. C., & Lindsay, N. (2021). Knowledge and innovation in start-up ventures: A systematic literature review and research agenda. *Technological Forecasting and Social Change*, 172, 121026. DOI: 10.1016/j.techfore.2021.121026

Guenaga, M., Mentxaka, I., Garaizar, P., Eguiluz, A., Villagrasa, S., & Navarro, I. (2017). Make world, a collaborative platform to develop computational thinking and STEAM. In *Learning and Collaboration Technologies. Technology in Education: 4th International Conference, LCT 2017, Held as Part of HCI International 2017, Vancouver, BC, Canada, July 9-14, 2017* [Springer International Publishing.]. *Proceedings*, 4(Part II), 50–59.

Guerrero, M., Liñán, F., & Cáceres-Carrasco, F. R. (2021). The influence of ecosystems on the entrepreneurship process: A comparison across developed and developing economies. *Small Business Economics*, 57(4), 1733–1759. DOI: 10.1007/s11187-020-00392-2

Guerrero, M., Urbano, D., Cunningham, J. A., & Gajon, E. (2017). Determinants of graduates' start-ups creation across a multi-campus entrepreneurial university: The case of Monterrey Institute of Technology and Higher Education. *Journal of Small Business Management*, 56(1), 150–178. DOI: 10.1111/jsbm.12366

GUEYE, TN. (2022). Role of social capital on entrepreneurial effects on economic growth in developing countries: An empirical analysis. *American Scientific Journal*, 3(15), 112–141.

GUEYE, TN. (2023). Impact of entrepreneurial dynamics on economic growth: Mediating role of social capital. *Economic Managerial Alternatives*, 5(1), 260–280.

Gulbrandsen, M., & Thune, T. (2017). The effects of non-academic work experience on external interaction and research performance. *The Journal of Technology Transfer*, 42(4), 795–813. DOI: 10.1007/s10961-017-9556-1

Guo, F., Restubog, S. L. D., Cui, L., Zou, B., & Choi, Y. (2019). What determines the entrepreneurial success of academics? Navigating multiple social identities in the hybrid career of academic entrepreneurs. *Journal of Vocational Behavior*, 112, 241–254. DOI: 10.1016/j.jvb.2019.03.003

Gupta, P., Chauhan, S., Paul, J., & Jaiswal, M. P. (2020). Social entrepreneurship research: A review and future research agenda. *Journal of Business Research*, 113, 209–229. DOI: 10.1016/j.jbusres.2020.03.032

Gupta, V., MacMillan, I. C., & Surie, G. (2004). Entrepreneurial leadership: Developing and measuring a cross-cultural construct. *Journal of Business Venturing*, 19(2), 241–260. DOI: 10.1016/S0883-9026(03)00040-5

Gurău, C., Dana, L.-P., & Lasch, F. (2012). Academic entrepreneurship in UK biotechnology firms: Alternative models and the associated performance. *Journal of Enterprising Communities: People and Places in the Global Economy*, 6(2), 154–168. DOI: 10.1108/17506201211228958

Guzman, J., & Stern, S. (2015). Where is Silicon Valley? *Science*, 347(80), 606–609. DOI: 10.1126/science.aaa0201 PMID: 25657229

Hair, J. F., Risher, J., Sarstedt, M., & Ringle, C. (2019). When to use and how to report the results of PLS-SEM. *European Business Review*, 31(1), 2–24. DOI: 10.1108/EBR-11-2018-0203

Hamari, J., Koivisto, J., & Sarsa, H. (2014). Does gamification work?-A literature review of empirical studies on gamification. In *2014, the 47th Hawaii International Conference on System Sciences* (pp. 3025-3034). IEEE.

Handel, M., & Levine, D. (2003). Editors' introduction: The effects of new work practices on workers. *Industrial Relations*, 43(1), 1–43. DOI: 10.1111/j.0019-8676.2004.00317.x

Hannah, D. P., & Eisenhardt, K. M. (2018). How firms navigate cooperation and competition in nascent ecosystems. *Strategic Management Journal*, 39(12), 3163–3192. DOI: 10.1002/smj.2750

Hansen, G. S., & Wernerfelt, B. (1989). Determinants of firm performance: The relative importance of economic and organizational factors. *Strategic Management Journal*, 1(5), 399–411. DOI: 10.1002/smj.4250100502

Hansen, L. P. (1982). Large sample properties of generalized method of moments estimators. *Econometrica*, 50(4), 1029–1054. DOI: 10.2307/1912775

Harraf, A., Ghura, H., Hamdan, A., & Li, X. (2020). Formal institutions and the development of entrepreneurial activity – the contingent role of corruption in emerging economies. *Journal of Entrepreneurship and Public Policy*, 10(1), 15–37. DOI: 10.1108/JEPP-06-2020-0033

Harris, P. A., Taylor, R., Thielke, R., Payne, J., Gonzalez, N., & Conde, J. G. (2009). Research electronic data capture (REDCap)—A metadata-driven methodology and workflow process for providing translational research informatics support. *Journal of Biomedical Informatics*, 42(2), 377–381. DOI: 10.1016/j.jbi.2008.08.010 PMID: 18929686

Hassen, T. (2022). A transformative state in the wake of covid-19: What is needed to enable innovation, entrepreneurship, and education in qatar? *Sustainability (Basel)*, 14(13), 7953. DOI: 10.3390/su14137953

Hayter, C. S. (2015). Public or private entrepreneurship? Revisiting motivations and definitions of success among academic entrepreneurs. *The Journal of Technology Transfer*, 40(6), 1003–1015. DOI: 10.1007/s10961-015-9426-7

Heartfield, J. (2007). Face of Fascism. Retrieved 10 17, 2019, from https://dome.mit.edu/handle/1721.3/19856

Heather, M. C. (2019). OECD SME and Entrepreneurship Outlook 2019.

He, D., Miao, P., & Qureshi, N. (2022). Can industrial diversification help strengthen regional economic resilience? *Frontiers in Environmental Science*, 10, 987396. Advance online publication. DOI: 10.3389/fenvs.2022.987396

Henderson, J. C., & Venkatraman, N. (1993). Strategic Alignment: Leveraging Information Technology for Transforming Organisations. *IBM Systems Journal*, 32(1), 4–16. DOI: 10.1147/sj.382.0472

Hendricks, K. B. (2018). The Balanced Scorecard: A Primer for Healthcare Organizations. *Journal of Healthcare Management*, 63(4), 256–263.

Henry, C., Hill, F., & Leitch, C. (2005). Entrepreneurship education and training: Can entrepreneurship be taught? Part I. *Education + Training*, 47(2), 98–111. DOI: 10.1108/00400910510586524

Herkenhoff, K., Phillips, G., & Cohen-Cole, E. (2016). The impact of consumer credit access on employment, earnings and entrepreneurship. National Bureau of Economic Research. https://www.nber.org/papers/w22846

Herron, L., & Robinson, R. B.Jr. (1993). A structural model of the effects of entrepreneurial characteristics on venture performance. *Journal of Business Venturing*, 8(3), 281–294. DOI: 10.1016/0883-9026(93)90032-Z

Hiebl, M. R. W. (2015). The Influence of Organizational Culture on Balanced Scorecard Usage: Evidence from the German Manufacturing Sector. *Journal of Management Control*, 26(4), 363–387.

Hindle, K. (2007). Teaching entrepreneurship at university: From the wrong building to the right philosophy. In Fayolle, A. (Ed.), *Handbook of research in entrepreneurship education* (pp. 104–126). Edward Elgar. DOI: 10.4337/9781847205377.00013

Hindu Nationalist's Historical Links to Nazism and Fascism. (n.d.). Retrieved 10 17, 2019, from https://www.ibtimes.com/hindu-nationalists-historical-links-nazism-fascism-214222

Holmes, P., & McGowan, F. (1998). Public service reform in the United Kingdom. Privatization, regulation and liberalization. *Science and Society*, 43(1), 93–109.

Hooi, L., & Chan, A. (2023). Does workplace digitalization matter in linking transformational leadership and innovative culture to employee engagement? *Journal of Organizational Change Management*, 36(2), 197–216. DOI: 10.1108/JOCM-06-2022-0184

Hopkins, T., & Feldman, H. (1989). Changing entrepreneurship education: Finding the right entrepreneur for the job. *Journal of Organizational Change Management*, 2(3), 28–40. DOI: 10.1108/09534818910145066

Hoskisson, R. E., Eden, L., Lau, C. M., & Wright, M. (2000). Strategy in emerging economies. *Academy of Management Journal*, 43(3), 249–267. DOI: 10.2307/1556394

Hossain, M. M. (2022, November 3). How far have we ensured judicial independence in Bangladesh? *The Daily Star*. https://www.thedailystar.net/supplements/50-years-our-constitution-original-idcals-vs-rcality/ncws/how-far-have-we-ensured-judicial-independence-bangladesh-3160231

House, R. J., Hanges, P. J., Javidan, M., Dorfman, P. W., & Gupta, V. (Eds.). (2004). *Culture, leadership, and organizations: The GLOBE study of 62 societies*. Sage publications.

Hsu, T. C., Chang, S. C., & Hung, Y. T. (2018). How to learn and how to teach computational thinking: Suggestions based on a review of the literature. *Computers & Education*, 126, 296–310. DOI: 10.1016/j.compedu.2018.07.004

Humam, M., & Hariadi, M. F. (2022). The Effect Of Social Capital Of Entrepreneurs In Entrepreneurial Process, *Journal of Innovation, Business and Entrepreneurship*.

Hu, N., Wu, J., & Gu, J. (2017). Cultural intelligence and employees' creative performance: The moderating role of team conflict in interorganizational teams. *Journal of Management & Organization*, 25(1), 96–116. DOI: 10.1017/jmo.2016.64

Hunter, E. M., Perry, S. J., & Currall, S. C. (2011). Inside multi-disciplinary science and engineering research centers: The impact of organizational climate on invention disclosures and patents. *Research Policy*, 40(9), 1226–1239. DOI: 10.1016/j.respol.2011.05.024

Huybens, E., & Smith, B. D. (1999). Inflation, financial markets and long-run real activity. *Journal of Monetary Economics*, 43(2), 283–315. DOI: 10.1016/S0304-3932(98)00060-9

Huyghe, A., & Knockaert, M. (2015). The influence of organizational culture and climate on entrepreneurial intentions among research scientists. *The Journal of Technology Transfer*, 40(1), 138–160. DOI: 10.1007/s10961-014-9333-3

Hwang, D.-W., Lee, Y.-W., & Kim, G. (2005). Large submarine groundwater discharge and benthic eutrophication in Bangdu Bay on volcanic Jeju Island, Korea. *Limnology and Oceanography*, 50(5), 1393–1403. DOI: 10.4319/lo.2005.50.5.1393

Imperatori, B., & Imperatori, B. (2017). Engagement and disengagement at work: what's new. *Engagement and Disengagement at Work: Drivers and Organizational Practices to Sustain Employee Passion and Performance*, 5-18.

Implementing RSS evil ideology - The Frontier Post. (2019). Retrieved 9 July 2020, from https://thefrontierpost.com/implementing-rss-evil-ideology/

Increasing Radicalisation in Bangladesh and its Impact on India's National Security – CENJOWS. (2024, June 24). https://cenjows.in/increasing-radicalisation-in-bangladesh-and-its-impact-on-indias-national-security/

India's maritime strategy: balancing regional ambitions and China. (n.d.). Routledge & CRC Press. https://www.routledge.com/Indias-Maritime-Strategy-Balancing-Regional-Ambitions-and-China/Upadhyaya/p/book/9781032089720?srsltid=AfmBOopx006emFuFa53VOrGItuff4pyU-69U-BhcxDUjDqDRI4LfRX5U

Indian society is the very center of Fascism: Sunny M. Kapicadu. (n.d.). Retrieved 10 17, 2019, fromhttp://roundtableindia.co.in/index.php?option=com_content&view=article&id=8731:if-you-say-it-s-Modi-who-brought-fascism-to-india-i-would-say-that-s-a-lie&catid=119&Itemid=132

Insights, C. B. (2020). *The Global Unicorn Club* [WWW Document]. URL https://www. cbinsights.com/research-unicorn-companies (accessed 6.4.20).

Iqbal, M., Warraich, I. A., & Haq, S. U. (2023). Impact of employee resilience and job engagement on project success: Mediating role of innovative work behavior. *Research Journal for Societal Issues*, 5(3), 234–257. DOI: 10.56976/rjsi.v5i3.144

Irani, Z. (2002). Information Systems Evaluation: Navigating through the problem domain. *Information & Management*, 40(1), 11–24. DOI: 10.1016/S0378-7206(01)00128-8

IRPJ = Intergovernmental Research and Policy Journal. (2022, March 28). *BANGLADESH LIBERATION WAR OF 1971: DECISIVE ROLE OF INDIA IN MEDIATION AND CONFLICT RESOLUTION; AND TRANSITIONAL JUSTICE IN BANGLADESH - IRPJ = Intergovernmental Research and Policy Journal*. https://irpj.euclid.int/articles/bangladesh-liberation-war-of-1971-decisive-role-of-india-in-mediation-and-conflict-resolution-and-transitional-justice-in-bangladesh/

Isenberg, D. (2011). *The Entrepreneurship Ecosystem Strategy as a New Paradigm for Economic Policy: Principles for Cultivating Entrepreneurship*. The Babson Entrepreneurship Ecosystem Project.

Islam, A. (2024, June 6). India's influence in Bangladesh: Support or meddling? *dw.com*. https://www.dw.com/en/indias-influence-in-bangladesh-support-or-meddling/a-68432609

Islam, S. (2024, July 16). Has Bangladesh lost its footing in the China-India Balancing Act? *The Diplomat*. https://thediplomat.com/2024/07/has-bangladesh-lost-its-footing-in-the-china-india-balancing-act/

Issue-I, T. A. (2024, May 15). *BIMSTEC and regional prosperity*. The Financial Express. https://thefinancialexpress.com.bd/views/opinions/bimstec-and-regional-prosperity

Izzatuddin, S., & Kusumastuti, R. (2021). Relationship between employee engagement and innovative behavior: Empirical study of pt bank bri syariah tbk in dki jakarta, west java, and banten. *Jurnal Administrasi Bisnis*, 10(2), 87–98. DOI: 10.14710/jab.v0i0.36684

Jacobides, M. G., Cennamo, C., & Gawer, A. (2018). Towards a theory of ecosystems. *Strategic Management Journal*, 39(8), 2255–2276. DOI: 10.1002/smj.2904

Jal, M. (n.d.). Rethinking Secularism in India in the Age of Triumphant Fascism. Critique, 43(3–4), 523–524. *Retrieved*, 10, 17.

Jay, J. (2012). Navigating paradox as a mechanism of change and innovation in hybrid organizations. *Academy of Management Journal*, 56(1), 137–168. DOI: 10.5465/amj.2010.0772

Jazeera, A. (2024, January 8). Sheikh Hasina: Once Bangladesh's democracy icon, now its 'authoritarian' PM. *Al Jazeera*. https://www.aljazeera.com/news/2024/1/8/sheikh-hasina-once-bangladeshs-democracy-icon-now-its-authoritarian-pm

Jcookson. (2024, January 18). *What Bangladesh's widely boycotted election reveals about its future*. Atlantic Council. https://www.atlanticcouncil.org/blogs/new-atlanticist/what-bangladeshs-widely-boycotted-election-reveals-about-its-future/

Jegourel, Y., & Chalmin, P. (2017). The Dynamics of the Price of Raw Materials and Industrial Strategies in African Producer Countries: What are the Challenges? International Development Policy| International Journal of Development Policy, 8.1.

Jelinčić, D. A., & Šveb, M. (2021). Financial sustainability of cultural heritage: A review of crowdfunding in Europe. *Journal of Risk and Financial Management*, 14(3), 101. DOI: 10.3390/jrfm14030101

Jenik, I., Lyman, T., & Nava, A. (2017a). Crowdfunding and financial inclusion. *CGAP (Consultative Group to Assist the Poor) Working Paper, 41.*

Jenik, I., Lyman, T., & Nava, A. (2017b). Crowdfunding and financial inclusion. *CGAP (Consultative Group to Assist the Poor) Working Paper, 41.*

Jennings, P. D., Greenwood, R., Lounsbury, M. D., & Suddaby, R. (2013). Institutions, entrepreneurs, and communities: A special issue on entrepreneurship. *Journal of Business Venturing*, 28(1), 1–9. DOI: 10.1016/j.jbusvent.2012.07.001

Jones, P., Huxtable-Thomas, L., Hannon, P., Hamidon, S., & Mohd Tawil, N. (2021). Introduction to entrepreneurial activity in Malaysia: A country-level perspective. In *Entrepreneurial Activity in Malaysia* (pp. 1–10). Palgrave Macmillan. DOI: 10.1007/978-3-030-77753-1_1

Jurvetson, S. (2000). Changing everything: the internet revolution and Silicon Valley. In Lee, C. M., Miller, W. F., Hancock, M. G., & Rowen, H. S. (Eds.), *The Silicon Valley Edge: a habitat for innovation and entrepreneurship* (pp. 124–149). Stanford University Press. DOI: 10.1515/9781503619180-012

Kafai, Y. B., Burke, Q., Chen, J., Fields, D., Nelson, B., & Robinson, K. (2014). Connecting the dots: Developing STEAM literacies through creative collaboration. *Teachers College Record*, 116(6), n6.

Kahoot! (2020). *Kahoot!*https://kahoot.com/

Kalliath, T., & Brough, P. (2008). Work–life balance: A review of the meaning of the balance construct. *Journal of Management & Organization*, 14(3), 323–327. DOI: 10.5172/jmo.837.14.3.323

Kalogiannakis, M., & Papadakis, S. (Eds.). (2020). *Handbook of research on tools for teaching computational thinking in P-12 education*. IGI Global. DOI: 10.4018/978-1-7998-4576-8

Kaminski, J., Hopp, C., & Tykvova, T. (2019). New technology assessment in entrepreneurial financing–Does crowdfunding predict venture capital investments? *Technological Forecasting and Social Change*, 139, 287–302. DOI: 10.1016/j.techfore.2018.11.015

Kanfer, A., Schechter, A., Veeraraghavan, K., & Zou, J. (2019). Inclusive design in the creation of computer science education tools. In *Proceedings of the 2019 CHI Conference on Human Factors in Computing Systems* (pp. 1-13).

Kanunjna, A. D. (2024, January 21). Bangladesh seeks careful balance between China and India. *dw.com*. https://www.dw.com/en/bangladesh-seeks-careful-balance-between-china-and-india/a-68023417

Kaplan, R. S., & Norton, D. P. (1992). Using the Balanced Scorecard as a Strategic Management System. *Harvard Business Review*, 74(1), 75–85.

Kaplan, R. S., & Norton, D. P. (1993). *Putting the Balanced Scorecard to Work. Harvard Business Review*. September-October.

Kaplan, R. S., & Norton, D. P. (1996). *The Balanced Scorecard: Translating Strategies into Action*. Harvard Business School Press.

Kaplan, R. S., & Norton, D. P. (2000). *The Strategy-Focused Organisation*. Harvard Business School Press.

Kaplan, R. S., & Norton, D. P. (2001). *The Strategy Focused Organisations: How Balanced Scorecard Companies Thrive in the New Business Environment*. Harvard University Press.

Kaplan, R. S., & Norton, D. P. (2004). *Strategy Maps: Converting Intangible Assets into Tangible Outcomes*. Harvard Business School Press.

Kaplan, R. S., & Norton, D. P. (2006). *Alignment: Using the Balanced Scorecard to Create Corporate Synergies*. Harvard Business School Press.

Kapoor, R. (2018). Ecosystems: Broadening the locus of value creation. *Journal of Organization Design*, 7(12), 1–16. DOI: 10.1186/s41469-018-0035-4

Karl, T. L. (1998). The Paradox of Plenty: Oil booms and petro -states. Journal of energy literature, 4, 65–65.

Kassean, H., Vanevenhoven, J., Liguori, E., & Winkel, D. E. (2015). Entrepreneurship education: A need for reflection, real-world experience and action. *International Journal of Entrepreneurial Behaviour & Research*, 21(5), 690–708. DOI: 10.1108/IJEBR-07-2014-0123

Kazanjian, R. K. (1988). Relation of dominant problems to stages of growth in technology-based new ventures. *Academy of Management Journal*, 31(2), 257–279. DOI: 10.2307/256548

Kearns, G. S., & Lederer, A. L. (2003). A Resource-Based View of Strategic IT Alignment: How knowledge sharing creates competitive advantage. *Decision Sciences*, 34(1), 1–29. DOI: 10.1111/1540-5915.02289

Keen, P. G. W. (1991). *Shaping the Future*. Harvard Business School Press.

Kefi, H., & Kalika, M. (2005). Survey of Strategic Alignment Impacts on Organisational Performance in International European Companies. *In Proceedings HICSS '05,38th Annual Hawaii International Conference.*

Kennerley, M., & Neely, A. (2003). Measuring performance in a changing business environment. *International Journal of Operations & Production Management*, 23(2), 213–229. DOI: 10.1108/01443570310458465

Kerr, W., & Nanda, R. (2009). *Financing constraints and entrepreneurship*. National Bureau of Economic Research. DOI: 10.3386/w15498

Khasru, S. M. (2024, August 18). *Bangladesh's student movement and Hasina's exit: the hard truth and India's hour of reckoning*. The Hindu. https://www.thehindu.com/news/international/bangladeshs-student-movement-and-hasinas-exit-the-hard-truth-and-indias-hour-of-reckoning/article68540639.ece

Killian, S., & O'Regan, P. (2019). Taxation and social enterprise: Constraint or incentive for the common good. *Journal of Social Entrepreneurship*, 10(1), 1–18. DOI: 10.1080/19420676.2018.1517103

Kim, D.-H., Lin, S.-C., & Suen, Y.-B. (2010). Dynamic effects of trade openness on financial development. *Economic Modelling*, 27(1), 254–261. DOI: 10.1016/j.econmod.2009.09.005

Kim, P. H., Wennberg, K., & Croidieu, G. (2016). Untapped riches of meso-level applications in multi-level entrepreneurship mechanisms. *The Academy of Management Perspectives*, 30(3), 273–291. DOI: 10.5465/amp.2015.0137

Kim, S., Arthurs, J., Sahaym, A., & Cullen, J. (2013). Search behavior of the diversified firm: The impact of fit on innovation. *Strategic Management Journal*, 34(8), 999–1009. DOI: 10.1002/smj.2038

Klopfer, E., Squire, K., & Jenkins, H. (2009). Environmental Detectives—The development of an augmented reality platform for environmental simulations. *Educational Technology Research and Development*, 57(6), 1–22.

Kofanov, O., & Zozulov, O. (2018). Successful development of startups as a global trend of innovative socio-economic transformations. *International and Multidisciplinary Journal of Social Sciences*, 7(2), 191–217. DOI: 10.17583/rimcis.2018.3576

Kohn, H. (n.d.). Nationalism. Encyclopedia Britannica. Retrieved 1 13, 2020, from https://www.britannica.com/topic/nationalism

Kolvereid, L. (1996). Prediction of employment status choice intentions. *Entrepreneurship Theory and Practice*, 21(1), 47–58. DOI: 10.1177/104225879602100104

Konsynski, B. R., & McFarlan, W. F. (1990). Information Partnerships: Shared Data, Shared Scale. *Harvard Business Review*, 68(5), 114–120. PMID: 10107083

Kopalle, P. K., Gangwar, M., Kaplan, A., Ramachandran, D., Reinartz, W., & Rindfleisch, A. (2022). Examining artificial intelligence (AI) technologies in marketing via a global lens: Current trends and future research opportunities. *International Journal of Research in Marketing*, 39(2), 522–540. DOI: 10.1016/j.ijresmar.2021.11.002

Korunka, C., Frank, H., Lueger, M., & Mugler, J. (2003). The entrepreneurial personality in the context of resources, environment, and the startup process—A configurational approach. *Entrepreneurship Theory and Practice*, 28(1), 23–42. DOI: 10.1111/1540-8520.00030

Kraft, K., & Lang, J. (2012). Profit sharing and training*. *Oxford Bulletin of Economics and Statistics*, 75(6), 940–961. DOI: 10.1111/j.1468-0084.2012.00714.x

Kudrati, M. (2019, December 16). Viral Post Claiming 96% Of Rape Offenders Are Muslims Is False. Retrieved July 16, 2020, from https://www.boomlive.in/fake-news/viral-post-claiming-96-of-rape-offenders-are-muslims-is-false-6293

Kukurba, M., Waszkiewicz, A. E., Salwin, M., & Kraslawski, A. (2021). Co-created values in crowdfunding for sustainable development of enterprises. *Sustainability (Basel)*, 13(16), 8767. DOI: 10.3390/su13168767

Kumar, H., & Raghavendran, S. (2015). Gamification, the finer art: Fostering creativity and employee engagement. *The Journal of Business Strategy*, 36(6), 3–12. DOI: 10.1108/JBS-10-2014-0119

Kuratko, D. F. (2016). Corporate entrepreneurship. *The Routledge Companion to the Makers of Modern Entrepreneurship*, 154.

Kuratko, D. F., Fisher, G., Bloodgood, J. M., & Hornsby, J. S. (2017). The paradox of new venture legitimation within an entrepreneurial ecosystem. *Small Business Economics*, 49(1), 119–140. DOI: 10.1007/s11187-017-9870-x

Lannegrand-Willems, L., & Bosma, H. A. (2006). Identity development-in-context: The school as an important context for identity development. *Identity*, 6(1), 85–113. DOI: 10.1207/s1532706xid0601_6

Lederer, A., & Salmela, H. (1996). Towrds a theory of strategic information systems planning. *The Journal of Strategic Information Systems*, 4(14), 1–50.

Lee, L., Kodama, C., Lee, J., Miyoda, Y., & Shiga, P. H. (2024, April 17). *Aligning values and interests: Japanese and Australian democracy support in the Pacific and Southeast Asia*. United States Studies Centre. https://www.ussc.edu.au/japanese-and-australian-democracy-support-in-the-pacific-and-southeast-asia

Lehner, O. M., & Harrer, T. (2019). Crowdfunding revisited: A neo-institutional field-perspective. *Venture Capital*, 21(1), 75–96. DOI: 10.1080/13691066.2019.1560884

Lerner, J., Schoar, A., Sokolinski, S., & Wilson, K. (2018). The globalization of angel investments: Evidence across countries. *Journal of Financial Economics*, 127(1), 1–20. .jfineco.2017. 05. 012DOI: <ALIGNMENT.qj></ALIGNMENT>10. 1016/j

Lester, J. (2015). Cultures of work–life balance in higher education: A case of fragmentation. *Journal of Diversity in Higher Education*, 8(3), 139–156. DOI: 10.1037/a0039377

Letchmiah, L., & Thomas, A. (2017). Retention of high-potential employees in a development finance company. *SA Journal of Human Resource Management*, 1(2). Advance online publication. DOI: 10.4102/sajhrm.v15i0.924

Levie, J., & Autio, E. (2008). A theoretical grounding and test of the GEM model. *Small Business Economics*, 2008(31), 235–263. DOI: 10.1007/s11187-008-9136-8

Levy- Tadjine, T. (2006). Immigrant entrepreneurship and its support in France. *Life & Economic Sciences*, 4, 31–45.

Liguori, E., Winkler, C., Vanevenhoven, J., Winkel, D., & James, M. (2020). Entrepreneurship as a career choice: Intentions, attitudes, and outcome expectations. *Journal of Small Business and Entrepreneurship*, 32(4), 311–331. DOI: 10.1080/08276331.2019.1600857

Liñán, F., & Fayolle, A. (2015). A systematic literature review on entrepreneurial intentions: Citation, thematic analyses, and research agenda. *The International Entrepreneurship and Management Journal*, 11(4), 907–933. DOI: 10.1007/s11365-015-0356-5

Lin, X. (2010). The diaspora solution to innovation capacity development: Immigrant entrepreneurs in the contemporary world. *Thunderbird International Business Review*, 52(2), 123–136. DOI: 10.1002/tie.20319

Liton, S. (2024, August 18). Making of a despot: How Hasina became all powerful. *The Business Standard*. https://www.tbsnews.net/features/panorama/making-despot-how-hasina-became-all-powerful-919086

Lockwood, J., & Mooney, A. (2017). Computational thinking in education: Where does it fit? A systematic literary review. *arXiv preprint arXiv:1703.07659.*

Long, R., & Fang, T. (2012). Do employees profit from profit sharing? evidence from canadian panel data. *Industrial & Labor Relations Review*, 65(4), 899–927. DOI: 10.1177/001979391206500406

Looi, K. H., & Maritz, A. (2021). Government institutions, entrepreneurship education and entrepreneurship education programmes in Malaysia. *Education + Training*, 63(2), 271–291. DOI: 10.1108/ET-07-2020-0217

Lopes Valadares, J., Emmendoerfer, L., Christina Resende, T., Morais, A., & Cerqueira, M. (2023). Leis Delegadas E Empreendedorismo Publico no Brasil: Analise À Luz DO Modelo DE Skowronck . Revista Jurídica (0103-3506), 2(74).

López-Núñez, M. I., Rubio-Valdehita, S., Aparicio-García, M. E., & Díaz-Ramiro, E. M. (2020). Are entrepreneurs born or made? The influence of personality. *Personality and Individual Differences*, 154, 109699. DOI: 10.1016/j.paid.2019.109699

Lubango, L. M., & Pouris, A. (2007). Industry work experience and inventive capacity of South African academic researchers. *Technovation*, 27(12), 788–796. DOI: 10.1016/j.technovation.2007.05.013

Lüdeke-Freund, F. (2020). Sustainable entrepreneurship, innovation, and business models: Integrative framework and propositions for future research. *Business Strategy and the Environment*, 29(2), 665–681. DOI: 10.1002/bse.2396

Lueg, R., & Radlach, R. (2016). The Balanced Scorecard: A review of its application in Germany. *European Management Journal*, 34(6), 573–586.

Lueg, R., & Vu, L. (2015). Success factors in balanced scorecard implementations – A literature review. *Management Review*, 26(4), 306–327.

Luftman, J. N. (2000). Assessing business IT-alignment maturity. *Communications of the Association for Information Systems*, 4(14).

Luftman, J. N., Lewis, P. R., & Oldach, S. H. (1993). Transforming the Enterprise: The Alignment of Business and Information Technology Strategies. *IBM Systems Journal*, 32(1), 198–221. DOI: 10.1147/sj.321.0198

Luftman, J., & Brier, T. (1999). Achieving and Sustaining Business–IT Alignment. *California Management Review*, 42(1), 109–122. DOI: 10.2307/41166021

Luftman, J., Kempaiah, R., & Nash, E. (2005). Key Issues for IT Executives 2005. *MIS Quarterly Executive*, 5(2), 81–101.

Mack, E., & Mayer, H. (2016). The evolutionary dynamics of entrepreneurial ecosystems. *Urban Studies (Edinburgh, Scotland)*, 53(10), 2118–2133. DOI: 10.1177/0042098015586547

Madzikanda, B., Li, C., & Dabuo, F. T. (2021). Barriers to development of entrepreneurial ecosystems and economic performance in Southern Africa. *African Journal of Science, Technology, Innovation and Development*, •••, 1–11.

Mahmud, F. (2024, February 7). 'India Out' campaigns simmer in Bangladesh amid election fallout. *Al Jazeera*. https://www.aljazeera.com/economy/2024/2/7/india-out-campaigns-simmer-in-bangladesh-amid-election-fallout

Maier, J. L., Rainer, R. K.Jr, & Snyder, C. A. (1997). Environmental scanning for information technology: An empirical investigation. *Journal of Management Information Systems*, 14(2), 177–201. DOI: 10.1080/07421222.1997.11518170

Maisel, L. S. (1992). Performance measurement: The balanced scorecard approach. *Journal of Cost Management*, (Summer), 47–52.

Mäkinen, E., & Esko, T. (2022). Nascent academic entrepreneurs and identity work at the boundaries of professional domains. *International Journal of Entrepreneurship and Innovation*, 24(3), 167–177. DOI: 10.1177/14657503211063896

Malina, M. A., & Selto, F. H. (2001). Communicating and controlling strategy: An empirical study of the effectiveness of the balanced scorecard. *Journal of Management Accounting Research*, 13(1), 47–73. DOI: 10.2308/jmar.2001.13.1.47

Maltritz, D., & Wüste, S. (2015). Determinants of budget deficits in Europe: The role and relations of fiscal rules, fiscal councils, creative accounting and the Euro. *Economic Modelling*, 48, 222–236. DOI: 10.1016/j.econmod.2014.12.001

Maltz, A. C., Shenhar, A. J., & Reilley, R. R. (2003). Beyond the balanced Scorecard: Refining the search for organisational success measures. *Long Range Planning*, 36(2), 187–204. DOI: 10.1016/S0024-6301(02)00165-6

Mannila, L., Dagiene, V., Demo, B., Grgurina, N., Mirolo, C., Rolandsson, L., & Settle, A. (2014, June). Computational thinking in K-9 education. In *Proceedings of the working group reports of the 2014 on innovation & technology in computer science education conference* (pp. 1-29). DOI: 10.1145/2713609.2713610

Marcolin, L., Miroudot, S., & Squicciarini, M. (2016). Routine jobs, employment and technological innovation in global value chains.

Marcotte, C. (2014). Entrepreneurship and innovation in emerging economies: Conceptual, methodological and contextual issues. *International Journal of Entrepreneurial Behaviour & Research*, 20(1), 42–65. DOI: 10.1108/IJEBR-09-2012-0089

Marques, V., & Berry, G. (2021). Enhancing work-life balance using a resilience framework. [Among Hybrid Entrepreneurs: A Comprehensive Review**]. *Business and Society Review*, 126(3), 263–281. DOI: 10.1111/basr.12237

Mars, M. M., & Rios-Aguilar, C. (2010). Academic entrepreneurship (re)defined: Significance and implications for the scholarship of higher education. *Higher Education*, 59(4), 441–460. DOI: 10.1007/s10734-009-9258-1

Martin, B. C., McNally, J. J., & Kay, M. J. (2013). Examining the formation of human capital in entrepreneurship: A meta-analysis of entrepreneurship education outcomcs. *Journal of Business Venturing*, 28(2), 211 224. DOI: 10.1016/j.jbusvent.2012.03.002

Marullo, C., Casprini, E., Di Minin, A., & Piccaluga, A. (2018). 'Ready for Takeoff': How Open Innovation influences startup success. *Creativity and Innovation Management*, 27(4), 476–488. DOI: 10.1111/caim.12272

Mason, C., & Brown, R. (2014). "Entrepreneurial Ecosystems and Growth Oriented Entrepreneurship." Background paper prepared for the workshop organized by the OECD LEED Program and the Dutch Ministry of Economic Affairs on Entrepreneurial Ecosystems and Growth Oriented Entrepreneurship, The Hague, Netherlands, 7th November 2013. Final Version: January 2014, 38 p. Available on: https://www.oecd.org/cfe/leed/entrepreneurial-ecosystems.pdf

Mason, C., & Brown, R. (2014). Entrepreneurial ecosystems and growth-oriented entrepreneurship. *Final Report to OECD*, Paris, 30(1), 77–102.

Mason, C. M., & Harrison, R. T. (2006). After the exit: Acquisitions, entrepreneurial recycling and regional economic development. *Regional Studies*, 40(1), 55–73. DOI: 10.1080/00343400500450059

Mason, C., & Brown, R. (2013). Creating good public policy to support high growth firms. *Small Business Economics*, 40(2), 211–225. DOI: 10.1007/s11187-011-9369-9

Mas-Verdú, F., Ribeiro-Soriano, D., & Roig-Tierno, N. (2015). Firm survival: The role of incubators and business characteristics. *Journal of Business Research*, 68(4), 793–796. DOI: 10.1016/j.jbusres.2014.11.030

Mata, F. J., Fuerst, W. L., & Barney, J. B. (1985). Information technology and sustained competitive advantage: A resource-based-analysis. *MIS Quartely*, (December), 487–504.

Matlay, H. (2010). Introduction: Contemporary perspectives on entrepreneurship education and training. *Journal of Small Business and Enterprise Development*, 17(4). Advance online publication. DOI: 10.1108/jsbed.2010.27117daa.001

Matt, M., & Schaeffer, V. (2012), The cooperative strategy of technology transfer offices: A longitudinal study. in Technology Transfer in a Global Economy, D. Audretsch, E. Lehmann, A., Link, A. Starnecker (Eds), special issue of the *International Handbook Series on Entrepreneurship* edited by Z. Acs and D. Audretsch, 55-72.

Matt, M., & Schaeffer, V. (2018). Building entrepreneurial ecosystems conducive to student entrepreneurship: New challenges for universities. *Journal of Innovation Economics Management*, 1(25), 9–32. DOI: 10.3917/jie.025.0009

Mayell, H. (2020, June 04). India's "Untouchables" Face Violence, Discrimination. Retrieved July 22, 2020, from https://www.nationalgeographic.com/news/2003/6/indias-untouchables-face-violence-discrimination/

McCaffrey, M. (2014). On the theory of entrepreneurial incentives and alertness. *Entrepreneurship Theory and Practice*, 38(4), 891–911. DOI: 10.1111/etap.12013

McDermott, G., Mudambi, R., & Parente, R. (2013). Strategic modularity and the architecture of multinational firm. *Global Strategy Journal*, 3(1), 1–7. DOI: 10.1111/j.2042-5805.2012.01051.x

McGrath, H., O'Toole, T., & Canning, L. (2019). Coopetition: A fundamental feature of entrepreneurial firms' collaborative dynamics. *Journal of Business and Industrial Marketing*, 34(7), 1555–1569. DOI: 10.1108/JBIM-10-2018-0287

Meijerink, J., & Keegan, A. (2019). Conceptualizing human resource management in the gig economy: Toward a platform ecosystem perspective. *Journal of Managerial Psychology*, 34(4), 214–232. DOI: 10.1108/JMP-07-2018-0277

Meliou, E., & Özbilgin, M. (2023). How is the illusio of gender equality in entrepreneurship sustained? a bourdieusian perspective. *Journal of Management Studies*, 61(4), 1536–1561. DOI: 10.1111/joms.12930

Memon, A. B., Meyer, K., & Tunio, M. N. (2022). Toward collaborative networking among innovation laboratories: A conceptual framework. *International Journal of Innovation Science*, 14(2), 282–301. DOI: 10.1108/IJIS-04-2021-0069

Meoli, A., Fini, R., Sobrero, M., & Wiklund, J. (2020). How entrepreneurial intentions influence entrepreneurial career choices: The moderating influence of social context. *Journal of Business Venturing*, 35(3), 105–982. DOI: 10.1016/j.jbusvent.2019.105982

Meoli, M., Rossi, A., & Vismara, S. (2022). Financial literacy and security-based crowdfunding. *Corporate Governance*, 30(1), 27–54. DOI: 10.1111/corg.12355

Microsoft. (n.d.). *Microsoft MakeCode*. https://www.microsoft.com/en-us/makecode

Miniaoui, H., & Schilirò, D. (2017). Innovation and entrepreneurship for the diversification and growth of the gulf cooperation council economies. *Business and Management Studies*, 1(1), 69. DOI: 10.11114/bms.v3i3.2594

Miralles, F., Giones, F., & Gozun, B. (2017). Does direct experience matter? Examining the consequences of current entrepreneurial behavior on entrepreneurial intention. *The International Entrepreneurship and Management Journal*, 13(3), 881–903. DOI: 10.1007/s11365-016-0430-7

Miscevic, N. (n.d.). Nationalism (Stanford Encyclopedia of Philosophy). Stanford University. Retrieved 1 12, 2020, from https://plato.stanford.edu/entries/nationalism/

Mishkin, F. S. (2007). Inflation dynamics. *International Finance*, 10(3), 317–334. DOI: 10.1111/j.1468-2362.2007.00205.x

Mishkin, F. S., & Schmidt-Hebbel, K. (2007). *Does inflation targeting make a difference?* National Bureau of Economic Research Cambridge. DOI: 10.3386/w12876

Mithas, S., Ramasubbu, N., & Sambamurthy, V. (2012). How information management capability influences firm performance. *Management Information Systems Quarterly*, 36(1), 25–49.

Mitra, D. (2024, August 6). Bangladesh Crisis: India's Silence so far, Implications and View from Dhaka. *The Wire*. https://m.thewire.in/article/south/bangladesh-crisis-indias-silence-so-far-implications-and-view-from-dhaka

Mizrahi, O. (2018). *The Gig Is Up: Thrive in the Gig Economy, Where Old Jobs Are Obsolete and Freelancing Is the Future*. Greenleaf Book Group.

Mohamad, N., Lim, H.-E., Yusof, N., & Soon, J.-J. (2015). Estimating the effect of entrepreneur education on graduates' intention to be entrepreneurs. *Education + Training*, 57(8/9), 874–890. DOI: 10.1108/ET-03-2014-0030

Mohammadi Khyareh, M., & Rostami, N. (2021). The impact of macroeconomic variables on entrepreneurship: Generalized Method of Moments (GMM). *Macroeconomics Research Letter*, 15(30), 34–61.

Mohammed Mian Soomro. (2020). *PR No. 31 Kashmir Solidarity Day Message By Patron-in-Chief Youth Forum for Kashmir/Federal Minister/Chairman Privatization: Islamabad.* Retrieved from http://pid.gov.pk/site/press_detail/12947

Mohammed, F. (2022). Impact of entrepreneurship development on employment generation in sabongari local government, kaduna state. *International Journal of Entrepreneurship and Project Management*, 7(1), 14–28. DOI: 10.47604/ijepm.1567

Mohanraj, G., Krishna, K. S., Lakshmi, B. S., Vijayalakshmi, A., Pramila, P. V., & Boopathi, S. (2024). Optimizing Trust and Security in Healthcare 4.0: Human Factors in Lightweight Secured IoMT Ecosystems. In *Lightweight Digital Trust Architectures in the Internet of Medical Things (IoMT)* (pp. 52–72). IGI Global. DOI: 10.4018/979-8-3693-2109-6.ch004

Mohanty, A., Venkateswaran, N., Ranjit, P., Tripathi, M. A., & Boopathi, S. (2023). Innovative Strategy for Profitable Automobile Industries: Working Capital Management. In *Handbook of Research on Designing Sustainable Supply Chains to Achieve a Circular Economy* (pp. 412–428). IGI Global.

Mohobbot, A. (2004). The Balanced Scorecard (BSC): A critical analysis. *Journal of humanities and social*, 18, 219-232.

Mommsen, H. (2001). National Socialism and Fascism. Retrieved 10 17, 2019, from https://sciencedirect.com/science/article/pii/b008043076702698x

Monecke, A., & Bredereck, R. (2021). The Balanced Scorecard and sustainability: Aligning performance measures with environmental goals. *Business Strategy and the Environment*, 30(5), 2425–2440.

Montecinos, C., Walker, H., & Maldonado, F. (2015). School administrators and university practicum supervisors as boundary brokers for initial teacher education in Chile. *Teaching and Teacher Education*, 49(1), 1–10. DOI: 10.1016/j.tate.2015.02.011

Mooraj, S., Oyon, D., & Hostettler, D. (1999). The Balanced Scorecard: A necessary good or an unnecessary evil. *European Management Journal*, 17(5), 481–491. DOI: 10.1016/S0263-2373(99)00034-1

Moraes, G. H. S. M., Fischer, B. B., Campos, M. L., & Schaeffer, P. R. (2020). University ecosystems and the commitment of faculty members to support entrepreneurial activity. *BAR - Brazilian Administration Review*, 17(2), 1–26. DOI: 10.1590/1807-7692bar2020190013

Mouazen, A., & Hernández-Lara, A. (2023). Entrepreneurial ecosystem, gig economy practices and women's entrepreneurship: The case of lebanon. *International Journal of Gender and Entrepreneurship*, 15(3), 249–274. DOI: 10.1108/IJGE-07-2022-0116

Moutinho, P., Fontes, M., & Godinho, M. (2007). Do individual factors matter? A survey of scientists' patenting in Portuguese public research organisations. *Scientometrics*, 70(2), 355–377. DOI: 10.1007/s11192-007-0207-4

Mubaraki, H., & Busler, M. (2014). The importance of innovation in Europe: Swedish case study. *International Journal of Innovation and Knowledge Management in Middle East and North Africa*, 3(1), 51–63. DOI: 10.47556/J.IJIKMMENA.3.1.2014.3

Mueller, S. (2011). Increasing entrepreneurial intention: Effective entrepreneurship course characteristics. *International Journal of Entrepreneurship and Small Business*, 13(1), 55–74. DOI: 10.1504/IJESB.2011.040416

Mueller, S., & Thomas, A. (2001). Culture and entrepreneurial potential. *Journal of Business Venturing*, 16(1), 51–75. DOI: 10.1016/S0883-9026(99)00039-7

Mumtaz, A. M., Ting, H., Ramayah, T., Chuah, F., & Cheah, J. H. (2017). Editorial, 'A review of the methodological misconceptions and guidelines related to the application of structural equation modelling: A Malaysian scenario'. *Journal of Applied Structural Equation Modeling*, 1(1), 1–13.

Munawar, M. (2019, May 30). *China's tryst with Hindutva's geopolitical agenda*. Daily Times. https://dailytimes.com.pk/403818/chinas-tryst-with-hindutvas-geopolitical-agenda/

Munir, K., & Javed, Z. (2018). Export composition and economic growth: Evidence from south asian countries. *South Asian Journal of Business Studies*, 7(2), 225–240. DOI: 10.1108/SAJBS-10-2017-0117

Munson, H. (2019, November 26). Sikh fundamentalism. Retrieved July 16, 2020, from https://www.britannica.com/topic/fundamentalism/Sikh-fundamentalism

Mustafa, M. J., Hernandez, E., Mahon, C., & Chee, L. K. (2016). Entrepreneurial intentions of university students in an emerging economy: The influence of university support and proactive personality on students' entrepreneurial intention. *Journal of Entrepreneurship in Emerging Economies*, 8(2), 162–179. DOI: 10.1108/JEEE-10-2015-0058

Mwatsika, C. (2016). Measuring the number of jobs created through entrepreneurship training. *International Journal of Academic Research in Business & Social Sciences*, 6(7). Advance online publication. DOI: 10.6007/IJARBSS/v6-i7/2243

N., S. P., Goritiyal, C., Ramana, N. V., Matcha, A., Sukania, P., & Boopathi, S. (2024). Economic Growth Study and Inferences From Developments in E-Mobility. In *Advances in Mechatronics and Mechanical Engineering* (pp. 178–199). IGI Global. DOI: 10.4018/979-8-3693-5247-2.ch010

Nair, A., & Tschang, F. T. (2022). Integrating digital transformation into the Balanced Scorecard framework. *Information & Management*, 59(2), 103–115.

Nambisan, S., & Baron, R. A. (2021). On the costs of digital entrepreneurship: Role conflict, stress, and venture performance in digital platform-based ecosystems. *Journal of Business Research*, 125, 520–532. DOI: 10.1016/j.jbusres.2019.06.037

Nam, C. W. (2022a). World economic outlook for 2022 and 2023. *CESifo Forum*, 23(03), 50–51.

Nandy, A. (1976). Adorno in India: Revisiting the psychology of Fascism. Retrieved 10 17, 2019, from http://psycnet.apa.org/psycinfo/1977-29404-001

Napier, G., & Hansen, C. (2011). *Ecosystems for Young Scaleable Firms*. FORA Group.

Narayanan, D. (2019, May 26). View: What shape will the BJP-RSS dynamics take under Modi 2.0? Retrieved July 16, 2020, from https://economictimes.indiatimes.com/news/politics-and-nation/view-what-shape-will-the-bjp-rss-dynamics-take-under-modi-2-0/articleshow/69498073.cms?from=mdr

Narayanan, V. K., & Shin, J. N. (2019). The institutional context of incubation: The case of academic incubators in India. *Management and Organization Review*, 15(3), 563–593. DOI: 10.1017/mor.2018.52

Neely, A., Gregory, M., & Platts, K. (2017). Performance measurement system design: A literature review and research agenda. *International Journal of Operations & Production Management*, 37(5), 581–610.

Neighbourly nudge: India-Bangladesh ties in Modi 3.0. (n.d.). India News Network. https://www.indianewsnetwork.com/en/20240630/neighbourly-nudge-india-bangladesh-ties-in-modi-3-0

Netra News. (2024, June 7). *Hasina's drift into conspiracy theories*. Netra News — . https://netra.news/2024/hasinas-drift-into-conspiracy-theories/

Network, D. F. (2019, June 04). Dalit 101 - Who are the Dalits? Retrieved July 22, 2020, from https://dfnusa.org/dalit-101-who-are-the-dalits/

Nightingale, P., & Coad, A. (2014). Muppets and gazelles: Political and methodological biases in entrepreneurship research. *Industrial and Corporate Change*, 23(1), 113–143. DOI: 10.1093/icc/dtt057

Niven, P. (2003). *Balanced Scorecard: Step-by-Step for Government and Nonprofit Agencies*. John Wiley & Sons, Inc.

Nnadi, M., & Soobaroyen, T. (2015). International financial reporting standards and foreign direct investment: The case of Africa. *Advances in Accounting*, 31(2), 228–238. DOI: 10.1016/j.adiac.2015.09.007

Nolzen, A. (2010). Genocide and Fascism: The Eliminationist Drive in Fascist Europe. German History, 28(1), 115-117. Retrieved 10 17, 2019, from https://academic.oup.com/gh/article/28/1/115/583276

Noorani, A. G. (2019). *RSS*. Delhi, India: LEFTWORD Books.

Norreklit, H. (2000). The Balanced Scorecard: A critical analysis of some assumptions. *Management Accounting Research*, 11(1), 65–88. DOI: 10.1006/mare.1999.0121

Norreklit, H. (2003). The Balanced Scorecard: What is the score? A rhetorical analysis. *Accounting, Organizations and Society*, 28(6), 591–619. DOI: 10.1016/S0361-3682(02)00097-1

Nørreklit, H., Mitchell, F., & O'Regan, N. (2016). The Balanced Scorecard in the public sector: A review. *Public Money & Management*, 36(2), 139–146.

North, D. C. (1990). A transaction cost theory of politics. *Journal of Theoretical Politics*, 2(4), 355–367. DOI: 10.1177/0951692890002004001

Novotny, A. (2017). The heterogeneity of the academic profession: The effect of occupational variables on university scientists' participation in research commercialization. *Minerva*, 55(4), 485–508. DOI: 10.1007/s11024-017-9321-5

Nowiński, W., Haddoud, M. Y., Lančarič, D., Egerová, D., & Czeglédi, C. (2019). The impact of entrepreneurship education, entrepreneurial self-efficacy and gender on entrepreneurial intentions of university students in the Visegrad countries. *Studies in Higher Education*, 44(2), 361–379. DOI: 10.1080/03075079.2017.1365359

Noworól, A. (2013, May). The role of hybrid partnerships in the management of development. In *NispaCEE Conference* (pp. 1-10).

O'Shea, R. P., Allen, T. J., Chevalier, A., & Roche, F. (2005). Entrepreneurial orientation, technology transfer and spinoff performance of US universities. *Research Policy*, 34(7), 994–1009. DOI: 10.1016/j.respol.2005.05.011

Obiamaka, OS (2011). The impact of human resources management (HRM) practices on organizational performance in Globalcom NIGERIA. Research Journal of Management Practice | ISSN, 2782, 7674.

OECD. (2010). *High-growth enterprises: What governments can do to make a difference,* Pugh, R., Schmutzler, J., & Tsvetkova, A. (2021). Taking the systems approaches out of their comfort zones: Perspectives from under explored contexts. *Growth and Change*, 52, 608–620. DOI: 10.1111/grow

OECD. (2013). *Studies on SMEs and entrepreneurship*. Organisation for Economic Cooperation and Development.

Ogbeibu, S., Emelifeonwu, J., Senadjki, A., Gaskin, J., & Kaivo-oja, J. (2020). Technological turbulence and greening of team creativity, product innovation, and human resource management: Implications for sustainability. *Journal of Cleaner Production*, 244, 118703. DOI: 10.1016/j.jclepro.2019.118703

Ogbeibu, S., Jabbour, C. J. C., Gaskin, J., Senadjki, A., & Hughes, M. (2021). Leveraging STARA competencies and green creativity to boost green organisational innovative evidence: A praxis for sustainable development. *Business Strategy and the Environment*, 30(5), 2421–2440. DOI: 10.1002/bse.2754

Ogwu, K., Hickey, P., Okeke, O. J.-P., Haque, A., Pimenidis, E., & Kozlovski, E. (2022). An integrated online/offline social network-based model for crowdfunding support in developing countries: The case of Nigeria. *Sustainability (Basel)*, 14(15), 9333. DOI: 10.3390/su14159333

Ohm, B. (2014). Contesting interpretational authority: Democracy and Fascism in the Indian 'empowered public'. Media international Australia, incorporating culture and policy, 152(152), 119-132. Retrieved 10 17, 2019, from https://search.informit.org/documentsummary;dn=568091844325867;res=iellcc

Ojaghi, H., Mohammadi, M., & Yazdani, H. R. (2019). A synthesized framework for the formation of startups' innovation ecosystem: A systematic literature review. *Journal of Science and Technology Policy Management*, 10(5), 1063–1097. DOI: 10.1108/JSTPM-07-2018-0071

Okah Efogo, F. (2020b). Does trade in services improve African participation in global value chains? *African Development Review*, 32(4), 758–772. DOI: 10.1111/1467-8268.12476

Okah Efogo, F., Wonyra, K. O., & Osabuohien, E. (2022). Foreign direct investment and participation of developing countries in global value chains: Lessons from the last decade. *International Review of Applied Economics*, 36(2), 264–284. DOI: 10.1080/02692171.2021.1962255

Oliveira, M., & Ferreira, J. J. (2019). Enhancing innovation capability with balanced scorecard approach. *Journal of Business Research*, 101, 706–716.

Oliveira, R., Ramalho, M., & Macedo, L. (2019). Balanced Scorecard and Performance Measurement: A review of the literature. *Journal of Business Research*, 101, 369–379.

Olve, N. G., Roy, J., & Wetter, M. (1999). *Performance Drivers*. John Wiley & Sons.

Orji, JO, & Opualla -Charles, S. (2022). The Unemployment–Inflation Dynamics: The role of Entrepreneurship Development in Nigeria. https://www.researchsquare .com/articlc/rs-1820633/latcst

Osabohien, R., Worgwu, H., Adediran, O., & Soomro, J. (2022). Social entrepreneurship and future employment in Nigeria. *International Social Science Journal*, 73(250), 927–937. DOI: 10.1111/issj.12360

Otley, D. (1999). Performance Management: A Framework for Management Control Systems Research. *Management Accounting Research*, 10(4), 363–382. DOI: 10.1006/mare.1999.0115

Oyelere, S. S., Agbo, F. J., & Sanusi, I. T. (2022, August). Developing a pedagogical evaluation framework for computational thinking supporting technologies and tools. [). Frontiers.]. *Frontiers in Education*, 7, 957739. DOI: 10.3389/feduc.2022.957739

Pandey, G. (2019, June 26). Indian MP Mahua Moitra's 'rising fascism' speech wins plaudits. Retrieved July 22, 2020, from https://www.bbc.com/news/world-asia-india -48755554

Pandey, I. M. (2005, January-March). Balanced Scorecard: Myth and Reality. *Vikalpa*, 30(1), 51–66. DOI: 10.1177/0256090920050105

Panikkar, K. N. (2003). *Before the night falls: Forebodings of fascism in India*. Books for Change.

Papageorgiou, A., & Papageorgiou, M. (2021). Employee Engagement and Organizational Performance: The Role of Balanced Scorecard. *Business Research Quarterly*, 24(2), 123–137.

Papcunová, V., Dvořák, M., Vavrek, R., Mižičková, J., Harasimová, P., Víchová, M., & Váňa, T. (2023). Availability and Quality of School Facilities as a Determinant of Local Economic Development: The Slovak. *Experimental Economics*, 11(2), 35.

Park, Y., Song, J., Yoon, S., & Kim, J. (2013). Learning organization and innovative behavior. *European Journal of Training and Development*, 38(1/2), 75–94. DOI: 10.1108/EJTD-04-2013-0040

Partovi, H. (2014). *Code.org*. https://code.org/

Passmore, K. (2014). Fascism: A very short introduction. Oxford: Oxford University Press. Retrieved 2020, from https://www.torontopubliclibrary.ca/search.jsp?Ntt= Fascism

Pasumarthy, R., Mohammed, S., Laxman, V., Krishnamoorthy, V., Durga, S., & Boopathi, S. (2024). Digital Transformation in Developing Economies: Forecasting Trends, Impact, and Challenges in Industry 5.0. In *Convergence of Human Resources Technologies and Industry 5.0* (pp. 47–68). IGI Global. DOI: 10.4018/979-8-3693-1343-5.ch003

Pathi, K., & Alam, J. (2024, January 3). *Elections: Sheikh Hasina once fought for democracy in Bangladesh. Her critics say she now threatens it | AP News*. AP News. https://apnews.com/article/bangladesh-elections-sheikh-hasina-opposition-bnp-485da99f50959e6cdf5b11e24fe6efe5

Pekarčíková, K., Vaněk, M., & Sousedíková, R. (2022). Determinants of economic growth: Panel data analysis of OPEC. *Resources Policy*, 79, 103129. DOI: 10.1016/j.resourpol.2022.103129

Peppard, J., & Ward, J. (2004). Beyond strategic information systems: Towards an IS capability. *The Journal of Strategic Information Systems*, 13(2), 167–194. DOI: 10.1016/j.jsis.2004.02.002

Peppard, J., & Ward, J. (2016). *Managing the Business of IT: What Every Executive Needs to Know*. Wiley.

Pérez, J., & Martínez, E. (2022). Aligning Strategic Initiatives with Technological Advancements: A Balanced Scorecard Approach. *Information Systems Research*, 33(1), 80–95.

Perkins, D., & Robbins, G. (2011). The contribution to local enterprise development of infrastructure for commodity extraction projects: Tanzania's central corridor and Mozambique's Zambezi Valley. Making Most of Commodities Program (MMCP) Discussion Paper, 9.

Pesqueux, Y. (2022). The tale of entrepreneurship in Africa. *Revue Organizations & Territoires*, 31(1), 1–10. DOI: 10.1522/revueot.v31n1.1442

Plagemann, J. (2021). Small states and competing connectivity strategies: What explains Bangladesh's success in relations with Asia's major powers? *The Pacific Review*, 35(4), 736–764. DOI: 10.1080/09512748.2021.1908410

Poernamasari, D.Dhonna Widya Poernamasari. (2023). The effect of profit-sharing on productivity of micro, small, and medium enterprises (msme) in indonesia. *Airlangga Journal of Innovation Management*, 4(2), 198–207. DOI: 10.20473/ajim.v4i2.48385

Politis, D., Winborg, J., & Dahlstrand, Å. L. (2012). Exploring the resource logic of student entrepreneurs. *International Small Business Journal*, 30(6), 659–683. DOI: 10.1177/0266242610383445

Porter, M. E. (1985). *The Competitive Advantage: Creating and Sustaining Superior Performance*. Free Press.

Powell, T. C., & Dent-Micallef, A. (1997). Information technology as competitive advantage: The role of human, business, and technology resources. *Strategic Management Journal*, 18(5), 375–405. DOI: 10.1002/(SICI)1097-0266(199705)18:5<375::AID-SMJ876>3.0.CO;2-7

Prasad, M. S. C., Dhanalakshmi, M., Mohan, M., Somasundaram, B., Valarmathi, R., & Boopathi, S. (2024). Machine Learning-Integrated Sustainable Engineering and Energy Systems: Innovations at the Nexus. In *Harnessing High-Performance Computing and AI for Environmental Sustainability* (pp. 74–98). IGI Global. DOI: 10.4018/979-8-3693-1794-5.ch004

President Alvi asks to pay attention to RSS, BJP agenda. (2019). Retrieved 9 July 2020, from https://nation.com.pk/16-Aug-2019/president-alvi-urges-world-to-pay-attention-to-rss-bjp-agenda

Pricopoaia, O., Busila, A. V., Cristache, N., Susanu, I., & Matis, C. (2023). Challenges for entrepreneurial innovation: Startups as tools for a better knowledge-based economy. *The International Entrepreneurship and Management Journal*, •••, 1–42.

Puniyani, D. (2017). *Fascism in India: Debating RSS-BJP politics*. Media House.

Putra, K. D., & Ofosu, S. D. (2024). FULL-TIME NOW OR LATER! Influence of Organizational Working Environment on Transition Intention.(Multi-case study of Hybrid Entrepreneurship in Indonesia).

Qian, H., Acs, Z. J., & Stough, R. R. (2013). Regional systems of entrepreneurship: The nexus of human capital, knowledge and new firm formation. *Journal of Economic Geography*, 13(4), 559–587. DOI: 10.1093/jeg/lbs009

Quatraro, F., & Vivarelli, M. (2015). Drivers of entrepreneurship and post-entry performance of newborn firms in developing countries. *The World Bank Research Observer*, 30(20), 277–305. DOI: 10.1093/wbro/lku012

Qu, M., McCormick, A. D., & Funck, C. (2022). Community resourcefulness and partnerships in rural tourism. *Journal of Sustainable Tourism*, 30(10), 2371–2390. DOI: 10.1080/09669582.2020.1849233

Rachman, T., Anindita, R., Izmi, N., Ewaldo, C., Rezki, F., & Andini, E. (2022). Fostering innovative work behavior of employees in the tourism industry: Strategies for successful remote tourism during the covid-19 pandemic. *Jurnal Manajemen Dan Pemasaran Jasa*, 15(2), 227–240. DOI: 10.25105/jmpj.v15i2.13573

Radinger-Peer, V., Sedlacek, S., & Goldstein, H. (2018). The path-dependent evolution of the entrepreneurial ecosystem (ee) – dynamics and region-specific assets of the case of Vienna (Austria). *European Planning Studies*, 26(8), 1499–1518. . 2018. 1494136DOI: <ALIGNMENT.qj></ALIGNMENT>10. 1080/ 09654313

Raffiee, J., & Feng, J. (2014). Should i quit my day job?: A hybrid path to entrepreneurship. *Academy of Management Journal*, 57(4), 936–963. DOI: 10.5465/amj.2012.0522

Rahamathunnisa, U., Sudhakar, K., Padhi, S., Bhattacharya, S., Shashibhushan, G., & Boopathi, S. (2024). Sustainable Energy Generation From Waste Water: IoT Integrated Technologies. In *Adoption and Use of Technology Tools and Services by Economically Disadvantaged Communities: Implications for Growth and Sustainability* (pp. 225–256). IGI Global.

Raja, I. (2020, February 28). Is India sleepwalking toward a Muslim Holocaust? Retrieved July 22, 2020, from https://www.dailysabah.com/opinion/op-ed/is-india-sleepwalking-toward-a-muslim-holocaust

Ramaharo, F., Razanajatovo, Y.H., & Aljaona, E.M. (2023). Macroeconomic models in use in Madagascar.

Ranasinha, R. (2010). South Asian broadcasters in Britain and the BBC: talking to India (1941–1943). South Asian Diaspora, 2(1), 57-71. Retrieved 10 17, 2019, from https://core.ac.uk/display/29900231

Ravisankar, A., Sampath, B., & Asif, M. M. (2023). Economic Studies on Automobile Management: Working Capital and Investment Analysis. In *Multidisciplinary Approaches to Organizational Governance During Health Crises* (pp. 169–198). IGI Global.

Ravisankar, A., Shanthi, A., Lavanya, S., Ramaratnam, M., Krishnamoorthy, V., & Boopathi, S. (2024). Harnessing 6G for Consumer-Centric Business Strategies Across Electronic Industries. In *AI Impacts in Digital Consumer Behavior* (pp. 241–270). IGI Global.

Rawhouser, H., Vismara, S., & Kshetri, N. (2023). Blockchain and vulnerable entrepreneurial ecosystems. *Entrepreneurship and Regional Development*. Advance online publication. DOI: 10.1080/08985626.2022.2162979

Rehman, S., & Roomi, M. (2012). Gender and work-life balance: A phenomenological study of women entrepreneurs in pakistan. *Journal of Small Business and Enterprise Development*, 19(2), 209–228. DOI: 10.1108/14626001211223865

Reich, R. (2001, December 19). Good and Bad Nationalism. Retrieved July 22, 2020, from https://prospect.org/article/good-bad-nationalism/

Reich, B. H., & Benbasat, I. (1996). Measuring the Linkage between Business and Information Technology Objectives. *Management Information Systems Quarterly*, 20(1), 55–81. DOI: 10.2307/249542

Reich, B. H., & Benbasat, I. (2000). Factors that Influence the Social Dimensions of Alignment between Business and Information Technology Objectives. *Management Information Systems Quarterly*, 24(1), 81–113. DOI: 10.2307/3250980

Reilley, G. & Reilley, R. (2000). Using a measure network to understand and delivery value. *Journal of Cost Management,* 5-14.

Reiner, S., Balkin, R., Gotham, K., Hunter, Q., Juhnke, G., & Davis, R. (2019). Assessing life balance and work addiction in high-pressure, high-demand careers. *Journal of Counseling and Development*, 97(4), 409–416. DOI: 10.1002/jcad.12289

Report, T. (2021, October 28). Bangladesh, India satisfied as 14 Lines of Credit projects completed. *The Business Standard.* https://www.tbsnews.net/bangladesh/bangladesh-india-satisfied-14-lines-credit-projects-completed-322333

Reporter, J., Kondo, M., Cicurel, D., Grant, B., Wolfisz, F., Oryszczuk, S., . . . Flacks-Leigh, J. (2020, August 20). The Canary editor criticised over 'Arbeit Macht Frei' tweet. Retrieved September 23, 2020, from https://jewishnews.timesofisrael.com/the-canary-editor-criticised-over-arbeit-macht-frei-tweet/

Resnick, M., Maloney, J., Monroy-Hernández, A., Rusk, N., Eastmond, E., Brennan, K., Millner, A., Rosenbaum, E., Silver, J., Silverman, B., & Kafai, Y. (2009). Scratch: Programming for all. *Communications of the ACM*, 52(11), 60–67. DOI: 10.1145/1592761.1592779

Reuer, J. J., Matusik, S. F., & Jones, J. (2019). The Interplay of Entrepreneurship and Collaboration. *The Oxford Handbook of Entrepreneurship and Collaboration*, 1-15.

Reuters_Tickers. (2024, August 5). Bangladesh's Sheikh Hasina falls from grace in nation her father founded. *SWI swissinfo.ch.* https://www.swissinfo.ch/eng/bangladesh%27s-sheikh-hasina-falls-from-grace-in-nation-her-father-founded/86108997

Reynolds, N. S., & Holt, D. (2021). Sustainable development and profit? A sense-making perspective on hybrid organisations and their founders. *Business Strategy and the Environment*, 30(4), 2147–2159. DOI: 10.1002/bse.2737

Riaz, S., Yanqing, W., Ishaq, M. I., Raza, A., & Siddiqui, R. A. (2024). Role of social networks and entrepreneurial success: Understanding the dynamics of knowledge acquisition and green entrepreneurial orientation. *Journal of Entrepreneurship & Innovation Management*, 1-23.

Rich, P. J., Bartholomew, S., Daniel, D., Dinsmoor, K., Nielsen, M., Reynolds, C., & Yauney, J. (2022). Trends in tools used to teach computational thinking through elementary coding. *Journal of Research on Technology in Education*, •••, 1–22.

Ries, E. (2011). *The Lean Startup: How Today's Entrepreneurs Use Continuous Innovation to Create Radically Successful Businesses*. Crown Business.

Rijo-García, S., Segredo, E., & León, C. (2022). Computational thinking and user interfaces: A systematic review. *IEEE Transactions on Education*, 65(4), 647–656. DOI: 10.1109/TE.2022.3159765

Rikhardsson, P., & Yigitbasioglu, O. (2018). Business intelligence & analytics in management accounting research: Status and future focus. *International Journal of Accounting Information Systems*, 29, 37–58. DOI: 10.1016/j.accinf.2018.03.001

Rocha, A. K. L. D., Moraes, G. H. S. M. D., & Fischer, B. (2021). The role of university environment in promoting entrepreneurial behavior: Evidence from heterogeneous regions in Brazil. *Innovation & Management Review*.

Roche, J. The Hybrid Nature of Social Enterprises - Exploring possible tensions and sources of mission drift. Louvain School of Management, Université catholique de Louvain, 2017. Prom.: Janssen, Frank. http:// hdl.handle.net/2078.1/thesis:10953

Rodríguez Gutiérrez, P. I., Pastor Pérez, M. D. P., & Alonso Galicia, P. E. (2019). University entrepreneurship: How to trigger entrepreneurial intent of undergraduate students. *Journal of Science and Technology Policy Management*, 10(4), 927–950. DOI: 10.1108/JSTPM-04-2018-0037

Roh, H. (2021). Enhancing organizational performance through effective communication strategies: Insights from the Balanced Scorecard. *Journal of Business Communication*, 58(4), 491–514.

Rompho, N. (2011). Why the Balanced Scorecard Fails in SMEs: A Case Study. *International Journal of Business and Management*, 6(11), 39–46. DOI: 10.5539/ijbm.v6n11p39

Roodman, D. (2009). How to do Xtabond2: An Introduction to Difference and System GMM in Stata. *The Stata Journal*, 9(1), 86–136. DOI: 10.1177/1536867X0900900106

Roundy, P. T., & Bayer, M. A. (2018). Entrepreneurial ecosystem narratives and the micro-foundations ofregional entrepreneurship. *International Journal of Entrepreneurship and Innovation*, 20(3), 194–208. DOI: 10.1177/1465750318808426

Rousseau, P. L., & Wachtel, P. (2002). Inflation thresholds and the finance–growth nexus. *Journal of International Money and Finance*, 21(6), 777–793. DOI: 10.1016/S0261-5606(02)00022-0

RSS ideology of Hindu supremacy will lead to suppression of Muslims in India and to targeting of Pakistan. (2019). Retrieved 9 July 2020, from https://www.dawn.com/news/1499293

S, B., & Gopi, S. (2024). Crafting Effective HR Strategies for the Modern Workplace: Navigating the Digital Frontier. In *Convergence of Human Resources Technologies and Industry 5.0* (pp. 23–46). IGI Global. DOI: 10.4018/979-8-3693-1343-5.ch002

Saeed, S., Yousafzai, S. Y., Yani-De-Soriano, M., & Muffatto, M. (2015). The role of perceived university support in the formation of students' entrepreneurial intention. *Journal of Small Business Management*, 53(4), 1127–1145. DOI: 10.1111/jsbm.12090

Şahin, F., Karadağ, H., & Tuncer, B. (2019). Big five personality traits, entrepreneurial self-efficacy and entrepreneurial intention: A configurational approach. *International Journal of Entrepreneurial Behaviour & Research*, 25(6), 1188–1211. DOI: 10.1108/IJEBR-07-2018-0466

Salati Marcondes de Moraes, G. H., Brandão Fischer, B., Guerrero, M., Lopes da Rocha, A. K., & Rücker Schaeffer, P. (2023). An inquiry into the linkages between university ecosystem and students' entrepreneurial intention and self-efficacy. *Innovations in Education and Teaching International*, 60(1), 134–145. DOI: 10.1080/14703297.2021.1969262

Sam Winter-Levy, N. (2018, June 26). Analysis | When is nationalism a good thing? When it unites an ethnically diverse citizenry. Retrieved July 09, 2020, from https://www.washingtonpost.com/news/monkey-cage/wp/2018/06/26/when-is-nationalism-a-good-thing-when-it-unites-an-ethnically-diverse-citizenry/

Sangh, R. S. (2012). Vision and Mission. Retrieved July 22, 2020, from http://rss.org/Encyc/2012/10/22/rss-vision-and-mission.html

Sangham: Birth and growth of Rashtriya Swayamsevak Sangh (RSS) [Television series]. (2014, October 12). India: Aaj Tak. Retrieved April 10, 2020, from https://www.youtube.com/watch?v=Fmo0TcWyXL0

Santillan, E., Santillan, E. T., Doringo, J. B., Pigao, K. J. F., & Mesina, V. F. C. (2023). Assessing the impact of a hybrid work model on job execution, work-life balance, and employee satisfaction in a technology company. *Journal of Business and Management Studies*, 5(6), 13–38. DOI: 10.32996/jbms.2023.5.6.2

Santoleri, P. (2019). Innovation and job creation in (high-growth) new firms. *Industrial and Corporate Change*, 29(3), 731–756. DOI: 10.1093/icc/dtz059

Santos, S. C., & Liguori, E. W. (2020). Entrepreneurial self-efficacy and intentions: Outcome expectations as mediator and subjective norms as moderator. *International Journal of Entrepreneurial Behaviour & Research*, 26(3), 400–415. DOI: 10.1108/IJEBR-07-2019-0436

Sassetti, S., Marzi, G., Cavaliere, V., & Ciappei, C. (2018). Entrepreneurial cognition and socially situated approach: A systematic and bibliometric analysis. *Scientometrics*, 116(3), 1675–1718. DOI: 10.1007/s11192-018-2809-4

Satalkina, L., & Steiner, G. (2020). Digital entrepreneurship and its role in innovation systems: A systematic literature review as a basis for future research avenues for sustainable transitions. *Sustainability (Basel)*, 12(7), 2764. DOI: 10.3390/su12072764

Saxenian, A. (2002). Silicon valley's new immigrant high-growth entrepreneurs. *Economic Development Quarterly*, 16(1), 20–31. DOI: 10.1177/0891242402016001003

Sayek, S. (2009). Foreign Direct Investment and Inflation. *Southern Economic Journal*, 76(2), 419–443. DOI: 10.4284/sej.2009.76.2.419

Schein, E. H. (2000). *Organizational Culture and Leadership* (2nd ed.). John Wiley and Sons.

Schillo, R. S., Persaud, A., & Jin, M. (2016). Entrepreneurial readiness in the context of national systems of entrepreneurship. *Small Business Economics*, 46(4), 619–637. DOI: 10.1007/s11187-016-9709-x

Schlosser, F., Wagner, H.-T., & Coltman, T. (2015). Reconsidering the dimensions of business-IT alignment. *The Journal of Strategic Information Systems*, 24(2), 98–112.

Schmude, J., Welter, F., & Heumann, S. (2008). Entrepreneurship research in Germany. *Entrepreneurship Theory and Practice*, 32(2), 289–311. DOI: 10.1111/j.1540-6520.2007.00227.x

Schmutzler, J., Andonova, V., & Diaz-Serrano, L. (2019). How context shapes entrepreneurial self-efficacy as a driver of entrepreneurial intentions: A multi-level approach. *Entrepreneurship Theory and Practice*, 43(5), 880–920. DOI: 10.1177/1042258717753142

Schneider, B., Ehrhart, M. G., & Macey, W. H. (2013). Organizational climate and culture. *Annual Review of Psychology*, 64(1), 361–388. DOI: 10.1146/annurev-psych-113011-143809 PMID: 22856467

Schneider, B., White, S. S., & Paul, M. C. (1998). Linking service climate and customer perceptions of service quality: Tests of a causal model. *The Journal of Applied Psychology*, 83(2), 150–163. DOI: 10.1037/0021-9010.83.2.150 PMID: 9577232

Schumpeter, J. A. (1976), Capitalism, socialism, and democracy. *George Allen & Unwin* Ltd [1943].

Schwartz, L., Maquil, V., Johannsen, L., Moll, C., & Hermen, J. (2023). Teaching computational thinking with a tangible development platform: An exploratory field study at school with Kniwwelino. *Education and Information Technologies*, •••, 1–33.

Scott, R. W. (2001). *Institutions and Organizations* (2nd ed.). Sage Publications.

Sen, A. (2000). A Decade of Human Development. *Journal of Human Development*, 1(1), 17–23. DOI: 10.1080/14649880050008746

Sénicourt, P., & Verstraete, T. (2000). Learn to undertake. Reflections and Perspectives, 39(10).

Setyawasih, R., & Buchdadi, A. (2022). Organizational culture and innovative work behavior in manufacturing company: The role of employee engagement as a mediator. *International Journal of Research and Review*, 9(1), 360–371. DOI: 10.52403/ijrr.20220143

Severino JM et al. (2021), New entrepreneurial dynamics in Africa.

Shahid, M. S., Imran, Y., & Shehryar, H. (2017). Determinants of entrepreneurial intentions: An institutional embeddedness perspective. *Journal of Small Business and Entrepreneurship*, 30(2), 139–156. DOI: 10.1080/08276331.2017.1389053

Shaikh, E., Tunio, M. N., Khoso, W. M., Brahmi, M., & Rasool, S. (2022). *The COVID-19 pandemic overlaps entrepreneurial activities and triggered new challenges: a review Study. Managing Human Resources in SMEs and Start-ups: International Challenges and Solutions*, 155-182.

Shaikh, E., Tunio, M. N., & Qureshi, F. (2021). Finance and women's entrepreneurship in DETEs: A literature review. Entrepreneurial Finance. *Innovation and Development*, , 191–209.

Shane, S. (2003). *A General Theory of Entrepreneurship*. Edward Elgar. DOI: 10.4337/9781781007990

Shane, S. (2009). Why encouraging more people to become entrepreneurs is bad public policy. *Small Business Economics*, 33(2), 141–149. DOI: 10.1007/s11187-009-9215-5

Shane, S. (2012). The importance of angel investing in financing the growth of entrepreneurial ventures. *The Quarterly Journal of Finance*, 2(02), 1250009. DOI: 10.1142/S2010139212500097

Shane, S., & Venkataraman, S. (2000). The promise of entrepreneurship as a field of research. *Academy of Management Review*, 25(1), 217–226. https://www.jstor.org/stable/259271. DOI: 10.5465/amr.2000.2791611

Shanker, R., Bhanugopan, R., Heijden, B., & Farrell, M. (2017). Organizational climate for innovation and organizational performance: The mediating effect of innovative work behavior. *Journal of Vocational Behavior*, 100, 67–77. DOI: 10.1016/j.jvb.2017.02.004

Shapero, A., & Sokol, L. (1982). *The social dimensions of entrepreneurship*. University of Illinois at Urbana-Champaign's Academy for Entrepreneurial Leadership Historical Research Reference in Entrepreneurship.

Sharma, A. (2020, June 10). On the Difference Between Hinduism and Hindutva. Retrieved July 16, 2020, from https://www.asianstudies.org/publications/eaa/archives/on-the-difference-between-hinduism-and-hindutva/

Shevchuk, A., Strebkov, D., & Bögenhold, D. (2024). Work values and hybrid careers in the gig economy: The evidence from an online labor market. *Economic and Industrial Democracy*, 45(1), 138–163. DOI: 10.1177/0143831X221140153

Shi, L., Yao, X., & Wu, W. (2020). Perceived university support, entrepreneurial self-efficacy, heterogeneous entrepreneurial intentions in entrepreneurship education: The moderating role of the Chinese sense of face. *Journal of Entrepreneurship in Emerging Economies*, 12(2), 205–223. DOI: 10.1108/JEEE-04-2019-0040

Shmueli, G., Ray, S., Estrada, J. M. V., & Chatla, S. B. (2016). The elephant in the room: Predictive performance of PLS models. *Journal of Business Research*, 69(10), 4552–4564. DOI: 10.1016/j.jbusres.2016.03.049

Shuaibu, M., Gwazawa, U., & Jega, A. (2018). Entrepreneurship development for diversification of nigerian economy. *Journal of Economics Management and Trade*, 21(6), 1–11. DOI: 10.9734/JEMT/2018/41679

Shukla, R. (2020, July 07). Aspects of male sexuality enmeshing with rise of fascism in India: Tentative psychoanalytical explorations. Retrieved July 10, 2020, from https://onlinelibrary.wiley.com/doi/epdf/10.1002/aps.1658

Siddiqui, K. (2017). Hindutva, Neoliberalism and the Reinventing of India. Retrieved July 22, 2020, from http://www.kspjournals.org/index.php/JEST/article/vicw/1280/1325

Siegel, D. S., & Wright, M. (2015). Academic Entrepreneurship: Time for a Rethink? *British Journal of Management*, 26(4), 582–595. DOI: 10.1111/1467-8551.12116

Silvius, G. A. J. 2007. Business and IT alignment in theory and practice. *In Proceedings of the HICSS '07,40th Annual Hawaii International Conference on System Sciences.*

Simmons, S. A., Wiklund, J., Levie, J., Bradley, S. W., & Sunny, S. A. (2019). Gender gaps and re-entry into entrepreneurial ecosystems after business failure. *Small Business Economics*, 53(2), 517–531. DOI: 10.1007/s11187-018-9998-3

Sinicki, A., Sinicki, & Ramachandran. (2019). *Thriving in the gig economy*. Apress.

Sitaridis, I., & Kitsios, F. (2020). Competitiveness analysis and evaluation of entrepreneurial ecosystems: A multi-criteria approach. *Annals of Operations Research*, 294(1), 377–399. DOI: 10.1007/s10479-019-03404-x

Smets, M., Aristidou, A., & Whittington, R. (2017). Towards a practice-driven institutionalism. In Greenwood, R., Oliver, C., Lawrence, T. B., & Meyer, R. (Eds.), *The Sage Handbook of Organizational Institutionalism* (pp. 384–411). Sage. DOI: 10.4135/9781446280669.n15

Smith-Hunter, A. E., & Boyd, R. L. (2004). Applying theories of entrepreneurship to a comparative analysis of white and minority women business owners. *Women in Management Review*, 19(1), 18–28. DOI: 10.1108/09649420410518403

Smith, M. (1998). *Measuring organisational e effectiveness*. Management Accounting.

Soffiantini, G. (2020). Food insecurity and political instability during the Arab Spring. *Global Food Security*, 26, 100400. DOI: 10.1016/j.gfs.2020.100400

Solesvik, M. (2017). Hybrid entrepreneurship: How and why entrepreneurs combine employment with self-employment. *Technology Innovation Management Review*, 7(3), 33–41. DOI: 10.22215/timreview/1063

Soltow, J. H. (1968). The entrepreneur in economic history. *The American Economic Review*, 58(2), 84–92.

Soomro, M. M. (2019, February 5). *PR No. 31 Kashmir Solidarity Day Message By Patron-In-Chief Youth Forum For Kashmir/Federal Minister/Chairman Privatization: Islamabad*. PID. http://pid.gov.pk/site/press_detail/12947

Spigel, B. (2013). Bourdieuian Approaches to the Geography of Entrepreneurial Cultures. *Entrepreneurship and Regional Development*, 25(9-10), 804–818. DOI: 10.1080/08985626.2013.862974

Spigel, B., & Harrison, R. (2018). Toward a process theory of entrepreneurial ecosystems. *Strategic Entrepreneurship Journal*, 12(1), 151–168. DOI: 10.1002/sej.1268

Spires, H. A., Hervey, L. S., Morris, G. K., & Stelpflug, C. (2012). Energizing project-based inquiry in computational thinking: The development of an online professional development community. *Journal of Science Education and Technology*, 21(1), 15–25. DOI: 10.1007/s10956-011-9290-4

Spivack, A. J., McKelvie, A., & Haynie, J. M. (2014). Habitual entrepreneurs: Possible cases of entrepreneurship addiction? *Journal of Business Venturing*, 29(5), 651–667. DOI: 10.1016/j.jbusvent.2013.11.002

Stadler, A., & Smith, A. M. J. (2017). Entrepreneurship in vocational education: A case study of Brazilian context. *Industry and Higher Education*, 31(2), 81–89. DOI: 10.1177/0950422217693963

Stam, E., & Spigel, B. (2017). Entrepreneurial Ecosystems, forthcoming in: Blackburn, R., De Clercq, D., Heinonen, J. & Wang, Z. (Eds) *Handbook for Entrepreneurship and Small Business*. London: SAGE.

Stam, E., & Spigel, B. (2018). Entrepreneurial ecosystems. Blackburn, R., De Clerq, C., Heinonen, J. (Eds.). *The SAGE Handbook of Small Business and Entrepreneurship*. SAGE, London, pp. 407–422. DOI: 10.4135/9781473984080.n21

Stam, E. (2010). Entrepreneurship, evolution and geography. In Boschma, R., & Martin, R. L. (Eds.), *The Handbook of Evolutionary Economic Geography* (pp. 307–348). Edward Elgar. DOI: 10.4337/9781849806497.00014

Stam, E. (2015). Entrepreneurial ecosystems and regional policy: A sympathetic critique. *European Planning Studies*, 23(9), 1759–1769. DOI: 10.1080/09654313.2015.1061484

Stam, E., & van de Ven, A. (2021). Entrepreneurial ecosystem elements. *Small Business Economics*, 56(2), 809–832. DOI: 10.1007/s11187-019-00270-6

Stephan, U., & Uhlaner, L. (2010). Performance-based vs. socially-supportive culture: A cross-national study of descriptive norms and entrepreneurship. *Journal of International Business Studies*, 41(8), 1347–1364. DOI: 10.1057/jibs.2010.14

Stephens, B., Butler, J. S., Garg, R., & Gibson, D. V. (2019). Austin, Boston, Silicon Valley, and New York: Case studies in the location choices of entrepreneurs in maintaining the technopolis. *Technological Forecasting and Social Change*, 146(4), 267–280. DOI: 10.1016/j.techfore.2019.05.030

Sternberg, R., Bloh, J., & Coduras, A. (2019). A new framework to measure entrepreneurial ecosystems at the regional level. *Zeitschrift für Wirtschaftsgeographie*, 63(2-4), 103–117. DOI: 10.1515/zfw-2018-0014

St-Pierre, J., Foleu, L., Abdul-Nour, G., & Nomo, S. (2015). the obstacles to the development of Cameroonian SMEs: what do entrepreneurs think? Kaldor, M. (2023). Commentary on Kögler: Analyzing the Ukraine war through a 'new wars' perspective. *European Journal of Social Theory*, •••, 136843102311688.

Stuetzer, M., Audretsch, D., Obschonka, M., Gosling, S., Rentfrow, P., & Potter, J. (2017). Entrepreneurship culture, knowledge spillovers and the growth of regions. *Regional Studies*, 52(5), 608–618. DOI: 10.1080/00343404.2017.1294251

Subscribe to read. (n.d.). Financial Times. https://www.ft.com/content/6961f171-d433-4fab-90c9-8fca790547d6

Suifan, T., Abdallah, A., & Janini, M. (2018). The impact of transformational leadership on employees' creativity. *Management Research Review*, 41(1), 113–132. DOI: 10.1108/MRR-02-2017-0032

Su, J., & Yang, W. (2023). A systematic review of integrating computational thinking in early childhood education. *Computers and Education Open*, 4, 100122. DOI: 10.1016/j.caeo.2023.100122

Sundar, R., Srikaanth, P. B., Naik, D. A., Murugan, V. P., Karumudi, M., & Boopathi, S. (2024). Achieving Balance Between Innovation and Security in the Cloud With Artificial Intelligence of Things: Semantic Web Control Models. In *Advances in Web Technologies and Engineering* (pp. 1–26). IGI Global. DOI: 10.4018/979-8-3693-1487-6.ch001

Sutrisno, S., Kuraesin, A. D., Siminto, S., Irawansyah, I., & Ausat, A. M. A. (2023). The role of information technology in driving innovation and entrepreneurial business growth. *Jurnal Minfo Polgan*, 12(1), 586–597. DOI: 10.33395/jmp.v12i1.12463

Szerb, L., & Trumbull, W. N. (2018). Entrepreneurship development in Russia: Is Russia a normal country? An empirical analysis. *Journal of Small Business and Enterprise Development*, 25(6), 902–929. DOI: 10.1108/JSBED-01-2018-0033

Taghouti, Y., & Abdelbaki, N. (2023). The determinants of territorial development in developing countries: Literature review. International Journal of Accounting, Finance, Auditing, Management and Economics, 4(1–1), 481–504.

Tallon, P. P., Kraemer, K. L., & Gurbaxani, V. (2000). Executives' perceptions of the Business Value of Information Technology: A Process-Oriented Approach. *Journal of Management Information Systems*, 16(4), 145–173. DOI: 10.1080/07421222.2000.11518269

Tallon, P. P., & Pinsonneault, A. (2011). Competing perspectives on the link between strategic information technology alignment and organizational agility: Insights from a mediation model. *Management Information Systems Quarterly*, 35(2), 463–486. DOI: 10.2307/23044052

Tallon, P. P., Queiroz, M., Coltman, T., & Sharma, R. (2016). Business process and information technology alignment: Construct conceptualization, empirical illustration, and directions for future research. *Journal of the Association for Information Systems*, 17(9), 563–589. DOI: 10.17705/1jais.00438

Tang, X., Li, G., Lv, L., Wang, P., & Zhu, R. (2024). Relationship between the informal social networks and entrepreneurial intentions of Chinese college students: The mediating role of entrepreneurial learning. *Education + Training*. Advance online publication. DOI: 10.1108/ET-08-2023-0338

Tang, X., Yin, Y., Lin, Q., Hadad, R., & Zhai, X. (2020). Assessing computational thinking: A systematic review of empirical studies. *Computers & Education*, 148, 103798. DOI: 10.1016/j.compedu.2019.103798

Tarafdar, M., & Tanriverdi, H. (2018). Impact of the information technology–human resource (IT-HR) alignment on performance: A study of IT and HR managers' perceptions. *Journal of Management Information Systems*, 34(2), 375–413.

Tchamanbe Djine, L., & Tchouassi, G. (2001). *Strengthening the entrepreneurial capacities of women through training: An analysis of the case of Cameroon*. University of Yaoundé II, Communication at the VII Scientific Days of the AUF Entrepreneurship Network on Entrepreneurship Training.

Tchouassi, G., & Tagne, J. S. (2020). Chapter 11 University incubators for young entrepreneurs. B. Boudarbat & AA Mbaye (Eds.), Economic Development and Employment in Francophone Africa: Entrepreneurship as a Means of Realization. University of Montreal Press.

Tchouassi, G., & Tchougon, EFJ (2022). Entrepreneurial education in higher education in Cameroon. The Education System in Francophone Africa: Challenges and Opportunities, 238.

Tchouassi, G. (2019). The specificity of the African socio-cultural model and the hiring process in Cameroonian companies. *Revue Congolaise de Gestion*, 2, 154–192. DOI: 10.3917/rcg.028.0154

Tchouassi, G., Ngwen, N., Tékam Oumbé, H., & Temfack, S. (2018). Entrepreneurial knowledge of young people and women and economic development. *International Review of Organization Sciences*, 1, 57–79.

Tchouassi, G., & Niyonzima, T. G. (2024). Effet de dynamique des prix et participation des pays Africains aux chaines de valeurs mondiales. *Revue Management Innovation*, 9(1), 165–191. DOI: 10.3917/rmi.209.0165

Terán-Yépez, E., Marín-Carrillo, G. M., del Pilar Casado-Belmonte, M., & de las Mercedes Capobianco-Uriarte, M. (2020). Sustainable entrepreneurship: Review of its evolution and new trends. *Journal of Cleaner Production*, 252, 119742. DOI: 10.1016/j.jclepro.2019.119742

Thaker, M., Thaker, H. B. M. T., Pitchay, A. B. A., & Khaliq, A. B. (2019). A proposed integrated Zakat-Crowdfunding Model (IZCM) for effective collection and distribution of Zakat fund in Malaysia. *Journal Website: Journal. Zakatkedah. Com. My*, 1(2), 1–12.

The Frontier Post. (2019, August 14). *Implementing RSS evil ideology*. The Frontier Post. https://thefrontierpost.com/implementing-rss-evil-ideology/

The Hindu. P. (2019, December 27). CAA, NRC may affect status of India's Muslim minority: Congressional Research Service. Retrieved April 25, 2020, from https://www.thehindu.com/news/international/caa-nrc-may-affect-status-of-indias-muslim-minority-congressional-research-service/article30409109.ece#:~:text=%E2%80%9CIn%20tandem%20with%20a%20National,on%20the%20amended%20Citizenship%20law

Therthani, S., Balkin, R., Perepiczka, M., Silva, S., Hunter, Q., & Juhnke, G. (2022). Assessing personality traits, life balance domains, and work addiction among entrepreneurs. *The Career Development Quarterly*, 70(3), 190–201. DOI: 10.1002/cdq.12296

Thomas, L. D. W., & Autio, E. (2014). The fifth facet: The ecosystem as an organizational field. *Proceedings - Academy of Management*, 2014(1), 10306. DOI: 10.5465/ambpp.2014.10306abstract

Thompson, J., & Bolton, B. (2024). *Entrepreneurs: Talent, Temperament, Opportunity, and Mindset*. Taylor & Francis. DOI: 10.4324/9781003385790

Thompson, T. A., Purdy, J. M., & Ventresca, M. J. (2018). How entrepreneurial ecosystems take form: Evidence from social impact initiatives in Seattle. *Strategic Entrepreneurship Journal*, 12(1), 96–116. DOI: 10.1002/sej.1285

Thornton, P. H., Ribeiro-Soriano, D., & Urbano, D. (2011). Socio-cultural factors and entrepreneurial activity: An overview. *International Small Business Journal*, 29(2), 105–118. DOI: 10.1177/0266242610391930

Thukral, E. (2021). COVID-19: Small and medium enterprises challenges and responses with creativity, innovation, and entrepreneurship. *Strategic Change*, 30(2), 153–158. DOI: 10.1002/jsc.2399

Tian, N., Poudyal, N. C., Augé, R. M., Hodges, D. G., & Young, T. M. (2017). Meta-analysis of Price responsiveness of timber supply. *Forest Products Journal*, 67(3–4), 152–163. DOI: 10.13073/FPJ-D-16-00017

timesofindia.com. (2019). Detention centres: All you need to know: India News - Times of India. Retrieved July 22, 2020, from https://timesofindia.indiatimes.com/india/detention-centres-all-you-need-to-know/articleshow/72938445.cms

Tornikoski, E. T., Viljamaa, A., & Varamäki, E. (2015). Hybrid entrepreneurship during retirement: Comparison of motives and aspirations. In *Entrepreneurship, self-employment and retirement* (pp. 187–208). Palgrave Macmillan UK. DOI: 10.1057/9781137398390_9

Trapp, C. T., & Kanbach, D. K. (2021). Green entrepreneurship and business models: Deriving green technology business model archetypes. *Journal of Cleaner Production*, 297, 126694. DOI: 10.1016/j.jclepro.2021.126694

Tseo, G., Sheng, H., Zhang, P., & Zhang, L. (2004). Employee ownership and profit sharing as positive factors in the reform of chinese state-owned enterprises. *Economic and Industrial Democracy*, 25(1), 147–177. DOI: 10.1177/0143831X04040105

Tunio, M. N. (2020). Role of ICT in promoting entrepreneurial ecosystems in Pakistan. [JBE]. *Journal of Business Ecosystems*, 1(2), 1–21. DOI: 10.4018/JBE.2020070101

Tunio, M. N., Chaudhry, I. S., Mughal, F., & Shaikh, E. (2022). Marketing Mode and Survival of the Entrepreneurial Activities of Nascent Entrepreneurs. In *Big Data Analytics* (pp. 1–18). Auerbach Publications. DOI: 10.1201/9781003307761-1

Tunio, M. N., Chaudhry, I. S., Shaikh, S., Jariko, M. A., & Brahmi, M. (2021). Determinants of the sustainable entrepreneurial engagement of youth in developing country—An empirical evidence from Pakistan. *Sustainability (Basel)*, 13(14), 7764. DOI: 10.3390/su13147764

Turker, D., & Selcuk, S. (2009). Which factors affect entrepreneurial intention of university students? *Journal of European Industrial Training*, 33(2), 142–159. DOI: 10.1108/03090590910939049

Tuytens, M., & Devos, G. (2011). Stimulating professional learning through teacher evaluation: An impossible task for the school leader? *Teaching and Teacher Education*, 27(5), 891–899. DOI: 10.1016/j.tate.2011.02.004

Unjhawala, Y. T. (2024, August 13). How India must respond to the crisis in Bangladesh. *Hindustan Times*. https://www.hindustantimes.com/opinion/how-india-must-respond-to-the-crisis-in-bangladesh-101723564304859.html

Upadhyaya, R., & McCormick, D. (2020). Entrepreneurial capabilities of successful firms: A study of small and medium-scale equipment manufacturers in Nairobi, Kenya. International Journal of Technological Learning. *Innovation and Development*, 12(3), 169. DOI: 10.1504/IJTLID.2020.112226

Urban, B. (2009). Opportunity recognition: delineating the process and motivators for serial entrepreneurs: analysis of survey data. *Suid-Afrikaanse Tydskrif vir Ekonomiese en Bestuurswetenskappe*, 12(4), 513–532. DOI: 10.4102/sajems.v12i4.192

Urbano, D., Aparicio, S., & Audretsch, D. (2019). Twenty-five years of research on institutions, entrepreneurship, and economic growth: What has been learned? *Small Business Economics*, 53(1), 21–49. DOI: 10.1007/s11187-018-0038-0

Urmetzer, S., & Pyka, A. (2020). Innovation systems for sustainability. In *Decent Work and Economic Growth* (pp. 600–611). Springer.

Van der Sijde, P., & Van Tilburg, J. (1998). Creating a climate for university spin-offs. *Industry and Higher Education*, 12(5), 297–302. DOI: 10.1177/095042229801200504

Van Praag, C. M. (1999).. . *De Economist*, 147(3), 311–335. DOI: 10.1023/A:1003749128457

Van Trang, T., Hung Do, Q., & Luong, M. (2019). Entrepreneurial human capital, role models, and fear of failure and start-up perception of feasibility among adults in Vietnam. *International Journal of Engineering Business Management*, 11, 1–11. DOI: 10.1177/1847979019873269

Vedula, S., & Kim, P. H. (2018). Marching to the beat of the drum: The impact of the pace of life in US cities on entrepreneurial work effort. *Small Business Economics*, 50(3), 569–590. DOI: 10.1007/s11187-017-9908-0

Vedula, S., & Kim, P. H. (2019). Gimme shelter or fade away: The impact of regional entrepreneurial ecosystem quality on venture survival. *Industrial and Corporate Change*, 28(4), 827–854. DOI: 10.1093/icc/dtz032

Venkateswaran, N., Vidhya, K., Ayyannan, M., Chavan, S. M., Sekar, K., & Boopathi, S. (2023). A Study on Smart Energy Management Framework Using Cloud Computing. In *5G, Artificial Intelligence, and Next Generation Internet of Things: Digital Innovation for Green and Sustainable Economies* (pp. 189–212). IGI Global. DOI: 10.4018/978-1-6684-8634-4.ch009

Vennila, T., Karuna, M., Srivastava, B. K., Venugopal, J., Surakasi, R., & Sampath, B. (2022). New Strategies in Treatment and Enzymatic Processes: Ethanol Production From Sugarcane Bagasse. In *Human Agro-Energy Optimization for Business and Industry* (pp. 219–240). IGI Global.

Verheul, I., van Stel, A., & Thurik, R. (2006). Explaining female and male entrepreneurship at the country level. *Entrepreneurship and Regional Development*, 18(2), 151–183. DOI: 10.1080/08985620500532053

Verstraete, T. (2000). *History of entrepreneurship: The realities of entrepreneurship*. EMS Editions.

Vijaya Lakshmi, V., Mishra, M., Kushwah, J. S., Shajahan, U. S., Mohanasundari, M., & Boopathi, S. (2024). Circular Economy Digital Practices for Ethical Dimensions and Policies for Digital Waste Management. In *Harnessing High-Performance Computing and AI for Environmental Sustainability* (pp. 166–193). IGI Global., DOI: 10.4018/979-8-3693-1794-5.ch008

Vijayakumar, G. N. S., Domakonda, V. K., Farooq, S., Kumar, B. S., Pradeep, N., & Boopathi, S. (2024). Sustainable Developments in Nano-Fluid Synthesis for Various Industrial Applications. In *Adoption and Use of Technology Tools and Services by Economically Disadvantaged Communities: Implications for Growth and Sustainability* (pp. 48–81). IGI Global.

Vision and Mission. (2012). Retrieved 9 July 2020, from http://rss.org/encyc/2012/10/22/rss-vision-and-mission.html

Vivarelli, M. (2004). Are all the potential entrepreneurs so good? *Small Business Economics*, 23(1), 41–49. DOI: 10.1023/B:SBEJ.0000026023.11752.a9

Vivarelli, M. (2013). Is entrepreneurship necessarily good? Microeconomic evidence from developed and developing countries. *Industrial and Corporate Change*, 22(6), 1453–1495. DOI: 10.1093/icc/dtt005

Vlačić, B., González-Loureiro, M., & Eduardsen, J. (2020). The process of the process of internationalization: Cognitive and behavioral perspectives in small ventures. *European Journal of International Management*, 1(1), 10027574. Advance online publication. DOI: 10.1504/EJIM.2020.10027574

Voelpel, S. C., Leibold, M., Eckhoff, R. A., & Davenport, T. H. (2005). The Tyranny of Balanced Scorecard in the Innovation Economy. In *Proceedings of 4th International Critical Management Studies Conference-Intellectual Capital Stream*. Cambridge University.

Vogel, P. (2013). "Building and assessing entrepreneurial ecosystems", Presentation to OECD LEED Program Workshop on Entrepreneurial ecosystems and Growth-oriented entrepreneurship, The Hague, 7 November 2013. Available on: https://fr.slideshare.net/OECDLEED/6-vogel-building-and-assessin

Voigt, F. (2019). Regional development and the transport system. Regional Development and Economic Sectors: Results of European Comparative Research on. *Lagging Regions of Industrialized Countries*, 8, 105.

Volkmann, C., Fichter, K., Klofsten, M., & Audretsch, D. B. (2021). Sustainable entrepreneurial ecosystems: An emerging field of research. *Small Business Economics*, 56(3), 1047–1055. DOI: 10.1007/s11187-019-00253-7

Von Graevenitz, G., Harhoff, D., & Weber, R. (2010). The effects of entrepreneurship education. *Journal of Economic Behavior & Organization*, 76(1), 90–112. DOI: 10.1016/j.jebo.2010.02.015

Vrontis, D., Chaudhuri, R., & Chatterjee, S. (2022). Adoption of digital technologies by SMEs for sustainability and value creation: Moderating role of entrepreneurial orientation. *Sustainability (Basel)*, 14(13), 7949. DOI: 10.3390/su14137949

Vuorio, A. M., Puumalainen, K., & Fellnhofer, K. (2018). Drivers of entrepreneurial intentions in sustainable entrepreneurship. *International Journal of Entrepreneurial Behaviour & Research*, 24(2), 359–381. DOI: 10.1108/IJEBR-03-2016-0097

Wales, W. J., Gupta, V. K., & Mousa, F.-T. (2013). Empirical research on entrepreneurial orientation: An assessment and suggestions for future research. *International Small Business Journal*, 31(4), 357–383. DOI: 10.1177/0266242611418261

Walsh, K., & Stephens, S. (2022). The Side-Hustle: An Emergent Typology of Entrepreneurs as Employees. *International Review of Entrepreneurship*, 20(2).

Walter, S. G., Parboteeah, K. P., & Walter, A. (2013). University departments and self-employment intentions of business students: A cross-level analysis. *Entrepreneurship Theory and Practice*, 37(2), 175–200. DOI: 10.1111/j.1540-6520.2011.00460.x

Ward, J., & Peppard, J. (2002). *Strategic Planning for Information Systems* (3rd ed.). John Wiley.

Waruguru, M., Bwisa, H., & Kihoro, J. (2017). An assessment of the opportunity component of entrepreneurship policy in the youth, women, and uwezo funds in Kenya. *International Journal of Academic Research in Business & Social Sciences*, 7(1). Advance online publication. DOI: 10.6007/IJARBSS/v7-i1/2606

Wegner, D., Thomas, E., Teixeira, E. K., & Maehler, A. E. (2020). University entrepreneurial push strategy and students' entrepreneurial intention. *International Journal of Entrepreneurial Behaviour & Research*, 26(2), 307–325. DOI: 10.1108/IJEBR-10-2018-0648

Weihe, G. (2006). *Drivers of Collaborative Advantage: On the Operational Dynamics and Social Dimensions of Public-Private Partnerships. Department of Business and Politics*. Copenhagen Business School.

Welcome to High Commission of India, Bangladesh. (n.d.). https://www.hcidhaka.gov.in/bilateral?id=eyJpdiI6IndYNXlWemJ3cE04Z3RyM3ZMVDlZanc9PSIsInZhbHVlIjoiRHFtWjZtQTU0d2Q0M2tVbjVZaXlkQT09IiwibWFjIjoiZGFhZmQ1YWIwMGM5NjFkZDIyZWU2MDVjMzcxZGJlZjFkZTIwMWFiYzMwZTRlYmQ0NDE0OGJiMjRhMWI2MGIwZCJ9

Welter, F. (2011). Contextualizing entrepreneurship – conceptual challenges and ways forward. *Entrepreneurship Theory and Practice*, 35(1), 165–184. DOI: 10.1111/j.1540-6520.2010.00427.x

Welter, F., Baker, T., Audretsch, D. B., & Gartner, W. B. (2016). Everyday entrepreneurship—A call for entrepreneurship re-s e a r c h t o e m b r a c e e n t r e p r e n e u r i a l d i v e r s i t y. *Entrepreneurship Theory and Practice*. Advance online publication. DOI: 10.1111/etap.12258

Westhead, P., & Solesvik, M. Z. (2016). Entrepreneurship education and entrepreneurial intention: Do female students benefit? *International Small Business Journal*, 34(8), 979–1003. DOI: 10.1177/0266242615612534

Whelan-Berry, K. S., Gordon, J., & Hinings, C. (2003). Strengthening organizational change processes. *The Journal of Applied Behavioral Science*, 39(2), 186–207. DOI: 10.1177/0021886303256270

Whittam, J. (1996). Italian nationalism and Fascism. Retrieved 10 17, 2019, from https://research-information.bristol.ac.uk/en/publications/italian-nationalism-and-fascism(8cde2546-edce-

Williams, N., & Vorley, T. (2014). Economic resilience and entrepreneurship: Lessons from the sheffield city region. *Entrepreneurship and Regional Development*, 26(3-4), 257–281. DOI: 10.1080/08985626.2014.894129

Wilson, F., Marlino, D., & Kickul, J. (2004). Our entrepreneurial future: Examining the diverse attitudes and motivations of teens across gender and ethnic identity. *Journal of Developmental Entrepreneurship*, 9(3), 177–197.

Winter-Levy, S., & Lalwani, N. (2018). When is nationalism a good thing? When it unites an ethnically diverse citizenry. Retrieved 9 July 2020, from https://www.washingtonpost.com/news/monkey-cage/wp/2018/06/26/when-is-nationalism-a-good-thing-when-it-unites-an-ethnically-diverse-citizenry/

Witter, M. (2011). Financing sustainable development in small island developing states. *Tools for Mainstreaming Sustainable Development in Small States*, 107

Wold, H. O. A. (1982). Soft modeling: The basic design and some extensions. In Jöreskog, K. G., & Wold, H. O. A. (Eds.), *Systems under Indirect Observations: Part II* (pp. 1–54).

Wong, A. E. T. (2024, August 6). *Sheikh Hasina: Bangladesh's pro-democracy icon who became an autocrat*. https://www.bbc.com/news/articles/cg3ee303yxpo

World Bank. (2020). World Development Report 2020: Trade for Development in an Era of Value Chain Globalization. In *Abridged*. World Bank.

Wright, M., Robbie, K., & Ennew, C. (1997). Serial entrepreneurs. *British Journal of Management*, 8(3), 251–268. DOI: 10.1111/1467-8551.00064

Wu, S. P. J., Straub, D. W., & Liang, T. P. (2015). How information technology governance mechanisms and strategic alignment

Wurth, B., Stam, E., & Spigel, B. (2021). Toward an Entrepreneurial Ecosystem Research Program. *Entrepreneurship Theory and Practice*. Advance online publication. DOI: 10. 1177/10422

Xi, G., Block, J. H., Lasch, F., Robert, F., & Thurik, R. (2017). Mode of entry into hybrid entrepreneurship: New venture start-up versus business takeover.

Xiao, J., Boschma, R., & Andersson, M. (2018). Industrial diversification in europe: The differentiated role of relatedness. *Economic Geography*, 94(5), 514–549. DOI: 10.1080/00130095.2018.1444989

Yu, F. Y., Lin, Y. C., & Luo, S. Y. (2018). A study on learning motivation and effectiveness using multimedia materials for virtual reality. *Journal of Educational Technology & Society*, 21(1), 220–231.

Zachariah, B. (2015). At the Fuzzy Edges of Fascism: Framing the Volk in India. South Asia-journal of South Asian Studies, 38(4), 639-655. Retrieved 10 17, 2019, from https://tandfonline.com/doi/full/10.1080/00856401.2015.1078948

Zahra, S. A. (2008). The Virtuous Cycle of Discovery and Creation of Entrepreneurial Opportunities. *Strategic Entrepreneurship Journal*, 2(3), 243–257. DOI: 10.1002/sej.47

Zain, O. F. (2009). Marginalization of Muslim Minority in India. *Pakistan Journal of Social Sciences*, 29(1), 101–106. Retrieved March 23, 2020, from https://pdfs.semanticscholar.org/be38/cad5042519594d9f4c20619d877108b13c9f.pdf

Zeeshan, M. (2024, August 6). The slow death of democracy in Bangladesh was always bad news for India. *The Diplomat*. https://thediplomat.com/2024/08/the-slow-death-of-democracy-in-bangladesh-was-always-bad-news-for-india/

Zhang, F., & Wang, C. (2018). Dynamic pricing strategy and coordination in a dual-channel supply chain considering service value. *Applied Mathematical Modelling*, 54, 722–742. DOI: 10.1016/j.apm.2017.10.006

Zhang, L. (2023). Examining the relationship between entrepreneurship education and job creation in china's post-pandemic economy. *Journal of Digitainability Realism & Mastery (Dream)*, 2(05), 45–52. DOI: 10.56982/dream.v2i05.119

Zhang, Y., Duysters, G., & Cloodt, M. (2014). The role of entrepreneurship education as a predictor of university students' entrepreneurial intention. *The International Entrepreneurship and Management Journal*, 10(3), 623–641. DOI: 10.1007/s11365-012-0246-z

Zhang, Y., Sun, J., Yang, Z., & Wang, Y. (2020). Critical success factors of green innovation: Technology, organization and environment readiness. *Journal of Cleaner Production*, 264, 121701. DOI: 10.1016/j.jclepro.2020.121701

Zhao, H., & Seibert, S. (2006). The big five personality dimensions and entrepreneurial status: A meta- analytical review. *The Journal of Applied Psychology*, 91(2), 259–271. DOI: 10.1037/0021-9010.91.2.259 PMID: 16551182

Zhao, H., Seibert, S. E., & Hills, G. E. (2005). The mediating role of self-efficacy in the development of entrepreneurial intentions. *The Journal of Applied Psychology*, 90(6), 1265–1272. DOI: 10.1037/0021-9010.90.6.1265 PMID: 16316279

Zhao, L., Trenberth, L., & Kelly, J. (2010). The development and implications of china's employee benefit systems. *Asia Pacific Journal of Human Resources*, 48(3), 287–301. DOI: 10.1177/1038411110378958

Zheng, L., Ding, T., & Li, J. (2015). Entrepreneurship and economic development in China: Evidence from a time-varying parameters stochastic volatility vector autoregressive model. *Technology Analysis and Strategic Management*, 27(6), 660–674. DOI: 10.1080/09537325.2015.1034676

Zimmer, O. (2003). Homeland Nationalism Gone Wild: Nationalism and Fascism. Retrieved 10 17, 2019, from https://link.springer.com/chapter/10.1007/978-1-4039-4388-0_5

Zohar, D., & Luria, G. (2005). A multilevel model of safety climate: Cross-level relationships between organization and group-level climates. *The Journal of Applied Psychology*, 90(4), 616–628. DOI: 10.1037/0021-9010.90.4.616 PMID: 16060782

Zucker, L. G. (1987). Institutional theories of organization. *Annual Review of Sociology*, 13(1), 443–464. DOI: 10.1146/annurev.so.13.080187.002303

Zwick, A. (2018). Welcome to the Gig Economy: Neoliberal industrial relations and the case of Uber. *GeoJournal*, 83(4), 679–691. DOI: 10.1007/s10708-017-9793-8

About the Contributors

Muhammad Nawaz Tunio Dr. Tunio's dedication to academic excellence is further evidenced by his teaching and administrative roles at various universities, where he has mentored students, organized international conferences, and contributed to developing curricula in Business Administration and Management.

***

Rohit is a Research Associate at College of Healthcare Management and Economics, Gulf Medical University, UAE. He has published research papers in international journals and participated in various international conferences, workshops, and seminars. He worked as a management trainee and intern in the Thumbay Hospital, United Arab Emirates (UAE); Decathlon, Zirakpur, India; and Bajaj Allianz General Insurance, India. He completed various MOOCs from Copenhagen Business School, University of New Mexico, University of California, Irvine, University of London, and many other. His areas of interest are Entrepreneurship, consumer behavior, marketing strategies and strategic management. He is inspired with thought leadership and a regular contributor to educational magazines, debates, and cultural activities. He can be reached at rohit27.sr@gmail.com

Ajay Chandel is working as an Associate Professor at Mittal School of Business, Lovely Professional University, Punjab. He has 14 years of teaching and research experience. He has published papers in SCOPUS, WOS, and UGC listed Journals in areas like Social Media Marketing, E-Commerce, and Consumer Behaviour. He has published cases on SMEs and Social Entrepreneurship in The Case Centre, UK. He also reviews The Case Journal, Emerald Group Publishing, and International Journal of Business and Globalisation, Inderscience. He has authored and developed MOOCs on Tourism and Hospitality Marketing under Epg-Pathshala- A gateway to all postgraduate courses (a UGC-MHRD project under its National Mission on Education Through ICT (NME-ICT).

Narayanage Jayantha Dewasiri, Ph.D., is a Chartered Manager at the Chartered Management Institute, UK. He conducts research at the Open University of Sri Lanka and the Sri Lanka Institute of Marketing. He is the founding Editor-in-Chief of the South Asian Journal of Marketing. His research interests are in corporate social responsibility, corporate governance, marketing and sales, management, and finance. He is working as the Head of Field Force at the HMD Global Inc., Sri Lanka. He also serves as a senior lecturer at University of Sabaragamuwa, Sri Lanka. He can be reached at dnjay@ou.ac.lk

Thomas Gahamanyi Niyonzima is a Congolese national, born on April 27, 1987, in Kisharu, Rutshuru Territory, North Kivu Province in the Democratic Republic of Congo, married with many children. In March 2022, he was accepted for a PhD in Economics and Management at the University of Yaoundé II Soa, Cameroon, in the field of Mathematical Economics, Statistics and Econometrics, where he is in his third year of PhD studies. His thesis research focuses on "Essays on the effects of price dynamics in Africa", under the supervision of Professor Tchouassi Gérard. He holds a Master diploma in Economics for SMEs since 2014 from the Centre international d'études supérieures spécialisées in canada, Edmundston, after completing his master's degree in Economics sciences at the University of Goma in the DRC from 2006 until 2011 in rural economics. Since April 2012, he has been a teacher-researcher at the Institut Supérieur de Commerce de Goma ISC -Goma in the DRC, where he teaches econometrics, macro and microeconomics, distribution logistics and public finance. Since May 2022, he has already taken part in several international symposium and conferences, in Dakar, Brazzaville, Marrakech, Kinshasa and Yaoundé. To date, he has three articles published in international journals, and two others are already with reviewers. In the professional world, he is a consultant in Finance and taxation for SMEs in transport companies and Logistics and customs clearance in the DRC.

Jorge Gomes is Professor of Strategy and Management at Universidade Lusófona and researcher at ADVANCE/CSG/ISEG - University of Lisbon. He holds a PhD in Management from ISEG and a Master's in Management Sciences from ISCTE-IUL, a postgraduate degree in Project Management from INDEG / ISCTE and a degree in Geographic Engineering from the Faculty of Sciences of the University of Lisbon. For the last 35 years he has worked as an engineer, project manager, quality auditor and consultant. His research interests include Strategy and

Operations, Benefits Management, Project Management, Project Success, Maturity Models, IS/IT Investment Management.

Preet Kanwal completed her Post-Doctoral Fellowship at the ESG, University of Quebec in Montreal, Canada, furthering research expertise in her field. During her Post Doctoral Fellowship, she worked on exploring demographic sensitivity and its impact on discrimination in HEIs while considering insights from Canada and India. Dr. Kanwal is an academician and researcher with over 20 years of experience in Human Resource Management. She holds a PhD in Human Resource Management from I.K. Gujral Punjab Technical University, Punjab, India, where she conducted an empirical study on the quality of work life in the textile industry of Punjab, India. She also has international experience teaching MBA students from Victoria University (Online), Australia, and Sunway University (Online), Malaysia. Dr. Kanwal's research interests revolve around the quality of work-life, work-life balance, industrial relations, labour laws, social security and labour welfare, organizational stress, and behaviour, particularly in the context of the textile industry. She has presented her research at numerous national and international conferences and published her work in Scopus-indexed and UGC-listed Journals. Additionally, she has authored several book chapters on related topics, underscoring her commitment to advancing knowledge in her field. Her contributions extend beyond teaching and research; she has been actively involved in organizing and leading training sessions, workshops, and conferences, both as a participant and as a session chair.

Shashank Mittal has done his FPM in Organizational behavior and Human Resource from Indian Institute of Management Raipur. He holds B. Tech from I.E.T. Lucknow. His post FPM work experience includes almost five years of industry and academics exposures in multiple roles. Prior to joining FPM, he has over two years of industrial experience and three years of teaching experience in various organizations. He has published multiple papers in ABDC ranked and SSCI indexed journals of international repute such as Journal of Knowledge Management, Journal of Behavioral and Experimental Finance, International Journal of Conflict Management, Journal of Management and Organization and Current Psychology. His current research interest includes Social identity, Knowledge exchanges, Status, Proactive helping, Employer branding, Organizational justice, and Humanitarian relief management. He enjoys badminton and cycling during leisure time.

Mário José Batista Romão is an Associate Professor of Information Systems at ISEG – University of Lisbon. He is Director of the Masters program in Computer Science and Management. He holds a PhD in Management Sciences by ISCTE-IUL and by Computer Integrated Manufacturing at Cranfiel University (UK). He also holds a MsC in Telecommunications and Computer Science, at IST - Instituto Superior Técnico, University of Lisbon. He is Pos-Graduated in Project Management and holds the international certification Project Management Professional (PMP), by PMI – Project Management International. He has a degree in Electrotecnic Engineer by IST

Parth Sharma, Associate Professor at the School of Law, University of Petroleum and Energy Studies, brings a wealth of expertise to his role. With a PhD in India-China relations from Aligarh Muslim University and a gold medal in his undergraduate studies, he has established himself as a leading scholar in the field of international politics. His research, published in highly regarded journals both nationally and internationally, has made significant contributions to the understanding of strategic affairs, political theory, and the politics of development. Dr. Sharma's qualifications extend beyond his academic achievements; he is a UGC (JRF-NET) qualified scholar in Political Science and has actively participated in workshops and conferences organized by prestigious institutions like the UGC, British High Commission, and Centre for Policy Research. His diverse interests encompass international politics, strategic affairs, political theory, the politics of development, and issues related to higher education, making him a valuable asset to the academic community.

Sandeep Kumar Singh is an associate professor in the area of Information Systems and Analytics at Jindal Global Business School, O.P. Jindal Global University, Sonipat. Prior to joining Jindal Global Business School, he worked as an Assistant Professor at JKLU Jaipur for two years. He has earned his Ph.D. in computational physics from Antwerpen University, Belgium. His PhD work focused on mathematical modeling and simulation of two-dimensional materials. Post to his PhD, he worked as a research scientist in Sweden for four years in energy storage systems, bioelectronics. He also did MTech in industrial mathematics and scientific computing from IIT Madras, Chennai. His current research interests are to apply complex mathematical modeling in the business and financial world.

Sanjay Taneja is currently an Associate Professor in Research at Graphic Era University, Dehradun, India. His significant thrust areas are Banking Regulations, Banking and Finance (Fin Tech, Green Finance), Risks, Insurance Management, Green Economics and Management of Innovation in Insurance. He holds a double master’s degree (MBA &M.Com.) in management with a specialization in Finance and Marketing. He received his PG degrees in Management (Gold Medalist) from Chaudhary Devi University, Sirsa, India in 2012. He earned his Doctor of Philosophy (Sponsored By ICSSR) in Banking and Finance entitled “An Appraisal of financial performance of Indian Banking Sector: A Comparative study of Public, Private and Foreign banks in 2016 from Chaudhary Devi University, Sirsa, India. He received his Post Doctoral Degree from faculty of Social Sciences, Department of Banking and Insurance, Usak University, Turkey entitled on "Impact of the European Green Deal on Carbon (CO2) Emission in Turkey" in 2023. He has published research papers in reputed SCOPUS/Web of Science/SCI/ABDC/UGC Care Journals. Prof. Taneja has more than fifty publications in total (Scopus/ABDC/Web of Science- 27)

Muhammad Usman Tariq has more than 16+ year's experience in industry and academia. He has authored more than 200+ research articles, 110+ case studies, 70+ book chapters and several books other than 4 patents. He is founder and CEO of The Case HQ, a unique repository for courses, narrative and video case studies. He has been working as a consultant and trainer for industries representing six sigma, quality, health and safety, environmental systems, project management, and information security standards. His work has encompassed sectors in aviation, manufacturing, food, hospitality, education, finance, research, software and transportation. He has diverse and significant experience working with accreditation agencies of ABET, ACBSP, AACSB, WASC, CAA, EFQM and NCEAC. Additionally, Dr. Tariq has operational experience in incubators, research labs, government research projects, private sector startups, program creation and management at various industrial and academic levels. He is Certified Higher Education Teacher from Harvard University, USA, Certified Online Educator from HMBSU, Certified Six Sigma Master Black Belt and has been awarded PFHEA, SMIEEE, and CMBE.

Gérard Tchouassi is a lecturer/researcher at the University of Yaoundé II-Soa in Cameroon. After obtaining his doctorate in economics in in economics in 1996 and a Doctorat d'Etat in economics in sciences in 2006 at the University of Yaoundé II-Soa, from December December 2008 to December 2011, of the Executive Committee of the Council for the of the Council for the Development of Social Science Research in Africa (CODESRIA). the Agence Universitaire de la Francophonie (AUF) scholarship for excellence de la Francophonie (AUF) and the Grand Lyon (France). He was project manager for the international colloquium on "Migrations et fuites des cerveaux africains à l'ère de la mondialisation", held at the CEREG held at the CEREG in Yaoundé on April 15, 16 and 17, 2010. He is Co-Responsible for the AUF's Inter-university Scientific Cooperation Project (PCSI). the AUF. He is a visiting professor at several universities, associate researcher and member of several laboratories and research networks in Cameroon and abroad. He is a resource person and consultant for several national and international organizations, including the United Nations Development Fund for Women (UNIFEM). His areas of research and expertise include include: Women's entrepreneurship, Microfinance, Fair trade,

Regional integration, Cross-border trade, Gender analysis, Gender-responsive budgeting, New Economy of migration and development, Human, environmental and naive resources. Development Aid, Formal and Informal Financial Systems, Pro-Poor Analysis, Economic Governance, Corruption, Economic and Territorial Attractiveness, Social and Solidarity Economy, Third-Sector Economy, Industrial Economy, Logistics and Transport, and Economic Philanthropy.

Mohit Yadav is an Associate Professor in the area of Human Resource Management at Jindal Global Business School (JGBS). He has a rich blend of work experience from both Academics as well as Industry. Prof. Mohit holds a Ph.D. from Department of Management Studies, Indian Institute of Technology Roorkee (IIT Roorkee) and has completed Master of Human Resource and Organizational Development (MHROD) from prestigious Delhi School of Economics, University of Delhi. He also holds a B.Com (Hons.) degree from University of Delhi and UGC-JRF scholarship. He has published various research papers and book chapters with reputed publishers like Springer, Sage, Emerald, Elsevier, Inderscience etc. and presented research papers in national and International conferences both in India and abroad. He has many best paper awards on his credit too. He is reviewer of various international journals like Computers in Human Behavior, Policing etc. His areas of interest are Organizational Behavior, HRM, Recruitment and Selection, Organizational Citizenship Behavior, Quality of work life and role.

Index

F

G

H

I

J

L

O

P

R

S

T

W

www.ingramcontent.com/pod-product-compliance
Lightning Source LLC
LaVergne TN
LVHW080351011026
849161LV00009B/2262